LED ZEPPELIN
THE CONCERT FILE

Picture research by Dave Lewis & Nikki Russell

ISBN: 1.84449.659.7
Order No: OP 50556

Exclusive Distributors
Music Sales Limited,
8/9 Frith Street,
London W1D 3JB, UK.

Music Sales Corporation,
257 Park Avenue South,
New York, NY 10010, USA.

Macmillan Distribution Services,
53 Park West Drive,
Derrimut, Vic 3030,
Australia.

To the Music Trade only:
Music Sales Limited,
8/9 Frith Street,
London W1D 3JB, UK.

Led Zeppelin

Typeset by MRM Graphics Ltd, Winslow Bucks
Printed and Bound in Singapore

A catalogue record for this book is available from the British Library.

Visit Omnibus Press on the web at www.omnibuspress.com

CONTENTS

Introduction 7

Notes and Acknowledgements 10

Prologue: The Early Performing Days of Jimmy Page, Robert Plant, John Bonham & John Paul Jones 13

The Led Zeppelin Concert File 20

Solo Appearances 355

The Concert File

LED ZEP CONCERT FILE PICTURE CREDITS
Pictures credits: Ara Ashjian, Atlantic Archives, Irwin Bieber/John Yaglinski Collection, Eddie Blower, Richard Aaron/Redferns, Alge, Anne Bjorndal Collection, Richard Borg Collection, Greg Chalk, J. T. Comerford, Fin Costello/Redferns, Andre Csillag, Mike Daily, Carl Dunn, Brian Evans, Howard Fields, Nigel Glazier, Globe Photos, Bob Gruen, Ross Halfin, Tom Hanley/Redferns, Alan Hare, William Heilemann, G. Irwin, William Hames/Idols, Hugh Jones Collection, Steve Kurasch, John Kink/Redferns, LFI, Dave Lewis, Tom Locke/TBL Archive, Kevin Mazur/LFI, Gary Merrin, Dean Messina, Philip Morris, Howard Mylett Collection, Photo Features, Robert Pistella, Barry Plummer, Norwood Price, Aubrey Powell/Hypgnosis, Neal Preston/Retna, Mike Putland, Chris Taylor/Q, Larry Ratner, Redferns, Retna, Rex Features, Ebet Roberts/Redferns, Pennie Smith, Star File, Syndication International, Tim Tirelli Collection, Jorg Tschirschwitz, Tyne Tees TV, Jan Way, Steve Way Collection, Dave Wilson/Camera Press, Graham A. Wiltshire, Jay Williams.

DEDICATION

This book is dedicated to the memory of Peter Grant, without whom ...
and to John Peel and Tommy Vance who believed in Led Zeppelin's music
at differing times and with equal effect.

INTRODUCTION

"When Led Zeppelin played a concert it wasn't just a concert. It was an event." – Peter Grant 1993.

Among the many remarkable sequences that can be found on surviving audience tapes of Led Zeppelin live in concert is one from the night of March 20, 1975, at a show in Vancouver.

Just as the band are launching into the middle section of 'Whole Lotta Love' – in the space of three minutes just before Jimmy Page's Theremin solo – Robert Plant leads them through a spontaneous version of James Brown's 'Licking Stick', which incorporates their own funk rhythm from the *Houses Of The Holy* track 'The Crunge', and follows that with a random war cry from the *Led Zeppelin III* opener 'Immigrant Song'. Then, with equal spontaneity, the Jones, Bonham & Page rhythm section interlock for a riff sequence that would be recalled some three years later for the track 'Ozone Baby' which eventually saw the light of day on the *Coda* album.

It was this air of unpredictability within their performances which made Led Zeppelin such an engrossing live act throughout their career. Their ten studio albums may represent one of the biggest selling and most influential back catalogues of all time – but they were only part of the story. "To me the records were just a staring point," recalls John Paul Jones. "The most important thing was always the stage show… so many great nights. At our worst we were still better than most. At our best we could just wipe the floor with the lot of them. It was just a very good live band."

Indeed, Led Zeppelin live was an extraordinary experience. From the very beginning no two performances were alike. Such was the creative spark between the four that the basic structures of their songs was repeatedly reworked, extended and improvised upon, making their studio counterparts almost unrecognisable. "The beauty of playing in the band," Jimmy Page reflected in a recent interview, "was that when we went onstage we never actually knew what was going to go on within the framework of the songs. They were constantly changing. New parts would come in on the night. The spontaneity was on the level of ESP, which meant it was always exciting."

Take the track 'No Quarter'. The studio version on *Houses Of The Holy* clocks in at a compact six minutes and fifty nine seconds. When they came to perform it live for the first time in 1973 it quickly became an instrumental showcase for John Paul Jones' keyboard work that extended to over fourteen minutes. Two years later it was further extended to twenty minutes while Page and Bonham ad-libed with Jones. They approached the middle section as the mood took them – one night it might emerge as a free form jazz arrangement, the next as a meandering pastoral guitar piece. By the advent of their 1977 US tour it was stretching to nearly thirty minutes in length with Jones incorporating elements of Rachmaninov and even a version of B. Bumble & The Stingers' 'Nut Rocker'.

Equally enthralling was the group's ability to turn itself into a human juke box, pulling out gems from their blues and rock'n'roll roots such as 'That's Alright Mama', 'Long Tall Sally', 'I'm Going Down', 'For What It's Worth', 'Blueberry Hill' and countless more, all of which added spice to their encores and medleys.

As Peter Grant observed, Led Zeppelin stopped giving mere concerts – their appearances were events. But they were also often less than perfect musically. Working spontaneously, there was always the risk that it could all go wrong. The fact is on any given night they could be incredibly inconsistent. As Robert Plant acknowledges: "We often used to take off and get lost. We were quite ramshackle at the best of times. People who tell you we were always good or always bad are wrong. It was always on a wing and a prayer."

For example, the night of May 22, 1977 in Fort

Worth. Plant, to the audience after the band has lost the tempo of the intro to 'In My Time Of Dying': "Tell you what we'll do, we'll start again. There's a few clowns up here too." Or in Zurich, June 29, 1980: "If anybody's bootlegging this you'll have to scratch the last number because it wasn't completely correct," Plant told the audience after a rather disorganised delivery of 'Kashmir'.

These glitches could often be attributed to the effects of their legendary road fever excess, the consequences of which often saw them in less than 100% physical fitness. Example: Kezar, San Francisco, June 2 1973: "Now that we've been awake for three hours we should start feeling like a rock and roll band," Plant told the audience after they had arrived nearly two hours late for this afternoon stadium date.

There was always a massive air of expectancy at a Led Zeppelin show. It could go either way – but when all the elements were in their favour and they were really feeding off the audience, then the results would invariably be spectacular. There's no finer example than their June 21 1977, performance at the LA Forum, preserved on a brilliantly atmospheric audience tape and issued on the CD bootleg *Listen To This Eddie*. Official or otherwise, this is one of the most authentic and inspiring live albums ever issued, a thrilling aural record that captures all the muscle and dynamism of being right there on the spot. It's a near perfect statement of intent by a band who at that time held America in the palm of its hand.

The series of concerts at the Fillmore venues in 1969, their tour of Japan in 1971, European dates in the spring of 1973 and the legendary five nights at London's Earls Court Arena in May 1975 are further examples of the band at the top of their game, as this book explains.

It is an attempt to tell the story of those 'Evenings with Led Zeppelin' as they were so often billed. Herein, their remarkable live history unfolds in the form of an exhaustive log of every known show they performed. It unravels the musical highs and lows of those touring days,

drawing from countless audience tapes that were recorded at the time. Despite tough management measures designed to prevent bootlegging, Led Zeppelin became one of the most bootlegged acts of all time. The fascination to collect and hear these live remnants is a modern day passion shared by countless enthusiasts throughout the world and, it has to be said, by the ex-members themselves.

Alongside the musical commentary are many on the spot reports drawn from original reviews and first hand reminiscences from those that were there at the time. These reports accurately portray Led Zeppelin's remarkable rise in stature from tour to tour, particularly in America. Reading through the various touring stages, many key events unfold within the shows: how they initially won over the US college circuit crowd supporting the likes of Vanilla Fudge and Iron Butterfly; how areas such as Boston, New York and Los Angeles developed special relationships with them; the initial lukewarm reception in England and the turning point at the Bath Festival in 1970; their incredible work rate during their first two years; and the unpropitious events that led to a gradual slowing down of their live schedule. Most striking perhaps is the first hand evidence of the latter day craziness that surrounded their stadium tours in the US, culminating in 1977 with a tour that in hindsight was just about the biggest both logistically, and in terms of their pulling power, undertaken by any group of their era. "Every time we went back more people wanted to see us and the gigs got bigger and bigger," remembers Page. "It was supply and demand."

The tragedies that befell Robert Plant would dictate a very different Led Zeppelin after that 1977 tour. The onset of punk saw them reviled in some quarters and though they fought bravely to reinvent themselves for the Eighties, the ultimate tragedy of John Bonham's death rent the group asunder as the Eighties began.

It may have been the end of Zeppelin as a group but Zeppelin as a lasting musical inspiration continues to flourish. The 1994 reunion of Jimmy

Page and Robert Plant for the *Unledded* concerts and subsequent world tour enabled them to reinvent the Zeppelin catalogue with the aid of the Egyptian Ensemble Orchestra, as well as offer the opportunity to approach numbers from their old repertoire which were rarely played live. A second tour in 1998 saw the pair returning again to the spontaneous medley tactic that had been such a feature in the old era. During 'How Many More Times' Plant randomly included snippets of 'We're Gonna Groove', 'In My Time Of Dying' and 'In The Light', with an impulsiveness to rival that celebrated night back in Vancouver in 1975.

Equally impressive has been John Paul Jones motivation to carve out his own solo career. His solo albums *Zooma* and *The Thuderthief* and accompanying live appearances were a vivid reminder of the bass guitar and keyboard dexterity which lit up so many Zep performances – proof again of his vital role within the band. Robert Plant has also continued to challenge himself and his audience: the release of his *Mighty ReArranger* album and tour with the Strange Sensation displaying a new creative urge and an ease with his past that allows him to pay homage to Led Zeppelin on his own terms.

For fans old and new though, the real watershed in recent years was was the release in 2003 of the *How The West Was Won* live CD and four hour *DVD* compilation. The sales and critical acclaim of these releases prompted a resurgence of interest in the group to a level reminiscent of their Seventies heyday.

Acknowledgement in movies such as *Almost Famous* and *School Of Rock*, Zep tribute bands treading the boards night after night, *Musicians Wanted* columns full of 'Guitarist required – Zeppelin influenced', and a back catalogue that is a permanent fixture in record stores from Marrakech to the misty mountains and back again – not to mention an abundance of busy Zeppelin web sites the world over – all ensure that Led Zeppelin is a name that remains very much in the present tense. This was acknowledged by the cover of *Q* magazine in March 2005 which proclaimed emphatically: "Led Zeppelin – The Most Important Band In The Word … Today!"

Like the DVD, *The Concert File* tells the Led Zeppelin story from the place where they functioned best. For their thousands of fans there was no more an exciting moment than when the arena darkened, Bonzo kick-started the bass drum, Page warmed up the Gibson and Plant delivered his trademark "Good Evening". It was the cue for three hours of stupendous, unpredictable, live rock entertainment, three hours you wish could last a lifetime.

And it has...

If you weren't there then, well you can be now. This book offers you a front row seat from which to experience the real deal of what this group was all about, lending their power to every audience they encountered. This is Led Zeppelin live on stage from 1968 through to 1980 in concert and beyond.

Dave Lewis
April 2005

Notes and Acknowledgements

The year-by-year gig listing that forms the bulk of this book has been compiled from painstaking research conducted over a number of years. Simon and I compiled the first edition of this book by listening to countless hours of live tapes and CDs, scouring hundreds of sources for original reviews and comments, and conducting interviews with many key personnel who witnessed the events at the time. At the time we thought we had made a reasonable job of the task.

Time moves on and new information continues to be unearthed. One of the luxuries we did not have back in the early Nineties was the Internet. The information cyber highway has proved to be an invaluable tool in discovering historical facts and insight into when and where Led Zeppelin played and exactly what happened. With the assistance and enthusiasm of fans across the globe, piecing info together over the past two years has improved the accuracy of the concert log many fold.

Some guidelines to the text: Alongside set list information and relevant details about the shows, this revised edition also contains, where applicable, relevant bootleg CD references. The bootleg listings are not intended to be comprehensive but offer a pointer to which shows have appeared on bootleg CDs. As previously noted, Zeppelin remain one of the most bootlegged acts of all time and, regardless of moral issues it throws up, this vast alternate catalogue has done much to shed invaluable perspective on the band's on-stage development through the years.

This revised edition also places a greater emphasis on tracking the visual references of the band. The release of the official DVD has opened up all our eyes and ears to exactly what footage was made during their concert appearances. This has led to a Visual References section that logs the source of all known Led Zeppelin video and cine film and it's availability, official or otherwise, on DVD.

As no official gig records exist for much of their early career gaining 100% accuracy of many dates has been difficult. Where no absolute verification could be sourced for a gig listing we have labelled the date 'Unconfirmed'. Suffice to say if anyone reading this has confirmation of any of these dates taking place please get in touch.

Alongside the tracking of their live gigs, there are details of guest appearances and relevant news items to unfold the story. Also included are all major significant TV and radio appearances the band or individual members made. Relevant studio recording data is also chronicled to add context to their ongoing career. Finally, the Solo Years appendix offers a summary of the touring and live appearances undertaken by Jimmy Page, Robert Plant and John Paul Jones as solo performers.

The end result is what we believe to be the largest and most accurate wealth of information of its kind ever collated into one Led Zeppelin book.

1997 CREDITS

The original book was put together with the assistance input and inspiration of many contributors. We would first like to single out the work of various past Zep chroniclers:

Hugh Jones – Former editor of the much-respected American Led Zeppelin collector journal *Proximity*. In his role as US co-ordinator of this project, his vast archive of American data and memorabilia helped fill many of the missing gaps.

Robert Godwin – Already acknowledged as one of the foremost compilers of Zeppelin discographies through his *Collectors Guide To Led Zeppelin* books, Robert's pioneering work in unearthing details of when and where Zeppelin played live greatly benefited this project. His unselfish sharing of such information has been an inspiration and this book would certainly be less accurate without his help.

Howard Mylett – Author of one of the first Zeppelin books and a long time collator of their work.

Luis Rey – Author of the chronology of live tapes *Led Zeppelin Live* . His often outspoken and illuminating opinions have been a constant source of delight and amusement for collectors over the years.

Many thanks for the generosity and support of the following who have been responsible for providing photographs and memorabilia: Mike Daily, Robert Pistella, Jorg Tchirschwitz, Norwood Price, Howard Fields, Steve Kurash, Larry Ratner, Graham A Wiltshire, Greg Chalk, Brian Knapp, Ger Arendsen, Tim Tirelli, Dave Rugg, Eric Sachs, Gary Davies, John Yaglinski, Henry Race, Matt Krol, Alge, Irwin Biber and Ted Tuksa, Anne Bjorndal, for bringing us closer to the early days.

Many thanks to the following who have also provided inspiration along the way: Paul Sheppard, Phil Tattershall, Mark Harrison, Julian Walker, Eddie Edwards, Dave Fox, Rudi O'Keefe, Larry Miller, Bob Langley, Kam Assi, Keith Dubrovin, Terry Boud, Mark J McFall, Dardo Simone, Chris Williams, Tommy Gammard, Danny Coyle, Elio Marena, Christophe Le Pabic, Benoit Pascal, Laura Whitten, Anne Marsden, Krys Jantzen, Mark Archer, Larry Bergmann Jnr., Tony Gold, Nigel Dorning, Geoff Adamson, Leo T Ishak, Russ Rees, Paul Hindess, Taylor, Bob Walker, Rick Barrett, Steve and Jan Way, Azumi Nakaya, Michael and Sharon Wolf, Terry Stephenson, Billy and Alison Fletcher, Andy Adams, Liz Hames, Debbie Bonham, the late Mick Bonham, Scarlet Page, Takashi and Yukio Yamamoto.

Charles Shaar Murray, Nick Kent, Roy Hollingsworth, Chris Welch, Roy Carr, Peter Doggett, Matt Snow, Phil Alexander, Phil Sutcliffe, David Clayton, Charles R Cross, Simon Robinson, Mark Lewishon, Patrick Humphries, Peter Robinson and Mark Timlin for journalistic motivation past and present.

The following periodicals for providing many sources of reference : *Melody Maker, NME, Disc, Sounds, Top Pops, Record Mirror, Let It Rock, Zig Zag, Beat Instrumental, Oz, Mojo, Q, Record Collector, Uncut, Word, Guitar Player, Guitar World, Guitarist* and Zeppelin fanzines past and present:

Tight But Loose, Zoso, Proximity, Wearing And Tearing, Winds Of Thor, Early Days And Latter Days, The Ocean, Pb, Runes, That's The Way, Four Sticks, In The Mood, The Only One, No Quarter.

Chris Charlesworth for the original concept, on the road reminiscences and much editorial advice.

2005 CREDITS

This 2005 revised edition of the book has benefited immensely from the knowledge of Mike Tremaglio. His own personal exhaustive logs of Zeppelin concerts has been a mine of information and has added crucial accuracy and detail to what went before. Mike – sincere thanks for making this book so much more complete.

Very special thanks are also due to: Gary Foy for editorial advice, Dave Linwood and Martyn Lewis for co-ordination of the *TBL* web site; also to Allessandro Borri, David Hope, Richard Borg, Phil Bushe, Hiroshi Miyagi, John Mangelschots, Mauri Mikola for providing continual updates and insights.

The following also waded in with info, feedback and inspiration along the way: Marshall Hall, Bill Eaglesham and Steve Ord for their Newcastle '68 research; Julian Walker, Gary Davies, Graeme Hutchinson, Mark Harrison, Keith Lambert, John Rutherford, Bab Mady, Ian Thompson, Scott Moffett, Tim Davies, Randell Morris, Simon Croom, Kurt Gedda, Ed Ortiz, Geoff Hunt, Jospeph, Robert Williams, Jo Schmidt, John Chesterton, Mike Rejsa, Andy Neill, Ian Avey, Paul Duggen, Gerard Sparaco, Doug Hinman, Andy Duncan, Peter Duffy, David F Brown, Steve Connolley, Paul Harper, Dan Tigerstedt, Shaun P McVaul, Liz Shipley, Jason Peters, Pete Badham, Sam Rappallo, Pete Harris, Hrannar Helgason, Brian Knapp, Samtos Haro, HP Newquist, Bill McCue ,Grant Burgess, Rick Willis, Benoit Pascal, John Hoff, Chris Hager, Roland Rimml, Michael Stark, Matt Jaffe, Michael Hobson, Adrian Pallett, Michael and Sharon Wolf, Jerry Bloom, Paul Groceau, Tim Behrans, Gavin Myers, Jason New, George Berbarien MD, Jeane-Francois Delepine, Charles Cioffero, Ian Thompson, Michael Frosty,

Stewart Guy, Simon Fisher, Eddie Lombardi, Wolfgang Mueller, Scott Applegate, Ian Dixon, Terry Boud, Steve (The Lemon) Sauer, Woody Wilson, Frank Melfi, Carolyn Longstaff, Mick Burlow, Andrew Ricci, Rich Williams, Andy Banks, Richard Chadwick at Opium Arts; Bill Curbishely, Andrea and Nicola at Trinifold Mangement; Cameron Crowe, Neal Preston, Andy Edwards, Paul Timothy, Pete Gozzard, Kevin Hewick, Steve Jones, Dave Marsh, Gary Woollard, Steve Beale, Keith Creek, Paul Kelvie, Mark Archer, Ian Green, Roly Thompson, Alan Cousins, Katherine Moore, Stuart Whithead; Joel, Tim, Jake and Jack at *Record Collector*; Sian at *Classic Rock*; Mark Blake at *Q*; Steve Jump, Kim Tanser, Roy Williams.

Kashmir French magazine (zeppat94@net-up com), Led Zeppelin Fan Club Italia (www.ledzeppelin.club it), Undergournd Uprising site (uuweb.led-zeppelin.us), Electric Magic site (www.ledzeppelin.com),

Fred Zeppelin, Whole Lotta Led, Simply Led, Letz Zep, Boot Led Zeppelin, Rubber Plants for keeping it live via tribute.

Max Harris, Phil Harris, Dec Hickey, Tom Locke and James Eaton for public house duties past, present and future, Shin and Suki at the post office, Chris and Nad at the Fox and Hounds, Nigel at the White Horse, Dave Smith, Simon B, Nathan ,Gareth, Marc, Emily, Tina, Darren and all at Virgin Mega MK.

Musical inspiration while writing this book: The music of Led Zeppelin, Robert Plant, John Paul Jones, Jimmy Page, Nick Drake, Joni Mitchell, Crosby Stills & Nash, The Rolling Stones, The Who, The Faces, The Beatles, Bob Dylan, Miles Davis, Dusty Springfield, Frank Sinatra and Elvis Presley.

Contact: Dave Lewis welcomes feedback, updates, corrections via e-mail to davelewis.tbl@virgin.net

Visit the *Tight But Loose* website at www.tblweb.com. for the most authoritative Zep related news service.

Subscribe to the *Tight But Loose* magazine, chronicling the world of Led Zeppelin since 1978: Dave Lewis, 14 Totnes Close, Bedford MK40 3AX

Simon Pallett would personally like to thank Jimmy Page, Ross Halfin and Geoff Campbell for constant inspiration and advice; Charles and Robert Pallett for constant support; Janet Pallett for endless patience love and understanding. To James Pallett and Mathew Pallett with love.

Dave Lewis would personally like to thank and acknowledge Gary and Carol Foy, Dave Linwood, Kevyn Gammond, Mike Warry, Martyn Lewis, John & Sally Lewis, Mervyn & Sheila Lewis, Justine & Simon, Ken & Betty, the late Trevor and Edith who heard and encouraged it all from the start.

In memory of Margaret Lewis 1949-2003.

Finally to Jan, Sam and Adam who live with it all – with such love, understanding and humour!

Dave Lewis June 2005

Led Zeppelin

PROLOGUE: THE EARLY PERFORMING DAYS OF PAGE, PLANT, BONHAM & JONES

Before Led Zeppelin Live, there was … Neil Christian & The Crusaders Live … The Tony Meehan Combo Live … Terry Webb & The Spiders Live … The Crawling King Snakes Live … The Band of Joy Live … and, most importantly, The Yardbirds Live …

JIMMY

For Jimmy Page live performing began in the late Fifties. His earliest live performances included a stint as backing guitarist to beat poet Royston Ellis and a spell with Red E. Lewis & The Redcaps. Lewis saw Page playing in his hometown of Epsom and invited the 15-year-old Page to join his rock'n'roll group. Their early dates included a support slot to Johnny Kidd & The Pirates. It was while working with The Redcaps that the young Page came to the notice of Neil Christian, who signed Page up for his group The Crusaders. The eighteen months that followed initiated Page into life on the road.

The vagaries of road life were not conducive to Jimmy's health and recurring bouts of glandular fever finally forced him to quit the group. He would later play on a number of Neil Christian's singles in his role as the youngest session guitarist on the scene. Page's guitar inspiration came from the likes of Presley sidemen Scotty Moore and James Burton, and The Everly Brothers' guitarist Johnny Day. He was also keen on the blues playing of B.B. King and Elmore James and the acoustic picking of Bert Jansch and John Renbourne.

After a spell at Croydon Art College, Page became was drawn into the jazz and blues circuit in the Richmond area where The Cyril Davies All Stars acted as mentors to The Rolling Stones. A guest spot during the interval of an R&B show at the Marquee Club in Central London led to an invitation to do sessions work, initially for Decca Records. One of his earliest sessions was for Jet Harris & Tony Meehan's 'Diamonds' at IBC Studios, with future Zeppelin engineer Glyn Johns working as tape operator.

Following brief stints with beat groups Mickey Finn and Carter Lewis & The Southerners (playing lead guitar and harmonica), Page became one of the most sought after session players in London, playing on literally hundreds of sessions for artists as diverse as Burt Bacharach, PJ Proby, The Who, The Kinks, Brenda Lee and Lulu. He was approached in 1965 to join The Yardbirds but turned the offer down, recommending instead his friend Jeff Beck. The pair enjoyed a healthy friendship and rivalry, and Beck gave Jimmy the

Jimmy Page with The Hilltop Five circa 1961

Jimmy Page with Neil Christian circa 1962

Fender Telecaster guitar that he would play with The Yardbirds and early Zeppelin.

A year later, fed up with the constraints of session work, Jimmy Page became a fully-fledged Yardbird. Originally taking over on bass (as seen in The Yardbirds cameo in Antonioni's *Blow Up* movie – even though Page actually played lead guitar on this recording!), when Paul Samwell Smith quit, Page soon formed a short-lived dual lead guitar partnership with Beck. The explosive results can be heard on the 'Happenings Ten Years Time Ago'/'Psycho Daisies' single issued in November 1966. By then Beck had left the group to commence a solo career. His first single, the hugely successful 'Hi Ho Silver Lining', was backed with Page's composition 'Beck's Bolero' cut in late '66 with a line-up that included Keith Moon, Nicky Hopkins, John Paul Jones (then a sought after session arranger) plus Beck and Page. It was on this session that Moon suggested they start up a group that would go down like a Lead Zeppelin. The phrase stuck with Page.

Jimmy Page carried on with The Yardbirds for the next eighteen months. Although the group experienced falling record sales and a frustrating time in the studio (fuelled by Mickey Most's inappropriate production), on stage – particularly in

America – this final line-up carved a strong reputation. This was further assisted by the astute management of Peter Grant, who saw the potential for hard rock in the US college and ballroom circuit and new venues such as The Fillmore East & West.

In keeping with the spirit of the era, The Yardbirds merged their R&B roots with the psychedelic sound predominant at the time. Page was in the forefront of this exciting hybrid and the experimental vision he brought to his playing hinted at a completely new sound. This can be heard clearly in the surviving live tapes of the group from this period, notably the poorly recorded attempt at an official live album *Live Yardbirds*, recorded at the Anderson Theatre in March 1968. This was issued by Epic in 1971 and hastily withdrawn on Page's insistence.

There is also a more authentic reminder, a bootleg titled *The Yardbirds Last Rave Up In LA*. This was recorded over two shows on May 31 and June 1, 1968, at the Shrine Auditorium in Los Angeles. A mere month before they called it a day. The set is packed with clues as to what would emerge as The New Yardbirds and Led Zeppelin just three months later.

There's the 'Dazed & Confused' bridge at the introduction to 'Train Kept A Rollin'' – their opening number that was retained for the early Zeppelin tours. Then there's 'Dazed & Confused' itself – based on an idea from Jake Holmes, a New

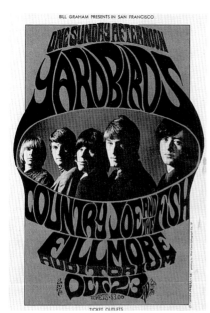

ground scene he was well poised to be at the helm of the new movement.

Listening to that final Yardbirds blow out in LA, it becomes apparent that much of the material performed during the first and second Led Zeppelin US tours was built around the framework of the last days of The Yardbirds. The faces and personalities had changed but the sound was predominantly Page – adopting the full frontal guitar heroics he had developed over the last two years.

It was presented with a mysterious and slightly menacing stage presence that lent itself perfectly to the mystique that would surround Led Zeppelin as they re-wrote the accepted rulebook of music business practise.

Page recalls: "I was actually in favour of keeping The Yardbirds together – I thought we had the potential to move on – we were getting into some very interesting fields with the improvisation on stage. But it wasn't to be, so I decided to start again from scratch."

York folk singer Page heard while touring, and adapted to feature the violin bow solo that would become a Zeppelin trademark. Only the lyrics would be changed for the version that subsequently appeared on Led Zeppelin's début album.

There are also several strung-out improvisations on 'I'm A Man' and a 'Smokestack Lightning' medley built around the guitar riff that would become 'How Many More Times'. This would drift into playful covers such as The Velvet Underground's 'Waiting For The Man', an open ended tactic that Page would develop with Robert Plant.

And there was Page's instrumental *tour de force* 'White Summer' – the beginning of the DADGAD tuning technique that would flower into 'Black Mountain Side' and 'Kashmir'. On stage during this period Page was in full psychedelic flight with painted Telecaster, a perm of curls and velvet attire. As psychedelia gave way to the under-

ROBERT AND BONZO

Around the same time as the demise of The Yardbirds, time was running out for young Robert Anthony Plant. The blues singer from the Midlands Black Country had given himself until he was 20 to make the big time. With only months to go, the big break was still eluding him. At that time Plant was dividing his time between a Midlands band known as Obstweedle and playing with Alexis Korner.

His passion for the blues dated back to his early teens. On leaving school he ditched a potentially promising career as a chartered accountant and

TIFFANIES: "It's Got To Be A Great Song" (Chess). Opens with a touch of Beethoven's Fifth Symphony, then develops into a typical U.S. girl-group sound. Mid-tempo, it's soloed with chanting. Sounds like the Toys.
ROBERT PLANT: "Long Time Coming" (CBS). An impassioned soul rockaballad, with brass, piano and gospel chanting — plus maracas setting up an underlying double-time shuffle beat. Very good of its kind.
OLIVER NORMAN: "Drowning In My Own Despair" (Polydor). As the title

became part of the Midlands blues scene. Spurred on by the influence of early blues masters Robert Johnson, Tommy McClelland, Howlin' Wolf and Otis Rush, he sang with a variety of bands including Andy Long & The Original Jurymen, The New Memphis Bluesbreakers, The Black Snake Moan, The Delta Blues Band, The Tennessee Teens and The Crawling King Snakes. The last outfit brought Robert Plant into contact with a drummer called John Bonham. "John came up to me," remembers Plant, "and said 'You're all right but you're only half as good a singer as I am a drummer'. It was his usual understatement and it led to us becoming great friends. We were always trying to prove something."

Bonham hailed from Redditch. His first live jobs were with The Senators, Terry Webb & The Spi-

ders and A Way Of Life. He quickly developed a reputation for being the loudest drummer around. Fairport Convention bassist Dave Pegg, who worked with Bonham in A Way Of Life, remembers: "If you were in a band with Bonzo, you knew you'd never get a rebooking wherever you played. But he was such a great player." His style was quite unique — incorporating the counter rhythm technique favoured by Ginger Baker but applied in a way that created a whole backbone of sound. His ability to create intricate bass drum patterns were quite innovative for the time.

Plant and Bonham went on to play in The Band Of Joy, an eclectic unit that went through several line up changes. Musically, they merged a blues approach with the free form experimental West Coast sound — taking influences from Buffalo Springfield and Moby Grape, and embracing the psychedelic trends of the era in much the same way as Jimmy Page was doing with The Yardbirds.

Their live shows were anything but conventional. Plant recalls them wearing face paint early on, and hilarious run-ins with Bonham over the billing of the band. "He always wanted it to be 'Robert Plant & The Band Of Joy featuring John Bonham' and we'd end up having fights over that." Their set list included covers of Tim Hardin's 'If I Were A Carpenter', Buffalo Springfield's 'For What It's Worth', Moby Grape's 'Hey Grandma', The Future's 'Part Time Love' and Prince Foster's 'Ten Commandments'. Other numbers were given bizarre arrangements, including Jefferson Airplane's 'White Rabbit' with 'March Of The Siamese Children' from The King And I in the middle.

Plant: "We had some crazy times on the road, like when Bonzo drove the van and reversed into some railings and took the door handle off!

MIDLAND BEAT

MEET THE GROUP

LISTEN

One of the most exciting groups to emerge from Birmingham for some time are Listen, a four-man outfit with an explosive sound. They are all set to make their disc debut with a number with the intriguing title "The Pakistani Rent-Collector," which is different enough to put them in the charts.

Apart from having one of the most unusual names on the local scene, Listen are also among the most colourful groups around, their mod fashions arousing almost as much comment as their wild, pulsating music. It's not surprising that their fan club is booming!

Managed by the shrewd, go-ahead Mike Dolan, Listen are becoming more and more in demand from promoters throughout the country, resulting in only occasional appearances in the Birmingham area for this up-and-coming group.

GEOFF THOMPSON (drums) was born on December 11, 1946, has light brown hair and blue eyes. He is 5 ft. 10½ ins. and plays guitar as well as drums. Girls and gambling are his hobbies and his 'favourites' are Solomon Burke (singer), cheese (food), rum and Coke (drink) and Joe Tex (composer). He likes mod clothes and unbreakable drum sticks, dislikes non-tipped cigarettes. Favourite music is 'commercial soul and harmony singing' with his personal ambition stated as 'to find a bass drum that does not slide away when I hit it.' Born in Cannock, Geoff's professional ambition is 'to be successful with Listen,' he names joining the group as the biggest break in his career and he lists his favourite groups as the Drifters and the Impressions.

ROGER BEAMER (bass guitar) was born on December 19, 1946, has auburn hair and green eyes. He is 5 ft. 8½ ins. and plays tabou as well as bass guitar. Motoring and sports are his hobbies and his 'favourites' are Blue (singer), Porterhouse steak (food), cider (drink) and Smokey Robinson (composer). He likes big, well-lit stages and appreciative audiences, dislikes small dressing rooms. Favourite music is 'commercial soul and Tamla Motown' with his personal ambition stated as 'to continue to be happy playing our style of music.' Born in Walsall, Roger's professional ambition is 'to be acknowledged for the type of music we play,' he names 'forming Listen' as the biggest break in his career and he names his favourite group as Geno Washington and the Ram Jam.

JOHN CRUTCHLEY (lead guitar) was born on March 11, 1947, has medium brown hair and is 5 ft. 11 ins. He plays rhythm and bass guitar and drums as well as lead. Girls and experimenting with new electronic and guitar sounds are his hobbies and his 'favourites' are brown and white (colours), Don Covay (singer), 'anything' (food), whiskey (drink) and Don Covay (composer). He likes travelling around the country and good parties, dislikes playing in very cramped conditions. Favourite music is jazz and commercial soul music with his personal ambition stated as 'just to carry on enjoying the life I now lead.' Born in Birmingham, John's professional ambition is to produce records for Listen, he names the Alan Bown Set as his favourite group.

ROBERT PLANT (vocalist) was born on August 15, 1948, has fair hair and brown eyes. He is 5 ft. 11½ ins. and plays harmonica and flute as well as being lead vocalist. Motoring and listening to soul records are his hobbies and his 'favourites' are blue (colour), Buffi Brewery (singer), dry biscuits (food), Brandy and Coke (drink) and Prince Buster (composer). He likes mod girls and ultra mod clothes, dislikes phoneys. Favourite music is modern jazz and commercial soul music with his personal ambition stated as 'to be accepted singing soul and jazz music.' Born in Birmingham, Robert's professional ambition is 'to have a successful record in the near future,' he names 'joining Listen' as the biggest break in his career and he names Jimmy James and the Vaga-bonds as his favourite group.

16

Robert Plant and the Band of Joy

ROBERT PLANT and the B.O.J. nearly made it into our special top three—but not quite. They were the runners-up. All the same, you'll be reading plenty about them in TOP POPS in the months to come.

The group, who all come from Birmingham, and specialise in West Coast music, issue their first single early in February, titled "Memory Lane". They wrote and produced it themselves.

Robert (above) told TOP POPS: "I have been confident that this group could do things, but being elected runners-up in the poll after such a short time on the road is a sign of great things. It is really too much!"

We had to open the door outside The Speakeasy with a shovel … and there's Keith Moon coming out of his Rolls. Bonzo went and hid in the truck. He could not be seen by one of his peers opening the door with a shovel! There were so many crazy times but we were good – I'll never forget the look on Alvin Lee's face when we blew off Ten Years After."

After establishing themselves in the Midlands, The Band Of Joy moved onto the London circuit playing The Marquee and Middle Earth clubs supporting Tim Rose, Fairport Convention and Ten Years After. In search of the elusive record deal, they recorded some demos at London's Regent Sound and there were vague plans to issue

a track called 'Memory Lane' as a single. Plant looks back on that acetate with much affection: "If you hear that, you hear Led Zeppelin. Bonzo's doing all those drum figures and fills that were influenced by Carmine Appice. It's identical to a lot of what followed."

By the spring of 1968 though, apathy from the major labels saw them call it a day. Bonham was offered the chance to tour with Tim Rose, then making a name for himself in the UK. Plant linked up with Alexis Korner for some recording work, alternating his time with a local band called Obstweedle. It was while playing with Obsweedle at a teacher training college in Birmingham in the late summer of '68 that he was visited by Jimmy Page and Peter Grant on the recommendation of Terry Reid. He more than exceeded their expectations.

A visit to Page's Pangbourne home to see if they could get on musically, confirmed his inclusion in The New Yardbirds line up. At this point the drum stool was still vacant with Procol Harum's BJ Wilson, Paul Francis and Aynsley Dunbar under consideration. Plant suggested Page check out Bonham and they went to see him backing Tim Rose at Hampstead Country Club. There was no doubt in Page's mind that this was the man for the job. Bonham, enjoying a steady wage with Rose and considering offers from Chris Farlowe & Joe Cocker, was initially reluctant to join. "I saw Bonzo with Tim Rose and he was playing 'Hey Joe' as an acoustic number. I could see the whole thing fitting together," recalls Page. After some persuasion from Grant, Bonham agreed. The line-up was nigh on complete. It's worth noting that alongside his acceptance to join Page's new group, Plant honoured his commitments with Aexis Korner recording with him and pianist Steve Miller at De Lane Studios in

London in September and taping a BBC braodcast session on October 11 at London's Aeolian Hall Studios.

Though there was an overriding Yardbirds influence attached to the early Zeppelin, Plant and Bonham also had their say. Plant's love of the West Coast and original blues was to influence many of the off-the-cuff choices that made it into their live repertoire. Arrangements such as Garnett Mimm's 'As Long As I Have You' and Spirit's 'Fresh Garbage' were all derived from Plant's suggestions. "On that first New Yardbirds tour we did include arrangements of things we'd covered in The Band Of Joy like 'I Can't Quit You Baby'," said Plant. "The Band Of Joy had been a real schooling for Bonzo and myself for taking material and stretching it, breaking down the general order of the pop song. So meeting Jimmy and Jonesy was like a gathering of souls because Jimmy had been doing that with The Yardbirds in a different form."

JOHN PAUL

All that was left was for them to be introduced to John Paul Jones (previously Baldwin). A seasoned session arranger, much respected for his work with The Rolling Stones, Lulu, Dusty Springfield and many others, John Paul came from a musical background. His father was a pianist who had played with the famous Ambrose Big Band, and by the time he had left school, John was already an accomplished bass and keyboards player. His first touring experience came from backing his father, following which he formed his own group, travelling around Army bases in England. He turned professional at 17, successfully auditioning for Jet Harris & Tony Meehan's backing band. This lasted for a couple of years and it was through Meehan's production work at Decca that he moved to the studio session scene. "He was always a very intelligent musician," recalled Meehan. "He could play rock or jazz more than competently."

"John Baldwin as he was known then was a great musician for his age," Jet Harris recently noted.

Jones spent a good five years arranging and contributing to countless albums and singles – The Stones, Yardbirds and Donovan all benefiting from his taste and style. It was on a session for Donovan's *Hurdy Gurdy Man* album that he first heard Page talking about forming a group. The two had often met on sessions in the studio – notably when Jones arranged the cellos on The Yardbirds' 'Little Games' single. By 1968 Jones was growing increasingly restless in the confines of a studio, and when he heard Jimmy was forming The New Yardbirds, he offered his services.

As Chris Dreja had opted out of the original line-up, Page had no hesitation in calling him.

John Paul Jones had little stage experience, other than a prestigious residency with Dusty Springfield at the Talk Of The Town. Compared to the other three, he was a relative newcomer to regular gigging but this mattered little. John Paul more than made up for it with the impeccable musicianship that became such an integral part of their chemistry. Jones: "I think they expected to see me smoking a pipe and wearing slippers. They heard about this session man and must have wondered what to expect. But once we got into that rehearsal room in Gerrard Street it was just instant. We just looked around and knew it was going to work … "

Clearly in those early days there was a stark divide between the more experienced Page and Jones and the fresh-faced boys from the Midlands. "It was remarkable how naïve Robert and Bonzo were," recalled Peter Grant. "Bonzo even offered to drive the van for an extra fifty quid a week. But once we got to America, well that's when their eyes were really opened and the fun began."

And for all Robert's later rock-god narcissism, initially he was often prone to being overcast by Jimmy's shadow. Grant remembers hiding bad reviews from him during their first year together, knowing it might reduce his confidence. However, by their third US visit in the summer of '69, America was beginning to fall for Robert Plant's increasingly dominant front man bravado. This was the point where The Yardbirds and The Band

Of Joy influences begin to evaporate and in their place came the Led Zeppelin sound; a unique blend of what Page and Plant would later describe as light and shade. Although they could be extremely derivative throughout their career, Led Zeppelin remained utterly distinctive. They were a band that lifted licks and lyrics often shamelessly without a nod or a credit … but they still managed to sound like no one else.

By 1969 the early apprenticeships in their previous live outfits had served their purpose. The way was clear for Led Zeppelin to take live rock music to a peak that had rarely been scaled before. But they never really forgot those early days and influences and as you will discover as you read on, they were never afraid to relive their pre-Zeppelin lives, pulling out old forgotten gems at a moment's notice during the lengthy medley numbers. It was a constant reminder of where they had come from and how important those early influences remained.

With this new Yardbirds line-up complete, there was an outstanding engagement to fulfil that was left over from the old Yardbirds' date sheet – a nine-date tour of Scandinavia. Still billed as The Yardbirds', the group that would become Led Zeppelin made their stage début on September 7 in Denmark. It's worth noting that there is little evidence of the group being dubbed New Yardbirds – this may have been a myth due to press coverage of the time.

"Standing by the side of the stage it was obvious that there was a chemistry," said Peter Grant. Robert recalled: "We were very green – it was a tentative start but we knew we had something."

The stage act for the début tour was based loosely on the set The Yardbirds had been performing on their final US tour. 'Train Kept A Rollin'' was the opener and 'Dazed & Confused' the centrepiece, with Page using the violin bow. Old blues chestnuts 'I Can't Quit You' and 'You Shook Me' were also delivered in the arrangements that would later appear on their first album. Early self penned numbers included 'Communication Breakdown' and 'How Many More Times' – the latter built around Howlin'

Wolf's 'How Many More Years'.

The act was fleshed out with a variety of covers – something that would remain a feature of their sets for many years to come. Elmore Gantry's 'Flames' and Garnett Mimm's 'As Long As I Have You' were early staples at this point. They also came up with a dynamic arrangement for the folk standard 'Babe I'm Gonna Leave You'. Page had played the Joan Baez version to Plant on their initial meeting. "I want to do a version of this but with a certain dynamic edge," he told his new singer.

It was obvious to them all that even on this début tour the line-up had an identity all of its own. Page: "We realised we were working under false pretences, the thing had quickly gone beyond where The Yardbirds had left off. We all agreed there was no point in retaining the New Yardbirds' tag so when we got back from Scandinavia we decided to change the name. It was a fresh beginning for us all."

Early photo sessions were held in Copenhagen including location shots in a park and on the street with local band The Beatniks.

Equipment Notes:

For the early Yardbirds' dates and into their first US tour, Jimmy used the Rickenbacker amp set-up left over from The Yardbirds' days. His main guitar was the Fender Telecaster painted in psyche-

Led Zeppelin

delic colours – a gift from Jeff Beck. He also carried with him a Gibson Les Paul that was gradually introduced and will later become his favoured instrument. For 'Babe I'm Gonna Leave You' and his 'White Summer' showcase, Jimmy used a black and white Dan Electro. John Paul Jones favoured a 1963 Fender Jazz bass on these early shows. John Bonham's drum set-up was a sparkle tinted Ludwig kit with a 24-inch bass drum and two floor tom-toms.

Saturday September 7 1968
Gladsaxe, Denmark
Teen Club Box 45
Set included: Train Kept A Rollin'/I Can't Quite You Baby/You Shook Me/Dazed And Confused/Babe I'm Gonna Leave You.

Billed as 'Yard Birds'. Support from Fourways and Bodies. Ticket price 5-7 DKr.

Local photographer Jorgen Angel became the first person to take photos of the new line up on stage. He told Hugh Jones' *Proximity* magazine: ''I took a number of photographs There weren't many actual lights on stage in those days – at least nothing you could use, so I used a flash. I used my mother's holiday camera and my father's old flash and I just snapped away. When I first knew of the gig I was disappointed even before the concert because I was looking forward to seeing The Yardbirds again and what we were getting was one Yardbirds member and three totally unknown guys. My disappointment was only up until they started performing because it was a great concert.''

Brondby, Norregard Hallen Copenhagen, Denmark
Brondby Pop Club
Billed as 'The Yard Birds'. Support from Day Of The Phoenix, The Eyes and Ham. Ticket price 4-8 DKr.

For the Scandinavian tours, the band were sometimes required to play two shows on the same day at different venues. After an early show, their minimal equipment would be transported to a late show.

Peter Grant recalls: "The first time I saw them play was in Scandinavia. I remember standing on the side of the stage and being amazed. And Bonzo was only on £50 a week and I recall him coming back afterwards and offering to drive the van for another fifty."

Sunday September 8 1968
Nykobing Lolland, Denmark
Raventlow Parken
Set includes: Train Kept A Rollin', I Can't Quit You Baby, You Shook Me, Dazed And Confused, How Many More Times.

Journalist Anne Bjorndal recalls: "It was a warm Sunday evening. The event was a harvest festival affair and they were supported by The Beatniks from Sweden and The Ladybirds. The Ladybirds were four go-go dancers dressed in hot pants, white boots and little else. By the time The New Yardbirds came on at 7pm the audience was quite drunk. Robert had to contend with some banter from the crowd. The set included 'Train Kept A Rollin'', 'Dazed And Confused' and they did a great version of 'You Shook Me', the next day Jimmy did an interview with the Danish

paper *Aktuel*."

Roskilde, Denmark
Fjordvilla Club Paramount
Support from Lady Birds, an all girl topless go-go dancing outfit, and Beauty Fools

Thursday September 12 1968
Stockholm, Sweden
Stora Scenen Grona Lund Amusement Park

Friday September 13 1968
Stockholm, Sweden
Inside Club
Billed as Yardbirds – support from local group Atlantic Ocean

Saturday September 14 1968
Knivsta Uppsala, Sweden
Angby Parkdans

Sunday September 15 1968
Gothenburg, Sweden
Stjarnscenen Liseburg Amusement Park
Billed as Yardbirds pop band

Tuesday September 17 1968
Malmö, Sweden
Klub Bongo
Page recalls: "In Scandinavia the songs began to stretch out and I thought we were working into a comfortable groove."

September 20 – October 10 1968
Barnes, England
Olympic Studios
Recording Sessions
Recording sessions for the first album took place over this period. Outtakes of 'Babe I'm Gonna Leave You', 'You Shook Me' and 'Tribute To Bert Burns' have surfaced on bootleg. 'Tribute To Bert Burns' was issued officially under the title 'Baby Come On Home' on the *Boxed Set 2* package issued in October 1993.

Known recording data: Friday, September 27, 1968 – Three takes of 'Babe I'm Gonna Leave You' (all outtakes), 'You Shook Me' take one; Thursday, October 10: 'Tribute To Bert Burns' (takes 1 to 3).
CD Reference: *Olympic Gold* (Scorpio)

Around this period Chris Dreja, ex-Yardbird bassist turned photographer, arranged a photo session with the band in a Putney studio which would produce the back cover photo for their first album.

October 1968
Barnes, England
Olympic Studios
Recording Sessions
There exist lengthy instrumental jams from this session featuring acoustic guitar and organ. Some sources claim Steve Winwood was involved.
Bootleg CD Reference: *Babe I'm Gonna Leave You*

UK CLUB GIGS 1968

The Yardbirds became Led Zeppelin just as they began their first tentative appearances in the UK. After rejecting Whoopee Cushion and Mad Dogs, Page recalled a phrase Keith Moon had used a couple of years earlier when there had been a vague plan to form a new group out of the sessions with Jeff Beck for 'Beck's Bolero'.

Page's tempestuous relationship with Beck reared its head during the launching of Zeppelin. It's often claimed that Page borrowed the formula Beck was establishing in his Jeff Beck Group (featuring Rod Stewart) at the time, right down to the appearance of 'You Shook Me' on Beck's recent *Truth* album and the first Zep album. Page had certainly observed Beck's popularity in the US with interest, checking them out – and the burgeoning US ballroom circuit – with Grant that autumn. Clearly there was a demand for the sort of pioneering rock sound both guitarists demonstrated. The difference was Page's determination to carry it through.

"Moon's joke was about going down like a lead zeppelin," recalled Grant. "In the circumstances the name seemed perfect. I got rid of the 'A'. I was doodling in the office and it just looked better and I also didn't want any confusion over the pronunciation in America."

They embarked on a series of one-nighters in October – often billed as 'The Yardbirds now known as Led Zeppelin' . Their first fee was a paltry £150.00 In between the club dates they went into Olympic Studios and recorded their first album in just 30 studio hours. "We had begun developing the arrangements on the Scandinavian tour and I knew what sound I was looking for. It just came together incredibly quickly' said Page.

With the album in the can, events moved speedily. In early November Grant secured a deal with the giant Atlantic Records in New York. He had made enquiries with Pye and EMI in the UK but to no avail. Atlantic had made their reputation on a series of legendary black soul and R&B artists and more recently they had begun to dabble in the white rock market, enjoying success with Vanilla Fudge, Iron Butterfly and Cream.

Atlantic supremos Ahmet Ertegun and Jerry Wexler saw the potential in this new English group, and were influenced by recommendations from Dusty Springfield and Van Morrison's producer Bert Burns, both of whom knew Page and Jones as consummate studio professionals. Grant was able to negotiate a shrewd deal with Atlantic, a five-year contract and $200,000 advance. He also had written into their contract various clauses giving them greater artistic control than any previous Atlantic act. A publishing company set up by Page and Grant under the subtle title Superhype made sure their song writing royalties also accrued independently.

With this satisfactory deal under their belts, it was a disappointment to Grant that initial UK reaction to his new act was relatively muted. "Before the album came out it was a joke in England," he said. "They just didn't want to know. I'd already set my sights on getting them over to America because I figured we'd be given a fair chance."

A début US tour was therefore quickly set up to begin on Boxing Day, December 26 1968. In the meantime Plant just about found time to marry Maureen, his Midlands girlfriend, on November 9, although there would be no honeymoon. That evening they played their first billed show at London's Roundhouse on an all-nighter that included one of Page & Plant's heroes, John Lee Hooker. A date at London's Marquee Club on 10 December earned them their first UK review in *Melody Maker*. "Led Zeppelin, the regrouped Yardbirds, played the Marquee last week," reported Tony Wilson. "They are now very much a heavy group with singer Robert Plant leading and ably holding his own against the powerful backing trio. Drummer Bonham is forceful – perhaps too much so and generally there seems to be a need for Led Zeppelin to cut down the volume a bit."

America would have no fears about the noise level …

Friday October 4 1968,
Newcastle, England
Mayfair Ballroom
Local newspaper *The Evening Chronicle* listed the gig as ''The Yardbirds featuring Jimmy Paige (sic) at last back from their USA tour''. Support acts were listed as Terry Reid's Fantasia (replaced nearer the time by New York Public Library),Junco Partners and Downtown Faction. Reid of course had turned down the opportunity to join Page's group.

It would appear this may have been an outstanding commitment gig owing from the Yardbirds early 1968 UK gigs.

No review of the gig appeared in subsequent editions of the local paper but there again neither was there any apology for any non-appearance. Via the *Undergound Uprising* Zep website fan David Hope revealed the following information: ''I was contacted by a person who claimed to have seen Zep in Newcastle in 1968. He told me he thought he was going to a Yardbirds show as that was how the gig was advertised. When the band took the stage no one knew who the singer was as

Led Zeppelin

he certainly did not look like Keith Relf. The singer informed the crowd The Yardbirds had split up and introduced the new group as Led Zeppelin and himself as Robert Plant. The music was shockingly different with .Dazed And Confused. the highlight and they played two encores"

If this show did take place, and there is strong indication to believe it did, it becomes the earliest British appearance of the group in the Page, Plant, Jones, Bonham line up. The Mayfair itself was demolished in 2000 to make way for a multiplex cinema.

Friday October 11 1968
London, England
Aeolian Hall, Studio 2
Radio broadcast for the World Service Rhythm & Blues show. Broadcast on Tuesday November 5. Producer: Jeff Griffin; engineer: Joe Young.

Guest Appearance: Robert honoured a BBC session engagement with Alexis Korner and Steve Miller, with whom he had been working prior to the formation of Led Zeppelin. He had also recorded with this line up at De Lane recording studios in London the previous month – cutting the track 'Steal Away'.

This radio broadcast featured Plant backing Alexis on harmonica on the following songs: You Don't Know/Do You Mind? /You Are My Sunshine/Streamline Train/Why Did You Waste My Time?

UNCONFIRMED
Tuesday October 15 1968
Guildford Surrey, England
Surrey University Halls
This date remains something of a mystery. If they did this gig on this date it's likely they were billed as The Yardbirds. It's also unlikely they would have returned to the same venue ten days later for the October 25th date. The *Melody Maker* ran a news story in their October 26 weekending issue that stated "Led Zeppelin, the group formed by Jimmy Page after the disbandment of The Yardbirds, make their debut at Surrey University tomorrow (Friday)." As the paper was published on a Thursday, that report would indicate the Surrey date was definitely on October 25 – a fact backed up by the discovery of a poster from the gig (see October 25 entry).

Surrey University would seem to think otherwise. On December 20, 2003, Jimmy Page returned to Guildford University to judge a Riffathon competition. Whilst there he unveiled a plaque that stated: "This plaque is to commemorate the debut performance of Led Zeppelin, University Hall, October 15 1968." There's enough indication to suspect that fact is wrong.

Friday October 18 1968
London, England
Marquee Club
Billed rather confusingly as 'The British Début of THE YARDBIRDS'. Support from Sleepy.

Saturday October 19 1968
Liverpool, England
Liverpool University

"Last appearance of Yardbirds," proclaimed news reports: "The Yardbirds make their last-ever appearance on Saturday at Liverpool University. None of the original Yardbirds remain. Only guitarist Jimmy Paige (sic) will stay to form a new group to be known as Led Zeppelin. The group are expected to sign with a leading British record label in the next week. Atlantic is being strongly tipped as their American outlet. A single is expected in December."

Friday October 25 1968
Guildford Surrey, England
Surrey University Halls

Previously it had been presumed that this was the first date they undertook billed as Led Zeppelin.

A news story in the *Melody Maker* at the time stated: 'Led Zeppelin, the new group formed by Jimmy Page after the disbandment of The Yardbirds, make their debut tomorrow at Surrey university".

However the emergence in 2003 of a seemingly genuine rare poster from this gig puts the name billing in doubt. Auction house Bonham's put this poster up for sale and made enquiries to gain its authenticity. The story goes that the vendor's family purchased a property in the west country and a quantity of posters were left behind when the house was vacated. The person who owned the property had been a booking agent in the Sixties and Seventies and booked many university gigs. He also owned a half share in a printing business and dabbled as an artist. This New Yardbirds

poster was amongst the posters found in the house.

On the matter of the billing – the poster states New Yardbirds as opposed to Led Zeppelin – it is feasible the poster was printed in advance of the gig. It's worth noting this is the only record of the group being billed New Yardbirds. Page and Grant's decision to switch to Led Zeppelin occurred in mid-October. By the time the decision was taken it's possible the Surrey University poster had already been designed.

The poster fetched £2,400. With it's quaint billing "First big dance of term" and typically late Sixties design, if genuine it can rightly be considered as one of the most important artefacts of Zep memorabilia, signalling the close of The Yardbirds era and the dawn of the Led Zeppelin age.

Just prior to the gig Jimmy Page told Chris Welch of *Melody Maker*: "It's refreshing to know that today you can go out and form a group to play the music you like and people will listen. It's what musicians have wanted for twenty years."

Saturday October 25 1968
Bristol, England
Bristol Boxing Club

Mick Farren and Russell Hunter, members of The Deviants, both reminisce about supporting Zeppelin in the book, *Days In The Life – Voices From The English Underground 1961 – 1971*. Hunter recalls: "We supported Led Zeppelin at one of their first gigs. It was a try-out for their big hype launch. It was at the local Bristol boxing club and the audience hated us and despised them. Somebody threw a beer glass at the stage and Sid Bishop, our guitarist, unfortunately threw it back and cut somebody's head. When Led Zeppelin came on, they got through a number and a half until the fire extinguishers, buckets, bricks and everything was being thrown at them."

Mick Farren: "All these farm boys in brown suits and haircuts, who had come into town on Saturday night looking to get laid, marched in. Page and Plant were cracking up in the dressing room after we'd come off, saying how terrible we

25

had been. They had got the same treatment because by now it was completely out of hand. We had to huddle inside the van while the farm boys bounced up and down on it and we didn't escape until two in the morning when it was safe to go home."

Farren later claimed this incident took place at a gig in Exeter (see December 19 entry)

*It's feasible Led Zeppelin undertook a short tour of the North around this period including the following venues:

UNCONFIRMED
Peterlee, England
Argus Butterfly

UNCONFIRMED
Hartlepool, England
Owton Manor Youth Club
Allegedly a young David Coverdale was in attendance at this show

UNCONFIRMED
Hull, England
Mecca Ballroom
Cancelled
In Chris Welch's biography of Peter Grant *The Man Who Led Zeppelin* (Omnibus Press) then Hull university booker Ed Bicknell (later to become manager of Dire Straits) recalled: "On the strength of seeing them at The Marquee I booked them to come up to Hull on a double bill with Jethro Tull who were the headliners. Jethro Tull got £400 and that was big money. They played the Mecca ball-room in Hull as it was too expensive to put them on in the Students Union hall. I still have the contract for the 'New Yardbirds' for £100 and I showed it to Peter years later. Peter had crossed out 'New Yardbirds' and written 'Lead Zeppelin' and singed it Peter Grant and then they cancelled. They didn't do the gig. They went onto America instead.

UNCONFIRMED
London, England
Elephant and Castle
In Chris Welch's biography of Peter Grant *The Man Who Led Zeppelin* (Omnibus Press), *New Musical Express* journalist of the time Keith Altham recalled:

"When Led Zeppelin first started Peter invited me to the Elephant And Castle to see his band playing one of their first gigs. So I went along and they were defeaning. Zeppelin was always loud but in a tiny pub they were over-powering. I lasted a few numbers and my ears were ringing. I couldn't stand anymore so I left. The following morning I got a call from Peter saying, 'Well what do you think of my band?'. So I said, 'To be honest with you Peter I thought they were far too loud. They are brilliant musicians but they sound like four guys put together to make a band.

"Of course every time I saw him after that it was 'Well my band's doing quite well despite what you said about them'. By which time they had become the biggest band in the world. 'Still too loud for you Keith' Peter would say."

Initial plans were made for Led Zeppelin to undertake a six-week US tour commencing in mid-November. They were also invited to return to Scandinavia for a further two-week tour in January. This schedule was then revised for Zeppelin to make their American début in late December, supporting Vanilla Fudge.

Led Zeppelin were also in line to appear in *The Rolling Stones Rock'n'Roll Circus* TV spectacular to be filmed at Intertel Studios, Wembley in December. After listening to an audition tape Mick Jagger felt their sound had too much emphasis on guitar and selected another up-and-coming group, Jethro Tull, instead. The show was never broadcast because the Stones were unhappy with their own performance. It was eventually released on DVD in 2004.

No official records exist for a majority of early Zeppelin gigs during this period and it's possible there were other shows which have yet to be verified.

Saturday November 9 1968
London, England
Roundhouse

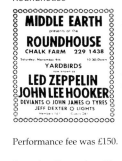

Billed as 'Yardbirds now known as LED ZEPPELIN'. Support from John Lee Hooker, Deviants, John James, Tyres and DJ Jeff Dexter. Admission fee was 16s (@80p in new money) for members and 26s (@£1.30) for guests.

Performance fee was £150.

Saturday November 16
Manchester, England
College of Science & Technology
Performance fee for this show was £225.

Robert Plant recalls: "We tried to get billed as Led Zeppelin, but they always put The Yardbirds on the posters, and they'd drag along the audience who'd come four years before to hear The Yardbirds. Of course we were doing stuff like 'Communication Breakdown'."

Saturday November 23 1968
Sheffield, England
Sheffield University

Friday November 29 1968
Richmond, Surrey, England
Crawdaddy Athletic Club

Tuesday December 10 1968
London, England
Marquee Club

Billed as 'LED ZEPPELIN (nee The Yardbirds)'. Support from Bakerloo Blues Line. Ticket prices: members' tickets 7/6d (35p) available in advance from December 3, non-members 10s (50p) on evening.

The contract for the show (signed on November 27) showed that "The Artiste agrees to appear on

The Concert File

THE VIOLIN BOW

The famous Page showmanship trademark – playing the guitar with a violin bow – dates back to the mid-Sixties. "It was first suggested by a session violinist. It just seemed to make a very interesting sound," was how Page recalled its origin. The session player in question was the father of David McCallum, best known for his role in *The Man From UNCLE*.

Page, however, was not the only guitarist to try this technique around this period. Eddie Phillips of The Creation also adopted this for their live act. Another member of that group, Kenny Picket, later joined the early Zeppelin road crew. The fact that both guitarists had the idea around the same time appears to be a coincidence. Page reckons he did one or two sessions using the violin bow though he can't remember which. He certainly used it on record and on stage with The Yardbirds. It can be heard on The Yardbirds *Little Games* album tracks, 'Tinker Tailor Soldier Sailor' and 'Glimpses'. On stage with The Yardbirds, Page initially used the bow on the lengthy 'I'm A Man'. He later incorporated it into the track 'I'm Confused' (later to be re-titled 'Dazed And Confused'), taking it into the Zeppelin set where it was also used for 'How Many More Times'.

It was 'Dazed And Confused', though, that became the best known vehicle for the violin bow showpiece as the track developed into a marathon performance. By clever use of Echoplex, Page was able to throw out the reverberated sound in a series of power chords as the violin bow struck the strings. This became a trademark of the Zeppelin set – as immortalised in their *Song Remains The Same* movie.

When 'Dazed and Confused' was dropped from the set after 1975, the violin was incorporated into the guitar solo that preceded 'Achilles Last Stand' for the 1977 US tour. It was subsequently used for the solo that introduced 'In The Evening' for the Copenhagen and Knebworth shows in 1979. For these appearances, a laser lighting effect was effectively employed on the bow itself. The 1980 European tour was the only Zeppelin tour where Page did not feature the bow solo.

Post-Zeppelin, Page retained the bow solo for The Firm, where it was incorporated in the *Death Wish II* track, 'The Chase'. The bow effect was used on the same track on the 1988 *Outrider* tour. Page brought the bow back into action again on the 1998 Page & Plant *Walking Into Everywhere* tour during 'How Many More Times.'

In 2002 Page returned to London's Royal Albert Hall for a one off performance of 'Dazed And Confused' at the Teenage Cancer Charity show – repeating the violin bow wielding antics the venue had first witnessed from him 32 years before.

Tuesday 10th December 1968 at a salary of 55% of the gross advance and door takings, less the cost of support group."

It also stated that "The band shall play for a maximum of one hour and 50 minutes. Dance to commence at 7.30pm and terminate at 11.30pm. Salary payable by cash to the group on night of engagement."

Tony Wilson filed their first ever UK live review for *Melody Maker*: "Led Zepplin (sic), the re-grouped Yardbirds, made their Marquee début last week. They are now very much a heavy group, with singer Robert Plant leading and ably holding his own against a powerful backing trio.

Amp troubles didn't help them on this particular occasion but there seemed to be a tendency for too much volume, which inevitably defeats musical definition.

"One of the best numbers of the set was 'Days Of Confusion' (sic) featuring interesting interplay of Plant's voice and Page's guitar on which he used a violin bow, creating an unusual effect. Drummer Bonham is forceful, perhaps too much so, and generally there appears to be a need for Led Zeppelin to cut down on volume a bit."

Friday December 13 1968
Bridge Nr Canterbury, England
Bridge Place Country Club
Billed as 'The Yardbirds'. A flyer for the club advises 'Ladies may come unescorted if they wish' – and many do.!

Monday December 16 1968
Bath, England
Bath Pavilion
Support from Yellow Brick Road. Fee for this show was a mere £75.

Zeppelin were a replacement for Jeff Beck – his name appeared on posters for the show.

Stewart Guy a member of the support act recalled: "This was our big moment in rock history. There we were playing through our set of covers when suddenly our drummer Nick put his pedal through the bass drum. Martin the drummer roadie ran on and changed the drums around. While all this was going on I noticed Jimmy and Robert watching from the wings. Robert looked at me and said 'Does your roadie always come on stage if things go wrong when you are playing?'
'All the time,' I answered. 'Jimmy we must remember that,' he remarked."

Thursday December 19 1968
Exeter, England
Civic Hall
Support from The Deviants and Empty Vessels (who went on to become Wishbone Ash) Performance fee was £125. This was a Christmas Ball for Exeter Art College.

Mick Farren recalled: "We opened for Zep at a few gigs in the West Country. This was before the first album came out. I remember clearly that that incident took place at Exeter Town Hall. The audience had thrown glasses at us and when we went back to the dressing room Planty and Page were having a real good laugh as us. They said 'You must have been awful'. We just replied 'Yeah you wait'. Anyway they went out and didn't get through one number before the barrage came. We knew Planty from doing a bunch of shows with him and his band around Birmingham and the Midlands. We didn't really know Page that much because he hadn't really done the underground club thing"

Friday December 20 1968
London, England
Wood Green, Fishmongers Hall
Billed as 'LED ZEPPELIN (formerly Yardbirds). Support ('By popular demand') from Closed Cell Sponge.

UNCONFIMED
Hanley Stoke On Trent, England
The Place
It's feasible they also made an appearance at this venue around this period. Research in the local Stoke book *The Place* lists the April 14, 1969, date and states "The band never forgot who gave them their first break and returned after a successful tour of the US".

Led Zeppelin

Led Zeppelin performed their first US concert in Denver, Colorado, on Boxing Day 1968. It was one of the few dates Peter Grant did not witness: "I had to ask them to fly out over Christmas and I felt bad about it. But they never queried it at all. They just knew it had to be done. Jimmy was really itching to get there."

Ironically, some of the dates were tentative bookings for Jeff Beck, then also managed by Peter Grant.

Coming off the back of the reputation The Yardbirds had built on the US college circuit, Grant hoped Jimmy Page's name would assist in establishing his new act – that and the strategic feeding of white label advance copies of their début album to key FM rock stations. The hunch more than paid off.

Fighting off the January blizzards, the group quickly took the opportunity to impress. Residencies at the Whisky-A-Go-Go and Bill Graham's Fillmore West and supporting fellow Atlantic acts Vanilla Fudge and Iron Butterfly had an immediate impact on the American audiences.

This was the first visit to America for both Robert Plant and John Bonham, as Plant recalls: "We were just babies really and we just couldn't believe the scene over there. Vanilla Fudge were great to us – I'll never forget it. They were great musicians with a very confident delivery. They encouraged us to open it up and

Bonzo became good friends with Carmine Appice."

Peter Grant flew over in time for their dates at the Fillmore West and was very pleased with progress. "I told them to go over there and make every performance something to remember and that's exactly what they were doing!" The début *Led Zeppelin* album was issued on January 17. It entered the *Billboard* chart at number 99, a humble beginning for what would quickly become the most talked-about album of 1969.

Their average fee for this opening US tour was around $1,500 a night. For one show they reputedly went on for just $320. "The Yardbirds had been getting $2,500 a night," recalled Grant, "but people like Bill Graham had faith in us and so too did the kids who saw it."

What they saw was a developing act that now incorporated numbers like Spirit's 'Fresh Garbage'. The 'The How Many More Times' finale was extended as on the first album with Albert Lee's 'The Hunter'. They even threw in a version of The Yardbirds' 'For Your Love' as the crowds began to call them back for more.

The tour included a two-night stint at the Fillmore East supporting Iron Butterfly and by then the reaction for Zeppelin easily outshone the headline act. Grant: "Iron Butterfly were very despondent about following us on stage. I knew that we had got a foothold – we were making an impression."

As they returned to England, their first album had climbed into the *Billboard* Top 40 where it would continue to ascend. But there were distinct signs that not everybody was enamoured of their instant success. John Mendelsohn, reviewing the album in the influential *Rolling Stone* magazine, claimed: "If they are to fill the void created by the demise of Cream, they will have to find a producer, an editor and some material worthy of their collective talents." It was to be the beginning of a long running battle between Zep and the US press, notably *Rolling Stone*. As Page commented:

"They saw this blast of publicity and heard all about the money being hyped and thought we were a capitalist group. After that review we became very wary of the press. We avoided them and perhaps they avoided us. In the end it was down to our live shows that our reputation spread."

Thursday December 26 1968
Denver, Colorado
Denver Auditorium

For their first US performance, Zeppelin opened the show for Vanilla Fudge. Spirit were also on the bill. Zeppelin's name did not even feature on advertisements.

"Rock Concert Is Real Groovy" read the headline in the *Rocky Mountain News* that provided their first Stateside review. Thomas MacCluskey reported: "The concert was cranked off by another heavy, the Led Zeppelin. Blues orientated (although not a blues band), hyped electric, the full routine in mainstream rock – done powerfully, gutsily, unifiedly, inventively and swingingly (by the end of their set).

"Singer Robert Plant – a cut above average in style, but no special appeal in sound. Guitarist Jimmy Page of Yardbirds fame – exceptionally fine. Used a violin bow on the guitar strings in a couple of tunes with resultant interesting, well integrated effects.

"Bassist John Paul Jones – solid, involved, contributing. John Bonham – a very effective group drummer, but uninventive, unsubtle and unclimactic in an uneventful solo."

Friday December 27 1968
Seattle, Washington
Center Arena

Page recalls: "In Seattle, Portland and those places where we weren't ever billed, we just walked out

and said 'Well actually, we're Led Zeppelin'. You can imagine the reaction of the crowd. They were quite warm receptions actually, but nothing like what happened later."

Saturday December 28 1968
Vancouver, Canada
Pacific Coliseum

Again unbilled support to Vanilla Fudge

Tuesday December 29 1968
Portland, Oregon

After the Portland show the band spent New Year's Eve driving through blizzards in an attempt to reach Seattle Airport to catch a flight to Los Angeles. When they finally arrived the airport was closed and to make matters worse, Bonzo and Robert were refused drinks at the airport bar because they are under-age.

Monday December 30 1068
Spokane, Washington
Kennedy Pavilion
Gonzaga University Gymnasium

Set included: Train Kept A Rollin'/I Can't Quit

Led Zeppelin

You/As Long As I Have You (inc. Fresh Garbage – Shake- Mockingbird)/Dazed And Confused/ White Summer/How Many More Times (inc. The Hunter)/Pat's Delight.

Elements of The Yardbirds' set were retained on these early US dates. 'Train Kept A Rollin'' flowed effortlessly into Willie Dixon's 'I Can't Quit You'. The first album had not yet been released and a variety of covers fleshed out the performance. Garnet Mimms' 'As Long As I Have You' was a perfect vehicle for the band to include some familiar blues references, such as Spirit's 'Fresh Garbage' and Otis Redding's 'Shake'. Tonight's medley even included the traditional lullaby and recent soul hit 'Hush Little Baby … Papa's Gonna Buy You A Mockingbird'.

The cold weather was noted by Plant: "You won't believe this, but I don't think either ourselves or the equipment is quite used to the temperature. It's taken about three hours of gas stoves under the equipment before we can ever get it together. Let's see if we can keep things going."

Jimmy, Robert and Bonzo had spent their first three days in America celebrating Christmas in sunny Los Angeles and the sudden climate change had a damaging effect. Plant: "We're all dying. I didn't know you got this 'flu thing here!"

'Dazed And Confused' included Jimmy's trade-mark violin bow solo (alongside 'How Many More Times'). The set also featured a Bonham drum solo entitled 'Pat's Delight'. Plant: "This is one for the women back overseas, waiting for their men to return." Pat was John Bonham's wife.

The group received a lukewarm reception but the majority of the audience had come to see Vanilla Fudge.

Bootleg CD References: *Gonzaga '68* (Capricorn), *Lifetime Guarantee* (Empress Valley), *Live At Gonzaga 1968* (Zep)

Thursday January 2 1969
Los Angeles, California
Whisky A Go-Go

Billed as 'LED ZEPPELIN featuring: Jimmy Page formerly of The Yardbirds'.

Four day stint with Alice Cooper.

Led Zeppelin's first appearance in the US city that would become almost their second home was

somewhat inauspicious. They were scheduled to play two sets each evening, but Jimmy had a fever. Page: "We got to Los Angeles and I was really, really ill. In fact, the doctor said I was insane to do the set. The first night I did it I had a temperature of over 104, but he'd given me all the shots and things so I was able to make it. We managed to finish the whole engagement without letting the guy down, but of course he docked us money because we only did one long set each night, we couldn't do two. It's not the greatest paying job in the world anyway, and when he knocked money off, we were all really down about that, as you can imagine. That was our first set of dates."

Alice Cooper recalled: "We had about 100 people there as nobody had heard of either of us. We got there and I said, 'Who wants to open? I know we'll flip a coin. You open tonight and I'll open tomorrow night.'"

Friday January 3 1969
Los Angeles, California
Whisky A Go-Go

Saturday January 4 1969
Los Angeles, California
Whisky A Go-Go

Sunday January 5 1969
Los Angeles, California
Whisky A Go-Go

Thursday January 9 1969
San Francisco, California
Fillmore West

Country Joe & The Fish headlined these four Fillmore shows with Led Zeppelin and Taj Mahal as support. Zeppelin performed two sets each evening.

Page recalls: "We got to San Francisco and I was feeling better and everyone else in the group was happy to see me better and we really started to play from that point on. We were playing all right before, but from that point it was really gelling more. The rest of the boys had gotten more accustomed to the American audiences; they had never been to America before, and they were able to gauge things a little better. They felt they could relax more on stage. So, right there is when it started happening. From then on we could see that there was some sort of reaction to us, but still, nobody ever expected it to get into a really big thing."

Peter Grant: "San Francisco was the first show that Jimmy played the Les Paul guitar on stage. He was playing a Fender before that. He'd had it for years, from being with The Yardbirds. There was something wrong with the pick-ups, and I remember every night he was there with the soldering iron, soldering the guitar."

Bootleg CD References: *Twinight* (Immigrant), *Whole Lotta For Your Love* (Pirate)

Friday January 10 1069
San Francisco, California
Fillmore West

Set 1: Train Kept A Rollin'/I Can't Quit You/As Long As I Have You (inc. Fresh Garbage – Shake)/Dazed And Confused/How Many More Times (inc. Dream Lover – The Hunter).

Set 2: White Summer – Black Mountain Side/Killing Floor/You Shook Me/Pat's Delight/Babe I'm Gonna Leave You/Communication Breakdown/For Your Love.

These Fillmore shows were the longest that Zeppelin had played to date and provided ample scope for experimentation. 'Babe, I'm Gonna Leave You' from the as yet unreleased début album and 'Killing Floor' were both now introduced into the set. 'Killing Floor' rapidly developed into 'The Lemon Song' an amalgamation of Chester Burnett's orignal lyrics and Page's riffs that would later be recorded for the second album.

The old Yardbirds' favourite 'For Your Love' was performed as a rare extra encore and introduced by Plant as "A thing Keith Relf had something to do with. Do you remember him? Works for Hammersmith Council now!"

Bootleg CD Reference: *For Your Love* (Silver Rarities), *Live Adventures At The Fillmore West* (Wendy), *Syonen Zep* (Akashic)

Saturday January 11 1969
San Francisco,
California
Fillmore West

Set 1: Train Kept A Rollin'/I Can't Quit You/Dazed And Confused/ You Shook Me/How Many More Times.

An excellent show. Robert introduced 'I Can't Quit You Baby' (a Willie Dixon song) as "An Otis Rush number that's on this album that's out in a couple of weeks." Jimmy experienced several guitar problems which caused long delays leading Robert to request, "Has anybody got a Les Paul? Jeff who? Tell him to bring it here then!"

Despite technical difficulties, this show highlighted their growing confidence. 'Dazed And Confused' included alternate lyrics and 'How Many More Times' was performed with the original Howling Wolf 'How Many More Years' lyrics.

The audiences at the Fillmore really took Zeppelin to their hearts and the band can felt it. Plant: "I tell you what! This is the third night and we've decided that we're gonna come and live here, 'cos you're so nice! If we don't make it, then the police in England would rather we'd stay there!"

Bootleg CD References: *Psycho Au Go Go* (Led Note), *Birth Of The Gods* (Balboas), *Anyone Got A Les Paul?* (Equinox)

Sunday January 12 1969
San Francisco, California
Fillmore West

Sets included: As Long As I Have You (inc. Mockingbird – Fresh Garbage)/I Can't Quit You/Dazed And Confused/Babe, I'm Gonna Leave You/Communication Breakdown/You Shook Me/White Summer – Black Mountain Side/Train Kept A Rollin'/Pat's Delight/How Many More Times (Inc. The Hunter)/Killing Floor.

Page: "We got standing ovations for each set for the four nights at the Fillmore West. It was really unbelievable."

Bootelg CD Reference: *California 1969* (Lemon Song)

Monday January 13 1969
San Diego, California
Fox Theatre

Wednesday January 15 1969
Iowa City, Iowa
University Of Iowa Memorial Union

Support from The Mother Blues.

The *Daily Iowan* reported under the headline "Led Zeppelin Replaces Basie": "Led Zeppelin, a rock instrumental and vocal group made up of four young English musicians will give a concert at the Universiy of Iowa. The appearance at 8pm wll be the group's first concert on an American college campus. The Led Zeppelin concert will take the place of the programme scheduled by Count Basie which has been cancelled."

During 'I Can't Quit You Baby' the show was interrupted by the Campus security removing a member of the audience who had not paid for his ticket. Plant then joked with the audience to pass a hat around to collect his bail.

Thursday January 16 1969
New Orleans, Louisiana

Friday January 17 1969
Detroit, Michigan
The Grande Ballroom
The band headlined The Grande Ballroom billed erroneously as 'Led Zeptlin'.

Linn County and Lawrence Blues Band were support.

Saturday January 18 1969
Detroit, Michigan
The Grande Ballroom
Support from Target.

Page: "It felt like a vacuum and we'd arrived to fill it. You could feel something happening … first this row, then that row. It was like a tornado, and it went rolling across the country."

Sunday January 19 1969
Detroit, Michigan
The Grande Ballroom
Support from Wind.

Monday January 20 1969
Wheaton, Maryland
Wheaton Youth Centre
On this date the band played for around 100 people for a fee of $250

Tuesday January 21 1969
Sewickley Pittsburgh, Pennsylvania
Hunt Armory
Billed as The Yardbirds for possibly the last time

Thursday January 23 1969
Boston, Massachusetts
Boston Tea Party
Set included: Train Kept A Rollin'/I Can't Quit You/As Long As I Have You (inc. Fresh Garbage – Bags Groove)/Dazed And Confused/You Shook Me.

Support from The Raven. This venue was once a house of worship and is now a condominium complex with a 7-11 convenience store at the front of the building.

Equipment problems plagued the first night in Boston. While Page attempted to sort out his guitar after 'Train Kept A Rollin'' Plant informed the audience: "It's great to be in Boston. According to

---

THE COMMUNICATION BREAKDOWN PROMO FILM

The earliest known film footage of Led Zeppelin is what appears to be a black and white promo film cut for 'Communication Breakdown'. A low budget, single camera affair, it captured the group in late 1968 or early 1969. They were still using the Rickenbacker amplifiers left over from The Yardbirds. The camera panned in on them in psychedelic fashion as they lip synced to the track. Bonzo could be seen indulging in some intricate stick twirling and Page joined in on backing vocals.

The film was first seen on Japanese TV in the Eighties, but its origin is unknown. It appears to have been shot before their one-off BBC *How Late It Is* appearance in March 1969, which is known to have been long since wiped from the archives. This promo film of 'Communcication Breakdown' differs from the other mimed footage of the track filmed for Swedish TV and used by Page on the official DVD.

Jimmy it's one of the best places he's ever played! I think, right now, in the shops there's an album called *Led Zeppelin*. I don't know whether it's out here yet. Is it out? You see, in one place it comes out one day and another place three weeks later. On this album we've tried to do a cross section of everything we've got into and we've included some blues because that's where it all comes from!"

Plant then introduced 'I Can't Quit You' but Page was still not ready, so Bonzo and Jones provided a rhythmic interlude. When they finally start the song, Plant's initial screams were mimicked perfectly by feedback, much to the amusement of the crowd.

Despite the sound problems this Boston debut was indication of the success to follow. Plant: "We've only been here for about four weeks and we never expected a reception like this. It's been a gas!"

Bootleg CD References: *Whiskey & Tea Party* (Ocean Recording), *Complete Boston Tea Party* (Arms), *Boston After Dark* (Empress Valley)

Friday January 24 1969
Boston, Massachusetts
Boston Tea Party

"After The Yardbirds Comes Led Zeppelin" – Ben Blummenberg for *Boston After Dark* analysed Zeppelin's style: "Rhythm changes abruptly, time patterns change abruptly, volume levels change abruptly, yet melodic lines and chord skeletons manage to merge kaleidoscopically as each member of the band feeds one another and in turn plays off the ideas thrown out. The entire approach is very loose and very improvisational. The result is surprising; intricacy develops out of a form that is usually considered to be quite simple. Yet the basic power is never lost.

"I expect the Led Zeppelin to be flying high for some time. They and the Jeff Beck Group are to rock what Formula One cars are to road racing. Their raw power is compelling and hypnotic while their complexity makes repeated exposure a pleasure. The LZ varies the arrangements of the same song on successive nights quite widely. As Jimmy Page said to me: 'If we can't do it live, we won't do it.' That idea hits me just right, as does the entire Led Zeppelin from stern to stern."

Saturday January 25 1969
Boston, Massachusetts
Boston Tea Party

"A Mountain Of Hard Rock," reported *Vibrations magazine*. "Page's group live is the same as the Beck Group in form but not in feeling. There is a mountain of hard rock and the old Yardbirds' Gothic Cathedral Theatre going up on the stage and the music comes out above the suspense the Zeppelin people are creating by their costume and motions. Zeppelin isn't simplifying; they play very complicated music. In an important way, Zeppelin is a kind of revenge for the declining years of The Yardbirds.

"It's hard to tell how much Beck has influenced Page and vice versa. Page plays dirty rock (close to blues) and Beck plays clean blues (close to rock). At one point, dirty rock and clean blues hold hands."

Sunday January 26 1969
Boston, Massachusetts
Boston Tea Party

Set included: Train Kept A Rollin'/I Can't Quit You/Killing Floor (Inc. The Lemon Song)/Dazed And Confused (inc. Shapes Of Things)/You

LED ZEPPELIN
THE RAVEN
JANUARY 23, 24, 25
THE BOSTON TEA PARTY
53 BERKELEY ST. 338-7026 LIGHTS BY THE ROAD

Tickets: Krackerjacks, Headquarters East, Bottega 2 George's Folly

that put everything into focus – was one that we played on our first American tour at the Boston Tea Party. We'd played our usual one-hour set, using all the material from the first album and Page's 'White Summer' guitar piece and, by the end, the audience just wouldn't let us off the stage.

"It was in such a state that we had to start throwing ideas around – just thinking of songs that we might all know or some of us knew a part of, and work it from there. So we'd go back on and play things like 'I Saw Her Standing There' and 'Please Please Me' – old Beatles favourites. I mean, just anything that would come into our head, and the response was quite amazing.

"There were kids actually bashing their heads against the stage – I've never seen that at a gig before or since, and when we finally left the stage we'd played for four and a half hours. Peter was absolutely ecstatic. He was crying and hugging us all. You know … with this huge grizzly bear hug. I suppose it was then that we realised just what Led Zeppelin was going to become."

A 90-minute tape of this show has surfaced – there are rumours that a complete tape exists but nothing has surfaced to date.

Bootleg CD References: *Tight But Loose* (Tarantura), *Killing Floor* (Cobla) *Whiskey & Tea Party* (Ocean Recording), *Filmore East* (Mad dogs)

Shook Me/Communication Breakdown/White Summer – Black Mountain Side/Babe I'm Gonna Leave You/Pat's Delight/How Many More Times (Inc. For Your Love)/Long Tall Sally/Something Else/C'mon Everybody/I Saw Her Standing There/Please Please Me/Roll Over Beethoven/Johnny B. Goode and others

This was the legendary four and a half hour show – one of the longest Zeppelin performances ever.

'Dazed And Confused' included a passage from 'Shapes Of Things', the old Yardbirds' number and Jimmy used the violin bow for another Yardbirds' song, 'For Your Love', during 'How Many More Times'.

John Paul Jones recalled the show: "As far as I'm concerned, the key Led Zeppelin gig – the one

Wednesday January 29 1969
Philadelphia, Pennsylvania
Electric Factory

Friday January 31 1969
New York, New York
Fillmore East
Set: Train Kept A Rollin'/I Can't Quit You/Dazed And Confused/Pat's Delight/How Many More Times (Inc. The Hunter)/You Shook Me/Communication Breakdown.

For both the New York dates, Porter's Popular Preachers opened the event, then Zeppelin took the stage prior to the headliners Iron Butterfly.

Birmingham band, The Move, were originally billed as the opening act, but dropped out. There were two shows each night, an early and a late show (8pm & 11.30pm). Psychedelic imagery was provided on a huge backdrop by the Joshua Light Show.

Promoter Bill Graham introduced the band: "Please welcome, from England, LED ZEPPELIN". A frantic performance earned two encores.

Under the headline: "Led Zeppelin Fly High – Iron Butterfly, Too". Fred Kirby reported for the influential trade magazine *Billboard*: "Led Zeppelin landed at Fillmore East and in the first of four weekend shows, the British quartet showed it could develop into the next big super group. Page, a former member of The Yardbirds, ranks with the top pop guitarists in the world and his performance substantiated his reputation. Plant is a blues-style screamer and wailer, whose vocalizing was wild. Iron Butterfly had a tough assignment in following Led Zeppelin."

Iron Butterfly waited a full 45 minutes before taking the stage after Zeppelin's frenzy. Hugh Jones of the Zep fanzine *Proximity* recalled: "When Iron Butterfly finally appeared it was anticlimactic to say the least. That night belonged to Led Zeppelin, and though they returned to the Fillmore in May and played even better, it was that January début that really blew people away, and made New York a 'Zeppelin Town' right from day one."

Peter Grant: "When Iron Butterfly's management found out Zeppelin were second on the bill, they wanted them off. They didn't want them near them! And they were right! Zeppelin did a fantastic set. The audience was still going 'Zeppelin, Zeppelin … ' when Iron Butterfly had started ed their set! Good band, not a bad band … but no match for Zeppelin."

Bootleg CD References: *Grande Ball* (Missing Link), *Psychedelic Raw Blues* (Immigrant), *New York In The Wind* (Empress Valley)

Saturday February 1 1969
New York, New York
Fillmore East
Two shows 8pm and 11.30
Set included: White Summer – Black Mountain Side/Train Kept A Rollin'/I Can't Quit You/Pat's Delight/How Many More Times (inc. The Hunter)/Communication Breakdown.

After Bill Graham's customary introduction, Plant made an announcement: "We're sorry about the delay but because we're all a bit stupid, we forgot the bass player's guitar! Would you believe that! So we're gonna open up without the bass player. We're gonna feature Jimmy Page. This is a thing that was very popular when he was with The Yardbirds."

An extended 'White Summer' followed until John Paul Jones was ready and they resumed with 'Train Kept A Rollin'.

A cry from the audience of 'To Hell With The Butterfly!' was echoed by many in attendance.

With only limited time available, Bonham's drum solo was surprisingly retrained. The show ended with a high speed version of 'Communication Breakdown' during which Plant split his trousers.

Bootleg CD References: *The Legendary Fillmore Tapes Vol. 1* (Savage Beast Music), *New York In The Wind* (Empress Valley)

Sunday February 2 1969
Toronto, Canada
Rock Pile
Set 1: Train Kept A Rollin'/I Can't Quit You/Dazed And Confused/You Shook Me/Killing Floor/How Many More Times (inc. Fever – The Hunter – Money).

Billed as 'Led Zeppelin featuring Jimmy Page'.

Support from Tee Garden and Van Winkle. Lights by Catharsis. Coincidentally Iron Butterfly were in Toronto on the same night playing in Toronto at the Massey Hall. Two sets were played.

Journalist Ritchie Yorke introduced the show: "Led Zeppelin is going to be doing two sets tonight … in between we've got Tee Garden and Van Winkle. Next Friday and Saturday night – Albert King, don't forget and B.B. King at Massey Hall on February 14 … but right now … their first Canadian appearance, and there's going to be a lot more of them … Atlantic recording stars – LED ZEPPELIN!"

'How Many More Times' included excerpts of the classics 'Fever' and 'Money'.

"Led Zeppelin: Fast becoming Cream of crop" read the headline in *The Globe and Mail*. Ritchie Yorke reported: "It was Page's night. One visual image easily stood out. It was the sight of Led Zeppelin's hero-worshipped guitarist, resplendent in avocado velvet suit, bent over as if in agony to the audience, his fingers working like a touch-typist's, his foot thumping like a kangaroo's tail, the sounds as clear and as piercing as a bedside phone in the stillness of 3am.

"Advance airplay and reviews of the début Led Zeppelin album (to be released on Atlantic shortly) brought over 1,200 people to the Rock Pile. They expected a lot, and few were disappointed."

In his enthusiasm Yorke confused the band personnel: "Bonham is not Jack Bruce but, likewise, he's on the right road. Jones is a fine drummer

with precision timing but Ginger Baker had that scene all wrapped up.

"Page came off as the finest group guitarist to emerge since Clapton. His spotlighted work, including the riffs with the violin bow, was executed expertly, without pomp or pretension. Singer Plant is from the English blues school – hard, angry, defiant, gutsy. He could well develop into one of the big name group singers of the year."

Bootleg CD References: *Absolutely Gems* (Sanctuary), *The Rock Pile Canada* 2/2/69 (Totonka)

Monday February 3, Tuesday February 4, Wednesday February 5 & Thursday February 6
Steve Paul's Scene Club, New York
CANCELLED

Billed as 'Jimmy Paige and England's most exciting new group'. All four of these shows were cancelled when John Bonham went back to England because his son Jason had been taken ill. The gigs were not rescheduled.

Friday February 7 1969
Chicago, Illinois
Kinetic Playground

This venue was demolished in November 2003.

Billed as Led Zepelin(sic) for their first shows in the windy city on a shared bill with Vanilla Fudge and Jethro Tull.

Peter Grant recalled: "We started at the Play-

ground at $7,500 and ended up at the end of the year on $12,500 a night. At that place some people tried to lay some amps on us. Jimmy told Richard to tell them we didn't like them but what he had us do was connect the new speakers into his old Orange and Fender gear! Typical Led Wallet!

"I remember we caught a guy fiddling there. Ahmet was there and I went out front to see what the crowds were like. The box office was on a corner. This guy was taking $5 from the guys in the queue. So I took my rings off, joined the line and as it came for my turn I shouted 'Gotcha!' and took him back to the dressing room and had him empty his pockets and took every last dime and nickel from him. He didn't do it again."

Saturday February 8 1969
Chicago, Illinois
Kinetic Playground

Monday February 10 1969
Memphis, Tennessee
State University
While in Memphis Page attempted to book them into the legendary Sun Records Studios

for a recording session but the studio was over-booked.

Friday February 14 1969
Sunny Isles Beach Miami, Florida
Thee Image Club
Set 1: Train Kept A Rollin'/I Can't Quit You/Dazed And Confused/Killing Floor (inc. The Lemon Song – Needle Blues)/Babe I'm Gonna Leave You (inc. Reflections On My Mind)/How Many More Times (inc. Roll Over Beethoven)
Set 2 includes: White Summer – Black Mountain Side)/As Long As I Have You (inc. Fresh Garbage – Bags Groove – Mockingbird)/You Shook Me/Pat's Delight.

The Thee Image was formerly a 32-lane bowling alley converted in to a rock venue. It is now a supermarket.
Bootleg CD References: *Thee Image Club* (Rag Doll Music), *Reflections On My Mind* (Image Quality), *Snowblind* (Scorpio), *Yellow Zeppelin* (Tarantura)

Saturday February 15 1969
Sunny Isles Beach Miami, Florida
Thee Image Club
Page: "I think that what did it for us was the stage thing. We were unknown, we did our number and the word got out that we were worth seeing. We tried as hard as we could on stage and it worked."

GUEST APPEARANCE
Monday February 24 1969
Wolverhampton, England
LayFayette Club
In his book *Bonham On Bonham*, John's brother Mick Bonham revealed that on this night a special party was staged for John Bonham's wife Pat's 21st birthday – all of the group were in attendance and took to the stage as the highlight of the evening.

March & April 1969 were among the most intensive months of the group's 1969 schedule and, in retrospect, possibly the most interesting. In March, between low key club dates such as The Hornsey Wood Tavern, they recorded two separate BBC sessions. These broadcasts for John Peel's *Top Gear* and Alexis Korner's *R&B Show* did much to spread the word on this up-and-coming new combo. On March 13 they flew to Scandinavia for a series of dates that ended with the recording of a 35-minute TV special for Danish TV (broadcast in England some 21 years later on BBC 2).

For a band known for shunning TV, this month saw them embracing the medium as they never would again. There were no less than four other film commitments in this period – TV mimed spots for the Swedish and German TV networks plus an appearance on the new BBC 2 series *How Late It Is,* where they played 'Communication Breakdown', and a performance of 'Dazed and Confused' filmed in a warehouse studio in Staines, Surrey, and seen later in the movie *Super-show.*

These early filmed sessions were part of Peter Grant's strategy to build awareness of the group (another TV appearance took place in June in Paris) but ultimately his dissatisfaction with the medium would lead him to make Zeppelin unavailable for TV again. "TV just doesn't do justice to our sound," was Grant's curt reply to subsequent offers of TV work, including offers from *The Tom Jones Show* and *Top Of The Pops.*

In stark contrast to the excitement of their American dates, late March and early April saw them complete a further round of low key club one-nighters in the UK, including London's Marquee and the Toby Jug in Tolworth. Again details from these shows remain somewhat sketchy .

There was still some way to go in building awareness at home. However, the headline greeting readers of Chris Welch's *Melody Maker* review

The Concert File

Led Zeppelin

of the first album (which received a belated UK release in late March) was a pointer to greater acceptance ahead. "Jimmy Page Triumphs," it proclaimed. "Led Zeppelin is a gas."

Saturday March 1 1969
Plymouth, England
Van Dike Club

Monday March 3 1969
London, England
Playhouse Theatre
RADIO ONE SESSION

BBC recording between 2pm and 6pm. Producer: Bernie Andrews: engineer: Pete Ritzema; tape operator: Bob Conduct. Broadcast date: Sunday March 23 on John Peel's *Top Gear* between 3pm and 5pm (also in session on the show are The Moody Blues, Deep Purple & Free). Tracks recorded: Communication Breakdown/Dazed And Confused/You Shook Me/I Can't Quit You (inc. Nineteen Years Old).

The début radio session for the BBC. Although Peter Grant was not keen on presenting his new act on TV, radio was more appealing: "I knew Bernie Andrews and I reckoned I could handle the BBC quite easily and *Top Gear* was the only outlet for our sort of artist."

This session was slotted in during a hectic round of UK one-night stands and was the first opportunity for home listeners to hear the material that would appear on the Led Zeppelin début album – then already issued in the US but due to be released in the UK at the end of the month. The importance of these BBC sessions cannot be overstated. They provided key exposure for the group and greatly enhanced their reputation.

This trial broadcast was passed unanimously by the BBC audition panel. "They were very loud but very good," remembers Andrews. Tape op Bob Conduct remembers the Playhouse as being ideal for recording loud groups … "because the irregular shape of the converted theatre with all its velvet upholstered seating absorbed a lot of volume even when it was empty."

The arrangements of the songs that Zeppelin

42

present on the radio were more in keeping with their live act than their studio counterparts. The take of 'You Shook Me' featured John Paul Jones on organ and a very different sounding Page solo; 'Communication Breakdown' contained an invigorating Page wah-wah funk section and 'I Can't Quit You' found Plant leading into the old blues standard 'Nineteen Years Old'. Only 'Dazed And Confused' was slightly restricted by the time allowed, clocking in at around six minutes 37 seconds in an arrangement similar to the début album.

The recordings of You Shook Me, I Can't Quit You Baby and Dazed And Confused would later be officially released on the 1997 BBC *Sessions* CD.
Bootleg CD references: *A Secret History* (Scorpio), BBC (LSD), *Complete BBC Classics* (Immigrant)

Wednesday March 5 1969
Cardiff, Wales
The Top Rank
A dress code requirement of shirt, tie and jacket led to a restricted attendance at this show. Page: "It was at one of those lush, chandelier ballrooms and at first they wouldn't let the group in because they didn't have ties. Robert Plant and John Bonham had to call the manager to get in. If it had been me I wouldn't have had anything to do with it. Then, there was a bloke who had come miles to see us and they wouldn't let him in because he was wearing a cravat. Robert got him in."

This incident remained a vivid memory for Plant as six years' later at the Earl's Court May 24 show he made reference to it: "Well we couldn't play in Cardiff – ah, Cardiff, does that ring a bell? When we played at the Locarno (sic), the equipment was set up and they wouldn't let us through the door because we didn't have a tie on – those were the days."

The gig itself was not without other problems. Page: "We'd been told that we'd have to do an exact 45-minute

spot, and if we went a minute over that was it. So we cut it down and when we started the last number, if we'd been allowed to complete it, it would have over-run by six minutes. They turned on the revolving stage as we were playing and the DJ came round. The audience was whistling and booing. It was a terrible shame because all they usually get in those places are Mickey Mouse groups and I'd played Cardiff before with The Yardbirds and they were great audiences. That sort of thing is just not fair to people who come along to see you. There would be more trouble in places like that if you played an encore than if you went off stage early. We won't be doing any more of them."

Friday March 7 1969
London, England
Bluesville 69 Club, 'The Hornsy Wood Tavern'
Advertised as Led Zeppelin – Back From Their Sensational American Tour!

Thursday March 13 1969
Leicester, England
De Montfort Hall Leicester University
Billed as 'Pyjama Dance' as a part of the University's Rag Week celebrations.

Zeppelin shared equal billing with Ferris Wheel and Decoys – admission 12 shillings (60p).

Fan David Hope researched this show and discovered that around 300 were in attendance but many stayed in the bar area, with only around 60 fans clustered around the stage. After the set the band signed autographs and mingled with the audience.

Friday March 14 1969
Stockholm, Sweden
Swedish TV
TV APPEARANCE
The start of a very busy day.

During the afternoon the band went into the local TV recording studio to promote their album. They mimed to 'Communication Breakdown' with John Bonham using the double Ludwig set up for this TV spot, one of the rare occasions he can be seen playing this type of kit. The footage was discovered in 1999 and acquired by Page, first for use as a CDROM bonus on the *Early Days Best Of Led Zeppelin Vol One* CD in 2000 and later as an extra item on the official DVD.

Visual References: *Early Days The Best Of Led Zeppelin Vol One* (Atlantic) – *DVD* (Warner Music Vision)

Friday March 14 1969
Stockholm, Sweden
Konserthuset
Set : Train Kept A Rollin'/I Got To Move/I Can't Quit You Baby/Dazed And Confused/White Summer- Black Mountain Side/How Many More Times

Shared billing with Country Joe & The Fish. This show took place at 7.30pm.

After the opening number Robert led the group into the rarely played 'I Got To Move' by Otis Rush because Jimmy broke a string. They performed the song without him. Part of this show was broadcast on Swedish radio.

Bootleg CD reference: *Missing Links* (The Diagrams Of Led Zeppelin), *Kicks* (Tarantura), *Stockholm* (Kaleidscopic), *Hampton Kicks* (House Of Elrond)

Friday March 14 1969
Uppsala, Sweden
Uppsala University Lecture Hall
Set included: Train Kept A Rollin'/I Can't Quit You Baby /Dazed And Confused/You Shook Me/White Summer/Black Mountain Side/Babe I'm Gonna Leave You/How Many More Times.

They then moved on to their second show of the night at the University Hall, arriving on stage around 11pm. Again with Country Joe & The Fish.

Saturday March 15 1969

Gladsaxe, Denmark
Teens Clubs Box 45

Set included: Train Kept A Rollin'/I Cant Quite You Baby/As Long As I Have You (incl Bags Groove- Fresh Garbage)/You Shook Me/Comminicaiton Breakdown

Support from The Ox and Uffe Sylvesters Badekat. Ticket price 10dr.

Bootleg CD reference: *Short Cuts* (Image Quality), *Rock Of Ages* (The Diagrams Of Led Zeppelin), *Led Zeppelin Is A Gas* (Empress Valley)

Saturday March 15 1969

Norregard, Denmark
Brondby Pop Club Norregardhallen

Set Included: Train Kept A Rollin'/I Can't Quite You Baby/Dazed And Confused/You Shook Me/White Summer-Black Mountain Side/Pat's Delight/Babe I'm Gonna Leave You/How Many More Times

Support from Keef Hartley Blues Band, Ham and a Swedish band Made In Sweden. Ticket price 4-10DKr.

This concert was reviewed in *Sydsvenska Dagbladet Snallposten* (the south Swedish daily newspaper) under the headline "The Supergroup in a gymnasium. Led Zeppelin attract a huge audience". The reviewer was not entirely complimentary about Jimmy: "Page has done his studies on Hendrix but has concentrated too much on sounding tricky. It's not funny listening to a guitarist who is standing there stroking the strings with a violin bow, not letting the amplifier rest for a second. Page has got talent but he doesn't reach the same class as Peter Green."

Bootleg CD Reference: *Denmark '69* (Deep), *Led Zeppelin Is A Gas* (Empress Valley), *Rock Of Ages* (The Diagrams Of Led Zeppelin)

Sunday March 16 1969

Copenhagen, Denmark
Tivolis Koncertsal, 'Super Sesssion'

Two performances at 4PM and 7PM. Support for both shows was Country Joe & The Fish and The Keef Hartley Blues Band. Attendance 1,700.

Journalist Anne Bjorndal: "The best of the Danish shows that I attended was the second Tivoli concert. The afternoon show was a little subdued but the evening show was really outstanding. The venue was quite a formal setting with rows of chairs."

Monday March 17 1969

Gladsaxe, Copenhagen, Denmark
TV Byen/Danmarks Radio/Danish
Broadcasting Corperation
TV RECORDING

Set: Communication Breakdown/Dazed And Confused/Babe I'm Gonna Leave You/How Many More Times (Incl The Hunter)

An afternoon appearance recorded for the Danish TV network. The group performed on a small stage surrounded by a polite audience. Filmed in black and white and produced by Edmont Jenson for the Denmark Radio network. This was first aired on May 19, 1969. Some 21 years later it was dusted down by the BBC and clips were used for their *Arena Heavy Metal* documentary and then in full for a one-off broadcast on January 1 1990.

Journalist Anne Bjorndal recalled: "By now they had built up quite a following in Denmark so some of the audience was made up of fans and friends who had seen them on previous dates. We all trooped over to the TV town of Gladsaxe – the entire recording took about an hour and a half including setting up the stage and lighting. Once in front of the cameras they really went for it."

Bootleg CD References: *Danish TV* (Cobra Standard), *Danish TV & Studio Sessions* (Watch Tower), *Denmark '69 (Deep)*

Visual References: Official *Led Zeppelin* 2003 DVD (Warner Vision), *Unofficial Early Visions* DVD (Celebration)

Wednesday March 19 1969

London, England
Maida Vale Studio, Delaware Road
WORLD SERVICE RADIO SESSION

BBC recording between 5.30pm and 9pm. Broadcast date: Monday April 14 on the BBC World Service show *Rhythm And Blues* (later re-titled *Blues Is Where You Hear It*). Tracks recorded: I Can't Quit You/You Shook Me/Sunshine Woman.

Producer Jeff Griffin offerred this spot, a blues showcase for a World Service programme hosted by Alexis Korner, on the strength of the début session. The tapes for this show have since been wiped and have thus been elevated to legendary status in collector circles due to the one-off performance of 'Sunshine Woman' – possibly a contender for *Led Zeppelin II* and never played live, the only known airing being this BBC recording. A rock'n'blues track driven by some barrelhouse piano from Jonesy and harmonica blowing from Plant, it is similar in pace to 'Bring It On Home'. The version of 'I Can't Quit You Baby' included a rare Plant ad lib sequence beginning with the lines 'I gotta fur coat for Christmas and a diamond ring".

Bootleg CD References: *Sunshine Woman* (Flagge), *Motor City Days* (Antrabata), *Ottowa Sunshine* (House Of Elrond)

Friday March 21 1969
London, England
BBC TV Studios
TV RECORDING

The group were invited at short notice to replace The Flying Burrito Brothers.

They duly tele-recorded 'Communication Breakdown' for *How Late It Is*, an arts programme introduced by Michael Wale. The track was recorded at 5.45pm in Studio G of the BBC Lime Grove Studios, and aired at 10.50pm that night. The master

tapes were subsequently wiped by the BBC.

Saturday March 22 1969
Erdington Birmingham, England Mothers' Club
Set included Train Kept A Rollin'/I Can't Quit You Baby/Dazed And Confused

Support from ex-Jethro Tull guitarist Mick Abraham's Blodwyn Pig.

In 2003 an audience recorded fragment of this show turned up on a 2-CD unofficial release from the Tarantura label. The recording featured 'Train Kept A Rollin'', 'I Can't Quite You Baby' and a snippet of 'Dazed And Confused'. Allegedly Bonzo was worse for wear throughout the show and did not make it for the encore. Blodwyn Pig's drummer Ron Berg took over to complete the gig.

Bootleg CD Reference: *Blighty* (Tarantura)

Sunday March 23 1969
London, England
Radio One Top Gear
RADIO BROADCAST

On this day Radio one broadcast the March 3 Playhouse theatre session. It was aired between 3 and 5pm on John Peel's *Top Gear*. Also on the show were Deep Purple and The Moody Blues.

Tuesday March 25 1969
Staines, England
FILMING SESSION

Filming for the movie Supershow . Director: John Crome; producer: Tom Parkinson. Original sound recording Brian Slott. Track filmed: 'Dazed And Confused'.

Over a two-day shoot at a disused lino factory in Staines, instigated by the Colour Tel film company

Led Zeppelin

(their recent credits included *The Rolling Stones Rock'N'Roll Circus* and *Jimi Hendrix At The Albert Hall*), artists from the world of blues, jazz and rock got together to be filmed separately and jamming. Zeppelin's involvement stemmed from Jimmy's friendship with the director. The whole project was planned with great secrecy and filming went ahead at a reputed cost of £100 per minute.

The Tuesday filming featured Led Zeppelin, Buddy Guy, Jack Bruce, Buddy Miles, Dick Heckstall-Smith and Chris Mercer. The jam session brought together Stephen Stills, Dallas Taylor, Buddy Miles and Jack Bruce.

Wednesday featured Eric Clapton, Colosseum, Buddy Guy and Roland Kirk. Allegedly, Jimi Hendrix was due to appear but missed the plane from New York.

Zeppelin's contribution was a vibrant 'Dazed And Confused'. The resulting film, complete with period piece zoom panning techniques remains one of their clearest colour filmed remants of this era. The original intention was for Zeppelin to perform two numbers, but Plant had problems with his voice so 'You Shook Me' was dropped.

The film itself, known as *Supershow*, received a limited run in London, premièring at the Lyceum in November 1969. It would emerge as an official video release by Virgin Vision in 1986. Page returned to it for inclusion in the 2003 DVD.

Peter Grant recalled: "A mate of Jimmy's buttonholed us into the *Supershow*. I wasn't that keen. I didn't even go down to the filming."
Bootleg CD References: *Riverside Blues* (Swinging Pig), *The Complete BBC Classics* (Immigrant)
Visual References: Official *Led Zeppelin* 2003 DVD (Warner Vision), *Unofficial Early Visions* DVD (Celebration)

Thursday March 27 1969
Bremen, Germany
Beat Club, *Bremen Ard*
TV RECORDING
Television recording directed by Michael Leeke-bosh – shot in black and white

The band's fifth TV appearance of the month

was a lightning visit to mime to 'Dazed And Confused' for the popular *Beat Club* German net-worked pop show. This slot was to fulfil a Yardbirds' booking held over from September 1968. Allegedly the producers were unimpressed with the performance and this mimed piece was never broadcast in its original form. However early the next year clips from this appearance were used in a collage video shot to accompany 'Whole Lotta Love' when the track became a big hit on the German singles charts. This often repeated clip was originally aired on March 28 1970.

Friday March 28 1969
Stansted Airport, England
AIR SCARE!
On the way home from Bremen, on March 28, the band were involved in an 'air scare' at Stansted Airport in Essex.

The April 4 edition of the *Hearts & Essex Observer* reported that: "A well known pop group the Led Zeppelin were among 87 passengers who took part in a dramatic escape down safety chutes after a British European Airways Comet made an emergency landing at Stansted Aiport last Friday. The Comet was on a flight from Hanover to Gatwick when the pilot Captain R. Park reported a fire warning light on one engine over the North Sea. After the landing one member of the group, John Bonham, said: 'We were told that the fire indicator on number four engine was showing red and that the light remained on after the extinguisher system had been operated. The next thing we knew we were coming down at Stansted I thought we were going to land in a field.'"

The group, the story revealed, had been appearing in a TV spot in Bremen and were on their way back to appear at a London night club.

The report included a picture of them at the airport with tour manager Richard Cole.

Friday March 28 1969
London, England
Marquee Club
A press release issued on March 26 headed "Led

ZEPPELIN IN AIR SCARE
Passengers left Comet by safety chutes

Zeppelin At Marquee" read: "Led Zeppelin, the most talked about (and raved about) British group of the moment, plays London's famous Marquee Club on Friday night. All eyes are on Led Zeppelin following the fantastic success of their first album, which in a matter of weeks in America climbed rapidly into the upper limits of *Billboard*, *Cashbox* and *Record World* charts. This album, entitled simply *Led Zeppelin*, was recently released in Britain and seems destined for similar success."

Support from Eyes Of Blue. Seemingly undaunted their 'air scare' experience earlier in the day, the group returned to the Marquee for an appearance that could have been captured for use on BBC2's then pop showcase *Colour Me Pop*. Peter Grant recalled: "When we did the Marquee, we offered BBC2 to film it and they didn't even turn up! I went out early afternoon from our office in Oxford Street to Wardour Street and thought 'Fuck me, what's this queue?' There were about 200 already lined up. That's when I knew that we just wouldn't need the media. It was going to be about the fans."

Saturday March 29 1969
Holland
TV RECORDING AIRED
On this date the Dutch TROS TV network aired 'Good Times Bad Times' on their Jam TV show. It is not known if it was a filmed segment -studio or live and no footage has been uncovered.

Saturday March 29 1969
Bromley Common, London, England
Bromley College Of Technology
Set included Communication Breakdown, You Shook Me, I Can't Quit You Baby, Dazed And Confused, How Many More Times and a cover of Eddie Cochran's Something Else.

Fan Peter Badham recalled: "I was made aware of the gig by a handout distributed in Bromley High Street that afternoon. They came on around 9.30. Page was directly in front of me in a black leather jacket. I'm pretty certain they played most of the first album. Stand outs included 'You Shook Me'. The encores were 'Something Else' and a reprise of 'Communication Breakdown'. I left slightly deaf but with a wide grin on my face knowing I'd been privileged to be in at the start of something special."

Sunday March 30 1969
Southall, England
Northcote Arms,
Farx Club

Billed as 'LED ZEPPELIN!' Support from Smokey Rice and Aphrodite's Rainbow Light Show.

The contract for this performance showed a fee of £75 or 60% of the door takings – whichever was greater – with payment to be made "In cash to bandleader on night of engagement".

Monday March 31 1969
Edmonton London, England
Cooks Ferry Inn
Photographer Graham Wiltshire recalled: "When I arrived I noticed two long haired chaps at the bar, Jimmy and Robert. A few minutes later they took the stage. 'Communication Breakdown' exploded from the amps. The stage was really cramped but it didn't deter Plant. His voice was amazing. A short potent set. Three days later my hearing had just about recovered."

UNCONFIRMED
Ravensbourne, England
Art College
It's possible they played this venue around this period but there is no confirmation

April
Barnes, England
Olympic Studios
RECORDING SESSIONS
Initial sessions for their second album commenced this month at Olympic. They began working on various new compositions, including 'What Is And What Should Never Be' and 'Whole Lotta Love'.

Tuesday April 1 1969
Hampstead, England
Klooks Kleek
Support from The End and Pale Green Limousine.

Jimmy Page: "We loved doing gigs in places like Klooks Kleek, but in the end they were turning away more people than could actually see the show."

Saturday April 5 1969
London, England
Dagenham Roundhouse
Jimmy was less than complimentary about the UK club scene in an interview with Nick Logan in *New Musical Express*.

Logan reported: "Having just returned from a sensational début tour of America, Led Zeppelin is currently playing British club dates before going back to the US again. Jimmy Page told me: 'In America the audiences get into their music more. They are more appreciative. They will listen to the sort of patterns you are playing. In Britain, all they are interested in is the way to the bar. And over in America they clap you, not because it is

the right thing to do, but because if you are trying to do something everyone in the audience is spurring you on and then it really gets to you. Most places here, they just go to have a dance or to have a drink, not to listen. They don't care who's on. There are a few exceptions like the Marquee, Middle Earth and Birmingham Mothers'.

"Jimmy tells me there are other reasons for the group's exodus to the States. 'The basic reason is the lack of exposure here. There just aren't the big venues in which to play. What we need is a club in every major city, something between the size of the Roundhouse and Marquee'."

Sunday April 6 1969
Nottingham, England
The Boat Club
Fan David Hope researched this show and discovered that the owner of the Boat Club, Keith Atkinson, had kept a copy of the contract. It was drawn up on 15/1/69 and awarded the group 60% of the gross advance and door takings. A minimum of £80 was guaranteed on the night. (£85 had been crossed out.) Zeppelin were engaged to play 2x30 minute spots.

Tuesday April 8 1969
Welwyn Garden City, England
Bluesville 69 Club, The Cherry Tree

Wednesday April 9 1969
Tolwortth, England
Toby Jug
This venue was demolished in 2004.

Monday April 14 1969
Hanley Stoke On Trent, England
The Place
This was possibly the second time they played this venue – see December 1968

Monday April 14 1969
London, England
World Service Rhythm And Blues
RADIO BROADCAST
On this day the World Service aired the March 19 Maida Vale session. It was broadcast on the *Rhythm And Blues* show with Alexis Korner.

UNCONFIRMED
Bolton, England
The Swan Hotel
They also played a date in Bolton around this time – Page made reference to it in an interview in *NME* in April. It's likely to have taken place on April 15 or 16.

UNCONFIRMED
Portsmouth, England
The Birdcage

UNCONFIRMED
Lancaster, England
Lancaster University

UNCONFIRMED
Colchester, England
Colchester University
*Claims have been made by various fans of attending dates around this period at the above three venues though no concrete proof has emerged

UNCONFIRMED
Thursday April 17 1969
Wolverhampton, England
Club Lafayette
It appears this gig was inserted in place of a date in Sunderland. In his book *A Promoter's Tale* (Omnibus Press) North East rock promoter Geoff Docherty tells how he had the group booked in for the Bay Hotel Sunderland on this date but was informed by Peter Grant that they would not be able to fulfil it due to going to the States the next day.

Local Wolverhampton records has this date listed as being advertised, but if it was played quite how they got there gear airlifted to the USA for the New York show the next day remains a mystery. It's therefore feasible they used borrowed gear for this show.

AMERICA SPRING 1969

Following the lukewarm reception at home, Led Zeppelin were eager to return to the States. This trip, designed to capitalise on the Top 20 success of the début album, crammed in 27 shows in just under six weeks. Such was the buzz from their début tour, they were now already sharing top billing with established acts such as Julie Driscoll, Delaney & Bonnie and Three Dog Night.

A planned four-date residency at the Fillmore West moved out for two nights to the larger Bill Graham-owned Winterland Ballroom, such was the demand. Along the way they begin sessions for a second album, booking time between their heavy schedule at studios such as Mirror Sound in Los Angeles and A&R in New York.

The stage act reflected their enthusiasm for creating new riffs and melodies. John Bonham incorporated a lengthy drum solo, then known as 'Pat's Delight' which soon evolved into 'Moby Dick'. Their version of 'Killing Floor', now played regularly live, would evolve into 'The Lemon Song' – a hybrid of the Chester Burnett standard and Page's riffing. It was the beginning of their much criticised practice of taking old blues tunes and calling them their own. Willie Dixon's 'You Need Love' was another example. Wrapped around a killer Page riff, it would soon be

A FIFTH MEMBER?

In early 1969 there seemed to have been a plan to take an extra guitarist on the road. Allegedly another ex-Yardbirds guitarist Anthony 'Top' Topham, who had been replaced by Eric Clapton in 1963, was in a dialogue with Grant and Page with a view to being involved. Telegrams were exchanged between Grant Page and Topham during February and March 1969 but nothing ever materialised.

A year later when it became apparent that studio material such as 'Thank You' and 'Since I've Been Loving You' would require John Paul Jones to play keyboards, there were talks again of adding a fifth member for live performances. Although the discussions never developed, Peter Grant remembers that Keith Emerson was mentioned as a possible candidate. "There was also a rumour that made Brian Lane, the manager of Yes, very paranoid," recalled Grant. "And that was that we were going to get Chris Squire to join on bass and move John Paul to keyboards permanently. That was never a serious consideration though."

As it turned out, JP was quite happy doubling up his role. "It was always a case of 'Oh, Jonesy will play that' if a new arrangement came up," remembers Jones.

unleashed as their anthem 'Whole Lotta Love', an early live incarnation of which they débuted at the Winterland Ballroom on April 26.

By then, the news of their success was beginning to filter back to England. In America though, they did themselves no favours in terms of acceptance by the mainstream media when a planned major feature for *Life* magazine fell through when author Ellen Sander fell victim to the band's increasingly boisterous road fever excesses.

Equipment Notes:

Around this period, Jimmy switched from the Telecaster to a 1959 Gibson Les Paul, his main guitar for all subsequent live work. For the early part of the tour photographic evidence shows he was still using the Telecaster. At some point during the early part of the year he also acquired a second Gibson Les Paul- a 1958 model sold to him by Joe Walsh. Walsh was a member of The James Gang who appeared on several bills with Zeppelin during the year. It was to became a lasting part of his guitar armoury. "It was a guitar I was meant to have. Joe Walsh told me I should buy this guitar," said Page years later. "He was right. It became my wife and mistress without the alimony!"

There was a change in amps, to a Marshall set-up. On the advice of Vanilla Fudge drummer

Carmine Appice, John Bonham changed to a maple wood Ludwig kit with a 26-inch bass drum. Side bongos are also added as well as a Paiste gong (used primarily for 'Dazed And Confused' and 'White Summer'). During the summer US tour, Bonham introduced a double bass drum for a short period, but returned to a single after complaints from the rest of the band that he was drowning them all out.

Friday April 18 1969
New York, New York
NY University Jazz Festival
Also on the bill are Dave Brubeck and Errol Garner.

Thursday April 24 1969
San Francisco, California, Fillmore West
Set included: As Long As I Have You (inc. Fresh Garbage – Shake – Mockingbird – You Can't Judge A Book By The Cover)/Killing Floor (inc. The Lemon Song and riff intro from Howlin Wolf's 1968 arrangement of Smokestack Lightning)/White Summer – Black Mountain Side/Babe I'm Gonna Leave You/Pat's Delight.

Support for all four Bill Graham shows from Julie Driscoll, Brian Auger & The Trinity and The Coldwell-Winfield Blues Band.

51

Led Zeppelin

Zeppelin started the tour proper with a residency in San Francisco, where the audience on their first tour had been particularly enthusiastic.

The highlight of this show was an extended 'As Long As I Have You' medley which included the rarely played 'You Can't Judge A Book By The Cover'. Halfway through the number, Jones' bass cabinet exploded and Plant ad-libed new lyrics: "I think we've got some trouble with our equipment, yeah … I think we're gonna get it together, yeah … I think we're gonna have a good time … I think we'd better the right key!" Page and Bonham continued to improvise until Jones was able to re-enter and finish the number. Plant comments: "We seem to have a cock-up every time we've been here!"

'White Summer' now included some accompaniment from Bonham on gong, and also included a new segment which would continue to develop before finally being recorded and released by The Firm in 1985 as 'Midnight Moonlight'.

Bootelg CD References: *Cracker Jack Blues* (Jelly Roll), *Blues Anytime* (Empress Valley), *Psychedelic Raw Blues* (Immigrant)

Friday April 25 1969
San Francisco, California
Winterland Ballroom
Set included: Train Kept A Rollin'/You Shook Me/Communication Breakdown/As Long As I Have You (inc. Fresh Garbage – Bags Groove).

This venue was demolished in 1982 and is now a condominium complex.

Peter Grant: "The reception at the Winterland shows was phenomenal and they played to capacity audiences both nights – in fact, they were on stage for three hours each night. Their album had already been out 16 weeks, but while they were there it sold 10,000 copies in San Francisco in one day alone."

Bootleg CD References: *Grande Ball* (Missing Link), *California '69* (Lemon)

Saturday April 26 1969
San Francisco, California
Winterland Ballroom
Set 1: Communication Breakdown/I Can't Quit You/Dazed And Confused/You Shook Me/How Many More Times (inc. Smokestack Lightning – Roll Over Beethoven – The Hunter).
Set 2: White Summer – Black Mountain Side/Killing Floor (inc. The Lemon Song – That's Alright Mama)/Babe I'm Gonna Leave You/Pat's Delight/As Long As I Have You (inc. Fresh Garbage – Bags Groove – Mockingbird)/Whole Lotta Love.

The biggest concert of the band's career so far. Plant: "I think last night we said that it was nice to be back. Well, there seems to be a lot more people here, so I hope the message is carrying on."

'Dazed And Confused' was now enhanced by Page's use of a Theremin (an electronic oscillator), to produce high pitched spacey psychedelic sound. This was probably the first time Page has used a Theremin in concert which would later be extensively deployed on live versions of 'Whole Lotta Love', At this show Page also used the device sparingly on 'How Many More Times', which included the riff from 'Smokestack Lightning' and some lyrics from Chuck Berry's 'Roll Over Beethoven'.

The second set opened with a virtuoso performance of 'White Summer', followed by a Hendrix-influenced version of 'Killing Floor' which included 'The Lemon Song' and 'That's Alright Mama'. The set closed with a riotous 'As Long As

'I Have You' medley incorporating their longest version of 'Mockingbird'.

Atlantic Records were now pushing for them to come up with a second album by the late summer – sessions for what would become *Led Zeppelin II* had already begun and this show featured an embryonic 'Whole Lotta Love' performed as the encore. The track was aired on a few subsequent occasions, eventually becoming part of the regular set in 1970.

Bootleg CD References: *Lead Set* (Tarantura), *Graham's Superb Vol 1* (IQ)

Avocado Club The Legendary Fillmore Series – West Vol. 1 (Empress Valley)

Sunday April 27 1969
San Francisco, California
Fillmore West

Set 1: Train Kept A Rollin'/I Can't Quit You/As Long As I Have You (inc. Fresh Garbage – Bags Groove – Cat's Squirrel – Cadillac No Money Down – I'm A Man)/You Shook Me/How Many More Times (inc. Feel So Bad – The Hunter – Mulberry Bush)/Killing Floor (inc. Sweet Jelly Baby).
Set 2: Babe I'm Gonna Leave You/White Summer – Black Mountain Side/ Sitting And Thinking/Pat's Delight/Dazed And Confused/Communication Breakdown.

After the two larger Winterland shows, they returned to the more intimate Fillmore for a final gig prior to leaving San Francisco. Plant's empathy for the Californian audiences was reflected in the ad-libbed lyrics of 'I Can't Quit You': "I'm so glad you came tonight ... but I think we're gonna leave this town for a little while ... I don't want to leave you people ... but I think we've got to leave San Francisco for a little while."

An extended 'As Long As I Have You' was packed full of obscure blues references, including Muddy Waters' 'I'm A Man'. 'How Many More Times' was a definite highlight including the rarely played 'Feel So Bad' and 'Here We Go Round The Mulberry Bush'. The first set encore of 'Killing Floor' featured some unusual 'Sweet Jelly Baby' lyrics.

The second set was more laid back affair with the electric/ acoustic start and bluesy finale. 'Sitting And Thinking', a Buddy Guy number was performed in its entirety for the only known occasion and the set closed with 'Dazed And Confused' – a rare finale delivery for the track.

Bootleg CD References: *Simplistic Atmosphere* (Jelly Roll), *Avocado Club The Legendary Fillmore Series – West Vol. 1* (Empress Valley), *Lead Set* (Tarantura),

Collage (TDOLZ), *Twinight* (Immigrant), *American Beauty* (Tarantura)

April 1969
Los Angeles California
A & M Studios
RECORDING SESSIONS

Whilst in Los Angeles the band booked studio time at A & M Studios to work on their second album. Photos from this session can be seen in *The*

Photographers Led Zeppelin book compiled by Ross Halfin

UNCONFIRMED
Tuesday April 29 1969
Los Angeles, California
Whisky A Go Go

UNCONFIRMED
Wednesday April 30 1969
Los angeles, California
Whisky A Go Go

Thursday May 1 1969
Irvine, California
U.C. Crawford Hall
Support from Lee Michaels.

Peter Grant: "It was a great night. They did five encores that night and although the hall was filled to capacity with over 3,000 people in the audience, there were over 700 people outside who couldn't get in. Fights broke out outside because people couldn't get tickets and when Jimmy heard about it he asked everyone to squeeze up, had the side doors opened and managed to squeeze the waiting people into the hall."

Disc reported: "Led Zeppelin has added unscheduled recording sessions to its second American tour in a hurry-up attempt by the group and Atlantic Records to get a second album on the market by mid-Summer.

"Members of the group were informed by Atlantic they should plan on going into a studio as soon as they arrived in Los Angeles. By the first of this week, the Zeppelin had spent four days in two studios recording half a dozen tracks. The recording activity is to continue in New York when the band arrive there. Atlantic wants the LP ready for release in July, following the label's annual sales meetings."

May 1969
Los Angeles, California
Mystic Sound Studios,
Los Angeles
RECORDING SESSIONS

Still on tour, the band booked into this small studio run by Chris Huston. Various tracks for *Led Zeppelin 2* were recorded here including 'Moby Dick' and 'The Lemon Song'. Page had previously used the studio on a session with Screaming Lord Sutch. Outtakes exist of the session for 'Moby Dick' which demonstrates how the solo was dropped in to the main riff part.
Bootleg CD Reference: *Olympic Gold* (Scorpio)

The band booked into various studios over this period to record *Led Zeppelin 2,* including Juggy Sound in New York and Quantum Studios in Los Angeles. Photographer Ron Rafaelli (known for his Rolling Stones cover for *Hot Rocks*) attended the latter recording sessions and took shots of Page in the studio which would later appear in the *Visual Thing* tour book sold on their fall US tour. Rafaelli also held group photo sessions at his studio in Hollywood. Around this time another memorable group photo shoot occurred at the Chateau Marmont Hotel in Hollywood. A photo from this session adorns the LP back cover sleeve of the *Remasters* compilation.

Friday May 2 1969
Pasadena, California
Rose Palace
Support for both Rose Palace shows from Julie Driscoll, Brian Auger & The Trinity.

Jerry Hopkins for *Top Pops* reported: "The band is busy selling out concerts. Four in San Francisco and two more at the Rose Palace in Pasadena. In that these ballrooms have huge capacities and no-one ever bothers to count heads as the audience enters, what 'Sold Out' means is the ballrooms have been crammed so full of people that the police on hand are beginning to squawk."

Peter Grant: "The group did some big jams almost every night. They went to the new club in Sunset Strip – The Experience – and did jams with Noel Redding, and Buddy Miles on organ. One night Lord Sutch came in and did his old act with Zeppelin – a medley of old rock tunes. Experience is the only place in Hollywood where you can get Watney's Red Barrel!"

Following this gig Page found time to jam with the Mike Pinero Band at a charity show.

Saturday May 3 1969
Pasadena, California
Rose Palace

Top Pops runs headline: "Jimmy Survives The Big Quake".

Peter Grant: "We flew to Los Angeles and there was a small earthquake. It registered 5.6 on the earthquake meter and a building fell down. Jimmy and his road manager Richard Cole were stopping in Jean Harlow's old suite in a hotel and Jimmy was reading up all the information he could about earthquakes. Jimmy was fascinated and scared. He'd read that most people who survived the big quake in the Thirties did so by sitting in a bath. Apparently a bath is the safest place because of the pipes it's attached to – if a floor collapses, the bath stays in place because of the fittings. So he insisted that the bathroom be free at all times and forbade anyone to use it at all. Poor Richard had to go to someone else's room every time he wanted to go to the toilet!

"Every time Jimmy heard a car bang or any loud noise he'd rush into the bathroom and stay put in the bath till the all clear was given."

Sunday May 4 1969
Santa Monica, California
Civic Centre

Monday May 5 1969
Santa Monica, California
Civic Centre

Wednesday May 7 1969
Portland, Oregon

Friday May 9 1969
Edmonton, Canada
Edmonton Garden

Support from the Angus Park Blues Band and Papa Bear's Medicine Show.

Due to an Air Canada strike it took them 12 hours to travel to Edmonton. The *Led Zeppelin* album was in the top three of the Canadian charts and the Canadian press were most complimenta-

ry. "Hot rock band loud, frenzied". Bob Harvey of *The Journal* reported: "Led Zeppelin is brutal. The hottest new band from Britain stalked on stage at the Gardens Friday and let loose an earthquake of sound and frenzy.

"The music's loud, almost to the point of pain, but they don't use volume to cover up deficiencies. The volume is part of their attack. They don't titillate, or tease audiences to share their inspiration. Instead they blast out with raw, jagged power, enough to bust a new door into your brain. They use their instruments like a brush and palette, creating frenzied visions that tumble through space and time.

"The visions have such deadly fascinations that you can't bear to blink an ear, but they're flung out like hammers, so that it's hard not to duck in self-protection. Led Zeppelin is probably the most aggressive, masculine rock group anywhere. They batter at the mind and ear, insisting that they will penetrate."

Saturday May 10 1969
Vancouver, Canada
PNE Agrodome
Support from Spring and Jaime Brockett. Papa Bear's Medicine Show were due to appear but were stranded in Alberta due to an Air Canada strike.

"Up, Up and Away With Zeppelin" – Bob Smith reviewed this show for the *Vancouver Sun*: "Nearly 4,000 young people accorded Led Zeppelin a wildly cheering standing ovation Saturday night in the PNE Agrodome. Zeppelin regard each audience as friendly adversaries to be bested or made love to and finally conquered.

"Zeppelin, a quartet, had registered a gradually accelerating, hill and dale performance of some 80 minutes when lead vocalist-harmonicat Robert Plant tried to say goodnight on behalf of his cohorts. But the crowd, heavily concentrated at floor level, pressed forward to the rim of the stage, some extending their hands, and literally begged for more.

"The group made a wise decision. It came back and reprised its last number for another 15 minutes. Like good shepherds, they were bringing their flock home."

While in Vancouver, Zeppelin also spent time in the local studio laying down harmonica tracks for the second album.

Sunday May 11 1969
Seattle, Washington
Green Lake AquaTheater
Three Dog Night, Jaime Brockett, Spring and Jimmy Winkler's Translove Airlines support. Concert 2pm to 6pm.

The Zeppelin show reopened the Aqua Theater which has been infrequently used in recent years.

The *Seattle Times* reported: 'The rock concert at the Aqua Theater yesterday afternoon was a smashing success. It had everything: sunshine, masses of people, The Led Zeppelin, Three Dog Night, and even Jimmy Winkler. The audience was everywhere. The benches in the Aqua Theater were filled to overflowing. There were persons in boats behind the stage, more on the roofs of buildings next door. Several energetic souls tread water in the pool between the stands and the stage. There were even two swim-suit clad fellows perched atop the roof of one of the diving towers. It was a large audience.

"The stars of the concert were Three Dog Night and Led Zeppelin. Both are brilliant bands. Zeppelin put on an instrumentally excellent performance. Jimmy Page is a superb guitarist and the rest of the group provides able backing too for his wild, fiery style. However, Three Dog Night stole the show. Their personality, their talent and their superb singing make them the hit of any show they play."

Tuesday May 13 1969
Honolulu, Hawaii
Civic Auditorium
This venue was demolished in 1974.

Zeppelin flew into Hawaii for one show and a few day's rest. They arrived at the airport clutch-

ing reels for the work-in-progress second album and were presented with garlands of exotic flowers as a welcoming gesture (an image that can be seen on page 139 of Ross Halfin's *The Photographers Led Zeppelin* book).

The show itself was only sparsely attended, and there were problems with the lights and the unbearable heat in the auditorium.

Ken Rosene of *Headlines* reported: "Led Zeppelin was the first major British rock group to appear in Hawaii, and I think most people at the Civic Auditorium last Tuesday will agree that we want more. The showmanship exceeded any rock performance (with the possible exception of Jimi Hendrix) here to date.

"The very British way of stage appearance really made for an interesting show. At times Robert Plant looked almost feminine (don't worry, he's married, has one kid and is only 20 years old), but he retained his masculinity with powerful gestures and a voice that was always clear – whether singing or screaming. Jimmy Page blew everybody out with his unbelievable guitar work. He is definitely one of the greats.

"Many thanks have to go to John Selby & Co. for bringing Zeppelin over. Because it was a Tuesday night, they probably lost money, but musically, Indica Music Productions put on the best rock show ever."

Friday May 16 1969
Detroit, Michigan
Grande Ballroom
Support from Sun Ra and Golden Earring. Two shows this evening, 7 and 10pm

Originally a concert was planned for this evening at the Olympia Stadium with Spirit and Illinois Speed Press as support, but this was cancelled in favour of the more intimate Grande Ballroom.

Saturday May 17 1969
Athens, Ohio
Ohio University Memorial Auditorium
For this appearance Zeppelin opened for Jose Feliciano, then riding on the back of his massive success with his cover of The Doors 'Light My Fire'. He recalled: "I was really keen to meet Jimmy Page but somehow missed him which I've always regretted."

Sunday May 18 1969
Minneapolis, Minnesota
Gutthrie Memorial Theater
After this show they flew to New York to continue work on the second album.

Saturday May 19 1969
Denmark
TV Byen/Danmarks Radio/Danish Broadcasting Corperation
TV RECORDING AIRED
The TV Byen special filmed on March 17 was Broadcast on Danish TV

Friday May 23 1969
San Jose, California
Santa Clara Pop Festival
The group performed two shows in one day with the help of the promoter. Peter Grant recalled: "The promoter of the San Jose Festival wanted them to play on the Friday. We were appearing in Chicago that night so he hired a Lear jet – it cost him 12,000 dollars to rent – and off we went to California. After the show he arranged to fly us back to Chicago and paid us 25,000 dollars for the festival appearance. A good deal, I thought."

The Sunday night bill at the festival was headlined by the Jimi Hendrix Experience.

Friday May 23 1969
Chicago, Illinois
Kinetic Playground
Support from Pacific Gas & Electric Co., and Illinois Speed Press.

Saturday May 24 1969
Chicago, Illinois
Kinetic Playground

Sunday May 25 1969
Columbia, Maryland
Merriweather Post Pavilion
Set includes: Whole Lotta Love.

The group name was spelt as 'Lead Zeppelin' on the tickets – which cost $3.50.

For tonight's show Zeppelin were second on the bill to The Who, the only occasion both bands appeared on the same bill though they were scheduled for another date the next week (see June 1 entry). Lenny Bruce-style comedian Uncle Dirty opened the show.

'Whole Lotta Love' was played again tonight in another new experimental version. The press reports however favoured The Who. "Who Steals The Show" read a local headline. Richard Cowan reported, "Zeppelin played a fairly orthodox show, mostly using material off their first album. Although guitarist Jimmy Page once again proved himself a fine musician, there wasn't much more to be said about the act as a whole. He and singer Robert Plant launched into innumerable transgressions of tonal question-answer games, more conducive to boredom than musically induced languor."

After this show the band headed back to New York for a gold record party the following day at the Plaza Hotel and yet another studio session.

There exists a brief reel of 8 mm cine footage of members of the Who and Zep backstage. The location is unknown.
Bootleg CD References: *Anybody Got A Les Paul?*, (Equinox), *Whole Lotta Love*

(Tarantura)

Tuesday May 27 1969
Boston, Massachusetts
Boston Tea Party
Set: As Long As I Have You (inc. Fresh Garbage – Shake – Mockingbird)/I Can't Quit You/Dazed And Confused (inc. Move On Down The Line)/You Shook Me/Pat's Delight/Babe I'm Gonna Leave You/How Many More Times (inc. For Your Love – The Hunter)/Improvisation – Communication Breakdown.

An unusual and interesting set. 'Dazed And Confused' had Plant working in the lyrics of 'Move On Down The Line'.

Surprisingly, 'How Many More Times' includes a section of The Yardbirds' 'For Your Love'. But the improvisation wasn't over yet. When Page broke a string before the encore, they switched into a harmonica, bass and drums jam before Page came back to lead them through 'Communication Breakdown'.
Bootleg CD References: *Complete Boston Tea Party* (Arms), *Whiskey And Tea Party* (Ocean), *Pat's Delight* (Tecumseh)

Wednesday May 28 1969
Boston, Massachusetts
Boston Tea Party
Support for all three Boston shows is Zephyr, whose line-up included future Deep Purple guitarist Tommy Bolin.

Thursday May 29 1969
Boston, Massachusetts
Boston Tea Party

Friday May 30 1969
New York, New York
Fillmore East
Set: Train Kept A Rollin'/I Can't Quit You/Dazed And Confused/You Shook Me/White Summer – Black Mountain Side/How Many More Times (inc. Boogie Chillun' – The Hunter)/Communication Breakdown.

Support for both nights was Woody Herman &

his Orchestra, Delaney & Bonnie & Friends, and The Joshua Light Show. Zeppelin performed two shows each night. 8pm and 11.30

'How Many More Times' included a snatch of John Lee Hooker's 'Boogie Chillun'' which will feature heavily in the medley sections in future years.

Bootleg CD Reference: *Early Days Latter Days* (Early Days), *The Legendary Fillmore Tapes Vol 2* (Savage Beast)

Saturday May 31 1969
New York, New York
Fillmore East

Two shows, 8 and 11.30pm

Billboard reported: "British rock quartet Led Zeppelin made a strong return to New York at a four-show concert at the Fillmore East last weekend. Woody Herman's Orchestra added the diversification of a big band sound and Delaney & Bonnie's set was marked by the surprise performance of pop-gospel singer Dorothy Morrison. The event grossed $45,000 with tickets scaled to $5."

Plant: "I think on the second tour people really started taking an interest in the other members of the group and not just Jimmy alone. Each of us has a different personality which is now coming to the fore."

After the New York shows, the band returned to England on June 1.

Sunday June 1st
St Louis, Missouri
Kiel Auditorium
WITHDRAWN APPEARANCE
The scheduled line up for this show was The Who, Led Zeppelin and Joe Cocker. The gig was duly advertised with Zeppelin as the second billing. However for reasons unknown, Zeppelin pulled out of the line up and the gig went ahead with just The Who and Joe Cocker.

UK TOUR – SUMMER 1969

This was the first proper scheduled UK tour (with Blodwyn Pig and Liverpool Scene supporting) arranged with the then rising booking agency, Chrysalis. After a slowish start, their reputation at home was now in the ascendent. Press reports from the US were hailing them as the most important group since Cream and the BBC radio sessions provided aural evi-

dence of their progress. During this month they recorded three additional BBC sessions. On June 27 they performed a pilot show at the BBC's Paris Theatre which would inaugurate the long-running Radio One *In Concert* series when it was broadcast on August 10. There were also sessions recorded on June 16 and 24 – the latter previewing 'Whole Lotta Love' and 'What Is And What

Should Never Be' from the new album and also featuring the unrecorded 'Travelling Riverside Blues' (which finally saw the light of day on the 1990 *Remasters* box set).

On the concert front there were prestige dates at the Bath Blues Festival where they played to 12,000 people and the tour finale – two shows as part of Vic Lewis's Pop Proms season at London's Royal Albert Hall. The final show that night ended in a chaotic jam session with members of the Liverpool Scene as the crowd howled for more, even with the house lights on. The UK audiences were definitely beginning to share what their American cousins had already discovered.

To round off another hectic schedule, during this tour they also booked studio time for the second album at Willesden's Morgan Studios and recorded what would be their last-ever TV appearance in Paris for *Tous En Scène*, as the musical segment in a French satire programme.

Friday June 13 1969
Birmingham, England
Town Hall

After rehearsals at Hanwell Community Centre, Zeppelin undertook their first proper British tour, featuring a set that would concentrate primarily on their own material from the *Led Zeppelin* album.

Record Mirror reported: "Led Zeppelin showed just why they have taken America by storm when they began their tour at Birmingham Town Hall on Friday. The more weird the electronic sounds created by Led Zeppelin, the more the crowd loved it, especially when guitarist Jimmy Page got going.

"The voice and harmonica playing of bare-footed Robert Plant were in perfect sympathy with the Page guitar. Bassist John Paul Jones and drummer John Bonham were also completely involved in their music."

Noted photographer Ron Raffaelli of the Visual Thing design company was in attendance at this show – the live photos of this gig would later appear in the *Visual Thing* Led Zeppelin tour book

which was sold during their Fall 1969 American tour.

Sunday June 15 1969
Manchester, England
Free Trade Hall

Billed as 'Led Zeppelin etc'

Monday June 16 1969
London, England
Aeolian Hall, Studio 2, Bond Street

RADIO ONE SESSION

BBC recording from 7.30pm to 11pm. Session commissioned by chief producer Paul Williams. Broadcast date: Sunday June 22, between 10am and 12 noon, on *Chris Grant's Tasty Pop Sundae*.(Also in session on the show were Marmalade and Vanity Fair). Tracks recorded: The Girl I Love She Got Long Black Wavy Hair/Communication Breakdown/Something Else/What Is And What Should Never Be/Group Interview with Chris Grant.

The first of three sessions for the BBC this month. This session was originally due to be aired on *Symonds On Sunday*, a popular Sunday morning show presented by Dave Symonds. During June, however, he was on holiday and replaced by a little known stand-in, Chris Grant (no relation to Peter!). He renamed the show *Chris Grant's Tasty Pop Sundae*. His ineptness was apparent from the hilarious unbroadcast interview conducted during the session. It's also clear from his over-the-top intros that this was not the most appropriate time slot for Zeppelin, especially in the company of pop/bubblegum acts such as Marmalade and Vanity Fair.

"It's nineteen minutes past the hour of ten o' clock … studio guests now … Led Zeppelin …

Alright boys let's go underground. The girl I love she got long black wavy hair … rigghtt!"

That was the inane talkover intro Chris Grant affords another of the rarest Zepp recordings – the sort of corny pop radio piffle that Page felt he had long since left behind. Nevertheless it provided Zeppelin with prime time airplay and the performance certainly left its mark on many listeners that particular mid-Summer morning.

This performance of 'The Girl I Love' was the only known occasion of Zeppelin performing this piece. It's possible that the track was being worked on at Morgan Studios for the in-progress *Led Zeppelin II* album. The riff was similar to 'Moby Dick', the Bonham showcase on the album, a typically strident mid-1969 riff laden exercise dominated by an incessant Page lead run.

The version of 'Communication Breakdown' had Chris Grant squealing "Oh yeah, Led Zeppelin!" over the final few seconds and another fabled intro: "Right now … Led Zeppelin … 'Communication Breakdown' … Tell me how it is!!"

A rare cover of Eddie Cochran's 'Something Else' was a definite highlight of this session with some excellent piano from John Paul and some posturing vocals from the increasingly confident Plant. Then it was back to that man Grant for the close: "Led Zeppelin … Underground sounds on Radio One."

Also recorded at this session was a preview of the *Zeppelin II* track 'What Is And What Should Never Be'. The fact that they would record a second BBC session version two weeks later clearly hints at their dissatisfaction with this cut – a simplistic take with none of the heavy phasing effects of the subsequent BBC recording. This take was never broadcast.

Also destined to remain on the cutting room floor was the six-minute group interview with all four members, during which Page can be heard strumming his guitar. This attempted question and answer session continually broke down as the engineer tried to get the balance right – and Grant continually fluffed the questions. For example:

Chris Grant: "Here we go boys, we've got the old red light up for you … In the studio we've got Led Zeppelin for you. Let's speak to John Paul Jones. Now I believe you are a musical arranger as well as a composer – true – yes?"

Jones: "No!"

Grant: "A composer as well as a musical arranger?"

Jones: "No. A musical arranger as well as a bass guitarist."

Grant: "Can we do this again?"

"Cut it! OK, here we go again …"

The versions of' Communication Breakdown', 'The Girl I Love', 'She Got Long Black Wavy Hair' and 'Something Else' would finally see the light of day on the official 1997 *BBC Sessions* CD

Bootleg CD References: *A Secret History* (Scorpio), *The Complete BBC Classics* (Immigrant), *Lost BBC Sessions* (Led Note)

Thursday June 19 1969
Paris, France
Antenne Culturelle Du Kremlin Bicetre
TV RECORDING

Tous En Scene French TV recording. Tracks broadcast: 'Communication Breakdown (rehearsal)'/'Communication Breakdown'/'Dazed And Confused'. Original broadcast September 5, 1969, on the French TV network.

According to the French magazine *Jukebox*, they performed 'Communication Breakdwn'/'Dazed And Confused'/'White Summer-Black Mountain Side'/'Good Times Bad Times'-'Whole Lotta Love'. If this is correct this would have been the first performance of 'Whole Lotta Love' in Europe.

This fleeting visit to Paris saw them appear in a bizarre French satire TV show. They arrived at Orly airport and booked into the Westminster Hotel.

The resulting 12 minutes of footage remains the only clear colour television film of the group. It was re-broadcast some 22 years layer in 1991 on the French cable TV channel Canal Jimmy. The group can be seen rehearsing 'Communication Breakdown' with the camera angles behind the drum kit providing a stunning portrayal of John Bonham at work – a percussive masterclass in itself. The programme was a bizarre concoction with scenes of bell boys pretending to be in a rock band all linked by a strange compere. The programme bill also had jazz and variety acts and even a Salvation Army band.

In the footage, Peter Grant can be seen ushering his boys onto the stage for the live recording. In front of a seated and rather bemused audience they duly delivered a stunning 'Communication Breakdown' with typical mid '69 verve. A section of 'Dazed And Confused' followed, edited in during the violin bow section. For Peter Grant this recording confirmed his doubts about TV as a medium for Zeppelin. "French TV was another difficult one. They never knew how to get the sound right in a TV studio and I realised it wasn't worth the effort."

In 2002 Jimmy Page acquired this footage and deployed the 'Communication Breakdown' and 'Dazed And Confused' clips as an extra item on the official Led Zeppelin DVD. Commenting about the Paris clip for the sleeve notes he noted,

"It's strange yes, but we wanted to show it because that's the reason we decided not to do any more TV after becoming disenchanted by the audio-video presentation that TV provided – so that suddenly makes it an important part of the story. It shows why we went off in the direction we did."

After the TV recording the band were also scheduled to perform a promotional date for their French record company allegedly in a boxing ring. This reception was hosted by Eddie Barclay in Le Bilboquet, a Parisian nightclub. Peter Grant recalled: "The thing I remember about this is that we didn't play because we couldn't get the gear in the place. Jimmy wanted to go so he could meet Brigitte Bardot. Anyway we didn't play live but all the papers gave us great reviews the next day, presuming we had. That was a laugh!"

While in Paris, the band also gave an interview on Jose Arthur's Pop Club on Radio France Inter.

Later that evening, Robert Plant and John Bonham visited the Rock'N'Roll Circus nightclub and jammed with Marc Tobaly and Jacques Grandet – the guitarist and bassist from the French group Variations.

Bootleg CD reference: *Hideaway* (Nienerwald)
Visual Reference: Official *Led Zeppelin* 2003 DVD (Warner Vision), *Unofficial Early Visions* DVD (Celebration)

Friday June 20 1969
Newcastle-On-Tyne, England
City Hall

Set included: Train Kept A Rollin'/I Cant Quit You Baby/Dazed And Confused/White Summer-Black Mountain Side/You Shook Me-Lemon Song/Pat's Delight/How Many More Times(Incl Over under Sideways Down-Oh Rosie-The Hunter/Communication Breakdown

A photo session from this date was used on a publicity postcard by Atlantic. Two of the shots also appeared as early portrait posters.

In 2002 part of this performance surfaced on an audience tape issued on the unofficial Tarantura CD set *Blighty*. Even in lo fi quality, it revealed the

band on scintillating form with Plant commenting: "You know we do a lot of shows in America and I think this is the best night we've ever had in England"

Bootleg CD Reference: *Blighty* (Tarantura)

Saturday June 21 1969
Bristol, England
Colston Hall
Blodwyn Pig were unable to support on this date.

Sunday June 22 1969
London, England
BBC Radio One Chris Grant's Tast Pop Sundae
RADIO BROADCAST
On this day Radio One aired the June 16 Aeolian Hall session. It was broadcast between 10am and 12 on *Chris Grant's Tasty Pop Sundae* . Also on the show were Marmalade and Vanity Fare.

Tuesday June 24 1969
London, England
Maida Vale, Studio 4
RADIO ONE SESSION
BBC recording from 2.30pm to 9.30pm. Producer: John Walters; engineer: Tony Wilson. Tracks recorded: Whole Lotta Love/Communication Breakdown/What Is And What Should Never Be/Travelling Riverside Blues/Jimmy Page Interview. Original broadcast: Sunday June 29 1969, between 7pm and 9pm, on *Top Gear* introduced by

John Peel. Also on the show in session are Pentangle, Savoy Brown Blues Band & Idle Race.

If the effect of their previous session had been dampened somewhat by the rather inappropriate Sunday morning scheduling, they had an immediate opportunity to hit their core audience with this session for *Top Gear,* recorded just eight days later. With John Walters producing (one of his first Peel shows) and Tony Wilson engineering, this session was easily their most advanced. Jimmy was allowed the luxury of adding several overdubs to the tracks during this seven-hour session. The truly excellent results mirror just how much ground the group had covered since their first BBC session in early March. "We did Led Zeppelin in mono and I still have the tape," recalls Walters. "Bearing in mind it was just an afternoon and evening in a very basic studio, it sounded great."

Cue John Peel: "7.30 on Radio One and I'd like to go on with Led Zeppelin and a song called 'A Whole Lotta Love'." In sharp contrast to the *Pop Sundae* approach, this was John Peel's no non-sense announcement for the radio première of the track which would soon emerge as their early anthem.

With the release of *Zep II* still four months away, it's a real surprise that they decide to pre-view 'Whole Lotta Love' to the radio audience, especially as it was so rarely played live at this point. This prototype version was dominated by Page stepping on the wah-wah pedal at regular intervals, culminating in a full-on effect for that famous solo which emerged out of the spacey middle section. During the fade, Plant was captured at his ad-libbing best, throwing in tongue in cheek references to his Black Country origins. This prompted Peel to comment on the song's close: "Got those old West Bromwich blues? You've got to be putting me on R Plant!"

This session was broadcast a day after their Bath Festival appearance on which Peel also comments: "This is Led Zeppelin who played very well at the amazing festival in Bath yesterday – and this is curiously titled 'What Is And What

Should Never Be' or something!"

The session was completed by an aggressive performance of 'Communication Breakdown'. (Peel: "I'd forgotten that track ends so suddenly!") and another rarity – 'Travelling Riverside Blues '69', a spontaneous blues rendition of Robert Johnson's original complete with obligatory lemon squeezing lyrics and dominated by some stirring Page slide guitar and amusing Plant ad-libs ("Why don't yer come in my kitchen?").

A quite magnificent performance only ever recorded for this session, and years later deemed important enough by Page to seek out and issue officially on the *Remasters* box set of 1990.

There was also a brief Jimmy Page interview recorded on the night of the session, conducted by Radio One DJ Brian Matthews in a much more accomplished fashion than Chris Grant's effort.

Possibly recorded for the World Service, Jimmy told Matthews that the new album was three-quarters finished. "We're finishing off the mixing in New York and it should be out in the first week of August." (It finally emerged in October). He also revealed that the title would be *Led Zeppelin II* and when asked to select a track that is representative of the album, he cited 'What Is And What Should Never Be', which was used as a link. This interview has still not been broadcast, at least on UK radio.

The reaction to the broadcast of this final prestigious *Top Gear* appearance, coupled with the success of the same weekend's Bath Festival and Albert Hall Pop Proms performances, ensured that Peter Grant could fly out to America in July for the third US visit, content in the knowledge that his act was now the most talked-about group of the moment. This surge of interest also succeeded in catapulting Led Zeppelin's début album into the top five of the UK album chart.

'Whole Lotta Love', 'What Is And What Should Never Be', 'Communication Breakdown' and 'Travelling Riverside Blues' would later be officially released on the 1997 BBC Sessions CD.

Bootleg CD Reference: *A Secret History* (Scorpio), *Radio Sessions* (Chapter One), *The Complete BBC Classics* (Immigrant)

Wednesday June 25 1969
Willesdon, London, England
Morgan Studios
RECORDING SESSIONS

The band cut the studio take of Ben E King/James Bethea's 'We're Gonna Groove' for possible inclusion on the second album. Despite being used as the set opener on their early 1970 dates, the track remained unreleased until it was revived for the *Coda* album. Also cut around this time was another outtake, 'Sugar Mama', which would later appear on bootleg.

Bootleg CD Reference: *Sugar Mama/Alternative Coda* (CG)

Thursday June 26 1969
Portsmouth, England
Guildhall

Friday June 27 1969
London, England
Playhouse Theatre
RADIO ONE SESSION

Set: Alan Black Introduction/Communication Breakdown (inc. It's Your Thing)/I Can't Quit You/Interview With Alan Black And Confused/Interlude with Adrian Henry, Mike Evans and Andy Roberts of The Liverpool Scene/White Summer – Black Mountain Side/You Shook Me/How Many More Times (inc. The Hunter – The Lemon Song).

BBC recording. Rehearsal 7pm. Recording 8.45Ppm to 10.15pm. Producer: Jeff Griffin; engineer: Tony Wilson.

This was a pilot show for what would emerge as the long-running BBC Radio One *In Concert* series. The idea stemmed from a conversation Page had with Radio One producer Jeff Griffin. He told Griffin that as much as the band enjoyed these sessions, he felt the BBC offered them limited time to showcase their act, and he would welcome the opportunity for the band to record a live session which allowed them to expand and improvise. Griffin had already had an idea for an in concert style show, so a pilot was arranged.

The date was set for June 27 during a particularly hectic week that sees them record the *Top Gear* session on Tuesday, cut the track 'We're Gonna Groove' at Morgan Studios the next day (considered for release on *Led Zep II* but subsequently dropped and eventually released on *Coda*) and play Portsmouth Guildhall on the Thursday.

Straight after the BBC recording, their gear was transported to the Bath Festival for their late afternoon stint before moving on to the Albert Hall Pop Proms for their afternoon and evening performances on Sunday, a quite astonishing pace even by their own work intensive 1969 standards.

The original plan was for the show to be aired live on the Friday, but this was shelved in favour of a later broadcast on Sunday August 10 as part of the second hour of John Peel's *Top Gear*. The Zeppelin special was well received and inspired Jeff Griffin to push ahead with the *In Concert* series which began in January 1970.

Despite their hectic schedule the band sound incredibly fresh on this recording. Following an impressive opening of 'Communication Breakdown' (which had Plant including a few lines from the Isley Brothers' hit 'It's Your Thing') and 'I Can't Quit You', Alan Black interviewed Jimmy and Robert.

"Well I don't think there was anything restrictive about that performance from Led Zeppelin. Well, we'll not only be hearing Led Zeppelin play tonight, we'll also be talking to them and I'd like to put a couple of questions to the two members who've joined me now, on my left Robert Plant and on my right Jimmy Page."

An interesting discussion followed in which Jimmy bemoaned the lack of specialist radio programmes: "There's only one outlet for our sort of band or Jethro Tull and Ten Years After and that's *Top Gear* and that's only two hours a week."

"Well we've talked a bit about creative freedom," adds Black, "so let's use some of it tonight and perhaps you would like to do one of your longer numbers – feel free to do anything you like!"

Plant: "And when we've finished that we'll be right out of breath, so we'd like to do a thing called 'Dazed And Confused'."

Following an excellent ten-minute version of the first album epic, an interval followed with members of the Liverpool Scene parodying commercial TV breaks of the period.

'White Summer – Black Mountain Side' followed. This take was issued years later on the 1990 *Remasters* set, without Black's quaint intro: "I know Jimmy Page was rather keen to do this one. It's by way of a contrast. I don't know if Jimmy would like to introduce the number but I can tell you the title is 'White Summer'."

The version of 'You Shook Me' that followed featured a lengthy organ solo – a rare occurrence for this period.

Finally, Black explained to the audience that Robert Plant … "is about to re-enact a typical Led Zeppelin stage show close, so listen carefully". A 12-minute delivery of 'How Many More Times' included the band introductions, 'The Hunter' and 'The Lemon Song', additions that were now an established part of this finale of the stage act.

Andy Roberts of the Liverpool Scene recalls that after the show … "We all adjourned to the Sherlock Holmes pub and I remember Adrian shouting across the bar to Jimmy Page 'Is it true you're known as Led Wallet!'"

This splendid early representation of their mid-1969 stage act was subsequently issued on a variety of bootlegs. It remains an authentic reminder of their growing on-stage confidence of the time and finally received an official release in edited form on the 1997 *BBC Sessions* double CD set.

Bootleg CD References: *Rock Hour* (Antrabata), *White Summer* (Swinging Pig), *The Complete BBC Classics* (Immigrant)

Saturday June 28 1969
Shepton Mallet, England
Bath Festival
Led Zeppelin, Ten Tears After, Fleetwood Mac

and John Mayall were the main attractions. Also on the bill were The Nice, Chicken Shack, Blodwyn Pig, Keef Hartley, Taste and The Liverpool Scene. John Peel compèred.

Zeppelin appeared in the early evening performing to a crowd of 12,000 – their biggest UK audience to date. A photo session from this show was later used for one of their first licensed colour posters distributed through Pace merchandisers.

Chris Welch of *Melody Maker* reported: "Nobody had coerced the youth of England into becoming Zep freaks, but there they were, cheering Page, Jones, Bonham and Plant, as the drums thundered and the guitars roared."

Sunday June 29 1969
London, England
Royal Albert Hall
Set included: Communication Breakdown/I Can't Quit You/Dazed And Confused/You Shook Me/How Many More Times/Long Tall Sally.

Advertised as "If you live around London … Your only chance to see … The amazing Led Zeppelin".

Two shows were performed at 5.30pm and 8.30pm under the banner of 'Pop Proms'. Support was from The Liverpool Scene and Mick Abraham's Blodwyn Pig. Top ticket price for the late show was 20 shillings (£1)!

The highlight of this first night of the Pop Proms was undoubtedly the final encore jam, when Zeppelin were joined on stage by members of Blodwyn Pig and The Liverpool Scene to perform 'Long Tall Sally'. *Melody Maker* reports: "The audience were on their feet shouting, stamping and clapping, flowers were thrown on stage and musicians jammed wildly."

Hugh Nolan, reviewing the show for *Disc* under the headline "Pop Proms – a riotous start" stated: "When Zeppelin came on and played at a good ten times the volume of everyone else – played very well indeed, mark you – the audience very nearly freaked completely. They stormed the stage, danced in the aisles and the boxes, and were screaming so hard that the band did three encores. Jimmy Page, ex-Yardbird who's got together one of the most exciting live bands playing anywhere now, blew some really mean and fine guitar solos."

The Royal Albert Hall show helped push the début album into the top five.

However there were still some who remained unimpressed with Zeppelin's style, as this example from the letters page of *Beat International*: "Dear Sir, At the first of the Pop proms, I was really disappointed to see the ridiculous antics of Led

BATH FESTIVAL
OF BLUES RECREATION GROUND   Nº 1

Saturday, June 28th
EVENING TICKET 6.30 on wa

12 Noon   10.30 pm | ADVANCE
                        BOOKING PRICE 1

PEDESTRIANS PLEASE ENTER GROUND VIA NORTH PARADE STREET ENTR
PLEASE SEE OVER RE CAR PARKING FACILITIES

Bath Festival, June 28 1969

Zeppelin, supposedly one of this country's great groups. It was too much to see singer Robert Plant making love to his microphone with Jimmy Page helping out with supposedly 'erotic' guitar a mere hour after The Liverpool Scene had been performing their Bobby & The Helmets number with Adrian Henri rolling around the stage with his mike, taking the go out of the Fifties rock acts. Adrian had 'Bobby Lives!' in large letters on his T-shirt. Judging by Robert Plant, Adrian's slogan is truer than you might think."

Robert and Jimmy later wore these 'Bobby & The Helmets' T-shirts on some of the US dates.

Sunday June 29 1969
London, England
BBC Radio One Top Gear
RADIO BROADCAST
Radio One broadcast the June 24 Maida Vale session between 7 and 9pm on John Peel's *Top Gear* show. Also on the show were Pentangle, Idle Race and the Savoy Blues Band

To keep the momentum going from their earlier visits, Peter Grant's next move was to book them on to an extensive US summer tour from the first week of July to the last day in August. Among the shows was a variety of high profile outdoor festival dates including the Atlanta Pop Festival, the Newport Jazz Festival and the Dallas International Pop Festival. This gave them a great opportunity to work alongside the likes of Chuck Berry, The Doors, Johnny Winter and B.B. King. It was an eye opening time for the young Robert Plant who, accepting Zeppelin's induction into the Hall of Fame in 1995, would pay acknowledgement to this period: "I'll never forget us playing with Janis and The Doors and so many amazing artists and hanging out with the Airplane and seeing Jonesy and Jack Cassidy disappearing up the corner to discuss the inner movements of a bass guitar. It was a wonderful time and all the way through our career I don't remember a single television set going anywhere."

In between this hectic touring schedule they continued to piece together their second album. "It was crazy really. We were writing the numbers in hotel rooms and then we'd do a rhythm track in London, add the vocal in New York, overdub harmonica in Vancouver and then come back to finish mixing in New York."

Led Zeppelin

KEEPING ZEPPELIN ON THE ROAD: ROADCREW/PERSONNEL

Led Zeppelin employed a small, loyal, band of technical and backroom staff throughout their career. From the beginning, Grant used Richard Cole who had previously worked with The Who, as road manager. Cole remained with Zeppelin up to the Knebworth shows. His version of events is well documented in the book *Hammer Of The Gods* and his own memoir *Stairway To Heaven*.

Clive Coulson was the other principal road crew member, supported by Henry "The Horse" Smith, Sandy McGregor, Kenny Pickett and Joe Jammer. Jammer was Jimmy's guitar tech and later went on to form his own band. Pickett had played with The Creation – he later went into jingle and song-writing, scoring a huge hit with the 1971 kiddies favourite 'Granddad', performed by Clive Dunn. He sadly died in January 1997. Coulson later became road manager for Bad Company.

By the mid Seventies, the road crew comprised Raymond Thomas (guitars), Brian Condliffe (bass and keyboards), Benji Le Fevre (vocals) and Mick Hinton (drums).

Lighting effects were stage-managed by Ian 'Iggy' Knight and Kirby Wyatt. The Showco sound technicians included Rusty Brutshe, Donny Kretzchmar, Alan Branton, and Joe Crowley. Tim Marten (guitars) and Andy Ledbetter (keyboards) were with them on the last European tour.

Personal assistants included Rick Hobbs (Jimmy's assistant), Phil Carlo (Europe '80), Brian Gallivan (1977 tour), Dave Northover (1977), John Bindon (1977), Dennis Sheehan (1977), Dave Moulder (Europe '80) and Rex King (Bonzo's assistant 1977 – 80). Rex later went on to road manage both Jimmy and Robert on their solo tours, as well as the 1995/96 Page/Plant tour.

PR staff included Bill Harry (*circa* 1969/70), B.P. Fallon (1972-1974), and Danny Goldberg (US only, 1973/75). Goldberg went on to an illustrious career in the music industry, running Geffen Records and managing Nirvana amongst other things.

Legal representatives were Joan Hudson Associates, London, and Steven Weiss, New York.

In 1977, the doctor was played by Larry Badgley.

Rather curiously, no new material from the second album was played in the live set that summer. The shows would still revolve around the tried and tested formula that had held them in such good stead so far, with 'How Many More Times' still acting as the basis for the medley and its nightly variations.

The third tour ended with them picking up a straight $13,000 for an appearance at the Texas International Pop Festival, part of their set being filmed for inclusion in the rarely seen *Texas International Pop Festival* documentary. The soundboard tape of this show surfaced years later on a bootleg and is one of the clearest remnants of the embryonic Zeppelin in all its late Sixties glory.

Saturday July 5 1969
Byron, Georgia
Atlanta International Pop Festival
The two day bill also included Janis Joplin, Chuck Berry, Johnny Winter, Spirit, Chicago, Blood Sweat & Tears, Delaney & Bonnie, Creedence Clearwater Revival and Joe Cocker.

Plant: "I think the atmosphere of the festivals in America manages to be so much different from the ones in England. They're so open and free in the States. In England even the press go with the completely wrong attitude towards the festival; the people just go with a different frame of mind. The Atlanta Festival where we played was a very

loose thing. You heard about the man who jumped on stage? Well, it was 100 degrees on stage, and this guy jumped on stage with nothing on and he was well … pleased with himself … he was tripping out … and instead of dancing in kind of a proper manner, he dived into the drum kit. But it was okay. You don't feel the restrictions you do at a concert."

The incident was reported in *Top Pops*: "Zeppelin had caused riots at the Atlanta Festival, appearing before 40,000 people. The ecstatic audience surged towards the stage and out of their midst leapt a naked man who jumped on stage and began to dance, to the delight of the crowd. Zep continued their act, but the man dived into John Bonham's gong. Picking himself up he continued his dance and then dived into John's drums, so the Zeppelin ejected him off the stage."

Peter Grant had other recollections from the festival: "We had a fall out with Blood, Sweat & Tears. They wouldn't come off. So I stood on the steps and nobody got through until they cleared off. But I used to say to the boys on those bills: 'Go out there and tear the place apart, take the roof or canvas off. I don't want to see you afterwards unless you succeed'. That normally got the required response."

Sunday July 6 1969
Newport, Rhode Island
Festival Field
Newport Jazz Festival
Set: Train Kept A Rollin'/I Can't Quit You/Dazed And Confused/You Shook Me/How Many More Times (inc. The Hunter – The Lemon Song)/Communication Breakdown/Long Tall Sally.

Zeppelin were scheduled to close the final night of a four-day festival which included acts as diverse as Sun Ra Solar Arkestra, Jeff Beck, Joe Turner, Herbie Hancock, Art Blakey Quintet, Sly & The Family Stone, Dave Brubeck, Errol Garner and Stephane Grapelli. However, a near riotous situation had developed on the second night ('the rock night') and local authorities, fearing a repeat of the incident, ordered that Zeppelin be pulled

from the bill, "in the interest of public safety".

Festival Promoter George Wein took the unwise step of announcing that Zeppelin would not be appearing due to illness of one of the group

On hearing this, Grant immediately flew to Newport with his lawyer and announced that Zeppelin would play. But the damage has already been done and thousands were leaving the arena as the band arrived. Plant: "We passed them coming – all going the other way, out of Newport!"

Page was not impressed with the situation: "You don't blow a date like this one. Not after all that. The Newport Jazz Festival was far too important to us to just cancel out and I'm very upset at the whole thing. Wein should have never announced one of us was ill."

Zeppelin finally took the stage at about 1am the following morning and delivered a powerful, energetic set, despite problems with the P.A. Plant was still annoyed and told the audience: "A lot of people thought that we weren't gonna come here today. There was a lot of talk that everyone was ill and bad. There was nothing wrong with us at all and we intended on playing. That's what we've come to America for. We were coming in the first place so don't get any hassles about what we were gonna do and what we weren't. We hope you'll enjoy everything we do tonight and have a ball."

They finally closed the festival with a rousing version of 'Long Tall Sally'.

In England, *New Musical Express* ran the headline "Great Zepplin (sic) closed Newport, despite ban!" – "Zeppelin showed up on Sunday anyway, following a knockout performance at the Atlanta Pop Festival, and at 1am Monday morning, pro-ceeded to go on stage and completely destroy the audience. Other acts ahead of Zeppelin seemed to ignore the time limit set on their performances. Page was uptight, but when he went on stage, that crowd out there was ready and waiting, and Led Zeppelin was prepared to sock it to me – regardless of the unfortunate set of circumstances."

John Paul Jones: "I remember seeing all three of James Brown's drummers stand around John Bonham at the Newport Jazz Festival in disbelief, wondering how one guy does what all three of them did."

Bootleg CD References: *Jazz* (NPJF 1001), *Tales Of 69* (Tarantura), *Newport Jazz Festival* (Empress Valley)

Tuesday July 8 1969
Miami, Florida

Wednesday July 9 1969
Tampa, Florida

Thursday July 10 1969
Jacksonville, Florida

Friday July 11 1969
Laurel Racecourse, Maryland
Laurel Jazz and Pop Festival
This took place at the Laurel Race Track- a horse racing arena.

Saturday July 12 1969
Philadelphia, Pennsylvania
The Spectrum
Spectrum Summer Pop Festival
Zeppelin headlined. The supporting bill consisted of Johnny Winter, Al Kooper, Jethro Tull, and Buddy Guy's Blues Band.

Top Pops reported: "At the Spectrum Stadium in Philadelphia where a three-day festival was in progress, there was a strict rule that no artist could perform an encore – they each had a 30 minute spot and that was that. After Zep left the stage the audience went berserk and screamed for more. They continued demanding an encore and the organisers finally had to let them reappear."

Sunday July 13 1969
New York, New York
Singer Bowl, Flushing meadow
GUEST APPEARANCE: A drunken John Bonham made an unscheduled and unwelcome appearance during The Jeff Beck Group's set. He interrupted their performance of 'Rice Pudding' by attempting to add the beat of 'The Stripper' as his clothes came off. He was quickly bundled off stage. Later during the Beck Group's encore, Plant, Page, Jones and Bonham all joined Beck for a genuine jam on 'Jailhouse Rock' with Glen Cornick of Jethro Tull, and Alvin Lee of Ten Years After. Eric Clapton watched from the side of the stage.

Tuesday July 15 1969
Rochester, New York

Wednesday July 16 1969
Detroit, Michigan

Thursday July 17 1969
Cincinnati, Ohio

Friday July 18 1969
Chicago, Illinoi
Kinetic Playground
Support for both nights was Savoy Brown and The Litter, with guest star Jethro Tull.

Saturday July 19 1969
Chicago, Illinois
Kinetic Playground
Top Pops reported: "Their gig at the Kinetic Playground in Chicago made them $20,000, and one end of North Clark Street, where the club is situated, was barricaded off from the crowd. The Promoters presented members of the group with gold engraved watches from Tiffany's."

Sunday July 20 1969
Cleveland, Ohio
Musicarnival
Set: Train Kept A Rollin'/I Can't Quit You/Dazed And Confused/White Summer – Black Mountain Side/You Shook Me/How Many More Times (inc. The Hunter – The Lemon Song). All seats $5

This show took place at the Musicarnival – a summer theatre tent in Warrensville Heights. The venue was closed in 1975. The James Gang were also on the bill, and Jimmy struck up a friendship with Joe Walsh who sold him a Gibson Les Paul guitar.

The gig itself was a rather below par performance married by equipment problems. Plant: "Once again, as last time in the State of Ohio, we find that the PA system is completely inaudible; but, nevertheless, we'd like to carry on … I think I'd better get out of the way … If we go up with a flash and a bang … "

Plant, jokingly, sings a few lines of 'You Make Me Feel So Young' during 'How Many More Times', otherwise a standard set.
Bootleg CD References: *Cleveland 1969* (The Diagrams Of Led Zeppelin), *The Destroyer 1969* (Tarantura)

Monday July 21 1969
New York, New York
Schaefer Music Festival,
Wollman Rink Central Park
Set: Train Kept A Rollin'/I Can't Quit You/Dazed And Confused/You Shook Me/White Summer – Black Mountain Side/How Many More Times (inc. Woody Woodpecker Song – For What It's

Ticket: Schaefer Music Festival in Central Park — Admission $1.50. ORCHESTRA — MON. EVE. 9:30 P.M. JULY 21 — SHOW 30

Worth – The Hunter – The Lemon Song)/Communication Breakdown.

Two shows tonight at 7pm and 9.30pm. Zeppelin shared the billing with B.B. King and were back on form for these important shows on the Wollman ice skating rink in Central Park.

Robert apologised to the crowd for the lack of new material: "We've got an album coming out in the second week in August, but at the moment there's a bit of a delay on it and there's been a bit of a delay in us getting the numbers together really for stage, because we're still doing the old ones." Both Page and Plant wore cowboy hats during show.

'How Many More Times' had lyrics from the theme to the *Woody Woodpecker Show*! Robert also graphically instructed the audience how to squeeze his lemons: "If you squeeze as hard as that, there ain't gonna be anything left for tomorrow … so do it gently!"

A US trade magazine reviewed the second set: "The band practically brought the house down and no kidding. By the end of the four encore colossus, the beam and erector set framework of the temporary stage was creaking under the strain as performers and audiences alike were swept into a rock'n'roll bacchanalia."

Bootleg CD References: *Complete Central Park 1969* (Sanctuary), *Twist* (The Diagrams of Led Zeppelin), *Schaefer Music Festival* (Rock Garden), *Superstars* (TNT Studio)

Friday July 25 1969
Milwaukee, Wisconsin
State Fair Grounds
Mid-West Rock Festival

Set: Train Kept A Rollin'/I Can't Quit You/Dazed And Confused/White Summer – Black Mountain Side/How Many More Times (inc. The Hunter – The Lemon Song)/Communication Breakdown.

This show deployed a flatbed trailer as a stage, set on the infield in front of the racetrack's grandstand. Zep performed a standard festival set. During the finale of 'How Many More Times', instead of "I've got you in the sights … ", Plant sang, in perfect cabaret style, "I've got you … under my skin" – much to the amusement of the crowd.

Bootleg CD References: Stroll On! (The Diagrams of Led Zeppelin), *State Fair* (Digger Productions)

Saturday July 26 1969
Vancouver, Canada
PNE Agrodome

"Led Zeppelin Flies Directly to the Nerve Ends" read the headline of the *Vancouver Sun*. Jurgen Hesse reported: "This heavy English rock group, which appeared Saturday to a capacity audience at the Agrodome, works on the principle of sensory overload – extreme volume, a screaming vocalist, brilliant musicianship, a harsh sound that goes

72

Woodinville, Washington
Goldcreek Park,
Seattle Pop Festival

Zeppelin performed on the final night of this three-day festival, taking the stage after The Doors. Other acts on the bill included Lee Michaels, Chuck Berry, Spirit, Albert Collins, Flying Burrito Brothers, Flock, The Guess Who, Ike & Tina Turner Revue, Vanilla Fudge. Bo Diddley and The Youngbloods.

Tellingly both Spirit and Vanilla Fudge, who headlined above Zeppelin at American gigs just seven months earlier, were now much lower down the billing than Zeppelin.

"Seattle Gives Peace A Chance" reported *Rolling Stone*. Ed Leimbacher observed: "Music, Love and Peace – that was the announced theme of Seattle's first annual Pop Festival, held at Woodenville's Gold Creek Park in a farm valley north-east of Seattle. Well, music there was a-plenty, and peace reigned supreme throughout the heat and sweat of the three day festival. As for love, let every man keep counsel with himself; my mama didn't raise no blabbermouths.

"The peace symbols, American flags, and bikinis were out in full force – 30,000 scenic wonders and up-from-unders, beer-drinkers and deep-thinkers, soda poppers and acid-droppers."

Leimbacher was equally as impressed with Zeppelin as he is with the atmosphere: "Robert Plant screamed his guts out; Jimmy Page bowed some phenomenal sounds from his guitar; the group even survived a momentary power breakdown. (The finest music, however, was Page's 8-minute almost-solo of 'White Summer'.)

"It was past midnight by then. Chuck Berry split in disgust at being delayed and the Seattle Pop Festival just slowly ground to a halt."

There exists an unmixed soundboard tape of many of the performances at this festival, allegedly including Zeppelin, apparently in the possession of a soundman who worked on the festival. The Flying Burrito Brothers' set and a few songs

directly to the nerve ends, and involvement with the audience.

"Led Zeppelin exists on the genius of lead guitarist Jimmy Page, whose baby face belies his musical message – that of jarring and unnerving the listeners with a fortissimo yowl that never lets up, never allows time for recovery. Only in a haunting, beautiful solo did Page show any compassion, any feeling for lyricism.

"Page is a street-corner philosopher who uses a loudhailer to speak to a little old lady asking for directions. One of his songs is titled 'Communication Breakdown'. He obviously believes that to reach people's hearts he has to slice through the layers of fat that hold emotions immobile.

"In rock parlance, Led Zeppelin is a very together group. It is made up of four individual musical artists attuned to each other's whims, capable of ensemble performance as well as separate forays into the jungle of lonely escapades."

from the Youngbloods surfaced but the only Zep related material to circulate was a snippet of conversation with Plant backstage.

The following day, The Edgewater Inn in Seatle was to become the scene of the most infamous tale of Zeppelin's increasingly rampant road fever – the 'Mudshark' incident. As legend has it, after a successful day's fishing in Puget Sound from their balconies at the Inn, road manager Richard Cole and various members of the Zeppelin and Vanilla Fudge entourages were reported to have tied up and sexually satisfied a willing red-haired groupie with a red snapper fish. Some reports have even suggested that the fish was a mud shark. Mark Stein of Vanilla Fudge is alleged to have filmed the incident for prosperity.

Tuesday July 29 1969
Edmonton, Canada
Kinsmen Field House
Zeppelin shared the bill with Vanilla Fudge. Attendance: 500

"Led Zeppelin's reluctant guitarist" – Bob Harvey reported: "Led Zeppelin wasn't quite as impressive Tuesday as they were at the Edmonton Gardens in May, but they were hampered by the sound system, as well as having to go on stage first. It would have been better if Vanilla Fudge had played first. Their music's more intellectual, and more jazz-influenced than the gutsy Zeppelin's.

"Tuesday's show at the Kinsmen Field House was probably the best of the year, and the size of the turnout probably caught the promoters – Concerts West of Seattle, and Dick Lodmell – by surprise. There weren't enough chairs to go around the crowd of 5,000, but otherwise the concert was the smoothest

and best-organized rock show here in a long time."

Wednesday July 30 1969
Salt Lake City, Utah
Terrace Lagoon Ballroom
Support from Vanilla Fudge.

Thursday July 31 1969
Eugene, Oregon
The band were each presented with a gold disc by Atlantic executive vice-president Jerry Wexler for sales in excess of a million dollars and half a million copies for their first album.

Page: "We didn't tell Bonzo that each of us would have gold records. He thought we were going to get one between us and we'd have to split it up, each of us getting it for three months at a time. I think he's speechless."

Friday August 1 1969
Santa Barbara, California
Santa Barbara Earl Warren Showgrounds
Zeppelin headlined over Jethro Tull and Fraternity Of Man

UNCONFIRMED
Saturday August 2 1969
Albuquerque, New Mexico
Civic Auditorium

UNCONFIRMED
Saturday August 2 1969
Austin, Texas
Civic Auditorium
Posters have appeared for both the Albuquerque and Dallas dates as a shared bill with Vanilla Fudge but it's more likely the Albuquerque date was played.

It was reported in *NME* (August 2) that Zeppelin would headline the Bilzen Jazz Festival in Belguim on August 22. They subsequently extended their US tour and did not fulfil this date – Deep Purple took their place.

Sunday August 3 1969
Houston, Texas
Houston Music Hall
Attendance: 3,000

UNCONFIRMED
Monday August 4 1969
Dallas, Texas
State Fair Coliseum
CANCELLED
Allegedly this show was cancelled in favour of the Texas International Pop Festival on August 31 – but ticket stubs do exist so it may have taken place.

Wednesday August 6 1969
Sacramento, California
Memorial Auditorium

Thursday August 7 1969
Berkely, California
Community Theatre

Friday August 8 1969
San Bernardino, California
Swing Auditorium,
Orange Showgrounds
Set: Train Kept A Rollin'/I Can't Quit You/I Gotta Keep On Moving/Dazed And Confused/White Summer – Black Mountain Side/You Shook Me/How Many More Times (inc. The Hunter – Every Little Thing I Do – Schooldays – Hail, Hail, Rock And Roll). Support from Jethro Tull.

Page again had string trouble after 'I Can't Quit You' and Plant filled in: "We're gonna carry on with a thing from the first album which I better tell you a bit about as Jimmy's doing a quick string thing. We did an album called *Led Zeppelin One*, but we left the 'One' off, 'cos we didn't know what to call it at the time. You must bear with me, 'cos it's on the spot co-ordination, so if you're ready to take it, I can give it!"

The jam gradually progressed into something resembling 'I Gotta Move' as played in Stockholm earlier in the year and when Page also broke a string.

The heat in the auditorium caused more problems for Page's guitar. Plant: "It's too hot y'see. All the strings keep going out of tune." Plant: "According to the guys that run this place, the place is gonna close in about a quarter of an hour, so we're gonna do our last number ... " 'How Many More Times featured sections of Chuck Berry's 'Schooldays' and 'Hail, Hail, Rock And Roll'.

Bootleg CD Reference: *Summer Of '69* (Rubber Dubber)

Saturday August 9 1969
Anaheim, California
Anaheim Convention center
Support from Jethro Tull.

Judy Sims, writing in *Disc*, was not impressed. "Jethro Tull were great, playing to a sold-out audience who really appreciated their efforts. Led Zeppelin, ostensibly stars of the show, came on for the second half. They were awful. Loud, pretentious, no subtlety, no nuance, just multi-decibel riffs, echoed by Plant's frenzied 'singing'. He has obviously been watching Roger Daltrey. It would be nice if he listened to Roger Daltrey. And the

IN CONCERT · ONLY L.A. APPEARANCE
LED ZEPPELIN
AND **JETHRO TULL**
Sat., AUG. 9, 8 P.M.
ANAHEIM CONVENTION CENTER

All seats reserved at $6.50, 5.50, 4.50
TICKETRON/TRS TICKETS Available at all TRS Outlets
(Dial TRS-1000 for nearest outlet)
Available at Anaheim Convention Center Box Office.
Sunset Agencies, Ali Wallich's Music Stores and United
Calif. Banks in Orange County. Mut Club's Anaheim
Convention Center, 800 W. Katella, Anaheim, Calif. 92802
For information call (714) 635-5000
PRODUCED BY CONCERT ASSOCIATES A KOMAN/SETTZMAN CO.

crowd loved it! Perhaps I shouldn't blame Page and co. for performing undemanding material when all they have to do is stand there and whack out mediocrity to receive the reward of thunderous appreciation that greeted their every move."

Sunday August 10 1969
San Diego, California
Sports Arena
Support from Jethro Tull.

Tracks reported: "All the conditions were there to make it an usual run-of-the-mill dull concert; it took place at the super-hype Sports Arena, a large

rent-a-Gestapo was present, and it was a sit down affair. When Zeppelin came on, several thousand music lovers ignored that stupid unwritten law which says you should sit perfectly still in your numbered seat like a respectable citizen, and converged to the floor area and felt free.

"Two encores cost the promoters an additional couple of grand and it was with their approval that the encores were permitted. Instead of the usual 11pm deadline the concert ended at 12.05."

During their stay in California they ventured to the Experience Club on Sunset Strip where Jimmy and Robert ended up jamming with Spencer Davis and Screaming Lord Sutch. It was here that Sutch asked Jimmy, along with John Bonham, to help him out on the recording of his new album. Their performances were duly issued as part of the *Lord Sutch And Heavy Friends* album released on Atlantic in 1970.

During this hectic schedule, Page also flew into New York to oversee the mixing of 'Bring It On Home' for *Led Zeppelin II* at A&R Studios. He met with Peter Grant, Eddie Kramer and journalist Ritchie Yorke. He played Yorke completed mixes of 'Living Loving Maid', 'Heartbreaker' and

THE ROCKPILE, TORONTO AUGUST 18 1969

The Rockpile, Toronto, August 18, 1969.

Led Zeppelin

'What Is And What Should Never Be'. Atlantic's much respected producer, Jerry Wexler, also heard this preview and stated: "On the strength of these three tracks, I would have to say this is the best white blues group I have ever heard." A day later Page was back with the group to resume the rest of the tour.

Sunday August 10 1969
London, England
BBC Radio One One Night Stand
RADIO BROADCAST
Radio One broadcast the concert recording taped at the Playhouse Theatre on June 27. It was aired between 8 and 9pm as part of John Peel's *Top Gear*. Also on the show was The Edgar Broughton Band.

UNCONFIRMED
Wednesday August 13 1969
Lubbock, Texas
Civic Center Music Hall
Some sources have this date as being a gig in Phoenix Arizona

UNCONFIRMED
Thursday August 14 1969
Austin, Texas
Municipal Auditorium

Friday August 15 1969
San Antonio, Texas
Hemisfair Arena
A handbill has emerged for this date listing a shared bill with Jethro Tull and Sweet Smoke. During their stay in Texas the band received abuse from the locals due to the length of their hair.

Saturday August 16 1969
Asbury Park, New Jersey
Convention Hall
Support from Joe Cocker. Two shows were played – 7.30 and 9.45pm.

This date took place the same weekend as the legendary Woodstock Festival in upstate New York. Zeppelin were initially approached to play the festival but Grant declined. "We were asked to do Woodstock and Atlantic were very keen, and so was our US promoter, Frank Barcelona. I said no because at Woodstock we'd have just been another band on the bill." Support for this show, Joe Cocker, did agree play at Woodstock and following his set flew to appear on the Sunday line-up, where he become one of the highlights of the weekend.

Sunday August 17 1969
Wallingford, Connecticut
Oakdale Musical Theater
Set included: Train Kept A Rollin'/I Can't Quit You.

This show was performed on a revolving stage, resulting in very uneven sound.
Bootleg CD References: *Tales Of '69* (Tarantura), *Red Snapper Deluxe* (Balboa)

Monday August 18 1969
Toronto, Canada
The Rock Pile
Two show, 8 and 11.30pm
Set 1: Train Kept A Rollin'/I Can't Quit You/Dazed And Confused/You Shook Me/How Many More Times (inc. The Hunter – The Lemon Song).
Set 2: Train Kept A Rollin'/I Can't Quit You/Dazed And Confused/White Summer – Black Mountain Side/You Shook Me/How Many More Times (inc. The Hunter – Trucking Little Mama – Needle Blues – The Lemon Song)/Communication Breakdown.

Billed as 'Mighty Monday', there were two shows. Edward Bear supported.

The first set was a hurried and frantic affair after coming on late. The second set was a much more relaxed, longer and satisfying performance, one of the best of the tour.

Plant: "It's very nice to be back, but we've got a lot of problems. We've just come from San Antonio in Texas, where all the geezers thought we should get our hair cut, and we've been through that and everybody's been feeling rather bad, so we're very pleased to be here one way or another. It's nice to be back. We'd like to say hello to anybody from the British Isles, including Scotland and two geezers who used to come from Birmingham in a group called The Yellow Rainbow. Nice to see you're still nicking gear! And so, if everybody can feel free and easy, we'd like to see what we can do."

Plant wound up the show with the band introductions: "We'd like to try to draw a conclusion to what's been a very hectic day. We'd like to tell you that Texas is still as it was when you last read about it and that England is still what it always will be, and we'd like to see you very shortly again, but if not you could all move to the Bahamas or something … on bass guitar, Hammond organ, and throne … King John Paul Jones, on drums John Henry Bonham and on lead guitar and as many chicks as he can find … Jimmy Page!" John Bonham then takes the microphone and introduces Robert as "straight from the Labour club at Cradley Heath."

'How Many More Times' was one of the longest versions on the tour. Riotous applause brought the band back for a sole encore of 'Communication Breakdown', introduced by Plant as "an old number by Bing Crosby."

"Led Zeppelin soars to the pop stratosphere" – Ritchie Yorke reviewed the shows for *The Globe And Mail*: "With the exception of the Toronto Pop Festival, last night's Led Zeppelin concert was the most significant pop event this year. Not only were the two shows completely sold out in advance, but at least 2,000 were turned away the management reported. They missed out on one of the finest shows ever to pour sweat onto the Rock Pile stage. Led Zeppelin proved itself not only to be one conceivable replacement for Cream, but at times I doubt if even Clapton, Bruce and Baker could have topped what Zeppelin offered!"

Yorke was still confused about the band's personnel and repeated the mistake from his review of the February concert: "Drummer John Paul Jones (sic) and bass player John Bonham (sic) are neither brilliant nor flashy, but as a rhythm team they're the toughest thing since cowhide chewing gum."

Bootleg CD References: *Absolutely Gems* (Sanctuary), *Complete Rockpile Show* (The Symbols), *Hideaway* (Nienerwald), *Long Tall Sally* (Tarantura)

Wednesday Auguast 20 1969
Schenectady, New York
The Aerodrome New York
Two shows at 8pm and 11pm. The venue was a converted bowling alley.

Thursday August 21 1969
Framingham Natick, Massachusetts
Carousel Theatre
Support from Orpheus. The show was presented by Frank Conley and held in a giant summer musical theatre tent with 2,600 in attendance. This venue is now the site of the Carousel Office Park. JJ Jackson introduced them on stage.

A local review stated: "They performed Willie Dixon's 'Down And Out Blues', 'I Can't Quite You Baby', 'Dazed And Confused' and 'White Summer' plus 'What Is And What Should Be' (sic) never before done on stage and Willie Dixon's 'You Shook Me'".

This was the first known live performance of what would emerge as the second track on *Led Zeppelin II*.

Friday August 22 1969
Dania, Florida
Pirates' World
Two nights at an outdoor amphitheater in an amusement park. This venue played host to many touring bands, including Johnny Winter, part of whose *And Live* album was recorded there. It was

also the location for the movies *Musical Mutiny* (with scenes featuring Iron Butterfly) and *Santa Claus And The Easter Bunny*. It was closed in 1975. Support both nights from The Echo, Royal Ascots and Brimstone. Zeppelin on at 9.30pm

"Spectacular Light Show – All Exciting Rides Free" proclaimed adverts for the event.

Saturday August 23 1969
Dania, Florida
Pirates' World

Sunday August 24 1969
Jacksonville, Florida
Veterans' Memorial Coliseum

UNCONFIRMED
Monday August 25 1969
Monticello, New York
Delano Motor Lodge
Triple C promotions exclusive area appearance. Two shows, 9pm and 11.30

Wednesday August 27 1969
Hampton Beach, New Haven
Casino Ballroom
Two shows at 8pm and 10pm

Rock archivist Doug Hinman recalled: "I went to the early show and vaguely remember being disappointed because the show started late and they only played around 35 minutes. Bonham had busted a snare drum which delayed the start. The opener was The Yardbirds' 'Train Kept A Rollin'."

Friday August 29 1969
Queens, New York
Flushing Meadows Park
State Pavillion
Singer Bowl Music Festival
Zeppelin headlined both nights of this two day 'Guitar Virtuoso Show'. Larry Coryell appeared on Friday and Buddy Guy appeared on Saturday.

Circus magazine reported: "Led Zeppelin fans are the first to pound on chairs in mad heat, but how spirited they actually are, is another thing. Take for instance, the concert at the Pavilion (a huge outdoor place) in New York. 10,500 fans all standing around, 3,000 more turned away outside. Since it's not closed in, the wind is blowing in from the bay, and there's Robert Plant, his golden locks streaming back in the breeze, his back all arched and his microphone cocked (no matter where he is or what he's doing, it looks like it's his Finest Hour). Thinking he's really got a thing, Plant yells at the crowd, 'Do you feel alright??!' About seven people muttered lustily. So Plant screams at them, 'THERE'S 10,500 PEOPLE HERE TONIGHT, DOES ANYBODY FEEL ALRIGHT?!' Nine people grumble ecstatically. At the top of his bird-on-the-wire gravel voice, 'THERE'S 10,500 PEOPLE HERE! DOES … ANYBODY … .' So much for feeling this man's blues."

Saturday August 30 1969
Queens, New York
Flushing Meadow Park
State Pavillion
Singer Bowl Music Festival
Second appearance at the Singer Bowl Festival

Sunday August 31 1969
Lewisville, Texas
Festival Field Dallas International Speedway
Texas International Pop Festival
Set: Train Kept A Rollin'/I Can't Quit You/Dazed And Confused/You Shook Me/ How Many More Times (inc. Suzy Q -The Hunter – The Lemon Song – Eyesight To The Blind – Bye Bye Baby – All Shook Up)/Communication Breakdown.

Zeppelin appeared on the second night of a three-day festival at Dallas International Motor Speedway. Also appearing were B.B.King, James Cotton, Delaney & Bonnie, Incredible String Band, Sam & Dave and Janis Joplin.

From the low key MC intro "Ladies and gentlemen. Please welcome the Led Zeppelin!", the band gave perhaps the outstanding performance of this year. 'Train Kept A Rollin'', moved into 'I Can't Quit You' for the last time.

Plant refers to their cancelled appearance at the State Fair Coliseum show on August 4: "It's very nice to be back in Texas. Last time we were here it was a near disaster when we said we weren't doing the festival and everything. This is the last date before we go back to England, so we'd really like to have a nice time … And you can help us."

Plant apologised for cutting the set short: "We've got to say goodnight according to the programme. Unfortunately, the programme has got a little delayed but there's nothing we can do about it!" However, they then embarked on one of the longest versions of 'How Many More Times' of the whole tour.

"Ladies and gentlemen. Please thank the Led Zeppelin."

This superb performance was thankfully captured on a clear soundboard tape that years later surfaced on bootleg.

Page: "This tour has been fantastic. But you can never be too sure. We've got to work even harder now. You can't rest on your laurels. It's easy to go down just as fast as you go up."

Bootleg CD References: *Texas International Pop Festival* (Last Stand Disc), *The Only Way To Fly* (Empress Valley), *Plays Pure Blues* (Whoopy Cat), *Plays Pure Bob* (Tarantura), *Don't Mess With Texas* (Oh Boy)

Visual References: Segments of their performance was shot on silent 8mm cine footage. The original intention was for a documentary of the whole festival to be released. This never materialised officially but a bootleg video titled *No Blues No Shoes* surfaced in 1992 via the Whoopy Cat label. Clips of 'You Shook Me', 'Dazed And Confused' and 'How Many More Times' can be seen on the unofficial DVD set *Early Visions* (Celebration)

August 1969
New York, New York
A and R Studios
RECORDING SESSIONS
Around this period Jimmy completed the mixing of the *Led Zeppelin 2* album with engineer Eddie Kramer. Snippets of monitor mixes of 'Hertbreaker', 'Whole Lotta Love' and' Ramble On' have emerged on bootleg.

Bootleg Reference: *The Lost Sessions Vol 4* (Empress Valley)

Friday September 5 1969
France
TV RECORDING AIRED
On this day the *Tous en Scene* TV show filmed on June 19 was broadcast in France.

After a relentless touring schedule, the band took a well deserved rest in September with Page holidaying in Spain and Morocco.

Just prior to another American visit the group made one-off appearances to promote the imminent release of *Led Zeppelin II*. Following dates in Holland and a trip to Paris they did a one-off Sunday night show at London's Lyceum Ballroom with Frosty Noses and Audience supporting. These Sunday night showcases were the brainchild of promoter Tony Stratton-Smith, who bravely attempted to turn the London venue into a British equivalent of America's Fillmore Auditoriums. The plan was for an act to showcase an entire new album and it was initially on that premise that Zeppelin were offered the date. As it turned out they presented their new stage act which incorporated just two numbers from the new album: 'What Is And What Should Never Be' and 'Heartbreaker'. UK audiences had to wait a further two weeks for the full recorded evidence of the group's remarkable 12-month rise when *Led Zeppelin II* was finally released and quickly shot to the top of the album charts on both sides of the Atlantic.

Friday October 3 1969
Scheveningen, Holland
Circus Theatre
Support from Steamhammer

Steamhammer's manager of the time Barry Taylor recalled: "I accepted these dates to tour with Zeppelin as I knew they were the most talked about new group of the year. This gig was in a seaside resort and the venue wasn't quite full. I bumped into John Paul Jones in the afternoon and found him an affable guy. Robert was very enthusiastic and sociable. Jimmy seemed quiet and a bit remote – I guess he'd seen it all before touring with The Yardbirds. As a fairly inexperienced manager I am taken aback with

the Grant/Cole management approach – insisting the slightly dodgy Dutch promoter paid in full before the gig and receiving it without argument!"

Saturday October 4 1969
Rotterdam, Holland
Grote Zaal de Doelen
Support from After Tea and George Cash

Sunday October 5
Amsterdam, Holland
Concertgebouw
Support from Steamhammer

Steve Davey, Steamhammer's bassist, recalled: "The second support slot we did with them was a complete sell out at a large venue similar to the Albert Hall. The dressing room looked out on to the stage and I had to walk down the staircase to face the audience and all I could hear was slow hand claps and cries of 'Zeppelin'. The seemingly hostile audience did warm to us as we got under way. After our set I recall admiring Bonzo's huge drum kit. John Paul Jones had one of the first Acoustic bass amplifiers I'd seen – in fact he had two of them. Jimmy had a pair of Marshall stacks and the PA was four Marshall column speakers on either side of the stage. That might seemed dated now but at the time it was well advanced as most of us took what we could fit into a Ford Transit van. Led Zeppelin though, as was evident during our time with them, were going places we would never attain. Looking back it was a huge thrill to be seen and be with them just before it really took off."

Tuesday October 7 1969
Stockholm, Sweden
Konserthuset
CANCELLED
Posters were produced and tickets sold, but the above date was cancelled and rescheduled for February 26 1970.

Wednesday October 8 1969
Goteborg, Sweden
Konserthuset
CANCELLED

Although booked and announced in the Swedish paper *Dagens Nyketer* it appears that this show was quickly cancelled

Thursday October 9 1969
Copenhagen
CANCELLED

UNCONFIRMED
Thursday October 9 1969
Harleem, Holland
Concertgebouw

This date was played this week – research has indicated it may have been October 10, though this conflicts with the date of the Paris show. It seems feasible it could have been on the day before

Visual Reference: Allegedly 12 minutes of colour footage of them performing 'Dazed And Confused' at this show was aired on the Dutch VARA networked TV show *Dit is het begin* on December 12, 1969. The programme also included Deep Purple performing 'Child In Time' in the studio. As yet this footage is yet to be found and may well have been wiped.

Friday October 10 1969
Paris, France
Olympia

Set: Good Times Bad Times-Communication Breakdown/I Can't Quit You Baby/Heartbreaker/You Shook Me/White Summer-Black Mountain Side/Dazed And Confused/Moby Dick/How Many More Times.

A special one-off date at the Paris Olympia, this show was recorded professionally but no tapes have surfaced. The band played for one and a half hours with no encores, during which Plant informed the audience that the second album would be titled *The Only Way To Fly*.

French fan Chrisophe Le Pabic discovered that the show was recorded by the French station French Europe 1 for a planned transmission on the Musicorama programme on November 2. However no evidence of the tapes being broadcast have surfaced. Photos from the gig in the book *Led Zeppelin Hexagonal Experiences* (Chrisophe Le Pabic/Benoit Pascal) show Plant on stage at the Olympia using two microphones, presumably one for the taping.

Sunday October 12 1969
London, England
The Lyceum, 'Sunday Scene'

Set included: Good Times Bad Times – Communication Breakdown/I Can't Quit You/Heartbreaker/You Shook Me/What Is And What Should Never Be/Dazed And Confused/How Many More Times (inc. The Hunter – Boogie Chillun').

Support from Frosty Noses and Audience.

The Lyceum show was the start of a series of Sunday night showcases, presented by promoter Tony Stratton-Smith. The original idea was for the headlining act to present an entire album in concert. Zeppelin declined and only two numbers from the new album were subsequently premièred.

The concert was a 2,000 capacity sell out and the group were paid what is thought to be the highest fee for a one night performance in the UK at that point. The deal with Stratton-Smith was for Led Zeppelin to receive the fee in cash the next day.

The band posed for a photo shoot with *Melody Maker's* Chris Walter in their dressing room before the show.

Nick Logan in *New Musical Express* reported: "It's a pity that with such a large audience present, Led Zeppelin should turn in one of their less inspiring performances. Having seen them at both the Marquee and the Albert Hall it seems the larger the venue the better it suits the Zeppelin's overpowering sound, although the Lyceum audience responded enthusiastically to everything they did. It was mainly the now familiar opening to their act – 'Communication Breakdown' etc. that suffered, Robert Plant's voice being drowned by the sheer volume of sound. Jimmy Page's guitar solo midway through was deservedly well received and when the group came in again on 'You Shook Me' and 'What Is And What Should Never Be' there was something of an improvement."

A young Freddie Mercury was in attendance at this show.

Bootleg CD References: *Ballroom Blitz* (World Productions), *The Lyceum Ballroom U.K. 10/12/69* (Totonka), Lyceum (Cobla Standard), *Triumphant UK Return* (Empress Valley)

AMERICA – AUTUMN 1969

Two appearances at the New York's Carnegie Hall kick-started their fourth US tour. They were the first pop act to play Carnegie Hall since June 1964, when The Rolling Stones caused a riot which resulted in the management banning rock at this prestigious venue. John Bonham was particularly pleased since the historic venue was noted for jazz (and classical) concerts.

These shows gave Grant the opportunity to set up a fourth US visit, even though the band were in need of a break after such an intensive workload. The 15 dates in three weeks saw them consolidate their position, ably assisted by the late October release of *Led Zeppelin II*. They were now, of course, the undisputed headline act for every show.

Atlantic also managed to persuade Grant to allow them to issue an edited version of 'Whole Lotta Love' as a single (the same idea was vetoed in the UK but not before a precious few hundred copies sneaked out). It's interesting to note that as 'Whole Lotta Love' began its climb towards *Billboard's* top five the song itself was not part of the current set – a prime example of their desire to please themselves and not always the audience (or their record company) when it came to deciding what to perform.

Final testimony to just how far they had come in the space of eleven months of American touring could be seen in their decision to play three nights at the close of the tour at Bill Graham's Winterland Ballroom in San Francisco. They would be supported by an eclectic bill of Roland Kirk and Isaac Hayes. Winterland was the alternate larger venue offered to acts that had outgrown the smaller Fillmore West. Another landmark occurred when they played before 15,000 at Boston Gardens, for which they copped a $45,000 fee.

"This performance makes me realise we can be bigger than The Beatles and the Stones," Grant told Richard Cole shortly after. He wasn't far wrong.

Atlantic Records obviously agreed. In December they amended the group's contract to ensure an annual minimum net royalty of $240,000 per year to run for the next ten years.

Friday October 17 1969
New York, New York
Carnegie Hall

Set included: Good Times Bad Times – Communication Breakdown/I Can't Quit You/White Summer – Black Mountain Side/Moby Dick/How Many More Times/Summertime Blues.

Two performances at 8.30pm and midnight.

Led Zeppelin took the stage at New York's Carnegie Hall, following in the footsteps of The Beatles and The Rolling Stones. Backstage visitors included *Zeppelin II* engineer Eddie Kramer, Traffic's Chris Wood, Dr. John and Screaming Lord Sutch.

Melody Maker's Chris Welch, making his first trip to America, travelled with them to file this report: "I met up with Bonzo and Robert at Euston Station and we met up with Jimmy, Peter Grant and John Paul Jones at London Airport. Some fans were there to see them off and Robert was really pleased to receive a copy of Paul Oliver's book *The Story Of The Blues* from them – which kept him engrossed on the flight.

"It was an incredibly exciting atmosphere in New York. My first LP, bought aged 15, was Benny Goodman's *Carnegie Hall 1938* concert so it was a terrific thrill to me to be standing on the side of the stage at the very same venue. 'This is it lads,' said Bonzo, eyeing his drum kit as the audience filed in. 'Gene Krupa and Buddy Rich – they've all played here so I'd better be good tonight.' At 8.30 the first set began. I was frankly amazed at the reaction. After, I talked with Jimmy and Robert at a Jewish delicatessen. Robert was drenched in sweat and blemished with a rash that had broken out. 'Somebody offered me a bottle of champagne after I'd played "White Summer" tonight', Jimmy told me. 'That's how involved in the music they are here!'"

Anne Moses reporting for *NME* observed: "The Zeppelin at Carnegie Hall and The Who all week at the Fillmore East has just been incredible. It was inevitable that both groups would come together at some point during the past seven days and they

did. A huge wham of a bash at Max's Kansas City in New York was the meeting place. The party was given by the Fillmore's Bill Graham for The Who following their opening on Monday night. The Zeppelin were down to watch and got into a long talk afterwards. During the week they met up again at a special birthday party at Ugano's where the Liverpool Scene have been playing.

"Led Zeppelin became the first rock act to play the Carnegie Hall since The Rolling Stones tore up the place some five years ago. Even up against Donovan at Madison Square Garden (a complete sell out) both the Zeppelin shows went clean, with tickets being scalped at the door for as much as twice their original price."

Saturday
October 18 1969
Detroit, Michigan
Olympia Stadium

Support from Lee Michaels and Magic Veil Light Show. This venue was demolished in September 1986. Now the location of an Army base.

Sunday
October 19 1969
Chicago, Illinois
Kinetic
Playground

Two performances – an afternoon and evening show. Support from Santana and Lighthouse.

Monday October 20 1969
Seattle, Washington
Paramount Theatre

Tuesday October 21 1969
Philadelphia, Pennsylvania
Electric Factory

Friday October 24 1969
Cleveland, Ohio
Public Auditorium
Support from Grand Funk Railroad. Advertisements stated: "One evening filled with music, love and peace. Bring own blanket – no chairs on floor".

Ticket sales were slow for this show and special adverts and posters were produced on the day to attract attendance.

Saturday October 25 1969
Boston, Masschusetts
Boston Garden
This venue was demolished in November 1997 when a new arena, The Fleet Center, was built next door. Support from Johnny Winter and MC5. Billed as Narragansett's "First Tribal Rock Restival".

The *Boston Herald* reported under the headline "Zeppelin Rock Rafters At Packed Boston Garden": Zeppelin entered to a standing ovation. Robert Plant talks warmly to the audience and with conviction. He was displaying this when the police enforced the curfew and abruptly curtailed the concert. WBCN's J.J. Jackson soothed the crowd and flashed the peace sign. The crowd flashed it back and exited in orderly fashion."

Peter Grant recalls: 'I realised they could be really big, at the first big gig they ever did, at the Boston Garden, to 16,000 people – and it's a sweat-

box, that place – and they absolutely pulverised them! I mean, they had it musically, and their performance was like … People in the audience used to tell me it was like a 'force'. It was in their heads for three or four days. I thought, 'There's no holding them now. There's no holding back'."

Sunday October 26 1969
Charlotte, North Carolina

Wednesday October 29 1969
Kent Ohio, JB'S
GUEST APPEARANCE
It was reported that Robert and Jimmy both performed with Joe Walsh at this venue.

Thursday October 30 1969
Buffalo, New York
Kleinhams Music Hall
Set: Good Times Bad Times – Communication Breakdown/I Can't Quit You/Heartbreaker/Dazed AndConfused/White Summer – Black Mountain Side/What Is And What Should Never Be/Moby Dick/How Many More Times (inc. The Hunter).

Support from The James Gang, who now featured Tommy Bolin and Joe Walsh in the line-up.

This concert nearly ended prematurely when a glass was thrown at Robert during 'I Can't Quit You'. Robert addressed the offender: "You're messing up a good concert you silly fool!" and then changed the lyrics of the next verse to: "If you think you're really very smart … Well, come on up here and do that thing again … Hear me talking to you."

Plant was obviously shaken by the incident and later sarcastically commented to the audience: "It's a great pleasure to be here tonight and we'd like to welcome our friend who's so used to throwing coconuts at a fairground. Thanks for the glass!"

The new *Led Zeppelin II* Bonham showcase 'Moby Dick' was now developed as the successor to 'Pat's Delight'.

"Led Zeppelin Soars And The Audience Is Loath To Leave" was the headline in the *Buffalo Evening News*. James Brennan reported: "Imagine the sound of a tin bucket spiralling down a well and caught by a string at the very last instant, leaving a maelstrom of whirling concordal sounds. Jimmy Page catches the bucket with the strings of his guitar and the sound discharged belongs to Led Zeppelin, in concert in Kleinhans Music Hall before a stand-ing-room only crowd which wanted to stay all night."

Bootleg CD References: *Buffalo Sixtynine* (New Plastic Records), *Pats Delight* (Tecumseh), *Long Tall Sally* (Tarantura)

Friday October 31 1969
Providence, Rhode Island
Rhode Island Auditorium
The Gansett Tribal Rock Festival promoted by Narragansett Brewing Company. Supporting acts were Dr. John The Night Tripper, and Taj Mahal.

Friday October 31 1969
Springfield Massachusetts
Springfield Municipal Auditorium
Second show of the day for the Narragansett Brewing Company – it can be presumed their Rhode Island performance was early on the festi-val billing.

Saturday November 1 1969
Syracuse, New York
Onondaga Memorial Auditorium

Sunday November 2 1969
Toronto, Canada
O'Keefe Center
Set included: Good Times Bad Times – Communi-cation Breakdown (inc. Bluebird)/I Can't Quit You/Heartbreaker/Dazed And Con-fused/White Summer – Black Mountain Side (inc. Still I'm Sad)/Babe I'm Gonna Leave You (inc. Be On My Side – Ramble On)/Moby Dick.

Two shows at 5PM and 8.30PM. Edward Bear supported.

The evening set was unusual and one of the best performances of the tour. 'Communica-tion Breakdown' included a section of Buffalo Springfield's 'Bluebird', and Jimmy Page incorpo-rated references to The Yardbirds' 'Still I'm Sad' in his 'White Summer – Black Mountain Side' show-piece.

Plant joked with the crowd: "We intend to try to do as much of the *Led Zeppelin IV* album as possi-ble, but we thought we'd cut it down by half and do *Led Zeppelin II*."

'Babe I'm Gonna Leave You' included sections of 'Be On My Side' and 'Ramble On'.

"Led Zeppelin: the hardest rock around" – Ritchie Yorke again reviewed the Toronto show: "Thrashing themselves and their equipment around on the O'Keefe Center stage last night, Led Zeppelin members demonstrated for the third time this year that theirs is the hard-est hard rock group in England or the United States.

"O'Keefe Center was packed to the brim for a couple of standing-room only, standing ovation shows with a total attendance of 6,470. There could have been more. I overheard a stage-door attendant telling two wailing young ladies who'd hitch-hiked from Syracuse that there was no way they could see the show."

Bootleg CD References: *Beast Of Toronto* (Immigrant), *Listen To My Bluebird* (Image Quality).

Led Zeppelin

COMING
TUESDAY, NOV. 4-8 p.m.

LED ZEPPELIN
plus
THE COPPER PENNY

KITCHENER MEMORIAL
AUDITORIUM

Tuesday November 4 1969
Kitchener, Canada
Memorial Auditorium
Support from The Copper Penny.

"The Zeppelinization of Kitchener" – Dave Fairfield reported: "The Led Zeppelin must rank among the super groups of our time. Robert Plant is a fine blues singer. He understands and follows Page's lead. At the same time, he is able to assert his own thoughts into the improvisation. Plant subtly combines his vocal talent with the gyrating tone of the guitar. He sings in harmony with, or in counter-point to it.

"The bassist and drummer deserve the same amount of credit. They enable Page to take the musical liberties that he does. Without their rhythmic skill the group might well have floundered in some instances.

"But it is Jimmy Page who sets the pace. He is the one who says so much. His virtuosity is incredible. He stuns and amazes you with the sporadic bursts of his guitar. His intellectualization of the psychedelic jumble has eased pop music one step further. A continuance with this type of expression promises much."

Wednesday November 5 1969
Kansas City, Kansas
Memorial Hall
Set included: Good Times Bad Times – Communication Breakdown/I Can't Quit You/Heartbreaker/Dazed And Confused/How Many More Times (inc. The Hunter – Boogie Chillun').

Two shows. Support from Morning Star, Bartok's Mountain, Spokesmen, Blues Garden and Bill Zickos. This venue was also known as the Soldiers and Sailors Memorial Hall and was the venue of country legend Patsy Cline's final performance

Zeppelin's equipment had been freighted direct from the previous show in Canada to San Francisco for the Winterland residency that began the following night, so they were obliged to perform tonight's show with unfamiliar gear.

Steve Weber of *The Kansas City Star* reports: "It is somewhat amazing – though not surprising – that the Led Zeppelin sounded as good as they did … considering the circumstances. They brought none of their own instruments, and were forced to use the instruments provided them by the promoters or borrow from other performers on the bill.

"The resulting sound was a tribute to their ability, really, for the need to adapt to unfamiliar instruments forced them to improvise more than they no doubt desired. Led Zeppelin, however, is made up of good and seasoned musicians who can overcome the limitations of their media …

Led Zeppelin

and for the most part that is what they did last night."

Bootleg CD References: *Birth Of The Gods* (Balboa), *Tales From '69* (Tarantura)

Thursday November 6 1969
San Francisco, California
Winterland Ballroom

Set: Good Times Bad Times – Communication Breakdown/I Can't Quit You/ Heartbreaker/ Dazed And Confused/White Summer – Black Mountain Side/What Is And What Should Never Be/Moby Dick/How Many More Times (inc. The Hunter – Boogie Chillun' – Move On Down The Line – High Flyin' Mama – The Lemon Song)/C'mon Everybody/ Something Else.

Roland Kirk and Isaac Hayes supported for all three shows.

The highlight of an otherwise standard set was the rare double encore of Eddie Cochran's 'C'mon Everybody' and 'Something Else'.

Bootleg CD References: *Room 2/3* (Image Quality), *Punk* (Tarantura), *Blow Up* (Immigrant), *The End Of '69* (Whole Lotta Live), *Winterland Party* (Wendy)

Friday November 7 1969
San Francisco, California
Winterland Ballroom

Set: Good Times Bad Times – Communication Breakdown/I Can't Quit You/ Heartbreaker/ Dazed And Confused/White Summer – Black Mountain Side/Babe I'm Gonna Leave You/What Is And What Should Never Be/Moby Dick/How Many More Times (inc. The Hunter).

Jimmy's ever evolving 'White Summer' showcase clocked in at just under 15 minutes.

88

Bootleg CD Reference: *Room 2/3* (Image Quality), *Winter Of Our Content* (Missing link)

Saturday November 8 1969
San Francisco, California
Winterland Ballroom

November 1969
Barnes, England
Olympic Studios
RECORDING SESSIONS
Work on their third album began around this period, Page taking in the multi-layered instrumental track dubbed 'Jennings Farm Blues' after Plant's then Midlands farm house. The basic structure of this track would later emerge as the acoustic 'Bron Yr Aur Stomp' on *Led Zeppelin 3*.
Bootleg Reference: *Jennings Farm Blues* (Scorpio)

NOVEMBER 1969
News story: Offers for a full scale Led Zeppelin World Tour to span much of 1970 are being considered by Peter Grant. These are said to include dates in both Europe and America as well as the Far East and Australasia. With offers continually being made for them to appear on TV, tentative plans are also underway for the group to appear in their own full colour TV spectacular – similar to the BBC radio special that was broadcast last August. Grant has also stated that he would like the group to appear in an additional colour TV show which would include several guest artists of their choosing.

Saturday December 6 1969
Paris, France
L'Ecole Centrale Chatenay-Malabry
Piston '70
A 45 minute set included Good Times Bad Times – Communication Breakdown, You Shook Me, How Many More Times, Whole Lotta Love, Heartbreaker.

Shared bill with The Pretty Things, Vibriations and Triangle.

Until recently no firm evidence of this show

taking place had emerged but French fan Chrisophe Le Pabic has researched the date and states: "I have met several people who were present on this night – executives from Barclay Records and Atlantic and a photographer working for Barclay, Daniel Decamps. I also met the guitarist Marc Tobaly from the support band and he also confirmed Zeppelin's appearance on this night."

The gig was at the Chatenay Malabry at the prestigious Engineering school Centrale. This special show was for the students only and not announced to the press. Part of the deal for them to appear was that they were booked into the George V hotel and had the use of black Citroen DS cars, the type used by General De Gaulle. Their fee was 16,500 francs.

Thursday December 20 1969
London, England
Savoy Hotel
NON PLAYING APPEARANCE
"Zeppelin is a gas!" say the government. *Disc* reported: "Led Zeppelin are gluttons for punishment. They are also something of a phenomenon. In just over a year of their existence, they have toured America four times, Denmark and Sweden twice, been to France and done nearly every club and Town Hall here. They have also managed to produce two albums clocking up more than £2 million worth of sales in America alone.

"We're doing a tour here in the New Year

before going back to America, and we're working on our third album at the moment," said John Paul Jones, speaking at a party in London's Savoy Hotel last week, to celebrate Led Zeppelin's record sales in America.

Mrs Gwyneth Dunwoody, Parliamentary Secretary to the Board of Trade, went along to thank them for their value as exports, and was kissed on the cheek by singer Robert Plant.

"You seem to be gas rockets rather than Led Zeppelins," said Mrs Dunwoody.

Jimmy Page, lead guitarist, didn't make it in time for the presentations. He had a car accident on the way up, but he arrived a little later, resplendent in white fringed satin. And after the party he nipped round to Berkeley Square to buy himself a Rolls-Royce.

There's no doubt about it, America has certainly taken Led Zeppelin to its heart, more so than this country.

"I don't know why we're so popular there," says John Bonham. "I suppose it's a combination of a good band and the time it broke. One can get fed up with touring, we've done an awful lot of it lately. It's all a mass of airports – that's all you ever see. But we've always had such good receptions, it's made it worth it. I don't know how we've managed to do so much in the last year. Looking back, none of us know how we've done it."

UK TOUR 1970

A timely UK outing which coincided with *Led Zeppelin II* toppling The Beatles' *Abbey Road* as the number one chart album. There were eight theatre dates and, not surprisingly, it was their London appearance that drew attention. Back at the famous Royal Albert Hall on Jimmy's 26th birthday they did much to enhance their reputation with an excellent show. This concert was filmed by the band under the direction of Stanley Dorfman and Peter Whitehead. Intended for a semi-documentary project, it never saw the light of day, allegedly because some of the film was shot at the wrong speed. A 40-minute cut was prepared and turned up as a much coveted bootleg years later.

All but one of these dates saw them perform with no support act – a trend that would continue on all subsequent tours.

The set list for these shows included a new set opener, a cover of Ben E. King's 'We're Gonna Groove'. This number was recorded in the studio for *Led Zeppelin II* but remained unreleased until it turned up on the posthumous *Coda* set in 1982.

On January 31, Plant suffered facial injuries when his Jaguar spun off the road after he was returning from a Spirit concert. This caused the cancellation of the proposed February 7 date at Edinburgh's Usher Hall, which was later rescheduled for February 17. A rare concert programme was distributed for this show and the accompanying blurb reveals that … "Although Led Zeppelin was created at the close of 1968, they are undoubtedly a group of the Seventies. THE group of the Seventies according to an opinion which is held world-wide."

During the early months of the new decade it was an opinion shared by all who were lucky enough to attend what would prove to be their only indoor UK shows of the year.

Equipment Notes:

Alongside the Gibson Les Paul and Dan Electro, Jimmy employed a Gibson Les Paul Custom 'Black Beauty' with tremolo arm fitted by Joe Jammer (this can be seen on various photos from the Albert Hall show and in the official DVD segment of the show). This guitar, which he had used back in his session days, was later lost on tour *en route* to Canada in August 1970. An advertisement was later placed in *Rolling Stone* for information leading to its return, but to no avail.

John Paul Jones significantly added the Hammond C3 organ to the set-up for 'Thank You' and 'Since I've Been Loving You'. The organ was run through a couple of Fender amps and speakers.

Bonzo retained the maple kit with a larger side bongo and timpani set-up used during the rock and roll medleys.

Wednesday January 7 1970
Birmingham, England
Town Hall

Although first played as far back as the Fillmore in San Francisco in April 1969, this was the first tour to feature 'Whole Lotta Love' as a set regular.

Thursday January 8 1970
Bristol, England
Colston Hall

Set: We're Gonna Groove/I Can't Quit You/Dazed And Confused/Heartbreaker/White Summer – Black Mountain Side/Since I've Been Loving You/Organ Solo – Thank You/Moby Dick/How Many More Times (inc. The Hunter – Boogie Chillun' – Move On Down The Line – High Flyin' Mama – The Lemon Song)/Whole Lotta Love/Communication Breakdown (inc. Good Times Bad Times).

The concert started over an hour late. Zeppelin

introduced a new set list for the new decade. Plant attempted several times to tell the audience a joke about the Lone Ranger and Tonto, but kept forgetting it. He also plugged their third album: "We've got an LP coming out in three months, and it's called *Led Zeppelin 19*. We're just gonna keep putting them out!"

John Paul Jones came to the fore on the Hammond organ for 'Since I've Been Loving You' and 'Thank You'. 'Since I've Been Loving You' was yet to be formulated fully in the studio and the live delivery was very much a work in progress. The lyrics had very little resemblance to those that would finally appear on *Led Zeppelin III*.

'How Many More Times' continued to be expanded with rock and blues tributes and 'Communication Breakdown' contained several bars of 'Good Times Bad Times' – an arrangement that

will be worked on again later this year in the US.

By the close of the set Robert finally remembered the punchline: "Tonto turned into a door and the Lone Ranger shot his knob off!"

Bootleg CD Reference: *Bristol Stomp* (No Label)

Friday January 9 1970
London, England
Royal Albert Hall

Set: We're Gonna Groove/I Can't Quit You/Dazed And Confused/ Heartbreaker/White Summer – Black Mountain Side/Since I've Been Loving You/What Is And What Should Never Be/Moby Dick/How Many More Times (inc. The Hunter – Boogie Chillun' – High Flyin' Mama – Leave My Woman Alone – The Lemon Song – That's Alright Mama)/Bring It On Home/Whole Lotta Love/Organ solo -Thank You/Communication Breakdown/C'mon Everybody/Something Else/Long Tall Sally (inc. Bye Bye Baby – Move On Down The Line – Whole Lotta Shakin' Going On).

A key Zeppelin appearance and very much a turning point in their standing in the UK. On the night of Jimmy's 26th birthday they played to their full potential to a fantastic audience and press reception.

Disc proclaimed 'Zeppelin rock and we rave!' Caroline Boucher reported: "Led Zeppelin proved on Friday that inside even the coolest hip audience there's a rocker screaming to get out. And at the end of two and a half hours the entire Albert Hall in London was on its feet jiving, stomping

and stripping. Jimmy Page is certainly a brilliant and reticent guitarist, but solo honours went to John Bonham who made a frantic 15-minute drum solo seem like five, with none of the embarrassment and boredom usually aroused by drum solos. Plant's vocals were adequate if a little disappointing. Both his movement and voice seemed suppressed. He never really let himself go. But what was so nice and refreshing was that the group ENJOYED playing, and actually WANTED to play more and more. That, in this age of dead-pan indifference from group and audience, is a valuable quality."

Jimmy Page: "It was just like it was at the Albert Hall in the summer, with everyone dancing round the stage. It is a great feeling. What could be better than having everyone clapping and shouting along? It's indescribable, but it just makes you feel that everything is worthwhile."

Backstage visitors included Roger Daltrey and his wife Heather. Jimmy was accompanied by Charlotte Martin, a French model with whom he would develop a long-term relationship and who would become the mother of his daughter Scarlet.

The show was professionally filmed on Grant's instructions under the direction of Peter White-head and recorded by Vic Maille on the Pye mobile studio. *Disc* later announced that Zeppelin would be seen on TV screens this year for the first time in a £25,000 film financed entirely by the group. "The movie, an hour-long semi-documen-tary, will show scenes for the Albert Hall, a section of a States tour, individual members of the group off-duty with their wives and families – and a lot of live action shots. Peter Grant stated 'A camera team will be travelling with them to Iceland and the whole thing should be tied up within a couple of months. I expect it to be shown in Britain by December'."

Some 33 years later the Albert Hall footage was finally given an official release on the *Led Zeppelin* DVD. Page had acquired the masters in 1999 and the film was painstakingly restored by director Dick Carruthers. "All the film was cleaned up frame by frame. It was all mute and we had to match the relevant visuals with the audio tapes," he revealed at the time of the DVD release in the spring of 2003.

Looking back on this footage at the time of the release of the DVD in 2003 Robert Plant reflected: "It was an absolute shock when I first saw the Albert Hall stuff. It's so disarming – not unnerving but kind of cute and coy and you see all the naivety and absolute wonder of what we were doing, and the freshness of it, because the whole sort of stereotypical rock singer thing hadn't kicked in for me."

Bootleg CD References: *Royal Albert Hall* (Monada), *Jimmys Birthday Party/Royal Dragon* (Taranutura), *Royal Albert Hall 1970* (Celebration), *Historical Birthday* (Shout To The Top)

Visual Reference: Official *Led Zeppelin DVD* (Warner Music 2003), *Early Visions* (Celebration), *Royal Albert Hall VHS* (Celebration)

Tuesday January 13 1970
Portsmouth, England
Guildhall

Thursday January 15 1970
Newcastle-on-Tyne, England
City Hall
Admission ranged from eight to twenty one shillings. Door take: £1,883

Friday January 16 1970
Sheffield, England
City Hall

Saturday January 24 1970
Leeds, England
Town Hall

Saturday February 7 1970
Edinburgh, Scotland
Usher Hall – **CANCELLED**
This show was postponed when Robert is involved in a road accident.
Disc reported: "Led Zeppelin's Robert Plant rushed to Kidderminster Hospital on Saturday suffering from broken teeth and severe cuts after his Jaguar involved in head-on collision. Plant discharged himself on Monday and is recuperating at Worcestershire home."

Tuesday February 17 1970
Edinburgh, Scotland
Usher Hall – **RESCHEDULED**
A Heriot Watt Entertainment promotion. Support from Barclay James Harvest. In the programme notes, promoter Alistair Adams revealed that the group turned down six other offers to appear at this Scottish University-staged event. As he proudly boasted: "You are watching the most expensive live action group in Britain and the top ticket price is 22 shillings."

LED ZEPPELIN
Concert scheduled for Saturday February 7 cancelled due to accident involving Robert Plant
CONCERT WILL NOW TAKE PLACE
TUESDAY, FEBRUARY 17
AT 7.30 P.M
All tickets valid Inquiries 225 3406 Anyone wishing refund of ticket money apply to Brown Square House Chambers St., Edinburgh 1

HERIOT WATT ENTERTAINMENTS
PRESENTS
LED ZEPPELIN
TUESDAY 17th FEB. 1970

(left margin) Led Zeppelin

EUROPEAN TOUR 1970

With Robert fully recovered the group were back on the road within a month, playing 12 dates in Europe. The most memorable date occurred on February 28 in Copenhagen where, before the show, they were confronted by one Eva Von Zeppelin. Claiming to be a direct descendant of the designer of one of the first airships, Count Von Zeppelin, she threatened to sue the band if they performed as Led Zeppelin, making the infamous statement: "They may be world famous but a group of shrieking monkeys are not going to use a privileged family name without permission." For their KB Hallen appearance they went under the name The Nobs, a playful pun on the name of their European promoter Claude Knobs and, of course, a thinly disguised reference to something else entirely. Little was heard of Eva's Von Zeppelin's claim again and they were back as Led Zeppelin for their next show.

Monday February 23 1970
Helsinki, Finland
Kulttuurialo

Set: We're Gonna Groove/I Can't Quit You/ Dazed And Confused/Heartbreaker/White Summer – Black Mountain Side/Since I've Been Loving You/ Organ Solo – Thank You/Moby Dick/How Many More Times (inc. The Hunter – Boogie Chillun' – Move On Down The Line – Fixin' To Die – The Lemon Song – Be-Bop-A-Lula)/ Whole Lotta Love.

The European tour was very much a continuation of the set list they had developed in the UK.

'How Many More Times' included renditions of Bukka White's 'Fixin' To Die' and Gene Vincent's 'Be-Bop-A-Lula'.

CD Bootleg References: *Fixin' To Die* (Mandala), *Valhalla I Am Coming* (Gold Standard), *Toccatta And Fuge* (Tarantura)

Wednesday February 25 1970
Gottborg, Sweden
Konserthuset

Thursday February 26 1970
Stockholm, Sweden
Gothernburg Koncerthause

This show was booked to replace the cancelled date on October 7 1969.

The Sewedish press reviewed this show favourably, Henrik Salender reporting: ''The audience thumped the stage and the rows of disco dressed girls looked like the devil had got hold of them. There is no doubt Led Zeppelin is an extremely professional group.''

While in Stockholm the band received gold discs at a reception and were also interviewed by Johan Zachrisson for a 15 minute segment on TV1. This footage has never surfaced

Friday February 27 1970
Amsterdam, Holland
Concertgebouw

Saturday February 28 1970
Copenhagen, Denmark
K.B.Hallen

Set: We're Gonna Groove/I Can't Quit You/Dazed And Confused/Heartbreaker/White Summer – Black Mountain Side/Since I've Been Loving You/Organ Solo – Thank You/Moby Dick/How Many More Times (inc. The Hunter – Move On Down The Line – High Flyin' Mama)/Whole Lotta Love/Communication Breakdown/C'mon Everybody/Something Else/Bring It On Home/Long Tall Sally.

New Musical Express reported: 'Zeppelin become Nobs!' "When Led Zeppelin plays a concert in Copenhagen tomorrow, it will be billed under the name of The Nobs. Reason is that Eva Von Zeppelin – relative of the airship designer – has threatened to sue the British group if it appears as Led Zeppelin in Denmark."

An initial muted audience response improved by the time they got to 'How Many More Times'.

Encores of 'Whole Lotta Love' and 'Communication Breakdown' prompted much calling for more. The rarely performed Eddie Cochran double-header of 'C'mon Everybody' and 'Something Else' led into a chaotic rendition of 'Bring It On Home'. Plant then told the audience: "We'd like to say thank you very much for receiving us back again, after last time we came here with Country Joe & The Fish. We've gotta say that I don't think we've changed much, but an incredible change in playing. We'd like to dedicate this to the wonderful clubs in Copenhagen, and until we come back

You/What Is And What Should Never Be/Moby Dick/How Many More Times (incl 'Jenny Jenny', 'Trucking Little Mama')

This was the beginning of Zeppelin's association with the Montreux Jazz Festival venue and close friendship with promoter Claude Knobs. The original venue was famously burnt to the ground in December 1971 during a Frank Zappa concert – the story of which was later immortalised in the Deep Purple song 'Smoke On The Water'.

"*Bon Soir*! Do ya feel alright?" was Plant's bilingual introduction to the crowd. The venue was to be a favourite of theirs and the scene for warm-up shows in 1971 and 1972.The highlights of the show included John Paul Jones' powerful and dramatic organ solo leading into 'Thank You' and a forceful 'Heartbreaker' complete with an opening riff similar in style to 'Walter's Walk'.

Bootleg CD References: *Intimidator* (Empress Valley), *Divinity* (Atlantic Ocean 208), *All That Jazz* (Diagrams Of Led Zeppelin), *The Dark Tower*

again this is how we'd like you to remember us." 'Long Tall Sally' completed an excellent show **Bootleg CD References:** *Dancing With Snow Queen* (BabyFace), *A Riot Going On* (Pot), *The Nobs* (Tarantura)

UNCONFIRMED
March 2 1970
Brussels, Belgium

Saturday March 7 1970
Montreux, Switzerland
Montreux Casino
Set included: We're Gonna Groove/I Can't Quit You/White Summer – Black Mountain Side/Dazed And Confused/Heartbreaker/Since I've Been Loving You/Organ Solo – Thank

(Tarantura)
Charisma (Tarantura)

Sunday March 8 1970
Munich, Germany
Circus Krone Bau
Fan Messmer Mathias recalled: "The show was delayed and they did not get on stage until after midnight. As there was no support act the promoter played Led Zeppelin album tracks over the PA during the delay."

Monday March 9 1970
Vienna, Austria
Konzerthaus
Set included: I Can't Quit You/Dazed And Con

fused/Heartbreaker/White Summer – Black Mountain Side/Since I've Been Loving You/Moby Dick/How Many More Times (inc. The Hunter – Boogie Chillun' – High Flyin' Mama – The Lemon Song).

Equipment problems marred this performance. Page had to call a stop and apologise to the audience when his Echoplex unit failed to work during his solo in 'Dazed And Confused'.

Bootleg CD References: *High Flyin' Zep* (Electric Magic), *Vienna 1970* (Metal Machine), *Live In Vienna 1970* (Ocean Sound Studio)

Tuesday March 10 1970
Frankfurt, Germany
Kongresshalle – **CANCELLED**
This show was cancelled, at a week's notice, after riots at the venue following an appearance by Jethro Tull on February 21. Riots at European concerts were rife at the time. particularly in Germany. There was widespread belief amongst young people that admission (particularly at large festivals) should be free.

Tuesday March 10 1970
Hamburg, Germany
Musikhalle
Set: We're Gonna Groove/I Can't Quit You/Dazed And Confused/Heartbreaker/White Summer – Black Mountain Side/Since I've Been Loving You/Organ Solo – Thank You/What Is And What Should Never Be/Moby Dick/How Many More Times (inc. The Hunter – Boogie Chillun' – High Flyin' Mama – Down By The River – Travelling Riverside Blues – Long Distance Call – The Lemon Song)/Whole Lotta Love.

With the short notice of cancellation of the Frankfurt show, this second Hamburg show was hastily arranged. There was a friendly relaxed atmosphere and the audience were rewarded with one of the most interesting performances of the tour.

'Heartbreaker' featured a new, delicate introduction adding to the dynamics of the piece. At the end of the song Plant segued into "With a purple umbrella …" from 'Living Loving Maid', humorously mimicking the sequence of the second album. Plant: "I think we're all getting a bit looser!"

'What Is And What Should Never Be' was now frequently added to the set list. 'How Many More Times' was again a stand out.

Plant: "I'd like to take this opportunity of introducing Led Zeppelin on the first of our two very lively nights in Hamburg." The singer proceeded to take the band through a brief history of the blues including Robert Johnson's 'Travelling Riverside Blues' (performed in its original style rather than Zeppelin's BBC session arrangement of 1969) and John Lee Hooker's 'Long Distance Call'. On a more contemporary note, he threw in a few lyrics from Neil Young's 'Down By The River'.
Bootleg CD References: *Mystery European Gig* (The Symbols), *Hamburg 1970* (Immigrant)

Wednesday March 11 1970
Hamburg, Germany
Musikhalle
Set: We're Gonna Groove/I Can't Quit You/Dazed And Confused/Heartbreaker/White Summer – Black Mountain Side/Moby Dick/How Many More Times (inc. Bolero – The Hunter – Boogie Chillun' – High Flyin' Mama – Long Distance Call – Shake 'Em On Down – Lemon Song)/Whole Lotta Love.

Another solid performance, the highlight of which was again the 'How Many More Times' medley which included Bukka White's 'Shake 'Em On Down', the structure of which would be transformed into 'Hats Off To Harper', a track on their third album. Page also added a few bars of Ravel's 'Bolero' prior to 'The Hunter'.

Bootleg CD Reference: *Everybody, Everybody* (Image Quality)

Thursday March 12 1970
Dusseldorf, Germany
Rheinhalle
Set included: Communication Breakdown/I Can't Quit You Baby/Dazed And Confused/Heartbreaker/White Summer/Black Mountain Side/Since I've Been Loving You/Thank You/Moby Dick/How Many More Times(inc. Bolero – The Hunter – Boogie Chillun' – Move On Down The Line – High Flyin' Mama – The Lemon Song)./Whole Lotta Love

The final night of the European tour saw the band beginning to tire, but they put in another spirited performance. 'How Many More Times' featured a 'laid back' jazz style introduction and Page again continued to develop the 'Bolero' theme.

Bootleg CD References: *Psychedelic Raw Blues* (Immigrant), *Dancing Days* (Aphrodite Studio), *Dusseldorf 1970* (Reel masters), *Loreley* (Moonraker)

Led Zeppelin

AMERICA – SPRING 1970

And the US tours kept on coming … This one was arranged to continue their push for mass acceptance in the US and saw them perform in venues of 10,000 capacity and upwards. It was a gruelling schedule that eventually took its toll on Plant's voice, the final date in Las Vegas being cancelled.

Stone The Crows were initially announced as the support act for the tour but then cancelled. From now on in, the shows were billed as 'An Evening With Led Zeppelin' and there were no support bands.

The political climate in the US was far from stable at this time. The shooting of four students on Ohio's Kent State University campus during a demonstration against the Vietnam War had exacerbated the already edgy relationship between the youth of America and its police. With their long-hair and wild appearance the Zeppelin entourage attracted unfavourable treatment from the authorities. Plant was more sensitive to the unpleasantness than his colleagues and his observations would later flower into the lyrics of the *Led Zeppelin III* standard 'That's The Way'. "We've seen much in America we don't agree with and our feelings of protest do reflect in the music," remarked Plant. "People may think we make a lot of bread but in some cities it's so rough – fans won't come to our shows. We've been threatened with arrest if we returned to the stage and our manager's had a gun pulled on him." It was during this tour that Page had his Gibson 'Black Beauty' Les Paul Custom guitar stolen during a flight change.

It wasn't all bleak news though – in Memphis they were made honorary citizens and they sold out the venues in almost every city they visited. The total gross of the tour was over $1,200,000 with record breaking attendances reported in Montreal and Vancouver.

Musically the act was developing as it had in the UK and Europe, with Jones's keyboards continuing to come to the fore on 'Thank You' and the as-yet unrecorded 'Since I've Been Loving You'. Following the tour's completion, it was obvious they were in need of a rest. Page and Plant took off for a relaxing holiday in a cottage where Plant had stayed while at school. Soon all roads were leading to Bron Yr Aur, a serene location that would inspire a change in musical direction. Just prior to that trip Jimmy Page made a rare solo TV appearance performing 'White Summer – Black Mountain Side' on the BBC 2 *Julie Felix Show*.

Saturday
March 21 1970
Vancouver,
Canada
Pacific Coliseum
Set included: We're Gonna Groove/Dazed And Confused/Heartbreaker/White Summer/Since I've Been Loving You/Organ Solo – Thank You/ What Is And What Should Never Be/Moby Dick/How Many More Times/Whole Lotta Love/Communication Breakdown (inc. Ramble On).

The band arrived at Vancouver International airport and gave a press conference in the afternoon at their hotel the Bayshore Inn. Hugh Jones of *Proximity* magazine revealed that the visit was substantially covered by the local *Richmond Review* newspaper at the time. The coverage included photos from the show. It was also reported that the band visited the Riverqueen and toured the city during their stay.

At the show itself Robert began inserting some alternative lyrics to 'Since I've Been Loving You' and 'Communication Breakdown', included lines from the rarely played 'Ramble On'. Overall the performance was somewhat erratic with Plant a little weak due to a sore throat.

The local Vancouver press reported: 'Zeppelin Pack 'Em In': "Led Zeppelin walked on stage at 8.30pm, took control and didn't stop through two and a half hours of glorious ear-splitting rock.

'"Never before in the history of Led Zeppelin has this happened,' Plant shouted mock-serious into the microphone, not knowing whether to be offended or flattered. When the stage was finally cleared, Led Zeppelin came back for two encores and a standing ovation that was a fitting tribute to one of the most talented rock groups in the business today."

"In Vancouver, where they played to 17,000, the group had to pay £600 for backstage damage to dressing rooms and buildings caused by over-zealous fans."

Back in the UK *New Musical Express* claimed the actual attendance to be in excess of 19,000, breaking The Beatles' record by 2,000.

This show holds the distinction of being the source for the first ever vinyl Led Zeppelin bootleg. Packaged in a plain brown cardboard cover bearing the name "Pb"(the chemical symbol for lead). It was later re-issued as *Mudslide* on the Trade Mark Of Quality label. The source was widely reported as being a radio broadcast but no evidence exists to confirm that. The 40-minute extract from the show was more likely the product of an enterprising person close to the venue's staff who taped the show direct form the soundboard. The raw unmixed sound with the vocals and drums up front but the guitar well buried would lend credence to that theory.

Bootleg CD References: *Mudslide* (Flying Disc), *Mudslide* (Diagrams Of Led Zeppelin)

Sunday March 22 1970
Seattle, Washington
Seattle Center Arena

Monday
March 23 1970
Portland,
Oregon
Memorial
Coliseum

Wednesday March 25 1970
Denver, Colorado
Denver Coliseum
Set: We're Gonna Groove/I Can't Quit You/Dazed And Confused/Heartbreaker/Since I've Been Loving You/Organ Solo – Thank You/Moby Dick/How Many More Times (inc. Ramble On – Bolero- The Hunter – Needle Blues – Boogie Chillun' – Move On Down The Line – Just Can't Be Satisfied – The Lemon Song)/Whole Lotta Love.

Plant: "About eighteen months ago, we played our very first ever gig in the United States in this Coliseum and so much has happened since then. We'd like to say that we really are pleased to be back." That statement wasn't entirely correct as the Coliseum was a different venue to the Auditorium Arena where they appeared in 1968. The Denver Rockets baseball team played at the Auditorium and then moved to the Coliseum.

The 'How Many More Times' medley featured 'Ramble On' and a very rarely performed version of Muddy Waters' 'Just Can't Be Satisfied'. 'Boogie Chillun' employed a new unique riff and solo, the riff being performed with 'Move On Down The Line' lyrics.

Bootleg CD Reference: *Denver 1970* (The Diagrams Of Led Zeppelin)

Thursday March 26 1970
Salt Lake City, Utah
Salt Palace
Salt Lake Tribune staff writer George Raine report-

ed: "Without question guitarist Jimmy Page is a virtuoso. He plays one of the fastest necks to be seen. His intonations, his vibratos and his sense of timing and syncopation are matched by only a handful of contemporary guitarists."

Friday March 27 1970
Inglewood Los Angeles, California
The Forum
Set: We're Gonna Groove/Dazed And Confused/Heartbreaker/Bring It On Home/White Summer – Black Mountain Side/Since I've Been Loving You/Organ Solo – Thank You/What Is And What Should Never Be/Moby Dick/How Many More Times (inc. Bolero – The Hunter – Needle Blues – I'm A Man – Boogie Chillun' – High Flyin' Mama – The Lemon Song)/Whole Lotta Love/ Communication Breakdown (inc. Down By The River).

Plant: "Good Evening. Everybody feel alright? Tonight we intend to get everybody looser than anybody's ever been loose … even with cod liver oil!"

One of the best shows of the tour. Los Angeles was rapidly becoming Zeppelin's second home.

'I Can't Quit You' had been dropped from the set structure, with 'What Is And What Should Never Be' now a permanent feature. Before 'Heartbreaker', Plant tried to calm down the movement of the crowd which was causing the security some concern: "The people who are standing in the aisles, can they sit on the floor or whatever. There's some people behind can't see. So if anybody knows they are obstructing somebody else's view, can they respect that fact or move, then everybody can see!"

Several numbers on, the crowd control was still over-zealous, prompting Plant to dedicate 'Since I've Been Loving You' to... "the little men with the suits on who keep pushing everybody back down the aisle. It's their big day, y'see. They can't understand it."

Plant was on humorous form for the introductions before 'How Many More Times'. The band was introduced as "the four survivors of the Graf Zeppelin", John Bonham as "for the benefit of Mr Kite!" and Jimmy Page as "the man who made rock, rock". Plant was definitely getting into the groove, urging everyone, even the policemen, to put their hands together.

'How Many More times' included an excellent version of Ravel's 'Bolero' by Page and Muddy Waters' 'I'm A Man', a number Page performed with The Yardbirds. Fearful of a riot, the staff turned on the house lights to monitor the situation, and Plant tried to get the house lights turned back down prior to the final number, 'Communication Breakdown'. As the audience shuffled out, the MC announced forthcoming events planned for the Forum: "April 25, the Forum presents Jimi Hendrix. If you wanna mail for tickets, mail them now! Tickets go on sale next Wednesday."

Back in the UK *NME* reported: "In Los Angeles, after their show before 20,000 at the Forum, 4,000 people hung around for half an hour after the show ended, hoping in vain for another encore. Zeppelin's personal gross from this concert was $71,000".

Bootleg CD References: *D'Ya Feel Alright?* (Mad Dogs), *LA Jive & Rambling Mind* (Holy Grail)

Been Loving You/Organ Solo – Thank You/What Is And What Should Never Be/Moby Dick.

Another good performance that thankfully lacked the tension and drama of the previous evening.

Page was now using an echo unit to good effect on the intro to 'Heartbreaker' and this number now segued into 'Bring It On Home' .

Bootleg CD Reference: *Texas, Two Steps* (The Diagrams Of Led Zeppelin)

Saturday March 28 1970
Germany
TV RECORDING AIRED
BEAT CLUB RADIO BREMEN ARD
'Whole Lotta Love' video collage – aired initially at 4.15pm

While the band were in the US, back in Germany 'Whole Love Love' was enjoying huge success as a single in Germany, and the German *Beat Club* programme put together a collage video to accompany the track. This featured a psychedelic female go-go dancer intercut with clips from the unused mimed 'Dazed And Confused' *Beat Club* filming shot exactly a year ago, superimposed onto her body. Unverified footage of another 1969 appearance was also used for this video. This was possibly from one of their Fillmore appearances in 1969 – promoter Bill Graham often filmed acts at the Fillmore East and West venues for his own archives and it's feasible he offered these to Grant who allowed *Beat Club* to use them.

Visual Reference: Unofficial *Early Visions* DVD (Celebration)

Saturday March 28 1970
Dallas, Texas
Memorial
Auditorium

Set included: We're Gonna Groove/Dazed And Confused/Heartbreaker/Bring It On Home/White Summer – Black Mountain Side/Since I've

Sunday March 29 1970
Houston, Texas
University of Houston
Hofheinz Pavilion

Set included: White Summer – Black Mountain Side/How Many More Times (inc. Bolero – Lickin' Stick – Needle Blues – For What It's Worth – Tobacco Road).

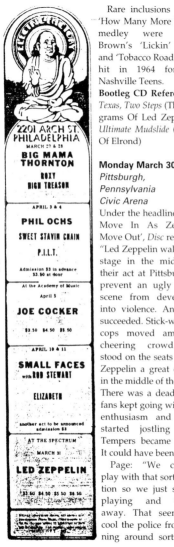

Led Zeppelin

Rare inclusions in the 'How Many More Times' medley were James Brown's 'Lickin' Stick' and 'Tobacco Road', a UK hit in 1964 for The Nashville Teens.

Bootleg CD References: *Texas, Two Steps* (The Diagrams Of Led Zeppelin), *Ultimate Mudslide* (House Of Elrond)

Monday March 30 1970
Pittsburgh, Pennsylvania
Civic Arena

Under the headline 'Cops Move In As Zeppelin Move Out', *Disc* reported: "Led Zeppelin walked off stage in the middle of their act at Pittsburgh to prevent an ugly crowd scene from developing into violence. And they succeeded. Stick-wielding cops moved among a cheering crowd who stood on the seats to give Zeppelin a great ovation in the middle of the show. There was a deadlock as fans kept going wild with enthusiasm and police started jostling them. Tempers became frayed. It could have been a riot."

Page: "We couldn't play with that sort of friction so we just stopped playing and walked away. That seemed to cool the police from running around sorting out the audience, and when we went back on stage after five or 10 minutes, there was no trouble. What we're finding so often on this tour of the States is that the relations between police and audiences are bad from the start, so it ends up with us having to cool things down."

'Led Zeppelin Give Really Poor Concert,' reported Tom Davis in a local paper. "The concert started badly. Jimmy Page and Robert Plant were on the stage wiggling their hips and acting like two complete jackasses. The only thing that was coming out of the amplifiers was a lot of graunch and fuzz

and feedback and the music was really poor. It went on like this for about twenty minutes and I was sitting there thinking how many Jeff Beck records I could buy with five dollars."

Tuesday March 31 1970
Philadelphia, Pennsylvania
The Spectrum

Philadelphia's *Evening Bulletin* reported: "For 15,800 cosmics who bought out the Spectrum last night to partake in the 150-minute, straight-run Led Zeppelin concert, it was all top shelf – pure and uncut. Without second-raters cluttering the bill, there was the rare opportunity at a rock concert for both performers and audience to interact and expand with each other. Both enjoyed the opportunity to 'really get into things'.

THE STOLEN GUITAR

Early in his career, Page's most precious guitar was a Gibson Les Paul Custom – Black Beauty model. Bought in 1962, it was one of his main guitars during the session era and in the early days of The Yardbirds. Though rarely used live, he did begin to feature it with Zeppelin during their early tours. Unfortunately it was stolen during a flight change *en route* to Canada in April 1970. Jimmy takes up the story: "The Gibson stayed with me until it was stolen in the States. I never took it on the road much but things were going so well I decided to start using it. It had a big tremolo arm and Joe Jammer custom wired it. I started to use it more then. It disappeared off the truck at an airport as we were on our way to Canada. We advertised for its return but no luck, even though it was very recognisable with all the custom work on it."

One of its last live outings was at the January 9 Royal Albert Hall show in 1970. The 'Wanted' advertisement for it was inserted into the July 19 1973 edition of *Rolling Stone*.

REWARD FOR RETURN OF BRITISH ROCK MUSICIAN'S LOST OR STOLEN BLACK GIBSON GUITAR LES PAUL CUSTOM WITH BIGSBY ARM NO. 06130 WITH EXTRA SWITCHES. MISSING IN U.S. FOR ABOUT ONE YEAR. NO QUESTIONS ASKED. CONTACT TED ROSENBLATT, 444 MADISON AVE., NY, NY 10022, (212) 752-1330.

"Last night's concert was like most others for Zeppelin on this tour. Big, big crowds, and even bigger money. If you're a promoter and you want the Zeppelin for a two-and-a-half-hour concert, then you've got to pay. Each concert on the tour carries a hefty $25,000 minimum."

Thursday April 2 1970
Charleston, West Virginia
Civic Center

Friday April 3 1970
Macon, Georgia
Macon Coliseum
NME reported: "In the Deep South state of Georgia, long-haired Jimmy Page has been taunted by people in hotel lobbies with remarks like 'What kind of girl are you?'"

Saturday April 4 1970
Indianapolis, Indiana
Indiana State Fair Ground
Coliseum

Sunday April 5 1970
Baltimore, Maryland
Civic Center
Set: We're Gonna Groove/Dazed And Confused/Heartbreaker/Bring It On Home/White Summer – Black Mountain Side/Organ Solo – Thank You/What Is And What Should Never Be/Moby Dick/How Many More Times (inc. Bolero – The Hunter – Needle Blues – Boogie Chillun' – Move On Down The Line – That's Alright Mama – My Baby Left Me – Honey Bee – The Lemon Song)/Whole Lotta Love.

At this show Plant's microphone cut out half way through 'We're Gonna Groove' and the number was completed as an instrumental.

'How Many More Times' included Elvis Presley's first single 'That's Alright Mama' and 'My Baby Left Me'.

Page: "A girl in Baltimore asked me if she could come backstage and watch the show from there. I thought this was the usual line from a girl just wanting to hang around with us. So I said: 'Why don't you go and sit in your seat and watch us?'

She said: 'Because last time at this place, the cops tear-gassed the place and I'm frightened of being out there.' That's the sort of tension we keep finding. There's such a lack of understanding and trust between the audiences and the police."

Bootleg CD Reference: *Some Things Never Pass* (Apple Jam)

Tuesday April 7 1970
Charlotte, North Carolina
Charlotte Coliseum

Set included: We're Gonna Groove/Dazed And Confused/Heartbreaker/Bring It On Home/White Summer – Black Mountain Side/Since I've Been Loving You/Organ Solo – Thank You/What Is And What Should Never Be/Moby Dick/Whole Lotta Love

A local review of this show mentioned they played a new song called 'When Will Be The Next Time'. This is most likely to have been the reviewer guessing at the title of 'What Is And What Should Never Be'.

Fan Butch Betts in attendance told *Proximity* magazine: "The Coliseum was around 75% full

and not sold out. The buzz after the show was electric. The only negative note being that some fans were disappointed with the deletion of the slide guitar lick during 'Whole Lotta Love'. It's hard to imagine but in 1970 that lick was something of a novelty as the record had been a big hit."

Wednesday April 8 1970
Raleigh, North Carolina
J.S.Dorton Auditorium

Set included: We're Gonna Groove/Dazed And Confused/Heartbreaker/Bring It On Home/White Summer – Black Mountain Side/Since I've Been Loving You/Organ Solo – Thank You/What Is And What Should Never Be/Moby Dick.

A very forceful 'We're Gonna Groove' opened the show. Plant: "That was a thing called 'Groove' which is just what we intend to do, and we hope you're gonna as well. So get loose!"

'White Summer' was now being extended further to include a delicate passage that will later be developed into 'Bron Yr Aur'. 'Since I've Been Loving You' now featured most of the lyrics that

will soon be recorded for the third album. John Paul Jones' organ solo at the start of 'Thank You' was now developing into a proper solo, rather than just an instrumental introduction to the piece.

Bootleg CD References: *American Accents* (Baby Face), *Fearsome Four Live On Stage* (Mandala), *Groove* (Tarantura)

Thursday April 9 1970
Tampa, Florida
Curtis Hixon Hall

Set included: Bring It On Home/White Summer – Black Mountain Side/Since I've Been Loving You/Organ Solo – Thank You/What Is And What Should Never Be/Moby Dick/ How Many More Times (inc. Bolero – The Hunter – Needle Blues – Boogie Chillun' – High Flyin' Mama – Mess O'Blues – My Baby – The Lemon Song)/Whole Lotta Love.

Ticket sales for this show were slow. The promoters placed adverts in local newspapers on the day of the concert.

Another excellent show. However Plant made public address announcements in between numbers to ask for calm and even to reunite some members of the audience with their friends. ("Will Carol Russell go to the front box office?").

'How Many More Times' included a unique funky intro. There are two rare additions to the medley – Elvis Presley's 'Mess O'Blues' and bluesman Little Walter's 'My Babe'. The former will be utilised extensively on future tours.

The venue for this show was demolished in 1986

Bootleg CD References: *Makundju* (Cobla), *Bring It On Home* (Pot), *First Choice* (Sugarcane), *Who's Birthday* (Tarantura)

Friday April 10 1970
Miami, Florida
Miama Beach Convention Hall

This venue hosted the popular Jackie Gleason TV show

Ticket sales were again surprisingly slow for this show and good seats were still available on the day of the performance.

The lcocal press report: "A Led Zeppelin Lands in Miami'. "Led Zeppelin, England's top-selling recording group, appear tonight at 8.30 p.m. They're doing the entire two-and-one-half-hour concert themselves, with no intermission.

"'We think people come to see us, not an unknown opening act,' says Jimmy Page, guitarist and group leader. 'So we play the whole thing.'

"Led Zeppelin has been described by a Virginia promoter as the only group he has seen in years which really loves to play. 'They promise two and one-half hours,' he said, 'and they do at least that, but three or four is more like it.'"

Saturday April 11 1970
St. Louis Missouri
Kiel Auditorium
Convention Hall

'Kiel Crowd Cheers British Rock Group' reported Harper Barnes. "Full of sound and fury, Led Zeppelin played long and hard Saturday night and drew repeated standing ovations from a crowd of about 9,000 at Kiel Convention Hall.

"Led Zeppelin is dominated by the technical proficiency of Jimmy Page on guitar and the screaming vocals of Robert Plant. Most of their performance was concerned with individual exhibition rather than music. Although there are flashes of fire that few other groups can duplicate, such as the heavy blues that had the crowd gyrating in

patent lack of rhythm in Zeppelin's noise.

"In a word: it's easy. An easy way to make a million bucks.

"Such miserable music would not be so offensive were it not for the fact that it is all so pretentious. Robert Plant is without talent as a singer or performer. He waves his arms uselessly, he clutches the microphone predictably. He cannot dance and his moves are graceless and tasteless. He seems to think he is very sexy, but he has absolutely nothing interesting or original to offer.

"Guitar companies must be pleased with Jimmy Page's work because all he is doing is demonstrating, with as much creativity as an encyclopaedia salesman, the range of sounds and gimmicks that can come out of an electric guitar. Listening to Page play was, for me, about as satisfying as watching a television picture signal.

"Obviously, Zeppelin fans loved the show. The group gave them what they wanted to hear. The credibility gap is here to stay."

front of the stage at the end, a Led Zeppelin concert overall is about as interesting musically as a long playing record of train whistles."

Sunday April 12 1970
Bloomingdale, Minnesota
The Met Center

Monday April 13 1970
Montreal, Canada
Montreal Forum

John Bonham: "Every concert has been fantastic, four or five encores. Everybody has been going sort of mad. In Montreal, the hall seats 13,800 and we drew 16,000. They sold all standing room and all the aisles."

The *Montreal Star* reported: 'Sell-out crowd greets Led Zeppelin, event of the year', but local reviewer Juan Rodriguez filed one of the most vitriolic attacks of their career: "To say that Led Zeppelin is an awful group is merely an understatement. 'Heavy' is the Zeppelin schtick. The volume is turned up high and each note sounds like an avalanche. False meaning is, thus, attached to each sound: listeners are conned into the belief that because Zeppelin is ridiculously loud, then they must necessarily play important music. Nothing could be further from the truth. The group is ridiculously monotonous. There is a

Tuesday April 14 1970
Ottowa, Canada
Civic Center

Set included: Dazed And Confused/Heartbreaker/Bring It On Home/White Summer – Black Mountain Side/Since I've Been Loving You/Thank You/Whole Lotta Love.

By now Jimmy had perfected the extended echo effect at the beginning of 'Heartbreaker' and the band experimented with a very mellow laid-back rendition of 'Since I've Been Loving You'.

Bootleg CD References: *Ottawa Sunshine* (House Of Elrond), *The Trade Mark Of Quality Masters* (Trademark Of Quality)

Thursday April 16 1970
Evansville,
Indiana
Roberts
Stadium

Friday April 17 1970
Memphis, Tennessee
Mid South Coliseum
Set: We're Gonna Groove/Dazed And Confused/Heartbreaker/Bring It On Home/White Summer – Black Mountain Side/Since I've Been Loving You/Organ Solo – Thank You/What Is And What Should Never Be/Moby Dick/How Many More Times (inc. Bolero – The Hunter – Needle Blues – Boogie Mama – High Flyin' Mama – Memphis Tennessee – For What It's Worth – Ramble On – Tobacco Rd – Honey Bee – Long Distance Call – The Lemon Song – That's Alright Mama)/Whole Lotta Love.

Plant: "We've waited for a long time to come to Memphis, in fact ever since we were born I think!"

On their arrival in town, Mayor Loeb held a reception for the band and made them honorary citizens of Memphis – a civic recognition awarded to only two other musicians – Elvis Presley and Carl Perkins.

There was a heavy security presence at the venue and, as is typical on this tour, the authorities overreacted to the sight of thousands of kids enjoying themselves. By 'How Many More Times', the house lights had been raised. Plant tried to diffuse the situation: "I want the policemen to put their hands together. Put those lights down! You're beautiful – even with the lights on!"

Events spiralled as the band launched into Chuck Berry's 'Memphis Tennessee'. Backstage, the promoter tried to coerce Peter Grant into pulling Zeppelin off the stage. When he refused, a gun was pulled and thrust at Grant's stomach. Grant's response is blunt and to the point: "You can't shoot me, ya cunt. They've just given us the fucking keys to the city."

Back on stage, Plant worked hard to calm things down: "All we wanna do is save our manager! Save Mr Peter Grant! Don't stand on the chairs 'cos they'll give you such shit! And also, please don't step on the rails, because your parents paid rates for them as well. They are yours but don't stand on them. They're for the hockey."

The band again attempted to continue with 'That's Alright Mama' but were forced to make another announcement. "Everybody must get off those chairs – really must! They're taking our manager away! Please get off the chairs – it's no joke!" Plant then threatened to leave the stage but the authorities keep pressurising him to make more announcements. "Listen, you must please respect the fact that we've come from England and everything and we weren't paid. Just please get off everything that might not be cool!" 'How Many More Times' was quickly concluded and the audience are left to calm down for a while.

Before the encore, Plant pleaded once more: "Listen, will you do us a favour. Before we do another one, please sit down. I'm sorry, I really am sorry. Please return to your seats and please remember, when anything happens, don't stand up for God's sake!"

'Whole Lotta Love' finally ended a dramatic night. "Thank you very much. God bless you and goodnight Memphis!"

Bootleg CD References: *Memphis 1970* (Zoso Label), *Memphis Underground* (Magnificent), *Memphis* (Neptune)

Saturday April 18 1970
Phoenix, Arizona
Veterans Memorial Coliseum
Set included: We're Gonna Grove/Dazed And Confused/Heartbreaker/Bring It On Home/White Summer/Organ solo/Thank You/Moby Dick/Whole Lotta Love

At this show Robert Plant collapsed on stage with exhaustion, causing the cancellation of the final show of the tour in Las Vegas.

Plant: "My voice packed up. In Phoenix the heat is so bad that it affects your voice terribly."

Bootleg CD References: *Desert Storm* (Empress Valley), *Phoenix* (Electric Magic)
The Nebula (Tarantura)

Sunday April 19 1970
Las Vegas, Nevada
Convention Center – **CANCELLED**
'Rock Concert Never Does Get Rolling Here'

reported *The Las Vegas Sun*. "A demonstration against the price of tickets was squashed before it got started last night when the concert prompting the protest was cancelled.

"Led Zeppelin was slated for an appearance in the Las Vegas Convention Center at $6 a ticket. Objecting to the price of tickets, 'Poor Limited', a group organised by high school students, planned to picket the concert because they claimed many youths could not afford to attend.

"The concert was cancelled after Robert Plant collapsed on Saturday night. 'There wasn't enough time to get a group equivalent to their calibre,' said Randy Dormio, music director of the radio station presenting the concert. 'So rather than offer an inferior programme, we cancelled it.'

"Response to the concert had been better than any other rock concert signed for Las Vegas. Dormio said that the tickets were priced fairly since Led Zeppelin is one of the most expensive rock groups ever to be booked for a Las Vegas concert."

Thursday April 23 1970
London, England
BBC TV Studios, Lime Grove
TV RECORDING

Jimmy Page performed 'White Summer – Black Mountain Side' on the *Julie Felix Show*. The show also featured The Hollies. The taping of the show occurred on Thursday April 23 and was broadcast at 11.10 pm the following Sunday (26th) on BBC1.

This rare TV appearance for Jimmy was arranged via Peter Grant's association with Mickie Most. Julie Felix, the US folk singer, was managed by Most whose RAR record label shared an office with Zep's Superhype publishing company. Julie was also a friend of John Paul Jones.

"My next guest this evening is a member of certainly the most successful group to come out of Britain in the last couple of years," announced Ms Felix. "Led Zeppelin LPs top both the British and American charts and the lead guitarist in that group is definitely a very talented and special musician. Ladies and gentlemen … Jimmy Page!"

Jimmy delivered a quite startling virtuoso performance of 'White Summer – Black Mountain Side' – a regular part of Zeppelin's live act up to that point. This version was something of a swan song for the piece, as it would not be played again until 1977.

His dexterity across the strings carried all the confidence of a musician at the very top of his profession. Significantly, for this TV version of the track, Page used an acoustic Martin guitar – it was usually played electrically on the Dan Electro model. This was the period where all roads were about to lead to the cottage in Wales, and the acoustic side to the group was about to flower as never before.

This episode of the *Julie Felix Show* was thought to be long lost, but it was rediscovered (with a slight line interference) in the BBC archives for showing at the 1992 Led Zeppelin Convention in London.

"I talked to the producer about getting Jimmy," Julie recalled. "It was mainly an acoustic programme though we did have other acts on like The Four Tops and Dusty Springfield. I know we went after him – the show was something of a cult. We had Spike Milligan, Leonard Cohen, Tim Buckley. People who didn't do a lot of TV. It had a bit of a reputation for being a connoisseurs' show and we did have artists on like Bert Jansch who Jimmy admired. So we asked Jimmy to do an acoustic slot. I knew John Paul Jones quite well, so that might have helped."

Bootleg CD References: *One More Daze* (Dynamite Studios), *Another White Summer* (Big Music),

The Complete BBC Classics (Immigrant)
Visual Reference: Unofficial *Early Visions* DVD (Celebration)

Late April/May
Machynlleth Gwynedd, Wales
Bron Yr Aur Cottage
REHEARSALS
Page and Plant, along with roadies Clive Coulson and Sandy Macgregor, spent time at this remote Welsh cottage composing and rehearsing material for their third album. Here they honed tracks such as 'That's The Way', 'Hey Hey What Can I Do', 'Poor Tom', Down By The Seaside', 'The Rover', and 'Bron Y Aur'.

Page's girlfriend Charlotte accompanied them, as did Plant's wife Maureen and daughter Carmen.

Bootleg Reference: *Another Way To Wales* (Black Swan), *Stairway To Heaven Sessions* (Zoso's Company)
Led Zeppelin III (Tarantura)

Wednesday May 6
Barnes, England
Olympic Studios
RECORDING SESSIONS
On this day the band recorded the track 'Poor Tom' for possible inclusion on their third album. It would eventually surface on *Coda*

MAY 1970
News Report
Granada TV producer Johnny Hamp is attempting to secure Led Zeppelin for a new series of half-hour TV specials. "I got the idea from Led Zeppelin, who didn't want the usual three-minute slot on TV. This series is planned to give groups who provide a good concert appearance a chance to develop on a wide scale. More than just plugging a single or track off an album. Most of the names are booked but I'm still negotiating for Zeppelin." This offer would come to nothing.

It was also rumoured that Jimmy Page and John Bonham would jam with members of The Grateful Dead at the Hollywood Rock Festival to be staged at Newcastle-under-Lyme in late May. Nothing materialised.

Sunday May 24 1970
Erdington Birmingham, England
Mothers' Club
GUEST APPEARANCE
Bonzo and Robert were persuaded to jam with a local band, Cochise.

May–June
Headley Grange, Hampshire,
England
Olympic Studios, Barnes England
RECORDING
More sessions for *Led Zeppelin 3* at Olympic and a run down mansion in Hampshire.

Headley Grange had come to Page's attention after hearing Fleetwood Mac had rehearsed there. It was large three-storey stone structure built in 1795, once a Victorian poor house, and Page made maximum use of the ambient sound possibilities within. Here they initially worked on tracks such as 'Out On The Tiles' (working title 'Bathroom Sound'), 'Immigrant Song', 'Since I've Been Loving You', 'Friends' (working title 'My Oh My'), 'Bron Yr Aur Stomp', 'Celebration Day', 'That's The Way' (working title 'The Boy Next Door') and a blues medley that would eventually emerge as '(Hat's Off) To Roy Harper'.

Bootleg CD References: *Studio Daze* (Scorpio)

Led Zeppelin

Page and Plant spent early May in the cottage known as Bron Yr Aur in south Snowdonia preparing material for their third album, which was duly recorded at Headley Grange, Olympic and Island studios over the next couple of months. There were massive offers to take them back to the States ($250,000 for dates in Boston and New Haven alone) but Grant saw more potential in Zeppelin reaffirming their position at home and wisely accepted an offer from promoter Freddie Bannister for them to headline the Bath Festival (second only in size and importance to the Isle of Wight gathering that year) at Shepton Mallet on 28 June. A year before, they had been further down the bill at the same festival.

Just prior to that they accepted an invitation to represent England in a cultural extravaganza organised by UK talent agent Jasper Parrott. Their June 22 show in Reykjavik was one of the few not attended by Peter Grant. It was during this visit Plant was inspired to re-write the lyrics for the new Zeppelin set opener 'Immigrant Song'.

That number was duly premièred at the beginning of their revised set at the massive Bath Festival four days later. Coming on just as the sun was setting (with a little help from Grant, who physically ensured the preceding act, Flock, vacated the stage on time to enable his boys to take full effect of the natural sunset), over the next couple of hours Zeppelin cemented their supremacy as the most popular rock act of the period in front of over 150,000 fans. Their reception was phenomenal – returning to the stage for multiple encores.

The success at Bath also helped foster an improved relationship with the UK press which universally acclaimed them as the hit of the whole weekend. "There have been one or two really magic gigs and Bath was definitely one of them," said Page, not long after.

A week later they travelled to Germany for a successful four-date tour, capitalising on their success in one of their most lucrative European

markets where the 'Whole Lotta Love' single had been a number one smash alongside the *Led Zeppelin II* album. It rounded off a very satisfying summer, and they returned to finish *Led Zeppelin III* at the new Island studios in July, with renewed confidence.

Equipment Notes:
For the acoustic set of this era, Jimmy used a six-string Harmony acoustic and introduced a cut-away twelve string Gretch on the US tour. Jones' contribution to the acoustic numbers came from a Gibson mandolin. John Bonham introduced a new green metal Ludwig kit.

Monday June 22 1970
Reykjavik, Iceland
Laugardalsholl Sports Center
This show was part of a cultural exchange extravaganza organised by the British government and promoted by international booking agent, Jasper Parrot. Led Zeppelin were the official representatives of the UK pop industry. The venue was later to host the famous 1972 world Chess Championship between Bobby Fischer and Boris Spassky

Rare black and white footage of their arrival in Iceland and performing 'Dazed And Confused' was discovered and cleaned up for use in the official Led Zeppelin DVD.

During this trip, Robert was inspired to write the lyrics for 'Immigrant Song'. Plant: "We went to Iceland and it was one of those times when you go to bed at night, but you don't sleep because the daylight's still there – a 24-hour day. There was just an amazing hue in the sky and it was one of those things that made you think of Vikings and big ships and John Bonham's stomach!"
Visual Reference: On stage and offstage clips of this visit can be seen as part of the menu links on the official *Led Zeppelin* DVD (Warner Vision)

Sunday June 28 1970
Shepton Mallet, England
Bath Festival
Set: Immigrant Song/Heartbreaker/Dazed And

Confused/Bring It On Home/Since I've Been Loving You/Organ Solo – Thank You/That's The Way (Boy Next Door)/What Is and What Should Never Be/Moby Dick/How Many More Times (inc. The Hunter – Needle Blues – Honey Bee – Long Distance Call – Boogie Chillun' – The Lemon Song – Need Your Love Tonight – That's Alright Mama)/Whole Lotta Love/Communication Breakdown/Long Tall Sally – Say Mama – Johnny B. Goode – That's Alright Mama.

Festival performance order: Donovan, Mothers Of Invention, Santana, Flock, Led Zeppelin, Hot Tuna, Country Joe, Jefferson Airplane (set aborted due to fear of electrocution), The Byrds (acoustic set), Moody Blues (unable to play), and Dr. John (acoustic again). The performances started at mid-day on Sunday and ended at about 6.30 AM on Monday morning.

After posing for a much used photo call backstage, Led Zeppelin took the stage at about 8.30 PM and launched straight into the freshly written 'Immigrant Song'. Plant ad-libbed the lyrics and they had little resemblance to those that would eventually appear on *Led Zeppelin III.*

'We're Gonna Groove' and 'White Summer' were now dropped from the set. 'Since I've Been Loving You' was well received by the crowd, considering that the song has not been heard in England previously. Plant struggled with the introduction of another new song: "We've got something a little different … if I can remember the words. This is called 'The Boy Next Door' for want of a better title." This track would be known

as 'That's The Way' at the time of its release on *Led Zeppelin III.* This was England's first real taste of acoustic Led Zeppelin and was met with polite applause.

They closed the set, as was the custom, with the extended 'How Many More

111

Times' medley. Plant made a speech to the crowd prior to the final encores: "We've been playing America a lot recently and we really thought that coming back here we might have a dodgy time. There's a lot of things going wrong in America at the moment, that are getting a bit sticky. It's really nice to come to an open-air festival where there are no bad things happening and everything's turned out beautiful.

Another medley of classic rock and roll brought to a close one of the most important shows of their career.

Just before they went on stage Peter Grant spotted some would-be bootleggers in the crowd. "I caught them under the stage. I couldn't find the promoter, so I thought 'Fuck it', and went and did it myself. I kicked the shit out of them and all the equipment. You know they have buckets of sand and water and all that, and an axe? I pulled the axe off the wall and steamed in and chopped it all up. Did a machete job on the machinery! I didn't get 'heavies' to do it, I did it myself. Then at least I knew it was done."

The performance was filmed on Peter Grant's instruction for possible future use, with no less than four different film crews in attendance. Peter Whitehead, who had worked with them at the Albert Hall, filmed the entire Zeppelin set for Grant but the film had the incorrect exposure and was unusable. No footage from this is believed to have survived.

British Lions Films were in charge of the Eidaphor TV projector screen at the festival and also recorded some acts on two-inch tape. They were refused permission to shoot Zeppelin. Another team Paradise/TVX recorded in black and white on one inch video tape. Again they did not shoot Zeppelin. Finally Gentle Giant Films recorded on colour 16mm. It's believed that this source produced the sole footage of Zeppelin at Bath that still exists though as yet it has not surfaced.

Melody Maker reported 'Five Encores For Zeppelin': "Led Zeppelin stormed to huge success at the Bath Festival. About 150,000 fans rose to give them an ovation. They played for over three hours – blues, rock and roll and pure Zeppelin. Jimmy Page, in a yokel hat to suit the Somerset scene, screamed into attack on guitar, John Paul Jones came into his own on organ as well as bass, and John Bonham exploded his drums in a sensational solo. And the crowd went wild demanding encore after encore … a total of five!"

John Bonham enjoyed his Bath night: "The atmosphere was fantastic really when you consider it was cold and windy. And even when it rained they sat through it and could still be happy. I didn't think you could get an atmosphere like that at a concert."

Peter Grant remembered later: "Bath was great. I went down to the site unbeknown to Freddie Bannister and I found out from the Met Office what time the sun was setting and it was right behind the stage and by going on at eight in the evening, I was able to bring the lights up a bit at a time. And it was vital we went on to match that. That's why I made sure Flock or whoever it was got off on time. Not that we had anything to lose as we'd been paid £20,000 up front!

"Bath was a turning point in terms of recognition for us. It was great and I remember Jonesy arriving by helicopter with Julie Felix and Mo (Jones' wife) and we had to get the Hell's Angels to help us get them to the site. I'd made a contract with the Angels in Cleveland in America with The Yardbirds, so we had no bother with them."

Bootleg CD References: *Bath 1970* (Le-Mon Recordings), *Bath Festival 1970* (Empress Valley)

Saturday July 11 1970
Studley, England
St Mary's Parish Church Vicerage Grounds
GUEST APPEARANCE
John Bonham attended the Studley annual Summer Fayre and signed autographs. John's wife Pat judged the fancy dress competition,

Thursday July 16 1970
Cologne, Germany
Sporthalle
For this brief German tour John Bonham filed a

diary report for *Record Mirror* under the headline 'Zep Zap Germans'. "We flew to Dusseldorf to start the tour and used the Inter-Continental Hotel as a base for the shows at Cologne and Essen. The flight in was a bit ropy. I'm not really the world's greatest flyer, but I particularly hate flying in Germany. There always seems to be such a lot of clouds, so much turbulence, and the plane can't ever seem to be able to fly above the weather. We played Cologne the first night. That was nice, and the act built nicely to a climax. We had to do two encores, which set the pattern for the whole tour."

Chris Welch of *Melody Maker* also travelled with them on these German dates and reported: "The first night was a warm-up. They played well – but not brilliantly. There were less crowds than had been expected – 4,000 instead of 7,000. And there were 1,000 outside demanding free admission. When this was refused they took to smashing windows causing DM 4,000 damage."

German promoter Fritz Rau: "After 9pm we let them in although 1,500 refused to buy tickets, even when we reduced them to six marks from 12. But they think all concerts should be free. Edgar Broughton came here and said all music should be free. It's a nice idea what Blackhill Enterprises is doing in London [holding free concerts in Hyde Park.], but the kids here don't understand about the cost of bringing over a group, and with all the damage, we probably won't be able to have pop concerts in this hall again."

While on tour, Welch filmed the group on his own personal cine-camera, capturing them on stage and travelling between shows. This footage was shown at the 1999 London Anniversary Daze convention. Clips of them offstage in Germany from Welch's home movie footage was also included in the 1997 'Whole Lotta Love' promo video to accompany the release of the track as a CD single in the UK.

Friday July 17 1970
Essen, Germany
Grugahalle
John Bonham: "Audiences are pretty much the

same everywhere, the only difference over here is that they didn't understand our stage announcements too good. You know, like in Essen on the second night, there were no seats in the hall, and the stage was very high, so Robert had to ask the kids at the front to sit down several times. Eventually he did get the message across, and the show got OK towards the end."

Chris Welch: "This was the noisiest of the four concerts, where Jimmy gave up trying to play his acoustic guitar feature. 'Christians to the lions,' said Jimmy as they went out to a storm of whistling. 'We have a problem,' said Robert. 'If you are going to make a noise, we might as well go away – so shut up!' He scolded them like children and he was greeted with cheers.

"Improving considerably on the night before, Jimmy played beautiful, inventive guitar, and Robert ranged from the familiar histrionics of *Led Zeppelin I* into blues harp and gentle vocals."

Saturday July 18 1970
Frankfurt, Germany
Festhalle
Set included: Immigrant Song/Heartbreaker/Dazed And Confused/Bring It On Home/That's The Way/Bron Yr Aur/Since I've Been Loving You/Organ Solo – Thank You/What Is And What Should Never Be/Moby Dick/Whole Lotta Love/Communication Breakdown/Rock And Roll Medley.

The transitional new set for the German tour was based around the nucleus of the Bath performance. However, the new instrumental 'Bron Yr Aur' (Welsh for 'Golden Breast') was inserted after 'That's The Way' to form the first proper acoustic set.

The band also took the potentially risky step of dropping the crowd-pleasing 'How Many More Times'. From now on 'Whole Lotta Love' would be the springboard for their rock and roll medleys. For this show they were joined on stage for 'Whole Lotta Love' by Chris Welch on timbales. Welch commented: "It was great fun. Faced with so many people there was a strong temptation to grab a microphone and order them to march forward to victory."

John Bonham: "Frankfurt on Saturday night was terrific. We played to 11,000 people at the Festhalle, which is something like an all-Germany record audience. They were really great, listened very hard and kept quiet throughout the act. Which is the way we like it now, as we have introduced some new acoustic songs into the act from the next album."

Allan McDougall of *New Musical Express* reported: 'Led Take-Over Germany!' – "Zeppelins of a Led variety went back to Germany last weekend and for four days took complete command of the country. Boy! Do Zeppelin get it on when they are in top gear. They really give crowds value for money. On stage they all look like chiefs of four different kinds. Plant, a giant, strutting Viking … Page with a red maxi-cardigan made from a curtain, looking like a Druid priest … Bonham, galloping along on his big, bright-green, pleasure-machine drums looks like a cross between Sinbad The Sailor and Bluebeard … and Jones moving around like a Hobbit with a bass guitar."

Sunday July 19 1970
Berlin, Germany
Deutschlandhalle
Set included: Immigrant Song/Heartbreaker/ Dazed And Confused/Bring It On Home/Since I've Been Loving You/Thank You/What Is And What Should Never Be/Whole Lotta Love (inc. Boogie Chillun' – Redhouse – The Lemon Song – Out In Virginia – Hoochie Koochie Man – Honey Bee – Long Distance Call – Needle Blues)/ Communication Breakdown.

Another fine performance. 'Whole Lotta Love' was well received as the new vehicle for improvisation. In this new arrangement, Page performed the Theremin section before the medley begins.

Bonham: "The audience tonight was fine, at the Deutschlandhalle. About 6,000 Berliners came to see us tonight, which is apparently more than have been to the last three rock concerts in this city put together."

Before tonight's show most of the group's entourage visited the Berlin Wall. Bonham: "Berlin is not the most exhilarating place in the world – some of us went to The Wall today, and that was a real downer." Page refused to go: "I've seen it before. The vibrations in Germany are making me sick enough without me getting more depressed."

New Musical Express reported: "There were hordes of police with water-cannons ready to quell the anticipated riots, but Zeppelin left the audience too limp from the sheer excitement of the two-and-a-half hour show. Even the police were toe-tapping and hand-clapping when Robert requested it! Led Zeppelin are really something else – they even made the tough Berlin police bop in the aisles."

Chris Welch again: "They played a superb set resulting in foot stamping, chants, cheers and whistles. Peter Grant was kept busy putting a stop to repeated attempts at pirate recording. Twice stereo microphone set-ups on boom stands were discovered, and disgruntled 'engineers' found their tapes being unceremoniously confiscated."
Bootleg CD References: *Checkpoint Charlie* (Immigrant), *Intimate* (Almost Mysterious), (Equinox)

The sixth USA visit in less than two years was easily their most ambitious so far. Advance orders for *Led Zeppelin III* were racking up by the day as Peter Grant negotiated what would be their largest grossing tour to date, in auditoriums of 15,000 plus. Now in a position to wield their power, the swing towards the artists instead of the promoter was firmly in their favour. With The Beatles now defunct and The Rolling Stones off the road, only The Who vied with Led Zeppelin as the world's top concert attraction.

After cancelling the first week of shows due to the ill health of John Paul Jones' father, Zeppelin were soon well into their stride. The new stage act, with 'Immigrant Song'/'Heartbreaker' as a stunning opening *tour de force*, slayed the audience at every stop-off. In Los Angeles, at the 18,000 capacity Inglewood Forum, they blasted through an astonishing set that was captured for all time on one of the first ever bootlegs – the infamous *Live On Blueberry Hill*.

When this double album started appearing in London in the autumn, Grant and Cole took it upon themselves to visit a known dealer and demand his stock. In retrospect, it was a futile gesture: that album is now on its sixteenth re-issue as a CD set alone – and all 35 years on.

Back in 1970 the tour continued with stops in Honolulu and a final leg that included their début at New York's Madison Square Garden where afternoon and evening shows on September 19 set the seal on a tumultuous tour. For those two dates alone they raked in a cool $100,000.

Back home, readers of the then influential *Melody Maker* voted them the top band in its annual poll – ending years of Beatles domination. "Zeppelin topple Beatles" headlines proclaimed.

However, there was a severe test of loyalty ahead when the controversial *Led Zeppelin III* was released in October. Although an instant number one on both sides of the Atlantic, it did not enjoy the sales longevity of the first two albums. The introduction of acoustic based compositions displayed a growing musical maturity some fans found hard to take.

Plant staunchly defended the album at the time: "You can just see the headlines, can't you. Led Zeppelin go soft on their fans or some crap like that. The point is that when you make an album, you never know how it will come out. We started rehearsing at the cottage to see what we wanted more clearly. Now we've done *Led Zeppelin III* the sky's the limit. It shows we can change. It means

The Chronicle Telegram / Teen-age page

Led Zeppelin concert wows Cleveland crowd

By JOHN KLEIN

If people left the Led Zeppelin concert Wednesday with any feeling short of musical ecstasy, they must have gone to be heard and not to hear.

Zeppelin burned their tunes into the half-filled Public Auditorium for nearly two hours while everyone dazedly moved only with the pulse coming from the stage.

THEY STARTED the concert with the tunes from their first two albums that everyone has heard many times, but no one seemed to care. They just listened and worked it out in their heads.

Where the early Zeppelin used noise, Jimmy Page picked and bowed his guitar as only he could, changing the noise of his old days into music that wouldn't quit. All the time lead vocalist Robert Plant wailed and moved as music was blasted to him.

The surprise of the night came as Plant, Page, and bass player John Paul Jones moved out in front with their acoustic strings. With Page on the guitar, Jones on the mandolin, and Plant on the microphone, they started in on the audience with Led Zeppelin III, their yet unreleased album. They displayed an honesty only music could as they dedicated this song to a friend that had just been killed in a motorcycle accident.

THEY FINISHED the regular part of their concert with Jones and a far-out organ on a little known Zeppelin tune called "Thank You," then hit with "Whole Lotta Love."

When they left the stage, the crowd clamoured for more, not letting up until there was music once more. Zeppelin returned with John Bonham featured on drums.

As the rest of the group left the stage, Bonham did everything possible to make his drums talk, plus a few things that weren't in the book.

WHEN THE REMAINING group members returned to the stage, Jones had split to England for family reasons and Plant said that was it; but as the audience pressed to the stage, they agreed to continue.

As they got set to do more, Page popped a string. To fill the gap Plant started to play his harp while Bonham started in on the tabla drums. When Page fixed his guitar, he joined in on the jam. They were then joined by a girl in a Belkin Production tee shirt who played bass to finish the night.

This time they left for good, leaving Led Zeppelin burned into everyone's mind, something you don't hear every day.

The Concert File

there are endless possibilities and directions for us to go in. We won't go stale and this proves it."

Wednesday August 5 1970
Cincvinnati, Ohio
CANCELLED

Wednesday August 5 1970
Los Angeles, California
Whisky A Go Go
GUEST APPEARANCE
John Bonham allegedly attended the performance of Irish rock band Skid Row featuring Gary Moore at this LA venue. They jammed on a version of 'Whole Lotta Love' and 'Got My Mojo Working'. The performance surfaced on a bootleg CD in 1999 titled 'Whole Lotta Love'.

August
Memphisis
Tennesse
Ardent Studios
RECORDING
SESSIONS
In between tour dates Page spent time at Ardent Studios in Memphis completing their third album. Working with engineer Terry Manning, a friend from his Yardbirds touring days, he overdubbed 'Since I've Been Loving You' and honed the album

from 17 tracks down to 10 and completed final mixes.

Thursday August 6 1970
Detroit, Michigan
CANCELLED

Friday August 7 1970
Cleveland, Ohio
CANCELLED

Saturday August 8 1970
Boston, Masachusettes
CANCELLED
(RESCHEDULED TO SEPTEMBER 9)

Sunday August 9 1970
Pittsburgh Pennsylvania
CANCELLED
The initial itinerary was amended several times for this tour.

The band were also erroneously billed to appear at the Strawberry Fields Festival at New Brunswick, Canada.

Tuesday August 11 1970
Charlotte, North Carolia
CANCELLED

Wednesday August 12 1970
Jacksonville, Florida
CANCELLED

Thursday August 13 1970
Tallahassee, Florida
CANCELLED

August 14 1970
Chestnut Hill,
Massachusetts
Boston College
Stadium
CANCELLED
Originally, Zeppelin were due to headline

the Boston College Eagle Rock Festival – a planned thirteen and a half hour marathon with support from Lighthouse, MC-5, The Stooges, The Allman Brothers, Catfish and The Amboy Dukes amongst others.

Boston College intended to put its share of the profits towards building a 7,000 seat 'dome' to house future rock concerts.

However, residents in the affluent suburb of Chestnut Hill, near the proposed site, objected to the festival and Major White, aware that pressure from the city's wealthiest residents could damage his campaign for governorship, revoked the College's licence only two days prior to the event. The promoters hastily rebooked Zeppelin for September 8 and then later changed the date to September 9.

Saturday August 15 1970
New Haven, Connecticut
Yale Bowl

Set: Immigrant Song/Heartbreaker/Dazed And Confused/Bring It On Home/Since I've Been Loving You/What Is And What Should Never Be/Moby Dick/Whole Lotta Love (inc. Boogie Chillun' – High Heeled Sneakers – High Flyin' Mama – Shake, Baby, Shake – Move On Down The Line – Moving On – Honey Bee – The Lemon Song – Needle Blues)/Communication Breakdown (inc. Good Times Bad Times).

Billed as 'Great & Solid Gold & Groovy' and sponsored by Silly Putty and promoted by The Greater New Haven Jaycees.

An excellent start to the tour with a performance that included many obscure references in the 'Whole Lotta Love' medley. 'Communication Breakdown' was now performed as the encore number and included sections of 'Good Times Bad Times'.
Bootleg CD Reference: *Rare Short Party* (Image Quality)

Monday August 17 1970
Hampton Beach, Virginia
Hampton Roads Coliseum
Set: Immigrant Song/Heartbreaker/Dazed And Confused/Bring It On Home/That's The Way/Bron Yr Aur/Since I've Been Loving You/Organ Solo – Thank You/What Is And What Should Never Be/Moby Dick/Whole Lotta Love (inc. Feel So Good Today – Boogie Chillun' – Movin' On)/Communication Breakdown (inc. Good Times Bad Times).

A rather unspectacular show. The version of 'Whole Lotta Love' was the briefest of the tour with very little improvisation.
Bootleg CD Reference: *Live In Hampton 1970* (Diagrams Of Led Zeppelin)

Wednesday August 19 1970
Kansas City, MI
Municipal Auditorium

Thursday August 20 1970
Oklahoma City, Oklahoma
City Fairgrounds Coliseum

117

Friday August 21 1970
Tulsa, Oklahoma
Tulsa Assembly Center
Set: Immigrant Song/Heartbreaker/Dazed And Confused (inc. White Summer)/Bring It On Home/That's The Way/Bron Yr Aur/Since I've Been Loving You/Organ Solo – Thank You/What Is And What Should Never Be/Moby Dick/Whole Lotta Love (inc. Boogie Chillun' – High Flyin' Mama – Matchbox – Who's Loving You Tonight? – Heartbeat – The Lemon Song – My Baby Left Me – That's Alright Mama)/Communication Breakdown (inc. Good Times Bad Times).

In contrast to Hampton, an excellent and unusual show. However, the situation in the States hadn't changed much since the spring and once again there were problems with the authorities.

The crowd reaction was exuberant throughout and during 'Heartbreaker' the security raised the house lights. Page stopped playing immediately: "Actually you can turn down the house lights now," said Plant. "Turn the lights off! Everybody sit still. Before we carry on, the lights go down. No listen, if we're gonna have a good time and you are, we're gonna have to work hand in glove with the so-called authorities. So, you sit down and they'll be cool and turn the lights off. So let's wait for them to turn off the lights."

Reluctantly, the authorities obliged. Plant is ever the diplomat. "That's not a victory – that's common sense, so don't take it as a victory!" Page then continued his solo, even adding an impressive mellow interlude, perhaps intended to calm down the crowd.

At the end of the number, Plant stated, "Let's hope we've reached an understanding with the electrical suppliers. That doesn't mean you can't take your ties off!"

'Dazed And Confused' included a rare electric interpretation of 'White Summer'. There was a delay in tuning the organ before 'Since I've Been Loving You' so the band humorously indulged in an impromptu 'hoe-down'.

'Whole Lotta Love' was the highlight of the show and included rare renditions of Carl Perkins' 'Matchbox', Buddy Holly's 'Heartbeat' and 'Who's Loving You Tonight?'
Bootleg CD References: *Tulsa Hillbilly* (Tarantura), *You Gotta Be Cool* (Whole Lotta Live), *Bottle Up And Go* (Scorpio), *The Lights Go Down* (The Diagrams Of Led Zeppelin)

Saturday August 22 1970
Fort Worth Texas
Tarrant County
Convention Centre

Sunday August 23 1970
San Antonio, Texas
Hemisfair Arena

Tuesday August 25 1970
Nashville, Tennessee
Municipal Auditorium
The local newspaper entertainment column announced: "Led Zapplin (sic), a local pop-rock vocal group, are to play at Municipal Auditorium on Tusday night". A local record store offered a deal on the first two Zeppelin albums on eight track cartridge to mark their appearance.

Wednesday August 26 1970
Cleveland, Ohio
Public Auditorium
Show start time was moved from 8.30 to 5.30, so JP Jones could return back to England for his fathers funeral. John left as planned after the main show. However when the band were called back for further encores they were joined on bass by a girl wearing a 'Belkin Productions' t-shirt. The local *Chronicle Telegram* reported: "When the remaining group members returned to the stage, Jones had split to England for family reasons and Plant said that was it, but as the audience pressed the stage, they agreed to continue.

"As they got set to do more, Page popped a

string. To fill the gap Plant started to play his harp while Bonham started in on the tabla drums. When Page fixed his guitar he joined in on the jam. They were then joined onstage by a girl in a 'Belkin Production' tee shirt who played bass to finish the night.

"This time they left for good, leaving Led Zeppelin burned in everyone's mind."

Milwaukee Journal
Thursday August 27th 1970

Due to a death in the family, the LED ZEPPELIN CONCERT has been postponed to Monday, August 31st.

Tickets on sale now at Arena ticket office and all Milwaukee area Sears stores. Concert time: 8 PM.

Thursday August 27 1970
Milwaukee, Wisconsin
Milwaukee Arena
CANCELLED
Concert cancelled due to the death of John Paul Jones's father. Jones returned home to England and the concert was rescheduled for August 31. The rest of the band moved to New York.

Friday August 28 1970
Detroit, Michigan
Olympia Stadium
'New acoustic material disappoints Led Zep freaks' read the local headline, highlighting the media's mixed reaction to their expanding repertoire. Pete Cain reported: "Jimmy Page and co wowed the audience in Detroit's Olympia with their expertise in the heavy idiom. Page in particular has a way of turning down his volume to a whisper (but only for a moment at a time) that puts the crowd right at the edge of their seats. Drummer John Bonham does the obligatory lengthy solo, as well as most rock drummers usually do it, but not any better. The crowd of course ate it up"

"But Led Zeppelin almost let the collective energy of the concert blow away when they put aside electric instruments to do acoustic material from their latest album. Page playing guitar and bassist Jones on mandolin couldn't possibly force their sound through a PA system entirely unsuited to subtlety. At any rate after two songs worth of squirming fans and frustrated musicians, Zep had to plug back in to rescue the evening, which they did with a vengeance."

Saturday August 29 1970
Winnipeg, Canada
Winnipeg Arena, 'Man Pop' Festival
Support from The Youngbloods, The Ides Of March, The Iron Butterfly and eight local acts.

The show was due to take place at the nearby outdoor Winnipeg Stadium. However, the weather was so bad on the day that the PA malfunctioned. The whole event was then transferred to the Winnipeg Arena, but the indoor arena had a lower capacity and 800 valid ticket holders were refused admission when capacity was reached.

Zeppelin eventually closed the show which ran until 3am the next morning. Their fee for this performance was $50,000.

Monday August 31 1970
Milwaukee, Wisconsin
Milwaukee Arena
Set included Immigrant Song/Heartbreaker/Dazed And Confused/Bring It On Home/That's The Way/Bron Yr Aur/Since Ive Been Loving You. Rescheduled date from August 27.

The *Milwaukee Journal* reported: "England's Led Zeppelin and an Arena audience of 6,000 became good friends in two hours Monday night. The audience loved the acid rock band for its musical talent. There were none of the old promotional tricks. No local disc jockeys. No local bands. Just the crowd and the Zeppelin. The group started slow, finished big and the crowd unwound with them. By the end of the show, the area in front of the stage was filled with hundreds of people who finally won out over the security guards. It was not teeny-bopper idolisation. These fans respected Zeppelin and Zeppelin respected them. Led Zeppelin is so much a part of today that it can easily transform into tomorrow. Its music cannot get much louder or its talent much better."

Bootleg CD References: *Milwaukee* (Akashic), *Milwaukee '70* (The Diagrams Of Led Zeppelin), *Latest Summer* (Jelly Roll)

Tuesday September 1 1970
Seattle, Washington
Seattle Center
Coliseum

A tense show. The audience were rowdy throughout Page was forced to stop the acoustic set and asked the crowd to stop whistling. Unusually but considering the crowd reaction, they did not return for an encore.

Wednesday September 2 1970
Oakland, California
Oakland Coliseum

Set: Immigrant Song/Heartbreaker/Dazed And Confused/Bring It On Home/That's The Way/Bron Yr Aur/Since I've Been Loving You/Organ Solo – Thank You/What Is And What Should Never Be/Moby Dick/Whole Lotta Love (inc. Boogie Chillun' – Boppin' The Blues – Ju Ju Rhythm – Lawdy Miss Clawdy – For What It's Worth – Honey Bee – Movin' On – Fortune Teller – That's Alright Mama)/Communication Breakdown (inc. Good Times Bad Times)/Train Kept A Rollin'/Blueberry Hill/Long Tall Sally.

A more enjoyable show with rare inclusions of 'Ju Ju Rhythm', 'Lawdy Miss Clawdy' and 'Fortune Teller', a number covered by both The Rolling Stones and The Who in recent years.

'Train Kept A Rollin'' (their set opener on their first tours) was recalled for a surprise second encore, and yet further encores featured Fats Domino's 'Blueberry Hill' and 'Long Tall Sally'.

Bootleg CD References: *Two Days Before* (Silver Rarties), *Another Night On Blueberry Hill* (Electric Magic), *Live On Bluberry Hill 2* (Tarantura)

Thursday September 3 1970
San Diego, California
Sports Arena

Set: Immigrant Song/Heartbreaker/Dazed And Confused/Bring It On Home/That's The Way/Since I've Been Loving You/Organ Solo – Thank You/What Is And What Should Never Be/Moby Dick/Whole Lotta Love (inc. Boogie Chillun' – Two And One Makes Three – Crosscut Saw – Since My Baby's Been Gone – Honey Bee – The Lemon Song – Needle Blues – Lawdy Miss Clawdy)/Communication Breakdown.

Another rampant crowd attended this show, constantly whistling, talking and shouting. There was a problem with Jimmy's guitar in the acoustic set and 'Bron Yr Aur' was eventually abandoned.

'Whole Lotta Love' featured some obscure references and was one of the most unusual versions of the tour.

Bootleg CD Reference: *Missing Sailor* (Immigrant), *Mad Dogs Box* (Mad Dog)

Friday September 4 1970
Inglewood Los Angeles, California
The Forum

Set: Immigrant Song/Heartbreaker/Dazed And Confused/Bring It On Home/That's The Way/Bron Yr Aur/Since I've Been Loving You/Organ Solo – Thank You/What Is And What Should Never Be/Moby Dick/Whole Lotta Love (inc. Boogie Chillun' – Movin' On – Redhouse – Some Other Guy – Think It Over – Honey Bee – The Lemon Song)/Communication Breakdown (inc. Good Times Bad Times – For What It's Worth – I Saw Her Standing There)/Out On The Tiles/Blueberry Hill.

Plant: "Good Evening. Nice to be back. This is gotta be about the sixth time."

Another landmark performance, elevated to

THE THEREMIN

The Theremin, the grandfather of electronic instruments, is the only musical instrument that can be played without being touched. It was named after Leo Theremin, a Russian physicist who patented it in the Twenties and whose great-niece, Lydia Kavina, is still one of the world's leading practitioners of the instrument. Its most notable use in the pop field in the Sixties was by The Beach Boys – it can be heard on their 1966 number one 'Good Vibrations'.

Jimmy Page first acquired the instrument in New York when Zeppelin were recording tracks for *Led Zeppelin II*. Its first known usage on stage was at the Fillmore East in San Francisco on April 26, 1969. The device was used sparingly in both 'Dazed And Confused' and 'How Many More Times' at this show, but was not introduced as a regular feature at this stage.

In the studio, its spiralling high pitched tone could be heard during the middle section of 'Whole Lotta Love'. When they adapted that number for regular live performance in January 1970, Page had the Theremin box set up by the side of the stage. By moving his hand towards the antenna of the instrument and varying distances and angles he was able to alter the tone of the sound and its duration. The high-pitched shrieks were then pitted against Plant's vocal screams. This call and response battle developed into a traditional part of 'Whole Lotta Love' live, preceding the rock'n'roll medley of the live arrangement.

When the pair reunited for the 1995 World Tour, the Theremin was recalled to the side of the stage and employed first as part of 'Shake My Tree' and later on in the tour, back in its old stomping ground in the 'Whole Lotta Love' medley. It was also present for the 'Whole Lotta Love' medley on the 1998 *Walking Into Everywhere* tour with Plant and on the 1999/2000 dates with the Black Crowes.

The Concert File

---

near legendary heights by the enterprising bootleggers who were on hand to capture the action as it unfolded. from DJ J.J. Jackson's introduction, right through to Plant's breathless delivery of 'Blueberry Hill'.

The first of the new acoustic numbers, 'That's The Way', was well received which pleased Plant: "It gives us great pleasure to hear that. We've had a bit of abuse in the Midwest, every time you sit on a chair and pick up a mandolin." Encouraged by this response, Plant went into great detail to explain the origins of the next acoustic number: "This is a thing called 'Bron Yr Aur'. This is the name of a little cottage in the mountains of Snowdonia near Wales, and 'Bron Yr Aur' is the Welsh equivalent of the phrase 'Golden Breast'. This is so, because of its position every morning as the sun rises and it's a really remarkable place and so after staying there for a while and deciding it was time to leave for various reasons, we couldn't really just leave it and forget about it. You've probably all been to a place like that, only we can tell you about it and you can't tell us." 'Since I've Been Loving You' and

'What Is And What Should Never Be' are both outstanding. 'Whole Lotta Love' is a very hard, in-your-face, rock version which ends with a massive firecracker explosion at the finale. "Led Zeppelin … Can you dig it?" asked J. J. Jackson.

"Who threw that firecracker? You ought to be locked up!" scolded Plant before launching into a unique version of 'Communication Breakdown' which not only included 'Good Times Bad Times' but also 'For What It's Worth' and The Beatles' 'I Saw Her Standing There'.

After one of the few live renditions of 'Out On The Tiles' from the new *Led Zeppelin III* album. Fats Domino's 'Blueberry Hill' closed the show and provided the title for the ensuing bootleg release, initially issued on the mysterious Blimp label as *Live On Blueberry Hill*. As the sleeve notes so accurately described it: "One hundred and six minutes and fifty three seconds of pure and alive rock."

Bootleg CD References: *Live On Blueberry Hill* (Cobra Standard), *Live On Blueberry Hill* (Sanctuary), *Live On Blueberry Hill* (Tarantura), *The Final Statements* (Antrabata), Return To Blueberry Hill (Immigrant)

Friday September 4 1970
Los Angeles, California
Troubadour Club
GUEST APPEARANCE

After making one of their most successful appearances at the Forum, the night continued. Zep moved on to an after gig rendezvous with Fairport Convention who were recording a live album, and Robert, Jimmy, John Paul and Bonzo all agreed to jam during their second set. Fairport's Dave Pegg remembers Page borrowing Simon Nicol's Gibson L5 and having trouble with it as it had a wound third string. Nichol recalls: "Dave Mattack's bass drum had been totally solid the whole night but I saw it jump forward three or four inches on Bonzo's first strike!"

Numbers played included 'Hey Joe', 'Morning Dew', 'Banks Of Sweet Primroses', 'Mystery Train' and 'That's Alright Mama'.

Fairport were recording the shows on Wally Hiedler's mobile and the tapes were rolling throughout the jam. Pegg recalls: "It was obvious there was a sound recording truck and I was just waiting for Peter Grant to go and break my legs or something, but he never said a dicky bird!"

The tape of the jam ended up in the hands of Peter Grant.

The party continued at the nearby Barney's Beanerie with a drinking contest involving Dave Pegg, Bonzo and Janis Joplin. Bonham was allegedly discovered a day later naked next to the hotel swimming pool.

Sunday September 6 1970
Honolulu, Hawaii
International Center Arena

First Set included: Immigrant Song/Dazed And Confused/Heartbreaker/Since I've Been Loving You/What Is And What Should Never Be/Moby Dick/Whole Lotta Love (inc. Boogie Chillun' – Messing Around My Heart – Redhouse – Some Other Guy)/Communication Breakdown (inc. American Woman).

Two shows at 7pm and 10.30pm. Ticket prices $6, $5, $4, and $3.

K-POI AM and FM present 'An Evening of Led Zeppelin'.

After the opening attack of 'Immigrant Song' there was a bizarre set change. Instead of segueing into 'Heartbreaker' as is the custom on this tour, John Paul Jones launched erroneously into 'Dazed And Confused'. The rest of the group had no choice but to follow.

When the song ends 15 minutes later, Plant was still confused: "What am I doing?" before he finally announced "This is one from the second album. It's about a mean woman – as they usually are!" 'Heartbreaker' followed.

There was some equipment problems prior to the next number and Plant announced: "The group's been renamed the Box Of Tricks – 'cos we don't know what these things really are, but they come with us everywhere we go."

The 'Whole Lotta Love' medley was performed at high speed and high energy, and the sole encore of 'Communication Breakdown' featured a funky John Paul Jones' bass solo and snatches of 'American Woman' by The Guess Who.

The Hawaii press reviewed both shows: "Times have been good to Led Zeppelin. They are making good money and good music. Page played well but there was a certain routine manner about his gig. Which is not to say it was bad. Page at his worst is better than most people. He plays extremely fast and accurately and has a fine sense of dynamics. He is one of the élite.

"So you wonder why they made John Paul Jones play that solo on the organ. Without qualification, it was the worst piece of garbage I have ever heard a major group put out. He knew it and they must have known it. He is obviously learning to play, which is good, but they ought to at least wait until he can use both hands.

"Just for the record, the second show was far superior to the first. The first featured Jimmy Page on bow, a 'Page speciality' I had hoped he would do it on the second show but he didn't.

"It was during the second show that Robert Plant stopped the show twice with his fast thinking. The first was a man having a seizure during the group's acoustic number. He called for a doctor and had the spotlight turned on the victim for more light. The second time came when a small fight broke out between ushers and spaced-out rock fans. By stopping the show, he stopped the fight. It takes a pretty aware cat to be able to do that.

"After two concerts I could have gone a third. It

was a night we will never forget."

A local photographer filmed a reel of 8mm cine film from the press pit. A few brief clips of this were used in the 1997 'Whole Lotta Love' promo video.

Bootleg CD Reference: *Holiday In Waikiki* (The Gold Standard), *Almost Son Of Blueberry Hill* (Shout To The Top), *Box Of Tricks* (Red Hot), *In Exotic Honolulu* (Akashic)

Visual Reference: The privately shot silent footage, mainly of Page and Plant, appeared on the *Early Visions* unofficial DVD set (Celebration)

AT BOSTON GARDEN

★★★★★★★★ The Incredible
LED ZEPPELIN
In two 2 1/2 hour solo performances
Sept. 9. 5:15 & 8:45 pm.

New Tickets On Sale
$4.50 5.50 & 6.50
Boston Garden Box Office   Freaque Boutique:
Krackerjacks   Out of Town Ticket Agency

Ticket exchanges for the Eagle Rock Fest.
at Boston College Roberts Center or P.O.
Box 800. Boston College. Chestnut Hill, Mass.

Wednesday September 9 1970
Boston, Massachusetts
Boston Garden

Set: Immigrant Song/Heartbreaker/Dazed And Confused/Bring It On Home/That's The Way/Bron Yr Aur/Since I've Been Loving You/Organ Solo – Thank You/What Is And What Should Never Be/Moby Dick/Whole Lotta Love (inc. Boogie Chillun' – Messing Around My Heart – Ramble On – For What It's Worth – Some Other Guy – Honey Bee – The Lemon Song)/Communication Breakdown.

The band were due to have an eleven day holiday break but this date was added to the itinerary in place of the cancelled Eagle Rock Festival on August 14. However, the promoters were still not happy. *Rolling Stone* reports: "Zeppelin were booked for two shows. They asked for and got, a guarantee of $87,000 against 65% of the gross. Had all gone well, Zeppelin could have walked away with as much as $110,000 for five hours' work.

"Five days before the concert, however, the early show had sold only 1,200 seats. On the night of September 5, Zeppelin called and tried to back out of the first show, claiming that American Airlines wouldn't ship their equipment on Labour Day (September 7); they said they couldn't possibly make it in time. American Airlines assured the promoters that they shipped 365 days a year and didn't even charge extra for it. Nonetheless, Zeppelin stuck to their story and refused to play the 5pm show. For the remaining show, Chernov (the promoter) offered Zeppelin a guarantee of $43,500. The group held out for $75,000 and threatened to cancel completely if they didn't get it. After repeated pleas from Chernov, the group finally settled for $61,000. Which meant that Chernov was out $12,000 and that Boston College lost $15,000. As for Zeppelin, they fell 1,400 seats short of selling out their one show."

Chernov later commented: "I have never seen anyone as vicious and money-minded. These guys are worse than G.M. ever thought of being. They had a school by the balls."

The show itself was as tense as the financial negotiations. There was a heavy police and security presence in the arena.

Firstly, an announcer took the stage and told the audience know what happened to the cancelled festival. He urged the audience to write to Mayor White to ensure future licences – one of which he mentioned could be for a concert by the newly estranged Beatle, Paul McCartney, next spring (this subsequently never materialises). Then, JJ Jackson of WBCN announced: "They haven't been here since last November, so can we have a big hand for LED ZEPPELIN."

From the start there were problems with the audience. Plant: "Can you move back and clear the aisles for a while, so we can get a good thing going." The crowd obviously felt pressured by the police presence but Robert tried hard to create some atmosphere. "There's a feeling here of too

much formality, which makes me think that people aren't very loose. If you don't get loose, we haven't a chance!" Robert addressed the security: "Can you move back a bit gents?" Not one of the best nights of the tour.

Zeppelin took a serious hammering from the press. "First there was the Hindenburg," writes Timothy Crouse. "The show was a bomb. There was some reflective clapping and a few scattered yells, but the audience response was mostly unenthusiastic, dead.

"Vocalist Plant, who is no slouch as a crowd engineer, knew exactly what to do. He blamed everything on the cops.

"Not that Zeppelin gave an off performance, but those of us who were not confirmed Zeppelin fans, could not quite understand the prolonged applause, the cheers and the V signs. To us, it seemed that Plant had tricked the audience into responding to the group as culture heroes. We felt slightly cheated."

Bootleg CD References: *Come Back To Boston* (Holy), *No Licence, No Festival* (Silver Rarities)

Wednesday September 16 1970
Savoy Hotel, London
Melody Maker Poll Awards
NON PLAYING APPEARANCE
The band returned to London to accept their *Melody Maker* poll awards at the Savoy Hotel. They also had a photo session with former Fairport Convention singer and fellow poll winner Sandy Denny in Kensington Gardens. Sandy would later duet with Plant on 'The Battle Of Evermore' on the band's fourth album. It's likely the first discussion about this duet occurred on this day.

Wednesday September 16 1970
Savoy Hotel, London
Melody Maker Poll Awards
Nationwide *BBC1*
TV APPEARANCE
Robert and Bonzo took part in a TV interview for BBC 1's news magazine programme *Nationwide*.

They were interviewed by Bob Wellings on the subject of toppling The Beatles' reign by being voted top world group. Brief clips from this interview turned up in 2004 on an American unauthorised DVD via Passport Video titled *A To Zeppelin – The Unauthorized Story Of Led Zeppelin*.

Saturday September 19 1970
New York, New York
Madison Square Garden

Afternoon set: Immigrant Song/Heartbreaker/ Dazed And Confused/Bring It On Home/That's The Way/Bron Yr Aur/Since I've Been Loving You/Organ Solo – Thank You/What Is And What Should Never Be/Moby Dick/Whole Lotta Love (inc. Boogie Chillun' – High Flyin' Mama – For What It's Worth – Honey Bee – The Lemon Song)/Communication Breakdown (inc. American Woman).

Evening set: Immigrant Song/Heartbreaker/ Dazed And Confused/Bring it On Home/That's The Way/Bron Yr Aur/Since I've Bbeen Loving You/Organ Solo – Thank You/What Is And What

Should Never Be/Moby Dick/Whole Lotta Love (Incl Boogie chillun'-Dust My Broom -Bottle Up And Go -Lawdy Miss Clawdy – Cinnamon Girl - Some Other Guy -Train Kept A Rollin' -I'm A King Bee -Baby Don't You Want Me To Go -CC Rider)/Out On The Tiles/Communication Breakdown incl Gallows Pole/The Girl Can't Help It/ Talking 'Bout You/Twenty Flight Rock/How Many More Time (incl Cadillac/ Blueberry Hill)

Prior to these shows Page and Plant gave a press conference at their hotel which was filmed. *Record Mirror* reported that: "Led Zeppelin will play two concerts at New York's Madison Square Garden on September 19. And in the event of a sell-out Zeppelin will make more than $100,000 for this date, around £30,000."

In fact, the afternoon concert was only about three-quarters full, but the evening concert was a sell-out.

The afternoon show featured excellent versions of 'Dazed And Confused' and 'Bring It On Home'. Before an emotional rendition of 'What Is And

What Should Never Be', Plant paid tribute to Jimi Hendrix who died the previous day. Plant: "I think it's really hard ever having to say something about something that's quite a delicate point. But yesterday something happened – Jimi Hendrix died and we're all very sorry because he contributed a lot to the current music thing, and we'd like to just hope that everybody thinks it's a real shame ... Jimi Hendrix!"

Lisa Mehlman of *Disc* reviewed the show under the headline: 'Zeppelin Play For The Tots': "Zeppelin certainly excited the crowds that were there. Very definitely the crowd was young. I saw many seemingly ten-years-old-and-under tots running around. I found the group sort of flashy but dull, somewhat contrived and certainly not high energy excitement. I must add that that was not the opinion of the audience, however, they loved them, rushing the stage at the end and all that. But to me, Led Zeppelin play loud, clean fun, with very little behind the surface chords and rhythm that they set up."

The evening show emerged on a good (for the time) audience tape in 2003 and was made available via various Zep web sites and duly on a variety of unofficial CDs. It revealed that they played a rare version of 'Gallows Pole' within 'Communication Breakdown'.

Plant also made reference to the untimely death of Jimi Hendrix the night before. After 'Bring It On Home' he told the audience: ''Before we go any further ... yesterday a rather uncomfortable thing happened yesterday for everybody and a great loss for the music world ... and we'd like to think that you as well as us are very sorry that Jimi Hendrix went ... I spoke to a close friend of his about half an hour ago and he said probably he would have preferred everybody to get on and have a good time rather that talk about it. So we'd like to get on and try and make everybody happy.''

Bootleg CD References: *Maui Wowie* (Missing Link), *American Woman* (The Diagrams Of Led Zeppelin), *RequiEm* (Empress Valley), *Have You Ever Experienced?* (Tarantura – 4 CD box set contains both shows), *Praying Silently For Jimmy* (Empress Valley)

Visual References: Footage from the press conference can be seen on the official *Led Zeppelin* DVD (Warner Vision) and unofficially on *Latter Visions* (Celebration)

Monday October 5 1970
Birmingham, England
Town Hall

News Report: "Plant almost joins Derek and Dominos". *New Musical Express* reported: "Robert Plant got pushed off the stage by a road manager at the Birmingham Town Hall on Monday – it was that sort of evening.

"Plant, along with nearly 2,000 others, had come to see a special off-tour booking of Eric Clapton's new group, Derek & The Dominoes. The Dominoes, though musically perfect, needed a good strong lead vocalist until Robert Plant casually wandered on to the stage.

"It was obviously unplanned. None of the group saw him. Few of the audience seemed to recognise him. And nor, apparently, did the roadie guarding one of the wing stage doors.

"Robert Plant was unceremoniously ushered back through the door, and the chance of a monster impromptu jam session was gone."

Friday October 16 1970
Savoy Hotel,
London, England
NON PLAYING APPEARANCE

Grant, Page, Plant and Jones attend an awards ceremony to honour sales of Led Zeppelin II and US sales of *Whole Lotta Love*. The gold and platinum discs are presented by Mr Anthony Grant - the Parliamentary Secretary to the Board of State He comments that the group have "contributed greatly to the country's balance of payments.

OCTOBER 1970

News Report: 'LED ZEPPELIN HAMMER BOOTLEGS' was the front page headline in *Melody Maker*. Richard Williams reported: "A

London record distributor said this week that two new Led Zeppelin albums will shortly be in the shops – both unofficial, illegal 'bootlegs'.

"One Zeppelin album is alleged to be studio recorded tracks, never released, and the other is a live album from Germany.

"Phil Carson, European general manager of Atlantic Records, who handle Led Zeppelin, told me: 'We will be taking positive legal action against anyone who is found pressing, marketing, or retailing these albums. In fact our people in Hamburg got onto it, and several people are in custody, awaiting trial. We'll be prosecuting them with a team of barristers. The kids think it's great to buy a bootleg album, but it's robbing the artists. In buying one, you're stealing the artist's lifeblood. It's a serious problem for a major company like ours.'

"And Zeppelin manager, Peter Grant declared this week: 'As far as I know there can be no tapes of Led Zeppelin available. After hearing some time ago that there was going to be an attempt to bootleg some tapes of the band, I flew to America. We've managed to retrieve all the tapes and we know of nothing in existence that can be issued'."

The previously mentioned bootleg album *Live On Blueberry Hill* (recorded at the LA Forum on September 4 1970) would be in selected shops within weeks.

NOVEMBER 1970

News Report – Led Zeppelin have scrapped plans for a short UK tour. They were due to play around four or five concerts at major venues in late November and early December.

However, Peter Grant has found some halls are not willing to accept the group because of apprehension over possible rioting. The Royal Albert Hall was one venue being sought but they have effectively banned Zeppelin and Ten Years After

following reported damage to the venue on previous bookings. Grant is now aiming at early 1971 for a UK return for the group: "At this point I don't know how many dates we will play. Some halls are known to be refusing to book rock concerts but I don't anticipate too much difficulty in finalising the right venue."

Zeppelin were also approached to perform a show in Germany on New Year's Eve 1970 that was to be relayed live via satellite, coast to coast across the US. The offer commenced at $500,000 and kept growing to $1,000,000 but Grant turned it down when he discovered the quality of such a link could be affected by bad weather. "They thought I was crazy," Grant recalled later. "A million dollars was a hell of a lot of money in 1970. But one of my strengths was being able to say 'No'. It was their arses on the line and I wasn't going to blow it, if the situation wasn't right."

Date Unknown
London, England
24 Hours BBC2
PETER GRANT TV INTEVIEW
Around this period Peter Grant took part in a documentary programme about the then topical business of bootlegging in the UK record industry. He relayed his run-in with UK bootleg dealer Jeffrey Collins.

October/November/December
Bron Yr Aur Cottage, Machynlleth Gwynedd Wales
REHEARSALS
Island Studios, London England
RECORDING SESSIONS
Page and Plant returned to the Welsh cottage for more writing and recording. They began recording their fourth album at Island Studios in December.

"The audiences are becoming bigger and bigger. Moving further and further away. We are losing contact, so by going back to places like The Marquee, we aim to re-establish our contact with the people who got us off the ground in the beginning. It will give the fans a chance to see a group which in the accepted tradition would be appearing only at large auditoriums for high prices." That was Jimmy Page's romantic vision of Led Zeppelin's Spring tour of the UK. The so-called 'Back To The Clubs' tour, in stark contrast to their last US tour, saw them returning to the club and university venues that had booked them in the early days. In a rare act of charity, Peter Grant charged the promoters concerned the same fee as they had done when they originally appeared on the scene – as a thank you for their original support.

The tour kicked off with a visit to trouble-torn Ireland where they played two excellently received shows in Belfast and Dublin – a brave move in the light of the conflict.

'Stairway To Heaven', the song that would become Led Zeppelin's anthem, was performed live for the first time on this trip to Ireland, in Belfast's Ulster Hall. Its début airing on radio followed on April 4 when the group previewed the song on a Radio One *In Concert* performance. Listeners to the show on that Spring Sunday evening could have no inkling they were privy to the very first public airing of a song that would rack up some 3,000,000 plays on radio around the world over the next 20 years.

The Radio One performance was a major coup for producer Jeff Griffin who had been cajoling them to return since their last session in 1969. It went on to become one of their most bootlegged performances. The actual date of recording was postponed from March 25 and rearranged for April 1 after Plant's voice showed signs of strain. A date at Liverpool University was also rescheduled for May.

A gap of nearly five months separated these shows from their last tour. They had spent much of January and February at Headley Grange recording their fourth album, and their desire to get back to performing on stage was evident in the urgency of these performances. They also offered the opportunity for UK fans to see the extended 'sit down' acoustic set which would be a permanent feature of their shows over the next year.

The decision to do a low key tour was viewed by them all as a good way to re-establish audience contact, but there were the inevitable complaints from fans unable to get tickets – a major influence in Grant's decision never to go back to this format again. There were rumours around this period that this tour would signal the end of Zeppelin as a touring unit (the future plan was apparently to split for solo projects and come together periodically to record an album). Such rumours were vehemently denied. During the first show in Belfast, Robert Plant announced: "A lot of these music papers that come across the sea say we are going to break up. Well … We're never gonna break up!"

Equipment Note:

For live performances of 'Stairway To Heaven', Page commissioned Gibson to supply him with a Gibson SG double-neck which would soon become a trademark of every Zeppelin show. This guitar model had also been used by the Mahivshna Orchestra's John Mclaughlin and Family's John Whitney. He also used the double neck for live performances of 'Gallows Pole' and 'Four Sticks'.

Jones brought in a Fender electric mandolin for 'Going To California' and also used a Fender Precision bass guitar alongside his more familiar Fender Jazz model. His keyboard set-up was extended with a Fender Rhodes 88 electric piano.

Zeppelin employed a 2,000 watt WEM PA system in Europe (they normally used a 3,000 watt JBL PA). Their regular equipment log at this stage included Hiwatt 100 watt amps (treble boosted)

Vox echo chambers, Echoplex echo chambers, a Sonic Wave, Marshall 100 watt amps and Shure Unidyne microphones.

Page's guitars included two Les Pauls, one Rickenbacker 12-string, one Telecaster and one Martin Jumbo 6-string. Ernie Ball Super Slinky strings were used.

John Bonham continued to use Ludwig drums and cymbals, including a 36-inch gong and stand. Ludwig tambourines were also used by Plant.

A Revox 2-track tape recorder was used to record rehearsals.

JANUARY 1971

News Report: Tentative negotiations are underway for Led Zeppelin to appear at a leading soccer stadium this summer. Charlton Athletic's ground in London is thought to be under consideration. Peter Grant is also looking at the possibility of their playing on Waterloo railway station. Nothing materialises.

Years later, Grant recalled the plan: "It was to be on that massive area before the platforms. We could have had Led Zeppelin specials coming in on the platforms. It was set to work but the station authorities said there was one late train that would get in the way. Shame, it could have been great. Led Zep at Waterloo Station – completely covered hall, good acoustics and a nice PA."

January/February
Headley Grange, Hampshire England
Recording Sessions
RECORDING SESSIONS
Intensive location recording at Headley Grange for their fourth album. Various alternate mixes and work in progress tracks have surfaced on bootlegs from these sessions over the years. These include alternate mixes of 'Black Dog', 'Four Sticks', 'Going To California', 'The Battle Of Evermore' and 'When The Levee Breaks' plus work in progress versions of 'Black Dog', 'No Quarter' and 'Stairway To Heaven'.
Bootleg CD References: *Stairway Sessions* (Silver Rarities), *All That Glitters Is Gold* (Celebration)

Saturday February 6 1971
Melody Maker's Chris Welch reported: "Led Zeppelin are going back to the clubs! They will perform a selection of dates at small clubs, pavilions and universities.

"Manager Peter Grant revealed: 'The boys came to me just after Christmas and talked about their next tour. We decided to do the clubs and forget about the bread and the big concert halls. We're going to play the universities and clubs and restrict prices to about twelve bob a ticket. When I rang The Marquee, the manager refused to believe it was me offering him Led Zeppelin so he had to call me back to be convinced. We are also planning to give a charity concert and give the entire proceeds to Release who are in trouble. I'm working it out with Caroline Coon. A lot of small clubs have disappeared because groups charged too much in the past. We want to prove the biggest of groups can go and play there.'

"Drummer John Bonham added: 'It'll be great because the atmosphere is always much better than in a big place like the Albert Hall. We wanted to do a tour where the greatest number of people could come and see us at the places that made us when we started out.

"The band are expected to charge just enough to cover the expenses of the tour. On April 4 they will broadcast on BBC radio's *Sound Of The 70's*."

Friday March 5
Belfasst, Northern Ireland
Ulster Hall
Set includes: Immigrant Song/Heartbreaker/Since I've Been Loving You/Black Dog/Stairway To Heaven/Dazed And Confused/Moby Dick/Whole Lotta Love (inc. Boogie Chillun')/Communication Breakdown.

Allegedly, to obtain a ticket for the Zeppelin show there was a stipulation that the purchaser also had to buy a ticket for the forthcoming Marc Bolan/T. Rex show at the venue. Ironically this show was subsequently cancelled due to the troubles.

A night of firsts … the first night of the tour, the

STAIRWAY TO HEAVEN

There was a time – although it's hard to believe now – when 'Stairway To Heaven' was viewed not as the Second Coming but merely as the longest track on their new album, albeit the most interesting one. It originally came into the set in a fairly low-key manner on the UK tour in the spring of 1971. The song's elaborate arrangement prompted Page to invest in the custom built Gibson SG double neck guitar, serial number 911117, that would become such a trademark; although in the studio the track was actually recorded on a Fender Telecaster.

Page can recall how the song was greeted with a standing ovation when it was performed in LA on the 1971 US tour. Over the next year, Atlantic were keen to issue it as a single but Peter Grant refused though promotional copies were pressed for US distribution. It was then that the song began to count up endless plays on US radio stations (three million & still counting!). This had something of a knock-on effect in England where it repeatedly topped radio station polls of listeners' all-time favourite songs.

By 1975 'Stairway' was installed in its rightful place at the finale of each Zeppelin show, but after their 1977 jaunt Plant began to tire of it. "There's only so many times you can sing it and mean it," he said. "It just became sanctimonious." It survived Knebworth and Over Europe and was a highlight of Live Aid. On their next reunion at the Atlantic '88 show, Plant was refusing to sing it right up to when they went on stage, relenting only at the very last moment.

Since then, of course, it's become the proverbial millstone around the neck, particularly for Plant. Couples married to it, guitar shops banned anyone playing it while trying out a guitar (or face a £5 fine) and ultimately Rolf Harris & Co. ridiculed it. It's a pity because the live arrangement has proved more durable than its studio counterpart.

Throughout the 250+ occasions when Plant sang the anthem, he would constantly add pleasing ad libs. "Does anybody remember laughter? – I hope so" and "I keep choppin' & changing" … these were all moments anticipated by the Zeppelin faithful as the song developed over the years.

The simple acoustic version Page and Plant performed at the Tokyo news station for Japanese TV in November 1994 did much to restore some credibility to the song, proving that in the hands of its original composers it could still retain its unique beauty.

'Stairway To Heaven' may have become something of a joke post-Rolf Harris, but when played live in the Zeppelin era it never outstayed its welcome, sanctimonious or not.

The inclusion of footage of the superb version performed on May 25 at Earls Court on the official DVD is now lasting evidence of the potency of the song in a live setting.

band's first visit to Ireland and the first public performance of 'Stairway To Heaven'.

Chris Welch reviewed the Irish shows for Melody Maker under the headline 'Ireland Unites Under Zeppelin': "A new kind of riot hit Ireland last weekend. A riot of fun, laughter and excitement, when Led Zeppelin paid their first visit to the troubled isle. The Britons who brought guitars

instead of guns were given an ecstatic welcome. Violence and explosions raged only half a mile away from their concert in Belfast on Friday night. But the young people of the town, unconcerned with ancient conflicts, used their energy to celebrate the worthwhile cause of peace, love and music.

"As for the gig itself, Zeppelin impressed from the first chord. The determined, battering, riff of 'Immigrant Song' shook stage and floor as the band steamed in. Robert Plant, impressive in black and red blouse, and golden hair with a demonic smile, echoed through the towering speaker columns.

"Another new song 'Stairway To Heaven' featured Jimmy on double necked guitar, which gives him a twelve string and six string sound on the same instrument. An excellent ballad, it displayed Robert's developing lyricism."

Page: "It's really good to be back playing gigs again. It was a kind of instant excitement on the first concert. I was wondering what it was going to be like. There's the danger that if the fans get too excited that you can't get the acoustic numbers across. That's all we ever want – the chance to get all of our music across. We've got four albums of material to choose from and I think that's a pretty good balance. 'Stairway To Heaven' is a good representation of what we're doing now. There are different moods to the song which lasts ten or twelve minutes."

Bootleg CD Reference: *Black Velvet* (Empress Valley)

Saturday March 6 1971
Dublin, Republic Of Ireland
National Boxing Stadium
Set: Immigrant Song/Heartbreaker/Since I've Been Loving You/Black Dog/Stairway To Heaven/Dazed And Confused/Going To California/What Is And What Should Never Be/Moby Dick/Whole Lotta Love (inc. Boogie Chillun' – Suzy Q – Some Other Guy – Honey Bee – Sugar Mama – Needle Blues – The Lemon Song – That's Alright Mama)/Communication Breakdown/Rock And Roll – Summertime Blues.

After the Belfast show the band drove across the border to Dublin. Bonham manages to get lost and accidentally drove through the Falls Road riot area. Bonham: "The street was covered in glass and there were armoured cars and kids chucking things. We just kept our heads down and drove right through."

Mick Hinton, Bonham's drum technician, recalled: "This was at the height of all the troubles and I remember coming out of the Ulster Hall and there was broken glass everywhere. I also recall some difficulty with papers in crossing the border in to Dublin and we had to drive around all the back roads to sneak in."

A bus strike hampered fans getting to the venue.

The set tonight built on the previous show with the addition of a rare jam as a final encore. Phil Carson of Atlantic records joined the band on bass to perform Eddie Cochran's 'Summertime Blues'.

Chris Welch again reported: "The Dublin concert was held in the boxing stadium and a new stage had to be specially constructed during the afternoon to accommodate all Zeppelin's equipment. It was another triumph, although Dublin was just a little slower than Belfast in getting into the spirit of the occasion. By the end of the evening, with Robert roaring into an improvised

Led Zeppelin

Southampton University, March 11 1971

rock medley, Dublin went just as berserk as their friends north of the border."

Page: "I enjoyed Ireland and wish we could come back."

Bootleg CD References: *Crazed Attack* (Crazy Dream), *Black Velvet* (Empress Valley)

UNCONFIRMED
Belfast Dublin Or UK March 1971
OFF STAGE CINE FILMING
On the official Led Zeppelin DVD Jimmy Page and Dick Carruthers deployed cine footage from the band's archives for the menu link to the Earls Court footage. This shows scenes of travelling along a busy road shot from a car and all four members walking across a road towards a pub.

It's possible this footage originates from their visit to Ireland although there is no confirmation of this. The cine footage is part of a reel that also had shots of them outside Headley Grange taken in January or February. Logically the next set of filming would have followed soon after. Therefore the segment is likely to have been shot in March 1971 during the UK tour.

Tuesday March 9 1971
Leeds, England
Leeds University

Wednesday March 10 1971
Canterbury, England
University Of Kent
Set included:Immigrant Song/ Heartbreaker/ Since I've Been Lving You/Dazed And Confused/Stairway To Heaven/ Going To California/What Is And What Should Never Be/Moby Dick/Whole Lotta Love/ Communication Breakdown.

Despite their good intentions with this tour, there were rumblings of criticism from the fans as well as the media. This was

reflected in the letters page of *Melody Maker*: "Are Zeppelin just so much hot air?" writes Warwick Jones of the University Of Kent ... "Led Zeppelin's failure to arouse any more than a token response from a long suffering Canterbury audience must be attributed to their stature as a 'super-structure' group – there being nothing beneath the glittering superficialities. Their previous reliance on volume to add false excitement to otherwise empty songs and a few catchy riffs was gone, exposing a group of barely adequate musicians, lacking in enthusiasm for what they were doing and expressing no warmth or emotion in their self-indulgent, quasi-sophisticated key and tempo changes.

"Reputation is not enough to ensure continuing interest and support in attempts at 'progression' in public, nor is image projection sufficient to cover creative and communicative inadequacy.

"Robert Plant's attempt to blame the 'communication breakdown' on the audience would have been funny if it had not been an arrogant and selfish attempt to justify a boring and frustrating performance."

The local student magazine also gave the show a thumbs down, but interestingly enough they noted that two drummers were on stage for

'Whole Lotta Love' – quite who and how was not reported.

Thursday March 11 1971
Southampton, England
Southampton University

Saturday March 13 1971
Bath, England
Bath Pavilion
Set includes: Immigrant Song/Heartbreaker/ Since I've Been Loving You/Black Dog/Dazed And Confused/Stairway To Heaven/Going To California/That's The Way/What Is And What Should Never Be/Moby Dick/Whole Lotta Love

(inc. Boogie Chillun' – Tobacco Road)/ Communication Breakdown.

Long term fan Paul Sheppard recalled: "The volume was incredibly loud for such a small venue. For the acoustic set, they sat on old canvas-backed metal chairs. Robert made a reference to The Mixtures who had a hit at the time with 'The Pushbike Song'. 'Tobacco Road' made an appearance in the 'Whole Lotta Love' medley."

Sunday March 14 1971
Hanley, Stoke, England
Trentham Gardens
Records in Stoke's reference library reveal that this date was moved from The Place venue (capacity 1500) to the larger 3500 capacity Trentham Gardens. Also of note is the fact Page's amp caught fire near the end of the show.

Tuesday march 16 1971
Liverpool, England
Liverpool University
CANCELLED

Plant had laryngitis which forced the cancellation of this show.

Thursday March 18 1971
Newcastle-On-Tyne, England
The Mayfair
In his book *A Promoter's Tale* Geoff Docherty revealed the band performed for 90% of the net receipts.

Friday March 19 1971
Manchester, England
Manchester University

Saturday March 20 1971
Sutton Coldfield, England
The Belfry
Set Included: Immigrant Song/Heartbreaker/ Since I've Been loving You/Black Dog/Dazed And Confused/Stairway To Heaven/Going To California/Whole Lotta Love/Communication Breakdown.

This date replaced the previously listed March 20 date set for Birmingham Stepmothers Club. The decision was taken to move the show to the larger Birmingham venue – well known as a major golf course. A flyer for the show stated 'Belfry presents Led Zeppelin Sat Mar 20 70 NP'' – the NP indicated new pence – the British currency had recently gone decimilised.

There was little press coverage of the Back to The Clubs tour – however two journalists did report on this show.

'Electrifying Zeppelin' – Tony McNally reported for *NME*: ''Well over a thousand people were packed into the dance hall of the Belfry for what

turned out to be the greatest rock concert ever seen there. Led Zeppelin put over the heaviest rock sound for three hours powering through new and old numbers. The well known riffs seem to possess an electrifying intensity as they reverberate from the massive stacks.''

''Zeppelin's rock in the Belfry' – Tony Stewart observed: ''Jimmy's exciting and fast playing blended well with the unpredictable bass lines. Robert has such a range that at times he seems like two vocalists. Even after three hours the applause was deafening and Zeppelin were lucky to leave the stage even then''

Sunday March 21 1971
Nottingham, England
Boat Club
Robert Plant: "The difference between Nottingham Boat Club and Birmingham Odeon is not that much. You create an atmosphere wherever you go if you are 'at one' with the crowd. Going back to the clubs is probably a move for conscience sake, to get back to where we started. But, it was almost a waste of time because it was so hectic and frantic."

Tuesday March 23 1971
London, England
Marquee Club
Set included: Immigrant Song/Heartbreaker/Black Dog/Dazed And Confused/Stairway To Heaven/Going To California/Whole Lotta Love/Communication Breakdown.

A nostalgic return to the Marquee Club. Demand for this date was predictably high. Tickets went on sale on March 1 with the box office set to open at 10 o'clock. Due to the extraordinary length of the queue, the box office was forced to open at 3.30 in the morning. The tickets were sold mainly to Marquee Club members on a strict one ticket per membership card holder system. Club manager Jack Barrie commented on the demand: "We asked the group if they could do two shows on the night or perhaps two or three other nights. But Zeppelin play a set of over two

Zeppelin gig swamps club

LONDON'S Marquee Club has been inundated with telephone inquiries, following MM's exclusive revelation last week that Led Zeppelin play there on March 23.

Jack Barrie, manager of the club said this week: " The 'phones haven't stopped ringing since the news came out. But we will obviously have to accommodate our members first, and tickets will go on sale at 10 am at the club on March 1, to members only. One ticket will be sold per membership card produced.

" Owing to the demand we asked the group if they could do two shows on the night, or perhaps two or three other nights. But Zeppelin play a set of over two hours and can't do more in one evening, and they already have other dates booked."

Barrie says that even if the postal strike is over, the club will not be able to handle postal applications.

hours and can't do more in one evening and they have already other dates booked."

Chris Charlesworth, in his *Melody Maker* review, questioned the wisdom of their move back to the clubs: "It was all very nostalgic for Led Zeppelin to play London's Marquee club, but was it such a good idea really? Naturally the place was packed to overflowing. Naturally the group was pretty good, though the sound suffered from the small surroundings. But how much better it might have been if Zep had chosen the Lyceum or the Roundhouse for the only London venue on the current tour.

"As it was, hundreds instead of thousands were able to see the group who a little over two years ago played here as the 'Former Yardbirds' and attracted little interest.

"Zeppelin are a group to be looked up to on a pinnacle for all to see. A group that can pack New York's Madison Square Garden just isn't right in the intimate atmosphere of the Marquee. The Marquee in all its long history has probably never seen a night like it, but I still doubt the wisdom of choosing the club in favour of a larger venue."

Thursday March 25 1971
London, England
Paris Cinema, Lower Regent Street
The initial date for the BBC *In Concert* recording was scrapped due to Robert's voice problems which had developed during the tour. Brinsley Schwarz and The Keef Hartley Band were late replacements.

Thursday April 1 1971
London, England
Paris Cinema, Lower Regent Street
RADIO ONE LIVE SESSION
Set: Immigrant Song/Heartbreaker/Since I've Been Loving You/Black Dog/Dazed And Confused/Stairway To Heaven/Going To California/That's The Way/What Is And What Should Never Be/Whole Lotta Love (inc. Boogie Chillun' – High Flyin' Mama – Fixin' To Die – That's Alright Mama – For What It's Worth – Mess O'Blues – Honey Bee – The Lemon Song)/Thank You/Communication Breakdown. BBC recording. Rehearsal 3PM – Recording 9PM to 10.45PM.

Original broadcast date: Sunday, April 4, 1971 between 7pm and 8pm on John Peel's Sunday *In Concert* programme (repeated as part of *Sounds Of The 70's* between 7pm and 8pm on Wednesday, April 7, 1971).

Actual broadcast: John Peel Introduction/Immigrant Song/Dazed And Confused/Stairway To Heaven/Going To California/That's The Way/What Is And What Should Never Be/John Peel Introduction/Whole Lotta Love Medley.

"This is something we've waited for a long time on the Sunday-repeated-on-Wednesday concert,

and I know it's going to be well worth the wait. Would you welcome please Led Zeppelin!" announced an unusually excited John Peel over the airwaves on Sunday April 4.

Since the start of the *In Concert* series Jeff Griffin had indeed been waiting for many months to secure a return visit for the original instigators of the *In Concert* format. "They seemed to be permanently busy in 1970, but I put it to them in early 1971 and Peter Grant immediately agreed to do it."

The group were commissioned for the show in March and it tied in conveniently with the month-long tour of the UK clubs that took them back to the same venues they were used to playing around the time of the first live BBC recording. Zeppelin's return to the *In Concert* slot was seen as a major coup, but the recording is not without its problems. Griffin had originally booked them for a Thursday March 25 date at the BBC's Paris Cinema, an old wartime theatre with a capacity of under 400 and a stage that stands barely a foot off the ground.

Just prior to the date Peter Grant warned Jeff of the possibility of being unable to make the recording due to Robert Plant losing his voice. A date at Liverpool University has already been blown out, and the singer was only able to fulfil their prestigious Marquee date with the aid of much medication.

Come the day of the recording and Grant has to

tell Griffin they couldn't do it. Hastily, Griffin booked Brinsley Schwarz and The Keef Hartley band to step in on the night with the promise that the audience would all l qualify for attendance at the rearranged date on April 1.

"I was the luckless person who had to go out and tell the first week's audience that the band wouldn't be appearing," remembered Griffin. "When Peter rang and told us the bad news, I asked if they could possibly rearrange the date and I was quite staggered when they agreed to do it so soon. In fact, so many people wanted to attend the next week, I'm sure we broke every fire regulation going to cram every one in."

"First I'd like to say sorry about last week. But we did 18 dates in about 6 days or at least 20 days and my voice just gave up completely. We hope it's all in condition tonight, if not, cheer because you're on the radio." That's the introduction (later edited out of the actual broadcast) that Plant made to the audience, explaining their non-appearance the previous week. It signalled the intro for 'Immigrant Song', complete with a twisting extended guitar solo from Page. This dovetailed into 'Heartbreaker' as was the custom. This piece, alongside 'Since I've Been Loving You' and the newly premièred 'Black Dog', was also left on the cutting room floor.

Their deletion provided the opportunity for a full airing of an 18-minute 'Dazed And Confused' with all the improvised trappings of Page's violin bow solo. A slight delay to adjust Jones' bass pedals preceded the first broadcast performance of 'Stairway To Heaven', played with a slight hesitancy as Page was still getting to grips with his newly acquired Gibson double neck.

"This is the time where we like to have a cup of tea, so I think we'd better sit down instead," said Plant as an introduction to their acoustic set. The BBC soundtrack is able to capture the rush of acoustic guitar and mandolin playing that dominates the as yet unissued 'Going To California' and 'That's The Way'.

A false start to 'What Is And What Should Never Be' was understandably edited out of the radio broadcast. Plant opened the song and complained that the band were in the wrong key "Completely finished!" he laughs. "I can see the headline in Mailbag!" (a reference to the letters column in *Melody Maker*).

After an acceptable take of that song, it was time for the finale. John Peel back on mike for the introduction: "I'm going to sing on the next one," he jokes with Plant, who also makes reference to Ray Steven's current hit 'Bridget The Midget', adapting its 'Do you feel alright?' catch phrase. A full 'Whole Lotta Love' medley followed with the usual indulgence in all manner of rock and roll fun.

"That's all we've got time for this week folks – next week Ted Ray!" quipped Plant, referring to a regular Fifties BBC radio comedy favourite.

The performance also featured two encores which were not broadcast: 'Thank You' minus the usual organ introduction and a frenetic 'Communication Breakdown'.

The day after the recording, Jimmy and Robert went back to the BBC studios to assist in the mixing down of the set for a one-hour broadcast on the Sunday. Jeff Griffin: "I do remember them taking an active interest in the mix down and suggesting certain edits in the long 'Whole Lotta Love' medley to accommodate the hour-long presentation. It really was a joy to work with them. Not only were they one of the most exciting live acts we ever recorded, it was their enthusiasm to do the pilot *In Concert* recording that really sent that brand of live radio on its way. When they agreed to come back for the 1971 show, I was just amazed because their mistrust of the media was very apparent. They never felt comfortable with doing TV or talking to the press, but they seemed very at home with the BBC and we were very privileged to play host to them. They were truly great sessions."

This 1971 BBC recording has gone on to be one of the most bootlegged BBC sessions in history. It has appeared on countless pressings over the years, though significantly none of them have emerged in the original format in which it was

137

aired. This is because the BBC tapes were quickly adapted to appear as an official BBC transcription disc. These were used by the BBC to export to particular radio stations world-wide who subscribed to their transcription service. The 1971 recordings were mixed down from the original source tape at the BBC's Transcription Studios in Kensington House, Shepherd's Bush. A session on May 11 was overseen by Jimmy Page when the tapes were mixed for stereo. The 12" disc that emerged carried a different line-up to the aired show with the unbroadcast encore 'Communication Breakdown' replacing 'Immigrant Song' as the opener and a voice-over proclaiming "And now, live from London, the BBC presents Led Zeppelin in concert". It's this disc, with a running order of 'Communication Breakdown', 'Dazed And Confused', 'Going To California', 'Stairway To Heaven', 'What Is And What Should Never Be' and 'Whole Lotta Love' (an edited version, spliced to finish at the end of their cover of 'Mess O'Blues') that was later dubbed to produce the Trademark Of Quality vinyl bootleg *BBC Broadcast*.

A later transcription pressing used for the 'BBC Rock Hour' export series in the Eighties consisted of yet another sequence from the show featuring 'Immigrant Song', 'Heartbreaker', 'Dazed And Confused', 'Stairway To Heaven', 'Going To California' and 'Whole Lotta Love (Edit)'.

The second source for the bootleg packages comes from the original BBC tapes that represented the complete performance including the unbroadcast tracks. Bootlegs such as *Ballcrusher* plundered these tapes, although it was the coming of the bootleg CD age that gave rise to the eventual appearance of an almost complete tape on the near definitive packages *BBC Zep* on the Tarantura and Antrabata labels.

The fact that Jimmy Page himself spent time mixing the tapes reaffirms the importance he placed on this concert, which captures the group at a significant stage in its career. Of course, this recording offers the first ever airing of 'Stairway To Heaven' on radio. Nobody present that evening, least of all the group themselves, could have predicted that the song would go on to log an estimated three million plays on radio over the next twenty years.

In 1997 Page finally mixed and edited the original tapes of this show to form disc two of the *Led Zeppelin BBC Sessions* CD set issued in November of that year. He re-edited the full concert tapes down to a compact 78 minute programme. At the time of the release studio engineer Jon Astley, who worked with Page on the project, revealed: "We used some of the bootlegs as reference points. Jimmy already had a few notes of things. We were listening to that *Stairway To Heaven* Cobla bootleg CD that came out recently to get the feel of the 1971 show."

John Paul Jones welcomed the eventual release of these sessions: "It's an excellent opportunity to hear the band in the making. The first session captures us just after coming back from America. It's good to compare that feel to some of our later stuff. It also shows just how good John Bonham was – and how vital to our sound his contribution was."

Bootleg CD References: *BBC Zep* (Antrabata), *Stairway To Heaven* (Cobla), *Thank You It's Complete* (Discurious), *BBC Zep* (Tarantura), *BBC* (LSD)

Sunday April 4 1971
London, England
Radio 1 In Concert
RADIO BROADCAST
On this day Radio 1 broadcast the April 1 Paris Cinema live recording edited down to a one hour presentation broadcast between 7 and 8pm on the John Peel Sunday *In Concert* slot. It was repeated on Wednesday April 6 in the same time slot as a part of the *Sound Of The Seventies* programme.

There was no let-up in the 1971 schedule. A further batch of isolated European shows were notable for their lack of general press coverage and on stage set list experiments. The Copenhagen show at KB Hallen on May 3 included rare live versions of the then unreleased 'Gallows Pole' and 'Four Sticks'. 'Misty Mountain Hop' and 'Rock and Roll' were also premièred on this tour.

The band were reticent to commit to a full scale tour due to Page mixing their fourth album and awaiting the birth of his daughter Scarlet.

Ultimately though, the 1971 European trek will be remembered for its abrupt end in Milan's Velodrome Stadium on July 5. This festival appearance in front of 15,000 was abandoned when tear gas wielding police attempted to curb so-called rioting fans. The group were forced to leave the stage as roadies tried to salvage equipment. "It was a frightening situation," said Page. "It was like a war and we never want to return again."

Monday May 3 1971
Copenhagen, Denmark
K.B.Hallen

Set: Immigrant Song/Heartbreaker/Since I've Been Loving You/Dazed And Confused/Black Dog/Stairway To Heaven/Going To California/That's The Way/What Is And What Should Never Be/Four Sticks/Gallows Pole/Whole Lotta Love (inc. Boogie Chillun' – High Flyin' Mama – Mess O'Blues – Honey Bee – Sugar Mama – The Lemon Song)/ Communication Breakdown (inc. Celebration Day)/Misty Mountain Hop/Rock And Roll.

The first show in Europe was a highly experimental performance. After 'Heartbreaker' Plant had to reprimand the crowd: "Whoa, stop! You stop! Tell him to stop – because any trouble and we go off! We can't play if there's gonna be this going on through every number, so somebody had better tell him in Danish what the score is! We cannot play if there's gonna be a constant passage of people moving. We'd rather people sit on the floor, sit down! We wanna give you a concert of music and we cannot do that if there's a lot of people running around."

'Dazed And Confused' featured some highly emotional and dynamic playing from Page, and Robert played with some alternative lyrics in 'Black Dog'. (NB: The ad-libbing of lyrics during 'Black Dog' becomes a characteristic of this era with Plant continually playing around with the verses, inserting references to 'Sweet jelly roll' among others.)

Plant: "There's a lot of people smiling tonight. There's four people here smiling anyway. This is a thing called 'Stairway To Heaven' off the next album and it goes on for some time and it gets nice … that's a profound statement!" 'Stairway To Heaven' is received to warm applause but there are technical problems in the acoustic set.

Plant got the set list confused before finally introducing 'Four Sticks', a brand new composition. Plant: "We're gonna try something that we have never ever tried before and there's every chance it'll fall apart. If it does, we'll stop and start again. This hasn't even got a title yet but we'll think of one as the night goes on!" 'Four Sticks' was a brave first attempt, but only receives polite applause and would rarely be performed again.

Another rarity, 'Gallows Pole', was performed next in rather chaotic fashion. 'Whole Lotta Love' featured Richard Cole jamming tablas and conga

The Concert File

139

drums. The first encore of 'Communication Breakdown' rather unusually included a section of 'Celebration Day'.

The crowd were still yelling for more and they were back on to present yet another new number, 'Misty Mountain Hop', which had also never been performed live before. 'Rock And Roll', announced by Plant under its working title of 'It's Been A Long Time', was the final encore.

The set tonight featured no less than six numbers from the upcoming fourth album. It would not be released for another six months, but Zeppelin had no qualms about playing the unfamiliar songs in public, such was their confidence in the strength of the new material.

George Sorensen reviewed the show for *New Musical Express* under the headline 'Led Zeppelin Even Better Now!' He reports: "Nearly 4,000 Danish fans were left with almost split eardrums in Copenhagen, when Led Zeppelin played 135 minutes of heavy, loud rock '71 – but everybody enjoyed the session and kept calling for more! Led Zeppelin is THE rock-'n'roll band in 1971, no doubt!"

The as yet unreleased 'Stairway To Heaven' was already creating an impression: "The title of the best new song was drowned by the applauding and cheering audience, but is called something like 'Stairways To Heaven', a beautiful number, starting softly with Jimmy Page on guitar and a silent Robert Plant, joined by John Paul Jones on organ and then building and building in force and speed into a breathtaking climax, where everybody went wild, a real inferno of sound."

Another significant performance thankfully privately recorded and years after made available on a variety of bootlegs.

Bootleg CD References: *Poles And Sticks* (Black Cat), *Loove* (Tarantura), *Copenhagen 1971* (Cobla), *Kb* (Image Quality), *Previews And Novelties* (Equinox)

Monday May 10 1971
Liverpool, England
Mountford Hall Liverpool University
RESCHEDULED DATE
Set included: Since I've Been Loving You/Black Dog/Dazed And Confused/Stairway To Heaven/Gallows Pole/Whole Lotta Love (inc. Mess O'Blues – It'll Be Me).

This show was a rescheduled date to replace the March 16 cancellation. The band were still experimenting with 'Gallows Pole' but problems with the arrangement prevented it from becoming part of the set long term. Jerry Lee Lewis's 'It'll Be Me' was a rare inclusion in the 'Whole Lotta Love' medley.

Barbara Drillsma, in her review of the show, reports: "After one cancellation and numerous 'They are returning' rumours, Led Zeppelin stormed into Liverpool on Monday evening. The city is used to crowds. Only the previous evening, 650,000 turned out to welcome home the football team from Wembley. And in comparison a gathering of 1,900 may seem like a drop in the ocean. But the 1,900 fans were crammed into the University – standing on window ledges, sitting in every available inch of floor space with not even breathing space. But was it worth it? Do Led Zeppelin get the hysterical response that they receive because they are still leading or because they are the band once acclaimed to be the greatest rock band alive? Their performance on Monday was, in parts, electrifying."

JUNE 1971
News Link: It's reported that Led Zeppelin are one of the names being sought for a series of charity concerts to aid relief in Pakistan. Edgar Broughton is the organiser of the events through the *Daily Mirror*. Zeppelin, John & Yoko Lennon and Ten Years After are all said to be interested in taking part. Nothing materialised.

Tuesday June 29 1971
Birmingham, England
Elbow Room
GUEST APPEARANCE

MILANESE

TUMULTUOSO ARRIVO DEL CANTAGIRO

Scontri fra teppisti e polizia al concerto dei «Led Zeppelin»

Ancora una volta una manifestazione di musica «pop» si è trasformata in un pretesto di guerriglia al Velodromo Vigorelli e nelle strade adiacenti - Sassaiole contro le forze dell'ordine: feriti due agenti, due arresti

Anche la tappa milanese del Cantagiro, al Vigorelli, ha purtroppo offerto spunto a una pretesto di guerriglia il sia manifestazione «pop» e della musica «pop» per scatenarsi di nuovo la guerriglia. Gruppi di giovani, tra i quali alcuni agitatori politici e mestatori a vario titolo, al sono scontrati con la polizia. Sassaiole da una parte e cariche dall'altra. Due agenti sono rimasti feriti e due «guerriglieri» sono stati arrestati.

Il bilancio sarebbe stato peggiore se la questura, memore dei tristi precedenti, non avesse predisposto un servizio d'ordine eccezionale. Fin dalla prima serata reparti di polizia e dei carabinieri coloro duemila uomini erano stati collocati ai punti strategici dello stadio che era praticamente circondato e sorvegliato anche da pattuglie automontate. Sino alle 21.30 la situazione è stata normale. Il pubblico, migliaia di persone venute ad ascoltare, oltre che i divi nostrani della canzone, il celebre complesso inglese dei Led Zeppelin, e affluito regolarmente. All'esterno circolavano solo gruppetti di giovani che probabilmente intendevano entrare senza biglietto e qualche estremista contestatore che distribuiva volantini riguar-

danti una manifestazione indetta per giovedi pomeriggio a Città Studi.

Alle 21.30 un gruppo più consistente, circa quattrocento persone, è comparso sul lato di via Arona e ha cominciato a ritmare con le mani il noto ritornello del «maggio francese» («Ce ne qu'un debut, continuons le combat») e a gridare «PS-SS». Sono volati sassi e un reparto della Celere ha caricato, disperdendo i giovani. Questi sono però tornati una decina di minuti più tardi e il vice-

questore dottor Vittoria ha fatto intervenire una colonna di jeep.

La battaglia si è spostata in corso Sempione, dove gli agenti hanno fatto uso di candelotti lacrimogeni, e si è presto estesa a quasi tutte le vie d'accesso al velodromo, ma i teppisti più irriducibili non hanno desistito. Alle 22.30 barricate con automobili sono state erette in via Domodossola e in via Giovanni da Procida. Reparti della Celere e

dei carabinieri hanno rinnovato le cariche in via Arona è stato circondato un gruppo di « guerriglieri » che stava tentando di lanciare bombe molotov. I rudimentali ordigni sono stati sequestrati.

AL CONSIGLIO PROVINCIALE

Critiche di Peracchi ai seminari di architettura

Al Consiglio provinciale, riunitosi ieri a palazzo Isimbardi, il presidente Erasmo Peracchi, ha parlato di alcuni recenti episodi di cronaca soffermandosi soprattutto sui fatti della facoltà di architettura.

Senza strumentalizzare questi episodi, come politici dobbiamo dire che « Milano non è certo la città che sogna una casa tranquilla » e che bisogna fare in modo che il giorno dato ogni qualche cosa. Anche agli occhi di chi non è marxista — ha proseguito il presidente della Provincia — appare contraddittoria la voluta rivoluzionaria di un gruppo studentesco poi a meno extraparlamentare dica in un lato, predica l'internazionalismo socialista e, dall'altro, si vuole per sopravvivere in un ghetto ideologico quale può essere una facoltà occupata. Le borghe che ha abbattuto il muro docente sono un fatto risolto, ma ha abbattuto il giusto che pagati. Il preside Portaghesi è solo giudice, la sentenza chiarirà le sue responsabilità. Avremmo ammesso delle ricerche da svolgere in alcune discutibili sperimentazioni didattiche seminariali

LE HOSTESSES FERROVIARIE

Sul Settebello «dama di cuori»

Il servizio inaugurato ieri alla Centrale - Graziose ragazze, in divisa rossa, si dedicheranno particolarmente ai bambini e agli anziani

---

John Bonham turned up to jam at a Rock Revival night featuring re-formed Midlands groups such as Danny King & The Mayfair Set, The Uglies, Ronnie's Renegades, Gary Levene & The Avengers, and Mike Sheridan & The Nightriders. Dave Pegg of Fairport Convention, Roy Wood, Jeff Lynne and Bev Bevan are also in attendance.

UNCONFIRMED
Sunday July 4 1971
Rome

A member of the Italian band Capitolo 6 claims his band supported Zeppelin at a date in Rome the day before the Milan show. No confirmation has come through of this.

Monday July 5 1971
Milan, Italy
Vigorelli Stadium
Set included: Black Dog/Dazed And Confused/Since I've Been Loving You/Moby Dick/Whole Lotta Love.

This show was a low point in Zeppelin's career. The performance was fine and the audience seemed to be enjoying the show but the inexperienced security staff was unable to appreciate the fact that than an enthusiastic audience was not necessarily intent on causing a riot. Police armed with tear gas waded into the captive crowd. Many fans were injured, the concert was abandoned and Led Zeppelin would never return to Italy.

They gave a press conference the next day to Italian newspaper reporters. *Ciao 2001* magazine reported: "Zeppelin came on at 10.40. Plant was telling the audience to cool it. He did this again after 'Since I've Been Loving You'. He tried to communicate with the audience in English saying 'Cool it, take it easy, sit down!' During Bonham's solo it really got out of hand and Peter Grant came on and stopped them playing."

Robert later tells the reporter: "Please tell your readers we wanted to play here for so long, but the Italian police forced us to stop. We have played all over the world but I've never seen anything as bad as this."

Mick Hinton, Bonham's drum technician, recalled: "We were on stage and suddenly all this tear gas was let off. I remember seeing Jimmy with tears streaming from his eyes and thinking it can't be that emotional! And then it hit me as well. The boys went off the stage and ran into an underground dressing room. The roadies stayed on to protect the stage. I got hit on the head with a bottle and Clive ushered me off stage and the next

The Concert File

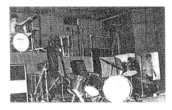

thing I knew I was on a stretcher. I remember we lost the hi-hat but aside from that, the kit was OK, incredibly."

News of the incident even reached the British press. 'Zeppelin hit by tear-gas as troops charge crowd' was the story line in the *New Musical Express*. "Led Zeppelin was involved in the worst riot of its career last weekend when – before a crowd of over 15,000 in Milan's Vigorelli Stadium – the group's act was disrupted by charging police and soldiers, wielding batons and lobbing tear-gas. Zeppelin had hardly commenced its act when the riot squad went into action, apparently sparked by some youngsters jumping to their feet and clapping their hands!

"London agent, Eddie Sandham, who was present at the concert, told the *NME*: 'Even before the show started, the stadium was ringed by hundreds of police and soldiers, sitting with their batons and shields, while outside there were truckloads of reinforcements. They went into action with scarcely any provocation and this led to a full-scale riot breaking out, during which some of the group's equipment – including the drums – was damaged'."

Peter Grant remembered: "I'd done four months in Italy with Wee Willie Harris back in the Fifties, so I knew what a dodgy place it could be. I got all the money up front and made sure we got the air tickets back in advance. Just as well because when we got to the gig there were water cannons and tear-gas. Everybody just went mad. So we had to flee and I'm not that good at running, but Mick Hinton and Richard got us out and we barricaded ourselves in the medical room and stayed there until it all cooled down.

"Years later I bumped into the promoter of that gig at the Cafe Royale. I went in the toilet to have a piss and this guy saw me and pissed all down himself because he thought I was going to have him. I'd forgiven him by then though. You can't account for the actions of the Italian police."

Bootleg CD References: *Short Cuts* (Image Quality), *Stepmothers Club* (Mad Dog)

Morale within the group took something of a dip after the riot in Milan. They were also experiencing problems with the mixing of the new album which they had hoped to release in time for the tour. A mixing session in LA during the early summer had proved disappointing and it had to be worked on again back in London – shelving release until the autumn. There was also a lengthy quarrel with Atlantic Records who were less than pleased that the group's intended design for the record jacket featured no group name or company logo. "We just didn't have time to sit down and get a balance on things," remarked Page at the time. "With all the touring you can lose proportion of what's happening. It was rough for a little while but now we intend to plan things a lot better. As for the album, there were so many hang ups. My senses have been battered to pulp. I've lived with it for so long – I can't hear it any more."

That statement was a throw back to the lack of confidence Page spoke of before the release of *Led Zeppelin II*. He needn't have worried.

Peter Grant was anxious that the band return to the US without delay. This was their longest break from touring to date – and in their absence the much hyped Grand Funk Railroad had made a major impression on the hard rock market. US radio stations were also heralding the dominance of soft rock, championed by James Taylor, Carole King and Crosby Stills Nash & Young. It's fair to say that both this tour and the subsequent 1972 visit proceeded with considerably less intemperance than that which surrounded their earlier US visits. Richard Cole confirms that the band was beginning to tire of the off stage indulgences that had provided so many crazy moments and left Led Zeppelin with a well earned reputation for excess.

Security was also stepped up as death threats and unsavoury backstage incidents grew more common. The audiences were also growing more frenzied and firecracker throwing was becoming a constant menace to their safety on stage.

Nevertheless, it was important they re-establish their live reputation on this month-long seventh visit. Two warm up shows in Montreux hinted at their prowess. The new material was received well by America; the well-heeled strut of 'Black Dog', the mellow 'Going To California' (the acoustic set mirroring the soft rock trend) and of course, 'Stairway To Heaven'. Page still recalls with pride the standing ovation they received when it was aired at the LA Forum for the first time that August.

As the rock and roll medley grew longer and the improvisations more extreme, their two and a half hour extravaganza proved conclusively they were in a different league from the likes of Grand Funk. The consistency achieved throughout this tour would ensure massive sales for the eventually released fourth album.

Saturday August 7 1971
Montreux, Switzerland
Montreux Casino

Melody Maker reported that: "Zeppelin played two unusual warm-up dates at Montreux Casino where dinner-jacketed diners mixed with Zeppelin fans."

The Orange amplifier company issue a press release reporting the Montreux dates as being the first to feature Orange amps as part of Jimmy Page's amplification.

Sunday August 8 1871
Montreux, Switzerland
Montreux Casino

Peter Grant: "I remember when we did Montreux. It was so packed, I had the idea of feeding the sound outside onto the lawns where loads of fans who couldn't get in had congregated. Claude (Knobs – the promoter) loved that."

Photographs of these dates can be seen in the book *The Montreaux Concerts* by Giles Chateau and Sam Rapallo

Visual Reference: Privately shot silent cine film of the crowd entering the arena and brief offstage shots of the group were included on the unofficial *Early Visions* DVD (Celebration)

Thursday August 19 1971
Vancouver, Canada
Pacific Coliseum

An eventful start to the tour proper.

The show was held at the city's ice hockey arena, but even the 17,141 seats in the venue could not accommodate everyone. By show time there were some 3,000 fans outside without tickets. The locked out fans began a brief battle with the police.

Inside the arena, there was other notable off stage action. A group of anti-pollution scientists set up equipment to monitor noise levels during the show. Peter Grant mistook them for bootleggers and their recording equipment was promptly smashed.

'Rock concert noise monitor beaten up, machine broken' is the headline of the *Vancouver Sun*. "A $2,500 sound measuring machine was smashed and its operator was beaten at the Led Zeppelin rock concert, conservationist Derek Mallard charged today.

"Mallard, executive director of the Scientific Pollution and Environment Control Society, said he sent the machine with operator Mac Nelson to measure the volume of sound in relation to its damage to human hearing. Nelson was able to take one reading from a corner of the stage. Then he was set upon and beaten up, he said.

"'The first reading was 116 decibels, well above the pain threshold,' Nelson told *The Sun*. 'I set the machine on a corner of the stage and someone kicked it to the ground. Then four men dragged me upstairs and started to beat me in the concourse. Apparently they thought I was recording their sound and giving tapes to someone outside'."

Further press reports stated that 35 youths and two officers were hurt as the crowd crashed the concert. "Twenty policemen, 12 of them equipped with riot helmets but no sticks, attempted to stop a crowd which police estimated at 3,000 from forcing its way into a concert by Led Zeppelin.

"'We held the crowd off at the start but then they started pounding and the promoters said to open the doors and let them in,' said Sgt. Eric Hodge. 'We couldn't do anything but try and keep things as quiet as we could. There were no arrests – we couldn't possibly arrest anyone. About two or three thousand got in after we let the doors open'."

The performance itself was considered a success. "Zeppelin getting better," writes Brian McLeod. "Led Zeppelin still plays music that sounds like a haunted cathedral singing the blues. Only now they play it better. In addition to their familiar pulsating pillars of rhythm, they have learned to penetrate every nook and corner of the sound spectrum, with a resulting versatility rarely found in a rock band."

Friday August 20 1971
Seattle, Washington
Seattle Centre Coliseum

Saturday August 21 1971
Inglewood, Los Angeles, California
The Forum

Set: Immigrant Song/Heartbreaker/Since I've Been Loving You/Black Dog/Dazed And Confused/Stairway To Heaven/Celebration Day/That's The Way/Going To California/What Is And What Should Never Be/Moby Dick/Whole Lotta Love (inc. Boogie Chillun'- Moving On – That's Alright Mama – For What It's Worth – Mess O'Blues – Got A Lotta Livin' To Do – Honey Bee – Sugar Mama)/Weekend/Rock And Roll/Communication Breakdown/Organ Solo – Thank You.

Unusually, Zeppelin hit LA at the start of the tour but their passion for the venue was well in evidence.

The audience are just as enthusiastic, forcing

Plant has to call for quiet: "This is one that requires a bit of silence actually because of the way it begins ... this is called 'Stairway To Heaven'." The first performance of 'Stairway To Heaven' in Los Angeles was received well, as was all the new as-yet unreleased material. Plant, however, had trouble recalling the correct lyrics to both 'Stairway' and 'Going To California'. The set list continued to grow, with the addition of 'Celebration Day' on this tour.

An unusual funky opening riff and a mass of firecracker explosions heralded the start of another 'Whole Lotta Love' medley, which included the rarely played Elvis classic 'Got A Lotta Livin' To Do'. Robert changed the lyrics of 'Boogie Chillun' to "I hear the Holiday Inn manager talking ..." The first encore was another rarity, a complete version of Eddie Cochran's 'Weekend', an appropriate choice for a Saturday night. Robert then introduced 'Rock And Roll' as ... "One off the next album. We haven't really got a title for it". 'Thank You' brought the evening's entertainment to an emotional finale.

Bootleg CD References: *Walk Don't Run* (Tarantura), *Firecrackers Explosion* (Empress Valley), *Wild Weekend* (The Diagrams of Led Zeppelin)

Sunday August 22 1971
Inglewood Los Angeles, California
The Forum
Set: Walk Don't Run/Immigrant Song/Heartbreaker/Since I've Been Loving You/Black Dog/Dazed And Confused/Stairway To Heaven/Celebration Day/That's The Way/Going To California/What Is And What Should Never Be/Moby Dick/Whole Lotta Love (inc. Boogie Chillun' – My Baby Left Me – Mess O'Blues – You Shook Me)/Communication Breakdown/Organ Solo – Thank You.

Tickets for the first show sold out so fast that adverts proclaimed: "By special request we're adding a second show."

The show opened playfully with The Ventures'

'Walk Don't Run', a Sixties instrumental, before returning to the standard set. 'Immigrant Song' included some terrible feedback whine, but this clears in time for an excellent 'Heartbreaker'.

'Dazed And Confused' was now featuring an extended funky interlude which sometimes threatened to develop into 'The Crunge'.

Plant again got the lyrics wrong to 'Stairway To Heaven' for the second night in a row, and his voice was a little ragged. "Tonight my voice is really fucked, so I don't think we're gonna do much harmonising. But we're gonna try – so, vibe on!"

The 'Whole Lotta Love' medley as well as a harmonica solo during 'You Shook Me' also featured 'My Baby Left Me', a number Jimmy recorded with Dave Berry way back in 1964.

'Communication Breakdown' was performed differently every evening and tonight included an extended bass solo from John Paul Jones and some improvised lyrics from Plant. Few concerts on the tour would match the magic and excitement of the Forum shows.

Bootleg CD Reference: *Freak Out* (The Diagrams Of Led Zeppelin), *Walk Don't Run* (Tarantura)
Visual Reference: Privately shot silent cine footage of the Forum show was included on the *Early Visions* unofficial DVD (Celebration). In March 2005 some of this footage was aired on Jonathan Ross's BBC *Secret Map of Hollywood* programme.

Monday August 23 1971
Fort Worth, Texas
Tarrant County Convention Center
Set includes: Immigrant Song/Heartbreaker/Since I've Been Loving You/Black Dog/Dazed And Confused/Stairway To Heaven/Celebration Day/That's The Way/Going To California/What Is And What Should Never Be/Moby Dick/Whole Lotta Love /Communication Breakdown/Organ Solo – Thank You.

Bootleg CD Reference: *Hot August Night* (Diagrams Of Led Zeppelin)

Led Zeppelin

Tuesday August 24 1971
Dallas, Texas
Memorial Auditorium

Wednesday August 25 1971
Houston, Texas
Sam Houston Coliseum
Venue switched from the Hofheinz Pavillion.
Visual Reference: An eleven-minute reel of 16mm colour silent audience shot footage exists from this show

Thursday August 26 1971
San Antonio, Texas
Hemisphere Arena
A reel of 16mm audience shot silent colour footage exists from this show

Friday August 27 1971
Oklahoma City, Oklahoma
Civic Auditorium

Saturday August 28 1971
St. Louis, Missouri
St. Louis Arena

Sunday August 29 1971
New Orleans, Louisiana
Municipal Auditorium

Tuesday August 31 1971
Orlando, Florida
Orlando Sports Stadium
Set: Immigrant Song/Heartbreaker/Since I've Been Loving You/Dazed And Confused/Black Dog/Stairway To Heaven/Celebration Day/That's The Way/Going To California/What Is And What Should Never Be/Moby Dick/Whole Lotta Love (incl Boogie Chillun-My Baby Left Me-Mess Of Blues)/Organ solo-Thank You

The start of this show held in an arena primarily used for wrestling was delayed while the authorities tried to control the crowd.

Announcer: "OK people, you've got to be like patient. Just relax 'cos you're not gonna make it happen any faster and it's gonna be a lot easier for everybody. If everybody at the back could just slide back about an inch to let these people breathe, it would be really nice. Just be patient and you will be truly rewarded."

The temperature in the venue was extremely high. 'Celebration Day' began slowly with an unusual riff and during the acoustic set Plant had to try to calm the frenzied crowd: "This is where we sit down. If we can ask you to try to please be as quiet as you can. Otherwise we're gonna be in the position where you can't hear and we can't even hear! You'll have to shut up a bit more. You'll have to be a little quieter please ... Stop whistling. For God's sake – SHUT UP!"

Page teased the audience with a few bars of The Kinks' 'You Really Got Me' before leading the band into 'What Is And What Should Never Be'.
Bootleg CD References: *Florida Sunshine* (Empress Valley), *Welcome To Disneyland Pt1 & Pt2* (Lemon), *Orlando Madness Pt1 & Pt2* (No Label)

Wednesday September 1 1971
Hollywood, Florida
Hollywood Speedway Park Sportatorium
Tonight's show was scheduled to take place at the Miami Jai Alai Fronton, but on the morning of the show *The Miami Herald* informed its readers that ... "The concert by the rock group Led Zeppelin, scheduled for 8 tonight at Miami Jai Alai Fronton, will be staged instead at the Hollywood Sportatorium."

No explanation is given for the change of venue.

Friday September 3 1971
New York, New York
Madison Square Garden

Set: Immigrant Song/Heartbreaker/Since I've Been Loving You/Black Dog/Dazed And Confused/Stairway To Heaven/Celebration Day/That's The Way/Going To California/What Is And What Should Never Be/Moby Dick/Whole Lotta Love (inc. Boogie Chillun'- My Baby Left Me – Mess O'Blues – You Shook Me)/Communication Breakdown/Organ Solo – Thank You/Rock And Roll.

Drum roadie Mick Hinton recalled: "The travelling was hard work so all the roadies shared the driving. We did a marathon run from Miami and headed for the Garden over a thousand miles away. Peter insisted that everything was just right for that date, with it being a big New York show. We hired additional trucks just in case the main ones broke down, and as it turned out, it was those that let us down nearly. And when we got to Madison Square Garden a circus was just packing up, so we had all these elephants clambering by the PA. Crazy!"

"Good Evening. How have you been? I think we're gonna get a bit warm tonight!"

Plant told the audience, as he has on every other show on the tour, rather optimistically, that the new album will be out in three weeks. He apolo-

gised for the delay and explained: "We got problems trying to get a record cover that looks how we want it."

'Communication Breakdown' was dedicated to a guy that threw something at Plant and Jimmy teased the crowd with a few licks of 'Train Kept A Rollin''. During 'Thank You', things really got out of hand when some members of the crowd climbed on the stage causing a section of it to collapse. Plant stopped the number: "You've gotta move back. Move back. Move back or we can't go on! Move right back! It's not fair to everybody else. Besides I'm scared of heights."

The band returned for one final brief encore of 'Rock and Roll' (still referred to as 'It's Been A Long Time'). Plant: "I gotta tell you, I can't hear a thing I'm saying. All the equipment's fallen out!" A chaotic end to a chaotic evening.

Bootleg CD References: *Mad Screaming Gallery* (Lemon Song), *How've Ya Been* (The Diagrams of Led Zeppelin), *Hard Company* (No label)

SATURDAY SEPTEMBER 4 1971
TORONTO, CANADA
MAPLE LEAF GARDENS

Set: Immigrant Song/Heartbreaker/Since I've Been Loving You/Black Dog/Dazed And Confused/Stairway To Heaven/Celebration Day/That's The Way/Going To California/What Is And What Should Never Be/Moby Dick/Whole Lotta Love (inc. Boogie Chillun' – My Baby Left Me – Mess O'Blues – You Shook Me)/Communication Breakdown/Organ Solo – Thank You.

Billed as 'Only Eastern Canadian Appearance', the group were introduced on stage by future biographer and supportive journalist Ritchie Yorke, a trend that continues on future visits to Toronto. Demand was not as high as anticipated and tickets are still available on the night of the show.

An average performance, excellent in places but uninspired in others, the group are not in a good mood tonight. They were beginning to tire of the nightly ritual of asking the audience for some quiet and respect during the acoustic set. Plant: "Listen. It really amazes me, because anybody who's been to England knows that when you go to a concert, there's such a thing as listening to what's going on! Unfortunately, we're faced with the problem in our free society where a lot of people come to listen, and there's a lot of people who are making a racket so nobody hears what's going on. We've got some things to say but every time I go to open my mouth, there's another spokesman … If the guy next to you is trying to listen, you've got to respect that and be quiet. So the whole thing's a big circular respect thing. So many of those big festivals fell apart because the respect

wasn't a uniform one, and the thing with these concerts is that they normally are!"

"Old reliable Zeppelin shows usual style" was the headline above Jack Batten's review. but he is not particularly impressed by the show: "Led Zeppelin performed for two and a half hours, playing, as usual, music that was heavy, bluesy, rhythmically stolid, filled with long but not necessarily unique improvisational passages. And the audience reacted in the customary style of Zeppelin audiences, which is to say with plenty of ovations (particularly on a very long and genuinely inept drum solo), a great rush to the stage (during the band's anthem 'Whole Lotta Love') and a tribute of matches lit up in every row of the Gardens (a beautiful and exciting sight).

"What else can you say about a Led Zeppelin show? That the band makes good music to get stoned by? Certainly, there was a nice haze of marijuana hanging over the Gardens and the people from the St. John's Ambulance had lots to do. Or you could say, on a purely simplistic level, that Led Zeppelin is at times the most overwhelmingly stupefyingly loud band around."

Bootleg CD References: *Live From The Midnight*

Sun (The Diagrams of Led Zeppelin), *In A Daze* (Keep Out), *Maple Leaf* (Baby Face), *Jennings Farm Blues* (Scorpio), *Farmhouse Blues* (Blue Kangaroo)

Sunday September 5 1971
Chicago, Illinois
Chicago International Amphitheatre

Monday September 6 1971
Boston, Massachusetts
Boston Garden
Set included: Immigrant Song/Heartbreaker/ Since I've Been Loving You/Black Dog/Dazed And Confused/Stairway To Heaven/Whole Lotta Love (inc. Killing Floor)/Communication Breakdown /Organ Solo – Thank You/Rock And Roll.

Another fraught concert. Boston was one of the worst places for crowd trouble on last year's tour, so it comes as no surprise to find that this time out the conflict is even worse.

"Where have you been for a year?" asked Plant, trying to establish some rapport with the audience.

Halfway through Page's solo in 'Dazed And Confused', Plant yelled "No! No! You gotta cool it!" and Page slowed things down to a standstill. Plant addressed the crowd: "Listen, I gotta put things straight. We had a bit of trouble in New York the other day, when so many people got on stage that it fell apart. Listen! Listen! LISTEN TO ME! … If everybody gets on the stage, then the police will stop the thing. So what we wanna do is play as much of the new stuff and old stuff as we can without it falling apart!"

This calmed the crowd momentarily but before 'Stairway To Heaven', Plant threatens: "If it becomes impossible to do it, then we'll stop!" Firecrackers distracted Plant's concentration during this song, causing him to miss an entire verse.

The band persisted, however, and on a positive note, included a 1969 arrangement of 'Killing Floor' in the 'Whole Lotta Love' medley. 'Communication Breakdown' featured some improvised "I've got a feeling" lyrics from Plant.
Bootleg CD References: *Killing Floor '71* (No Label), *Listen To Me*, *Boston* (Tarantura), *Boston Garden Party* (Magnificent)

Thursday September 9 1971
Hampton Beach, Virginia
Hampton Roads Coliseum
Set included: Immigrant Song/Heartbreaker/ Since I've Been Loving You/Black Dog/Dazed And Confused/Stairway To Heaven/Celebration Day/That's The Way/Going To California/What Is And What Should Never Be/Moby Dick.

There were no problems with the crowd tonight. In fact, before the acoustic set, Plant commented: "Right, you're sitting down and so are we. Far out! This is the part where we usually ask people to stop falling out of the spotlights for a bit. Fortunately, there's no trouble tonight."

'Celebration Day' featured some powerful playing from Jones, whose general performance had been consistently good throughout the whole tour. Plant sang a line from 'High Heeled Sneakers' – "Put on your red dress, baby, 'cos we're going out tonight!" – as a prelude to 'What Is And What Should Never Be'.
Bootleg CD References: *Hampton Kicks* (House Of Elrond), *Inspired* (Antrabata), *Jim's Picks* (Tarantura), *Hampton 1971* (Cannonball)

Friday September 10 1971
Syracuse, New York
Onondaga County War Memorial Auditorium

Saturday September 11 1971
Rochester, New York
Rochester War Memorial Auditorium
Set: Immigrant Song/Heartbreaker/Since I've Been Loving You/Black Dog/Stairway To Heaven/Celebration Day/That's The Way/Going To California/What Is And What Should Never Be/Moby Dick/Whole Lotta Love (inc. Boogie Chillun' – Hello Mary Lou – Mess O'Blues – You Shook Me)/Organ Solo – Thank You.

The version of 'Black Dog' saw them get lost during the middle section and the song nearly came to a complete stop. Page managed to save the situation by improvising his way straight into the solo. 'Celebration Day' was introduced as "something for New York City, a place not too far away from here" and Plant instructed the crowd: "Everybody move a little bit back. A little bit of do unto your brother and sister!" Obviously he's wary after the recent problems in New York and does not want a repeat of that situation tonight.

The arrival of the acoustic set was accompanied by the token pleas: "We're gonna sit down. If we're gonna sit down, I reckon you oughta sit down, so the people behind you can see what's going on … Y'see, the essence of these numbers we wanna do now, is silence – remember that! The crying of voices doesn't really take us back to the Welsh mountains. Now cool it! If you do a big out-cry, none of us are gonna get anywhere at all. So please be quiet!"

Bootleg References: *Mad Screaming Gallery* (Lemon), *Live At Leeds* (LA)

Monday September 13 1971
Berkeley, California
Community Theatre

Set: Immigrant Song/Heartbreaker/Since I've Been Loving You/Black Dog/Dazed And Confused/Stairway To Heaven/Celebration Day/That's The Way/Going To California/What Is And What Should Never Be/Moby Dick/Whole Lotta Love (inc. Boogie Chillun' – Hello Mary Lou – Mess O'Blues – You Shook Me)/Communication Breakdown (inc. Gallows Pole).

Another triumphant return to California. 'Dazed And Confused' continued to expand in length and clocked in at over 22 minutes long. 'Whole Lotta Love' was also expanded tonight. Prior to 'Boogie Chillun'', Page inserted a new funky interlude and Plant ad-libbed "Just want a little bit". This section would be retained through future tours. The ever-changing 'Communication Breakdown' included lyrics from 'Gallows Pole'.

Bootleg CD References: *Going To California II* (Tarantura), *Back On The West Coast* (Mad Dogs)

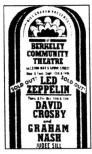

Tuesday September 14 1971
Berkeley, California
Community Theatre

Set included: Immigrant Song/Heartbreaker/Since I've Been Loving You/Black Dog/Dazed And Confused/Stairway To Heaven/That's The Way/Going To California/Whole Lotta Love (inc. Boogie Chillun' – Hello Mary Lou – My Baby Left Me – Mess O'Blues – You Shook Me – The Lemon Song).

Another superb performance with Plant very talkative between songs. "You should have come last night. Last night there were several bowler-hatted beatniks. There was a pollution alert today and I lost my voice This is one from millions and millions of years ago, just when the good things were checking themselves out." That was the introduction to a transitional 'Dazed And Confused' changed yet again to feature the MC5's 'Livin' In The USA' ad-libs from Plant. 'Stairway To Heaven' was as impressive as on any night on the tour and features the unique line: "You are the home of the children of the sun".

There were tuning problems during the acoustic set, so Plant provided a lengthy introduction to 'Going To California' – "This is quite a moving night for me. This is a thing that got together … I was going to say in the Scottish Highlands, or the Welsh mountains, but I think it was something like the Gorham Hotel, West 37th Street. Here's to the days when things were really nice and simple and everything was far out, all the time. On that theme, it's not a very good cup of tea you get over here!"

This concert was immortalised on an early dou-ble album bootleg release from the Trade Mark Of

Quality label, under the title *Going To California*, complete with original sleeve caricatures by William Stout, now a renowned artist. Another much loved and essential vinyl issue that lines up alongside *Live On Blueberry Hill* as a brilliantly authentic example of their live prowess of this era.
Bootleg CD References: *Going To California* (Shout to the Top), *Going To California* (Electric Junk)

Thursday September 16 1971
Honolulu, Hawaii
Civic Auditorium
Set included – Immigrant Song/ Heartbreaker/ Since I've Been Loving You/Black Dog/Dazed And Confused/Stairway To Heaven/Celebration Day/Moby Dick/Whole Lotta Love (inc. Hello Mary Lou)/ Communica-tion Breakdown.

The critics were not convinced: 'Led Zeppelin Is Shot Down' reported the *Honolulu Star-Bulletin*. Don Weller stated: "The show was marred by a generally sloppy performance on the part of the group, rather noisy behaviour on the part of some of the 4,000 people in attendance, and a hot and sweaty atmosphere on the part of the good ol' poorly ventilated Civic Auditorium.

"From the very first note it was obvious that these guys were simply not into what they were doing. Rhythms were off, Plante's (sic) vocals were relatively impotent, and the overall group enthusiasm was missing. You couldn't help but get the impression that these guys were tired and looking forward both to the end of the evening and also to the end of their present road tour.

"There was some totally selfish and obnoxious noisy behaviour on the part of a number of people in the audience. Aside from someone yanking down one of the microphones during the last part of 'Since I've Been Loving You', yelling into it and basically ruining the effect the band was trying to create, another clown jumped up on stage and started yelling some four-letter gems into the stand-up mike. The band should be commended for their ability to put up with such obstacles."

Friday September 17 1971
Honolulu, Hawaii
Civic Auditorium
John Bonham: "The American tour was good. It was quite strange because we hadn't been to America for almost a year. To be perfectly honest ... I was scared. But we played really well and had some great things happen. The Los Angeles Forum sold out in one day, so we did another concert there and we really didn't expect such a demand. I think I enjoyed it more than any other tour of America."

JAPAN 1971

A new territory and new on-stage developments. Zeppelin had long harboured plans to play in the Far East. A visit to Japan as part of 'Expo 70' had been touted a year earlier. This three-city, five-concert stop-off on the way back from America, saw them present some of their most relaxed performances. Away from the glare of the press and the growing madness of America, this was the perfect opportunity to lay back and stretch out. This they did, notably with extended versions of 'Dazed And Confused' and the medley-filled 'Whole Lotta Love'. Cover versions of 'Please Please Me', 'Bachelor Boy', 'We Shall Overcome' and 'Smoke Gets In Your Eyes' may have raised eyebrows in more familiar territories, but in front of the adoring Japanese, anything went down.

Off stage they greatly enjoyed the hospitality

history. These include *Complete Live In Japan* (Last Stand Disc), a limited edition 27-CD boxed set featuring their entire Japanese tours from 1971 and 1972, and *Live In Japan 1971* (Last Stand), a 13-CD boxed set of just the 1971 concerts.

Equipment Notes: Page was using a Harmony Sovereign acoustic and Bonzo used bongos with sticks for the September 29 live performance of 'Friends'.

Thursday September 23 1971

Tokyo, Japan
Budokan Hall

Set: Immigrant Song/ Heartbreaker/Since I've Been Loving You/Black Dog/ Dazed And Confused/ Stairway To Heaven/ Celebration Day/ That's The Way/Going To California/What Is And What Should Never Be/Moby Dick/ Whole Lotta Love (inc. Boogie Chillun' – Hello Mary Lou – Mess O'Blues – I'm A Man – Tobacco Road – Good Times Bad Times – How Many More Times – The Hunter – You Shook Me)/ Communication Breakdown.

An excellent first show in Japan

During 'Immigrant Song' Jimmy broke a string. While the string was being changed, Robert took the opportunity to address the Japanese audience for the first time. "I understand that in Japan not many people speak English. Anyway, every day it's getting better. We'd like to say that so far we've had an incredible time, a wonderful time. We haven't even played a concert yet and we've all ready been having a ball. I'm gonna do my best to make this the best time we've ever had, because it seems to be such a difference to America. America doesn't seem to be so good anymore,

on offer and endeared themselves to the people by performing a benefit show in Hiroshima, for which they were presented with a letter of appreciation and the city medal, by the local mayor. There was plenty of road fever going down as well, including an incident where Plant allegedly punched Bonham before the encores of one of the shows. The drummer was to temporarily go missing during their acoustic set at Osaka on September 29.

Though Cole claims they came out of this tour with little profit, it was a triumphant diversion from the norm. "It was a fantastic place to play," Bonham told journalists on their return. "The people were so friendly and we had the best promoter looking after us." A return visit was provisionally booked for the following year.

Over the years Japanese bootleggers have surpassed anything that the rest of the world has thrown up, with beautifully produced boxed sets that reflect Led Zeppelin's entire Japanese touring

unfortunately. Maybe it'll get better." Plant also informs the audience that the new album will be out in four weeks (it keeps getting put back).

The Japanese audience were polite but very enthusiastic. The acoustic set began with a few bars of 'Bron Yr Aur Stomp' but Page aborted it, leaving Plant alone to finish the first verse. After 'That's The Way', Plant explained 'Going To California' : "A long time ago in 1967, there was a place called San Francisco and San Francisco was responsible for many good things, including everybody's head. Right on, man! I dunno what happened after 1967, maybe it was the truck drivers. Anyway, it's still there and it's in California."

The undisputed highlight of the show was the 'Whole Lotta Love' medley. After some of the restrained versions played on the US tour, the band threw caution to the wind and produce one of the longest renditions ever, featuring complete versions of 'Tobacco Road', 'Good Times Bad Times' and even 'How Many More Times' – once of course a medley in its own right.

During the 'Communication Breakdown' encore, Plant had to stop the song to prevent some members of the crowd climbing on the stage.

Bootleg CD References: *Reflection >From A Dream* (TDOLZ), *Tales of Storms* (Aphrodite), *Storm Of Fanatics* (Mud Dogs), *First Attack Of The Rising Sun* (Empress Valley), *Meet The Led Zeppelin* (Wendy), *Timeless Rock* (Watchtower)

Friday September 24 1971
Tokyo, Japan
Budokan Hall
Set: Immigrant Song/Heartbreaker/Since I've Been Loving You/Black Dog/Dazed And Confused/Stairway To Heaven/Celebration Day/That's The Way/Going To California/Tangerine/What Is And What Should Never Be/Moby Dick/Whole Lotta Love (inc. Boogie Chillun' – Cocaine – Rave On – Your Time Is Gonna Come -I'm A Man – The Hunter – Hello Mary Lou – Pretty Woman – How Many More Times)/Organ Solo – Thank You/ Communication Breakdown.

The second and final show in Tokyo was an afternoon performance and continued in much

the same vein as yesterday's show. They continued to experiment and the set was full of surprises. 'Heartbreaker' contained a snatch of Simon & Garfunkel's '59th Street Bridge Song (Feelin' Groovy)', a trend that will continue, and Plant dedicated all the new songs to Cliff Richard.

'Dazed And Confused' was continuing to evolve. Plant ad-libbed some new lyrics and Page included a few licks from The Rolling Stones' 'Honky Tonk Women'. Plant threw in a few lines from 'Friends' but it was not performed in full. However, 'Tangerine' from the third album was performed on stage for the first time to much hand clapping from the audience.

Plant introduced John Bonham as "The only person who could do it. The only person who was in his pyjamas 10 minutes before the show. The right honourable John Bonham."

'Whole Lotta Love' was again a standout performance. After Page teased the crowd with a jerky stop-start introduction they ran through versions of 'Cocaine' ('rollin' round my brain'), Buddy Holly's 'Rave On' and Albert King's 'Pretty Woman'. Plant also threw in lines from the previously rarely performed 'Your Time Is Gonna Come' from the Led Zeppelin I album.

Allegedly. just before the encores Bonham and Plant had an argument in the dressing room, resulting in Jones performing the organ solo and 'Thank You' as they cooled off.

The 155-minute concert ended with a version of 'Communication Breakdown' that found Plant ad libbing lyrics from 'Hey, Hey What Can I Do?' – 'I gotta little girl, she won't be true!'

After the show the entourage visited a geisha house, dressed up in traditional geisha costumes.
Bootleg CD References: *Light And Shade* (Diagrams Of Led Zeppelin), *Pretty Woman* (Tarantura), *Afternoon Daze* (Mud Dogs), *Hard Rock Night* (Wendy)

After the Tokyo shows the band travelled to Kyoto for one night. They spent the day sightseeing. Later at a night club John Paul Jones was reported to have played 'Green Onions' on the

electric organ. They then moved on to a rock club called Saturday and borrowed instruments from the Japanese band who played at the club. Page, Jones and Bonzo performed an impromptu jam without Plant that lasted about 40 minutes. A photo of this can be seen on the bootleg sleeve of the CD *The Storm of Fanatics*.

Monday September 27 1971
Hiroshima, Japan
Shiei Taikukan Municipal Gymnasium
Set: Immigrant Song/Heartbreaker/Since I've Been Loving You/Black Dog/Dazed And Confused/Stairway To Heaven/Celebration Day/That's The Way/Going To California/Tangerine/What Is And What Should Never Be/Moby Dick/Whole Lotta Love (inc. Boogie Chillun' – Let's Have Fun – Be-Bop-A-Lula)/Communication Breakdown.

The band arrived at Hiroshima Station on September 26. They visited the Memorial Dome and went to the atomic bomb library located inside Peace Park.
For this show 'Dazed And Confused' was extended yet further by the inclusion of another instrumental interlude and clocked in at over 27 minutes. 'Tangerine' was now a regular feature of the acoustic set and John Bonham's 'Moby Dick' solo was now extended to 19 minutes.

A few bars of Frank Sinatra's 'The Lady Is A Tramp' was used to introduce 'Whole Lotta Love'. The medley was kept surprisingly short but did include rarities such as 'Let's Have Fun' and Gene Vincent's 'Be-Bop-A-Lula'. Just before the 'Boogie Chillun' section, Page went into a riff sequence later to be used on the *Physical Graffiti* track, 'In The Light'.

There was another threatened stage invasion during 'Communication Breakdown' and Plant had to stop the song in the middle of Jimmy's solo. Plant: "Whoa, you must stop it! Please do not come on the stage. Stay here and be cool. Please sit down. Sit on the floor mate!" Page then picked up the solo exactly where he left off.

This show, attended by over 6,000, was a chari-

Tuesday September 28 1971
Osaka, Japan
Festival Hall

Set: Immigrant Song/Heartbreaker/Since I've Been Loving You/Black Dog/Dazed And Confused /Stairway To Heaven/Please Please Me – From Me To You/Celebration Day/Bron Yr Aur Stomp – That's The Way/Going To California/We Shall Overcome/Tangerine/ Down By The Riverside/What Is And What Should Never Be/Moby Dick/Whole Lotta Love (inc. Boogie Chillun' – Biology – Bachelor Boy – C'mon Baby – Maybeline – Hello Mary Lou/C'mon Everybody/High Heeled Sneakers/ Communication Breakdown.

"Arigato!" Plant attempted his first word in Japanese. "Tonight you will be happy!" he informed the audience.

Another very relaxed show one of their best performances in Japan packed with set list surprises. Plant threw in ad hoc verisons of The Beatles' 'Please Please Me' and 'From Me To You'. The first verse of 'Bron Yr Aur Stomp' was played prior to 'That's The Way'. Prior to 'Tangerine', Robert led the crowd in a sing-along of the protest song 'We Shall Overcome', 'Down By The Riverside', the gospel/folk classic was another surprise insert to a lengthy acoustic set.

'Whole Lotta Love' again featured more rarely performed classics including Cliff Richard's 'Bachelor Boy', Chuck Berry's 'Maybeline' and a full version of 'Biology'.

The encores brought more surprises. 'High Heeled Sneakers' was played in its complete form and a chaotic delivery of 'C'mon Everybody' featured roadie Clive Coulson sharing the vocals, and Atlantic vice-president Phil Carson on bass.

Carson recalled later: "We had a good relationship and I got to jam with them on stage quite a lot. John Paul Jones would play keyboards, I would be on bass guitar and we would sail through seven or eight old rock songs. It was great. Having John Bonham kicking away behind you on drums was just an amazing feeling. We never rehearsed – we never knew what Robert

ty concert for the benefit of the victims of the atom bomb. During their visit to Hiroshima, the band presented the Mayor with a check for 7,000,000 yen – their earnings from the show and in return they were presented with peace medals.

Plant: "I read about the tragedy of Hiroshima in a history book. I would like to do something for the people of Hiroshima."

At the presentation of peace medals the mayor gave the members the Civil Charter, thanking for this contribution. Plant, representing Led Zeppelin, told the mayor: "We were born after the atomic air raid. We are not in a position to blame anybody, as it just happened in the past history and it was a human being who did it. It is not our fault, but our 'past' should be blamed. We would like to express our sincere apology about it. In this regard, we would like to help any victims who have been suffering from the bombing. Music can bring peace and joy to you. We, the musicians, will feel honorable if we can be of help to anybody."

Bootleg CD References: *Peace* (Tarantura), *Message To Love* (Lemon), *Live Peace In Horishima 1971* (Wendy), *Peace Of Mind* (Mud Dogs)

was going to sing next anyway. But they did lean towards the things I would be most comfortable with! Eddie Cochran songs were very high up on my list for playing. Normally we played 'C'mon Everybody' and old Elvis things like 'Blue Suede Shoes' and Johnny Kidd & The Pirates' 'Shaking All Over'. It was great fun."

Bootleg CD References: *Osaka Woman* (Cobla), *C'mon Everybody* (Mud Dogs), *Please Please Me* (Tarantura), *Please Please Me* (Wendy)

Wednesday September 29 1971
Osaka, Japan
Koseinenkin Kaikan Festival Hall

Set: Immigrant Song/Heartbreaker/Since I've Been Loving You/Black Dog/Dazed And Confused /Stairway To Heaven/Celebration Day/That's The Way/Going To California/ Tangerine/Friends/Smoke Gets In Your Eyes/ What Is And What Should Never Be/Moby Dick/Whole Lotta Love (inc. Boogie Chillun' – I Gotta To Know – Twist And Shout – Fortune Teller – Good Times Bad Times – You Shook Me)/ Communication Breakdown/Organ Solo – Thank You/Rock And Roll.

The final show was heralded by Plant's on stage comments: "We spent two weeks in wonderful, glorious Japan which has been incredible. Great hotels, great bars, great people and without giving you any bullshit, this is our last night in Japan and we're gonna have a good time and I think you will!"

'Dazed And Confused' was the longest version so far – over 30 minutes long and tonight included a false start plus a brief excerpt from the Forties standard, 'Pennies From Heaven'. Plant joked about the well behaved, respectful crowd: "You're too quiet. Much too slow, too silly and fast asleep."

The acoustic set was disrupted by some strange off stage antics. Page played a few bars of 'Rudolph, The Red-Nose Reindeer' prior to 'That's The Way'. Bonham went missing for most of the acoustic set and Plant lead the crowd in a pantomime style chant of 'Mr Bonham'. Plant

speculated that 'Mr Bonham go with geisha!' He adds: "Japan is a wonderful place and you're too much. You're putting up with a lot. We don't usually do things like this!"

Bonham finally returned and took to the tom-toms for the first-ever live rendition of 'Friends' from the third album. Plant followed that with a few bars of 'Smoke Gets In Your Eyes'.

Bonham again tried to escape without playing 'Moby Dick'. Before the solo, he can be heard saying to Robert off-mike, 'I don't wanna play it! I'm fed up playing it!' He finally made it through a mere 11 minutes of his solo.

'Whole Lotta Love' included 'I Gotta Know', 'Twist And Shout' and 'Fortune Teller'.

A suitably chaotic performance to end a truly outstanding tour.

Years later Peter Grant threw light on Bonzo's erratic behaviour: "There were rows… one bloody amazing one in Japan when Robert came off stage with a split lip. It was over some dispute over some money from some tour. He still owed Bonzo some petrol money, seventy quid or something, but that's how it was!"

Some of the Japanese shows were recorded at the insistence of Atlantic's Japanese Warner Pioneer label. Grant recalls: "There was this six track transistorised board. Jimmy was a bit worried about this, so the deal I made was that they could record it if we could have the tapes and take them back to England and approve it. So Jimmy listened to them and found them to be terrible. So he took the tapes back and wiped over them and used them again. So it was goodbye *Live In Japan*."

Page did in fact rediscover some of these tapes when researching their tape archive in 1997, but they were not considered good enough to warrant official release when it came to sourcing material for the DVD and live album in 2003.

Plant: We've recorded ourselves at the Farm on just an ordinary Revox, and achieved a far better sound."

After the last show in Japan, Robert and Jimmy, together with Richard Cole, travelled home via Thailand, Hong Kong and India. Peter Grant, John

Led Zeppelin

Bonham and John Paul Jones come back via Moscow.

Plant recalled: "We all bought cameras in Japan and became sweaty photographers – Page must have lost about two pounds rushing around taking pictures in the red light district. In Bangkok, all the kids followed us calling 'Billy boy, Billy boy' which means 'queer' (because of our hair), but they're laughing and happy all the time."

These cameras would be used to film the Peace gardens in Hiroshima and would later be used by friends and roadies to film parts of their Australian visit in early 1972. Years later this home movie footage would be recovered and used as part of the 'Immigrant Song' live sequence on the official DVD set.

Bootleg CD References: *A Cellarful Of Noise* (Noise Generator), *Live In Japan* (Cobla), *Smoke Get In Your Eyes* (Mad Dogs), *Nine Two Nine* (The Diagrams Of Led Zeppelin), *You Were There In Spirits* (Empress Valley), *Complete Geisha Tape* (Tarantura)

UK – WINTER 1971

To round off a most satisfying year, Peter Grant booked a 16-date UK tour that tied in with the release of the 'four-symbols' fourth album. The tour confirmed their supremacy in the UK rock marketplace. Tickets for most shows went on sale on November 5 – only six days before the start of the tour, such was their immediate selling power. The 9,500 tickets for the November 20 show at Wembley sold out in just 54 minutes. A second show was quickly added and there was enough demand for a third. A second Manchester date at Belle Vue was also added after fans queued over 18 hours to snap up tickets for the Manchester Free Trade Hall date.

The highlight of the tour was undoubtedly the two London Empire Pool Shows. Now a traditional stop-off for all major touring acts in the capital (it's known as Wembley Arena nowadays), this venue had previously been used to host the annual *NME* Poll Winners' concerts but no rock act had ever performed there on their own. Grant set a precedent that would open the floodgates for others to quickly follow, notably Marc Bolan's T. Rex, the following spring.

And they did it in style, presenting 'Electric Magic' – two five-hour shows that, as well as support acts, included the Grant co-managed Stone The Crows and mixed vaudeville circus acts with performing pigs and plate spinners. Zeppelin's two sets were hugely acclaimed and led to one of the best reviews of their career. Roy Hollingworth's 'Zapped By Zeppelin' report in *Melody Maker* confirmed the affection in which they were now held by critics and fans alike. Around the country it was a similar story as they showcased the new album with supreme confidence. Five selections from the new set were unveiled and much to Atlantic's relief, fans had no trouble identifying the nameless artwork of the new record as it sailed to the number one spot.

Once again, the Zep mystique had captured the imagination of their following and whatever title applied (*The New Led Zeppelin/Zoso/Four Symbols/Nameless/ Untitled/Led Zep IV* were all used in the press at the time to acknowledge its release), it was the quality of the music that made it THE album to be seen with over the Christmas period of 1971.

Led Zeppelin

Wembley Empire Pool, November 20 1971

Equipment Notes:

This period saw the introduction on stage of the four symbols from the fourth album sleeve. Jimmy's so-called 'Zoso' symbol was added to one of his Marshall speaker cabinets. Bonzo had the three linked circles on the Ludwig bass drum. Jones had his symbol draped across the Fender Rhodes keyboard, and Robert's feather symbol is painted on a side speaker PA cabinet. Only Page and Bonham's symbols would be retained after the 1972 US tour.

By this stage, Plant was regularly using Shure S545/S57/S58 microphones.

Fashion note:

For some dates on this tour, Page wore a specially knitted jumper featuring his 'Zoso' symbol, which was sent to him by a fan. Just before the tour they did a photo session in London with Page wearing this jumper. Plant wore a polka dot scarf and Bonham was pictured drinking a pint of beer.

Thursday November 11 1971
Newcastle-on-Tyne, England
City Hall

Set included: Immigrant Song/ Heartbreaker/ Black Dog/ Since I've Been Loving You/Rock And Roll/Stairway To Heaven/That's The Way/ Going To California/Tangerine/Dazed And Confused/What Is And What Should Never Be/Celebration Day/Whole Lotta Love Medley/ Communication Breakdown.

"Good evening! Well, here we are again!"

A fine opening night. Plant's voice was still in great shape and Page's playing as inspired as ever. The audience were very vocal and cheered wildly when Robert introduced tracks from the new album.

Plant: "Now then, today's the day of the Teddy Bear's picnic, and to go with it, the new album came out. I know what they say about the length of time between the two, and I'm sure you can read all sorts of reports and toss a coin!"

'Rock And Roll' was now added to the main set and finally had its correct title. 'Dazed And Confused' was moved to later in the set, as was 'Celebration Day'. 'Moby Dick' was strangely absent from most shows.

Throughout this concert Plant made references to Bonham's love of Newcastle Brown Ale, to roars of approval from the crowd. Plant: "He's become a connoisseur of every area we go to."

As usual the critics got their snipes in. Under the headline 'Zeppelin – good, bad, or indifferent?', Stu Bennett for *Disc* absolutely slated the gig. "The group that has brought the rock back to rock and roll were, for me at least, awful. The tragedy of it all was this band can play, and Plant can sing to rival any group in the world. They proved this with one new track, 'Stairway To Heaven'. But, alas, the mediocrity of the rest of the gig could easily be seen. Plant immediately sank to rock bottom in my estimation. True enough, Page did some amazing things with that guitar. But only spasmodically."

In his book *A Promoters Tale*, Geoff Docherty revealed the band performed for 90% of the net receipts.

Bootleg CD References: *Teddy Bear's Picnic* (No Label), *Newcastle Brown Ale* (Empress Valley Supreme), *Transitional Magic* (Electric Magic)

Friday November 12 1971
Newcastle-on-Tyne, England
Mecca Ballroom

Tickets were sold in advance for a show at The Locarno in Sunderland tonight, but at short notice the venue was changed to the Mecca Ballroom in Newcastle. Original tickets for Sunderland were valid for the Newcastle show.

The Concert File

Saturday November 13 1971
Dundee, Scotland
Caird Hall
Set included – Immigrant Song/Heartbreaker/Black Dog/Rock And Roll/Since I've Been Loving You/Stairway To Heaven/that's The Way/Bron-yr-Aur Stomp/Tangerine /Dazed And Confused/What Is And What Should Never Be/Moby Dick/Whole Lotta Love
Bootleg CD reference: *The Road And The Miles To Dundee* (Led Note)

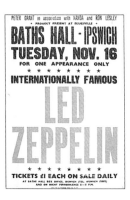

Tuesday November 16 1971
Ipswich, England
St. Matthew's Baths Halls
Set included – Immigrant Song/Heartbreaker/Black Dog/Since I've Been Loving You/Rock And Roll/That's The Way/Tangerine/Dazed And Confused/What Is And What Should Never Be/Celebration Day/Whole Lotta Love (inc. Boogie Chillun' – Hello Mary Lou – Mess O'Blues – Honey Bee – Going Down Slow)/Weekend/Gallows Pole

The show was promoted by Ron and Nina Lesley who staged many local gigs at the Baths Hall in St Matthew's Street during the winter and at the local Manor Ballroom when the baths was being used as a swimming pool. The Baths Halls was used for a variety of events with

a wooden floor covering the pool during the winter season.

Fan Richard Jarratt recalled: "I saw Robert and Jimmy arrive in a green Rolls Royce. After a quick wave to the waiting fans they disappeared to the back of the hall."

The show began with a dedication. Plant: "Good evening! It's really far out to be back. Last time we were here, we were with Jimmy James. We'd like to dedicate this show to Delroy Wilson and his good, good band."

This concert was held on temporary flooring over a swimming pool and Plant was obviously wary of this and makes references to it throughout the concert. "I don't know whether the 12-foot end's this one or that one. God help us! I'm sure you must have had a Town Hall! It's gonna be a silly night tonight. We'd like you all to feel at home. Just think of the drop beneath you and the drop that might come eventually!"

'Heartbreaker' again included 'Feelin' Groovy', which now became a regular feature. During the acoustic set, Page attempted the opening bars of 'Bron Yr Aur Stomp' but gave up on the idea. Plant explained that there were a lot of new songs that they'd like to try, but instead "We're gonna try to keep it very serious and Marc Bolan!"

They performed a truly inspired, very experimental version of 'Dazed And Confused'. "Wonderful," commented Plant at its conclusion.

The extra songs in the 'Whole Lotta Love' medley were standard for this tour, but the delivery was always outstanding. The real surprise came with the final encores – a rare run through of Eddie Cochran's Weekend and an even rarer stab at 'Gallows Pole'. The latter two songs came to light on a complete audience recorded cassette tape that emerged in 2000 – it was duly issued on the Empress Valley set *Feelin' Groovy Definitive Edition*.

Bootleg CD References: *Ipswich 1971* (Diagrams of Led Zeppelin), *Over The 12 Foot End* (No label), *Feeelin' Groovy Definitve Edition* (Empress Valley).

Wednesday November 17 1971
Birmingham, England
Kinetic Circus

Thursday November 18 1971
Sheffield, England
Sheffield University

Saturday November 20 1971
London, England
Wembley Empire Pool

Set includes – Immigrant Song/ Heartbreaker/ Black Dog/ Since I've Been Loving You/Rock And Roll/ Stairway To Heaven/ Dancing Days/Going To California/That's The Way/Tangerine/ Bron Yr Aur Stomp/ Dazed And Confused/Celebration Day/What Is And What Should Never Be/Moby Dick/Whole Lotta Love (inc. Boogie Chillun' – Hello Mary Lou – Mess O'Blues – Honey Bee – Going Down Slow).

Support from Bronco and Stone The Crows. Bronco's line-up includes Robbie Blunt who would later team up with Plant in 1981.

The Wembley concerts were the centrepiece of the tour and were five hour events with the live acts interspersed with variety circus acts. This included a plate spinning attempt by Olley Grey who had previously performed on a Royal Festival Hall bill with Roger Chapman's Family. There was also an exhibition of prize performing pigs complete with hats and ruffles around their necks – they did little else but mope about the stage.

Despite being nervous at being back in London both nights were very well received, earning them some of the best reviews of their career.

"Are you cold?" was Plant's opening words on a freezing November weekend.

Following a brutal opening of 'Immigrant Song'/'Heartbreaker', Plant asked for the house lights to be turned on the audience. "Right, if you're gonna keep warm, you better keep doing things like that!"

Commenting on the pigs' inactivity he told the audience: "I expected a bit more from the pigs! Did you? I could have brought some goats!"

There was one very rare addition to the set list: an as yet unrecorded track known as 'Dancing Days' was premièred after 'Stairway To Heaven'. This track was later recorded at Olympic Studios the next spring and played live again on the 1972 US tour. Its studio release on the *Houses Of The Holy* album followed in March 1973.

'Bron Yr Aur Stomp' was finally introduced to the set as a regular addition to the acoustic set. 'Celebration Day' was moved further up the set list, and 'Moby Dick' was reintroduced prior to 'Whole Lotta Love'. However, there was a delay and Plant commented: "He's gone for a piss – second night in a row!" He is subsequently introduced as "the very short-bladdered John Bonham!"

Roy Hollingworth's led the plaudits for this show in *Melody Maker* under the headline 'Zapped By Zeppelin': "We are at home with Led Zep, comfy on a cold perishing English night. Even the elderly stewards are enjoying it. 'I've been here years,' says one, 'And I've never known such happy, polite people. Everyone says 'please' and everyone says 'thank you'. I want to see this group The Zeppelin!' This was an English band playing like crazy, and enjoying every minute they stood there on stage. They played non-stop for the best part of three hours. Enormous. They played about everything they've ever written. Nothing, just nothing, was spared. This was no job, this was no 'gig'. It was an event for all. So they get paid a lot of bread, Well, people paid that bread, and I'll reckon they got every penny's worth. It was a great night."

Bootleg CD Reference: *Electric Magic Show*

The Concert File

(Electric Magic), *Magick* (Tarantura) *The Electric magic Show* (Mud Dogs)

Sunday November 21 1971
London, England Wembley Empire Pool

Set included – Immigrant Song/Heartbreaker/ Black Dog/Since I've Been Loving You/Rock And Roll/Stairway To Heaven/Dancing Days/Going To California/That's The Way/Tangerine/Bron Yr Aur Stomp/Dazed And Confused/Celebration Day/What Is And What Should Never Be/Moby Dick/Whole Lotta Love

Stone The Crows were featured again tonight. Home replaced Bronco as the opening act. In what must have been an in-joke, the guitarists with both support acts used violin bows in their sets.

Richard Branson's newly inaugurated Virgin Records retail outlet set up a stall on both nights of the shows to exclusively sell the fourth album. There was no official programme but instead a beautiful full colour poster was available for just 30p. This now sells at auction for over £600.

This show was the first experience of the group live for co-author Dave Lewis: "It was incredibly loud but very clear," he recalled. "There was a great sense of occasion in the air and those in attendance knew they were witnessing yet another milestone in the group's evolution.

"DJ Jeff Dexter warmed up the audience with records from the charts of the day including Redbone's 'Witch Queen Of New Orleans' and Issac

Hayes' 'Shaft' (which Page would quote from a few days later during 'Dazed And Confused' live in Manchester). Frequent cries of 'Wally' echoed across the arena, a then concert-going in joke reference to a Who roadie. Promoter Ricki Farr made a brief announcement and then on they came to rapturous applause. It was evident how loud it was going to be when Bonzo rattled around the kit and Jimmy flexed the Gibson. Then 1-2-3-4 Blam! I was watching Led Zeppelin perform 'Immigrant Song' in front of my own eyes … and nothing would ever be the same again.''

Peter Grant: "It was a chance to do something different and we had the circus acts and the pigs and we had them dressed up in policemen's helmets. One of them shit backstage and I turned to Robert and said 'Don't worry, he's just nervous – it's the first time he's played a big gig!'"

Tuesday November 23 1971
Preston, England Public Hall

John Bonham's brother Mick recalled in his book *Bonham On Bonham* how he was tricked into playing congos on stage at this show. "Mick Hinton came over and said that John wanted a pint of mild and he wanted me to fetch it. I crouched down and tried to get there without being noticed John grabbed my arm and pointed to a set of congos behind his kit and shouted 'Play them!' Before I could reply 'How?' the opening riff of /Whole Lotta Love/ kicked in. Though I say so myself I thought I was doing OK.''

Wednesday November 24 1971
Manchester, England Free Trade Hall
Set: Immigrant Song/Heartbreaker/Black Dog/Since I've Been Loving You/Celebration Day/Stairway To Heaven/Going To California/That's The Way/Tangerine/Bron Yr Aur Stomp/Dazed And Confused (inc. Theme >From Shaft)/What Is And What Should Never

'til half past six, and it's nice to be back ... I dunno, where are we? In Manchester. Manchester, right! It's good to be back."

'Celebration Day' was again advanced its position in the set and was played after 'Since I've Been Loving You'. 'Dazed And Confused' continued to evolve and Page even included a section from 'The Theme From Shaft', currently a popular movie and a hit single for Isaac Hayes. The 'Whole Lotta Love' medley included 'Rave On', the only known performance of this Buddy Holly classic.

Bootleg CD Reference: *Rave On* (The Diagrams Of Led Zeppelin)

Thursday November 25 1971

Leicester, England
Queens Hall, Percy
Gee Building
Leicester University

Set: Immigrant Song/ Heartbreaker/ Black Dog/ Since I've Been Loving You/ Celebration Day/ Going To California/ That's The Way/ Tangerine (including false start)/ Bron-Yr-Aur Stomp / Dazed And Confused (incl. Theme From Shaft)/ Stairway To Heaven / What Is And What Should Never Be/ Whole Lotta Love (include. Just A Little Bit/ I'm Going Down/ Boogie Woogie/ Mary Lou/ Rave On/ Mess O' The Blues/ Squeeze My Lemon)/ Rock And Roll/ Communication Breakdown.

Local Leicester musician Kevin Hewick (then 14) attended the show with his uncle Joe: "My uncle managed to smuggle in his ITT tape recorder. He told me afterwards that he saw the security guys stomping on some machines that were discovered. He managed to tape the whole gig stopping for a change of cassette during 'Whole Lotta Love'. The surviving tape also has a few minutes of post-gig banter between my uncle and his friends. The dialogue runs like this. "The sound wasn't bad was it'?

"No not as bad as The Pink Fairies. When I saw The Who it was all light show and that. Tonight they just walked on and looked like four human beings. The violin bow sounded like Yoko Ono

Be/Rock And Roll/Whole Lotta Love (inc. Boogie Chillun' – Rave On – Hello Mary Lou)/Thank You.

With the pressure of the London Empire Pool shows behind them, they began to loosen up and produced one of the most enjoyable shows of the tour, to a very appreciative audience.

The show started with an apology. "We're sorry about the delay, but there was some ice on the motorway, and John Paul Jones wanted two helpings of apple pie!"

Plant complained of having a cold: "Gosh I think I got that flu that's going about. I was in bed

wailing. That's what she does. It was a bit crammed in there though not as bad as The Who. Overall it was really good. Mind you the *Melody Maker* said not to expect too much. 'Stairway' was really good. Wish they'd done 'Friends 'and 'Gallows Pole' though.''

Bootleg CD References: *Mystical Majesties Request* (Electric Magic), *Best For Hard 'N' Heavy* (Empress Valley Supreme)

Monday November 29 1971
Liverpool, England
Liverpool Stadium

Fan Andy Duncan recalled: ''My brother went to this show and it was at the stadium – this was regularly used as a venue for wrestling. Plant made a comment about that at this show a year later at the Liverpool Empire. During the 'Boogie Chillun' intro you can hear him sing 'One night I was laying down … I believe we told you this when we went to that place where they did the wrestling'.''

Tuesday November 30 1971
Manchester, England
King's Hall Belle Vue

This show was added to the original itinerary after the Free Trade Hall show had sold out.

After the first encore, the crowd invaded the stage bringing an abrupt end to the show.

Thursday December 2 1971
Bournemouth, England
Starkers, Royal Ballrooms

Set: Immigrant Song/Heartbreaker/Black Dog/ Since I've Been Loving You/Stairway To

Heaven/Going To California/That's The Way/Tangerine/Bron-yr-Aur Stomp/ Dazed And Confused/What Is And What Should Never Be/Rock And Roll/ Whole Lotta Love (incl. Just a Little Bit, Hideaway, Trucking Little Mama, Boogie Chillun', (small cut) Heartbeat, Hello Mary Lou, Lawdy Miss Clawdy, I Can't Quit You)/Communication Breakdown/Weekend/ It'll Be Me

This show was promoted by Mel Bush who would go on to be one of the most ambitious UK concert promoters of the era and would link up with Peter Grant to present Led Zeppelin at Earls Court four years later.

A rather chaotic show. 'Rock And Roll' was performed late in the set tonight, after a request from a member of the audience. There was an equipment problem in the middle of the number and the whole band stopped playing, leaving Plant alone singing the lyrics.

'Whole Lotta Love' featured the only known rendition of Buddy Holly's 'Heartbeat'.

Bootleg CD References: *Heartbeat* (H-Bomb Music), *Rock And Roll Magic* (Electric Magic)

Thursday December 9 1971
Coventry, England
Locarno Ballroom

This low-key show was added at the last minute, but was most eventful. After three numbers, resident DJ Pete Waterman (later to become successful as a member of the Stock, Aitken & Waterman production team and *Pop Idol* TV talent spotter) went on stage and advised everyone to clear the building as there had been a bomb scare.

Fan Simon Croon recalled: ''The concert was interrupted by a bomb scare – this was at the height of the IRA campaigns. However, the half arsed efforts at evacuation by security and police simply allowed many of us to move down the front!''

The show was later restarted. During 'Dazed And Confused' Jimmy lost his grip on the violin bow and saw it fly into the crowd.

Wednesday December 15 1971
Salisbury, England
City Hall – **CANCELLED**
This date was cancelled after Jimmy went down with flu and rescheduled for the following week. However there was a gig here tonight thanks to Peter Grant who, due to the late cancellation, paid for the hall so that support acts Jerusalem and Marble Orchard could perform.

Tuesday December 21 1971
Salisbury, England
City Hall

The rescheduled date was the final show of an eventful and fulfilling year. 'Lawdy Miss Clawdy' and 'Mystery Train' were featured in the 'Whole Lotta Love' medley.

AUSTRALIA – NEW ZEALAND 1972

Peter Grant dispatched tour manager Richard Cole to check out the venues for this Australasian adventure in late 1971. The original plan was for them to stop off en route for a date on February 14 in Singapore but the authorities there refused them entry due to local regulations banning long hair. Unless they cut their hair, there would be no concert. Needless to say they did not comply.

Instead, the band travelled via Air India, stopping off in Bombay. The six-date tour, comprising mostly open air shows, was a big success with record breaking attendances. Some 25,000 came to see them in Auckland, with trains specially chartered in from the islands. The set list broadly picked up where they had left off last year with an ever expanding rock and roll medley, extending to include such numbers as Elvis' 'Let's Have A Party'. Surprisingly, 'Rock And Roll' was dropped from the main set and only performed occasionally. Zeppelin enjoyed generally good press coverage and snatches of the Sydney show and a press party were filmed and shown on national television. Overall this was a highly successful visit to a new territory.

On the way back from the tour Jimmy and Robert stopped off in Bombay again and recorded 'Friends' and 'Four Sticks' with the Bombay Symphony Orchestra in the local EMI studios. It was these arrangements (never officially released) that would be the basis for the MTV *Unledded – No Quarter* reunion versions by Page & Plant some 22 years later.

Equipment Notes:
During this period John Paul Jones began to use a fretless Fender Jazz bass for 'Bron Yr Aur Stomp'. Jimmy continued using the cutaway Gretsch for acoustic numbers, including 'Tangerine'. For the Australian trip, Bonzo used a new green Ludwig set-up with white rims, returning to his more familiar kit for the US tour.

Just prior to the Australian trip Peter Grant received an invitation for "Led Zeppelin and his musicians" to participate in the annual Midem Music Festival, a music industry gathering held in Cannes every January.

It would seem that despite their worldwide success, the organisers of the world's biggest music trade fair had failed to grasp that "Led" wasn't a solo singer with backing musicians. In a clever and cynical response, Grant caused maximum embarrassment by reprinting their letter of invitation in full under the headline "Mr Zeppelin regrets …" in a full page advert in the music trade

MR. ZEPPELIN REGRETS......

paper *Record Retailer* during Midem week. "I mean... Bernard Chevry, the guy who sent it, was a prat," said Peter.

Just prior to leaving for the tour, the band held a photo session in a Baker Street photo studio with Chris Dreja, the former Yardbird who had taken the back cover photo of the first Zeppelin album.

Sunday 6 February 1972
Wolverhampton, England
Lafayette Club
GUEST APPEARANCE

Robert and Bonzo jammed with Fairport Convention at an impromptu gig. Fairport press officer Frances Van Staden stated: "Officially Fairport with their new guitarist Roger Hill were not planning any appearances together until later this month in Holland and Belgium."

Tuesday February 14 1972
Singapore, Hong Kong
CANCELLED

Record Mirror reported: "Plans for a concert in Singapore by Led Zeppelin have had to be abandoned – because of their long hair!

"But the group Middle Of The Road have decided to take a middle course by getting theirs cut for their Singapore engagement.

"The Singapore authorities will not admit anyone with long hair into their territory and the concert promoters told Zeppelin that they must have their hair cut short or there could be no concert.

"Instead the group are visiting Bombay for two days on their way to Australia. They may call at Bombay again on their way home to do some recording. A spokesman for Middle Of The Road said that when the three boys in the group heard about the Singapore hair stipulation they agreed to conform by getting comparatively short back and sides."

Wednesday February 16 1972
Perth, Australia
Subiaco Oval

This first concert in Australasia led to A run in with the authorities. At the concert, there were skirmishes between police and fans and in the early hours of the following morning, at the White Sands Hotel, the group were victims of an unsuccessful raid by the local drugs squad.

'Mêlée At Pop Show' read one news report. "About 500 youths were involved in a mêlée outside the Subiaco Oval last night during a concert by pop group Led Zeppelin. About 4,000 people who were unable to gain entry to the concert milled outside the main gates of the Oval and lit fires. Many of the people who were unable to buy tickets to the concert climbed the fences, cut holes in fence wire and pulled gates from their hinges in an attempt to join the 8,000 people already in the ground. People living in the areas from Leederville to Wembley telephoned the central police and Newspaper House last night to complain about the noise."

'Heavy Rock With Discipline' read another report: "Perth has probably never heard a concert quite like it. Certainly a Festival of Perth has never been so 'heavy'. The Led Zeppelin rock group's only concert at Subiaco Oval last night was unique. The 8,000 people who went enjoyed every minute of the two and a half hour performance.

"Soon after the concert began, Robert Plant told the audience: 'We took 36 hours to get here, so we are going to have a good time.' That drew a wild cheer from the audience. The sound produced by amplifiers placed on each side of the stage was at times painfully loud. Perhaps for the older eardrums, a few less decibels would have been appreciated."

According to other newspaper reports Zeppelin were the victims of an 8am drug raid. "Four drug police today raided the visiting English group, Led Zeppelin. The raid was carried out at a Scarborough hotel where the group was staying. Police woke the musicians and searched their baggage and belongings. No drugs were found. The raid followed last night's riot at Subiaco Oval. The group's lead guitarist, Jimmy Page, said he and the rest of the group were furious. They thought the raid was in retribution for the concert trouble."

It was also reported that the Australian Premier would look into the raid. 'Tonkin Will Order Report on Drug Raid', read a headline. "The Premier, Mr Tonkin, said last night that he would call for a report on a raid by Drug Squad police on the visiting English pop group, Led Zeppelin. No drugs were found and no police action was taken. Mr Tonkin said last night that some aspects of the police raid puzzled him. 'I am wondering that as they had not been able to find any drugs, what information they acted on,' Mr Tonkin said.

"The Subiaco City Council announced yesterday that in future it would enforce a clause that restricted the sound output produced by pop groups at performances at the Oval."

After the Perth concert, the band visited a local nightclub and ended up jamming some old rock-'n'roll favourites including 'Teddy Bear'.

Plant: "Nothing really happened in Perth. I think it's what they call 'all in the mind'. There was a concert, a very successful concert. At the same time there was the usual element of people who are part of every corner of society who decided they'd bring wire-cutters and cut their way in, and I also found that the police over here haven't really sorted out ways of handling situations like this. I don't know whether they can even be handled.

"But anyway, although we were playing we didn't even know it was happening. There were people coming over the fences and all that and there were people phoning the Mayor and saying this is too much. Somewhere, someone along the line is worried that these things can take place. I'm worried about the fact that they can be abused because the basic idea is to have a wonderful time and see everyone glow, really glow."

While in Perth the band recorded a series of interviews and promo trailers for the 3XY radio station.

Saturday February 19 1972
Adelaide, Australia
Memorial Drive
Set: Immigrant Song/Heartbreaker/Black Dog/Since I've Been Loving You/Stairway To Heaven/Going To California/That's The Way/Tangerine/Bron Yr Aur Stomp/Dazed And Confused/Moby Dick/Whole Lotta Love (inc. Boogie Chillun – Hello Mary Lou – Let's Have A Party – That's Alright Mama – Going Down Slow – The Shape I'm In).

This concert was originally scheduled to take place on February 18, but was postponed by one day, on the day of the gig, due to a buckled stage and damp amplification equipment.

The concert had previously been in jeopardy when it was realised that Creedence Clearwater Revival were also playing in town at the Apollo Stadium on February 17 and 18. After negotiations between the promoter, Trevor Hunt, and the managers of the two bands, a compromise was reached whereby Creedence would play only on February 17 and Zeppelin on February 18.

It was another strong performance despite some vocal problems for Plant.

Page led into 'Dazed And Confused' with a few licks of Hendrix's 'Voodoo Chile'. 'Dazed' was shorter tonight (only 20 minutes!) but intense and featured a new high speed solo from Page. Elvis' 'Let's Have A Party' was now added to the 'Whole Lotta Love' medley and would be one of the highlights of all the Australian shows.

Fan David F. Brown recalled: "I was lucky enough to see this show and attend the soundcheck. At the same time they were doing that there was a cricket match going on at the Adelaide Oval. Apparently the Zeppelin soundcheck started to seep into the live cricket commentary which led to some frantic calls to the ABC network! I remember that prior to them coming on for the gig the music played over the PA was The Allman Brothers' *Live At The Fillmore* album. Towards the end of the show the small crowd who had gathered outside the venue pushed down a wire fence and gatecrashed the last few songs."

Press reaction to the show was favourable. "Led Zeppelin Is Shattering Rock Experience – The Led Zeppelin concert at Memorial Drive on Saturday was a shattering experience of some of the world's heaviest and wildest rock. The controlled violence with which the UK group produced many of its sounds, hurled out of two giant banks of speakers at the 8,000 strong crowd, has never been seen before. From the start, all eyes were on brilliant lead guitarist, Jimmy Page. His electric guitar work was extraordinary. At one stage, using a bow, he smashed out a string of piercing notes only to end with a delicate run of sitar-sounding music. Thunderous applause followed all his work."

Robert Plant: "Adelaide was a bit like a sort of mid-west cow-town in America. It's a shame really because my voice was a bit rough. We'd been travelling a lot and not sleeping and everything like that and I went on – there were people shrieking and shouting and fights ten feet from the stage and I was getting really upset because this is the last thing any of us in the group like to see, because we're pretty intent in what we're doing, especially as we've got a good following here. And there was all that going on in front of us, and no organised security. Well, there was a little guy of about 80 with a flash-lamp and that was about it.

"Every time you call to the cops over here 'Get a barrier line so we can get off' or make sure everything's OK, everybody turns their head and ignores you."

Bootleg CD References: *Voodoo Drive* (Akashic), *Voodoo Drive* (Tarantura), *Oooh My Ears, Man* (Diagrams Of Led Zeppelin), *Thunder Downunder Australia Tour 1972* (Equinox)

Sunday February 20 1972
Melbourne, Australia Kooyong Stadium

Set includes – Immigrant Song/Heartbreaker /Black Dog/Since I've Been Loving/Stairway To Heaven/Going To California/That's The Way/Tangerine/Bron Yr Aur Stomp/Dazed And Confused/Rock And Roll/Whole Lotta Love (inc. Boogie Chillun' – Let's Have A Party).

The show kicked off to a great start with Page in a playful mood adding 'Feelin' Groovy' to the 'Heartbreaker' solo. Plant took time to dispel some rumours: "You might have heard about Perth. It was all a lie! I tell you, you've got to watch it. We've all got to watch it. Time is running short. They'll send me to a penal colony for saying that."

Before a wild and fluent 'Dazed And Confused' they light-heartedly played some of the theme music to BBC Radio's *Workers' Playtime* programme.

During 'Dazed', the skies opened and water began to gather on the uncovered stage. Plant changed the lyrics of the final verse to "Well, it's started to rain, I think it's time we gotta go. If we don't go now, we're gonna die, I don't wanna know!" The band then left the stage.

The rain subsided after a while and Zeppelin returned for a fast and frantic 'Rock And Roll'. They attempted the 'Whole Lotta Love' medley but were forced to cut it short after 'Let's Have A Party', when the rain poured down. Plant: 'Thank you very much. We gotta go and you gotta go too, otherwise we'll all blow up! We can't do it because electricity and water don't get together at all, but we've had a wonderful time. Good day!"

Australian Press reports included: "The Sounds of a Zeppelin – Ears are probably still ringing following yesterday's pop concert at the Kooyong Stadium. More than 12,000 pop fans crowded the stadium yesterday afternoon and had their ears blasted by one of the world's most popular rock groups, Led Zeppelin. The sound from the group's wall of amplifiers and speakers not only filled the stadium in Glenferrie Road, Kooyong, but could be heard miles away. Many pop fans saved themselves the price of a ticket and listened to the music from outside the stadium. Several others saved themselves the price of a ticket by jumping over fences to get into the arena."

Under the headline 'So loud, even rain backed off', Issi Dy for *Weekender* wrote: "Robert Plant's voice took everybody's breath away at the sheer power and guts. It was the biggest P.A. I'd ever seen. Apparently the equipment brought out by the group weighed 5 tons! Although Plant's erotic movements and brilliant singing won the audience completely, it was easy to see who led the group. Guitarist Jimmy Page kept the group tightly in rein and played some of the best guitar patterns yet heard in this country. He changed guitars several times to produce the right effects,

varying from acoustic blues to wild-feedback rock'n'roll.

"About three-quarters of the way through the show it began raining and the group stopped playing for fear of an electric short circuit. The audience screamed for more. However, 10 minutes later, as if even the clouds were shaken by the tremendous volume, Led Zeppelin came back with 'Whole Lotta Love' and had the crowd standing on the seats, yelling approval. Bathing my ears later that night I hoped that we will see Led Zeppelin again – soon!"

After the show, the band attended a gold record reception at Melbourne's Southern Cross Hotel where they were staying.

Plant: "I thought the Melbourne audience were about the warmest thing I've felt in Australia yet – warmer even than the climate, really good. I think Perth was the best we've played yet – we'd just landed and we were full of Bombay and full of travelling, but nevertheless, today was warmer. You could see the people and you could see the colours. Everybody was grooving and everybody was smiling. Even the elements couldn't hold it back."

The photo on the front cover of the original, large format edition of this book was taken from this show.
Bootleg CD References: *Acoustically* (The Diagrams Of Led Zeppelin), *The Wet Head Is Dead Downunder 1972* (Empress Valley)

Friday February 25 1972
Auckland, New Zealand
Western Springs Stadium
Set included – Immigrant Song/Heartbreaker/ Black Dog/Since I've Been Loving You/Stairway To Heaven/Going To California/That's The Way/Tangerine/Bron Yr Aur Stomp/Dazed And Confused/Moby Dick/Whole Lotta Love/ Communication Breakdown

Peter Grant: "Fantastic gigs! New Zealand was the biggest public gathering in the history of the island."

A special 'Led Zeppelin' train was chartered from Wellington to bring fans to the concert – an idea Grant would later apply to the staging of the 1975 Earl's Court shows.

Rolling Stone reported: "The arrival of Zeppelin brought a near-catatonic reaction from the country's rock freaks, who descended on Auckland from as far away as Dunedin (the other end of the country: about 900 miles) for the open-air concert. Seats sold at $3.10 and $4.10 and somewhere between 20,000 and 25,000 filled the Western Springs Stadium (a couple of miles from Auckland city and usually used for stock cars).

After the Auckland show, the band visited a strip-club. One of the strippers followed the band back to the White Heron Hotel and was duly thrown in the pool at 5am.

Bootleg CD References: *Going To Auckland* (Tarantura), *Going To Auckland* (Akashic), *Live In Aukland* (Genuine Masters)

Sunday February 27 1972
Sydney, Australia
Sydney Showground

Set included – Immigrant Song/Heartbreaker/ Black Dog Since I've Been Loving You/Stairway To Heaven/Going To California/That's The Way/Tangerine /Bron Yr Aur Stomp/Dazed And Confused/ What Is And What Should Never Be/Moby Dick/Rock And Roll/Whole Lotta Love medley (incl Boogie Chillun'-Hello Mary Lou/The Rover-Lets Have A Party-Lawdy Miss Clawdy-Going Down Slow)/Communication Breakdown/Organ Solo/Thank You.

By this show Page appeared newly clean shaven, having shaved off the beard he had grown since the summer of 1970.

Plant laid down some ground rules from the start: "Now listen! We've already come across the one problem we were told about. Now, there's been a lot of mistakes about this thing, but we don't want to make any mistakes and neither do you, right? So don't come past this barrier, otherwise there's gonna be some shit. And why don't you sit down … and if it rains, we're gonna have to stop. That's a fact, it'll blow up! Take a seat!"

The highlight of the show occurred during the 'Whole Lotta Love' medley. After 'Hello Mary Lou', Plant lost his way for a moment so Page filled the gap with an instrumental version of 'The Rover'. This was a work in progress composition intended for their fifth album but subsequently held over to surface on the *Physical Graffiti* double album. It was the only known full version of the song performed live.

Australian press reported: 'Pop Goes the Showground': "Ecstatic young fans filled five stands, the concourse beneath the stands and nearly half of the Show-ground arena yesterday for a concert by the English group Led Zeppelin. The official crowd figure was stated as being between 26,000 and 28,000 – the largest audience for a Sydney pop concert. This tally exceeded recent big concerts in Sydney – Deep Purple and The Bee Gees."

'Balloon Goes Up On Led Zeppelin': "The balloon went up when thousands of excited fans surged over a five-foot fence at the Showground to mob the visiting English pop group, Led Zeppelin. Police and security guards rushed to stop the fans but had to give up. The lead singer of the group, Robert Plant, pleaded with the crowd to sit down and shut up. This appeal succeeded where police efforts had failed. The three-hour show led to major traffic jams in Anzac Parade as the crowd made its way home about 5am."

While in Sydney, the band visited Bonaparte's and Chequers night-clubs.

Silent colour cine film of this show was shot by a roadie for the band's personal archive. It included scenes of the empty arena, fans arriving and live footage shot at the side of the stage. Page used some of this footage on the official DVD cut to the June 27 Long Beach version of 'Immigrant Song'.

Bootleg CD Reference: *Ayer's Rock* (Tarantura)
Visual References: Official *Led Zeppelin* 2003 DVD (Warner Music Vision), *Early Visions* (Uno-

fficial- Celebration), *The Rovers Return* (Genuine Masters)

February 1972
Sydney, Australia
GTK ABC TV
TV APPEARANCE
While in the Australia the band did make themselves more available to the media. They allowed a press reception and interviews to be filmed by Australian Broadcasting Corporation for broadcast in black and white on the weekly Sunday night programme GTK. Held in Sydney by the record company, it included footage of a young Germaine Greer mingling with Plant and Jones. Plant talked in a very broad black country accent about the Perth police raid. JPJ discussed George Harrison's recent Bangla Desh benefit shows and asked if they would consider making a film, he tellingly replied "Undoubtedly we will get around to it". Bonzo came over as very articulate when commenting on the changes on their music.

ABC also filmed parts of the Sydney concert, including a snippet of 'Whole Lotta Love', all of 'Rock And Roll' and 'Let's Have A Party' plus footage of them making their way off stage.

This footage would eventually be salvaged and edited for use as an extra five minute item on the official DVD.

Visual References: Official *Led Zeppelin* 2003 DVD (Warner Music Vision), *Early Visions* (Unofficial – Celebration), *The Rovers Return* (Unofficial-Genuine Masters), *1970-1972* (Unofficial – Cosmic Energy)

Tuesday February 29 1972
Brisbane, Australia
Festival Hall
Set: Immigrant Song/Heartbreaker/Black Dog/Since I've Been Loving You/Celebration Day/Stairway To Heaven/Going To California/That's The Way/Tangerine/Bron Yr Aur Stomp/Dazed And Confused/What Is And What Should Never Be/Moby Dick/Whole Lotta Love (inc.

Boogie Chillun' – High Flyin' Mama – The Wanderer – Hello Mary Lou – Let's Have A Party – Going Down Slow – The Shape I'm In).

The tour ended with the only indoor show of the tour and a fine performance before a boisterous crowd. During the 'Whole Lotta Love' medley they turned in a version of Dion's 'The Wanderer' – another one off performance.

Bootleg CD Reference: *Stompin In Surfers Paradise* (Cobra)

March 1972
Bombay, India
EMI Studios
RECORDING SESSIONS

On the way back from Australia Page and Plant stopped off in Bombay to record a session with the Bombay Symphony Orchestra. They recorded versions of 'Friends' and 'Four Sticks'. Though never officially released, tapes from these sessions have appeared on bootlegs.

Bootleg References: *All That Glitters Is Gold* (Celebration), *Lost Sessions Vol 2* (Empress Valley)

April/May 1972
Stargroves, Newbury, Berkshire, England
Olympic Studios, Barnes, England
RECORDING SESSIONS

Sessions for their fifth album commenced on location at Mick Jagger's county house Stargroves. Working with engineer Eddie Kramer they took to the open air to record 'Black Country Woman' which would eventually surface on *Physical Graffiti*. A photo of this session can be seen in the booklet for the *Latter Days The Best Of Led Zeppelin Vol Two* CD.

At Olympic tracks such as 'Dancing Days', 'The Song Remains The Same', 'Walters Walk' and 'No Quarter' took shape.

Bootleg Reference: *Sugar Mama Alternative Coda* (CG)

In 2004 Eddie Kramer put up for auction early mix reel-to-reel tapes from this era. One of the tapes was a completed 7-inch reel of the *Houses Of The Holy* album for which the track 'Over The Hills And Far Away' was listed under the title 'Many Many Times'. The tapes attracted bids of over $700,000 dollars.

AMERICA 1972

This month-long 19-date stretch that followed two little-publicised warm-up dates in Holland and Belgium may have been the lowest profile tour of all Led Zeppelin's American visits but as the belated official live set *How The West Was Won* revealed years later – in performance terms it was possibly the best.

Vastly overshadowed by The Rolling Stones' US tour of the same period, they found themselves performing some of their most adventurous shows to little press acclaim. The exception was a perceptive piece by Roy Hollingworth for *Melody Maker* which went out under the headline 'Led Zeppelin – The Forgotten Giants?'

It was around this period that Peter Grant began to implement his 90% of the gate receipts policy. The group's stature was such that he was able to pull off this major swing with little resistance from the agents and promoters. Any deal with Led Zeppelin was better than no deal at all, they decided. As a consequence Led Zeppelin's treasure chest began to pile up at an even faster rate.

While in New York in June, they spent time

mixing down tracks that had been recorded at Olympic Studios in England the previous month. The track 'Houses Of The Holy' was also laid down at the New York sessions though it did not make the final fifth album selection. The tour itself had plenty of preview extracts from this 'work in progress' fifth album – 'The Ocean', 'Dancing Days', 'The Crunge' (inserted in 'Dazed And Confused'), and 'Over The Hills And Far Away'. 'Black Country Woman' (later to appear on *Physical Graffiti*) also receives a try out – a policy that was in stark contrast to the inflexibility of the sets of their latter era. With the acoustic segment still intact, the shows were beginning to run to three hour marathons. The off-the-wall song selections of these dates made for some of the most interesting of their entire career, particularly in light of the fact that much of the tour went unrecorded in the press.

Being ignored by the press was certainly not lost on them and in a rare interview at the time John Paul Jones summed up their frustrations. "Here we are slaving away constantly getting incredible reactions and nobody back home seems to care," he said. John Bonham added: "It's the Stones this... the Stones that ... it made us feel we were flogging our guts out and for all the notice we were being given we might as well have been playing in Ceylon. Kids in England didn't even know if we were touring the States. It comes across as though we're neglecting them, which of course we're not."

It would be an entirely different story on their next visit in 11 months time. Grant began to realise that it was time to hire a proper PR team and recruited BP Fallon in the UK and, later, Danny Goldberg from the respected Solters, Roskin & Sabinson agency, for the US.

This may have been a low key tour but in hindsight it produced some of their most interesting set lists and consistently excellent performances. They may not have been receiving the press acclaim they felt they were due but this visit certainly had a lasting impression on all those in attendance – one that would inspire remarkable crowd scenes when Zeppelin returned twelve months later. Some 30 years on every Led Zeppelin fan would have first hand evidence of just how good they were at this stage of their career when Page compiled the *How The West Was Won* live set from the Los Angeles and Long Beach shows.

Saturday May 27 1972
Amsterdam, Holland
Oude Rai

Set included – Immigrant Song/Heartbreaker/ Black Dog/Since I've Been Loving You/ Celebration Day/Stairway To Heaven/Bron Yr Aur Stomp/Dazed And Confused/What Is And What Should Never Be/Moby Dick/Whole Lotta Love (inc. Everybody Needs Somebody – Boogie Chillun – Hello Mary Lou – Running Bear – That's Alright Mama – Hoochie Coochie Man – Going Down Slow – The Shape I'm In)/Rock And Roll/Communication Breakdown.

The first of two warm-up shows for the forthcoming US tour. The band were somewhat rusty, resulting in situations such as Plant trying to sing over Page's solo in 'Celebration Day'. Page was excellent in 'Dazed And Confused', adding riffs from 'The Crunge' which has just been recorded the month before at Stargroves.

'Whole Lotta Love' now included an instrumental version of Solomon Burke's 'Everybody Needs Somebody' prior to 'Boogie Chillun''. This would be greatly expanded on in the future. The medley also featured the rare additions of Johnny

Preston's 'Running Bear' and 'Hoochie Coochie Man'.

Bootleg CD Reference: *Running Bear* (Gold Standard), *Dancing Bear* (Tarantura) *Amsterdam 1972* (MMachine)

June 1972
Amsterdam, Holland
Hard Rock Heaven CCTV
TV APPEARANCE

While in Amsterdam, Zeppelin were filmed by for the local CCTV network. The black and white footage included scenes of them entering their hotel, Richard Cole opening a briefcase full of cash and talking to the promoter and a short excerpt of them performing 'Immigrant Song' at the concert. This was screened on a programme called *Hard Rock Heaven*.

Visual Reference:
Early visions DVD (Unofficial – Celebration), *1970-1972* (Unofficial – Cosmic Energy)

Sunday May 28 1972
Brussels, Belgium
Vorst Nationaal

Set included- Immigrant Song/ Heartbreaker/ Black Dog/Since I've Been Loving You /Stairway To Heaven/ Going To California/That's the Way/ Bron-Y-Aur Stomp/Dazed & Confused/ What Is & What Should Never Be/ Whole Lotta Love (includes Everybody Needs Somebody to Love, Boogie Woogie, Hello Mary Lou, Running Bear, Lawdy Miss Clawdy, Heartbreak Hotel, Dont Be Cruel, Millionaire Blues, Going Down Slow, Shape Im In)

Bootleg CD References: *Burning Ticket* (Babyface), *Belguim Triple* (Empress Valley)

Tuesday June 6 1972
Detroit, Michigan
Cobo Hall

Wednesday June 7 1972
Montreal, Canada
Montreal Forum

Set includes – Immigrant Song/Heartbreaker/ Black Dog/Since I've Been Loving You/ Stairway To Heaven/ Going To California/ That's The Way/ Tan-gerine/Bron Yr Aur Stomp/Dazed And Confused/What Is And What Should Never Be/Moby Dick/Whole Lotta Love (inc. Boogie Chillun').

As in America, the Canadian crowd bordered on the unruly, with firecrackers a constant threat.

Plant: "I can hear it. It really doesn't sound so good. Everywhere we go around the country, everybody wants somebody else to stand up or sit down and every time I say anything about one thing or the other, there's lots of chaos. So can you sit down?"

'Since I've Been Loving You' had an almost jazzy solo tonight and 'Dazed And Confused' now included an instrumental section based on 'Walter's Walk' – another new number recorded the previous month at Olympic Studios and eventually released in 1982 on the *Coda* set.

Bootleg CD Reference: *Red Snapper Deluxe* (Balboa Productions)

UNCONFIRMED
Thursday June 8 1972
Boston, Massachusettes
Boston Garden

No hard evidence of this show taking place has surfaced.

Friday June 9 1972
Charlotte, North Carolina
Charlotte Coliseum

Set: Immigrant Song/Heartbreaker/Celebration Day/Black Dog/Since I've Been Loving You/Stairway To Heaven/Going To California/That's The Way/Tangerine/Bron Yr Aur Stomp/Dazed And Confused/What Is And What Should Never Be/Moby Dick/Whole Lotta Love (inc. Everybody Needs Somebody)/Rock And Roll/Communication Breakdown.

A relaxed show found the band getting into their stride. 'Celebration Day', which had been dropped from the set list, surprisingly appeared as the third number for this show. It would not be played again on this tour.

Before 'Stairway To Heaven', the band jokingly ran through 'Knees Up Mother Brown', a Cockney sing-along. "Actually, that's on the next album!" quipped Robert.

'Dazed And Confused' was rather chaotic. The audience have started to sway backwards and forwards and Plant ad-libbed the lyrics: "Cool It! Cool It! Don't do it, if you don't want no trouble!" Plant: "What we gotta try to do is reach some form of rapport with the officialdom. So, whatever you do, don't collapse the stage. Don't sit on the stage, otherwise we're all gonna blow it. OK?"

'Whole Lotta Love', surprisingly, had no medley. After a brief jam on the 'Everybody Needs Somebody' riff, Robert teased the crowd pretending to go into 'Boogie Chillun', but instead headed straight for the finale.

Bootleg CD References: *Charlotte 1972* (The Diagrams Of Led Zeppelin), *Knees Up Mother Brown* (Image Quality), *Acoustic Tales In Charlotte* (Continental Sounds)

Saturday June 10 1972
Buffalo, New York
Memorial Auditorium
Before this show, the group attended Elvis Presley's early evening performance at Madison Square Garden.

After the Buffalo show, they ventured on to New York's Bitter End club to watch Paul Gurvitz and later called in at the infamous Nobody's, a Greenwich Village bar often frequented by visiting English musicians. It was reported they livened the place up with vocal renditions of 'Blue Moon' and 'Roll A Bowl A Ball A Penny A Pitch'.

Sunday June 11 1972
Baltimore, Maryland
Civic Center
Set: Immigrant Song/Heartbreaker/Black Dog/Since I've Been Loving You/Stairway To Heaven/Going To California/That's The Way/Tangerine/Bron Yr Aur Stomp/Dazed And Confused/What Is And What Should Never Be/Moby Dick/Whole Lotta Love (inc. Everybody Needs Somebody – Boogie Chillun' – I Need Your Love Tonight – Hello Mary Lou – Heartbreak Hotel – I'm Going Down – Going Down Slow – The Shape I'm In)/Rock And Roll/Communication Breakdown.

This show got off to a bad start with Robert having trouble with the lyrics to 'Immigrant Song' and repeating the first line twice, but it developed into the best night of the tour so far.

'Since I've Been Loving You' was introduced as 'a song of love, a triangle of love' and was an outstanding performance. "This is conceived in a moment of blindness – when blindness meets the dark!" was Robert's rather pretentious introduction to 'Stairway To Heaven'.

Before the acoustic set, Robert told the crowd about the Elvis concert: "We went to see Elvis Presley. That guy did so much for music – long time ago, mind you! His voice has gone down about two or three tones and seemed to have changed a bit and his waist is a bit bigger."

Bonham joined the band on vocals for 'Bron Yr Aur Stomp'. Plant: "We'd like to put a spotlight on our percussionist who's singing. This is the ninth tour of America and we finally got him to a microphone. Weighing 204 pounds, the good times have put their toll on him!"

There was no 'Crunge' section tonight in 'Dazed And Confused', but Plant added jazz-like scat vocals to the 'Walter's Walk' segment.

'Moby Dick' was the longest of the tour tonight, clocking in at 28 minutes and 'Whole Lotta Love' had some rare inclusions in the form of 'I Need Your Love Tonight' and 'I'm Going Down'. Obviously inspired by their recent concert visit, Elvis' 'Heartbreak Hotel' was also added to the repertoire.

Bootleg Cd References: *Baltimore 1972* (Immigrant), *Baltimore Jack* (The Diagrams of Led Zeppelin), *Nutty And Cool* (Baby Face)

Led Zeppelin

Tuesday June 13 1972
Philadelphia, Pennsylvania
The Spectrum
This show was added to the original itinerary. Tickets went on sale May 25.

Wednesday June 14 1972
Uniondale, New York
Nassau Coliseum
Set included: Immigrant Song/Heartbreaker/ Black Dog/Since I've Been Loving You/Stairway To Heaven/Going To California/Tangerine/Bron Yr Aur Stomp/Dazed And Confused (inc. The Crunge)/What Is And What Should Never Be/Moby Dick/Whole Lotta Love (inc. Everybody Needs Somebody – Boogie Chillun' – High Flyin' Mama – Hello Mary Lou – Lawdy Miss Clawdy – Going Down Slow – The Shape I'm In)/Rock And Roll/Communication Breakdown (inc. The Lemon Song)/Weekend/Bring It On Home.

Zeppelin were on excellent form by the time they hit New York and this time around they

played at the 16,000 capacity Nassau Coliseum. Plant: "I tell you what, I feel a lot better than I did at Madison Square Garden!"

The audience were responsive and well-behaved, and were rewarded with bonus encores including Eddie Cochran's 'Weekend' and a wild 'Bring It On Home' which had the whole auditorium joining in. Plant: "I wanna hear you louder than us!"

'Stairway To Heaven' tonight included the first ever Plant 'Do you remember laughter?' ad-lib.

Roy Hollingworth of *Melody Maker* reviewed the band's triumphant return to New York under the headline 'Whole Lotta Led': "It was one of the most amazing concerts I'd seen from any band, at any time. Nothing had gone missing, it had been the complete act. There had been power, climax after climax, beauty, funk, rock, boogie, totally freaked passages, and such constant, snarling energy that on this evening Led Zep could have provided enough human electricity to light half of America."

Plant: "Something has really happened this time. Something has really clicked. It's fantastic, the spirit within the band is just fantastic."

Bootleg CD Reference: *Sometime In New York City* (Image Quality)

Thursday June 15 1972
Uniondale, New York
Nassau Coliseum

Set included – Immigrant Song/Heartbreaker/ Black Dog/Since I've Been Loving You/Stairway To Heaven/Going To California/That's The Way/Tangerine/Bron Yr Aur Stomp/Dazed And Confused (inc. The Crunge)/What Is And What Should Never Be/Moby Dick/Whole Lotta Love (inc. Boogie Chillun' – Willie And The Hand Jive – Hello Mary Lou – Money Honey – Heartbreak Hotel – Trucking Little Mama – Going Down Slow)/Organ Solo (inc. Amazing Grace) – Thank You.

From this tour, prior to taking the stage, Zeppelin pumped a deep mysterious hum through the PA that built and built until the frantic opening chords of 'Immigrant Song' slash the tension. The performance tonight was even better than the previous night and turned into another one of those special nights.

Page cut a searing, aggressive solo in 'Black Dog' and 'Since I've Been Loving You' was again excellent. Every solo seems inspired tonight.

'Stairway To Heaven' was introduced by Plant as 'a song that amazed us really. A real gas, even though you do it every night. One of those things you can never get fed up singing …" He would change his mind in time.

'Tangerine' was dedicated to … "the good times. The days of Tintagel and Camelot – and that's not a motel somewhere in Connecticut!"

'Whole Lotta Love' was the highlight of tonight's amazing performance and included the rarely performed 'Willie And The Hand Jive' by Johnny Otis and Elvis' 'Money Honey' which was originally recorded by The Drifters. The crowd were in ecstasy at this stage and the authorities raised the house lights so they could check on them. Plant responded by adding the line "You better put those house lights down" to 'Heartbreak Hotel'.

Roy Hollingworth reported back: "The excitement was thick as 16,000 people were made ready. There was that hum, that frightening hum. An electrical tone was started. It sounded like the rising drone of a bomber. It got louder, louder, till it filled the whole place and the band walked out onto the stage. The place collapsed, and the band, without hesitation, kicked into rock. Page stabbed out a riff, and Plant yelled and squealed, and glory, all Hell broke loose.

"In the limousine afterwards, Plant shakes his head and tells me 'They'd never believe how good it is here back home. They'd just never believe what happened tonight'."

Bootleg CD References: *Tangerine* (Mud Dogs), *Long Island Line* (IQ), *Welcome Back* (Tarantura)

Saturday June 17 1972
Portland, Oregon
Memorial Coliseum
Set included Immigrant Song/Heartbreaker/ Black Dog/Since I've Been Loving You/ Stairway To Heaven/ Going To California/ That's The Way/Dazed And Confused/(including Walter's Walk-The Crunge)/What Is And What Should Never Be/Moby Dick/Whole Lotta Love (inc Boogie Woogie/Boppin' The Blues)

Sunday June 18 1972
Seattle, Washington
Seattle Coliseum

Set included – Immigrant Song/Heartbreaker/ Black Dog/Since I've Been Loving You/Stairway To Heaven/Going To California.

Zeppelin originally intended to play in Vancouver this evening, but this plan was thwarted by the Canadian authorities. Buses were therefore chartered to bring the fans from Canada down to Seattle. The start of the concert was delayed because the buses were stuck in traffic.

Plant: "Well, what can we say! Somebody tried to do a lot of damage in Vancouver, I believe; breaking doors down and all that old shit! It's pretty unfortunate really when we try to stand for an alternative idea to the system that goes on now, and we're talking about love and peace and somebody's smashing everything up. I don't really know the situation, but I know that we couldn't go this year. We couldn't even go across the border. So, anybody from Vancouver here? Well, that's a nice one! We've always had such a good time there."

Ironically, crowd problems started to develop during the acoustic set. Plant: "I think the people at the front should sit down, so the people at the

back can see and please don't kick any policemen! If we're to get anywhere, it's no good kicking them. They don't even know what they're doing."
Bootleg CD References: *Sub Zep* (No Label), *Trouble In Vancouver* (Gold Standard)

Monday June 19 1972
Seattle, Washington
Seattle Coliseum
Set: Immigrant Song/Heartbreaker/Black Dog/The Ocean/Since I've Been Loving You/Stairway To Heaven/Going To California/Black Country Woman/That's The Way/Tangerine/Bron Yr Aur Stomp/Dazed And Confused (inc. The Crunge)/What Is And What Should Never Be/Dancing Days/Moby Dick/Whole Lotta Love (inc. Everybody Needs Somebody – Boogie Chillun' – Let's Have A Party – Hello Mary Lou – Only The Lonely – Heartbreak Hotel – Going Down Slow – The Shape I'm In)/Rock And Roll/Organ Solo (inc. Amazing Grace – Everyday People – Louie Louie – Let's Dance) – Thank You/Money/Over The Hills And Far Away/Dancing Days.

A truly outstanding show. The best of the tour and one of Zeppelin's finest ever – certainly one of their most surprising in terms of the set list. The band were loose and in an experimental mood. The first surprise came after just three numbers, with the live début of 'The Ocean' from the forthcoming *Houses Of The Holy* album. This rendition was very close to the final album version and Robert remembered nearly all the lyrics.

During the acoustic set, a between-song jam lead into 'Black Country Woman' – another live début of a song recently recorded but destined not to be released until 1975 on *Physical Graffiti*. 'Dancing Days' was also added to the set at this show. Plant introduced it as 'a song of summer' and commented: "Well, that's the first time I believe we've ever done it. All being well we're gonna get this album out before the summer goes!" He continued: "We've come over here for about 22 days and we're working 19 of them or something like that and we're all pretty wasted; but our percussionist has decided to lose weight at the same time. So, John Bonham – at the beginning of the tour 210 pounds, right now, 175 pounds – 'Moby Dick!'"

'Whole Lotta Love' was another monumental performance and included a very impromptu version of Roy Orbison's 'Only The Lonely'. Plant led the way into the song and eventually they all picked up on it.

Plant: "You've had a good time and so have we. I don't think there's any band anywhere in the world that has as much fun as we do and I think it rubs off on you!"

The encores just kept on coming. After 'Rock And Roll', John Paul Jones commenced an epic organ solo that led into another medley of surprises. First 'Amazing Grace', then Sly And The Family Stone's 'Everyday People'. Next up is 'Louie Louie' (originally performed by the Seattle band, The Kingsmen), then Chris Montez's 'Let's Dance', before finally heading into 'Thank You'.

The audience response was wild, so the band just continued. 'Money' the Barrett Strong classic was next, followed by 'Over The Hills And Far

Away', yet another début from the *Houses Of The Holy* album. Plant tried to tell the audience it's time to go home: "We're only contracted to do 50 minutes in the first place and it's now three hours and 20 minutes since we started. This is one you might have heard about two hours ago. We like it so much, we're gonna do it again!" Remarkably, the show closed with a second rendition of 'Dancing Days'.

"Three and a half hours of Led Zeppelin," wrote Brian Smith for the local newspaper. "The English rock quartet last night played a very complete performance, which in three and a half hours encompassed many of their old hits, an acoustic set, a 25-minute drum solo and several mid-Fifties rock'n'roll numbers."

Bootleg CD References: *The Evergreen* (The Diagrams Of Led Zeppelin), *Sizzles In Seattle* (Lemon Song), *Let's Do It Again* (Badgeholders)

Wednesday June 21 1972
Denver, Colorado
Denver Coliseum

Thursday June 22 1972
San Bernardino, California
Swing Auditorium
Set: Immigrant Song/Heartbreaker/Black Dog/Since I've Been Loving You/Stairway To Heaven/Going To California/That's The Way/Tangerine/Bron Yr Aur Stomp/Dazed And Confused (inc. The Crunge)/What Is And What Should Never Be/Moby Dick/Whole Lotta Love (inc. Everybody Needs Somebody – Boogie Chillun' – Let's Have A Party – Hello Mary Lou – Going Down Slow – The Shape I'm In)/Rock And Roll.

After the Seattle extravaganza, the band returned to the standard set. However, the performance was still excellent. The band were now really in their stride.

During a totally Page dominated 'Dazed And Confused', Robert yelled out "C'mon all you white folks – Do The Crunge!" and John Bonham's weight continued to fluctuate – tonight he's introduced as being 168 pounds.

The only negative aspect of tonight's show was the fact that the audience persisted in throwing firecrackers which only serveed to irritate Plant: "All those firecrackers – that's a load of shit!"

Audience shot 16mm silent colour cine film exists from this show.

Bootleg CD References: *Berdu* (Cobra Standard), *Born To Be Wild* (Whole Lotta Live), *Route 66* (Tarantura), *Swining In San Bernadino* (Empress Valley)

Visual Reference: *Early Visions* DVD (Unofficial – Celebration), *1970-1972* (Cosmic Energy)

Friday June 23 1972
San Diego, California
Sports Arena

Saturday June 24 1972
Berkeley, California
Community Theatre

Sunday June 25 1972
Inglewood Los Angeles, California
The Forum
Immigrant Song/Heartbreaker/Over The Hills And Far Away/Black Dog/Since I've Been Loving You/Stairway To Heaven/Going To California/That's The Way/Tangerine/Bron Yr Aur Stomp/Dazed And Confused (inc. The Crunge)/What Is And What Should Never Be/Dancing Days/Moby Dick/Whole Lotta Love (inc. Everybody Needs Somebody – Boogie Chillun' – Let's Have A Party – Hello Mary Lou – Heartbreak Hotel – Slow Down – Going Down Slow – The Shape I'm In)/Rock And Roll/The

Ocean/Louie Louie /Thank You/Communication Breakdown/Bring It On Home.

Another excellent performance. The new material from *Houses Of The Holy* has now been added as regular inclusions in the set. Plant: "Good Evening! It's been a long time again. We finally saved up the air fare to get back. We'd like to try a number off the new album. We haven't really decided what we're gonna do at the end of it yet, so you'll have to bear with us! This is a thing called 'Over The Hills And Far Away', which is always a good place to be."

Robert again assured the audience that 'Black Dog' has "nothing to do with a chick in Detroit" and predicts: "I think we're gonna have a good time. In fact, I can't ever remember coming here when it's been bad."

'Since I've Been Loving You' really shone tonight and a most eloquent 'Stairway To Heaven' received the longest ovation so far. Unfortunately,

by this stage, disruptions were beginning to break out between elements of the audience and the authorities. Plant attempted to calm the crowd: "The best vibes of the tour so far have been in strange places, and we've been known to play for 12 and a half hours … and then after that we went to the gig."

Introducing 'Dancing Days', Plant informed the audience that the new album … "is not gonna be called *Led Zeppelin Five*, it's got every possibility of being called *Burn That Candle*." This title was never used by Zeppelin; however, some 20 years later, the enterprising bootleggers revived the title for a bootleg CD of this show slightly amended to *Burn Like A Candle*.

'Whole Lotta Love' was dedicated to LA and includes all the usual references used on this tour, as well as the unique performance of Larry Williams' 'Slow Down'.

After the first encore of 'Rock And Roll', Plant spotted someone in the crowd fighting: "Hey, big man, cool it! Let me tell you something. Before there's any blows start. You start blowing blows

and we'll go, right? And let me tell you something else – it's no good antagonising them either. If everybody keeps cool, we can stay here all night!"

After repeated hints from Plant that this would be a long show, Zeppelin kept to their word. 'The Ocean' was next, followed by a powerful keyboard riff from John Paul Jones that introduced a rocking version of 'Louie Louie' featuring Jimmy Page on backing vocals. 'Thank You' closed this segment of encores.

The crowd were frantic and Zeppelin were quickly called back to the stage. "You don't even give us a chance to have a cigarette, do ya? I was thinking of the other variety actually," joked Plant.

'Communication Breakdown' and a boisterous 'Bring It On Home' drew to a close another spectacular marathon performance.

In their review of the show, *Phonograph Record Magazine* drew many favourable comparisons with other supergroups. "People paid six and a half dollars for an hour and twenty minutes of the Stones. Zep fans spent seven and a quarter dollars, top, to see their group for THREE HOURS." The finale of the show was particularly impressive: "The last hour had to it a feeling of 'specialness' that had been lacking in the preceding portion of the show, as good and audience pleasing as that portion may have been."

Danny Holloway for the *NME* reported: "All in all, there were five encores because the audience screamed and stomped like spoiled babies until they got what they wanted. I'm told that the group have performed ten gigs of this calibre over the last two weeks. It's easy to understand America's love for the group and vice versa. I heard after the show that Plant's voice was beginning to go and Page had to stay in bed on doctor's orders. It means a lot when you see a group as big as they are putting so much into their stage act."

The soundcheck earlier in the afternoon was also quite special. Plant: "When we did the LA Forum, we made some recordings of the rehearsal, and we did about an hour's run through which ended up getting an echo set going. I think we played every number on *Elvis' Golden Discs Volume One*. It's amazing that you can stir yourself enough to get all the lyrics from that far back, and Jimmy managed to do all the solos as well. It was completely spontaneous."

Official CD Reference: *How The West Was Won* (Atlantic)

Bootleg CD References: *Burn Like A Candle* (Smoking Pig), *LA Forum* (Cobla Standard Series), *Burn Like A Candle*(Empress Valley), *Burn That Candle* (Equinox), *A Night In The Heartbreak Hotel* (Missing Link)

HOW THE WEST WAS WON

When Jimmy Page began searching the Zeppelin archives for footage for the DVD project he stumbled upon master tapes of two US dates from the 1972 tour – this June 25 Los Angeles appearance and the following night's show in Long Beach. Both shows were familiar to Zep collectors. The LA date had long been held in high esteem via an excellent audience recording released on a bootleg CD under the title *Burn Like A Candle*. Long Beach had surfaced via a lesser quality tape issued on Cobra Standard's *Wild Beach Party*.

The existence of a full official tape of the Long Beach date had been hinted at via soundboard snippets from the June 27 gig that had surfaced on the Scorpio label's *Studio Daze* bootleg CD which featured 'What Is And What Should Never Be' and 'Dancing Days' and the *One More Daze* CD that included 'Moby Dick'.

Page set to work with engineer Kevin Shirley and cleverly merged both shows to form a seamless live album. Titled *How The West Was Won* and issued simultaneously with the DVD in late May 2003, it became a huge seller, entering the *Billbaord* US chart at number one. Finally Zeppelin fans had the official live album they had always craved.

"Playing the West Coast was always fantastic," Page said at the time of the album's release. "Each member of the band was playing at their best during those 1972 performances. And when the four of us were playing like that, we combined to make it a fifth element. That was the magic- the intangible."

Tuesday June 27 1972
Long Beach, California
Long Beach Arena
Immigrant Song/Heartbreaker/Black Dog/Over The Hills And Far Away/Since I've Been Loving You/Stairway To Heaven/Going To California/That's The Way/Tangerine/Bron Yr Aur Stomp/Dazed And Confused/What Is And What Should Never Be/Dancing Days/Moby Dick/Whole Lotta Love (inc. Everybody Needs Somebody – Boogie Chillun' – Let's Have A Party – Hello Mary Lou – Blueberry Hill – Going Down Slow – The Shape I'm In)/Rock And Roll.

Yet another superb show. Plant commented on the previous show at the Forum: "That was too much. That was really great!"

'Over The Hills And Far Away' was now coming into its own. Page's solo was fluent and dynamic and Plant sang the whole song in an unbelievably high key. Afterwards, Plant gasped: "I think I better have some lemon and honey!" There was only so much a human voice could stand.

Before the acoustic set Plant informed the audience: "As you probably heard, we gotta sit down because we got such a tight schedule and itinerary, we can't really carry on too long standing up. Don't tell me you believe that!" During 'Going To California' when Plant sang of "a girl with love in her eyes and flowers in her hair" he ad-libbed "I ain't seen too many this time."

Plant: "It seems every time we come to the States, we do something that you ain't heard before and can't identify with – this is one of those. This is one off the new album and all being well, we should have it out before the nights start drawing in, because it's a summery album really." 'Dancing Days' followed and was well received.

'Whole Lotta Love' tonight included the Fats Domino classic 'Blueberry Hill', played in a much higher key than when Zeppelin last performed it at the same venue in 1970.
Official CD Reference: *How The West Was Won* (Atlantic)
Bootleg CD Reference: *Wild Beach Party* (Led Note)

Wednesday June 28 1972
Tucson, Arizona
Community Center
Set list: Immigrant Song/Heartbreaker/Black Dog/Over The Hills And Far Away/Since I've Been Loving You/Stairway To Heaven/Bron-yr-Aur Stomp/Dazed And Confused/What Is And What Should Never Be/Dancing Days/Moby Dick/Whole Lotta Love/Rock And Roll

Jimmy Page: "We just seemed to keep adding numbers and adding more numbers, so that what started out as an hour just grew into three hours. We got really fatigued by it, what with all the travelling as well, every night after the gig. I got back from that tour and for a week I just didn't know where I was."

The band returned to the UK on June 30. Further often-quoted US dates did not occur.
Bootleg CD Reference: *Crashing Revelry* (Empress Valley)

June 1972
New York, New York
Electric Lady Studios
RECORDING SESSIONS
While in New York they worked again with Eddie Kramer on their fifth album. The track 'Houses Of The Holy' was mixed down at this session but would not make the final album – it was eventually released on *Physical Graffiti*.

After completing work on *Houses Of The Holy* the group paid a return visit to Japan, playing six shows over a nine-day period.

This tour signified a long overdue overhaul of their set, with 'Rock And Roll' now installed as a particularly appropriate set opener. Four new compositions were presented – the previously played 'Over The Hills And Far Away' and 'Dancing Days' and the new coupling of 'The Song Remains The Same' with 'The Rain Song'. The latter coupling was introduced by Plant on different occasions under the working titles of 'The Campaign', 'The Overture' and 'Zep'. As with their last Japanese visit, they were not afraid to introduce some off-the-wall cover versions for the Japanese audiences. A version of Ben E. King's 'Stand By Me' in Osaka on October 9 emerged as one of the highlights of the tour.

Equipment Notes:

Some radical introductions. Jones begins using the Mellotron 216 for 'Stairway To Heaven', 'The Rain Song', and 'Thank You'. This primitive version of a sampler is prone to going out of tune. Jones also introduced an Arco stand-up bass, allegedly pur-

Arriving in Tokyo, October 1 1972

The Concert File

chased "for about 10 dollars in Newcastle in 1969" as Robert explained at their Cleveland April 27 show in 1977. Jimmy begins using the Gibson double-neck for 'The Song Remains The Same'/'The Rain Song' live sequence.

Monday October 2 1972
Tokyo, Japan
Budokan Hall
Set: Rock And Roll/Over The Hills And Far Away/Black Dog/Misty Mountain Hop/Since I've Been Loving You/Dancing Days/Bron Yr Aur Stomp/The Song Remains The Same/The Rain Song/Dazed And Confused (inc. The Crunge)/Stairway To Heaven/Whole Lotta Love (inc. Everybody Needs Somebody – Boogie Chillun' – My Baby Left Me – Killing Floor – I Can't Quit You)/Heartbreaker/Immigrant Song/Communication Breakdown.

After a lengthy introduction from Mr Goro Itoi, the MC for the Tokyo shows, the band unveiled a dynamic new set structure – the basic format upon which later tours would be based.

'Rock And Roll' was chosen as the new set opener. 'Misty Mountain Hop' was now installed in the set and flowed directly into 'Since I've Been Loving You'. 'The Song Remains The Same' also segued straight into 'The Rain Song'.

'Dazed And Confused' continued to grow in stature and complexity, but the highlight of the set was still the extended 'Whole Lotta Love' medley, which tonight included a rare regression back to 'Killing Floor' – a favourite from their 1969 tours. 'Communication Breakdown' was played tonight for the only time on the tour.

Bootleg CD References: *Live At The Big Hall Budokan Oct 2 1972* (The Diagrams Of Led Zeppelin), *Budokan Oct 2 1972* (Patriot), *The Overture* (Sanctuary), *No Use Greco* (Tarantura)

Tuesday October 3 1972
Tokyo, Japan
Budokan Hall
Set: Rock And Roll/Black Dog/Over The Hills And Far Away/Misty Mountain Hop/Since I've Been Loving You/Dancing Days/Bron Yr Aur Stomp/The Song Remains The Same/The Rain Song/Dazed And Confused (inc. The Crunge)/Stairway To Heaven/Whole Lotta Love (inc. Everybody Needs Somebody – Boogie Chillun' – Let's Have A Party – You Shook Me)/Immigrant Song/The Ocean.

"It is very good to be back. When group come to Tokyo – group have fun! We should clap you!"

The band were experimenting with set variations at these shows. From tonight, 'Black Dog' and 'Over The Hills' exchanged places in the set. 'Dancing Days' from the new album was introduced as "a song about summertime and all the good things that happen". 'Bron Yr Aur Stomp' was "a song that requires the honourable Led Zeppelin to sit down and features the transvestite vocal chords of John Bonham!" The acoustic set has now been reduced to one song.

Plant was still unsure how to introduce 'The Song Remains The Same'. "Last night it was called 'Zep', tonight we'll call it – 'The Overture'."

'Everybody Needs Somebody' (finally with lyrics) and 'You Shook Me' were established into the 'Whole Lotta Love' repertoire and 'The Ocean' makes a rare appearance as a second encore.

A privately audience reel of poor quality distant silent cine footage exists from this show.

Bootleg CD References: *2nd Night in a Judo Arena* (Tarantura), *Live At The Big Hall Budokan Oct 3 1972* (The Diagrams of Led Zeppelin)

Wednesday October 4 1972
Osaka, Japan
Festival Hall
Set: Rock And Roll/Black Dog/Over The Hills And Far Away/Misty Mountain Hop/Since I've

THE MELLOTRON

The Mellotron was an early electronic keyboard instrument that came to prominence in the mid-Sixties – notably on The Beatles' 'Strawberry Fields Forever'.

Les Bradley was largely responsible for its introduction to the UK, working from a patent made by an American called Harry Chamberlain.

It worked on the principle that it was able to reproduce various sounds – mainly string instruments, by pressing relevant keys. The sounds were stored on tape loops that rewound into position after use.

John Paul began using a 216 model during the recording of 'The Rain Song' for the *Houses Of The Holy* album in the spring of 1972. Later that year, it was taken on the road for their Japanese tour. It remained a part of the keyboard set up until the 1977 US tour. It was used for 'The Rain Song', 'Kashmir' and 'Stairway To Heaven' – inspiring on stage Plant quips such as "John Paul Jones was the rather cheap orchestra". Its major flaw was that it had a tendency to go out of tune – forcing John Paul to eventually invest in the superior Yamaha GX1 keyboard set up. This was used for the Copenhagen/Knebworth dates in 1979, through the Over Europe 1980 jaunt – complete with the presence of a mysterious telephone.

Been Loving You/Dancing Days/Bron Yr Aur Stomp/The Song Remains The Same/The Rain Song/Dazed And Confused (inc. San Francisco – The Crunge)/Stairway To Heaven/Whole Lotta Love (inc. Everybody Needs Somebody – Boogie Chillun' – Got A Lotta Livin' To Do – Let's Have A Party – You Shook Me – Lemon Song)/Heartbreaker/Immigrant Song.

In contrast to the energetic and frantic performances of the 1971 Japanese Tour, the 1972 shows were much more relaxed and laid back affairs. The group seemed tired at times, particularly Plant who sometimes failed to hit the high notes.

During the ever expanding 'Dazed And Confused', Page played an instrumental version of Scott Mackenzie's 'San Francisco (Be Sure To Wear Some Flowers In Your Hair)'. This theme would be much more expanded in later concerts.

Presley's 'Got A Lotta Livin' To Do' was a rare inclusion in the 'Whole Lotta Love' medley.

The band took some time to appear again to perform 'Immigrant Song' and some members of the audience had already left the hall.

Bootleg CD References: *Dancing Geisha* (Tarantura), *Live At Festival Hall* (Power Archives), *Stand By Me* (Apollonian)

Thursday October 5 1972
Nagoya, Japan
Kokaido

Set: Rock And Roll/Black Dog/Misty Mountain Hop/Since I've Been Loving You/Dancing Days/Bron Yr Aur Stomp/The Song Remains The Same/The Rain Song/Dazed And Confused/Stairway To Heaven/Whole Lotta Love (inc. Everybody Needs Somebody – Boogie Chillun' – Feel So Good – Let's Have A Party – You Shook Me)/Organ Improvisation (inc. Cherry Blossom)/Thank You.

"It is very nice for English boys to be in Nagoya."

The highlight of tonight's show was the rare encore of 'Thank You', complete with a lengthy Mellotron improvisation by John Paul Jones, which includes samples of some traditional Japanese music.

'Over The Hills And Far Away' had been temporarily dropped from the set for tonight.

Bootleg CD References: *D.R.A.G.O.N.* (Flagge), *Sakura, Looking Up! Great Discovery* (Jelly Roll), *Rock 'N' Roll Springtime* (Image Quality), *The Geisha Boys* (Akashic)

Monday October 9 1972
Osaka, Japan
Festival Hall

Set: Rock And Roll/Black Dog/Over The Hills And Far Away/Misty Mountain Hop/Since I've Been Loving You/Dancing Days/The Song Remains The Same/The Rain Song/Dazed And Confused (inc. Down By The River – The Crunge)/Stairway To Heaven/Moby Dick/Whole Lotta Love (inc. Everybody Needs Somebody – It Must Be Love – Milk Cow Blues – Leave My Woman Alone – Lawdy Miss Clawdy – Heartbreak Hotel – Wear My Ring Around Your Neck – Going Down Slow – The Shape I'm In)/Stand By Me/Immigrant Song.

Plant: "We've just come back from Hong Kong. We went to Hong Kong for a few days and we're well knackered!" Nevertheless, this is a truly exciting show and probably the best of the tour.

Robert again struggled with a title for 'The Song Remains The Same'. "We can't find a name for it. We'll call it … 'The Campaign'."

'Dazed And Confused' was beginning to evolve into an even longer epic than ever before – Page's pre-violin bow sequence was the foundation for Plant to ad-lib lines from Neil Young's 'Down By The River'. By the time they reached London in December, it would be the regular spot for the previously mentioned 'summer of love' anthem, 'San Francisco (Be Sure To Wear Some Flowers In Your Hair)'.

Tonight there was an added bonus, courtesy of John 'Samurai' Bonham. This was the only show of the Japanese tour to feature Bonham's 'Moby Dick' drum solo and after tonight it would not be played again until the summer 1973 US tour.

The highlight of the concert was yet again the 'Whole Lotta Love' medley, which was reminiscent of the marathons from last year's tour. Tonight, the band delved deep to produce some really rare and obscure references, including 'Milk Cow Blues', 'Leave My Woman Alone' and 'Act Naturally'. Page even played a few riffs from the Stones' 'Satisfaction' after 'It Must Be Love'.

A full version of Ben E. King's 'Stand By Me' was an unusual but pleasing choice as a first encore, followed by a storming version of 'Immigrant Song' – always a crowd pleaser in Japan.

Bootleg CD References: *Let Me Get Back To 1972* (H-Bomb Music), *Tapes From The Darkside* (H-Bomb), *Magical Dreams* (Wyvern Legend), *Live-Japan Warm Ups* (Tarantura)

Tuesday October 10 1972
Kyoto, Japan
Kaikan #1 Hall
Set: Rock And Roll/Black Dog/Misty Mountain Hop/Since I've Been Loving You/The Song Remains The Same/The Rain Song/Dazed And Confused/Stairway To Heaven/Over The Hills And Far Away/Whole Lotta Love (inc. Everybody Needs Somebody – Boogie Chillun' – That's Alright Mama – Let's Jump The Broomstick – Going Down Slow – The Shape I'm In)/Immigrant Song.

The final concert in Japan was something of a lacklustre affair.

'Dazed And Confused' was played straight tonight with none of the regular additions. 'Over The Hills And Far Away' was performed late in the set, introduced as "very honourable track off fifth LP".

'Whole Lotta Love' had a bizarre funky intro and the whole finale to the show had a rather hurried feel. Brenda Lee's 'Let's Jump The Broomstick' was the only rare inclusion in the medley.

When they began to perform 'Whole Lotta Love' a Japanese girl and well known groupie was seen to step on stage dancing frantically. One of the reasons the show was hurried was because the band did not want to miss the last bullet train from Kyoto to return to Tokyo.

Bootleg CD References: *The Last Night In Japan* (The Diagrams of Led Zeppelin), *Miyabi – Live In Kyoto 1972* (No Label)

A 14-disc box set titled *The Campaign* includes recordings of the complete 1972 Japanese tour (Tarantura).

UK TOUR WINTER 1972/1973

Their longest-ever UK tour was preceded by two shows at the Montreux Casino, continuing their long-standing relationship with promoter Claude Knobs. After a couple of days' rehearsal at London's Rainbow Theatre, the tour kicked off in Newcastle-on-Tyne on November 30. The original 110,000 tickets for the 24 dates sold out within four hours of box offices opening simultaneously on November 10. "When I heard that it just made me feel very humble," said Page. Grant, more than anxious to re-establish them back home stated: "I would have staked everything I've got on getting this tour right." Ticket prices were pegged at £1 for all shows, except Manchester Hardrock which was £1.25.

The tour took in two nights at London's Alexandra Palace. This attempt to open up another new venue in the capital did not prove entirely successful, the sound mix barely reaching the first 30 rows.

As 1973 began, Robert caught the flu after the car that he and Bonzo were travelling in broke down on the way to a date in Sheffield. This caused the postponement of dates in Bradford and Preston, both of which were re-scheduled. An additional date was added at Southampton University on January 22.

For once they encouraged the presence of UK press with *NME*'s celebrated Nick Kent joining the entourage and filing favourable reports.

Four numbers from the new album were performed: 'Over The Hills And Far Away', 'The Song Remains The Same', 'The Rain Song' and 'Dancing Days'. The acoustic set was again restricted to just 'Bron Yr Aur Stomp'. Trouble with the cover artwork, now a regular occurrence,

JOHN & TONY SMITH BY ARRANGEMENT WITH PETER GRANT PRESENT

LED ZEPPELIN

DECEMBER 1972				JANUARY 1973		
NEWCASTLE	CITY HALL	November	Thursday 30th	SHEFFIELD	CITY HALL	Tuesday 2nd
NEWCASTLE	CITY HALL		Friday 1st	PRESTON	GUILDHALL	Wednesday 3rd
GLASGOW	GREENS PLAYHOUSE		Sunday 3rd	BRADFORD	ST GEORGE'S HALL	Thursday 4th
GLASGOW	GREENS PLAYHOUSE		Monday 4th	OXFORD	NEW THEATRE	Sunday 7th
MANCHESTER	HARD ROCK		Thursday 7th	LIVERPOOL	EMPIRE	Sunday 14th
MANCHESTER	HARD ROCK		Friday 8th	STOKE	TRENTHAM GARDENS	Monday 15th
CARDIFF	CAPITOL		Monday 11th	ABERYSTWYTH	KING'S HALL	Tuesday 16th
CARDIFF	CAPITOL		Tuesday 12th	SOUTHAMPTON	GAUMONT	Sunday 21st
BIRMINGHAM	ODEON		Saturday 16th	ABERDEEN	MUSIC HALL	Thursday 25th
BIRMINGHAM	ODEON		Sunday 17th	DUNDEE	CAIRD HALL	Saturday 27th
BRIGHTON	DOME		Wednesday 20th	EDINBURGH	KING'S THEATRE	Sunday 28th
LONDON	ALEXANDRA PALACE		Friday 22nd			
LONDON	ALEXANDRA PALACE		Saturday 23rd			

ALL TICKETS — FIRST COME FIRST SERVED

£1 Except Hardrock £1.25

ALL BOX OFFICES OPEN 9 AM FRIDAY 10TH NOVEMBER
ALEXANDRA PALACE TICKETS AVAILABLE FROM HARLEQUIN RECORDS
HAYMARKET/OXFORD STREET/DEAN STREET (SOHO RECORDS)

SOLD OUT

and their popularity has undoubtedly waned

CHRIS CHARLESWORTH
MELODY MAKER LAST WEEK

delayed the release originally planned for early January.

Overall, this lengthy set of dates reaffirmed their status in the UK. It would however prove to be the last opportunity for British audiences to see Led Zeppelin in their homeland at such close quarters. Venues such as the Aberystwyth Kings Hall with its capacity of under 800 would soon be a thing of the past. The stadium era beckoned.

October 1972
Finsbury Park London, England
Rainbow Theatre
REHEARSALS

The band moved into the popular London venue to warm up for the UK tour.

Saturday October 28 1972
Montreux, Switzerland
Montreux Pavilion

Set includes – Rock And Roll/Black Dog/Over The Hills And Far Away/Misty Mountain Hop/Since I've Been Loving You/Dancing Days/Bron Yr Aur Stomp/The Song Remains The Same/The Rain Song/Dazed And Confused/Stairway To Heaven/Whole Lotta Love (inc. Let's Have A Party – I Need Your Love Tonight – Heartbreak Hotel)/Heartbreaker.

Also on the bill: Ray Charles and Three Dog Night.

The band were introduced by promoter Claude Knobs as "The greatest rock and roll band in the world."

"Led the good times roll!" Chris Charlesworth of *Melody Maker* reviewed both 4,000 capacity warm-up shows and reported: "Zeppelin are a tremendous live force. They've lost none of the energy that characterises a band who need to work to gain recognition, but the energy has matured into a confidence that allows them to spring off into spontaneous directions during their shows.

"A nod, a wink, a drum roll or a wave of a fret-board and Zeppelin can turn a number back on its heels into songs totally unexpected. Who would imagine, for example, that 'Whole Lotta Love' could end up as 'Heartbreak Hotel'? It can, and it does when Zeppelin fly."

Sunday October 29 1972
Montreux, Switzerland
Montreux Pavilion

Set includes – Rock And Roll/Black Dog/Over The Hills And Far Away/Misty Mountain Hop/Since I've Been Loving You/Dancing Days/Bron Yr Aur Stomp/The Song Remains The Same/The Rain Song/Dazed And Confused/Stairway To Heaven/Whole Lotta Love)/Heartbreaker

Chris Charlesworth again: "Sunday's concert at

Montreux followed the same pattern as Saturday's and, if anything, was better for the experience of the previous day.

"The decision to play these 'warm-up' gigs augers well for some Zep shows here soon. If they do come off, take my advice, go and see them. They will reshape your values about what is genuine and what is not. They just have to be the best heavy band this country has produced."

Thursday November 30 1972
Newcastle-on-Tyne, England
Newcastle City Hall

Rock And Roll/Over The Hills And Far Away/Black Dog/Misty Mountain Hop/Since I've Been Loving You/Dancing Days/Bron Yr Aur Stomp/The Song Remains The Same/The Rain Song/Dazed And Confused (inc. The Crunge)/Stairway To Heaven/Whole Lotta Love (inc. Everybody Needs Somebody – Boogie Chillun' – Let's Have A Party – Going Down Slow – The Shape I'm In)/Immigrant Song/ Heartbreaker/Organ Solo – Thank You.

A reasonable performance for an opening night, although somewhat sluggish in places. A 2,300 capacity sell out with a door take of £2,219.

The set for the British tour was similar to the Japanese and Swiss shows, except 'Over The Hills And Far Away' had now been promoted in the running order to second place. Tonight, both 'Black Dog' and 'Misty Mountain Hop' were introduced by Plant as 'My Brain Hurts'! – a reference to a Monty Python sketch. John Bonham wore a suitably silly mask at times to add to the lunacy of the evening.

'Dazed And Confused' contained an instrumental passage that was beginning to develop into 'San Francisco', but otherwise was a bit rambling and uninspired, and also considerably shorter than most versions on the tour. 'Stairway To Heaven' was dedicated to Roy Harper, who was in hospital.

The crowd were warm and responsive. Zeppelin's former opening salvo of 'Immigrant Song' and 'Heartbreaker' was the surprise choice for a first encore, before John Paul Jones concluded the evening with a brief organ solo leading into 'Thank You'.

The stage area itself is littered with flower arrangements left over from a recent Lord Mayor's ball.

Plant: "I tell you we were as nervous as hell before going out there."

Page: "I can tell you we were really nervous tonight. When you haven't played England for some time, not only do you want things to be spot on, but you always get a little frightened that you'll somehow disappoint the kids. For a first night, the reaction was just tremendous."

"Zeppelin – The Last Laugh" – Roy Carr reviewed the performance for *New Musical Express*: "Promoter Tony Smith steps up to the microphone and announces: 'What can I say, except Led Zeppelin!' A Newcastle Brown Ale-induced roar fills the air, Bonzo Bonham thunders out the pistol shot intro to 'Rock And Roll' and in one outburst of nervous fury Pagey and John Paul Jones tear into the riff. Plant screams, his head pushed back into his shoulders, silver rock'n'roll shoes stamping out the beat, the mike chord stretched across his bare chest. The crowd leaps to its feet with a primeval grunt of approval."

Roy Hollingworth for *Melody Maker* reported: "One has to own up. If you wanna dance, if you REALLY wanna hear a rock'n'roll band, wipe off that bloody silly make-up and go see Led

Zeppelin. Of course, if you haven't got a ticket now, you'll never get one because they've sold out all the British dates. No hype and no mean achievement."

Bootleg CD References: *Newcastle Symphony* (Image Quality), *Nice Starter* (The symbols)

Friday December 1 1972
Newcastle-On-Tyne, England
Newcastle City Hall
Set includes – Rock And Roll/Over The Hills And Far Away/Black Dog/Misty Mountain Hop/Since I've Been Loving You/Dancing Days/Bron Yr Aur Stomp/The Song Remains The Same/The Rain Song/Dazed And Confused (inc. The Crunge)/Stairway To Heaven/Whole Lotta Love (inc. Everybody Needs Somebody – Boogie Chillun' – I Need Your Love Tonight – For What It's Worth – Heartbreak Hotel).

Another sell out with a door take of £2,221.

An improvement on last night's show. 'Dazed And Confused' and 'Whole Lotta Love' were the highlights of the set. Unusually, the medley section ended with 'Heartbreak Hotel' instead of the usual blues selection.

Sunday December 3 1972
Glasgow, Scotland
Green's Playhouse

Monday December 4 1972
Glasgow, Scotland
Green's Playhouse
Set: Rock And Roll/Over The Hills And Far Away/Black Dog/Misty Mountain Hop/Since I've Been Loving You/Dancing Days/Bron Yr Aur Stomp/The Song Remains The Same/The Rain Song/Dazed And Confused (inc. The Crunge)/Stairway To Heaven/Whole Lotta Love (inc. Everybody Needs Somebody – Boogie Chillun' – Let's Have A Party – Stuck On You – I Can't Quit You)/Heartbreaker/Immigrant Song/Communication Breakdown (note last two numbers unverified – these are listed as being played in the Martin Millar book, see right)

Zeppelin were now beginning to relax and experiment more. 'Dazed And Confused' was very progressive with Page testing new riffs and Plant ad-libbing at will.

The audience reaction tonight was outstanding. Glasgow audiences were renowned for being very receptive, but tonight they were ecstatic. Plant recalls a recent quote from the British music press: "There was a story by someone who worked for *Melody Maker* … Chris Charlesworth … and he said our 'popularity had obviously waned' – thank you very much!"

The 'Whole Lotta Love' medley tonight included the rarely played 'Stuck On You', which Plant delivered in true Elvis parody.

In 2002 author Martin Millar published *Suzy, Led Zeppelin And Me* (Codex Books), a highly entertaining novel built on his experiences of seeing Led Zeppelin in Glasgow on this night. He recalled: "I remember the gig in 1972. The Greens Playhouse was a big old cinema. I queued up all night in the bitter cold to get a ticket. During the gig I recall the audience bursting into sustained applause when Jimmy got the violin bow out. When the band did a little synchronised dance step during 'The Crunge' part of 'Dazed' they all stood in line and kicked one leg out. A great touch. I'm not certain why I had the urge to write about it but the memories have remained vivid. The novel stretches back over a lot of years and has other aspects aside from Zeppelin. However the main story is built around the gig which was a

Led Zeppelin

very important part of my life when I was growing up."

Bootleg CD Reference: *Stuck On You* (The Diagrams Of Led Zeppelin)

Thursday December 7 1972
Manchester, England
Hard Rock

Friday December 8 1972
Manchester, England
Hard Rock

Set: Rock And Roll/Over The Hills And Far Away/Black Dog/Misty Mountain Hop/Since I've Been Loving You/The Song Remains The Same/The Rain Song/Dazed And Confused/Stairway To Heaven/Whole Lotta Love (inc. Everybody Needs Somebody – It's Your Thing – High Flyin' Mama – Boogie Chillun' – Say Mama – Let's Have A Party – I Can't Quit You – The Shape I'm In)/Heartbreaker/Immigrant Song/Communication Breakdown.

Tonight's show got off to a sluggish start, but soon settled into a comfortable groove. Plant was struggling in places and seemed to be deliberately aiming at a lower register so as not to force his voice too much – only reaching for the high notes on a few occasions.

Plant: "This is what they call one step up from Belle Vue … which I think might be right about." The audience tonight were extremely loud and noisy. Plant commented, in his best mock Manchester accent: "Every time we come to Manchester, there's a lot of people shouting out."

Page's playing was extremely loose, verging on sloppy in places, particularly on 'The Song Remains The Same'. 'Dazed And Confused' was overflowing in energy, leading to near chaos in several instances. Page even attempted several runs deploying riffs later to be used on 'Hots On For Nowhere'.

'Whole Lotta Love' was also outstanding and included a version of the Isley Brothers' 'It's Your Thing'.

Bootleg CD References: *The Rovers Return* (Empress Valley Supreme), *Hard Rock* (Sanctuary)

Monday December 11 1972
Cardiff, Wales
Capitol Theatre

Set includes – Rock And Roll/Black Dog/Misty Mountain Hop/Since I've Been Loving You/Bron Yr Aur Stomp/The Song Remains The Same/The Rain Song/Dancing Days/Dazed And Confused/Stairway To Heaven/Whole Lotta Love (inc. Blue Suede Shoes – Let's Have A Party – Boogie Chillun' – Be-Bop-A-Lula)/Heartbreaker/The Ocean/Organ Solo – Thank You.

As the tour continued, the band felt looser and more improvisation developed. Tonight, the constantly-changing 'Whole Lotta Love' medley even included Elvis Presley's 'Blue Suede Shoes' and Gene Vincent's 'Be-Bop-A-Lula'. 'The Ocean' was played for the first time on British shores and from now on would be used as an occasional bonus encore.

"Hail Hail Rock N'Roll" – Nick Kent reviewed the show for the *New Musical Express* and reported: "The big surprise of the tour is Page, who's up and rockin' alongside the Lemon Squeeze Kid.

"While Plant tends to move in curves with the emphasis on the hips, Page seems more deranged, doing knee-bends, thrusting out and using the guitar-neck as a bayonet. He even moves like a demon when playing his weighty twin-neck guitar, flashing weird evil grins when the mood takes him."

Nick Kent would recall this show four years later when panning *The Song Remains The Same* movie: "It's not a patch on my memories of that night at the Cardiff Capitol. No 27-minute 'Dazed And Confused' that night, I can tell you. Not one drum solo, either. Just a great band playing visionary rock'n'roll propelled by its own passion and adrenaline. Anyone know any good bootlegs going of that night?"

Tuesday December 12 1972
Cardiff, Wales
Capitol Theatre
Set includes: Whole Lotta Love (inc. Let's Have A Party – Heartbreak Hotel – I Can't Quit You – The Shape I'm In)/Old MacDonald's Farm/ Immigrant Song/Heartbreaker/Organ Solo – Thank You.

A continuation of last night's party. When they returned for the first encore, they even indulged in a few choruses of 'Old MacDonald Had A Farm' before launching into the opening attack of 'Immigrant Song'.

Bootleg CD Reference:

Saturday December 16 1972
Birmingham, England
Birmingham Odeon
Set includes: Rock And Roll / Over The Hills And Far Away / Black Dog / Misty Mountain Hop / Since I've Been Loving You / Dancing Days / Bron -yr-Aur Stomp / The Song Remains The Same / The Rain Song/Dazed and Confused / Stairway To Heaven / Whole Lotta Love

Bootleg CD Reference: *Sweet Brummy Roll* (Empress Valley)

Sunday December 17 1972
Birmingham, England
Birmingham Odeon

Wednesday December 20 1972
Brighton, England
Brighton Dome
Set includes: Rock And Roll / Over The Hills And Far Away / Black Dog / Misty Mountain Hop / Since I've Been Loving You / Dancing Days / Bron -yr-Aur Stomp / The Song Remains The Same / The Rain Song/Dazed and Confused / Stairway To Heaven / Whole Lotta Love

The set included a bonus encore medley of traditional Christmas tunes.

Alexandra Palace, December 22 1972

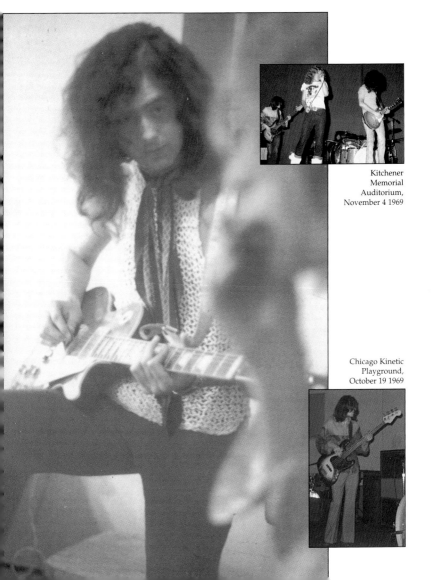

Kitchener
Memorial
Auditorium,
November 4 1969

Chicago Kinetic
Playground,
October 19 1969

Bath Festival, June 28 1970

Melody Maker Poll Awards, Savoy Hotel London, September 16 1970

Frankfurt, July 18 1970

Withdrawn poster, Southampton University,
January 22 1973 gig

Sydney Showground, February 27 1972

Shepperton Studios filming, August 1974

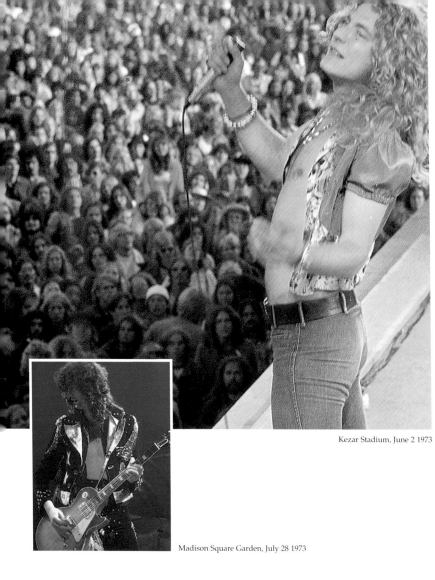

Kezar Stadium, June 2 1973

Madison Square Garden, July 28 1973

Chicago Stadium,
January 21 1975

Cleveland Ohio,
January 24 1975

Earl's Court London, May 23 1975

Earl's Court, May 23 1975

Earl's Court, May 23 1975

Earl's Court,
May 18 1975

Earl's Court, May 18 1975

L A Forum, May 23 1976

The Omni Atlanta, April 23 1977

USA 1977

L A Forum, June 23 1977

Madison Square
Garden, June 14 1977

The Omni Atlanta, April 23 1977

Madison Square Garden,
June 14 1977

Oakland, July 23 1977

Oakland, July 23 1977

Oakland, July 24 1977

Madison Square Garden, June 14 1977

Knebworth, August 4 1979

Knebworth, August 4 1979

Knebworth, August 11 1979

Over Europe, 1980

Over Europe, 1980

Berlin, July 7 1980

Knebworth, June 30 1990

John Paul Jones, Mid 1980s

Mannheim July 3 1980

Madison Square Garden, May 14 1988

Marquee, February 3 1988

New York Hall of Fame, January 12 1995

Live Aid Philadelphia, July 13 1985

The Firm, 1984

US Arms Tour, December 1983

February 1993

Zeppelin author Howard Mylett recalled: "I managed to get to speak to Jimmy and Robert backstage after the show. However, in the rush to do so, I managed to miss them performing a special medley of Christmas numbers."

Bootleg CD Reference: *Sweet Brummy Roll* (Empress Valley)

Friday December 22 1972
London, England
Alexandra Palace

Set: Rock And Roll/Over The Hills And Far Away/Black Dog/Misty Mountain Hop/Since I've Been Loving You/Dancing Days/Bron Yr Aur Stomp/The Song Remains The Same/The Rain Song/Dazed And Confused (inc. San Francisco)/Stairway To Heaven/Whole Lotta Love (inc. Everybody Needs Somebody – Boogie Chillun' – Let's Have A Party – Heartbreak Hotel – I Can't Quit You – The Shape I'm In)/Immigrant Song/Heartbreaker/Organ Solo – Thank You.

A moderately successful return to London – hindered by the poor acoustics of the venue.

Plant: "It's a bit warmer than the last gig we managed to pull off – that was at that notorious Wembley place. Well, I think we must install the warmth of our bodies into this place very quickly, before we all freeze! It's always the same – freezing!"

Robert explained that they've had a bit of trouble on this tour, and dedicated 'Misty Mountain Hop' to "Manchester CID, and may they have a very merry Christmas!" 'Dancing Days' was described as "a song about summer, inebriation and good times" and Plant repeatedly ad-libbed the line "Let's go back to high school!"

'Bron Yr Aur Stomp' again included backing vocals from John Bonham. Plant explained: "He's now turned into a vocalist. He first started off with an old Conway Twitty number, 'It's Only Make Believe', which was accidentally missed off the last album."

Plant was full of Christmas spirit. "You lucky people. It's getting very close to Christmas and if we were all as straight as we used to be, we

should be at the office party now. Nevertheless, this is something that takes us nearly as far back as that." An excellent version of 'Dazed And Confused' featured some outstanding call and response duels between Page and Plant. The 'San Francisco' section now also included lyrics.

'Whole Lotta Love' was very loose, and during 'Boogie Chillun'', Plant ad-libbed: "I was brought up on strong religion, and all I did was keep on givin'… Our little boy's come to the age of 24 years, and he's learnt to sing in American … a hard language to learn to sing after a war."

Zeppelin's decision to perform at Alexandra Palace was an attempt to open up a new London venue, as they had with the Empire Pool. However, problems with the sound and the cold atmosphere hampered the success of the event. "It sounded great on stage," said Plant afterwards, "but beyond the first ten rows the sound was atrocious."

Chris Charlesworth reviewed the London return for *Melody Maker*: "Alexandra Palace was never built to rock. The atmosphere inside this giant hall seemed cold and forbidding. It would have been possible to fit twice as many fans inside but fire regulations don't permit that so there was an abundance of space around the throng who crowded into the centre.

"And for those who didn't get into the centre, seeing and hearing Zep was a chancy business. If you were tall you could probably see over a sea of heads, but even then there was a diminishing sound that flew up into the rafters and returned as a disjointed series of echoes. My guess is that only about a half of the fans heard the music as it should have been heard."

Bootleg CD References: *Riot Show* (Cobla), *Flawless Performance* (Image Quality), *Riot House* (Chad)

Saturday December 23 1972
London, England
Alexandra Palace

Set: Rock And Roll/Over The Hills And Far Away/Black Dog/Misty Mountain Hop/Since

I've Been Loving You/Dancing Days/Bron Yr Aur Stomp/The Song Remains The Same/The Rain Song/Dazed And Confused (inc. San Francisco)/Stairway To Heaven/Whole Lotta Love (inc. The Crunge – Everybody Needs Somebody – Boogie Chillun' – Let's Have A Party – Heartbreak Hotel – I Can't Quit You- The Shape I'm In)/Heartbreaker.

A cartoon, shown on a large screen, preceded the live music. Leaflets were distributed on the night offering a free official Zeppelin poster. Ticket holders were asked to send off their ticket stub to Peter Grant's office. The poster itself was a four sided, fold out, colour item that now commands a serious price tag on the collectors' market. A bootleg show souvenir programme proved to be another sought after item.

Due to the crowd fire limit, the audience were clustered in the centre of the hall, leaving the back area open-spaced. This hampered the atmosphere, and the second show at Alexandra Palace was not as good as the previous night, although the band were still full of festive cheer. Plant: "Good Evening. A merry 23rd of December! Tonight we've got Father Christmas himself with us – John Bonham! Tin Pan Alley's answer to Father Christmas."

Robert again tried to install some atmosphere into the frosty environs. "A long time ago we used to play in places like Wood Green Tavern and all the haunts that have really got some good vibes about them – on those little stages where you got concussion every time you moved! We'd like to get that same thing going tonight, ladies and gentlemen."

'Misty Mountain Hop' was again dedicated to Manchester CID. Plant: "They wondered who left the bathroom taps on all night after we'd gone!" 'Dancing Days' was now also a song about "Christmas cheer" – as well as summertime. Plant commented: "I have never seen so many drunk people in one town as I did on the way here and I've been to Dublin … and Bombay."

'The Song Remains The Same' was introduced as "a song off the new album which comes out …

any time next year. The new album could possibly be called … a number of things, so we'll have to tell you later. It might be called Led Zeppelin Four!"

During 'Dazed And Confused', the then infamous London superfan known as 'Jesus' (a regular at all the capital's major festival/big name shows), stripped off naked and played a tin whistle.

The audience tonight were also full of the spirit of Christmas, or spirits of some sort! Their constant noise-making forced Robert to call a halt to 'Stairway To Heaven' during the soft intro: "Listen, I gotta tell you something before you all start shrieking about. First, it is the 23rd December and it is supposed to be the season of goodwill. So, if you all sit down, there's people at the back who prefer to sit, 'cos really it's one of the hardest numbers to do without a monkey house going crazy!" 'Stairway To Heaven' then continued without further incident.

One member of the audience kept calling out for John Bonham's solo. Robert explained: "He doesn't do 'Moby Dick' anymore. He's writing a new one. It's called 'The Titanic'." 'The Crunge', previously played during 'Dazed And Confused', now showed up in the 'Whole Lotta Love' medley just before Page's Theremin section. The sole encore of 'Heartbreaker' was dedicated to "an ardent rock and roller – Roy Harper" and included a playful instrumental snatch of 'Mama's Little Baby Loves Shortening Bread'.

"Farewell London. Nice One. Merry Christmas to you all. See you … someday" were Plant's parting words.

Bootleg CD References: The Titanic (Image Quality), Merry Christmas Mr. Jimmy (Lemon)

Tuesday January 2 1973
Sheffield, England
Sheffield City Hall

Set: Rock And Roll/Over The Hills And Far Away/Black Dog/Misty Mountain Hop/Since I've Been Loving You/Dancing Days/The Song Remains The Same/The Rain Song/Dazed And Confused (inc. San Francisco)/Stairway To Heaven/Whole Lotta Love (inc. Everybody

Needs Somebody – Boogie Chillun' – Let's Have A Party – Heartbreak Hotel – I Can't Quit You – Going Down Slow)/Heartbreaker.

Robert and Bonzo drove to the show in Bonham's Bentley which broke down on the way. The pair were forced to hitch-hike to Sheffield in the rain. Plant caught a cold and the following two dates were postponed.

Plant was obviously suffering for the whole of tonight's show. His voice was almost completely gone and he didn't even try to hit any high notes. He knew his limitations and apologised to the audience.

Zeppelin persisted with the show and Page seemed to try extra hard to compensate for his companion's sickness. To their credit, only one number, 'Bron Yr Aur Stomp', was dropped from the set, otherwise the full show was performed.

Wednesday January 3 1973
Preston, England
Preston Guild Hall
CANCELLED

Thursday January 4 1973
Bradford, England
St. George's Hall-
CANCELLED

Sunday January 7 1973
Oxford, England
New Theatre
Set includes – Rock And Roll/Over The Hills And Far Away/Black Dog/Misty Mountain Hop/Since I've Been Loving You/Dancing Days/Bron Yr Aur Stomp/The Song Remains The Same/The Rain Song/Dazed And Confused (inc. San Francisco)/Stairway To Heaven/Whole Lotta Love (inc. Everybody Needs Somebody)/Heartbreaker.

Plant's vocals benefited immensely from the few days rest and although his voice still broke occasionally, it had recovered reasonably well.

The show started late tonight. In fact, Zeppelin were still on stage soundchecking when the audi-

ence were admitted to the auditorium.

Plant talked about the new album and said that it was due out "any time between now and August". 'Bron Yr Aur Stomp' returned to the set, although Bonham was absent from backing vocals. 'Dazed And Confused' was extended to 28 minutes and Page was particularly adventurous, including snatches from both 'Walter's Walk' and 'Hots On For Nowhere'.

'Whole Lotta Love' was dedicated to… "Any of our road managers that didn't get arrested in Sheffield. This really is a bit heathen for a Sunday night".

Geoff Hunt of the tribute band Whole Lotta Led recalled: "This was the only Zep show I attended and I'm sure they came back to play 'Heartbreaker' as an encore as this sticks in my memory as I recall Page playing the guitar with one hand. I am also sure they played 'The Ocean' although at the time I didn't recognise it as the album wasn't out yet. I remember Bonzo counting in the intro."

Bootleg CD References: *Oxford Blues* (Flying Disc), *Oxford 73* (The Diagrams Of Led Zeppelin), *Made In England* (Tarantura)

Sunday January 14 1973
Liverpool, England
Liverpool Empire
Set: Rock And Roll/Over The Hills And Far Away/Black Dog/Misty Mountain Hop/Since I've Been Loving You/Dancing Days/Bron Yr Aur Stomp/The Song Remains The Same/The Rain Song/Dazed And Confused/Stairway To Heaven/Whole Lotta Love (inc. Everybody Needs Somebody – Boogie Chillun' – Baby I Don't Care – Let's Have A Party – I Can't Quit You with references to Stones In My Passway – The Shape I'm In)/Heartbreaker/The Ocean.

Plant: "Another Sunday evening and everything stops at ten to ten. Amazing."

Despite Robert suffering the after-effects of flu, tonight's show was one of the most varied and exciting of the whole tour. Plant started by explaining the delay with the new album:

195

"Unfortunately, it's nothing to do with us. It takes such a long time to get these things finished. Usually, record companies are always involved in silly sketches of some sort." Nevertheless, the new material was played with passion and was well received by the receptive crowd.

'Dazed And Confused' continued to extend. Page inserted a new funky riff and Robert ad-libbed "Do the James Brown!" 'San Francisco' was performed in a dreamy haze and Page's bow solo was so soft and gentle that it was barely audible. An unusual Eastern feel prefaced the wild 'call and response' ending; light and shade contrasting to produce pure genius.

Whole Lotta Love' followed and once again rock and blues standards combined, resulting in frenzy. Bonham excelled himself with some furious hammering at the start of the boogie section and during 'I Can't Quit You', Plant ad-libbed a few bizarre lyrics: "If you hear me howling in your pantry rider, please open the door and let me in!"

"Here's one for the M6," yelled Plant at the start of 'Heartbreaker' and 'The Ocean' was dedicated to the audience – "all of you!" Plant: 'It's been a very nice Sunday night – see you again one day."

Bootleg CD References: *Elvis Presley Has Just Left The Building* (no label), *Live In Liverpool '73* (The Diagrams Of Led Zeppelin), *Days Of Heaven* (Tatytura), *The Fabulous Four* (Tarantura)

Monday January 15 1973
Stoke, England
Trentham Gardens
Set includes – Rock And Roll/Over The Hills And Far Away/Black Dog/Misty Mountain Hop/Since I've Been Loving You/Dancing Days/Bron Yr Aur Stomp/The Song Remains The Same/The Rain Song/Dazed And Confused (inc. The Crunge – San Francisco)/Stairway To Heaven/Whole Lotta Love (inc. Voodoo Chile – Everybody Needs Somebody – Boogie Chillun' – Baby I Don't Care – Let's Have A Party).

Another relaxed and enjoyable performance.

Plant stated that 'Black Dog' was about "a Labrador that used to come with us when we went shooting people … we don't shoot animals!" and that 'Misty Mountain Hop' was a song about "what happens if you walk through the park and there's a load of hairies sitting in a circle – dedicated to Rizlas".

'Dazed And Confused' contained both 'San Francisco' and 'The Crunge'. Afterwards, Plant sighed: "Well, that wasn't a bad 20 minutes, was it? There's very few bands that play for three hours and we are nearly ready for the old age pension."

Page began 'Whole Lotta Love' with a few riffs from Jimi Hendrix's 'Voodoo Chile', before Plant got carried away with 'Everybody Needs Somebody' – "I wanna tell all you soul brothers that just came from The Place. That this is where it's really at. This is where soul started!" – Soul started in Stoke!

During 'Boogie Chillun'', Plant ad-libbed "Do you notice that the windows are so steamed up that it must be good" Unusually, the final blues section was not performed tonight.

Fan Robin Dearden, who attended the show, was sure they performed 'Four Stick's as an extra encore though no recorded evidence has surfaced to back up the claim.

Bootleg CD References: *The Stoker* (Tarantura), *Broken Fingers* (Image Quality), *Dedicated To Rizzlers* (Equinox), *Live In Stoke England* (LZ), *Trentham Gardens* (Music With Love)

Tuesday January 16 1973
Aberystwyth, Wales
King's Hall
The band's deep-felt affinity with Wales lead them to play at this small, 800-capacity, sea-front venue. However, surprisingly, the group were not received as well as expected. The audience

remained in their seats throughout the whole show and offered only polite applause.

Page: "It's good to have one concert that is strange and a bit unnerving."

Thursday January 18 1973
Bradford, England
St. George's Hall

Set: Rock And Roll/Over The Hills And Far Away/Black Dog/Misty Mountain Hop/Since I've Been Loving You/Dancing Days/Bron Yr Aur Stomp/The Song Remains The Same/The Rain Song/Dazed And Confused (inc. San Francisco)/Stairway To Heaven/Whole Lotta Love (inc. Everybody Needs Somebody – Boogie Chillun' – Baby I Don't Care – Blue Suede Shoes – Let's Have A Party – I Can't Quit You with references to Stones In My Passway – The Shape I'm In)/Heartbreaker/Immigrant Song.

Tonight's show was the rescheduled date from the January 4 cancellation due to Plant's influenza.

Another excellent performance, climaxing in 'Whole Lotta Love'. During 'Everybody Needs Somebody', Plant excelled in sexual innuendo, ad-libbing "We all need someone to cream on! I really need someone to cream on" – a reference to The Rolling Stones' track, 'Let It Bleed'.

As the band left the stage, Plant cried: "Elvis Presley has just left the building!"

Plant: "I think we've got a lot of friends in England. I remember Bradford when the audience were superb. The raunchiness is in everybody; that below-the-belt surge that everybody gets at some time or another. Everybody gets their rocks off, I suppose, and we supply a little bit of music to that end."

Bootleg CD References: *Bradford 73* (The Diagrams Of Led Zeppelin), *Heart Attack* (Toasted Condor)

Sunday January 21 1973
Southampton, England
Gaumont Theatre

The soundcheck for this show included a run through some Elvis numbers including 'Love Me', 'Frankfurt Special' and 'King Creole'. Robert took to the drums at one point.

Howard Mylett recalls: "On arriving in the afternoon, I saw Robert's Range Rover parked outside with its feather symbol on the side. The soundcheck featured some Elvis numbers and Robert also played on the drums. The show itself was excellent."

CD Reference: *Elvis Has Just Left The Building* (LZ; includes snippets of the soundcheck), *Hiawatha Express* (Toasted)

Monday January 22 1973
Southampton, England
The Old Rectory, Southampton University

Set: Rock And Roll/Over The Hills And Far Away/Black Dog/Misty Mountain Hop/Since I've Been Loving You/Dancing Days/The Song Remains The Same/The Rain Song/Dazed And Confused/Stairway To Heaven/Whole Lotta Love medley inc: Everybody Needs Somebody To Love -I Cant Quite You Baby-Let's Have A Party/Heartbreaker/Organ solo/Thank You/How Many More Times/Communication Breakdown.

Tonight's show was a late addition to the itinerary and was professionally recorded on Page's instructions. The show itself took place on a small carpeted stage.

A bizarre poster for the event was distributed and displayed within the University, and allegedly withdrawn by Grant who took offence at the Nazi association the poster depicted.

In 2002 Page salvaged the tapes for this show for consideration for release for what would become the *How The West Was Won* official live set. Engineer Kevin Shirley did mixdown some of the performances from this show for possible use but ultimately they decided to issue the 1972 Los Angeles and Long Beach recordings.

Thursday January 25 1973
Aberdeen, Scotland
Aberdeen Music Hall

Set: Rock And Roll/Over The Hills And Far Away/Black Dog/Misty Mountain Hop/Since I've Been Loving You/Dancing Days/Bron Yr Aur Stomp/The Song Remains The Same/The Rain Song/Dazed And Confused (inc. San Francisco)/Stairway To Heaven/Whole Lotta Love (inc. Everybody Needs Somebody – Boogie Chillun' – Baby I Don't Care – Let's Have A Party – I Can't Quit You – The Shape I'm In)/Heartbreaker/What Is And What Should Never Be/The Ocean

Plant: "Good Evening! And after 490 miles, it had better be a good evening."

Zeppelin were still on form and delivered another fine performance. However, the set was beginning to become a bit predictable. 'Whole Lotta Love' was not as varied as on previous tours and was now following a set pattern from which there was little deviation. The encores, however, included a surprise in 'What Is What Should Never Be' and a preview of 'The Ocean'.

Fan John Rutherford recalled: "The first concert I ever attended was this gig on Burns Night – still the most exciting performance I've witnessed in 32 years. Page was wearing a white suit which bore resemblance to the Osmonds stage gear. Before they kicked off with 'Rock And Roll' you could see Page doing a mock Osmonds 'Crazy Horses' dance! At the climax of 'Stairway' Plant threw his tambourine sideways and there was a comical crawling race between a roadie and a fan to recover the instrument – the roadie won."

Zeppelin had hoped to book a show at the Ayr

Ice Rink which Page remembered playing years back. However, it proved unavailable.

Bootleg CD Reference: *A15* (The Diagrams Of Led Zeppelin)

Saturday January 27 1973
Dundee, Scotland
Caird Hall

Set includes: Rock And Roll/Over The Hills And Far Away/Black Dog/Misty Mountain Hop/Since I've Been Loving You/Dancing Days/Bron Yr Aur Stomp/The Song Remains The Same/The Rain Song/Dazed And Confused/Whole Lotta Love (inc. Everybody Needs Somebody – Boogie Chillun' – Baby I Don't Care – Let's Have A Party – I Can't Quit You – The

Shape I'm In – Ramble On)/Heartbreaker/
Communication Breakdown.

The quality performances continued with Plant fully recovered. During 'Everybody Needs Somebody', the crowd surged back and forth causing Plant to ad-lib: "Mr Security Man, put your hands together. Now, we're so happy to be here tonight and we came all the way from Aberdeen to do some groovin ... I'd like to introduce you to my good friends down here, these are called the heavies! You watch these heavies, 'cos they get too heavy! Last time we came here, I seem to remember all the trouble going on down the front, and we don't want that to happen again 'cos it makes me cry, cry."

'I Can't Quit You' was performed with soul tonight and Plant even threw in a line from 'Ramble On' – "Leaves are falling all around ... time I was on my way."

Blistering versions of 'Heartbreaker' and 'Communication Breakdown' complete the onslaught.

Bootleg CD References: >*From Boleskine To Alamo* (Flying Disc)*, Nasty Music* (Tarantura) *TheRoads And Miles To Dundee* (Led Note)

Sunday January 28 1973
Edinburgh, Scotland
King's Theatre
Set includes: Black Dog/Bron Yr Aur Stomp/The Song Remains The Same/The Rain Song/Dazed And Confused/Stairway To Heaven/Heartbreaker/Thank You

John Anderson reviewed the performance in

Sounds: "Any thoughts of Led Zeppelin's stamina giving out on Sunday, on what was the second last gig of their exhausting two months' British tour, were promptly dispelled before a full-and-running overfanatical crowd of 1,472.

"'Stairway To Heaven' was one of Plant's frequent triumphs and John Bonham's percussive heroics throughout held everything beautifully in place. John Paul Jones' keyboard work provided an effective symphonic background to 'Rain' (sic) but for total impact with this audience nothing popped Page's athletics on guitar."

The Edinburgh Corporation were in attendance to monitor the crowd reaction. This was the first time the venue had played host to a rock event. Any damage and the doors would be firmly shut for future events. However, the standing room only audience behaved impeccably.

Tuesday January 30 1973
Preston, England
Guildhall **RESCHEDULED**
Set list: Rock And Roll / Over The Hills And Far Away / Black Dog / Misty Mountain Hop / Since I've Been Loving You / Dancing Days / Bron-yr-Aur Stomp / The Song Remains The Same / The Rain Song/Dazed And Confused / Stairway To Heaven / Whole Lotta Love/Heartbreaker

This show was rescheduled to replace the January 3 concert cancelled due to Plant's influenza.
Bootleg CD Reference: Plant's Influenza (Empress Valley), Strange Affinity (Electric Magic)

EUROPEAN TOUR 1973

There was no real let-up in their hectic touring schedule during this period. Barely four weeks separated the lengthy UK trek from this month long visit to Europe. There were security problems in France when rioting fans at Lyons caused dates in Marseilles and Lille to be cancelled. Musical developments included the constantly evolving 'Dazed And Confused' marathon that would further extend in the US and 'Whole Lotta Love', the continuing spring-

board for all manner of rock and roll fun. Zeppelin were clearly enjoying themselves – even if the delayed release of *Houses Of The Holy* had met with some indifferent response in the press.

In an interview at the George V hotel during their two-show residence in Paris, Plant defended the album. "So there's some buggers who don't like the album. Good luck to 'em. I like it and a few thousand other buggers too." And in a comment that would have a hollow ring about it in future years, Plant went on to state: "We're playing better than we've played before. It's working that does it. The British tour, then three weeks off and then a solid blow over here. It's easy to get stale and some bands reach a peak and think that's it. The old country house bit and a year off. It doesn't work that way. There's only one way to function and that's on stage. We've reached a high and we ain't going to lose it. And no bad album review is going to change that."

Friday March 2 1973
Copenhagen, Denmark
K.B.Hallen
The previous day the band attended a record company press reception at an art gallery called Galerie Birch. Photographer Jorgen Angel recalls that there

was some horseplay and one of the hanging paintings was smeared, causing a tense atmosphere.

Sunday March 4 1973
Goteborg, Sweden
Scandinavium Arena
Set List included: Rock And Roll/Over The Hills And Far Away/Black Dog/Misty Mountain Hop/Since I've Been Loving You/Dancing Days/Bron Yr Aur Stomp/The Song Remains The Same/The Rain Song/Dazed And Confused/Whole Lotta Love (Incl Everybody Wants Somebody To Love-Boogie Woogie).

Bert Gren in the *Goteborgs-Posten* reported: "To experience Led Zeppelin last Sunday felt like a bit like seeing a really bad Italian western movie. Or rather like sex without either erotics or love. For the music was tough, cold and hard. I mostly found it terribly cold and without feeling."

Tuesday March 6 1973
Stockholm, Sweden
Kungliga Tennishallen Stockholm
Set: Rock And Roll/Over The Hills And Far Away/Black Dog/Misty Mountain Hop/Since I've Been Loving You/Dancing Days/Bron Yr Aur Stomp/The Song Remains The Same/The

Rain Song/Dazed And Confused (inc. San Francisco)/Stairway To Heaven/Whole Lotta Love (inc. Everybody Needs Somebody – Boogie Chillun' – Baby I Don't Care – Let's Have A Party – I Can't Quit You)/Heartbreaker/The Ocean.

After a powerful opening, Robert introduced 'Black Dog' as 'Chien Noir'. Robert also revealed tonight for the first time that the new album would be called *Houses Of The Holy* and not 'Led Zeppelin Five'."

Prior to 'The Song Remains The Same', Page teased the crowd with a few riffs from the Rolling Stones' 'Satisfaction'. 'Dazed And Confused' featured an unusual funky section and the Swedish audience rather bizarrely stamped their feet during Jimmy's bow solo.

'Whole Lotta Love' was preceded by a few bars of the 'Hokey Cokey' and 'Everybody Needs Somebody' included a brief riff that would later be used for 'In The Light'.

Bootleg CD Reference: *(I Can't Get No) Satisfaction* (The Diagrams Of Led Zeppelin)

Wednesday March 7 1973
Stockholm, Sweden
Kungliga Tennishallen Stockholm

Saturday March 10 1973
Oslo, Norway
Ekeberghallen
CANCELLED
Allegedly, concerts in Norway were repeatedly cancelled during the early Seventies due to resistance for the authorities.

Wednesday March 14 1973
Nuremburg, Germany
Messe- Zentrum Halle
Set: Rock And Roll/Over The Hills And Far Away/Black Dog/Misty Mountain Hop/Since I've Been Loving You/Dancing Days/Bron Yr Aur Stomp/The Song Remains The Same/The Rain Song/Dazed And Confused (inc. San Francisco)/Stairway To Heaven/Whole Lotta

Love (inc. Everybody Needs Somebody – Boogie Chillun' – Baby I Don't Care – Let's Have A Party – I Can't Quit You – Lemon Song)/Heartbreaker.

The general standard of the whole European tour was very high. Many fans still consider that these shows represent Zeppelin at their technical best, in particular Page, whose playing reached a new level.
Bootleg CD Reference: *Nuremburg 1973* (The Diagrams Of Led Zeppelin)

Friday March 16 1973
Vienna, Austria
Wiener Stadthalle
Set: Rock And Roll/Over The Hills And Far Away/Black Dog/Misty Mountain Hop/Since I've Been Loving You/Dancing Days/Bron Yr Aur Stomp/The Song Remains The Same/The Rain Song/Dazed And Confused (inc. San Francisco)/Stairway To Heaven/Whole Lotta Love (inc. Boogie Chillun' – Baby I Don't Care – Let's Have A Party – I Can't Quit You – Lemon Song)/Heartbreaker.

Introduced as the "Rock Sensation of the Year" – this was an outstanding night, despite the fact that John Paul Jones was apparently feeling unwell. Plant: "Mr Jones has colic – must be careful! So all your spiritual feelings must go straight to Mr Jones' stomach."

Page was flying now. 'Since I've Been Loving You' was performed with an amazing aggression and fluency. Plant complimented the audience: "It's very nice to be here in Vienna … you've even got some good groupies!" 'Dancing Days' was introduced as "a song about little schoolgirls, not too young mind you, and my love for them … remembering what happened to Jerry Lee Lewis, I think I'll take it easy."

'Dazed And Confused' was another triumph for Page and afterwards Plant sang "Happiness is a warm gun" from The Beatles' 'White Album'. 'Stairway To Heaven' also benefitted from Page's new found energy, as he delivered a breathtaking final solo. For the 'Heartbreaker' encore, Jimmy provided a spontaneous new opening arrangement, never to be aired again, but thankfully captured by the bootleggers.

Dave Hopkinson of *Melody Maker* wrote: "The historic city of Vienna, normally bulging at the seams with Strauss waltzes and grand operas, played host on Friday night to Led Zeppelin at the enormous Wiener Stadthalle.

"Robert Plant strode around with chest bared and hair flailing, thrusting his pelvic girdle at the audience, while Jimmy Page, wearing his Les Paul low-slung, crashed out well-amplified chords. John Bonham hammered the skins for all he was worth, and John Paul Jones provided some superb orchestral effects on the Mellotron.

"The opening bars of 'Stairway To Heaven' were greeted with a huge roar, and when the band finally broke into 'Whole Lotta Love' that was the cue for a general stampede towards the front of the stage."

Bootleg CD References: *Led Poisoning* (Flying Disc), *Zig Zag Zep* (Tarantura), *Vienna 1973* (Diagrams Of Led Zeppelin), *Lead Poisoning* (Cobla), *A Night At The Opera* (Electric Magic)

Saturday March 17 1973
Munich, Germany
Olympiahalle
Set: Rock And Roll/Over The Hills And Far Away/Black Dog/Misty Mountain Hop/Since I've Been Loving You/Dancing Days/Bron Yr Aur Stomp/The Song Remains The Same/The Rain Song/Dazed And Confused (inc. San Francisco)/Stairway To Heaven/Whole Lotta Love (inc. Everybody Needs Somebody -Boogie Chillun' – Baby I Don't Care – Let's Have A Party – I Can't Quit You – Lemon Song – Going Down Slow)/Heartbreaker.

The storm raged on despite an unruly and noisy crowd. Tonight the rest of the band tried to keep up with Jimmy. Bonham was firing on all cylinders and even took the lead in places. Plant tested the limits of his vocal capacity at every available opportunity.

'Dazed And Confused' began tonight with a gentle, soft intro, but soon exploded into life, Page displaying a superhuman sense of dynamics, his playing fluid to perfection.

'Whole Lotta Love' included 'Going Down Slow', rarely performed on this tour.

Bootleg CD References: *Sturm Und Drang* (Led Note Label), *Lunatics In Munich* (Holy Grail), *Olympiahalle 1973* (Immigrant)

Monday March 19 1973
Berlin, Germany
DeutschLandhalle
Set: Rock And Roll/Over The Hills And Far Away/Black Dog/Misty Mountain Hop/Since I've Been Loving You/Dancing Days/Bron Yr Aur Stomp/The Song Remains The Same/The Rain Song/Dazed And Confused (inc. San Francisco)/Stairway To Heaven/Whole Lotta Love (inc. Everybody Needs Somebody – Boogie Chillun' – Baby I Don't Care – Let's Have A Party – I Can't Quit You – Lemon Song).

Robert's voice was a bit harsh tonight and the show got off to a slow start. The audience were very apathetic, and Plant did his best to rouse them. Plant: "Well, it is very good to be back in another happy town. We believe everywhere we go is happy. This surely is good times, ya? Everybody is happy? The first four rows is happy, ya?" Plant persists in sarcastically referring to the Germans as "happy people!" throughout all the German dates.

After 'Bron Yr Aur Stomp', there was a brief delay and the crowd began to handclap.

'Dazed And Confused' lasted over 30 minutes and included a new relaxed section over which Plant ad-libbed: "I got a feelin' … feelin' won't be wrong." After 'Stairway To Heaven', Plant sang a few lines of The Beatles' 'Please Please Me', before the next introduction: "Here's a song that really invokes the finest physical feelings for a person, without violence, it's usually called sex. Tomorrow we go to Hamburg … to the Reeperbahn where things are beautiful all the time. This is one for the Eros Centre."

'Whole Lotta Love' was a bit ramshackle tonight and Robert's mike kept cutting out during 'Let's Have A Party'. Page saved the number with a superlative solo on 'I Can't Quit You'.

Plant's final remark "Elvis Presley has now left the building!" was now becoming something of a catchphrase for these shows.

Bootleg CD References: *Air Raids Over Europe* (Tecumseh), *Let's Have A Party* (Arms), *Majestic Holies* (Immigrant)

Tuesday March 20 1973
London, England
TV Appearance
The Old Grey Whistle Test *BBC2*
Bob Harris presented an exclusive preview of the forthcoming *Houses Of The Holy* album. This took the form of 'No Quarter' cut to a very weird film, with striking strobe effects and negative images of naked women.

Wednesday March 21 1973
Hamburg, Germany
Musikhalle
Set includes – Black Dog/Misty Mountain Hop/Since I've Been Loving You/Dancing Days/Bron Yr Aur Stomp/The Song Remains The Same/The Rain Song/Dazed And Confused (inc. San Francisco)/Stairway To Heaven/Whole Lotta Love (inc. The Crunge – Everybody Needs Somebody – D'yer Mak'er – Boogie Chillun' – Baby I Don't Care – Let's Have A Party – I Can't Quit You – Lemon Song).

Zeppelin returned with another fine performance. Tonight the whole band were playing in total unison.

Bonham was on peak form, playing with uncontrollable energy. During 'Dazed And Confused' he practically duelled with Page, then added a marching refrain. 'Whole Lotta Love' continued the excitement. A Theremin battle lead into 'The Crunge', as Plant ad-libbed "Do the James Brown!" and 'Cold Sweat'. 'Everybody Needs Somebody' surprisingly included some

'D'yer Mak'er' lyrics.
Bootleg CD References: *Suspended Animation* (Image Quality), *Baby I Don't Care* (Turtle), *April Fools Day* (LZ), *1st April (A Paris Affair)* (Oh Boy)

Thursday March 22 1973
Essen, Germany
Grugahalle
Set: Rock And Roll/Over The Hills And Far Away/Black Dog/Misty Mountain Hop/Since I've Been Loving You/Bron Yr Aur Stomp/The Song Remains The Same/The Rain Song/Dazed And Confused (inc. San Francisco)/Stairway To Heaven/Whole Lotta Love (inc. Everybody Needs Somebody – Boogie Chillun' – Baby I Don't Care – Let's Have A Party – I Can't Quit You – Lemon Song).

Another inspired performance, despite the fact that there were persistent problems with Page's Les Paul. Robert: "We must ask you to cool everything for about three minutes 'cos James's guitar is a bit fucked". After 'Black Dog', Robert thanked the audience in Spanish – "Gracias!"

'Since I've Been Loving You' was outstanding and featured some spine-chilling screams from Plant. 'Dancing Days' was described as a song about "the innocent love of little schoolgirls and my perversion toward it. We love little schoolgirls, fourteen … or fifteen!" 'Dazed And Confused' was once again amazing. The interaction between Bonham and Page, above Jones's rock solid foundation, was truly spectacular. The speed and dexterity of both players was breathtaking. Plant joined in and ad-libbed "Do the James Brown!" and 'Cold Sweat' during the funky section. The transition into 'San Francisco' was now slick and professional. Jimmy included snatches of 'Walter's Walk' later in the piece.

'Whole Lotta Love' was the climax of the show. Although there was now little variation in the numbers which are included in the medley, the delivery of those songs was always challenging.
Bootleg CD References: *Essentially Led* (Live), *Gracias!* (Empress Valley), *Essen 73* (Savege Beast),

Essential Led (Flying Disc)

notes."

Saturday March 24 1973
Offenburg, Germany
Ortenauhalle
Set: Rock And Roll/Over The Hills And Far Away/Black Dog/Misty Mountain Hop/Since I've Been Loving You/Dancing Days/Bron Yur Aur Stomp/The Song Remains The Same/The Rain Song/Dazed and Confused (inc. San Francisco)/Stairway To Heaven/Whole Lotta Love (inc. Cold Sweat – Everybody Needs Somebody – Boogie Chillun' – Baby I Don't Care – Let's Have A Party – I Can't Quit You – Lemon Song)/Heartbreaker.

The last concert in Germany was probably the best of the tour. The band turned in a highly accomplished performance which included the most complete version of 'Cold Sweat' during a highly energetic 'Whole Lotta Love' medley.

Bootleg CD References: *Custard Pie* (Cobla Standard), *Sweet At Night* (The Diagrams Of Led Zeppelin)

Monday March 26 1973
Lyons, France
The Palais De Sports
Set includes – Dazed And Confused (inc. San Francisco)/Whole Lotta Love (inc. I Can't Quit You – Lemon Song)/Heartbreaker.

In 'Dazed And Confused' 'San Francisco' now featured a meandering section and 'I Can't Quit You Baby' was a masterclass of improvisation; however, in general the show fell short of recent standards.

The French regional shows proved problematic. They were badly organised and security was virtually non-existent, threatening the general safety of both group and audience.

Mick Hinton recalls: "We had some trouble in France with the promoter. And it was there we travelled by train. In fact I know I ran out of money and can remember running after Peter as the train ran off shouting 'I've got no money!' and Peter throwing me a wad of

Tuesday March 27 1973
Nancy, France
Parc des Expositions
Set includes : Rock And Roll/ Over The Hills And Far Away / Black Dog / Misty Mountain Hop / Since I've Been Loving You / The Song Remains The Same / The Rain Song/Dazed And Confused / Stairway To Heaven / Whole Lotta Love includes(Everybody Needs Somebody to Love, Boogie Chillun', (Your So Square) I Don't Care, Let's Have A Party, I Can't Quit You)

Plant: "France was chaotic. Promotion people are absolutely nuts over there and the kids are more interested in using a concert as an excuse to be leery, most of the time. I don't really like that, I don't consider that I've gained anything or given anybody anything when I see that there's a lot of fools fighting."

Lack of confidence in organisation and an increase in violence caused the two final provincial French dates to be cancelled. Zeppelin returned to England, but agreed to undertake the final shows of the European tour in the more controlled environment of the French capital.

Bootleg CD Reference: *Heavy Machinery* (Empress Valley)

Thursday March 29 1973
Marseilles, France – CANCELLED

Saturday March 31 1973
Lille, France
CANCELLED

Sunday April 1 1973
Paris, France
Palais des Sports de Saint Ouen

Set: Rock And Roll/Over The Hills And Far Away/Black Dog/Misty Mountain Hop/Since I've Been Loving You/Dancing Days/Bron Yr Aur Stomp/The Song Remains The Same/The Rain Song/Dazed And Confused (inc. San Francisco)/Stairway To Heaven/Whole Lotta Love (inc. Everybody Needs Somebody – Boogie Chillun' – Baby I Don't Care – Let's Have A Party – I Can't Quit You – Lemon Song).

The Paris concerts saw them back to form and this show was a triumphant way to end a highly successful tour.

With the forthcoming US tour pending, Grant made enquiries about hiring a major PR agent. Danny Goldberg of Lee Solter's agency was flown to Paris, interviewed by Grant and the whole band and quickly hired. Goldberg recalled: "Lee and I flew to Paris to see them. To stand on the side of the stage and watch Jimmy was very impressive. I was particularly impressed with how good he was on the acoustic guitar because it was different than the image you were expecting with 'Whole Lotta Love'."

Bootleg CD Reference: *Viva La France* (The Diagrams Of Led Zeppelin)

Monday April 2 1973
Paris, France
Palais des Sports de Saint Ouen
Set: Rock And Roll/Over The Hills And Far Away/Black Dog/Misty Mountain Hop/Since

I've Been Loving You/Dancing Days/Bron Yr Aur Stomp/The Song Remains The Same/The Rain Song/Dazed And Confused /Stairway To Heaven/Whole Lotta Love (inc. Everybody Needs Somebody – I'm Going Down – Boogie Chillun' – Baby I Don't Care – Let's Have A Party – I Can't Quit You – Lemon Song)/Heartbreaker.

"Vive le Zeppelin!" – Roy Hollingworth of *Melody Maker* reported: "Zeppelin kicked a great hole in the night, splitting it all open down at the city's massive Palais des Sports stadium where they finished their European tour. And the Frenchies wet themselves with frightening passion. It was all very astonishing.

"Zeppelin conquered again last night. They turned an audience that resembled dumb figures at the start into a terrifying mass of hysteria. The roar of approval from ten thousand kids was enough to pump the adrenalin through a nun, let alone a rock'n'roller."

Bootleg CD Reference: *Vive Le Zeppelin* (Empress Valley Supreme Disc)

Led Zeppelin

With this tour Led Zeppelin graduated from being a mere rock band to something of an institution in America. By the end of the exhausting two-legged, three month trek (for which they grossed over $4,000,000), few kids in the United States would not have heard of the four Englishmen now breaking attendance records previously set by The Beatles.

Grant did his groundwork with this one, hiring PR consultant Danny Goldberg to ensure that this time around nobody took the spotlight away from his boys. He also knew that the demand to see their live show was bigger than ever, and he booked stadium venues without hesitation.

The two opening dates established the trend: 49,236 at Atlanta Braves Stadium on May 4, and 56,800 at Tampa Stadium a day later. This latter show smashed The Beatles' 1965 Shea Stadium attendance record for a single act performance.

Goldberg did his job by securing a well documented quote after the May 4 date from the Mayor of Atlanta: "This is the biggest thing to hit America since the première of *Gone With The Wind*." The attendance records quickly came to the attention of the US mainstream press. They also hired their own luxury jet, a Boeing 720B known as The Starship, which came complete with LED ZEPPELIN emblazoned on the fuselage.

Their stage show was further developed with the introduction of laser effects, dry ice, backdrop mirrors, hanging mirror balls and even a Catherine wheel pyrotechnic effect for Bonzo's gong at the show's climax. "We felt the denim jeans trip had been there for a long time," said Plant. "It was time to take the trip a little further and these ideas fit perfectly with the mood of the new songs and the excitement of the old."

On-stage developments included rapturous nightly receptions for 'Stairway To Heaven' due to increased audience awareness of the song from massive FM radio air play. Jones'

'No Quarter' was developing into a showpiece all of its own and the no-nonsense medleys in 'Whole Lotta Love' made for breathless finales.

From the start, the tour developed into one of their most enjoyable visits. George Harrison caught up with them in LA and was amazed by the length of their show. "Fuck me! … With The Beatles we were on for 25 minutes and could get off in 15!" he told the band.

Plant suffered some vocal problems in early July but in general their performances throughout the tour were consistent. The confident mood within the camp inspired them to decide to film the latter stages of the tour. "It all started in the Sheraton Hotel, Boston," remembered Grant. "We'd talked about a film for years and Jimmy had known Joe Massot was interested – so we called them and over they came. It was all very quickly arranged."

Massot's film crew duly chronicled the final week of the tour, leading to the last three nights at Madison Square Garden, New York. This footage would later form the basis of their *The Song Remains The Same* movie.

Welcome Back

LED ZEPPELIN

May 4. Atlanta Braves Stadium, Atlanta
May 5. Tampa Stadium, Tampa
May 7. Civic Center Arena, Jacksonville
May 10. University of Alabama, Tuscaloosa
May 11. Kiel Auditorium, St. Louis
May 13. City Auditorium, Mobile
May 14. Municipal Auditorium, New Orleans
May 16. Sam Houston Arena, Houston
May 18. Memorial Auditorium, Dallas
May 19. Convention Center, Fort Worth
May 22. Hemisphere Arena, San Antonio
May 23. University of New Mexico, Albuquerque
May 25. Coliseum, Denver
May 26. Salt Palace, Salt Lake City
May 28. Sports Arena, San Diego
May 30 & 31. Forum, Los Angeles
June 1. Kezar Stadium, San Francisco

The cameras were also around during the only real sour note of the tour – the theft by persons unknown of $180,000 of the group's money from a safe deposit box at the Drake Hotel in New York, discovered just before their final show on July 29. By that time they were almost past caring.

The final word on this record breaking '73 jaunt came from Plant: "We all went over the top on that tour, but 99.5 of the gigs were great. New Orleans was like home and LA felt like that too. It was a little hard for me to get back into the second part of the tour but when we got to the Garden we were peaking again. I just hope the cameramen got us from the right angles."

Equipment Notes:

For this US tour Bonzo switched to a clear Vistalite Ludwig kit, retaining the three linked circle symbol on the bass drum. Jones adds a five-string Fender Precision bass for this tour alongside his regular Fender Jazz bass. Jimmy added a Cherry Red Gibson Les Paul which is used for Theremin work.

Fashion Notes:

In line with the more flamboyant stage set, their dress attire takes on a more flamboyant nature. Page favoured a hummingbird jacket and handmade trousers with sewn-on silver motifs. For much of the tour, Plant wore a cut-off blouse. Bonham was often seen in a distinctive spider web design T-shirt. Jones had a bizarre Spanish matador jacket for the Madison Square Garden shows.

April 1973
London, England
Shepperton Studios
Shepperton England
Old Street film Studios

REHEARSALS

The band rehearsed a new stage and lighting act in preparation for the forthcoming tour.

The emphasis was on the new light show. Page: "We've had lighting before on occasions when people have turned up and just done it for us. This time we routined all the lighting before we came over. It took three or four days rehearsing to get it really tight, so that it augmented the set."

May 1973
America
Unconfirmed Venue and Date

Led Zeppelin's soundchecks were infrequent and usually employed to work on new ideas and run through some rock'n'roll songs, usually from the Elvis catalogue.

A soundboard recording exists from a 1973 soundcheck which is often erroneously cited as having been taped prior to the July 6 Chicago date. From the quality of Plant's vocals (which were in poor shape at the beginning of the second leg of the US tour), it's evident it's from the first leg of the tour, possibly from the day before the May 4 show. Another school of thought is that due to the abundance of songs from *Physical Graffiti* it derives from the rehearsal prior to the US tour held at the Met Center, Minnesota on January 17 1975.

The surviving bootlegged tape reveals remarkable insight into the evolution of numbers such as 'Night Flight', 'The Rover' and 'The Wanton Song'. All were rehearsed at this soundcheck but not played live on the tour, and they would not be issued until the 1975 double set *Physical Graffiti*.

They also performed versions of Chuck Berry's 'School Days', 'Nadine' and 'Hey Hey Rock'n'Roll', Johnny Kidd & The Pirates' 'Shaking All Over' and 'I'll Never Get Over You' and Cliff Richard's 'Dynamite' and 'Move it'.

The tape is a rare and remarkable insight into how they warmed up for their live performances.
Bootleg CD Reference: *Round And Round* (Ghost), *Magical Mystery Tape* (Tarantura), *Tribute To Johnny Kidd And The Pirates* (Scorpio), *The Smithereens* (Akashic)

Led Zeppelin

Friday May 4 1973
Atlanta, Georgia
Fulton County Stadium/Braves Stadium

Set: Rock And Roll/Celebration Day/Black Dog/Over The Hills And Far Away/Misty Mountain Hop/Since I've Been Loving You/No Quarter/The Song Remains The Same/The Rain Song/Dazed And Confused (inc. San Francisco)/Stairway To Heaven/Moby Dick-Heartbreaker- Whole Lotta Love

Zeppelin opened the tour in a truly spectacular way, with two massive outdoor shows in front of 49,236 people – the largest crowd in the history of Georgia, and grossed $246,180. A closed circuit TV system projected the concert onto giant screens for the benefit of distant spectators.

"Zeppelin take the States by storm," reported Ritchie Yorke. "The latest Led Zeppelin tour is proving yet again that this is the top rock'n'roll band in the world. There's never been anything like it. I am now convinced that Zepp could out-draw the Stones, Alice Cooper, Carole King or Elvis Presley in any US city you care to mention.

"So much for the cynics who doubted if Zepp still had US drawing power. And for the critics who arrogantly said the album sucked. Led Zeppelin reign supreme and it's high time many more members of the media realised it."

The *Atlanta Constitution* had a front page lead story on the event: "The manicured grassy fields at Atlanta Stadium may never be the same after a Friday night rock concert attracted a record 50,000 crowd. What was once the domain of athletes and hot dog chewing baseball fans became centre stage for Led Zeppelin, a British group wired for sound and worshipped by the teenage legions. Police towed away an estimated 100 cars left on the side of the Interstate highways."

Saturday May 5 1973
Tampa, Florida
Tampa Stadium

Set: Rock And Roll/Celebration Day/Black Dog/Over The Hills And Far Away/Misty Mountain Hop/Since I've Been Loving You/No Quarter/The Song Remains The Same/The Rain Song/Dazed And Confused (inc. San Francisco)/Stairway To Heaven/Moby Dick-Heartbreaker- Whole Lotta Love (inc. Boogie Chillun')/The Ocean/Communication Breakdown.

Modestly billed as "An event … The supershow of the year".

Led Zeppelin attracted 56,800 to today's show and broke the single concert attendance record set by The Beatles in 1965. The show grosses an estimated £309,000.

"Hello. It seems between us we've done something nobody's ever done before … and that's fantastic!" was Plant's triumphant opening comment. Robert's voice was a bit hoarse at first but overall it's a fine performance for so early in the tour. The set list had some major changes for the American shows. 'Celebration Day' was recalled and now followed directly after 'Rock And Roll'. 'Over The Hills And Far Away' was moved back in the run

THE STARSHIP

Travelling between venues was always considered a major chore by Zeppelin. Neither Page nor Grant had any love of flying, and Bonham was often known to require a drink or two to calm his nerves before take-off. However, in a country the size of America, air travel was a necessity.

From the 1972 US tour onwards, Grant had hired a small private Falcon Jet to transport the band and their closest associates, but these aircraft were comparatively light and susceptible to air turbulence. After performing a show at Kezar Stadium on June 2 1973, Zeppelin encountered bad turbulence on a flight back to Los Angeles. This unnerving incident persuaded Grant that since flying was inevitable, then they would do it with as much style, comfort and safety as possible – regardless of the cost.

During the break in that tour, tour manager Richard Cole leased The Starship at a cost of $30,000 for just over three weeks. This was a full sized Boeing 720B passenger jet as used by commercial airlines which had been reduced to forty seats and was specially customised on the whim of its clients. The fuselage of the plane was re-sprayed with LED ZEPPELIN emblazoned down the side. Inside, the main cabin contained seats and tables, revolving arm chairs, a 30-foot long couch running along the right hand side of the plane opposite the bar, a tel-

evision set and video cassette player. An electronic organ were also built into the bar and at the rear were two back rooms, one with a low couch and pillows on the floor, the other a bedroom, complete with a white fur bedspread and shower room. Clients could order in advance whatever food they wished and this would be served, together with copious amounts of alcohol, by a couple of attractive stewardesses.

Flying in The Starship, Zeppelin found that they didn't need to change hotels so often. They could base themselves in large cities such as Chicago, New York, Dallas, and Los Angeles and fly to and from concerts within an hour or two's flying distance. After the final encore the four members of Led Zeppelin would be wrapped in red bathrobes, hustled into waiting limousines, rushed to the airport and in the sky before their audience had left the venue.

The Starship was again used throughout the whole 1975 US tour, by which time Bonzo liked to occupy the co-pilot's seat. "He flew us all the way from New York to LA once," Peter Grant told a startled Chris Charlesworth on one tour. "He ain't got a licence, mind ... "

In 1977, the Starship was grounded at Long Beach Airport due to engine problems, so Zeppelin were forced to find a comparable alternative. Cole eventually chartered 'Caesar's Chariot', a Boeing 707 owned by the Caesar's Palace Hotel in Las Vegas.

ning order to fourth place. 'Black Dog' was now performed with a few bars of 'Bring It On Home' as an introduction. 'Dancing Days' and 'Bron Yr Aur Stomp' were both dropped from the standard set. John Bonham's solo 'Moby Dick' was reintroduced, although in a much truncated form. 'Whole Lotta Love' was also now much shorter, losing most of the medley section – only 'Boogie Chillun'' was regularly retained.

The sheer size of the crowd tonight caused problems at the front of the stage. After 'Since I've Been Loving You', Robert appealed for calm: "Listen, as we've achieved something between us that's never been done before, will you just cool it on the barriers here. Because otherwise a lot of people might get poorly, right? So, if you have a little respect for the person who's standing next to you, then possibly we can have no problems, 'cos we don't want no problems, do we? It's bad enough with the balance of payments!" The situation didn't improve however, so after 'The Rain Song' Plant addressed the crowd again: "We want this to be a really joyous occasion. I gotta tell you three people have been taken to hospital and if you keep pushing on that barrier, there's gonna be stacks and stacks of people going. We are animals, but we can move back a little bit because it's the only way."

Robert commented that 'Dazed And Confused' takes him back to when he was 19 … "before I got the clap or anything" A power packed 11-minute version of 'Moby Dick' flowed straight into 'Heartbreaker' which is in turn linked non-stop

into 'Whole Lotta Love'. This is the only occasion where these pieces were linked in such a manner. Plant made references to beating The Beatles' record during the 'Boogie Chillun'' section.

The first encore of 'The Ocean' was complete with Bonham's spoken introduction and 'Communication Breakdown' closes the show. Then 200 white doves were released as the band left the stage.

Peter Grant recalled: "The thing with Tampa is that I didn't tell them really how big it was going to be but when we drew up Robert was going 'Fucking hell G, where did all these people come from?' And I just said, 'Don't worry son. I know you're still on probation with the band but you'll be alright', which of course he was. I was confident they could handle it. In fact, I knew they would rise to the occasion."

Plant: "I think it was the biggest thrill I've had I pretend – I kid myself – I'm not very nervous in a situation like that. I try to bounce around jus like normal. But, if you do a proportionate thing it would be like half of England's population.

"It was a real surprise. Tampa is the last place I would expect to see nigh on 60,000 people. It's no the country's biggest city. It was fantastic. One would think it would be very hard to communicate; with 60,000 people some have got to be quite a distance off. There were no movie screens showing us, like in Atlanta. The only thing they could pick on was the complete vibe of what music was being done.

"It's a bit like amyl nitrate. It's like a rush tha you're not ready for. I didn't know how many people were going to be there. I had no idea wha it would look like. There was nobody else but Lec Zeppelin, four of us, and all those people as far as the eye could see. But the minute we walked ou there, there were so many little matches held up that the whole place was glowing and that is a start. When you get that sort of reception as a start, you know the medium is set."

Bootleg CD References: *Pigeon Blood* (Flagge) *56'800 In The Ocean* (Silver Rarities), *First Day* (ARMS), *Tampa Stadium* (Tarantura)

Monday May 7 1973
Jacksonville, Florida
Jacksonville Coliseum

Thursday May 10 1973
Tuscaloosa, Alabama
Memorial Coliseum University of Alabama

Friday May 11 1973
St. Louis, Missouri
Kiel Auditorium

Sunday May 13 1973
Mobile, Alabama
Municipal Auditorium

Set includes: Rock And Roll/Celebration Day/Black Dog/Over The Hills And Far Away/Misty Mountain Hop/Since I've Been Loving You/No Quarter/The Song Remains The Same/The Rain Song/Dazed And Confused (inc. San Francisco)/Stairway To Heaven/Moby Dick-Heartbreaker- Whole Lotta Love (inc. Boogie Chillun')

Plant made references to 'Acapulco Gold' in 'Over The Hills And Far Away' and afterwards commented "Malacum Salaam! – It's a bit of Indian," he explained.

'Since I've Been Loving You' was outstanding. "That was something we will always play as long as we're in existence," vowed Plant. "It seems so early really to do a concert. We only got out of bed around 2.30, so I just finished me bacon and eggs and here we are. What's the name of this place … Mobile?" he jokes prior to introducing a wild version of 'The Song Remains The Same'.

Plant commented that the English tax authorities were ripping Zeppelin off and John Bonham was humorously introduced as … "a rather fat chubby happy fellow – full of shit and speed!" 'Moby Dick' was now beginning to expand in length and tonight clocked in at just under 15 minutes.

Plant: "In this band we're very lucky that everybody is more enthusiastic as time goes on. There is no fatigue or boredom musically at all. There's a bit of boredom when you're stuck in Mobile, Alabama, or places like that. A few lamp standards may fall out of the windows – things like that – but we move on and we keep playing that music."

Bootleg CD References: *Goin' Mobile* (Midas Touch), *Upwardly Mobile* (Ghost), *Mobile Dick* (Ghost), *Night Flight* (Metal Mania)

Monday May 14 1973
New Orleans, Louisiana
Municipal Auditorium

Set: Rock And Roll/Celebration Day/Black Dog/Over The Hills And Far Away/Misty Mountain Hop/Since I've Been Loving You/No Quarter/The Song Remains The Same/The Rain

LED ZEPPELIN AMERICAN TOUR 1973   LIST & DIMENSIONS OF EQUIPMENT

Qty	Item	Dimensions
1	Accessory Trunk	48 x 20 x 26
1	Accessory Trunk	36 x 20 x 20
1	Accessory Trunk	30 x 20 x 16
1	Accessory Trunk	32 x 16 x 12
1	Accessory Trunk	30 x 18 x 12
1	Accessory Trunk	32 x 12 x 12
2	Accessory Case	16 x 12 x 8
3	Acoustic Cabinets	26 x 20 x 50 each
3	Acoustic Amplifiers	26 x 12 x 8 each
4	Marshall Amplifiers	32 x 14 x 12 each
4	Marshall Cabinets	34 x 18 x 38 each
2	Orange Cabinets	32 x 15 x 28 each
2	Orange Amplifiers	23 x 18 x 12 each
1	Fender Piano in Case	50 x 14 x 27
1	Accessory Case	40 x 20 x 12
2	Drum Accessory Cases	17 x 24 x 15 each
1	Tympani Drum	33 x 33
1	Tympani Drum in Case	36 x 36 x 30
4	Ludwig Bass Drums	30 x 20 each
2	Ludwig Floor Tom Tom	22 x 18 each
2	Ludwig Floor Tom Tom	20 x 18 each
2	Ludwig Top Tom Tom	18 x 11 each
1	Case with 2 Snare Drums	20 x 18
2	Cymbal Cases	24" Diameter each
2	Gong Case	43 x 43 x 8
1	Gong Ring	50 x 2
1	Mellotron	40 x 30 x 35
3	Cases with Tapes	23 x 24 x 5 each

EQUIPMENT LIST / Continued...

Qty	Item	Dimensions
2	Fender Bass Guitars	50 x 5 x 15 each
2	Gibson Les Paul Guitars	42 x 5 x 14 each
1	Gibson Double Neck Guitar	46 x 20 x 5
1	Drum Board	85 x 36 x 2
1	Wooden Step	36 x 16 x 8
4	Trunks	4'x 3'x 2' approx. 150 lbs.
2	Wooden Sections	6' x 4' approx. 150 lbs
2	Half Circle Sections	8' x 4' approx. 150 lbs.
1	Colour Wheel	3' Diameter 14 lbs.
4	Follow Spots	5' x 2' x 2' approx.100lbs
3	Stands	4' x 2' approx. 14 lbs. each
3	Dry Ice Machines	4' x 1' x 1½'approx. 150lbs each

TOTAL NUMBER PIECES - 77
ALL DIMENSIONS IN INCHES UNLESS OTHERWISE INDICATED.

Song/Dazed And Confused (inc. San Francisco)/Stairway To Heaven/Moby Dick/ Heartbreaker/Whole Lotta Love (inc. The Crunge – Boogie Chillun')/Communication Breakdown (inc. Cold Sweat).

Another excellent show. The crowd were wild with anticipation and erupted as soon as Zeppelin hit the stage. The authorities turned on the house light so security could see what's going on. Plant: "We've got to get these house lights down. It's pretty pointless us bringing our own lights, if we've got these things going on. Mr Cole, can you take your dress off and get these lights turned down please?"

After 'Over The Hills And Far Away', Plant explained: "We've got three poor policemen here trying to do their duty, so why don't we all sit down – those people in the gangways – then these guys can cool it and dig the show too That's pretty reasonable. It's what they call live and let live."

Before 'Moby Dick' Plant said: "I once heard a song called 'The Witch Queen Of New Orleans'. Well, tonight, I'm pleased to announce that John Bonham is 'The Drag Queen Of New Orleans'!" Page laughs so much that he enters the piece late, but even so, Bonham is relaxed and extends the solo to nearly 21 minutes.

'Whole Lotta Love' featured a funky 'Crunge' section prior to the Theremin solo. Robert adlibed 'Do the James Brown!' and added a few lines from 'Cold Sweat'. During the final refrain of 'Whole Lotta Love', Robert kept repeating the line 'Ain't nothing but a hound dog!' in true Elvis parody. The sole encore of 'Communication Breakdown' again includes some lines from 'Cold Sweat'.

"Good Night, New Orleans – the best city in the States!"

At an aftershow party at Cosimos Studios John Paul Jones jammed on organ in a line-up that included Atalntic's Phil Carson and Jerry Greenberg on drums. Earlier Ernie K Doe had performed a set.

Robert Plant: "Next to my home town in the Midlands, New Orleans is my favourite city. The combination of the incredible music and the beautiful balconies in the French quarter is just great."

Years later he reflected: "New Orleans was always a highlight of Zep tours. Ahmet Ertegun would come down and throw a big party for the band. We'd have the Neville Brothers, Ernie K Doe, Lee Allen – Bob Doggett came and played Hammond organ and did honky tonk."

"It's only May but it's the year's best," wrote Lisa Robinson for *Disc*. "Page was moving around the stage with his guitar like a dancer ... his guitar playing is so consistently great. Perhaps he only hears the differences each night; to us mortals it just sounds SO bloody GREAT."

Bootleg CD References: *New Orleans '73* (The Diagrams Of Led Zeppelin), *Live & Led Live Pt1 & Pt2* (Flying Disc), *Longest Night* (Satellite), *Johnny Piston & The Dogs* (TM 005/006), *The Drag Queen* (Tarantura)

Wednesday May 16 1973
Houston, Texas
Sam Houston Coliseum

Set: Rock And Roll/Celebration Day/Black Dog/Over The Hills And Far Away/Misty Mountain Hop/Since I've Been Loving You/No Quarter/The Song Remains The Same/The Rain Song/Dazed And Confused (inc. San Francisco)/Stairway To Heaven/Moby Dick/ Heartbreaker – Whole Lotta Love (inc. I'm Going Down – Boogie Chillun')/Communication Breakdown.

Not quite as effective as the previous shows, but they were still on excellent form. They were playing very loose tonight but with a seemingly never-ending supply of energy.

"So what have you been doing for two years?" asks Robert. 'Misty Mountain Hop' is introduced as ... "about what happens when you take a stroll on a Sunday afternoon with a packet of cigarette papers and some good grass and ... I'm not advocating it ... just telling the story!"

Bootleg CD References: *Going Down* (Watch Tower), *Two Nights In May* (Celebration)

Friday May 18 1973
Dallas, Texas
Memorial Auditorium

Set includes – Rock And Roll/Celebration Day/Black Dog/Over The Hills And Far Away/Misty Mountain Hop/Since I've Been Loving You/No Quarter/The Song Remains The Same/The Rain Song/Dazed And Confused (inc. San Francisco)/Stairway To Heaven.

In contrast not one of the best shows of the tour.

Equipment problems resulted in a rather chaotic start to the set. In 'Celebration Day' Plant honed in on the sound problems, adlibbing: "Give me some monitors, Rusty!" Also, John Paul Jones was not feeling so good tonight. Plant explained: "John Paul Jones has got two fractured ribs and he's still managing to stand. I think that's fantastic! That's not really funny at all … we thought he'd got the clap."

Bootleg CD References: *Four For Texas* (Diagrams Of Led Zeppelin), *Discover America* (Tarantura), *Fractured Ribs* (Toasted Condor), *Heartattack* (Toasted Condor), *Thunder Rock* (Great Dane)

Saturday May 19 1973
Fort Worth, Texas
Tarrant County Convention Center

Set includes – Rock And Roll/Celebration Day/Black Dog/Over The Hills And Far Away/Misty Mountain Hop/Since I've Been Loving You/No Quarter/The Song Remains The Same/The Rain Song/Dazed And Confused (inc. San Francisco)/Stairway To Heaven.

John Paul Jones seemed to have made a remarkably quick recovery and the band were back on their game.

After 'Black Dog', Robert chastised the audience for not joining in: "What happened to you on the Ah! – Ah!'? You were jerking off. What happened?" There were technical problems again and tonight Plant incorporated the line "Give me some more monitors if you please!" into 'Since I've Been Loving You'.

After a brief fanfare, Robert dedicated 'Dazed And Confused' to an old friend of his – 'The Butter Queen'. Plant: "The Butter Queen – Fantastic! Do you know what it's like? Far out … she is too much really."

Jimmy Page: "In Texas they've got the richest groupies in the world. Some of the groupies followed our private jet in their private jet!"

Bootleg CD References: *Tympani For The Butter Queen* (Midas Touch), *A Worthwhile Experience* (Flying Disc), *From Boleskine To The Alamo* (Flying Disc), *The Butter Queen* (Unbelievable)

Tuesday May 22 1973
San Antonio, Texas
Hemisfair Arena

Wednesday May 23 1973
Albuqueruqe, New Mexico
The Pit University Of New Mexico

Friday May 25 1973
Denver, Colorado
Coliseum

Saturday May 26 1973
Salt Lake City, Utah
Salt Palace

Set includes – Rock and Roll/Celebration Day/Black Dog/Over The Hills And Far Away/ Georgia On My Mind/ Misty Mountain Hop/Since I've Been Loving You/No Quarter/The Song Remains The Same/ The Rain Song/Dazed AndConfused/ Stairway To Heaven/ Heartbreaker/Whole Lotta Love/ Communication Breakdown

The medley in 'Whole Lotta Love' was dropped for this show.

Bootleg Cd References: *Salt Lake City 1973* (Watch Tower), *The Dirty Trick* (Empress Valley)

Monday May 28 1973
San Diego, California
Sports Arena

Set: Rock And Roll/Celebration Day/Black Dog/Over The Hills And Far Away/Misty Mountain Hop/Since I've Been Loving You/No

Quarter/The Song Remains The Same/The Rain Song/Dazed And Confused /Moby Dick /Stairway To Heaven/Heartbreaker – Whole Lotta Love (incl. The Crunge, Honey Bee, Boogie Chillun', Going Down)/The Ocean

'Led Zeppelin Hits Peak At Sellout'. Carol Olten reported: "The culmination of all rock'n'roll of a decade appears to have occurred with Led Zeppelin and the crowning achievement capable of its star instrument, the guitar, seems to be the possession of Jimmy Page.

"Appearing Monday night before a sold-out house of 16,000 persons, Led Zep attested to all the praises that have preceded its performance here, namely sold-out concerts all around the country and gold record sales that continue to mount.

"Essentially, the set was as powerful as rock-'n'roll ever gets. Raunchy. Flashy. And full of the fuzzy, sheet metal noise that has brought a musical form to its culmination."

Bootleg CD References: *San Diego 1973* (Watch Tower), *Three Days Before* (Empress Valley), *San Diego 1973* (Empress Valley)

Wednesday May 30 1973
Inglewood Los Angeles, California
The Forum – **CANCELLED**

News Report: "Page Hurts Hand: But How? – The Wednesday night concert was postponed until Sunday after Jimmy Page sprained his finger and the band's physician insisted he couldn't play that night. Quite an inconvenience for thousands of fans who were on their way to the Forum when they heard the news over the radio.

"How did Page sprain his finger? Incredible rumours about that were rampant around the Sunset Strip including that the boys were busy throwing beer bottles and finally a table – out of the windows of the ninth floor of the Continental Hyatt House Hotel into a Lincoln convertible in the parking lot – just for fun, you know. Page's finger got in the way and you know the rest. Led Zeppelin has stayed at the Continental several times before and their frolicking has resulted in

repair expenses being tacked on the bill, but they are always contrite afterwards and seemingly are always welcome guests at this hostelry of the rock kingdom."

Thursday May 31 1973
Inglewood Los Angeles, California
The Forum

Set: Rock And Roll/Celebration Day/Black Dog/Over The Hills And Far Away/Misty Mountain Hop/Since I've Been Loving You/No Quarter/The Song Remains The Same/The Rain Song/Dazed And Confused (inc. San Francisco)/Stairway To Heaven/Moby Dick/Heartbreaker – Whole Lotta Love (inc. The Crunge – Boogie Chillun')/The Ocean/ Communication Breakdown.

Both concerts at the LA Forum were sold out in just two hours, breaking the Stones' record at the Forum.

As ever, Los Angeles was Zeppelin's favourite stomping ground and tonight they were truly on fire, despite Page's injured finger. 'Rock And Roll' was absolutely storming and sets the pace for the rest of the concert.

There were a few problems with firecrackers and monitor malfunctions, but nothing could stop Zeppelin enjoying themselves as it was Bonzo's birthday. Robert informed the crowd: "Today, John Bonham is 21 – he's always 21! I've known the birthday baby for about 15 years … and he's been a regular bastard all the time!"

'Stairway To Heaven' was dedicated to Bonham, who is in fact 25-years old, and before 'Moby Dick' Plant announced: "It's the gentleman's birthday. I think it's only fair that we should let him bang his balls out, right?' Bonham's solo was powerful and energetic, so he kept it down to a mere 16 minutes. Afterwards Plant led the Forum crowd through a few choruses of "Happy Birthday dear Bonzo!"

At the end of the show, Robert also paid tribute to Jimmy: "Jimmy sprained his finger two days ago and we had to cancel last night. He's been playing tonight and putting his hand in a bowl o

214

cold water to keep the swelling down – I think that's great! He was playing that bit in 'Heartbreaker', and if you could have felt what he must have felt … We're rock and roll veterans!"

"Zeppin' Out" was the headline for Charles Shaar Murray's review in *New Musical Express:* "One of the first things one notices about Zeppelin's audiences is their calm and serenity. They got their rocks off all right, and they shook and twitched till they were as sweaty and exhausted as the band, but not once did anybody give off a violent vibe. For all its enormous volume and energy, Zeppelin's music is inappropriate music to split skulls to.

"Now I always knew Zeppelin were good, but it had been three years since I'd last seen them and no way was I prepared for this. The pure, clean power of Zeppelin's performance and sound is even more extraordinary than it might otherwise appear. They just play the music, loud and proud.

"Where Zeppelin score over other bands is that they keep all the bases covered. Everything that's part of the show is meticulously polished until it's as good as it can possibly get. Nothing sags, nothing is second-rate, nothing is skimped. The LA Forum gig was pretty damn good. It blew me out completely."

Plant: "The gig was a magic one because the people were so relaxed. It was as if I'd known them for years."

After the show, there was a birthday party for Bonzo in Laurel Canyon. He arrived dressed in only a T-shirt, plimsolls and a pair of swimming trunks. This set the mood for the rest of the party and by the end of the evening Bonzo had thrown virtually everybody into the swimming pool. Peter Grant recalls: "We get to the party and they're all watching Deep Throat in tuxedos and smoking little joints with clips on. There's this cake like a wedding cake and George Harrison picks up the top and pushes it into John Bonham's face. Then the colour drained from George's face. He knew he'd dropped a clanger. There's no lateral thinking with John: it's boom, wallop! So George runs outside and John gets hold of him and throws him in the swimming pool. Patti (Harrison's wife) comes running out screaming and she gets thrown in. Then everybody got thrown in. Wonderful night. Wonderful!

"Everybody got thrown in the pool – except for me. Nobody ever dared throw me in a swimming pool."

Bootleg CD References: *Bonzo's Birthday Party* (Empres Valley), *Bonzo's Birthday Party* (Cobla Standard), *Bonzo's Birthday Presents* (Celebration Definitive Masters)

Bonzo's Birthday Party (Sanctuary), *Bonzo's 25th Birthday* (Arms)

Saturday June 2 1973

San Francisco, California

Kezar Stadium

Set: Rock And Roll/Celebration Day/Black

Led Zeppelin Zooms High at Kezar

By Philip Elwood

Britain's noisy Led Zeppelin rock group drew close to 50,000 fans yesterday afternoon in Kezar Stadium and probably set an American concert gross receipts record by bringing about $320,000 through the box office.

A month ago in New York's Shea Stadium the group grossed $309,000 to shatter the 1966 Beatles' mark.

Some Zeppelin fanatics had arrived in Golden Gate Park Thursday to assure themselves choice seats. There were no reserved seats, and dedicated Zeppelin followers like to be close in — to let the mammoth amplified sounds swallow them whole.

The shouting vocals of Robert Plant and the screaming guitar of Jimmy Page were easily audible at the eastern stretches of the Panhandle, a half mile away, and crowds of listeners were piled on rooftops five or six blocks up the hill from the stadium.

The entire Kezar turf was carpeted with young people and all but the backside bleacher seats (behind the stage) were jammed like a 49ers-Packers game of old. [illegible] stage was set over the western end zone section of the football field.

The wildest aspect of the audience seemed represented by exotic costumes, although some dancing livened the areas where there was space to move. And there certainly was more grass in hand than under foot.

First Aid

The first-aid tent on the stadium floor, staffed by the Haight-Ashbury Medical Clinic, reported "normal activity," which means a lot of kids on various drug trips, and one broken leg, a result of a stairway tumble.

There was not the audience warmth for Led Zeppelin that was evident last weekend when the Grateful Dead and friends christened Kezar as a supershow rock arena.

A substantial number of yesterday's crowd (perhaps half) had bought tickets in agencies away from the immediate Bay Area and they were here to have a high time with the Zeppelin, not necessarily to generate the communal-like atmosphere that distinguishes performances by locally based groups.

The Zeppelin arrived on stage after a nearly two hour intermission which followed a spirited performance by Lee Michaels. That long a break brings an audience down and generally encourages restlessness, although the patience of Bay Area rock crowds is astonishing.

Even after they had finally begun, Zeppelin had electronic troubles (Page's guitar plug broke a wire) and another delay occurred.

Lacked Spark

The quartet's performance lacked the dynamic spark of earlier local presentations. Plant's vocals and bodily gyrations seemed tired and routine, and drummer John Bonham and bassist John Paul Jones had trouble solidifying their [illegible] going.

Led Zeppelin [illegible] better than $1000 a minute for their two-and-a-half hour show. [illegible] the lawn on a sunny Saturday afternoon.

Dog/Over The Hills And Far Away/Misty Mountain Hop/Since I've Been Loving You/No Quarter/The Song Remains The Same/The Rain Song/Dazed And Confused (inc. San Francisco)/Stairway To Heaven/Moby Dick/Heartbreaker – Whole Lotta Love (inc. The Crunge – Boogie Chillun')/Communication Breakdown/The Ocean.

This show was an afternoon festival appearance with support from Roy Harper, The Tubes and Lee Michaels. Despite arriving late the band turned in a superb performance, one of the most memorable outdoor appearances of their career, captured via some striking photographic images by Jeff Mayer and Neal Preston which can be seen in the books *The Photographers Led Zeppelin* (compiled by Ross Halfin) and *Led Zeppelin: A Photographic Collection* (Neal Preston)

There was some confusion over timings and Zeppelin arrived at the show late and rushed straight to the stage, only to find that the equipment wasn't working properly and Robert had to fill in: "As we've been awake for a total of about two and a half hours, it doesn't really seem that we should be doing what we're doing right now, but I believe there's something to do with lightness and darkness, so we'll try a bit of lightness! Actually, I feel quite healthy. It's quite an amazing feat to be awake in the daylight … Now, if I was cool, I should put the mike in the stand and clear off until everything works right. Well, thank you very much for a great show, we'll see you in five minutes."

'Rock And Roll' finally commenced the proceedings. The band were a bit sluggish to start with, but don't take long to warm up. Plant: "It's feeling alright, isn't it? I thought the vibes were a bit weird as we drove in, in the big black limousine, but I know now that everything's alright … apart from the fact that I got TB."

Introducing 'Misty Mountain Hop', Robert was overcome by the smell of pot coming from the audience. "Smells good up here! It's all blowing in the right direction". Somebody at the front then threw a huge joint onto the stage. "Ah, bless you! I'll save it for afterwards if you don't mind!" was Plant's response.

Robert later criticised a certain West Coast music publication, without mentioning any names, and dedicated 'The Song Remains The Same' to the musical papers who think … "that we should remain a blues band!"

Returning for the first encore, Plant commented: "We've just had a bit of a water confrontation with a few people round the back, which keeps our name alive. We'd like to thank Bill Graham for getting it all together. That man has given you more music in eight years than anybody else has ever given music anywhere else in the world. I'm glad you realise it … I hope he pays for us to get home now … he never pays us any money!"

A fierce 'Communication Breakdown' and a playful 'The Ocean' closed the festival. Robert's parting shot was: "I gotta tell you, this is the best vibes since the first time we played the Fillmore five years ago. Vibes are real!"

Page was allegedly responsible for Zeppelin being nearly two hours late on stage. "They knew the billboards said they would be on stage at 2pm," commented promoter Bill Graham, "and the contract stresses that clearly - but this is Led Zeppelin so there's nothing you can do!" The concert over-runs the scheduled time and caused some concern in the neighbourhood, putting future Kezar events in jeopardy.

Rolling Stone reported: "Zeppelin are back doing what they do best – converting heavy metal into dollars. The gross revenue at Kezar was an estimated $325,000, topping the $309,000 the band pulled in at Tampa. Fifty cents off the top of each ticket went to the city's fund to pay for improvements at Candlestick Park, the baseball and football stadium across town. It replaced Kezar last year as the home of the 49ers. Kezar is tucked in the southeast corner of Golden Gate Park, and is bordered on two sides by evergreens and on the other two by city streets. It is blocks away from the Haight-Ashbury. Hundreds of persons drank beer and lolled in the sun on the rooftops of flats and apartment houses nearest the stadium. Since Led Zeppelin plays at a volume slightly below earthquake level, the rooftoppers had no trouble hearing the two and a half hour show. It is reported that the band could be heard up to a half-mile away, along the Panhandle. And three blocks up the hill at the University of California Medical Centre, patients complained they couldn't nap."

'Led Zep – a limp blimp'. Todd Tolces for the local press reported: "I never thought I'd see the day when anyone could outdraw The Grateful Dead in their home town. After all, the Dead ARE San Francisco! But this weekend, Led Zeppelin outdrew the Dead at the same Kezar Stadium they filled the week before with 20,000 and almost tripled the attendance to an amazing 53,000.

"The crowd was aching for rock'n'roll. Zeppelin complied contractually for almost three hours at a volume twice as loud as the Dead's but certainly not as good. Bonham did a terribly boring solo for 25 minutes with the guy at the mixer doing most of the work. And Page got his share of feedback garbage in during his solo in every song they did. The mix as a whole was lousy.

"But for all their faults there were sparks of life in the limp blimp. Plant's voice is still amazing!'

Charles Shaar Murray for the *New Musical Express* reported: "How can I tell you about that show? Led Zeppelin and 50,000 San Francisco people got together to provide one of the finest musical events I've ever had the privilege to attend. There may be bands who play better, and there may be bands who perform better, and there may be bands who write better songs, but when it comes to welding themselves and an audience together into one unit of total joy, Zeppelin yield to nobody.

"Altogether a magical concert. I suppose legions of die-hard Zep freaks have known this all along, but for me it was a revelation. All hail, Led Zep. Hosannas by the gram. If there's any excitement still left in this ego circus we call rock'n'roll, a sizeable portion of it derives from you. Be

proud."

Three minutes of colour newsreel from this show exists.

Bootleg CD references: *Takka Takka* (Tarantura), *The Vibes Are Real* (Continental Sounds), *Two Days After* (Immigrant), *Imperial Kezar* (Electric Magic), *Who's Next* (The Diagrams Of Led Zeppelin)
Visual Reference: Unofficial *Latter Days* DVD

Sunday June 3 1973
Inglewood Los Angeles, California
The Forum

Set: Rock And Roll/Celebration Day/Black Dog/Over The Hills And Far Away/Misty Mountain Hop/Since I've Been Loving You/No Quarter/The Song Remains The Same/The Rain Song/Dazed And Confused (inc. San Francisco) /Stairway To Heaven/Moby Dick/Heartbreaker – Whole Lotta Love (inc. The Crunge – Boogie Chillun' – I'm Going Down – I'm A Man- The Hunter)/The Ocean/Communication Breakdown /Organ Solo – Thank You.

Tonight's concert, arranged to replace the cancelled show on May 30, was the final gig of the first leg of the tour and the band went out in style

217

with an excellent show, nearly three hours in duration.

'Misty Mountain Hop' was dedicated to Bonzo tonight as he'd … "managed to make 25 years without falling over and as he's 25 years and three days old now."

After a highly dramatic 'Dazed And Confused' featuring some blistering solos from Page, Robert again paid tribute to Jimmy: "You shouldn't have been here tonight and we should have been in England! As you know, the concert you originally had to come to was cancelled because of Jimmy's finger. Now, this finger is very susceptible to strain and ligament pulling. Jimmy's had his finger in a bucket of cold water offstage, completely, the whole of the time since the concert was cancelled. I think he's doing really well and that's a fact. It's no fun"

'Whole Lotta Love' was where the real fun started. During the 'Boogie Chillun'' section, Plant sang "I believe that boy's going down!" repeatedly until Page launched into a full version of 'I'm Going Down'. This led into the old Yardbirds' stage favourite 'I'm A Man', before Plant sang the lyrics to 'The Hunter' which they used to perform in the 'How Many More Times' medleys; an exciting performance of true spontaneity.

After the standard encores of 'The Ocean' and 'Communication Breakdown', Zeppelin returned once more. "There's something else we'd like to say," comments Plant, as John Paul Jones began the organ solo, leading into an epic version of 'Thank You' featuring some beautifully constructed Page solos. In an emotional moment that crystallises the band's affinity with their Los Angeles fans, Plant extends the final line: "There would still be you and me!" adding spontaneously. "And you … and you … and you …"

Bootleg CD References: *Three Days After* (Cobra Standard), *Trade Mark Of Quality Masters* (Trade Mark Of Quality)

News Story: As the first leg of the US tour drew to a close, *New Musical Express* speculated in a news story 'Zeppelin For Lincoln?': "Led Zeppelin are at present considering an offer to appear at an open-air venue in Lincoln during the summer. Promoter Tony Lyne has offered the group £10,000 for the gig and has been told that they are considering the proposition. Grant decided against the idea and there would be no further UK performance in 1973.

June 1973
San Francisco
Radio One Scene and Heard
RADIO INTERVIEW
Just before leaving San Francisco Robert and Jimmy were interviewed by Michael Wale for the Radio One magazine programme *Scene And Heard*. They talked about their current US success and Plant had a few words to offer about Slade and Noddy Holder.

Friday July 6 1973
Chicago, Illinois
Chicago Stadium
Set: Rock And Roll/Celebration Day/Black Dog/Over The Hills And Far Away/Misty Mountain Hop/Since I've Been Loving You/No Quarter/The Song Remains The Same/The Rain Song/Dazed And Confused (inc. San Francisco)/Stairway To Heaven/Moby Dick/Heartbreaker – Whole Lotta Love (inc. The Crunge – Boogie Chillun')/Communication Breakdown.

After a month's break, the first show of the second leg was below par. There were problems with the PA, sections of the audience were continually fighting and Robert's voice was in poor shape.

After 'Over The Hills And Far Away' Plant made his first appeal to the crowd: "I'd really be obliged if you could cool all that! There's no need to be fighting. I'm sure there's plenty of fights to watch outside!"

After 'Stairway To Heaven', security staff waded into the crowd to attempt to break up the fighting. "There is some sensible reason why these people are doing this," commented Plant. "I have never seen so much leeriness and violence, so cool it! Can you dig that?"

RIFFS AND ROCK'N'ROLL ON THE ROAD LEADING TO SONGS IN THE STUDIO

The improvisational aspect of Zeppelin's live work often led to the genesis of fragments of riffs which were later used in the studio. In 1972 an early arrangement of 'The Rover' was played in Sydney Australia as part of the 'Whole Lotta Love' medley prior to the track being worked on during the spring. The marathon versions of 'Dazed And Confused' also became a breeding ground for new riffs and ideas to develop. Evidence of this includes the structure of 'The Song Remains The Same' (working title 'Plumpton And Worcester Races') coming through in on the road versions in 1972 . They also used 'Dazed' to develop two work-in-progress *Houses Of The Holy* tracks, 'The Crunge' and 'Walter's Walk', the latter of which was left off the album and eventually surfaced on *Coda*. Elements of 'Ozone Baby' recorded at Polar Studios in 1978 and eventually issued on *Coda* can be detected in the 1975 live version medleys of 'Whole Lotta Love'. The descending riff pattern of 'Hots On For Nowhere' from *Presence* can also be heard during the 1972 'Dazed And Confused' middle instrumental improvisations.

'Tea For One' was another track Jimmy previewed, albeit briefly – the opening riff section can be heard as Page tuned up before going into 'Tangerine' at the May 25 1975 Earls Court show.

The remarkable bootlegged soundcheck recording that surfaced from the 1973 US tour contained run downs of 'The Wanton Song' (working title 'Desiree'), 'Night Flight' and 'The Rover', three numbers which would surface on *Physical Graffiti*. That soundcheck remnant also reflected their affinity for running through old rock'n'roll tracks – Plant paying homage to Chuck Berry ('Round And Round', 'Hail Hail Rock'nRoll') and home grown rockers Johnny Kidd ('Shakin' All Over') and early Cliff Richard 'Please Don't Tease'). It would seem they may have had a plan to officially release a rock'n'roll set as they committed to master tape a studio session containing various rock'n'roll tracks cut at Headley Grange in late 1973. That session is thought to be still lining their archive. alongside other unheard unreleased songs such as 'St Tristans Sword' (first worked on in July 1970 and again for the fourth album) and 'Lost In Space', another *Graffiti* era outtake allegedly with John Paul Jones on vocals.

A sole encore of 'Communication Breakdown' was rushed through with only a few 'Crunge' references. Not a good start to the second leg.

'Only the fans could mar Led Zeppelin's performance' was the headline in the *Chicago Sun-Times*. April Olzak reports: "Led Zeppelin is quite possibly the best rock group in the world. In a sell-out concert Friday night at the Chicago Stadium (18,000 occupied seats and another 18,000 sold for tonight), they dispelled every bad word ever written about them, came through soaringly over the rotten acoustics in the Stadium, and in general, overcame every conceivable obstacle that might have marred their music. Except the audience.

"Robert Plant paused at the start of several numbers to remark, pleasantly enough, that he'd never seen so many fights at a concert, and, please, cool it. Zeppelin takes no glee in ringside chaos. Crowd antics to them are like asking George Shearing to play 'Melancholy Baby'."

Bootleg CD References: *Second City Showdown* (Midas Touch), *Chicago 1973* (LZ),

Saturday July 7 1973
Chicago, Illinois
Chicago Stadium
Set: Rock And Roll/Celebration Day/Over The Hills And Far Away/Misty Mountain Hop/Since

I've Been Loving You/No Quarter/ The Song Remains The Same/The Rain Song/ Dazed And Confused/Stariway To Heaven/ Moby Dick/Heartbreaker/Whole Lotta love/ Communication Breakdown.

While in Chicago, Robert, Jimmy and Bonzo visited The Burning Spear club to see Bobby Bland. Bonham felt like playing and, apparently uninvited, climbed on stage and began to strike up a beat. After an initially frosty reception to this intruder on stage, he finally left to a standing ovation.

Bootleg CD References: *In the Windy City II* (Empress Valley*), Untouchable* (Electric Magic)

UNCONFIRMED
Sunday July 8 1973
Indianapolis, Indiana

This date had previously been reported as being played at the Market Square Arena. However this venue did not open until 1974, and there is no evidence to suggest they played a date in Indianapolis on this day.

Sunday July 9 1973
St. Paul, Minnesota
Civic Centre

Set: Rock And Roll/Celebration Day/Bring It On Home/Black Dog/Over The Hills And Far Away/Dancing Days inro/Misty Mountain Hop/Since I've Been Loving You/No Quarter/The Song Remains The Same/The Rain Song/Laurel And Hardy Theme/Dazed And Confused (Incl San Francisco)/Stairway To Heaven/Moby Dick/Heartbreaker/Whole Lotta Love (Incl Boogie Chillun)/Communication Breakdown

Firecrakers again blighted this show. Page played the intro of 'Dancing Days' but did not go into the song. A joke run through the Laurel and Hardy theme preceded 'Dazed And Confused'.

Press reports: "Led Zeppelin Concert: The Long Wait to be the First in Line – The first of an anticipated 18,500 rock music fans showed up at the St. Paul Civic Center at 2am Sunday for a Led Zeppelin concert at 8pm tonight.

"'There should be 3,000 to 4,000 people here by noon,' said Jim Crabbe, 20. "Everybody is going to be smashed up against the doors by the time the doors open at 6pm." Crabbe is one of five youths who have been camped since Sunday morning. The reason the group arrived so early is to be assured of front row seats. Tickets to the concert are being sold on a first come, first served basis. No reservations have been taken for the $5.50 seats."

Michael Anthony wrote: "When 18,500 young folks stomp and shout 'more' for a full three minutes, a band, exhausted though the players may be, has no choice but to trudge back for an encore.

"If Monday night's concert at the new St. Paul Civic Center proved anything, it is that Twin Cities rock audiences are no different from any others. The St. Paul show sold out in two days early in June.

"One has to admit that, for the most part, all the hoopla is justified, for this was an exciting, well-conceived show, aided in no small part by provocative lighting and staging."

Bootleg CD References: *Complete Performance In Minnesota* (The Diagrams Of Led Zeppelin)

Tuesday July 10 1973
Milwaukee, Wisconsin
Milwaukee Arena

Set includes – Rock And Roll/Celebration Day/Black Dog/Over The Hills And Far Away/Misty Mountain Hop/Since I've Been Loving You/No Quarter/The Song Remains The Same/The Rain Song/ Dazed And Confused (inc. San Francisco)/Stairway To Heaven/Moby Dick.

"Good Evening. It's very nice to be back. When did we come here last? 1969, was it? Do you remember that fes-

tival where it rained all day? Well, anyway, a lot of things have changed since then, and we've had a few experiences as well."

Plant's voice had recovered well but the group was still not matching the standard of the first leg. Again, there were problems with firecrackers. Introducing 'Misty Mountain Hop', Plant commented: "This is a song that doesn't involve firecrackers, except the ones you put in cigarette papers!"

'Zeppelin Flying High' reported the *Milwaukee Journal*. Damien Jaques wrote: "The Led Zeppelin soared high over Milwaukee Tuesday night. One of the granddaddies of hard rock groups thoroughly entertained about 11,000 at the Arena.

"The group is on one of those monster concert tours that reportedly has them carting money away by the carload. The four musicians supposedly are drawing better crowds and making more money than The Beatles, Rolling Stones or Alice Cooper ever did.

"Milwaukee rock fans should be happy that the Arena was included in the bonanza."

Bootleg CD References: *One More For The Road* (Red Hot), *Rock And Roll Bonanza* (Electric Magic)

Thursday July 12 1973
Detroit, Michigan
Cobo Hall
Set: Rock And Roll/Celebration Day/Black Dog/Over The Hills And Far Away/Misty Mountain Hop/Since I've Been Loving You/No Quarter/The Song Remains The Same/The Rain Song/Dazed And Confused (inc. San Francisco)/Stairway To Heaven/Moby Dick/Heartbreaker – Whole Lotta Love (inc. The Crunge – Boogie Chillun' – I'm Going Down)/Communication Breakdown/The Ocean.

A much improved show. Plant did a good job plugging the *Houses Of The Holy* album which … "Can be found on the shelves of your local record shop – rush out and buy a copy."

Yet again the problem of firecracker needed to be addressed: "Don't throw any more firecrackers, 'cos that's silly! It breaks the concentration, of

which we've got very little left." 'Misty Mountain Hop' is then dedicated to … "the loss of brain cells".

'The Song Remains The Same' was described as … "about the experiences you get when you travel around places … India … Japan … Bangkok … Hong Kong … all the brothels!" 'Whole Lotta Love' included 'I'm Going Down' and 'Communication Breakdown' also contained lines from 'The Crunge'.

'The Ocean' was dedicated to … "the people inside *The Houses Of The Holy*". In true Keith Moon style, Bonham lumbered up to the microphone and explains that … "On this track I was allowed to shout" before delivering his enthusiastic count-in.

Bootleg CD References: *Detroit Rock City* (Lemon Song), *Motor City Daze* (Antrabata), *Going Down To Detroit* (Zeppelin Live Achieve)

Friday July 13 1973
Detroit, Michigan
Cobo Hall
Set: Rock And Roll/Celebration Day/Black Dog/Over The Hills And Far Away/Misty Mountain Hop/Since I've Been Loving You/No Quarter/The Song Remains The Same/The Rain Song/Dazed And Confused (inc. San Francisco)/Stairway To Heaven/Moby Dick/Heartbreaker – Whole Lotta Love (inc. The Crunge – Boogie Chillun')/Dancing Days.

Another enjoyable show for the band and audience alike.

John Bonham was introduced as … "somebody who never stops getting better and better. I've known him for ten years and he still keeps getting better and better and unbelievably better. The only white whale in show business!" 'Moby Dick' tonight lasted for a massive 28 minutes and varied from breathtaking excitement to sheer tedium. Afterwards, Plant commented: "John Henry Bonham – The only drummer in rock! Not that we're conceited or anything!"

Page included a few Chuck Berry riffs in 'Heartbreaker' and in 'Whole Lotta Love', Plant did some of his best 'Crunge' ad-libs – "Where's that confounded bridge?" The encore tonight, surprisingly, was 'Dancing Days', its only known performance on this tour.

Zeppelin attempted to arrange a third night in Detroit but transportation difficulties prevent this.
Bootleg CD References: *Babe I'm Gonna Leave You* (Dynamite Studios), *Monsters Of Rock* (Tarantura)

Sunday July 15 1973
Buffalo, New York
War Memorial Auditorium
Set: Rock And Roll/Celebration Day/Black Dog/Over The Hills And Far Away/Misty Mountain Hop/Since I've Been Loving You/No Quarter/The Song Remains The Same/The Rain Song/Dazed And Confused (inc. San Francisco)/Stairway To Heaven/Moby Dick/Heartbreaker – Whole Lotta Love (inc. The Crunge – Boogie Chillun')/The Ocean.

The band took to the stage late and Plant apologised for the delay, explaining that ... "Jimmy's got a guitar strap that's made of cement!" Apparently, there had been an accident with his main guitar and he had to use his second model. Plant was not amused when someone let off a flash bomb in the auditorium. "That's one guy who's not on the same journey." The bangs continued during 'Dazed And Confused'. "I don't know who the sadist is who let off the bomb ... what a jerk off. You've got to live with him every week!"

The concert really took off during 'Heartbreaker' where Page excelled himself on the solo and started to dominate the rest of the show. Page's Theremin work on 'Whole Lotta Love' was superb. Encouraged by Page's new found energy, Plant pushed himself during the 'Boogie Chillun'' section. He even threw in a few 'Hangman!' cries from 'Gallows Pole'.

The *Buffalo Evening News* reported 'Led Zeppelin Kneads Crowd To Silly Putty'. Dale Anderson wrote: "Led Zeppelin doesn't give concerts; they perform physical transformations. They kneaded the full-house crowd in Memorial Auditorium into silly putty Sunday night with two hours 50 minutes of massive sensory massage."
Bootleg CD References: *Where The Zeppelin Roam* (Midas Touch), *In Concert & Beyond* (The Diagrams Of Led Zeppelin), *Misty Mountain Crop* (Flying Disc)

Tuesday July 17 1973
Seattle, Washington
Center Coliseum
Set: Rock And Roll/Celebration Day/Black Dog/Over The Hills And Far Away/Misty Mountain Hop/Since I've Been Loving You/No Quarter/The Song Remains The Same/The Rain Song/Dazed And Confused (inc. San Francisco)/Stairway To Heaven/Moby Dick/Heartbreaker – Whole Lotta Love (inc. The Crunge – Boogie Chillun')/The Ocean.

Tonight's concert began with an announcement: "Led Zeppelin has asked if we can get a few things straight here tonight. Nobody around here digs any fireworks – please cool the fireworks Please also, we have an area right here in front of the stage where we have so many optic effects that we need to get off tonight, that we can't have any chance of anybody bumping the stage 'cos it'l completely ruin them. Their show usually runs about one hour and forty-five minutes. If you can keep the fireworks down and keep everything of the front, Led Zeppelin would like to thank you and do about three hours tonight! So, sit back and stay cool and we'll have a long great show this evening!"

The show that followed was one of the mos enjoyable of the tour. Bonham played very heavy Plant's voice was low and quite rough, but stil surprisingly effective. Page's playing was fierc and fluent, his speed on 'Since I've Been Lovin You' breathtaking. Tonight was also a show o excesses. 'Dazed And Confused' was expanded to 35 minutes and 'Moby Dick' lasted for a staggering 33 minutes, pushing the boundaries of human endurance.

'Stairway To Heaven' was one of the show's highlights. Page's solo was tense and dramatic, ensuring that the number received a well-deserved lengthy standing ovation. 'Heartbreaker' and 'Whole Lotta Love' also contained moments of pure inspiration from Page.

The concert ran for 182 minutes, enabling Zeppelin to keep their pre-show promise.

'Led Zeppelin – rock as extravaganza' was the headline in the *Seattle Times*. Patrick MacDonald writes: "The Stones first developed massive light and sound systems for the huge halls rock groups now play and Alice Cooper expanded the idea by turning concerts into spectacles but nobody so far has reached the level of extravaganza shown by the Led Zeppelin in concert last night at the Seattle Center Coliseum. Smoke, fire, strobes, sparklers and rockets filled the stage at one time or another during the group's non-stop three hours of music. Not to mention the three-story banks of lights and speakers that surrounded the four performers and the mirrored panels behind them.

"The sound system was such that at any point in the hall the music was visceral – it could be felt more than heard. For me this took some getting used to but once acclimatised it was strangely pleasurable, as if the constant vibration activated some pleasure center."

Bootleg CD References: *V1/2* (Last Stand), *Complete Seattle* (The Diagrams of Led Zeppelin), *V1/2* (Cobla), *Grandilquence* (Antabata)

Wednesday July 18 1973
Vancouver, Canada
Pacific Coliseum PNE
Set includes: Rock And Roll/Celebration Day/Black Dog/Over The Hills And Far Away/Misty Mountain Hop/Since I've Been Loving You/No Quarter/Dazed And Confused/Stairway To Heaven

In contrast to the previous evening, tonight's show was below par due to Robert Plant falling ill. It was obvious Robert was having difficulties. He even paused during one of his introductions and gasped: "Oh dear – I'm tired"

Plant praised those who travelled to Seattle last year: "Thanks for the faith! Nice one!" and attemptd to make a deal with the crowd: "We'll play our balls off if you promise no firecrackers, right? You can have our balls, we don't want your firecrackers!"

'No Quarter' was now beginning to develop further – tonight's version lasted over 14 minutes. John Paul was experimenting more with the keyboards and there was more interplay between him and Page. Plant's poor health led to them leaving the stage without returning for any encores.

The show was called to a halt without any encores. A stage announcer apologised to the crowd and asked them to stay in their seats. This was to allow the limos a clear access to get Plant to the hospital. He was treated for exhaustion but was declared fit enough to continue the tour.

'Early finish fortunate for Led Zep' was the headline of the *Vancouver Sun*. Don Stanley reported: "Led Zeppelin promised three hours of music but called it a night at slightly over two, with no encore. It was explained to an almost surly Coliseum audience that lead singer, Robert Plant, was being taken to hospital and would we please leave in an orderly manner.

"It was unfortunate for Plant (if the report was true) but fortunate for the band that they left the stage early. Their concert was terrible, unbelievably inept for the top draw in contemporary rock."

Bootleg CD References: *No Firecrackers* (Electric Magic), *Cut In The Seventies* (The Diagrams Of Led Zeppelin), *Canada Dry* (Tarantura)

Friday July 20 1973
Boston, Massachusetts
Boston Garden

Set: Rock And Roll/Celebration Day/Black Dog/Over The Hills And Far Away/No Quarter/The Song Remains The Same/The Rain Song/Dazed And Confused (inc. San Francisco)/Stairway To Heaven/Heartbreaker – Whole Lotta Love (inc. The Crunge – 'Boogie Chillun'').

A wild uncontrollable audience wrecked havoc with tonight's show. Plant's voice was still quite weak also and had not fully recovered yet.

Plant: "Easy! You don't want to break those things down, so please stop pushing forward! If you don't stop pushing forward we're gonna have to stop until everybody moves back a bit. Is that understood? Can you push back? Every time we come to Boston we have such a good time with so many good people! Listen, there are people at the front who are gonna get hurt!"

In order to calm the crowd, Zeppelin dropped 'Misty Mountain Hop' and 'Since I've Been Loving You' and cut straight to the relatively mellow 'No Quarter'. However, the crowd would not be subdued and, as a result, were not rewarded with an encore. An announcement was made: "Thank you and good night! Led Zeppelin are gone!"

While in Boston, a decision was taken to film the end of the tour. Director Joe Massot was called and instructed to assemble a team immediately.

Bootleg CD Reference: *War Cry* (No label)

Saturday July 21 1973
Providence, Rhode Island
Civic Center

Set: Rock And Roll/Celebration Day/Black Dog/Over The Hills And Far Away/Misty Mountain Hop/Since I've Been Loving You/No Quarter/The Song Remains The Same/The Rain Song/Dazed And Confused (inc. San Francisco)/Stairway To Heaven/Moby Dick/Heartbreaker – Whole Lotta Love (inc. The Crunge – Boogie Chillun')/The Ocean.

Plant: "I was gonna say it's nice to be back, but I don't think we've been here before – I could be wrong!"

Tonight's show was something of a return to form. Robert's voice was still hoarse and he hit some painful notes during 'Rock And Roll', but it improved drastically as the show progresses.

When disturbances started to erupt in the crowd, Robert laid down ground rules in no uncertain terms: "Listen! We've come 5,000 miles and we really haven't come to dig a lot of silliness. Please just cool it, 'cos otherwise we can't play. Last night was a complete menagerie and tonight we want it to be really good 'cos we're playing a lot better! So just move back and appreciate what has to be done. Normally we would just forget it, but last night there was so much chaos. You can't expect Jimmy to play a great solo if there's bull-shit! If you start pissing about, it's no good, we're gonna finish!"

The crowd responded to Robert's wishes and he began to feel guilty about his harsh words: "I did-n't want to offend anyone, and just to prove it, we're gonna play really fantastically!"

Robert kept his promise and the rest of the show was incident free. 'No Quarter' was again one of the highlights with Page and Bonham's jazzy improvisations setting the foundations for the mammoth arrangements of future tours.

"Providence – you've been very nice. Good one!"

Bootleg CD References: *LZ Rider* (Tarantura), *LZ Rhoder* (no label)

Monday July 23 1973
Baltimore, Maryland
Civic Center

Set: Rock And Roll/Celebration Day/Black Dog/Over The Hills And Far Away/Misty Mountain Hop/Since I've Been Loving You/No Quarter/The Song Remains The Same/The Rain Song/Dazed And Confused (inc. San Francisco)/Stairway To Heaven/Moby Dick/Heartbreaker – Whole Lotta Love (inc. The Crunge – Boogie Chillun')/The Ocean.

Zeppelin were regaining their confidence and tonight's show was a further improvement. They were less tense and there was more improvisa-tion.

During 'The Rain Song', Plant ad-libbed "Sit down! Please sit down!", but there were very few problems with the crowd. In 'Dazed And Confused', Page got totally lost and performed most of the sections out of their usual sequence – 'San Francisco' was played towards the end of the piece.

Backstage, a row erupted after a member of Zeppelin's road crew discovered a dealer selling pirate photographs of the group inside the audi-torium. Grant accused the local promoter of sanc-tioning this for a cut of the proceeds and the dis-pute was captured on film by Joe Massot's crew. This marvellous piece of cinema *verité* shows Grant in all his fury, unleashing a tirade of abuse at the unfortunate promoter who vainly protests his innocence.

Bootleg CD Reference: *Baltimore Jack* (The Diagrams Of Led Zeppelin)

Tuesday July 24 1973
Pittsburgh, Pennsylvania
Three Rivers Stadium

Set: Rock And Roll/Celebration Day/Black Dog/Over The Hills And Far Away/Misty Mountain Hop/Since I've Been Loving You/No Quarter/The Song Remains The Same/The Rain Song/Dazed And Confused (inc. San Francisco)/Stairway To Heaven/Moby Dick/Heartbreaker – Whole Lotta Love (inc. The Crunge – Boogie Chillun')/The Ocean.

The band and entourage flew out from New York for this show accompanied by photographer Bob Gruen. As they bordered the Starship 1 plane, on Plant's request Gruen took some group shots of them by the wing. This memorable image can be seen in the books *The Photographers Led Zeppelin* (compiled by Ross Halfin) and *Led Zeppelin Bob Gruen's Works*.

A rain date was held for July 25, in case of inclement weather.

The resurrection continued. Another fine per-formance, Plant's voice had nearly made a full recovery. During 'Since I've Been Loving You', Robert ad-libbed "Don't send me to heartbreak hotel!" He apologised for the lack of video screens and vowed somebody's head will roll… "I prom-ise … it's only 'cos we're vain!"

'Led Zeppelin draws 40,000 in Three Rivers' – Rex Rutkoski writes: "One of the largest crowds – 40,000 – to attend a concert in Pittsburgh's Three Rivers Stadium, saw Led Zeppelin perform a three hour continuous show last night.

"There were some minor incidents involving only a small percentage of the throng including an unsuccessful gate-crashing attempt at gates A and B – guards employed water hoses to subdue the effort; the arrest of five youngsters who tried to scale a stadium wall with a ladder to gain entry; injuries to over-enthusiastic fans who leaped the roofs of the baseball dug-outs, seeking to obtain a closer view of the band. These episodes, though, did nothing to mar the concert, to which most of the young people brought a general festive mood.

"Zeppelin utilised a variety of lighting techniques to enhance the show. The foursome's finale brought fireworks from the stage and the release of a flock of doves. The birds had trouble orienting themselves on the dark fields and flew into speakers and the crowd. Many people attempted to grab the birds.

"Led Zeppelin earned $119,763 for their efforts last night. Patrons paid $4.65 and $6.65 for tickets.

"A large traffic tie-up resulted after the concert, which attracted customers from throughout the tri-state area."

Cine footage shot by a roadie from the side of the stage was later used in the official 1997 'Whole Lotta Love' promo video.

Bootleg CD References: *Hello Pittsburgh* (Image Quality), *Early Days Latter Days* (Early Days), *The Resurrection* (Electric Magic)

Friday July 27 1973
New York, New York
Madison Square Garden
Set: Rock And Roll/Celebration Day/Black Dog/Over The Hills And Far Away/Misty Mountain Hop/Since I've Been Loving You/No Quarter/The Song Remains The Same/The Rain Song/Dazed And Confused (inc. San Francisco)/Stairway To Heaven/Moby Dick/Heartbreaker – Whole Lotta Love (inc. The Crunge – Boogie Chillun')/The Ocean.

The tour culminated with three prestigious shows at Madison Square Garden which were filmed and would eventually form the on-stage sequences of *The Song Remains The Same* movie.

Tickets were sold by mail order only with a maximum allocation of six tickets per letter. The three shows, promoted by Concerts East, are reported to have grossed an aggregate $390,000 at a $7.50 top ticket price.

Zeppelin rose to the occasion with a storming show. The audience were wild and Plant tried to restrain them: "Let's get one thing straight – stop acting like kids! Cool it a little bit."

Introducing 'Stairway To Heaven', Plant commented: "I think this is a song of hope ... and it's a very quiet song, so shut up!" 'Dazed And Confused' was one of the most professional and tightest versions ever. Page really pushed his performance. During 'The Ocean', Plant sang the line "Carmen's only four years old ... ', referring of course to his daughter.

'Led Zeppelin Rocks To a Close at Garden' reads one review: "I saw the Friday opening of the Led Zeppelin concert from backstage, feeling the weight and response of the packed Madison Square Garden. It was possibly the best place to test the power of the British rock group, making the final dates of its current and very successful American tour.

"And power it is – Led Zeppelin provides a kind of tent-show hard-rock revivalism, healing and providing succour to the faithful, on a stage that throughout the evening became cluttered with smoke, dry-ice fumes and that most privileged of rock'n'roll people, the film-maker."

Plant: "'Stairway To Heaven' is quite a moving thing. At the Garden, I sang well away from the mike and I could hear 20,000 people singing it.

mean, 20,000 people singing 'High Heeled Sneakers' is one thing, but 20,000 people singing 'Stairway To Heaven' is another. People leave satisfied after that."

Audience shot silent cine from this show exists.
Bootleg CD References: *The Safecracker's Show* (Midas Touch), *Discover America* (Tarantura), *Grandiloquence* (Antrabata)
Visual References: *The Song Remains The Same* (Warner Home Video), Official 2003 *Led Zeppelin* DVD (Warner Music Vision), *1973* (Unofficial – Cosmic Energy)

Saturday July 28 1973
New York, New York
Madison Square Garden
Set: Rock And Roll/Celebration Day/Black Dog/Over The Hills And Far Away/Misty Mountain Hop/Since I've Been Loving You/No Quarter/The Song Remains The Same/The Rain Song/Dazed And Confused (inc. San Francisco)/Stairway To Heaven/Moby Dick/Heartbreaker – Whole Lotta Love (inc. The Crunge – Boogie Chillun')/The Ocean.

Plant: "Well, we had a really good one last night. What we intend to do is to try to get it better every night and only with your co-operation can we do that!"

However, firecrackers soon broke Plant's concentration. "Another point to be made before we start taking the building into the stratosphere is that we must eradicate the firecrackers, because that is no longer clever!"

Zeppelin were requested to wear the same stage clothes for all three concerts to assist in the editing together of footage from different nights. Everyone complies except John Paul Jones who insists on wearing something completely different for each show.

Plant: "Playing in New York does have a psychological sort of impression on me. Despite the fact that we can play for 18,000 people in Chicago, it's far more important to do better in New York. I think it's only psychological really. New York audiences are no different to

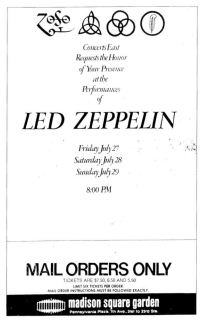

Concerts East
Requests the Honor
of Your Presence
at the
Performances
of

LED ZEPPELIN

Friday July 27
Saturday July 28
Sunday July 29

8:00 PM

MAIL ORDERS ONLY
TICKETS ARE $7.50, 6.50 AND 5.50
LIMIT SIX TICKETS PER ORDER.
MAIL ORDER INSTRUCTIONS MUST BE FOLLOWED EXACTLY.

madison square garden
Pennsylvania Plaza, 7th Ave., 31st to 33rd Sts.

people anywhere. Last night at the Garden was superb."

'Zeppelin havoc' ... Barry Taylor reviews the show for *New Musical Express*. "Zeppelin have had this city in a frazzle. The fledging scene-makers were out *en masse* three days before the concert. Outside the Garden, tickets are being hawked for as much as $70 a pair and long hairs are being randomly accosted by leering opportunists with trunkloads of *Led Zeppelin On Blueberry Hill*, a bootleg two-record set of a three-year old concert.

"Zeppelin had their audience sussed and started by laying it on thick. But the impact of their flash began to wear thin. It seemed that Page was sometimes getting his fingers caught in the strings. Plant had either lost his voice somewhere along the tour or he was tired and decided to save it for the right moments. Jones and Bonham are still as indestructible a rhythm machine as ever, though there were moments of hesitation when the delayed echo, used to boost the vocals, seemed to ricochet off the walls and throw things slightly out of sync."

Ten minutes of audience shot 8mm silent colour cine film exists from this show shot by *Proximity* Zep magazine editor Huge Jones. Parts of this footage was deployed by Jimmy Page for the official DVD interspersed with the band's archived Madison Square Garden footage.

Bootleg CD References: *Tour De Force* (Tarantura), *Another Magic Night Vol 1 & Vol 2* (Dynamite Studio), *Electric Magic* (Scorpio), *MSG* (Cannonball), *The Effect Is Shattering* (Empress Valley)

Visual References: *The Song Remains The Same* (Warner Home Video), *Official 2003 Led Zeppelin DVD* (Warner Music Vision), *1973* (Unofficial - Cosmic Energy)

Sunday July 29 1973
New York, New York
Madison Square
Garden

Set: Rock And Roll/Celebration Day/Black Dog/Over The Hills And Far Away/Misty Mountain Hop/Since I've Been Loving You/No Quarter/The Song Remains The Same/The Rain Song/Dazed And Confused (inc. San Francisco)/Stairway To Heaven/Moby Dick/Heartbreaker – Whole Lotta Love (inc. The Crunge – Boogie Chillun' – Bonham Solo)/The Ocean/Organ Solo – Thank You.

Plant: "I gotta put you straight on a couple of things. This year in America we decided to work extra hard, so we did two tours and this is the last night of the last tour"

The final show of the tour was slick and professional. It's been an intense tour. Zeppelin were battling with exhaustion and giving their all.

There was no 'Moby Dick' tonight (last night lasted 28 minutes), and instead Bonham performed an energy charged five minute workout at the end of 'Whole Lotta Love', accompanied by a fire-eater who sets fire to his gong.

The second leg climaxed, as the first leg did in Los Angeles, with an emotional performance of 'Thank You'.

Ritchie Yorke reported: "Zeppelin played for almost three hours – a set that had the audience of nearly 25,000 blasé New Yorkers bursting into unanimous standing ovations after almost every song.

"What they do is completely unique. Few groups of any variety have interwoven shades and patterns of hard and light so expertly as Zeppelin. Certainly Led Zeppelin are a dazzling visual band but their astonishing musical expertise is the most potent weapon in their arsenal."

'Zep and the faithful 60,000' … Lisa Robinson writes in *Disc*: "If Zeppelin has had some highs on this tour, the final concert at the Garden had to be one of the very best. Jimmy, forgetting his earlier fatigue was in magnificent form this night – his solos were inspired.

"At the end of 'Whole Lotta Love' out comes fire-eater Mike Quashie – a West Indian resplendent in some robes; gold and red drag bearing several torches ablaze with fire. Jimmy and Robert are completely delighted as the fire-eater sets Bonzo's gong on fire as well as one of his drumsticks. Bonzo is going crazy banging the gong with the drumstick and it's a wonder he doesn't set himself on fire."

Jimmy Page: "It's really been an incredible tour, but we're all terribly worn out. I went past the point of no return physically quite a while back but now I've gone past the mental point. I've only kept going by functioning automatically. We've kept up a ridiculous pace."

Robert Plant: "It certainly has been an incredible tour but so were all the others. We'll just have to wait and see if we can top this one."

There was drama offstage too. A reported $203,000 was stolen from the group's safety deposit box at the Drake Hotel. (It later transpired that the actual sum was $180,000.) Richard Cole discovered the money is missing at 7.15pm, just

prior to the gig and is immediately interrogated by police as a suspect. After the show, Zeppelin did not return to their hotel but were taken to a party organised by Ahmet Ertegun, where he presented them with personal gifts and gold records for *Houses Of The Holy*.

Grant also assisted the FBI in their enquiries, and was later involved in another incident at the hotel and arrested for assaulting *New York Daily News* photographer Charles Ruppmann and stealing his film. Grant recalls: "The safety deposit box in the hotel had been robbed and everything had gone; $180,000 all in brand new notes from Madison Square Garden. I got back to the hotel about three in the morning and there's a photographer there. He took a flash and hit the back of my head with his camera. I said, 'Give us your bleedin' film', so he did and I threw it in the gutter. And the next day I got arrested!"

The theft placed Zep in a Catch 22 situation. If they appeared unconcerned, the press would suggest cynically that they were too rich to care; if they show undue concern the press would snarl that all they cared about was money.

Zeppelin later sued the Drake hotel and obtained a reasonable settlement. However, it was one of the few sour moments on a tour that had produced so many outstanding performances. Page: "It had got to the point where we couldn't care too much. I mean if the tour had been a bummer then that would have been the last straw. But it wasn't. I remember when I heard the news that it had happened I was just about to go on stage. We still played a good gig. A far worse sit-

uation was cutting my hand before the LA shows!"

Backstage footage from the Madison Square Garden stint was used as a menu link for the Madison Square Garden sequence on the official Led Zeppelin DVD

Official CD Reference: Soundtrack from the film *The Song Remains The Same* (Swan Song)

Bootleg CD References: *Missing Doll* (Tarantura 2000), *Madison Square Garden 1973* (Fire Power), *Grand Finale* (Empress Valley)

Visual References: *The Song Remains The Same* (Warner Home Vision), Official *Led Zeppelin* 2003 DVD (Warner Music Vision)

Friday July 31 1973
New York, New York
NBC Nightly News
TV APPEARANCE

This edition of the NBC Nightly News included an item on the US music business and claims of payola, drug dealing and mob connections. Presented by John Chancellor and reported by Betty Rolin, it included footage of Led Zeppelin and their entourage boarding the Staship plane at JFK Airport. It also showed Page and Bonham singing along to 'I Do Like To Be Beside The Seaside' accompanied by Jonesy on the in plane organ. Plant was briefly interviewed, stating: "I'm a bit upset there's not a pool table on board but apart for that is the best way to travel!"

After the lengthy non-stop touring schedule of 1972/3, Led Zeppelin took stock of their situation and began an 18-month sabbatical from live appearances. "We've been coming to different conclusions and decisions and we've got mixed up in a rather gargantuan film," commented Plant at the time. "Nothing's preconceived right now. We'll work a bit and then we'll take a break. That's the way it works – that's Led Zeppelin right now."

During the autumn of 1973, Joe Massot and his film crew spent time with all four group members and Peter Grant to film location sequences. Each of Zeppelin acted out a fantasy role. Grant and Richard Cole were portrayed as Mafia style henchmen; Page re-enacted the Tarot card illustration from their fourth album sleeve, climbing a mountain near Loch Ness in December; Plant went to Raglan Castle in Wales to film a King Arthur-style scene; Jones cavorted around his Sussex home as a ghostly Lord of the Manor; and Bonham, somewhat less pretentiously, was featured drag racing at Santa Pod and riding his Harley around Blackpool.

The first and only personnel problem of their career occurred when they reassembled at Headley Grange for initial recording sessions for the next album. John Paul Jones told Grant that he was becoming disillusioned with his role and the constant rigours of touring. He'd been seriously thinking of quitting and had even considered applying for the job of choir master at Winchester Cathedral. Grant hushed up the crisis, told Jones to take a few weeks to think about it and gave the studio time over to Bad Company so they could record their début album. Grant recalls: "It was kept low key. I told Jimmy, of course, who couldn't believe it. But it was the pressure. He was a family man, was Jonesy. By that time the security thing in the US was getting ridiculous. We started getting death threats. It got very worrying after that and I think that's how we lost a little of the camaraderie. Eventually I think he realised he was

doing something he really loved. It was never discussed again."

John Paul agreed to take part in the rescheduled album sessions. Musical inspiration immediately followed with the initial recording of a Bonham/Page demo titled 'Driving To Kashmir', which would become known simply as 'Kashmir'. This Eastern influenced epic would develop into a centrepiece of their future stage set.

As was often the custom, the band warmed up for the new recording sessions by running through vintage rock'roll tracks. A recording was made of one of these sessions from Headley Grange, dated October 17 1973, with Ron Nevison engineering on 16-track, containing the following numbers: 'Baby I Don't Care' (takes 1 & 2)/'Jailhouse Rock' (takes 1 & 2)/'One Night'/'Don't Be Cruel' (takes 1 & 2)/'The Girl Of My Best Friend'/'Jailhouse Rock' (takes 1, 2 & 3)/'Money Honey' (takes 1 & 2)/'Summertime Blues'. Whether this reel was logged for their own reference or was intended to be released in some format is unknown.

At the time a return to the live arena was still a long way off. Grant decided it would be best not to tour at all in 1974. Instead they busied themselves with the completion of a sixth album and continued working on the film. Peter Clifton took over the project after the band grew dissatisfied with Massot's original rushes. Massot signed off with the famous comment: "They thought it was my fault Robert Plant had such a big cock!"

Grant also renegotiated their Atlantic deal and set up their own Swan Song record label, with Zeppelin, Bad Company, Maggie Bell and The Pretty Things as the initial stable of artists. This was inaugurated with launch parties in New York and Los Angeles in the early summer on 1974. In LA they met Elvis Presley after his Forum concert. A UK launch duly followed in the autumn at Chiselhurst Caves.

There was no shortage of concert offers during the lay-off. Promoter Freddie Bannister jumped the gun by announcing he had secured Zeppelin

VOICE PROBLEMS

The young Robert Plant was not a professionally trained vocalist. He sang from the heart and from the depths of his soul, but the wild unchecked use of his voice in the early years would eventually lead to vocal problems. During 1973 the sheer length of the Zeppelin set list, coupled with the amount of touring they were undertaking, began to tell. Robert's voice was now prone to considerable strain and recurring hoarseness. The 'flu that caused them to cancel shows in January 1973 may also have been a contributing factor, and it's notable that Robert often dropped an octave on various numbers as they progressed that year.

Two clear examples are the arrangements of 'Over The Hills And Far Away' and 'Stairway To Heaven'. The former was sung faithful to the *Houses Of The Holy* album version on its introduction to the set in late 1972. By the time of the US tour the following year, Plant was favouring a lower register for the chorus, thus reducing the strain on his voice. The finale of 'Stairway To Heaven' ("And as we wind on down the road") was given similar treatment.

Contradicting some of the more piquant observations in *Hammer Of The Gods*, Plant was often quoted as saying he was tucked up in bed – looking after his voice. "The real lame thing is – the singer often went to bed. There was a lot to be said for trying to keep the voice in shape. I've used that as a cop out but at the same time it was a fact," was how he remembered it in 1988.

During the 1973 US tour his voice could be very erratic – perfectly illustrated by shows such as the Chicago (July 6) date where his voice from the start is almost completely shot. This state of affairs may also have been a contributing factor to their lay-off in 1974. Listening to the studio versions of 'Trampled Underfoot', 'Sick Again', 'Wanton Song' and 'Kashmir', it's clear his voice was still hoarse during the initial sessions for *Physical Graffiti*. His performance on these cuts, whilst certainly not lacking in commitment, is noticeably less clear than on the *Houses Of The Holy* album. Asked in an interview with *The Scotsman* in 1988 how he looked after his vocal chords, Plant revealed that ... "15 years ago I had an operation on my throat and couldn't speak for three weeks". No news of such an operation leaked out to the press at the time, but it now seems likely that the operation took place around late '73 to early '74, and this contributed to the lay-off.

Listening to tapes of the 1971/2 touring era, when Plant's vocal performances were consistently excellent, it's clear his voice underwent some considerable changes as their schedule took its toll. From 1975, Plant was careful to pace himself, employing the aid of a Harmoniser to moderate the more extreme vocal gymnastics.

to headline the first Knebworth Festival, due to be staged on July 20, only for Grant to decide otherwise. An offer to headline a festival in Munich on July 29 for a show that would be relayed via satellite to 10,000 theatres in America by ABC TV was also given the thumbs down.

However, the group members were not entirely out of view on the live front. There were a few jam sessions and cameos, mostly with old friend Roy

Harper and Swan Song label mates Bad Company. All the group were in attendance at the Wembley Stadium show headed by Crosby, Stills, Nash & Young which featured Plant favourite Joni Mitchell. Page and Bonham later jammed with Stills and Young at an after-show party at London's Piccadilly.

By late September the new album had been mixed and completed, and Page revealed it would

be a double set: "We have more material than would fit in with a single album. So we figured it was time to put out a double set and include some tracks we have in the can. It seems like a good time to do that now."

With Swan Song now active, the feature film project on the back burner (soon to be dubbed by Grant as "The most expensive home movie ever made"), and a major new double album ready for release, Grant began piecing together a major new touring schedule for 1975.

As *NME*'s Nick Kent astutely observed after meeting up with them at initial rehearsals at the Liveware Theatre in London's Ealing in late November: "The barley has been harvested. The heifers too have been put out to pasture and the Scalextrix sets have been stored away for the time being. Led Zeppelin are once again fully operative, girding their collective loins for another American tour after what has undisputedly been their longest period of musical inactivity. Atlantic Records is excited, and every juvenile devotee throughout the USA who teethed his taste for rock on those first Zep outings is excited … "

October/November
Hampshire, England
Headley Grange
RECORDING SESSIONS

Initial recording sessions for their sixth album. Working with engineer Ron Nevison they began working on new compositions, including 'Trampled Underfoot', 'Kashmir', 'In The Light'

and the instrumental "Swan Song". They employed Ronnie Lane's mobile unit for the recording, Nevison having built the studio for Lane.

Monday December 3 1973
London, England
Royal Albert Hall
GUEST APPEARANCE:

Jimmy Page joined Roy Harper at his London showcase gig. Page played on one number, 'Male Chauvinist Pig Blues'. The concert was professionally filmed, but has never been released.

Wednesday December 12 1973
London, England
BBC TV Centre, Shepherds Bush
GUEST APPEARANCE:

John Paul Jones played bass guitar in the backing group for Madeline Bell's TV appearance on the BBC2 music show *Colour My Soul*. Jones's involvement stemmed from his long-standing friendship with Ms Bell, culminating in his producing and co-writing her recent solo album *Comin' Atcha* at his Dormouse Studios.

January/February
Hampshire, England
Headley Grange
RECORDING SESSIONS

An intensive period of recording that produced eight new songs 'Custard Pie', 'In My Time Of Dying', 'Trampled Underfoot', 'Kashmir', 'In The Light', 'Ten Years Gone', 'The Wanton Song' and 'Sick Again'.

These songs would form the main bulk of *Physical Graffiti* – the decision was taken to add various completed songs lining their archives to extend the record to a double set. Seven tracks were added – 'The Rover' (Stargroves 1972), 'Houses Of The Holy' (Stargroves/Electric Lady 1972), 'Bron Y Aur' (Island 1970), 'Down By The Seaside' (Island 1971), 'Night Flight' (Island 1971), 'Boogie With Stu' (Headley Grange 1971) and 'Black Country Woman' (Stargroves 1972)

Further mixing sessions took place at Olympic Studios with engineer Keith Harwood replacing Ron Nevison who was contracted to work on The Who soundtrack for *Tommy*. Sadly Keith Harwood died in 1977.

The 1973/4 *Graffiti* sessions spawned various outtakes and work in progress versions which have surfaced on bootlegs.

Bootleg CD References: *Brutal Artistry* (Midas Touch), *Control Monitor Mixes* (Watch Tower)

Friday February 1 1974
Radio One Rockspeak
RADIO BROADCAST

On this day Radio One's *Rockspeak* programme broadcast an interview with John Paul Jones conducted by Michael Wale. JP talked about his involvement with Madeline Bell's album *Comin' Atcha* and other Zep plans – including his tongue-in-cheek quest to be the choirmaster at Winchester Cathedral.

Thursday February 14 1974
London, England
Rainbow Theatre
GUEST APPEARANCE

Jimmy Page, Robert Plant and John Bonham all attended Roy Harper's St. Valentine's Day concert. Jimmy, resplendent in a Chinese jacket decorated with hummingbirds, joined Roy's all star band comprising Keith Moon (drums), Ronnie Lane (bass) and Max Middleton (keyboards) for numbers including 'Same Old Rock' (playing a Martin acoustic), 'Male Chauvinist Pig Blues' and 'Home' (playing the Gibson Les Paul) and 'Too Many Movies'. 'Home' included a cameo appearance from John Bonham who came on strumming an acoustic guitar, dressed in a red jacket and black tights and sporting a pork pie hat. Finally, Robert Plant strolled on at the end to act as MC to declare to the crowd: "Ladies and Gentlemen – Roy Harper!!"

Some of this set was later issued on Roy's *Flashes From The Archives Of Oblivion* double album. Harper dubbed this one-off line-up as The

Intergalactic Elephant Band.

Jimmy Page: "We maybe played a few wrong notes here and there, but what the hell! The spirit of the thing was great."
Bootleg CD Reference: *Bizarre* (Tarantura)

Tuesday May 7 1974
New York, New York
Four Seasons Hotel/Uris Theater
Broadway
NON PLAYING APPEARANCE

All the group plus Peter Grant, Richard Cole and new label mates Maggie Bell and Bad Company attended the official launch of their new label Swan Song records.

In the evening, Page, Plant, Bonham and Mick Ralphs attended Mott The Hoople's show at the Uris Theater on Broadway (Ralphs was a former member of Mott). This could have developed into a guest appearance as *NME* reported: "Bonham insisted on playing and a scuffle broke out with Ian Hunter and Dale 'Buffin' Griffin. It seems Bonham wanted to play on 'All The Young Dudes'. He told Hunter 'I know all the breaks'. Hunter was having none of it, insisting it was Mott's night. Apparently, there was more unpleasantness between the Zeppelin and Mott roadies. Page later apologised. The Zeppelin entourage moved on to East 4th Street and called in on Club 82 – the latest after hours drag bar discotheque."

Saturday May 11 1974
Los Angeles, California
Inglewood Forum

c/o Harlequin Records,
32, Gt. Pulteney Street,
London, W.1.

We regret that Led Zeppelin are not now appearing at the Knebworth Park Concert on July 20th. However, the concert is still taking place with the following artists:

The Allman Bros. Band
The Van Morrison Show
The Doobie Bros.
The Mahavishnu Orchestra
Tim Buckley

Tickets are priced £2.75 inc, VAT. Should you still require tickets, please return your original order in the s.a.e. provided and we will be pleased to forward tickets by return post.

Sincerely,

FREDERICK BANNISTER PROMOTIONS LTD

was at the swish Bel Air Hotel in LA. Guests included Groucho Marx, Mickey Dolenz, Bill Wyman, Lloyd Bridges and Bryan Ferry.

During their stay at the Continental Hyatt House, the group dressed up in drag to be photographed by BP Fallon. These pictures later adorned the peep-hole inserts of the *Physical Graffiti* cover.

June 1974

News Report: Led Zeppelin have turned down an offer to top a one day festival at Knebworth – the first to be held in the grounds of the Hertfordshire stately home. Promoter Freddie Bannister jumps the gun slightly by announcing that Zeppelin will headline over the Allman Brothers Band, Van Morrison and The Mahavishnu Orchestra on Saturday July 20. Peter Grant announced days later that filming and recording commitments will prevent the group from making any live appearances this year.

Bannister issued a statement that reads: "We had a very definite arrangement with Led Zeppelin's manager Peter Grant for the band to appear on July 20. I very much regret that I am left with no alternative but to resort to legal action to exonerate my reputation."

Grant's reply was simple: "We never signed a contract in the first place."

Bannister's threat of legal action was subsequently dropped.

There was strong criticism of their alleged Knebworth withdrawal in the letters pages of the UK music press. "Led Zeppelin seem to have little more respect for their fans than a dog has for the lamp post!" read one such complaint. "It's a sad state of affairs when the supposed world's best group cannot spare a day or so to appear at this concert. You can correct yourself lads by appearing in Hyde Park for free."

This sentiment was not entirely lost on John

All the band attended Elvis Presley's show at the LA Forum. Afterwards promoter Jerry Weintraub arranged for Led Zeppelin to meet Elvis.

Peter Grant: "They said we would only get 20 minutes and we ended up staying two hours. It was then that I managed to sit on Elvis' father, Vernon! He was perched on the end of the settee and I just didn't see him. Bonzo and Elvis were talking about hot rods. This thing about how much kick back you can get. And John was calling him El and he says 'I've had one El that kicked back real hard' and he pushes Elvis's shoulder and knocks him back and all the minders jump up. Elvis laughs 'What did you do that for?' and John replies, 'I gotta tell you El, I was in reverse at the time!' It was a great thrill for us all that night."

Other highlights of the meeting included Plant singing the opening to 'Love Me' – "Treat me like a fool … " – and Elvis responding with the next lines, and Elvis asking for their autographs for his daughter Lisa Marie.

NON PLAYING APPEARANCE
Monday May 13 1974
Los Angeles,
California
Bel Air Hotel
The West Coast launch for the Swan Song label

Paul Jones – who soon does just that.

Saturday August 31 1974
London, England
Hyde Park
GUEST APPEARANCE:
John Paul Jones joined Roy Harper for his free concert in London's Hyde Park. He formed part of Harper's backing band along with Pink Floyd's Dave Gilmour and Steve Broughton of The Edgar Broughton Band. Their performance included a new Harper composition 'The Game', the studio version of which was subsequently issued with Jones as a guest musician on his *HQ* album in 1975.

August 1974
Shepperton, England
Shepperton Studios

Not an actual gig – but a re-enactment of one they had already played. Working with new director Peter Clifton, the group decided to re-shoot close-up scenes for their in-progress feature film which will emerge two years later as *The Song Remains The Same*.

A complete stage replica of their three night stint at Madison Square Garden in July 1973 was assembled at Shepperton Studios and the group spent a week re-enacting scenes from the concerts.

These sessions were a closely guarded secret and remained so except for a leak to *Let It Rock* magazine. They reported: "Let's turn to a film that nobody knows much about – the as-yet untitled Led Zeppelin musical. The resulting footage from their Madison Square Garden shows was apparently punctuated with blank spaces. Not to be outdone, they sacked original producer Joe Massot and hired Australian director Peter Clifton. He recently rebuilt the concert stage at Shepperton Studios and got the group to re-enact their stage performance of the time – thus filling the blank spaces. Apparently, the session produced a memorable confrontation between the super efficient music business and the pathetic dregs of the British film industry old guard. The filming was one of the last to be shot at Shepperton in its former guise and there was tension galore. Clifton however completed the task and is now re-editing the entire footage for release as a full length feature film next year."

Sunday September 1 1974
Austin, Texas
Texas Jam Festival
GUEST APPEARANCE:
Jimmy Page joined Bad Company for an encore performance of 'Rock Me Baby'. He played a borrowed Gibson guitar.

"It was really great playing in Austin," commented Page afterwards. "I wouldn't have wanted to do it as an ego thing or if the band hadn't asked me to. But I must admit it was so great to get up on stage again."

Wednesday September 24 1974
New York, New York
Central Park,
Schaefer Music Festival

GUEST APPEARANCE:

Jimmy was again the guest of Bad Company when he attended their Schaefer Festival show with Peter Grant. 'Rock Me Baby' was again chosen as the encore jam.

Lisa Robinson, reporting in *New Musical Express*: "Following the first encore of 'The Stealer', Paul Rodgers yelled to the crowd 'Do you want another one?' and they screamed for more. Peter beckoned to Jimmy and a roadie handed him a guitar (a Sunburst Fender Stratocaster) as Paul announced to the audience 'Here's a good friend of ours, and I think a good friend of yours as well – Jimmy Page!'

"The audience, already hysterical, rushed the stage and went berserk. Jimmy took off his maroon jacket and joined the band. He was grinning so wide as he took a few solos but it wasn't a superstar ego thing, he just played with the band. He hugged Paul at the end and they went off to a roaring ovation."

Foghat, obliged to follow Bad Company, couldn't believe their bad luck.

Saturday September 14 1974
London, England
Quaglino's Restaurant, St. James' Place
GUEST APPEARANCE:

Following the Crosby, Stills, Nash & Young show at Wembley which is attended by all four group members, Jimmy Page and John Bonham joined an all star jam at the after-show party. The line-up of Page on guitar (using a borrowed Les Paul copy), Bonham on drums, Tim Drummond on bass, Stephen Stills on guitar, Neil Young on guitar and Graham Nash on vocals jammed on versions of Young's 'Vampire Blues' and 'On The Beach'. At one point, Stills took over from Bonzo on drums. The video footage of the entire Crosby, Stills, Nash & Young Wembley concert surfaced on an unofficial DVD in 2004. It was filmed by the same video company later employed for Zeppelin's Earls Court shows.

Thursday October 31 1974
Surrey, England
Chislehurst Caves
NON PLAYING APPEARANCE:

The official UK launch of Swan Song Records took place at Chislehurst Caves in Kent. All the group were in attendance plus Bad Company, Maggie Bell and new signing, The Pretty Things.

Alan Freeman, Bob Harris and Roy Harper also attended and music was provided by Bob Kerr's Whoopee Band and John Chiltern's Feetwarmers with George Melly. Topless ladies, cigar chewing monks and inebriated nuns mingled with the guests, making it a bizarre Hallowe'en occasion in the grand Zeppelin tradition.

Tuesday November 26 1974
Ealing London, England
Liveware Theatre
REHEARSALS

Their formal return to activity began with initial

rehearsals for the 1975 tour. *NME's* Nick Kent visited them to conduct an interview with Page. He reported that during the afternoon and evening they ran down 'Trampled Underfoot', 'In My Time Of Dying', 'When The Levee Breaks', 'Sick Again', 'Custard Pie', 'Don't Be Cruel' and 'Hound Dog'. 'Custard Pie' one of the new tracks from *Physical Graffiti,* though rehearsed here, was never performed live. *NME* Photographer Pennie Smith took a few shots of the four of them standing in the foyer of the hall, one of which was featured in the December 7 edition of the paper.

Thursday December 19 1974
London, England
Rainbow Theatre
GUEST APPEARANCE:
Another Bad Company jam. Jimmy Page and John Paul Jones joined Duster Bennett and the rest of Bad Company for an encore performance of 'Rock Me Baby'.

(DRIVING TO) KASHMIR

Written on the road to Tan Tan and demoed by Page and Bonham in late '73 when it had a working title 'Driving To Kashmir', this track had all the potential for growing in stature when played live. When they premiered it in early '75, 'Kashmir' did not disappoint. It was another occasion where the four were able to add an extra ingredient which the studio version had only hinted at. Jones cleverly adapted the brass arrangement for the Mellotron, playing the hypnotic riff behind Page's guitar. John Bonham made ample use of the 26-inch bass drum miked for maximum impact, while Robert produced one of his most effective vocal performances. He became engrossed in the lyric, following every twist and turn of the journey and ad-libbing additional lyrics, notably the "Woman talking to ya!" tag at the end of the middle section. Coupled with some very effective lighting, 'Kashmir' was a definite highlight of every 1975 show, no more so than when they performed it on home turf in London SW5 in May that year.

Subsequently, the track was merged with Jimmy's 'White Summer – Black Mountainside' solo spot (employing the Dan Electro as opposed to the Gibson Les Paul as was customary in 1975) for the US '77 and Europe '80 arrangements, which perhaps stripped it of its earlier impact.

Because of its hypnotic and repetitive construction, 'Kashmir' was also prone to onstage errors and the band members frequently lost their way during the middle section.

It was revived somewhat disastrously for the 1988 Atlantic reunion but given new life in the Nineties when rearranged with the Egyptian Ensemble for the 1995/6 Page &Plant *Unledded* Tour. It also gained renewed prominence in 1998 when Page collaborated with rapper Puff Daddy on the track 'Come With Me' for the soundtrack to the film *Godzilla*. This incorporated the riff structure of 'Kashmir' reworked by Page and took the song close to the top of the UK charts. This arrangement was also used as background music to the BBC's World Cup soccer coverage during the summer of the same year.

'Kashmir' remains a very vivid part of their live history, past, present & future and has been described by Robert Plant as 'The pride of Led Zeppelin'.

The Concert File

"1974 didn't happen. 1975 will be better." – Jimmy Page, November 1974.

The lay-off had been their longest to date – but a vital one. Armed with a new double album set, *Physical Graffiti*, ready to be issued on their newly inaugurated label Swan Song, Led Zeppelin began a new chapter in their history with the announcement of a long-awaited US tour.

This tenth US visit was a lengthy two-leg affair, preceded by two warm up dates in Rotterdam and Brussels. In line with the developing rock concert presentation, this tour was on a much grander scale and incorporated a massive light show with neon lit 'Led Zeppelin' backdrop. Krypton laser effects were employed for Page's violin bow interlude. For the first time, Bonzo was on a high-rise rostrum.

The early part of the tour was dogged by ill health. Jimmy was forced to develop a three finger technique after slamming his hand in a train door prior to leaving England. Plant also struggled with a bout of 'flu while Bonham suffered stomach pains. Only Jones survived intact. "Nothing exciting ever happens to me!" he dryly commented at the time.

Due to Page's hand restrictions, 'How Many More Times' was drafted in as a replacement for 'Dazed And Confused' up until early February. After it returned at Madison Square Garden on February 3, Plant began using the spacey middle section – previously reserved for their version of Scott Mackenzie's 'San Francisco (Be Sure To Wear Some Flowers In Your Hair)' – as a vehicle for other bizarre interpretations. As the tour progressed these would include Joni Mitchell's 'Woodstock' and Ben E. King's 'Spanish Harlem'.

This new stage show also featured plenty of new material, with 'Kashmir' and 'Trampled Underfoot' quickly established as live standards. The set list was constructed to represent, as Plant would put it: "Every colour of the spectrum" – a cross section of their six and a half year development. 'Stairway To Heaven', now established as the most in-demand track on US radio, closed every performance.

Off stage, there were the by-now-customary rumblings, even before the tour commenced. A proposed February 4 date at the Boston Gardens was cancelled by the local Mayor after fans rioted as they waited in line for tickets. A headlining appearance due for March 8 at Florida's West Palm Beach Speedway was also thwarted by officialdom.

Refreshed by a twelve day break in mid-February, Zeppelin really hit their stride during March. By that time, *Physical Graffiti* was ensconced on top of the *Billboard* chart and their five other albums also re-entered the Top 200 – confirmation of their now undisputed position as the world's top rock attraction.

The final flurry of shows, culminating in three nights at their old stomping ground, the LA Forum, saw them scale new heights of on-stage improvisation with the set now stretching to three hours. "My voice was getting so good by the end, I felt I could sing anything!" observed Plant shortly after the tour ended.

It was another hugely successful conquest of America; even if the early part had been hindered by their physical state. As they left the stage for the final time on the last night in LA, Plant excitedly announced: "If there's anyone here from England ... Well, we're coming back, baby!"

Equipment Notes:

John Paul Jones' equipment set-up was further extended here with a Steinway grand piano (for 'No Quarter'), and a Hohner Clavinet D6 (used for 'Trampled Underfoot'). With the introduction of 'In My Time Of Dying', Page brought back the Dan Electro (last used in 1970 for 'White Summer'). This guitar was also used for 'When The Levee Breaks' early on in the tour. Around this period, Page also began bringing along an additional 1959 Les Paul Standard (acquired from Joe Walsh), which was periodically used as a back-up to his Number One Gibson model (notably for 'Kashmir' on this tour).

Fashion Note:
Plant took to wearing a cherry adorned wrap-around number for much of the tour. Page premiered his famous dragon suit for the LA shows in March and retained it for the Earl's Court run. For the US tour, John Bonham donned a *Clockwork Orange* style white boiler suit.

Saturday January 11 1975
Rotterdam, Holland
The Ahoy

A predictably nervous return to the stage saw Plant forget the lyrics to 'Stairway'.
He gave an interview to *Musik Express* the next day in the lounge of their hotel in Hague, and mentioned how embarrassed he was at forgetting the lyrics at the Rotterdam show. "It was only OK last night but it should be better in Brussels and America should be really good. Maybe we played too many songs. We just came here to see what it would sound like live again."

Talking about the forthcoming release of *Physical Graffiti*, he revealed: "We only did the final mixing last November. We were waiting for some Indian violinists we wanted to use on a couple of tracks."

Sunday January 12 1975
Brussels, Belgium
Vorst National
Set: Rock And Roll/Sick Again/Over The Hills And Far Away/When The Levee Breaks/The Song Remains The Same/The Rain Song\Kashmir/The Wanton Song/No Quarter/Trampled Underfoot/In My Time Of Dying/Stairway To Heaven/Whole Lotta Love · Black Dog/Communication Breakdown.

Before the show Robert conducted a backstage interview with Bob Harris for broadcast the following ~~follwoing~~ week on BBC2's *Old Grey Whistle Test*.

In line with previous pre-tour shows in Europe, this concert was used for experimentation. New material from *Physical Graffiti* was given its first public airing here, alongside an arrangement of the never before played live 'When The Levee Breaks' from the fourth album.

Under-rehearsed and experiencing problems with Page's damaged fingers, this show was rough, chaotic and less than two hours in length. A minimal show with no space for improvisation – 'Dazed And Confused' and 'Moby Dick' were both absent from the set list.

For these warm-up dates, the full new lighting rig and stage design was passed up in favour of what will be their last relatively simple stage set up.

Bootleg CD References: *It's Time To Travel Again* (Diagrams of Led Zeppelin), *The Belgium Triple* (Empress Valley)

Friday January 17 1975
London, England
The Old Grey Whistle Test *BBC 2*
TV APPEARANCE
The interview conducted by Bob Harris with Robert prior to the Brussels show was aired in full on the evening's edition of *The Old Grey Whistle Test*. Plant was seated on an equipment flight case and talked about *Physical Graffiti*, the film project, Swan Song and their plans to play in the UK. At the close of the clip Bob Harris announced, ''The singer with the best rock'nroll band in the world. The band's new album is out soon and I heard some new things from it at the gig and they sounded amazing. In about two or three week's time we'll have some exclusive music from it.''

A three minute edit of the interview was used by Page as an extra item on the official DVD. The full version was included on *The Old Grey Whistle Whistle Test* 2001 compilation issued via BBC DVD

Visual References: *The Old Grey Whistle Test* (Warner Music Vision), *1975* (Unofficial – Cosmic (BBCDVD), Official *Led Zeppelin* 2003 DVD Energy)

NORTH AMERICA 1975

Led Zeppelin

Saturday January 18 1975
Bloomington, Minnesota
Met Center
This venue was demolished in 1994.

The previous evening was spent at the venue rehearsing the new show (with tour photographer Neal Preston in attendance, capturing some rare rehearsal images), resulting in a concert that was, in Plant's view, "Good for an opening night!"

"First-night kinks mar Zeppelin show," wrote Jon Beam for the local press: "The group's two and a quarter hour concert, Saturday, was more art form than art. Marred by many opening night kinks, it was merely a likeable performance – certainly not as satisfying as the band's excellent, three-hour show in St. Paul in 1973.

"Vocalist Robert Plant, who perceptively labelled the performance 'rusty', slipped off-key many times; his screaming voice was obviously not in mid-tour form to provide the promised three-hour concert. Guitarist Jimmy Page, the creative force of the six-year-old band, was hampered by a broken finger on his fretting hand. Nonetheless, the guitarist was impressive, especially on the blues riffs. John Paul Jones' overloud bass was less distinguished than his occasional work on Mellotron. Drummer John Bonham provided steady support, although his unimaginative, 15-minute solo during 'Moby Dick' was the low point of the evening.

"When the house lights went on, the heretofore mild-mannered listeners, most of whom had paid $8.50 for tickets, booed vociferously, expecting

another hour of music. However, Led Zeppelin, after a few days of rehearsal here and a passable show, was ready to leave the Twin Cities, $90,000 to $100,000 richer."

Monday January 20 1975
Chicago, Illinois
Chicago Stadium
Set: Rock And Roll/Sick Again/Over The Hills And Far Away/When The Levee Breaks/The Song Remains The Same/The Rain Song/Kashmir/The Wanton Song/No Quarter/In My Time Of Dying/Trampled Underfoot/Moby Dick/How Many More Times/Stairway To Heaven/Whole Lotta Love – Black Dog/Communication Breakdown.

Plant's bare-chested arrival at Chicago's O'Hare airport ensured that he added to the group's problems by catching influenza. Page's finger, however, was starting to improve and 'How Many More Times' has been recalled to the set to allow space for guitar improvisation. As Page tells Chris Charlesworth of *Melody Maker*: "We've had to cut 'Dazed And Confused' from the set and substitute 'How Many More Times' which we haven't played for four years. I'm still doing the violin bow routine but we've had to alter even that and I can't do it as well as I'd like to. I can tell it's not as good as it usually is but the audience don't seem to notice. We almost can-

Rehearsals - Minneapolis January 17 1975

celled the tour, but we couldn't as we'd sold all the tickets and a postponement would have meant chaos."

In addition to these problems, the sound system was defective, ensuring that press reviews are not all entirely favourable.

'Led Zeppelin: malfunctions reduce power' reported Al Rudis: "Led Zeppelin is alive, but not well. Robert Plant's 'flu-ridden voice hurt the British band in its concert Monday. Jimmy Page was nursing a broken finger too. What was worst of all was the old bugaboo of rock and roll: defective sound equipment. In Zeppelin's case, it's understandable that the group wouldn't want to be burdened with maintaining its own sound system if it only tours every year and a half; but they're the ones who rented the system used Monday night, so they must be held responsible.'

'Kinky Led Zeppelin still king of the funky' wrote Jack Hafferkamp: "For its part, the band played a new variation on its standard heavy-heavy, super-loud, bare-chested, Victorian decadent, fingernail polish and lipstick, kiss-me-because-I'm-really-funky, cartoon performance. Two hours worth.

"Still there were a few surprises. My companion, for example, noted she owns a blouse just like the one Robert Plant was wearing. John Bonham played what must have been the longest drum solo in the history of mankind. And Plant revealed over, and over, and over again that he has the flu. He said that almost as many times as he mentioned the title of the band's new record. In fact, I think the final score was New Record 8, Flu 5."

Bootleg CD References: *Live At The Chicago Stadium* (Cobra Standard), *Luftschiffe* (Tarantura), *Live On The Levee* (Silver Rarities)

Tuesday January 21 1975
Chicago, Illinois
Chicago Stadium

Set: Rock And Roll/Sick Again/Over The Hills And Far Away/In My Time Of Dying/The Song Remains The Same/The Rain Song/Kashmir/The Wanton Song/No Quarter/In My Time Of Dying/Trampled Underfoot/Moby Dick/How Many More Times/Stairway To Heaven/Whole Lotta Love – Black Dog/Communication Breakdown.

An early set list change saw 'When The Levee Breaks' replaced by 'In My Time Of Dying'. 'Levee' would not be performed live again by Zeppelin.

The second night in Chicago was a marked improvement, as Lisa Robinson in *New Musical Express* reported: "Fifteen seconds onstage and

241

everyone knows it's going to be HOT. They've been truly depressed and confused all day about the first Chicago show. No matter, tonight they're playing with that old black Zeppelin magic again, and the audience go wild. It sounds as if The Beatles battled the Stones in a parking lot – and Zeppelin won!"

Some 15 minutes of excellent colour cine film from this show exists, clips of which were used in the 1997 official 'Whole Lotta Love' promo video
Bootleg CD References: *Live At The Chicago Stadium* (Cobra Standard), *Luftschiffe* (Tarantula), *Live On The Levee* (Silver Rarities)
Visual Reference: *Chicago '75* (Toasted -Unofficial video), *1975* (Unofficial- Cosmic Energy)

Wednesday January 22 1975
Chicago, Illinois
Chicago Stadium
Set: Rock And Roll/Sick Again/Over The Hills And Far Away/In My Time Of Dying/The Song Remains The Same/Kashmir/The Wanton Song/No Quarter/Trampled Underfoot/Moby Dick/How Many More Times/Stairway To Heaven/Whole Lotta Love – Black Dog/Communication Breakdown.

Press reaction continued to improve. Chris Charlesworth, in his review for *Melody Maker*

reports: "It's cold outside, freezing, sub-zero and bitter, but inside Chicago Stadium 20,000 Led Zeppelin fans are roaring in unison as if some giant orgasm has overtaken each and every one."

Lisa Robinson of *New Musical Express* asked: "What can you say about a six-year old band that has America in the palm of its hand. It's just begun, really – and yet Zeppelin has already managed to make every other rock/news/concert/ whatever pale by comparison."

Friday January 24 1975
Richfield, Ohio
Richfield Coliseum
Set: Rock And Roll/Sick Again/Over The Hills And Far Away/In My Time Of Dying/The Song Remains The Same/The Rain Song/Kashmir/The Wanton Song/No Quarter/Trampled Underfoot/Moby Dick/How Many More Times (inc. The Hunter)/Stairway To Heaven/Whole Lotta Love – Black Dog/Communication Breakdown (inc The Lemon Song).

This venue was demolished in 1999

A powerful performance. Page now seemed comfortable with his new playing style and began to experiment. However, Plant's voice was starting to show signs of strain again.

'Zeppelin: Slow To Start, But Hot' – Bob Von Sternberg reviews the show in the following day's press: "Led Zeppelin spent their first hour on stage at the Coliseum Friday night playing music that was howlingly loud, but soggy and spiritless. It may have been the effects of guitarist Jimmy Page's intermittent slugs on a Jack Daniels whisky bottle or they might have needed to get some adrenalin moving but after that first hour the band caught fire and soared through the rest of the concert."
Bootleg CD Reference: *Ultraviolence* (Holy Label

Saturday January 25 1975
Indianapolis, Indiana
Market Square Arena
Set includes: Rock And Roll/Sick Again/Ove

The Hills And Far Away/The Song Remains The Same/The Rain Song/Kashmir/The Wanton Song/No Quarter/Trampled Underfoot/Moby Dick/How Many More Times/Stairway To Heaven/Whole Lotta Love – Black Dog.

Page's guitar work continued to improve, but Plant's voice had deteriorated causing serious problems.

Bootleg CD Reference: *Condition Breakdown* (Holy Label)

Monday January 27 1975
St. Louis, Missouri
Missouri Arena – **CANCELLED**
This show was cancelled due to Plant's influenza. Plant rests at their Chicago base, while the rest of the band and entourage take the Starship to Los Angeles for a few days' holiday.

Chris Charlesworth: "There was a band meeting to decide where to go. They paid for the Starship on a daily basis whether they used it or not and nobody wanted to stay in Chicago because it was so cold. John Paul Jones wanted to go to the Bahamas, and Bonzo fancied Jamaica. Jimmy wanted to see some girl in LA. Then the pilot stepped in and pointed out that the plane wasn't licensed outside of continental America, so Jimmy got his way. All the way to LA we got roaring drunk and sang old English songs with John Paul on the electric organ. Peter Grant loved it … he was singing 'Any Old Iron' … songs like that. We stayed in the Hyatt House and just partied."

Wednesday January 29 1975
Greensboro, North Carolina
The Coliseum
Set: Rock And Roll/Sick Again/Over The Hills And Far Away/In My Time Of Dying/The Song Remains the Same/The Rain Song/Kashmir/No Quarter/Trampled Underfoot/Moby Dick/How Many More Times/Stairway To Heaven/Whole Lotta Love – Black Dog/Communication Breakdown.

Another very lacklustre performance, possibly

due to Jimmy, John Paul and Bonzo having had to rise very early and fly coast to coast (against the time changes) from Los Angeles to reach Greensboro in time. Robert, who flew in from Chicago, would probably have benefited from another day in bed. The show was now condensed even further by the removal of 'The Wanton Song' from the set list.

Ticket problems and violence erupted once more. Chris Charlesworth: "About five hundred fans attempted to storm the rear of the building, throwing broken bottles, stones and pieces of scaffolding. Three of the group's five limousines were severely damaged, and the drivers of the other two – which were parked inside the building – wanted to take their cars away. Peter Grant wasn't having that … oh no! He actually offered to buy them on the spot for cash, but after a 'discussion' the drivers had no alternative but to let him have them.

"The group and entourage had to make a very quick getaway within seconds of the final encore. Grant took the wheel of the first limo with the band and Richard Cole inside, and everybody else piled into the second. With a Police escort, sirens blazing, at speeds of up to 70 mph in a heavily built-up area, Grant led the way, driving through red lights and on the wrong side of the road.

"It was incredible to be involved in scenes like that … Peter was just unflappable. When we got to the plane he got out and kicked the car really hard. 'Fucking useless pile of junk!' he shouted. 'Way off tune … my old Bently goes twice as fast!' We all just stood there laughing … totally exhilarated by it all. Then we flew back to New York and the band checked in the Plaza. It was a very tiring day. Unforgettable!"

Bootleg CD References: *A Quick Get Away* (The Diagrams Of Led Zeppelin), *Footstomping Graffiti* (No label)

Friday January 31 1975
Detroit, Michigan
Olympia Stadium
Set: Rock And Roll/Sick Again/Over The Hills And Far Away/In My Time Of Dying/The Song Remains The Same/The Rain Song/Kashmir/No Quarter/Trampled Underfoot/Moby Dick/How Many More Times (inc. The Hunter – The Lemon Song)/Stairway To Heaven/Whole Lotta Love – Black Dog.

"Good evening! It's our great pleasure to be just about back!" Plant's opening comment summed up the gig quite accurately. Zeppelin were returning to form slowly but there was still considerable room for improvement. Page displayed momentary flashes of brilliance, notably in 'Sick Again' and 'Over The Hills And Far Away', but Plant was still very raspy.

Plant explained the problem with Jimmy's finger and joked that … "The bone on his wedding ring finger is bust and that's a real drag because if he was to get married now, he couldn't get a ring on."

Bonzo was introduced tonight, as he would be many times on the tour, as "Mr Ultraviolence!", a reference to the *Clockwork Orange* style suits that both he and his assistant Mick Hinton wore throughout the tour.

The band seemed to tire early tonight and the last portion of the show was something of an anticlimax. 'How Many More Times' was particularly slow and unexciting, with Plant barely able to keep up with the lyrics.
Bootleg CD Reference: *Tune Up* (Immigrant)

Saturday February 1 1975
Pittsburgh, Pennsylvania
Civic Arena

UNCONFIRMED
Sunday February 2 1975
Pittsburgh, Pennsylvania
Civic Arena
No evidence exists of this show being played – it was not listed on the original press tour itinerary.

However some sources say it was added after the original date sold out very quickly.

Monday February 3 1975
New York, New York
Madison Square Garden
Set: Rock And Roll/Sick Again/Over The Hills And Far Away/In My Time Of Dying/The Song Remains The Same/The Rain Song/Kashmir/No Quarter/Trampled Underfoot/Moby Dick/ Dazed And Confused (inc. San Francisco)/Stairway To Heaven/Whole Lotta Love – Black Dog/Jam – Communication Breakdown (inc. The Lemon Song).

Plant: "Whatever happened to nice warm weather. It's so cold. Never mind, I think we can overcome it tonight."

They seemed determined to impress on this first New York date. Plant's voice was still hoarse but they quickly developed a good rapport with the audience, resulting in one of the best shows so far.

Significantly, 'How Many More Times' was dropped – Page now feeling strong enough to recall 'Dazed And Confused' for its first performance since July 29, 1973, at the very same venue. A truncated version was played, some of the sections still proving painful, but nevertheless an important step on the road to Page's full recovery.

Unusually, tonight, just before the final encore Page and Plant indulged in a brief jam consisting of an old Yardbirds number 'I Wish You Would' and a few lyrics from 'The Crunge'.

'There's Art in Led Zep's Heavy Meta Hullabaloo'. The *New York Times* reported "Teenage devotion to Led Zeppelin has continued to increase. On Friday evening, February 3, an army of fans, equipped with sleeping bags and food, braved freezing weather to camp in front of

Madison Square Garden and wait for the ticket windows to open the following morning, and smashed by fans a few hours later, by which time Madison Square Garden had experienced the fastest sell-out in its history."

'Led Zeppelin Excites Crowd at Garden But Somehow Delirium Wasn't There'. The *New York Times'* John Rockwell is not convinced about Zeppelin's performance. "The climax of last night's two-and-three-quarter hour show was curiously muted from the audience's standpoint. Yes, people were standing up and clapping. But they simply weren't delirious.

"In the end, there is still something missing, and that is, to put it bluntly, creative significance. Led Zep isn't original enough to make a really important statement in its music. The four of them can produce songs that epitomise the contained aggression of the seventies and they can hint very strongly indeed toward what rock is all about. But they simply don't reach way down deep inside their audiences. And to judge from the reaction at the end of last night's concert, the audiences know it."

Atlantic Records held an aftershow party for the group at the Garden's Penn Plaza Club. Andy Warhol, Keith Moon, William Burroughs and Amanda Lear were among attending. *People* magazine was out on the news stands claiming "Led Zeppelin are bigger than The Beatles". John Lennon had allegedly heard 'Stairway To Heaven' and loved it. ("He's only just heard it!" is Plant's typical comment.)

Bootleg CD Reference: *Heavy Metal Hullabaloo* (The Diagrams Of Led Zeppelin)

Tuesday February 4 1975
Uniondale, New York
Nassau Veterans Memorial Coliseum

Set includes – Rock And Roll/Sick Again/Over The Hills And Far Away/In My Time Of Dying/No Quarter/Trampled Underfoot/Moby Dick/Dazed And Confused (inc. San Francisco).

A concert was originally scheduled in Boston this evening, but after riots over ticket sales, the show was cancelled by the local authorities. However, Boston fans didn't miss out since tickets were distributed to Boston fans by mail order for this extra date. All mail with Massachusetts post-marks received preferential treatment.

'Led Zep Concert Banned in Boston': "Mayor White cancelled the Led Zeppelin concert after some 3,000 fans ran amok in a January 6 pre-ticket-sales camp-out, causing $30,000 damage to the arena. The Garden allowed fans to bivouac inside the arena to keep them out of the blustery New England night. But the kids (average age 14) looted concession stands, got bombed on stolen beer, turned on fire-hoses, broke doors and seats and, in the biggest blasphemy of all, wrecked the surface of the ice hockey court, making it necessary to reschedule a Bruins game."

Bootleg CD Reference: *Sometime In New York City* (IQ)

Thursday February 6 1975
Montreal, Canada
Montreal Forum

Set: Rock And Roll/Sick Again/Over The Hills And Far Away/In My Time Of Dying/The Song Remains The Same/The Rain Song/Kashmir/No Quarter/Trampled Underfoot/Moby Dick/Dazed And Confused (inc. San Francisco)/Stairway To Heaven/Whole Lotta Love – Black Dog/Heartbreaker

A mixed performance, inspired in places but incredibly poor in others. Plant's voice seemed to have taken a turn for the worse again. The winter weather was constantly hindering his recovery.

During 'Over The Hills', Page's guitar lead packed up and Plant filled in above the rhythm

section. After 'The Rain Song', Robert lectured the crowd on the Mellotron: "It's a very peculiar instrument because every time we take it somewhere, it goes out of tune. It's built and comprises of tapes inside the box, and to simulate violins is not an easy job when you're travelling to North America. In fact, we're gonna try to simulate some Eastern violins now." 'Kashmir' was growing more powerful with each performance and was rapidly turning into one of the highlights of the show.

Bonham's solo was now stretching to 25 minutes and tonight Plant called Bonzo "Karen Carpenter", a reference to a recent poll in *Playboy* magazine which placed Carpenter as 'Best Drummer', above Bonzo. Bonham's first hand response was captured in an interview with Lisa Robinson: "Karen Carpenter couldn't last ten fucking minutes with a Zeppelin number!"

'Dazed And Confused' included a very delicate version of 'San Francisco' and was now recapturing some of its former glories. Page's solo on 'Stairway To Heaven' was also developing a previously unknown intricacy.

A bizarre siren heralded the end of the show and tonight, instead of 'Communication Breakdown', the Canadians were treated to a ragged version of 'Heartbreaker' as a second encore.

"Montreal – you are the best! Maybe the snow has melted all around the hall," was Plant's parting comment.

Melody Maker run the headline 'Zep's inspiration breakdown': "Zeppelin may be one of the few rock bands left who haven't blown their credibility, but they have their ups and downs too. The show started off with the pile-driving 'Rock And Roll' but faltered quickly when it turned out that Robert Plant is touring with only half a voice. Plant came down an octave on all the high notes, cutting off the top range of the piece and seriously constricting it. But Zep rallied! Jimmy Page got into the act, and if his playing isn't as committed as it once was, there was the odd snatch of brilliance."

After the show, the group flew back to New York. They were set to attend a party for The Jackson 5, but arrived too late. Instead, Jones and Plant hung out with David Bowie at the Plaza Hotel.

Excerpts from three songs filmed from the press pit by a reporter on 16mm colour film with sound exist from this show.

CD Bootleg References: *The 1975 World Tour* (Cobra), *When The Levee Breaks* (TNT Studio)
Visual Reference: *Latter Visions* DVD (Unofficial – Celebration)

Friday February 7 1975
New York, New York
Madison Square Garden

Set: Rock And Roll/Sick Again/Over The Hills And Far Away/In My Time Of Dying/The Song Remains The Same/The Rain Song/K a s h m i r / N o Q u a r t e r / T r a m p l e d U n d e r f o o t / M o b y Dick/Dazed And Confused (inc. San Francisco)/Stairway To Heaven/Whole Lotta Love – Black Dog/Heartbreaker

Robert's voice was still in poor shape but seemed to improve as the show progressed. Introducing 'In My Time Of Dying', Plant commented: "Strangely enough, due to the state of our health, it's quite an apt title." Plant confirmed that *Physical Graffiti*, the long awaited and much overdue new album was "sooner or later gonna come out"

Bootleg CD References: *Trampled Under Foot*

246

(Cobla Standard), *Strangely Enough* (Electric Magic)

Saturday February 8 1975
Phioladelphia, Pennsylvania
The Spectrum

Set: Rock And Roll/Sick Again/Over The Hills And Far Away/In My Time Of Dying/The Song Remains The Same/The Rain Song/Kashmir/No Quarter/Trampled Underfoot/Moby Dick/Dazed And Confused (inc. San Francisco)/Stairway To Heaven/Whole Lotta Love – Black Dog/Heartbreaker

Plant's voice was beginning to mend at last, and he offered a now standard opening speech informing the audience of Zeppelin's intention to perform a cross-section of the music they have recorded over the last six and a half years. With regard to *Physical Graffiti,* Plant commented: "As usual, it's late. But we don't want to do too much in case you get fed up with it."

Robert tried periodically to calm down the crowd. "Can we advocate that people stay in their seats? It's not very pleasant to see situations like that right under your nose, so can we all keep cool?"

'Dazed And Confused' continued to improve with every performance. Plant sighed: "We really enjoyed that, and we were glad you were here as well!"

Twelve minutes of excellent silent cine film exists from this show.

Bootleg CD References: *Philadelphia Special* (LZ), *Phildelphia Spectrum* (Electric Magic)
Visual Reference: *1975* (Unofficial DVD – Cosmic Energy)

Monday February 10 1975
Landover, Maryland
Capitol Centre

Set: Rock And Roll/Sick Again/Over The Hills And Far Away/In My Time Of Dying/The Song Remains The Same/The Rain Song/Kashmir/No Quarter/Trampled Underfoot/Moby Dick/Dazed And Confused (inc. San Francisco)/Stairway To Heaven/Whole Lotta Love – Black Dog/Heartbreaker

This venue was demolished in 2002.

Though Plant still couldn't reach some notes his enthusiasm and passion made up for it. 'Moby Dick' was particularly enjoyable tonight as Bonzo expanded the syn-drum section to include the riff from 'Whole Lotta Love'. Plant persisted with his Karen Carpenter jibes.

'Heavy Zeppelin'. Larry Rohter writes: "18,800 young and extremely passionate fans last night witnessed a concert marred by more than 20 arrests and sporadic outbursts of violence inside and outside of the Capital Center Arena.

"Simplicity and loudness are the two features that last night's concert goers will remember longest. It is not surprising that these elements characterize the Led Zeppelin sound for, like it or not, Led Zeppelin is what rock'n'roll in 1975 is all about."

Silent cine footage of 'Heartbreaker' from this show exists
Visual Reference: *1975* (Unofficial DVD- Cosmic Energy)

Wednesday February 12 1975
New York, New York
Madison Square Garden

Set: Rock And Roll/Sick Again/Over The Hills And Far Away/In My Time Of Dying/The Song Remains The Same/The Rain Song/Kashmir/No Quarter/Trampled Underfoot/Moby Dick/Dazed And Confused (inc. San Francisco)/Stairway To Heaven/Whole Lotta Love – Black Dog/Heartbreaker (inc. That's Alright Mama).

An excellent show, performed in the middle of a snow storm. Plant: "We came four blocks in the

snow to get here … you realise that? People were calling me on the telephone today and saying 'Is it gonna be on?' For a minute I was wondering about my anatomy, then I realised there was some discrepancy about the weather. Isn't it good though that it snows? Doesn't it change the vibe of the city? I think it's great!"

This was the best show of the tour so far. Plant referred to 'In My Time Of Dying' as a folk standard and asked: "Can you ever imagine 'Whole Lotta Love' ending up like that!" Plant also interrupted his usual introduction to 'The Song Remains The Same' to point out: "There's a guy selling T-shirts there". 'Dazed And Confused' continued to expand, and tonight included a section from 'Walter's Walk'.

During the final encore of 'Heartbreaker', Page and Plant led the band through an almost drunken impromptu version of 'That's Alright Mama' – a perfect end to a perfect party. Plant: "Ladies and gentlemen of New York … you're too much … and we ain't so bad ourselves!"

While in New York, for recreation, Jimmy went to see Linda Ronstadt in New Jersey with ex-James Gang member Joe Walsh, and Robert visited the city's night-clubs and record stores.

Writer Cameron Crowe travelled with the band with a view to arranging a cover story for *Rolling Stone* magazine. Crowe managed to build up a good rapport with the group (he later contributed the sleeve notes to *The Song Remains The Same* soundtrack album) and interviewed all four members, finally capturing Page at the Plaza Hotel during their Madison Square stint. Page, though none too happy with the paper's previous cover-age of the group, reluctantly agreed to a group photo session.

Cameron Crowe remembers: "Time was running out but I got Ben Fong Torres at the magazine's office to hold the cover. Photographer Neal Preston reserved a room at the Plaza and set up a backdrop. It was the band's day off (February 11). The members were informed of the afternoon shoot but mysteriously that morning Page disappeared from the hotel. Plant was first to arrive at 4pm, his shirt 'accidentally' open, his hair 'accidentally' perfect, then Jones and Bonham. Joe Walsh was there with his then manager Irving Azoff to help their friend Jimmy through this most tender ordeal. Page was still nowhere to be seen.

"Finally, Page arrived. In his arms were two bouquets of dead roses – his defiant statement for the cover of *Rolling Stone*. He explained his delay: 'I was looking for black roses. They exist you know!' He looked around the room. 'Let's do this quickly!'

"The session began. Three of the four members of Led Zeppelin struck a conciliatory pose, but the fourth Jimmy Page – held roses and stared through the camera. It was his chilling look that made the photo. The film was rushed to the lab and I flew home to San Francisco to write up the story. I had decided it would be a question and answer feature – that's how good the interviews were.

"The call came early next day. There had been an equipment malfunction. The film was unusable; barely exposed was a dark silhouette of what might have been a *Rolling Stone* cover to rival the best. The cover was hastily switched to a tinted live Preston shot. That turned out nicely – and the issue with Zeppelin on the cover was a huge seller. It's just a shame Page's defiant stance was never seen."

An excellent quality soundboard sourced recording of this show surfaced in 2002 initially released as *Flying Circus*.

Bootleg CD References: *Flying Circus* (Empress Valley), *Can't Take Your Evil Ways* (Diagrams Of

Led Zeppelin), *Heartbreakers Back In Town* (TNT Studio), *Ladies & Gents* (Tarantura), *MSG 1975* (Last Stand Disk), *That's Alright* (Electric Magic)

Thursday February 13 1975
Uniondale, New York
Nassau Veterans Memorial Coliseum
Set: Rock And Roll/Sick Again/Over The Hills And Far Away/In My Time Of Dying/The Song Remains The Same/The Rain Song/Kashmir/No Quarter/Trampled Underfoot/Moby Dick/Dazed And Confused (inc. San Francisco)/Stairway To Heaven/Whole Lotta Love – Black Dog/Roll Over Beethoven/Communication Breakdown.

Another fine performance. 'Dazed And Confused' contained much improvisation. Page's injured finger was obviously causing less problems now. 'Whole Lotta Love' tonight included the Theremin for the first time during a funky interlude prior to leading into 'Black Dog'.

The only jam with other musicians of the whole tour occurred when Ron Wood of The Rolling Stones joined Zeppelin for the final encore of 'Communication Breakdown'. Robert sang a few lines of Chuck Berry's 'Roll Over Beethoven' while the guitars were being sorted out. 'Communication Breakdown' itself was greatly extended with both guitarists taking solos.

Bootleg CD References: *Trampled Underwood* (Image Quality), *The New Faces* (Jelly Roll), *Fighting Back At The Coliseum* (Empress Valley)

Friday February 14 1975
Uniondale, New York
Nassau Veterans Memorial Coliseum
Set: Rock And Roll/Sick Again/Over The Hills And Far Away/In My Time Of Dying/Since I've Been Loving You/The Song Remains The Same/The Rain Song/Kashmir/No Quarter/Trampled Underfoot/Moby Dick/Dazed And Confused (inc. San Francisco)/Stairway To Heaven/Whole Lotta Love – Black Dog/Heartbreaker.

Plant's voice was again very hoarse at the beginning of the show, but there was a good atmosphere in the venue and a forceful, high energy performance ensured another memorable evening.

Plant announced: "Today is one of the last of the pagan traditions that is carried on into the 20th Century. It's the day for sowing the wild seeds. In fact, now they call it St. Valentine's Day … so, happy St. Valentine's Day. I think we should dedicate this whole show to St. Valentine." He continued: "Tonight, we intend to take a knife and cut right through the glorious ice cream of Led Zeppelin. You get a little bit of vanilla, a little bit of chocolate, a little bit of coloured and a little bit of everything."

'Since I've Been Loving You' was a surprise addition. Plant: "Who knows what it's gonna sound like, but it's something we really used to dig playing."

Plant stated that this was Zeppelin's last night in New York and … "Despite our depleted physical forms, we intend to shake this building … and as you're fully aware, we can't shake this building by ourselves."

'No Quarter' featured John Paul Jones at his

best, his improvisations taking the number to 20 minutes in duration.

Fan Mike Tremaglio recalled: "One of my friends saw this show from the 14th row. Unfortunately he could not score tickets for my brother and I – not that I held it against him as I got him tickets for the June 7, 1977, New York show. We asked him to log down all the details of the Nassau show and we did get a blow by blow account of the new songs from *Physical Graffiti* a full two weeks before it was released in the US. His recall was tremendous and I can remember him describing 'In My Time Of Dying' and 'Kashmir' in real detail."

Bootleg CD References: *Nassau 1975* (The Diagrams Of Led Zeppelin), *St. Tangerine's Day* (Image Quality), *St. Valentine's Day Massacre* (Off Beat)

Sunday February 16 1975
St. Louis, Missouri
Missouri Arena
Set: Rock And Roll/Sick Again/Over The Hills And Far Away/in My Time Of Dying/The Song Remains The Same/The Rain SongKashmir/No Quarter/Trampled Underfoot/Moby Dick/ Dazed And Confused (inc. San Francisco)/ Stairway To Heaven/Whole Lotta Love – Black Dog/Heartbreaker.

Date rescheduled from January 26

An energetic performance with Plant's voice back on form. With a break approaching the morale was high and this was reflected in some lengthy improvisation. During the pre-violin bow sequence in 'Dazed And Confused' Page threw in the intro chords of 'Train Kept A Rollin' which was picked up by Plant for a brief moment.

An excellent quality soundboard sourced recording of this show surfaced in 2004.

Bootleg CD Reference: *St. Louis Blues* (Empress Valley)

Following this gig the band took a two week break. Jones and Bonham returned to the UK. Page and Plant holidayed on the Caribbean island of Dominica.

Friday February 21 1975
Londdon, England
The Old Grey Whistle Test *BBC2*
TV APPEARANCE
Bob Harris presented two exclusive previews from the *Physical Graffiti* album, 'Houses Of The Holy' and 'Trampled Underfoot' cut to abstract films. The latter, compiled by Philip Jenkinson of Filmfinders, deployed old black and white footage of 1920's dancers and would be an often repeated item on the programme.

Saturday February 22 1975
London, England
Radio One Alan Freeman Rock Show
RADIO BROADCAST
During his Saturday afternoon show Alan Freeman broadcast an exclusive preview of five tracks from *Physical Graffiti* – 'Custard Pie', 'Down By The Seaside', 'Night Flight', 'The Wanton Song' and 'Sick Again'.

Thursday February 27 1975
Houston, Texas
Sam Houston Coliseum

Thursday February 27 1975
Houston, Texas
Sam Houston Coliseum

Friday February 28 1975
Baton Rouge, Louisiana, Louisiana State University Assembley Center
Set: Rock And Roll/Sick Again/Over The Hills And Far Away/In My Time Of Dying/The Song Remains The Same/The Rain Song/Kashmir/No Quarter/Trampled Underfoot/Moby Dick/ Dazed And Confused (inc. Woodstock)/ Stairway To Heaven/Whole Lotta Love – The Crunge – Black Dog.

The second leg of the US tour got off to a much better start than the first, but there were still problems with Plant's voice. Tonight, he deliberately sang in a lower register so as not to strain it. Page, Bonham and Jones were on good form.

Plant commented that *Physical Graffiti* had finally been released: "The egg has been laid … or is it the guy who got laid?" Plant waffled a lot tonight and there were a few unusual dedications. A heavy and dramatic version of 'Kashmir' was dedicated to "Mr Royston and Mr Harold who are travelling with us" and 'Trampled Underfoot' was dedicated to "Sam Martel – a wild cat". John Bonham was introduced as "The man with a bicycle clip caught in his sock … the greatest percussionist since Big Ben!"

'Dazed And Confused' clocked in at 33 minutes and just kept getting better and better. The 'San Francisco' section had now been dropped and instead Joni Mitchell's 'Woodstock' was performed. 'Whole Lotta Love' now included a Theremin/'Crunge' section prior to the link with 'Black Dog'.

Plant: "Baton Rouge – a really good audience … and Led Zeppelin, just a fun-lovin' bunch of boys. It's been more than our pleasure."

Bootleg CD References: *Freeze* (Tarantura), *Led Astray* (Silver Rarities), *Bon Soir, Baton Rouge!* (Capricorn Records), *Blaze* (Immigrant), *Hang On To Your Heads* (The Diagrams Of Led Zeppelin)

Monday March 3 1975
Fort Worth, Texas
Tarrant County Convention Center

Tuesday March 4 1975
Dallas, Texas, Memorial Auditorium – Dallas Convention Center
Set: Rock And Roll/Sick Again/Over The Hills And Far Away/In My Time Of Dying/The Song Remains The Same/The Rain Song/Kashmir/No Quarter/Trampled Underfoot/Moby Dick/Dazed And Confused (inc. Woodstock)/ Stairway To Heaven/Whole Lotta Love – The Crunge – Black Dog.

Plant: "Dallas. Are you receiving us … 'cos if you ain't, we're gonna make sure that you will and we've got two nights to do it."

The first night in Dallas was a rather lacklustre affair. The audience were unresponsive and the band's playing was merely average. After 'Over The Hills', Plant commented: "I'd like to bid you all good health … I'd like to bid myself good health!" He then added sarcastically: "Anyway, don't get too atmospheric, don't get too vibey too quick!"

'The Rain Song' was described as "an honest to goodness song of love and love can be one of the most fulfilling things in the world!" Plant was very talkative again tonight. After 'Kashmir' he added: "John Paul Jones played Mellotron, a very cheap form of orchestration … and he doesn't cost that much to rent either! John Paul, since he's had his hair cut, has taken to watching Liberace on the TV. He also plays at Blackpool on the summer season in England."

Plant kept trying to inject life in the audience: "Why don't you wake up, c'mon!" Later, he added: "I'm sorry if we seem to be very happy. It's terrible to look out into an audience where everyone is very flat faced. These days there isn't enough smiling going on!"

John Bonham was introduced as "The man with only two cavities … one of the finest musical sights you're likely to experience within the next 15 minutes!"

A complete soundboard tape from this show surfaced in 2003 under the title *Chasing The Dragon*. This superseded the 92-minute tape featured on various CD bootlegs such as 'Over The Hills And Far Away' and 'Dallas '75'.

A few minutes of silent 8mm colour cine footage of this show exists.

Bootleg CD References: *Chasing The Dragon* (Empress Valley), *Dallas 1975* (Last Stand Disk), *Over The Hills And Far Away* (Great Dane), *Live In Dallas Volume One/Two* (Rock), *Solid Guitar* (Tarantura)

Wednesday March 5 1975
Dallas, Texas, Memorial Auditorium – Dallas Convention Center
Set: Rock And Roll/Sick Again/Over The Hills And Far Away/In My Time Of Dying/The Song Remains The Same/The Rain Song/Kashmir/No Quarter/Trampled Underfoot/Moby Dick/

Dazed And Confused (inc. Woodstock)/ Stairway To Heaven/Whole Lotta Love – The Crunge – Black Dog.

A much improved performance. Plant kept plugging the new album … "which according to the business side of things seems to have sold more than 10 copies so far this week, and we're very grateful and happy about it."

'Trampled Underfoot' was hard and heavy tonight. At the end of the number Robert related some of the lyrics with pride: "Come to me for service every hundred miles … baby let me check your points, fix your overdrive!"

Bonham was introduced as "A man who can go for hours without stopping … but he's a lousy lay."

Plant commented: "We'd like to say what a great pleasure it is being back in Texas, even if me and Pagey have been flying back to New Orleans every night. But tonight … who knows? Whatever happened to the Butterqueen? She got margarine instead."

Bootleg CD References: *Chasing The Dragon* (Empress Valley), *Live in Dallas* (The Diagrams Of Led Zeppelin), *Dallas Second Night* (No label)

UNCONFIRMED
Friday March 7 1975
Austin, Texas
Events Center

No evidence of this show taking place has surfaced. The venue is also in doubt. It's more likely to have occurred at the Austin Municipal Auditorium if it happened at all.

Saturday March 8 1975
West Palm Beach, Florida
The Raceway
CANCELLED

David Rupp, owner of the West Palm Beach Speedway, cancelled the 'Florida Rock' festival in late February. His reason for cancellation was the failure of the promoters, Connecticut Concerts Corporation, to make essential improvements to the property.

Swan Song issued the following press statement: "Led Zeppelin Expresses Disappointment Over Cancellation Of 'Florida Rock' Festival. Danny Goldberg, vice-president of Swan Song commented: 'The group and their manager Peter Grant are very disappointed that they will be unable to play Florida on this tour due to a circumstance utterly beyond their control. I know that they have a very special feeling for Florida, due in part to the fact that the biggest concert they ever played was in Tampa in 1973.'"

The press release continues: "Following the cancellation, a variety of ideas for other dates for Zeppelin to play in Florida were reported in the Florida press. It was reported that the Mayor's office in Miami was attempting to make the Orange Bowl available for a proposed concert by Zeppelin which would benefit the Paediatric Center in Florida. On February 26, Steven Weiss, Zeppelin's attorney, sent the following telegram to the Mayor's office: 'Dear Mr Cobo, No definite proposal for Led Zeppelin to play Orange Bowl on March 8 or any other date has been received either from Paediatric Center or any other party and therefore there is not even anything for me to submit to President of Swan Song and group manager for his consideration. Efforts of Miami Mayor to make Orange Bowl available for Led Zeppelin concert are much appreciated and the charity is undoubtedly a worthy one. However, since nothing concrete has been submitted, it is now no longer feasible from time point of view to put together a proper and artistic concert for March 8 even if a firm offer was now received Further there is no other feasible open time period available on remainder of 1975 tour to play Orange Bowl so therefore any consideration of Led Zeppelin playing Orange Bowl this tour no longer feasible. Hope that the Orange Bowl will be made available for next tour. Florida is a very special place for the Led Zeppelin and they like playing Florida very much I believe they would be most interested in a charity concert at the Orange Bowl on their next tour.'"

Monday March 10 1975
San Diego, California
Sports Arena

Set: Rock And Roll/Sick Again/Over The Hills And Far Away/In My Time Of Dying/The Song Remains The Same/The Rain Song/Kashmir/No Quarter/Trampled Underfoot/Moby Dick/Dazed And Confused (inc. Woodstock)/Stairway To Heaven/Whole Lotta Love – The Crunge – Black Dog.

"It's been so long San Diego!" sang Plant during 'Rock And Roll'. Zeppelin were back on the West Coast and in party mood, but there were problems with the crowd and Plant was constantly urging them to move back to stop people being crushed at the front.

Plant changed the opening line of 'The Rain Song' to: "This should be the springtime of your loving … "

'Dazed And Confused' and 'Stairway To Heaven' were the highlights of a strong performance – despite the unruly audience.

Ten minutes of silent cine footage exists from this show.

Bootleg CD Reference: *Symphony In a Thousand Parts* (The Diagrams Of Led Zeppelin)
Visual Reference: *1975* (Unofficial DVD – Cosmic Energy)

Tuesday March 11 1975
Long Beach, California
Long Beach Arena

Set: Rock And Roll/Sick Again/Over The Hills And Far Away/In My Time Of Dying/The Song Remains The Same/The Rain Song/Kashmir/No Quarter/Trampled Underfoot/Moby Dick/Dazed And Confused (inc. Woodstock)/Stairway To Heaven/Whole Lotta Love – The Crunge – Black Dog.

Plant: "We must apologise for the slight delay, but we couldn't get into the building and we hadn't got any tickets! It's a fact. We saw a well known scalper, but we blew it … and it was blown!"

The concert got off to a slow start, but the group were in a buoyant mood and determined to have fun. Plant commented that, "We're feeling invigorated by the English weather you're having. Watch out. If you intend to sit still, forget it."

'The Song Remains The Same' was hampered by guitar tuning, and afterwards Plant added: "For the benefit of anyone who was making a bootleg then – the 12-string was out of tune!"

There were many equipment problems. The keyboards were continually buzzing and humming and the roadies created a terrible noise trying to fix them. Plant: "The drumming and hammering is courtesy of the Acme Quaalude Company Ltd. In the background there's a guy building a chicken pen … can you hear it?" "He's building a shit house!" joked Bonham.

'Dazed And Confused' was the highlight of the show, lasting 29 minutes. During 'Stairway To Heaven', Plant ad-libbed "I remember laughter!" and 'The Crunge' featured full lyrics.

Plant: "Ladies and gentlemen of Long Beach … sleep well! Half a Quaalude with water."

Silent cine footage exists from this show

Bootleg CD References: *Long Beach Arena Complete* (Confusion Records), *Pussy And Cock* (Tarantura), *Long Beach 75* (LSD)
Visual Reference: *1975* (Unofficial DVD- Cosmic Energy)

Wednesday March 12 1975
Long Beach, California
Long Beach Arena

Set: Rock And Roll/Sick Again/Over The Hills And Far Away/In My Time Of Dying/The Song Remains The Same/The Rain Song/Kashmir/No Quarter/Trampled Underfoot/Moby Dick/Dazed And Confused (inc. Woodstock)/Stairway To Heaven/Whole Lotta Love – The Crunge – Black Dog/Heartbreaker (inc. I'm A Man).

From this part of the tour onwards they really began to hit their stride.

Plant: "Sorry about the delay, but there's treacherous conditions on the roads. There's snow storms back in Hollywood! Was anybody here last night? You mean you could sleep after that!"

'In My Time Of Dying' was described as "An old work song. A long time before Mr Zimmerman listened to it in the Village back in the Sixties."

Plant referred to all the songs as 'pieces' tonight. "I used to call them numbers – but that's when you're in Vegas." Jimmy breaks a string at the start of 'The Song Remains The Same' and Plant calls a halt to the piece: "Hang on. Hold it a minute! They didn't tell me it was like this in Valhalla! Yes, it happened for the first time in six and a half years! Does anyone remember laughter?"

After 'The Rain Song', Plant commented: "I think Andy Williams is gonna do it next," and 'Kashmir' is inexplicably dedicated … "to anybody who got divorced today."

John Paul was introduced as 'Mr Liberace' and after 'No Quarter', Plant gasped: "That was thoroughly enjoyable – better than a good chick … almost!" 'Trampled Underfoot' was introduced bizarrely as 'Trampled Under Jimmy's Foot'! and 'Dazed And Confused' was dedicated to Roy Harper: 'Wherever you are Roy, don't stay in that state too long!"

Plant sang a few lines of The Rolling Stones' 'Have You Seen Your Mother Baby', then added: "The vibes are really good tonight, better than last night, too many reds! By the time we get to the Forum, we should be sky high."

'Whole Lotta Love' was dedicated to their attorney, Steve Weiss, whose birthday it was, and the final encore of 'Heartbreaker' included a rare impromptu performance of 'I'm A Man'.

"Thank you very much. A bicycle clip was caught in our sock!" was Plant's cryptic parting comment.

Bootleg CD References: *Standing In The Shadow* (Diagrams of Led Zeppelin), *Trampled Under Jimmy's Foot* (Silver Rarities)

Friday March 14 1975
San Diego, California
Sports Arena
Set: Rock And Roll/Sick Again/Over The Hills And Far Away/In My Time Of Dying/The Song

Remains The Same/The Rain Song/Kashmir/No Quarter/Trampled Underfoot/Moby Dick/ Dazed And Confused (inc. Woodstock)/Stairway To Heaven/Whole Lotta Love – The Crunge – Black Dog/Heartbreaker.

This date was added to the itinerary after the Monday San Diego date sold out very quickly.

An excellent quality soundboard sourced recording of this show surfaced in 2004

Bootleg CD Reference: *Conspiracy Theory* (Empress Valley)

Monday March 17 1975
Seattle, Washington
Seattle Center Coliseum
Set: Rock And Roll/Sick Again/Over The Hills And Far Away/In My Time Of Dying/The Song Remains The Same/The Rain Song/Kashmir/No Quarter/Trampled Underfoot/Moby Dick/ Dazed And Confused (inc. Woodstock)/Stairway To Heaven/Whole Lotta Love – The Crunge – Black Dog.

This was a superb performance with the band totally on top of their game.

Hugh Jones, editor of *Proximity*, recalled: "The start of the show was extremely aggressive, and it was evident almost immediately that they were 'on'. Nothing sluggish about this performance. Robert's voice sounded surprisingly low, but he was singing well, and the whole band sounded very tight.

"The sound was terrific. It was incredibly loud yet at the same time sparklingly clear. Every nuance of the playing could be clearly heard, with this incredible power over-riding the whole thing.

"After 'Sick Again', Robert greeted us with the traditional 'Good Evening!' He only shouted it once, apparently satisfied with the response, and then claimed that 'For once in our career we started early, because we didn't want to keep you waiting'. This drew a cheer, but then he really set the tone for the evening by saying: 'As you can imagine, it's more than a pleasure to be back in this coastal town … a town of great fishermen, including our drummer.

"The line was delivered with casual sincerity, none of the hysterical rock star bit. It sounded as if he really meant it – which of course he did. The reference to Bonzo fishing (at the Edgewater Hotel) was an 'in' joke that everybody got, and a perfect example of how Robert interacted with the audience and why the band was so renowned for their crowd rapport."

Some 12 minutes of silent colour cine film of this show exists.

Bootleg CD References: *Seattle Won't You Listen* (The Diagrams Of Led Zeppelin), *The Hammer Of The Gods* (Tarantura), *Gallery Of Soldiers* (Power Chord), *Seattle '75* (Empress Valley)

Wednesday March 19 1975
Vancouver, Canada
Pacific Coliseum
Set: Rock And Roll/Sick Again/Over The Hills And Far Away/In My Time Of Dying/The Song Remains The Same/The Rain Song/Kashmir/No Quarter/Trampled Underfoot/Moby Dick/Dazed And Confused (inc. Woodstock)/Stairway To Heaven/Whole Lotta Love – The Crunge – Black Dog.

"Ladies and gentlemen … the Canadian return of Led Zeppelin" boomed from the speakers as the band took to the stage, firing on all cylinders. 'And how is Vancouver. Is it full of beans?" asks Plant. 'In My Time Of Dying' was excellent and Plant extended the ending with vocal gymnastics.

'Kashmir' was dedicated to … "Richard Cole, our tour manager – a good upright British citizen. This a song from Physical Vancouver – the new LP."

An extended 'No Quarter' was once again a highlight. Bonham was introduced as "the king of jazz – one of the finest percussionists in Led Zeppelin today". After 'Moby Dick', Plant commented: "The blow job by the way was fantastic!"

'Dazed And Confused' was then dedicated to … "our manager, Peter Grant, who's made so many things possible. He's the man who gives us the blow job in the dressing room."

'Dazed And Confused' was the best version of the tour so far and ran to 38 minutes. Page inserted an intricate classical interlude prior to the 'Woodstock' section.

Bootleg CD References: *Prisoners Of Rock 'n' Roll* (The Diagrams Of Led Zeppelin), *Physical Vancouver Farewell* (Tarantura), *Ladies And Gentlemen* (Sanctuary)

Thursday March 20 1975
Vancouver, Canada
Pacific Coliseum
Set: Rock And Roll/Sick Again/Over The Hills And Far Away/In My Time Of Dying/The Song Remains The Same/The Rain Song/ Kashmir/ No Quarter/ Trampled Underfoot/ Moby Dick/Dazed And Confused (inc. Woodstock)/Stairway To Heaven/Whole Lotta Love – Heartbreaker.

Another outstanding performance. The pace was set by an aggressive stomp through 'Rock And Roll' and never let up.

Plant shared his thoughts on the disastrous 1973 Vancouver show which had ended rather suddenly with Plant reportedly being taken to hospital: "Last time it was quite a peculiar show actually. Something strange happened to me that evening. I found the light show to be amazing and I wondered what the name of the group was! So I should dedicate this ('Kashmir') to that state of mind. Long may it come at my moments of ease."

'No Quarter' was now reaching epic proportions, tonight extended to 26 minutes. Bonham was strangely introduced as "a man who's a stinking rotten dirty pig!" 'Whole Lotta Love' was highly improvised tonight and included brief snatches of James Brown's 'Lickin' Stick', as well as a Plant war cry from 'Immigrant Song' and the riff from 'Ozone Baby'. After a fierce Theremin battle with Plant, Page then led straight into 'Heartbreaker'. 'Black Dog' was not performed tonight.

Bootleg CD References: *Pleeese* (Silver Rarties), *Prisoners Of Rock 'n' Roll* (The Diagrams Of Led Zeppelin), *Ladies And Gentlemen* (Sanctuary), *Physical Vancouver Farewell* (Tarantura)

Friday March 21 1975
Seattle, Washington
Seattle Center
Coliseum

Set: Rock and Roll/Sick Again/Over The Hills And Far Away/In My Time Of Dying/The Song Remains The Same/The Rain Song/Kashmir/No Quarter/Since I've Been Loving You/Trampled Underfoot/Moby Dick/Dazed And Confused (inc. For What It's Worth – Woodstock)/Stairway To Heaven/Whole Lotta Love – The Crunge- Black Dog/Communication Breakdown – Heartbreaker.

Then it was back to Seattle for another stellar show with much improvisation. 'No Quarter' was a highlight with Jones and Bonham randomly incorporating a jazzy rhythm during the solo improvisation. 'Trampled Underfoot' now included some lyrics from 'Gallows Pole'. 'Dazed And Confused' included snatches of Buffalo Springfield's 'For What It's Worth' as well as 'Woodstock', and the longest encore section of the tour was performed tonight.

Hugh Jones of *Proximity* recalled: "Following 'No Quarter', Robert called for a change in the programme, causing a little confusion on stage. 'There's one song that we've done twice in, in ... I suppose since we got ripped off for all that bread in New York, ages ago. And because we really dig playing here, and for no other reason, we're gonna do it again now. I don't think anybody else in the band knows about it yet, it's a little bit of change in the ... sorry about that, John! You see, right on the spot! It could be 'Louie Louie' but instead it's a thing from the third album ... 'Since I've Been Loving You'.

"Following a brutal 'Trampled Underfoot' and Bonzo's marathon 'Moby Dick', more confusion appears to be occurring onstage. Robert shouts for an ovation for Bonzo, then asks in a casual tone, 'Is everybody, uh, enjoying themselves?' Jimmy is talking urgently with a group of people just off stage, and at one point seems to lift his guitar in the air as if to throw it down, obviously perturbed about something. Unfazed and still in his conversational tone, Robert observes 'Mr Page is having a fit'. Apparently, we found out later, a local fan made Jimmy a gift of a beautiful Les Paul guitar, which turned out to be stolen from a high school music teacher. During the evening the instrument was confiscated at Sea-Tac airport as it was being shipped back to the UK (or so the story goes), and for some reason Page was interrupted during the show to be informed of this."

Three minutes of silent colour cine footage exists from this show

Bootleg CD References: *214 & 207.19* (Cobla Standard), *No Quarter* (H-Bomb Music), *Hammer Of The Gods* (Last Stand Disc), *Seattle '75* (Empress Valley)

Visual Reference: *1975* (Unofficial DVD – Cosmic Energy)

Monday March 24 1975
Inglewood Los Angeles, California
The Forum

Set: Rock And Roll/Sick Again/Over The Hills And Far Away/In My Time Of Dying/The Song Remains The Same/The Rain Song/Kashmir/No Quarter/Trampled Underfoot/Moby Dick/ Dazed And Confused (inc. Woodstock)/Stairway To Heaven/Whole Lotta Love – The Crunge - Black Dog/Heartbreaker.

"Good Evening! My name is J. J. Jackson o KWLOS. We're all here to welcome back to the LA area ... Led Zeppelin!" A mass of firecrackers her alded the band's arrival on stage.

The Forum had long been one of Zeppelin's favourite venues and once again they revelled in the surroundings. Plant: "This is the place, this is the one. These are the last three gigs on our American tour and so we intend them to be something of a high point for us. Obviously, we don't achieve that without a little bit of a vibe, that I can already feel, and a few smiles."

After 'Over The Hills', Robert remarked: "A gram is a gram is a gram!" Ambiguous and humorous remarks were rife tonight. Plant continued: "Since we saw you last time there have been a few developments in the camp and a few camps in the development – Bonzo decided not to have the sex change after all!" 'The Song Remains The Same' is about "places where the red light still shines for two rupees, places where there's a magical feeling in the air … rather like Paul Rodgers' bedroom when he takes his shoes off."

Plant described the Mellotron as "A rather cheap, nasty, improvised version of an orchestra, but unfortunately with the tax and overheads, we can't afford to take an orchestra with us anymore."

Plant introduced Billy Miller – "Elvis Presley's right hand man" – and sang a few lines from 'Love Me'. After 'Moby Dick', Plant commented: "What a wonderful drum solo and a wonderful head job in the dressing room … thank you Ahmet Ertegun!"

'Dazed And Confused' was described as "The first thing we had a go at, apart from the secretary" but was rather uninspired in places tonight. 'Stairway To Heaven' was dedicated to "All our English friends that have arrived at the Continental Riot House. This is for the foundations of the Continental Riot House and for you people who have made this a good gig." The whole band performed impeccably on 'Stairway', turning in one of the most impressive single performances of the tour.

Plant: "Children of the sun. Good night!"

As far as the press were concerned, the new additions to the set were now beginning to steal the show. *Disc* reported: "All the newer material

was well received, although it seems that 'Kashmir' is set to become the star track and another classic. It was also while the group performed this number that I think the lights and effects were used to their best advantage."

During the LA stint John Paul Jones and Richard Cole visited Elvis Presley at his rented Bel Air mansion. The King was playing a residency at the Las Vegas Hilton and evidently requested Jones' company "because he's so quiet". During the visit Elvis swapped watches with the pair, taking Jones' Mickey Mouse watch and replacing it with a double dial Lapis Baume and Mercier model.

Colour cine footage from this show exists from two sources.

Bootleg CD References: *Fire Crackers' Show* (The Diagrams Of Led Zeppelin), *Trampled Under Gallows* (Zero)

Visual Reference: *1975* (Unoffical DVD Cosmic Energy), *Deep Throat* (Unofficial DVD Empress Valley)

Thursday March 25 1975
Inglewood Los Angeles, California
The Forum

Set: Rock And Roll/Sick Again/Over The Hills And Far Away/In My Time Of Dying/The Song Remains The Same/The Rain Song/Kashmir/No Quarter/Trampled Underfoot/Moby Dick/Dazed And Confused (inc. Spanish Harlem – Woodstock)/Stairway To Heaven/Whole Lotta Love – Lickin' Stick – The Crunge – Black Dog.

Yet another excellent performance – even better than the previous night.

Plant: "Last night we had a really good time. We had a great concert. It was one of the finest we've had in California for a long time!"

'Kashmir' was outstanding and Plant described it as being about "the wasted, wasted lands … and it's not the lobby of the Continental Hyatt either!" 'No Quarter' was extended to truly epic proportions, lasting nearly 27 minutes with Jones and Bonham again favouring the jazz improvisation they adopted in Seattle four days ago.

'Trampled Underfoot' was dedicated to … "All the good ladies of America who've helped us get rid of the blues from time to time on the road … that boils down to about two!" Page's solo was masterful and commanding. Plant ad-libbed "drive on – feels pretty good" and again extended the number with lyrics from 'Gallows Pole', even throwing in a few cries of 'Hangman'.

Bonham was introduced tonight as … "The man who broke every window in room 1019 … the man who smashed wardrobes … the man who set fire to his own bed … the amazing man with only two cavities … Mr. Quaalude!"

'Dazed And Confused' was another stand out extended to 39 minutes. Page inserted a gentle Spanish sounding passage which led into Ben E King's 'Spanish Harlem' before running into 'Woodstock'. 'Stairway To Heaven' shone once more. Page's playing was sharp and decisive as the tension builds with each note. John Paul Jones was superlative.

'Whole Lotta Love' once again included a snatch of James Brown's 'Lickin' Stick' and Plant ad-libbed "Like a sex machine!" Page even included a few riffs from the never performed 'Night Flight' prior to the Theremin section.

Plant: "People of the Forum. We've had a good time … It is the summer of our smiles … "

Colour and black and white cine film from this show exists.

Bootleg CD References: *A Gram Is A Gram Is A Gram* (Image Quality), *Cosmic Crazy* (Arms), *The Revenge Of The Butterqueen* (Ghost), *The Sex Machine* (Lemon Song)

Visual Reference: *1975* (Unofficial DVD – Cosmic Energy), *Deep Throat* (Unofficial DVD Empress Valley)

Thursday March 27 1975
Inglewood Los Angeles, California
The Forum

Set: Rock And Roll/Sick Again/Over The Hills And Far Away/In My Time Of Dying/The Song Remains The Same/The Rain Song/Kashmir/Since I've Been Loving You/No Quarter/Trampled Underfoot/Moby Dick/Dazed And Confused (inc. Loving You) /Stairway To Heaven/Whole Lotta Love – The Crunge – Black Dog.

Deep Throat porn star, Linda Lovelace introduced the band for the final show of the US tour. Plant returned the compliment: "I'd like to thank Linda Lovelace for coming on and making an appropriate speech about our presence, and we'd like to apologise for being late, but one of the cars didn't crash!"

Bonham and Page were outstanding during 'Over The Hills And Far Away', and although the band seemed a little tired in places, overall the concert was a triumph. Plant commented that he was glad the final show was in LA, because last time the tour ended in New York which was … "not the most pleasant place to be. There's some nice ladies on 83rd Street. But the rest of it … no!"

During 'In My Time Of Dying', Plant ad-libbed "please Lord, don't leave me dazed and confused!" and then added some of 'You Shook Me' before the number fell apart. He speculated that they may end up in the Fall doing a gig in the Sahara desert, due to their love of the East, and 'Kashmir' was once again spectacular.

'Since I've Been Loving You' was a late addition to the set and warmly appreciate by the crowd 'Trampled Underfoot' was now referred to as 'Trampled Under Gallows' due to Plant's persistent injection of lyrics from 'Gallows Pole'. 'Dazed And Confused' was one of the longest versions of the tour tonight, with a very spacey middle section as Plant repeatedly ad-libbed 'Loving You'.

This show clocked in at nearly three and a half hours and completed a run of some of the finest in the history of the band.

'Led Zeppelin At Its Peak In L.A. Forum reported *Billboard*. Bob Kirsch wrote: "'Zeppelin has two major strong points. It has mastered the technique of combining musical excellence with mind-boggling volume. And it is able to operate either as a unit or each can move into a subordinate role for whoever happens to be soloing at the time.

"Zeppelin has long been the target of critical barbs for crashing volume and the seeming sameness of its material. Yet in an age when headline acts are often boring, sloppy and create no excitement at all, this British quartet stands out as a masterful example of what rock and roll was meant to be."

Colour silent cine footage from this show exists

Bootleg CD References: *Tour De Force L.A.* 1975 (Rabbit Records), *Remainz* (Akashic Records), *Psychical Graffiti* (Flying Disc), *The Final Show In The Forum 1975* (Jelly Roll), *Electric Orgasm* (Jolly Roger Records); all three nights can be found on the CD box sets *Get Back To La* (Tarantura) and *Deep Throat* (Empress Valley)

Visual Reference: *1975* (Unofficial DVD – Cosmic Energy), *Deep Throat* (Unofficial DVD Empress Valley)

EARL'S COURT 1975

"What we want to do is find somewhere where we can make it into a bit of an event. And if we can find the right venue, possibly in early summer, then we'll go to town on it in true style."

Robert Plant's early 1975 hint of what the UK could expect when it came to Led Zeppelin's long awaited return home wasn't too far off the mark. Rather than attempt a trek around the UK – a logistic nightmare with the current size of the PA and stage set up – Grant decided on one central location where fans could travel in to view their show all in the best possible setting. That setting was the Earl's Court Arena in London.

Initially booked for three nights on May 23, 24 and 25, due to what promoter Mel Bush described at the time as 'Demand unprecedented in the history of rock music', two further dates were added for May 17 & 18, making the total audience 85,000. Bush negotiated with British Rail to advertise the ease with which Inter City trains could bring fans in. 'The Zeppelin Express Physical Rocket' was how it was dubbed. A memorable advertising campaign with a poster designed by Peter Grainey depicting the Stephenson Rocket captured the whole magnitude of the event in store.

At vast expense, the whole of their so-called American show was airlifted over. They spent three days at Earl's Court in early May, testing the various lighting effects. A huge Ediphor screen which showed the action as it was being filmed was erected above the stage, one of the first occasions when such a device was used for a rock show in England. The whole affair was a huge success. The three hour plus performances, with the inclusion of the acoustic set and marathon versions of 'No Quarter' and 'Dazed And Confused', were some of the longest ever performed by the group.

"Statistics are always misleading," wrote Tony

259

Palmer in the May 18 edition of *The Observer*. "With Zeppelin statistics are irrelevant – except they are truly astonishing. No pop group in history, no entertainer, no opera singer has ever attracted such an audience."

Earl's Court was a testament to just how far Peter Grant had taken their career – from the Marquee Club to what was then the biggest Exhibition Centre in the UK. As Plant observed: "It got to the point in 1975 where [Grant] said 'Look, there's nothing else I can do for you guys. We've had performing pigs and high wire acts. There's no more I can do, because now you really can go to Saturn'."

Earl's Court can be viewed in hindsight as the last of Led Zeppelin's glory days before they were beset by tragedy. It was one of the most important series of shows they ever performed and, unsurprisingly, is still held in the highest esteem by collectors and enthusiasts the world over.

Immediately following theses dates, Page and Plant split for a holiday that would take them across Africa and on to Agadir and Marrakech. Page also spent some time in New York, working on mixing the soundtrack to their planned *The Song Remains The Same* movie. He also hung out with Bad Company who were on tour.

They were all due to meet up in Paris in early August to commence rehearsals for a second trip to the States that would take in a series of outdoor stadium dates. Events would dictate otherwise, however, but in the meantime there was the spectacle of Earls Court to savour.

Equipment Notes:

Page deployed the Gibson double-neck for the rare Earl's Court version of 'Tangerine', and for the reintroduction of the acoustic set, he used a Martin D28. He also introduces a Lake Placid blue Fender Stratocaster during the first weekend of Earl's Court shows for 'Over The Hills And Far Away' and 'No Quarter' – the first time this guitar had been used on stage. Jones used a Harmony mandolin for 'Going To California' plus an upright Framus bass for 'Bron Yr Aur Stomp'.

April 1975
New York, New York
Midnight Special
TV APPEARANCE
During a promotional visit to work on Swan Song business with Jimmy, Robert appeared on the popular TV show interviewed by DJ Wolfman. Swan Song exec Danny Goldberg and The Pretty Things Phil May were in attendance at the filming but did not appear.

Saturday April 5 1975
News Story: "Show a little respect, Zep!"

Led Zeppelin are criticised in the letters page of *Melody Maker* for not playing any dates outside London and also for the poor organisation of queues when the tickets were put on sale at Earl' Court.

One reader wrote: "Living as I do, reasonably near London, I perhaps have the least right to complain, but it is an absolutely absurd situation whereby fans of the group have to travel from as far away as Scotland to see them – at least a couple of concerts in Glasgow would have shown some concern on the part of Zeppelin's management. Surely little more respect for your British fans would be in order Messrs Plant, Page, Jones and Bonham?"
UNCONFIRMED

UNCONFIRMED
GUEST APPEARANCE
Philadelphia, Pensylvania
The Main Point
While on Swan Song business in the early spring – possibly in late April – Jimmy jammed on stage with the Pretty Things

Late April/Early May
Shepperton Studios
Shepperton, England
Earl's Court, London
Earl's Court Arena
REHEARSALS
The band had their vast PA flown over and set up in Shepperton in preparation for the UK dates. Various lighting tests were made to ensure the laser lights worked effectively. The band rehearsed an extended new set to include acoustic numbers.

Saturday May 17 1975
Earl's Court, London
Earl's Court Arena
Set: Rock And Roll/Sick Again/Over The Hills And Far Away/In My Time Of Dying/The Song Remains The Same/The Rain Song/Kashmir/No Quarter/Tangerine/Going To California/That's The Way/Bron Yr Aur Stomp/Trampled Underfoot/Moby Dick/Dazed And Confused (inc. Woodstock)/Stairway To Heaven/Whole Lotta Love, The Crunge – Black Dog.

"We'd all like to welcome back to Britain … Led Zeppelin!!" was compère and Radio 1 DJ, Bob

Harris' simple introduction. Each Earl's Court show was introduced by a popular DJ.

As on the US tour, 'Rock And Roll' opened the proceedings and Plant ad-libbed "It's been so long England … what can I say?" However, all was not well. Jimmy's guitar kept cutting in and out and it was obvious there were problems with the PA. Plant commented: "You wouldn't believe that after all the trouble and messing about to try to get this unearthly monster with us … the first number gets blown by a sixpenny jack plug. Anyway, it's a pleasure to be playing to so many people in England. We couldn't make Nottingham Boat Club this time, but nice to get here!"

'In My Time Of Dying' was dedicated to Dennis Healey, the Chancellor Of The Exchequer, who was taxing large earners heavily at the time. "We're about a foot away from the chain gang with our dear Dennis!" Plant also referred to stories in a certain music paper back in February 1973 and assured the crowd that rumours of the band breaking up were untrue.

The set lists for the Earl's Court shows were similar to the previous US tour with the unexpected addition of an acoustic set. Zeppelin seemed slightly nervous tonight and the arrival of the acoustic set was described by Plant as "One small step for your ears but a giant step for our confidence." 'Tangerine' featured four part vocal harmony on stage for the first time and was well received. The remainder of the acoustic set was plagued with tuning problems and seems under-rehearsed and slightly rusty. For 'Bron Yr Aur Stomp', Plant even had to read the lyrics from a piece of paper.

'Moby Dick' clocked in at 19 minutes and the vivid laser effects lit up 'Dazed And Confused', a more compact 26 minute delivery. John Paul Jones played a brief sample of 'The Teddy Bears' Picnic' prior to an epic version of 'Stairway To Heaven' which formed the climax of the show. Plant was now regularly adding the line "That's all we got!" to the final verse prior to Page's solo. 'Whole Lotta Love' was shorter than the US version and contained only a few riffs from 'The Crunge' prior to Jimmy's Theremin battle.

Plant ended the first homecoming concert by saying thank you and goodnight in Welsh.

'Led Zeppelin blitz London!' was the title of a four page special in *Melody Maker*. Chris Welch reviewed the opening night's show under the headline 'Avenging Angels': "Laser beams, green pencils of light, cut through the smoke surrounding Jimmy Page, as the master guitarist of rock flailed a violin bow against the strings, filling the cavern of Earl's Court with an eerie howl of gothic horror. It was one of the most vivid moments etched on the memory of a remarkable *tour de force*, when Led Zeppelin came among us like avenging angels at the weekend. Their marathon performances were unique demonstrations of the state of the rock concert art. And the band showed how they have come of age, grown in scope and stature. They played and played on Saturday night, piling up pressure, easing away and blasting back. The balance between anticipation, surprise and satisfaction kept the show a three hour cauldron of events."

Bootleg CD References: *Join The Blimp* (Tarantura), *Arabesque & Baroque* (Antrabata), *Complete Earls Court Arena '75* (Immigrant), *Devil's Banquet* (Power Chord)

Sunday May 18 1975
Earl's Court, London
Earl's Court Arena

Set: Rock And Roll/Sick Again/Over The Hills And Far Away/In My Time Of Dying/The Song Remains The Same/The Rain Song/Kashmir/No Quarter/Tangerine/Going To California/That's The Way/Bron Yr Aur Stomp/Trampled Underfoot/Moby Dick/Dazed And Confused (inc. Woodstock)/Stairway To Heaven/Whole Lotta Love – The Crunge – Black Dog.

For the second night at Earls Court Zeppelin were introduced by Raio 1 DJ Johnnie Walker. On one of the audience tapes of the show you can hear Walker state: "You've waited a long time … " followed by a member of the audience shouting ''Too fucking right!''

The band seemed more confident and relaxed for the second outing which resulted in a far better performance. Plant: "We're more than overjoyed to be allowed back into the country. The equipment you're now seeing amassed above our heads in rather precarious positions took about three weeks to get through Customs. They had a dossier that thick on Led Zeppelin … nothing to do with personal effects or prison sentences! So not only are we pleased to be here to play but to have all the equipment we anticipated to give you our best."

Robert also plugged the new album … "on the magnificent Swan Song label … great design … picture of Jimmy there on the label after his operation in Cairo!" 'Kashmir' was about the "wasted, wasted, wasted land!" and featured John Paul Jones who Robert described as "the only man who wears onions on his shoulders that I've ever met in my life!"

'No Quarter' was introduced as "another song about a journey – a journey that has no end, rather perilous one where they give … No Quarter". Tonight's version was beautifully constructed and would later feature on the rare vinyl bootleg bearing the same name on the Red Devil label.

Robert was very talkative and explained a new development: "We decided that there were things way way back that we really dug playing and never really got it on onstage. And so we decided

262

to develop, for at least one number in our career, four part harmony. Can you believe that? We can do 'Bus Stop' by The Hollies next time!"

'Tangerine' got better each night as did the acoustic set. Robert commented that they wrote a lot of songs west of Offa's Dyke explaining "Offa's Dyke is not a chick in New York". However, Robert encountered a problem with 'Bron Yr Aur Stomp': "I'm in a bit of a pickle. If you really wanna know the problem … No, I'm too embarrassed to tell you … I believe the press is here tonight so I can't tell you… I'm gonna sack whichever road manager has burnt the lyrics to the next song. It was a long time ago that we wrote it."

'Trampled Underfoot' was powerful and included some lyrics from 'Gallows Pole'. John Bonham was introduced as "one of the finest rhythm men this side of Basutoland. In fact, there's rumours that he did come from Basutoland. A man with no taste … no manners … no friends … my best friend, the man who always kicks me when I'm down … John Bonham!"

'Dazed And Confused' was an improvement on the previous night with Bonham and Jones in forceful syncopation. Page chopped recklessly at the chords. 'Stairway To Heaven' was again outstanding and 'The Crunge' section of 'Whole Lotta Love' was further extended and now included lyrics.

'This gig is scarred on my brain for life' was the headline in *Sounds*. Pete Makowski wrote: "In six and a half years Led Zeppelin are THE biggest and, judging by the excellence of their performance at Earl's Court last Sunday, one of, if not the most exciting live act in the world. I guess I came on the right night. It was one of those gigs that will remain scarred on my brain for life. It is difficult to describe the magic or the atmosphere of that Sunday."

'They can rock you, they can roll you, 'til your back ain't got no bone … but can they kiss you goodnight' was the headline of a review in *New Musical Express* which cast some doubts on Zeppelin's performance. However, Charles Shaar Murray's review was mostly complimentary: "By Zeppelin's own standards, it was a mediocre gig, though apart from The Who and the Stones – I can't think of many bands who could've put on anything like it, produced moments like 'Trampled Underfoot' during which it seemed that the entire stage was just gonna roll forward and crush everybody in the hall. Maybe the key to Led Zeppelin is this: they're like a vibrator. It can get you off something ridiculous, but it can't kiss you goodnight."

Even the *Financial Times* got in on the act – Antony Thorncroft reporting: "When I first saw Led Zeppelin over five years ago they were a very good, very exciting, rock band: now they must

rate a paragraph in any social history of the twentieth century. They are no longer judged in musical terms but as an entertainment industry phenomenon."

Bootleg CD References: *Red Devil* (The Diagroams Of Led Zeppelin), *Argenteum Astrum* (Tarantura), *No Quarter* (Empress Valley), *Complete Earl's Court Arena '75* (Immigrant), *Arabesque & Baroque The 2nd Night* (Antrabata)

Friday May 23 1975
Earl's Court, London
Earl's Court Arena
Set: Rock And Roll/Sick Again/Over The Hills And Far Away/In My Time Of Dying/The Song Remains The Same/The Rain Song/Kashmir/No Quarter/Tangerine/Going To California/That's The Way/Bron Yr Aur Stomp/Trampled Underfoot/Moby Dick/Dazed And Confused (inc. San Francisco)/Stairway To Heaven/Whole Lotta Love – The Crunge – Black Dog.

Before this show the band held a photo call backstage – they were photographed in front of their dressing room caravan within the Earls Court Arena

"Good Evening! Welcome to the show. After an absence of something like two years, I guess we're all ready for a little *Physical Graffiti*. Please welcome to Earl's Court ... Led Zeppelin!" David 'Kid' Jensen was tonight's guest DJ.

Plant: "Last weekend we did a couple of warm-up gigs for these three. We believe these were the first three gigs to be sold out, so these must be the ones with the most energy stored up. You've been waiting!"

Zeppelin's performance continued to improve and the audience reacted accordingly. Tonight, Robert explained that his left arm was swollen because he's just had inoculations for cholera and smallpox in preparation for a trip when they go "hunting in the jungle for new words and new songs for a new album". 'Kashmir' was written on one such trip and is growing in stature with each show. Tonight's rendition was very heavy and Bonham-dominated.

During the acoustic set Robert introduced Mick Hinton who he claimed "was arrested for swearing at passers-by in a tube station six months ago. He was then arrested three months later for driving up a traffic island. Really gets about Mick does – costs Bonzo a fortune! He's now limping 'cos Bonzo's just given him a dead leg!"

The acoustic set helped create an intimate and relaxed atmosphere, much needed in the cavernous recesses of the arena. A rapport was built between band and audience. Robert stated that Roy Harper came to see them every night and added: "Roy – please buy some tickets next time."

After 'That's The Way', Robert noticed a hazard on stage: "The lemon tea is now mingling very nicely with the electrical points down by John Paul's keyboards. It's looking very good down there John, actually. I can see it just about to blow you right out of this world ... I thought I'd tell you, 'cos you always have been a good bloke, even when you played with Jet Harris and Tony Meehan."

'Dazed And Confused' began with wild screams from Plant and tonight surprisingly

264

included 'San Francisco' instead of 'Woodstock'.

Plant reacted to Charles Shaar Murray's review of the previous week's concert by dedicating 'Stairway To Heaven' to him and adding, "I believe there's a psychiatrist on the way, Charles. Just hang on." 'Stairway' was again powerful, tense and emotional, a worthy set closer.

Plant: "And did those feet in ancient times … Thank you very much England, Wales, Scotland and Northern Ireland … and may the best team win!"

Bootleg CD References: *Arabesque & Baroque, The Third Night* (4CD, Antrabata), *Physical Express* (Jelly Roll), *Welcome To The Show* (Diagrams Of Led Zeppelin), *Thunderstorm* (Tarantura), *The Awesome Foursome* (CG)

Saturday May 24 1975

Earl's Court, London
Earl's Court Arena
Set: Rock And Roll/ Sick Again/ Over The Hills And Far Away/ In My Time Of Dying/The Song Remains The Same/The Rain Song/Kashmir/No Quarter/Tangerine/Going To California/That's The Way/Bron Yr Aur Stomp/Trampled Underfoot/Moby Dick/Dazed And Confused (inc. Woodstock)/Stairway To Heaven/Whole Lotta Love – The Crunge – Black Dog.

Nicky Horne: "Welcome to Earl's Court. For the next three hours … your mother wouldn't like it!"

One of the most famous, acclaimed performances of their entire career.

'Kashmir' was now building into a stand out moment. Plant joked: "If you go along the A449, past Droitwich, take the third turn off on the right, Kashmir is just up there – it's got a white fence around it."

'No Quarter' was again a stand out performance – one of the very best deliveries of the John Paul Jones opus with Page emerging from the dry ice to deliver a superbly understated solo.

'Tangerine' was dedicated to "families and friends, and people who have been close to us through the lot. It's a song of love in its most innocent stages". Afterwards, Plant informed the crowd about the rare use of four part harmony, but added: "Mind you, we have been doing a summer season here at Earl's Court, so we're getting quite used to it now."

After 'That's The Way', Plant sang a few lines from Neil Young's 'Old Man' and jested: "This is all a preview for the talking shows we're gonna do in the fall … when we've really made it."

'Trampled Underfoot' was absolutely breathtaking and after the finale, Robert, unaccompanied, led into Little Richard's 'Rip It Up'. He pauses to ask: "I'm not upstaging anybody, am I?"

Prior to 'Moby Dick', Robert complimented Bonzo's son, Jason: "He's a better drummer than 80% of rock group drummers today … and he's only eight years old"

'Dazed And Confused' was dedicated to Dennis Healey: "We gotta fly soon. Y'know how it goes with Dennis … dear Dennis. Private enterprise … no artists in the country anymore … he must be dazed and confused!" Tonight, 'Dazed' was an absolute treat – thirty four minutes of musical genius. 'Woodstock' was back for this performance and the heavy use of echo on the "We are stardust" refrain created an eerie spacey interlude. The number climaxed with a final flurry of vocal onslaught from Robert.

Jimmy performed one of his best ever solos in 'Stairway To Heaven', building slowly before taking off on a seemingly never-ending spiral of virtuosity. In response, Plant pushed himself so much that he was left hoarse for later.

When they returned for the encores, Bonzo felt compelled to share his opinions on sport: "I'd like to say at this point that I think football's a load of bollocks!" Plant retorted: "I'd like to say that soccer's a wonderful sport, the best sport" 'Whole Lotta Love' tonight included James Brown 'Sex Machine' ad-libs and 'Let Your Love Light Shine On Me'.

Steve Lake's negative review in *Melody Maker*

prompted an angry response in the paper's Mailbag letters page. "I think it's about time Steve Lake stayed at home and reviewed records, not concerts," wrote Jack Haynes. "How can anyone who went to one of the Led Zeppelin gigs at Earl's Court try and put the experience into words. I am still excited by the mere thought of the concert and have to say that future concerts by any group will be a let down. For £2.50 I would say three and a half hours of Zeppelin is better than five hours of The Grateful Dead or The Allman Brothers any day. We Zeppelin fans are not greedy."

Bootleg CD References: *To Be A Rock And Not To Roll* (Watch Tower), *Graf Zeppelin* (Tarantura), *Odysseus Earl's Court 75 4CD* (Celebration Records), *Arabesque & Baroque The Fourth Night* (Antrabata), *Bron-Y-Aur Stomp* (BGS/Great Dane Records), *Your Mother Wouldn't Like It!* (TDOLZ)

Visual References: *Latter Days The Best Of Led Zeppelin Vol 2* (Atlantic), Official *Led Zeppelin* 2003 DVD (Warner Music Vision), *Earls Court Defintive DVD* (Unofficial – Celebration), *Earls Court* (Unofficial DVD – Cosmic Energy)

Sunday May 25 1975
Earl's Court, London
Earl's Court Arena
Set: Rock And Roll/ Sick Again/Over The Hills And Far Away/ In My Time Of Dying/The Song Remains The Same/ The Rain Song/Kashmir/No Quarter/ Tangerine/Going To California/That's The Way/Bron Yr Aur Stomp/Trampled Underfoot/ Moby Dick/Dazed And Confused (inc. San Francisco)/Stairway To Heaven/Whole Lotta Love – The Crunge – Black Dog/Heartbreaker/ Communication Breakdown (inc. D'yer Maker).

Alan 'Fluff' Freeman: "What I wanna know is … are you ready? Let's hear some hands! I wanna tell you something, we are here tonight because you and I have great taste!"

The fifth and final show at Earl's Court was also the longest, lasting over three and a half hours. Another memorable performance.

The emergence of a clear soundboard tape of the show in 2001 was proof of just how at ease they were on this final night. Free from the pressure of the opening gigs, clearly looking forward to the summer break and their forthcoming travels, and content in the knowledge that their public acclaim at home had reached new heights – they were able to sit back and enjoy it. That's exactly what they did, performing with a sense of on stage camaraderie and unity that defied the critics and delighted the fans.

The opening numbers were delivered at a remarkable pace, almost as though the band were determined to give their all for this last show. Plant: "Good evening. Welcome to the last concert in England for a considerable time … *Quelle dommage*! But who knows … there's always the 1980's."

'In My Time Of Dying' included some lyrics from 'You Shook Me' and Plant ad-libbed "Keep shakin' it for me babe!" Afterwards, Plant joked: "Who said the blues didn't come from West Bromwich?" 'The Song Remains The Same' was played at almost double speed and seemed like a race to the finish. A pure adrenaline rush.

During 'That's The Way', Robert sang about the 'girl next door' for a change. He also threw in a few lines from 'Friends' and Robert Johnson's 'Judgement Day' prior to 'Bron Yr Aur Stomp'. 'San Francisco' was included in 'Dazed And Confused' again, although there was little other improvisation. This was the last time that 'Dazed And Confused' was played live by Zeppelin.

Robert dedicated 'Stairway To Heaven' to his daughter: "Carmen – this song's to a little girl who sits there probably wondering what it's all about … So, where is the bridge? Well, Carmen, here's your chance to find out where the bridge is … and if you know, please let me know after the show." Again, there was no holding Jimmy back tonight. He soloed as though his life depended on it.

As it was the final show of the tour, Zeppelin threw in some extra encores. First, 'Heartbreaker' then absolutely finally they concluded with a remarkable version of 'Communication Breakdown' which led into a reggae inspired jam with a few 'D'yer Maker' lyrics.

Plant: "Thank you Great Britain for five glorious days! Thanks for being a great audience and if you see Dennis Healey … tell him we're gone!"

Page recalled later: "We were so determined to do the same sort of show and more than what we'd been doing in America that in the end we came out of it with just a few hundred pounds over the five days; but it didn't matter because the vibe was so electrifying."

Plant recalled: "We'd been to America for a long time and we were very tired, but the whole idea of coming back when we were that hot and just going out and doing it for five nights was very exciting and it worked perfectly. It worked in every way – everybody enjoyed it."

Peter Grant: "Earl's Court was fantastic. Nobody sat behind the stage. We had the whole Showco set up. It took half a jumbo jet to get it over. Mel Bush did a super job in promoting those gigs. He presented us with souvenir mirrors afterwards, depicting the advert. Mel told me that we had enough ticket applications to have done ten shows that month."

The final comments on the Earl's Court come from Bonzo in an interview with Chris Welch from June 1975. "I enjoyed those concerts. I thought they were the best shows we've ever put on in England. I always get tense before a show and we were expecting trouble with such a big audience. But everything went really well and, although we couldn't have the laser beams on full power, I thought the video screen was well worth doing. It cost a lot of bread, but you could see close-ups you'd never be able to see normally at a concert. It was worth every penny!"

* After years of being the most sought after footage of the band by fans around the world, the almost complete video of the Earls Court May 24 performance surfaced on bootleg in 1999 via a Russian mail order website. It was subsequently issued on DVD via the Celebration and Cosmic Energy bootleg labels. Some 50 minutes of the May 25 performance later surfaced on the *London Calling* and *Latter Days* DVD bootlegs.

Footage from both the May 24 and 25 shows was edited for the 49-minute Earls Court selection on the official DVD. Footage of 'Kashmir' was also used for the CD-ROM of the track included on the *Latter Days* CD *Best Of Vol 2*. This has the studio track cut to Earls Court footage. This volume was subsequently packaged with the first volume to form the slip-cased *Very Best Of Led Zeppelin* issued in 2003.

Bootleg CD References: *Conquistador* (Watch Tower), *Arabesque & Baroque – The Final Night* (Antrabata), *Great Taste Last Night* (Image Quality), *Earl's Court 1975* (Mud Dogs); all five shows can be found on the 22-CD box set *Demand Unprecedented In The History Of Rock Music (The Complete Earls Court Tapes)* (Empress Valley)

Visual References: *Latter Days – The Best Of Led Zeppelin Vol 2* (Atlantic), *The Very Best Of Led Zeppelin* (Atlantic), *Official Led Zeppelin 2003 DVD* (Warner Music Vision), *Latter Visions* (Unofficial DVD Celebration), *London Calling* (Unofficial DVD Sugar Mama)

Led Zeppelin

On August 4, 1975, the hired car in which Robert Plant was travelling spun off the road on the Greek island of Rhodes. He suffered multiple fractures of the ankle and elbow, and his wife Maureen was also seriously injured. Plant was quickly airlifted back to the UK and then, when it was established that a long stay in England would adversely affect his tax exile status, to the tax haven of Jersey.

The immediate result of the accident was the cancellation of the group's proposed summer stadium tour of the US. Dates in Oakland, California (where 100,000 tickets had already been sold), Pasadena's Rose Bowl, and further shows in Kansas, Louisville, New Orleans, Tempe, Denver and Atlanta were postponed indefinitely. There was also a plan to play warm-up dates in Europe including an announced date in Helsinki. This would have preceded further dates to follow in South America and a return to the UK and Europe in the spring of 1976.

Instead the group and entourage based themselves in Jersey and subsequently Malibu, where they took the decision to use Plant's convalescence period to work on a new album, "the wheelchair album" as Plant would later call it. After rehearsals at Hollywood's SIR studio, the group flew to Munich and recorded the whole album at Musicland Studios in a mere three weeks.

In December Zeppelin were back in Jersey where Plant began to shuffle around a little more, venturing out to the local night spot, Beehan's West in St. Hellier. It was there on December 10 that Led Zeppelin performed an impromptu forty-five minute set with resident pianist Norman Hale.

On New Year's Day, Plant took his first few steps unaided since the fateful August day. "It was a new year, so I took a step … one small step for man, one giant step for six nights at Madison Square Garden."

The whole period put incredible strain on them all and the resulting album, *Presence*, mirrored the urgency, both lyrically and musically. With Page

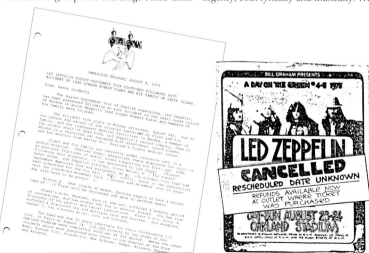

THE SONG REMAINS THE SAME: THE FIRST OFFICIAL LIVE RELEASE

When Peter Grant sanctioned the filming of the latter stages of Led Zeppelin's 1973 US tour, it was obvious they would need to record the concerts professionally. Engineer Eddie Kramer was brought in to record the three shows at Madison Square Garden on July 27, 28 & 29, using the Wally Heider Mobile Studio truck.

Over the next three years Page and Kramer mixed the material down at New York's Electric Lady and London's Trident studios to provide the soundtrack for the film. In October of 1976 the results were issued as the double album set *The Soundtrack From The Film The Songs Remains The Same*.

By Page's own admission the end product was hardly the best representation of Led Zep as a live band.

"Obviously we were committed to putting this album out, although it wasn't necessarily the best live stuff we have," he commented. "I don't look upon it as a live album ... it's essentially a soundtrack." Page actually assembled each track from the three available nights' recordings, often splicing in differing solos and vocals from each night to create the best hybrid recording.

Despite the attempt to present the album as a condensed live show from 'Rock And Roll' through to 'Whole 'Lotta Love', the set is seriously flawed. 'Dazed And Confused' is lumbering and the 12-minute 'Moby Dick' needs the film visuals to sustain interest. The omission of several key songs from the film – notably 'Black Dog', 'Since I've Been Loving You' and 'Heartbreaker' – is also very apparent. Perhaps a three-album set would have been a better option.

When Jimmy Page came to remaster the Led Zeppelin catalogue in the early Nineties he ignored this soundtrack album. Aware that it was not wholly representative of their live act, he finally redressed the balance by compiling the 1972 live set *How The West Was Won*.

However the improved quality of the 1973 New York footage and accompanying audio used on the DVD (notably 'Black Dog' and 'The Ocean') hinted that there was still scope to upgrade the 1973 tapes used for the original *Song Remains The Same* movie soundtrack and re-issue them in improved sound and the correct sequence.

firmly taking control, the basic guitar/drum/vocals line-up made for some exhilarating results - spearheaded by the extraordinary 'Achilles Last Stand', the ten minute opening track that told of Page and Plant's travels across Africa prior to the crash. The album topped the charts again in the US and UK, but was not one of their biggest sellers. In retrospect, it has emerged as their most underrated effort, a starkly honest statement capturing the uncertainty of the period.

Despite the turmoil, the recording of the album acted as a tonic for the injured Plant and the entire group. As Page noted, "The whole testament of the Munich album is that it proved once and for all that there is no reason for the group to split up. I can't think of too many groups that have been

around as long as we have and still retain that spontaneity. We started screaming in rehearsals and never stopped."

As for live work, Plant was tentative in interviews early in the year. "I could do with just sitting down with all my family and thanking the gods I've got one that I'm part of. That doesn't mean to say I've lost the grease at the bottom of my shoes. It means I've got to go back to my corner for a while."

However, he was back up on stage in Los Angeles as early as May, when he and Page joined Bad Company for a two song encore jam at the Forum. Back in the UK, there were continual reports that Zeppelin would play at least one show in the UK in the summer. One rumour revolved around them turning up as the mystery guests on the bill at London's Marquee Club on May 27. As it turned out, this date was taken by label mates The Pretty Things with Jones jamming on the encore. There were also offers to play Wembley Stadium in July but again Grant turned them down.

Instead this period was used to complete the long running film project which was finally premièred in the autumn. A 137-minute epic known as *The Song Remains The Same*, both the film and accompanying album proved to be an ultimately unfulfilling experience and a rare compromise by the group. However, the film successfully filled the void in the absence of the real thing as it opened across the UK and US, following much publicised launch premières in New York, Los Angeles and London.

This uncertain period was certainly not without its downside. Page's drug problems began to escalate during the year and he was attacked in the press by film director Kenneth Anger for reputedly failing to come up with the soundtrack for the movie *Lucifer Rising*.

Once again though, the spirit of camaraderie within Led Zep won through, and when they met up for rehearsals for a planned world tour due to begin in early 1977, Page was more optimistic for their future. "So much of this year has been taken up with petty time consuming things. It's not been so much a static period as an unsatisfying one. It's been like trying to sort out a year's problems in a month and not finding the process as simple as that. It's changing now though – something epic is really going to happen on this next tour."

In rehearsal they did not reacquaint themselves musically by running through Elvis covers, as was their custom. They went straight back into the fray by attempting to restructure the heavily studio overdubbed 'Achilles Last Stand' for live performance.

It was that number that Jonh Ingram, in his ecstatic *Sounds* review of *Presence*, had noted would be "a motherfucker played live". America and the world awaited …

Saturday August 23
Sunday August 24 1975
Oakland, California
Alameda County Coliseum
CANCELLED
These shows were part of Bill Graham's Day On The Green events. Joe Walsh and The Pretty Things were due to support.

Friday August 29 1975
Kansas City MO
CANCELLED

Sunday August 31 1975
Atlanta
Atlanta Stadium
CANCELLED

October 1975
Hollywood, California
SIR Studios
REHEARSALS

With no chance of appearing live now due to Robert's injuries, the band channelled all energies into making an album instead. Pre-production began at the SIR Studios in Hollywood. Here they ran through some initial ideas, including early stabs at 'Tea For One' and 'Royal Orleans'. A rehearsal tape surfaced with them working on 'Tea For One' which included a jam on 'Don't Stop Me Talking'/'Hoochie Coochie Man'.

Page: "We started screaming in rehearsals and never stopped."

Bootleg CD Reference: *Midnight Rehearsal* (Gejm), *Brutal Artistry Vol 2* (Midas Touch)

Wednesday November 5 1975
Helsinki, Finland
UUSI Messehalli
CANCELLED

The August issue of the local Suosikki magazine announced: "The invincible number one Rock'n' Roll band Led Zeppelin will perform at the Uuisi Messuhalli in Helsinki on November 5. The concert will be the most remarkable ever staged in Finland. Zeppelin will bring along their 350,000 watt sound system that is unique in the world and will play the same four-hour set as in London's Earls Court where an ecstatic audience of 85,000 witnessed their performances. Led Zeppelin will be the first act to perform in this new concert venue with a capacity of around 4,000."

Though unpublicised in the UK at the time, the above confirms that they intended to perform in Europe following the US dates. These plans, of course, were shelved after Robert's accident.

November 1975
Munich, Germany
Musicland Studios
RECORDING SESSIONS

With a batch of songs ready to record they flew to Munich to make what would become their sev-

enth album *Presence*. It was recorded within three weeks with Page taking the lead role, often packing in 18-hour stints to complete the overdubbing.

"I think *Presence* has got some of the hottest moments Led Zeppelin ever had – agitated, uncomfortable, druggy, pained," said Robert Plant in 2005.

Wednesday December 3 1975
Jersey
Behan's Park West
GUEST APPEARANCE

The band were based in the tax haven of Jersey for the past few weeks as Robert recuperated from his accident. They began to venture out to the local night-spots, and on this evening John Paul Jones and John Bonham attended a rock'n'roll night at the local Jersey dance hall. Resident pianist Norman Hale, formerly of The Tornados, invited them up on stage for a jam. They promised to return next week with the rest of Zeppelin.

Wednesday December 10 1975
Jersey
Behan's Park West

This venue was also known as West Park Pavillion and Inn On The Park. It was demolished in November 2001.

And they are as good as their word. All four members convened for an impromptu 45-minute set with Norman Hale on piano which included 'Blue Suede Shoes', 'My Baby Left Me', 'It'll Be Me' plus some of their own material.

Their last live show in front of an audience was attended by 17,000 at Earl's Court back in May. Just 350 witnessed this unexpected low key return to the stage. Page used the Lake Placid blue Stratocaster that he had favoured for the Munich *Presence* recording sessions over the past few weeks.

Plant: "You see the possibility of performing and who can avoid it, you know. It was like rock-'n'roll night at this dance hall that was like some place ten years gone by, in the best English tradition. Bonzo said 'C'mon man, let's plan on going!'

And I said 'Look, I can't even walk for God's sake, don't embarrass me. I can't hobble across the dance floor and onto the stage'. He said we'd go through the side door and then up the back steps. And with amazing grace, that's what I did and I found myself plunked on a stool. But I was really shy. Every time I went to hit a note, I stood up. Not putting any weight on my foot, but just sort of standing. Oh, they got some great photos! You know those guys in holiday areas with the cameras who come and take your photo and then you have to call midday the next day and show up at the pier where he will present you with whatever snaps he took the night before, and you find out how silly you looked or how drunk you were for an extortionate price? I gave the guy a free hand to shoot like crazy ... shoot all these shots of Led Zeppelin in this antiquated ballroom. It was a really exciting experience – rock'n'roll in the most basic sense.

"Of course, I made sure I sat almost behind Bonzo, wedged between the piano and the drums, but then I felt myself edge forward a little bit Then after the third number I was wiggling the stool past the drums and further out. And once we got going, we didn't want to stop. They kept flashing the lights on inside the place – 'Get them off stage, they've done enough!'

"Bad Company played the same place after us – so this tiny little dance hall is getting the pride of English musicians for nothing, just for the hell of playing!"

Friday January 23 1976
New York, New York
Radio City Music Hall
GUEST APPEARANCE

Not quite a musical contribution – John Bonham attended Deep Purple's concert at Radio City and, somewhat inebriated, addressed the crowd at the end of the show. "Hi! I'm John Bonham from Led Zeppelin and we've got a new album out soon." Bonham had a run-in with guitarist Tommy Bolin but apologised at a party later at the Rainbow Grill. Page and Plant were also in New York. Page

mixed the soundtrack for their forthcoming film while Plant gave a series of interviews. In February Bonzo could be seen hanging out with ex-Free guitarist Paul Kossoff in Los Angeles. Kossoff would tragically die the following month.

Saturday April 3 1976
London, England
Radio One Alan Freeman Rock Show
RADIO BRAODCAST

During his Saturday afternoon show Alan Freeman presented an exclusive preview of the entire *Presence* album with only a break to turn over the album.

Tuesday April 6 1976
London, England
The Old Grey Whistle Test *BBC 2*
TV APPEARANCE

Bob Harris presented a track from the just released *Presence* album,
'Achilles Last Stand' cut to vintage black and white footage of a bizarre 1920's film.

Wednesday May 23 1976
Inglewood Los Angeles, California
The Forum
GUEST APPEARANCE

Robert Plant and Jimmy Page joined Bad Company for an encore performance of 'I Just Wanna Make Love To You'.

John Bonham was also in attendance but an injured hand prevented him from joining in. "I didn't feel I could do much and if I was going to get up I wanted to do it properly."

Page had his regular Les Paul on hand. The

walked onstage after Bad Company's first encore to an ecstatic reception. "I'm sure you recognise this gentleman and this one," was Rodger's simple introduction. To their second home of LA they need no formal introduction. For Plant it was the real beginning of the grand comeback. 'What I wouldn't give for it to be all of us playing tonight. I want to get back on stage again so much."

Bad Company guitarist Mick Ralphs commented: "Jimmy is one of the few guitarists I can play with on stage. He's never into a big ego trip. I've played with other guitarists who are trying to outdo you. But Jimmy isn't like that. He tries to make the song happen rather than himself."

Afterwards, the combined Zep/Bad Co. Swan Song entourage attended a party in Beverley Hills thrown by Ahmet Ertegun.

Thursday May 27 1976
London, England
Marquee Club
GUEST APPEARANCE
John Paul Jones sits in with The Pretty Things playing some boogie-woogie piano at the end of their encore.

Prior to the show, this evening's programme had been billed as "Another Marquee Mystery Band. Seeing is believing. Please come early!" A hot rumour ran around London that the mystery band will be none other than Led Zeppelin or at least two of their members on a bill with label mates The Pretty Things. A further twist to the story was perpetrated by *The Sun* the day before the gig in a news item concerning frolics that caused an in-flight run-in between members of Led Zeppelin and TV *Kojak* cop actor Telly Savalas, as they travelled from Los Angeles. The story reports that "The Zeppelin group are in London to make a promotional film and play at The Marquee".

As a result, hundreds of hopeful fans descend

on Wardour Street hoping to catch this rare on stage sighting. Eventually the police have to be called to disperse the crowd.

The "Marquee mystery band" turned out to be The Pretty Things in a showcase gig laid on by Swan Song. In a goodwill gesture, John Paul Jones appeared at the end. Page, Plant and Bonham were conspicuous by their absence. However, the appearance of Ahmet Ertegun did suggest that something much bigger may have been on the agenda at one point.

JUNE 1976
News Report: Following their non-appearance at The Marquee, it was reported that Led Zeppelin had been offered one of this summer's three available dates at Wembley Stadium – July 3, July 31 or August 21.

Swan Song's reply to the offer: "Zeppelin would love to get back on stage and there is an imminent possibility of them doing so now that Robert Plant is nearly back to full fitness. No specific dates or venues have been arranged. When they are good and ready, they'll announce something."

Sunday September 12 1976
Montreux, Switzerland
Mountain Studios
RECORDING SESSIONS
John Bonham recorded an all percussive track that would eventually surface as 'Bonzo's Montreux' on *Coda*.

OCTOBER 1976
News Story: Led Zeppelin are preparing for a lengthy world tour to commence in America early next year. It is understood they will be undertaking a number of dates in the UK. An informed source revealed that they intend to play "quite a lot of dates in Britain and not just a string of concerts at Earl's Court or another London venue". They will begin rehearsing in London during November.

Tuesday October 5 1976
London, England
The Old Grey Whistle Test *BBC 2*
TV APPEARANCE
Bob Harris presented an exclusive clip of 'Black Dog' from the forthcoming *The Song Remains The Same* movie.

This was the first filmed footage of the band live on stage to be screened on UK TV since the long lost *How Late It Is* clip in 1969.

Saturday October 16 1976
London, England
Radio One Alan Freeman Rock Show
RADIO BROADCAST
In his afternoon show Alan Freeman exclusively previewed two tracks 'No Quarter' and 'Whole Lotta Love' from the soon to be released *The Song Remains The Same* soundtrack album.

THE LIVE CHRONOLOGICAL ALBUM PROJECT

The idea of presenting a live album set in chronological order was first discussed with Led Zeppelin after the Earl's Court shows. By that time they had amassed a number of concerts in their tape archive, and over the next five years it was a project that Page would often consider but ultimately never complete.

It was no secret they had made several attempts at recording themselves properly – as far back as the Royal Albert Hall in 1970. As it turned out, the release of *The Song Remains The Same* movie dictated that a live album drawn from the filmed gigs at Madison Square Garden in July '73 had to be made available as a soundtrack. As Page put it in 1977: "It's an honest soundtrack but a live chronological album is something I've always fancied. There's great stuff there – a winning version of 'No Quarter' from Earl's Court, 'I Can't Quit You' from the Royal Albert Hall, 'How Many More Times' is also pretty good. It's great hearing those old numbers that we'll probably never do again. We've also got numbers from Southampton University and some other clubs."

The idea was certainly given serious thought after their forced lay-off due to Robert's tragedy. Page had a home studio installed at his Plumpton home – the console

of which was taken from the Pye Mobile Recording unit which had been used to record the group at the Royal Albert Hall and other artists' live albums during the Seventies, including The Who's *Live At Leeds*.

There was no further development until the need for a posthumous Zeppelin album surfaced in 1981. Page again offered to compile a chronological live album. Plant was reticent and instead the studio archives were trawled to produce *Coda*. Page, however, did use the Royal Albert Hall tapes for the inclusion of 'I Can't Quit You Baby' from their soundcheck.

In the Eighties, Page was often asked in interviews about the possibility of a live album. Plant's continued reluctance and the flood of live CD bootlegs curbed his enthusiasm. "There's no point me taking time to wade through hours of tapes if somebody doesn't really want it out," is how he summed it up in 1993.

In 2002 he finally got his wish: the four-hour official DVD drawn mainly from the Albert Hall 1970, Madison Square Garden 1973, Earl's Court 1975 and Knebworth 1979 shows. The accompanying live album *How The West Was Won* – drawn from 1972 performances at Long Beach and Los Angeles – was a more than acceptable compromise as regards Page's wish to capture the real spirit and adventure of Led Zeppelin live – a quest that had spanned some 27 years.

Wednesday October 20 1976
New York, New York
Cinema 1, Ritz Theater, Manhattan
NON-PLAYING APPEARANCE
All the band attended the charity world première of their *The Song Remains The Same* movie, with proceeds going to the Save The Children fund. Swan Song threw a lavish party afterwards at the Pierre Hotel with Carly Simon, Mick Jagger, Ron Wood and Linda Ronstadt among the guests.

While in New York, the band staged a rare photo session for their cover story in *People* magazine. The shoot saw Jones and Bonzo wearing smart jackets and Plant in a woollen jumper. Back in the UK they held another studio photo session to promote the film. This group portrait showed Page in a raincoat.

Photos from this session were used as an official promo hand out by Swan Song.

Saturday October 23 1976
New York, New York
NBC TV
Don Kirshner's Rock Concert
TV APPEARANCE
On this day the popular US TV rock show screened two clips, 'Black Dog' and the 'Dazed And Confused' bow sequence, from the forthcoming *The Song Remains The Same* movie. This was the first occasion Led Zeppelin had been seen playing live on stage in full on US television.

Tuesday November 2 1976
London, England
The Old Grey Whistle Test *BBC 2*
TV APPEARANCE
Bob Harris presented a filmed interview of Robert Plant and Peter Grant. This was shot on the River Thames a week earlier on a boat called *Swanage Queen* with *Whistle Test* producer Michael Appleton filling in for Bob who had gone down with flu at the time. The pair talked about the making of the film. The interview was followed with an exclusive screening of part of Jimmy Page's violin bow sequence in 'Dazed And Confused' from the film – prompting Harris to comment, "That's a stunning piece of film" at the close.

Thursday November 4 1976
London, England
Warner West End 2/ABC 1 Cinemas
NON-PLAYING APPEARANCE
The double European première of *The Song Remains The Same* was attended by all the band. A party followed at The Floral Hall, Covent Garden with Billy Connolly, Paul & Linda McCartney, Alan Freeman, Rick Wakeman and Roy Harper among the guests.

Thursday November 4 1976
London, England
Capitol Radio Your Mother Wouldn't Like It
RADIO BROADCAST
Capital Radio's *Your Mother Wouldn't Like it* programme broadcast an interview with Jimmy Page conducted by Nicky Horne, discussing *The Song Remains The Same* movie and other Zep plans.

November 1976
London, England
Ezyhire Studios
REHEARSALS
The band reconvened for their first rehearsals for the forthcoming US tour. They immediately got down to working on a live arrangement of 'Achilles Last Stand'. Page: "We could have just eased into familiar stuff but we went straight in to the deep end by trying out 'Achilles'. I thought I'd have to use the twin-neck but it actually sounded better with the six string using different effects. When we did that first rehearsal it just all clicked all over again. Something epic is going to happen musically – that's the way I feel with this next tour."

Saturday December 25 1976
News report: The Christmas issue of *Melody Maker* runs the front page headline: "ZEP MEN: 3 SHOWS", and reports: "Led Zeppelin's Robert

Plant and John Bonham are re-joining their old group, Band Of Joy, next month for three special shows. The band, who built a strong reputation in the Midlands during the late Sixties, have reformed. And their first three concerts – with Plant and Bonham as guest artists – will be benefit shows for the relatives of The Possessed, the Birmingham-based band killed in a motorway crash last month.

"None of the dates have yet been set, but two of the shows will be at Birmingham Barbarella's and Wolverhampton Civic Hall at the end of January.

"Band Of Joy will open each concert by themselves, before being joined by Plant and Bonham at the end of the shows."

Nothing more is ever reported on these shows.

AMERICA 1977

Led Zeppelin

In the autumn of 1976 Led Zeppelin regrouped to prepare for their first tour since Robert's enforced lay off. After all the promotional interviews for *Presence* and *The Song Remains The Same* film, the socialising at movie premières and the vacationing in the South of France, Led Zeppelin were returning to the scene of their greatest triumphs – the arenas of America.

Rehearsals for the tour moved from north London to Fulham's Manticore studios early in 1977. Initial plans were for the dates to open in America in the early spring and move to Canada and South America before the band made their way back to the UK. At Manticore, they worked on an entirely new set, reviving the long deleted full acoustic section and arranging 'Ten Years Gone' and 'The Battle Of Evermore' for their début live performances. They also rehearsed 'Custard Pie', 'Babe, I'm Gonna Leave You' and 'Candy Store Rock' but these numbers would not be featured in the set. Surprisingly little of their most recent album *Presence* was worked on, with only 'Achilles Last Stand' and 'Nobody's Fault But Mine' finding their way to the stage. This brought into question the group's overall enthusiasm for the *Presence* album.

Written as it was during a period of turmoil, Plant probably felt that some of it was too personal for live performances.

During the rehearsals they ventured out to check on the emerging punk scene at London's Roxy club, mixing with The Damned and Eater to the bemusement of the now punkish music press. The energy of the punk movement was a throwback to their own primitive beginnings.

Everything was ready for a February 27 start in Fort Worth, Texas, when Robert contracted laryngitis and the schedule was postponed for a month. At one point, Toronto was earmarked for the new starting date of April 1, but this was changed in favour of opening in Dallas that night. In the UK, promoter Mel Bush tried to persuade Peter Grant to book Zeppelin as the top attraction at a planned one day festival due to be staged at Wrotham Park in Potters Bar. He was unsuccessful.

Forty-nine concerts were eventually scheduled over a three-leg period and even by their own standards this tour was something special for Led Zeppelin. As they lined up to take the stage at the Dallas Memorial Auditorium on their first live show in nearly two years, many questions

Led Zeppelin "Tour 77"

April 1	Memorial Auditorium, Dallas, Tex.
April 3	The Myriad, Oklahoma City, Okla.
April 6, 7, 9,10	Chicago Stadium, Chicago, Ill.
April 12	Metropolitan Sports Center, Minneapolis, Minn.
April 13	Civic Center, St. Paul, Minn.
April 15	Blues Arena, St. Louis, Mo.
April 17	Market Square Arena, Indianapolis, Ind.
April 19, 20	Riverfront Coliseum, Cincinnati, Ohio
April 23	The Omni, Atlanta, Ga.
April 25	Kentucky Fairgrounds & Exposition Center, Louisville, Ky.
April 27, 28	Coliseum, Richfield, Ohio
April 30	Silverdome, Pontiac, Mich.
May 18	Coliseum, Birmingham, Ala.
May 19	L.S.H. Assembly Hall, Baton Rouge, La.
May 21	The Summit, Houston, Tex.
May 22	Tarrant County, Convention Center, Ft. Worth, Tex.
May 31	Coliseum, Greensboro, N.C.
May 25, 26, 28, 30	Capital Center, Largo, Md.
June 3	Tampa Stadium, Tampa, Fla.
June 7, 8, 10, 11, 13, 14	Madison Square Garden, New York, N.Y.
June 19	Sports Arena, San Diego, Cal.
June 21, 22, 23, 25, 26, 27	Los Angeles Forum, Los Angeles, Cal.

Led Zeppelin albums are available on Swan Song Records & Tapes.

remained unanswered. Would Robert's injured foot take the strain? Would the long gap between rehearsals and the gig affect them? Would America still crave for Led Zeppelin as they had done in previous years?

They needn't have worried. From the moment Page slayed across the double-neck to pick out the chords of the opening number, 'The Song Remains The Same', it was clear that America's love affair with the group was far from over.

From Dallas the tour moved to a four day stint in Chicago, and from there the statistics began to blur: 40,000 in Cincinnati over two nights; 36,000 in Cleveland, a remarkable 76,229 at the Pontiac Silverdome – a new record for a single act performance, beating the 56,800 they themselves had attracted in Tampa in 1973. In June, there were six nights at both Madison Square Garden and the LA Forum. These shows were immortalised on two bootlegs, *For Badgeholders*

Only and *Listen To This Eddie*, which preserve for all time some of their most remarkable live performances.

Behind the scenes it wasn't all plain sailing. Offstage excesses and road fever took on a darker shade as the drug abuse continued, and Richard Cole had unwisely brought along John Bindon, a London villain, to look after security. Jimmy Page was far from healthy, and a performance in Chicago was curtailed when he went down with food poisoning. An open air return to Tampa was rained off after three numbers, causing a near riot. Whatever craziness was happening around them, on stage Led Zep were still producing remarkable performances, none more so than the LA stint which takes its place alongside Earl's Court as perhaps the best ever sequence of Zeppelin shows.

On July 23 in California, the dark undercurrent within their entourage boiled to the surface in an unsavoury flashpoint incident, a backstage row between a member of promoter Bill Graham's staff and Peter Grant. Cole, Bindon and John Bonham were also involved. Graham's man was severely beaten and charges were made against the four. The second show the next day went ahead only after Zeppelin's lawyers persuaded Graham to sign an agreement indemnifying the group against damages. Graham signed knowing that the document had no legal binding.

Three days later, in New Orleans, Robert Plant received the tragic news that his five-year-old son Karac had died of a mysterious stomach virus. Plant flew back to London immediately and the rest of the tour was cancelled

Back in England in early October, Jimmy Page gave a series of interviews to dispel rumours that this latest misfortune would signal the end of the group. "Robert will work again when he's ready. I'm sure of that," he said.

It was a tragic ending to a tour that had begun with much optimism and produced some stunning performances. From here on in, the song would never really be the same.

Equipment Notes:

For this final US jaunt, John Paul Jones switched allegiance to two new Alembic bass guitars, a four-stringed and eight-stringed model (the latter causing concern for Page who feared it might drown him out). The Fender bass was used only rarely, notably at their Madison Square Garden run. The Framus stand up bass was used for 'Black Country Woman'/'Bron Yr Aur Stomp'. On the first leg of the US tour, John Paul used a twelve-string Ovation guitar for 'Ten Years Gone' and 'Battle Of Evermore' plus a Harmony mandolin on 'Going To California'. By the time they came back to the US in May '77, Jones has his custom-built three-necked guitar crafted by Andy Manson, offering a mandolin, six string acoustic and twelve string acoustic in one instrument, plus bass pedals. This was used for 'Ten Years Gone'. The keyboard set-up now featured a black Yamaha CP 70B Grand Piano, the Honer Clavinet and an upgraded Mellotron 400.

Page's guitar set-up had increased to accommodate the newly revamped set list – Gibson doubleneck for 'The Song Remains The Same'/'Sick Again' and 'Stairway To Heaven'; the Dan Electro for 'In My Time Of Dying' and 'White Summer'/'Kashmir'; a Botswana brown Fender Telecaster was introduced for 'Ten Years Gone'; a Gibson mandolin for 'Battle Of Evermore' and 'Going To California'; a Martin D28 for 'Black Country Woman'/'Bron Yr Aur Stomp'. The Cherry Red Les Paul was periodically employed (notably on 'Over The Hills And Far Away'/'No Quarter'/ 'Guitar Solo'/ 'Achilles Last Stand'), while the regular 1958 Les Paul covered the rest.

John Bonham introduced a new Ludwig metallic kit for this tour

and all dates up to the 1980 Europe tour – now without the symbol on the bass drum.

The sound system, as with previous American tours, was handled by Showco of Dallas, Texas, under the guidance of Rusty Brutsche. The indoor system used on this tour was capable of delivering up to 30,000 watts and was hung on a three level suspended rig. The outdoor system was more than twice as powerful and required ten personnel plus sixteen stage hands to set it up in the required time. 150 Crown amps are employed, including twenty for the monitor system. No compressors, limiters or noise reduction systems were used. The monitors were suspended twenty feet above the stage. No floor monitors were used so as to allow as much free space as possible on the stage.

Shure SM 548 microphones were used on Page's amps and all the drums except for the overheads which use a pair of unidirectional AKG 451Es. An amazing amount of effort was taken to get the drum sound right. Every single drum head was miked, including timpani and gong. The snare, hi-hat, and bass drum were even miked front and back. A total of 15 microphones were used for the drum kit alone.

The mixing desk had thirty full capacity inputs and all thirty were used for the Zeppelin sound, fifteen for the drums, four for keyboards, bass and guitar, three for acoustic instruments, four vocal mics and four effects returns. The shows were recorded from the board on a Nakamichi 550 cassette deck.

Rusty Brutsche handled the main mix personally, while Benji Le Fevre took care of Plant's vocal effects which include echo, delay and harmoniser

Original US Tour Itinerary:

The initial itinerary for the US tour prior to the cancellation read: Feb 27 Fort Worth (re scheduled to May 22)/Feb 28 Houston (re scheduled May 21)/March 1 Baton Rouge (re scheduled May 19)/March 3 Oklahoma City (re scheduled April 3)/March 4 Dallas (re scheduled April 1)/ March 6 Tempe Arizona(re scheduled July 20)/March 8

San Diego(re-sheduled June 19)/March 9-12-13 The Forum Inglewood 9 (re scheduled June 21-22-23)/March 14 15 16 The Forum Iinglewood (re-scheduled June 25-26-27)/April 1 Toronto (not re-scheduled)/April 3-4 Montreal (not re-scheduled)/April 22 Dayton Ohio (not re-scheduled)/May 20 Birmingham Alabama (re-scheduled May 18)/May 21 Atlanta (re-scheduled April 23/Greensboro (re-scheduled May 31)

Lisa Robinson in *Hit Parader* magazine reported a slightly differing itinerary that quoted the dates being "From the 27th February Fort Worth – Houston – Baton Rouge – Oklahoma City – Dallas – Tempe – San Diego – Los Angeles through the 13th of March then after a two week break in April further gigs in the mid west and Canada and after another break the 19th of May as follows: May 20 Tuscaloosa/May 21 Charlotte/May 23 Greensboro/May 25-26-28 Washington/June 3 Tampa/June 7-8 (maybe more) New York – plus more gigs in outdoor stadiums in the summer."

January/February 1977
Fulham London, England
Manticore Studios
REHEARSALS

During January the band moved their equipment into the Manticore Studio complex owned by Emerson Lake & Palmer. Here they spent time perfecting a new stage show for the American tour. Visitors to the rehearsals included *NME's* Roy Carr who conducted an interview. He reported that Billy Idol of punk band Generation X was briefly in attendance. Photos taken by Kate Simon of them rehearsing here can be seen in the cover booklet for the *Latter Days/The Best Of Led Zeppelin Vol Two* CD. These shots show Page using a pedal steel guitar which was subsequently not employed for the tour.

NME photographer Pennie Smith also took a number of group shots for *NME*. These showed Bonham and Plant in Fifties drape jackets.

Steve Marriot was another visitor, then in the throes of reforming The Small Faces. "We ended up signing Muddy Waters songs," remarked

Plant. "He is still the master of white contemporary blues."

Friday April 1 1977
Dallas, Texas
Dallas Memorial Auditorium – Dallas Convention Center

Set: The Song Remains The Same/Sick Again/Nobody's Fault But Mine/In My Time Of Dying/Since I've Been Loving You/No Quarter/Ten Years Gone/The Battle Of Evermore/Going To California/Black Country Woman – Bron Yr Aur Stomp/White Summer – Black Mountain Side/Kashmir/Moby Dick/Page Solo/Achilles Last Stand/Stairway To Heaven/Black Dog/Rock And Roll.

One of the most crucial performances in the band's history given all the problems of the previous two years. As they nervously gathered backstage ready to go on (an image captured by photographer Neal Preston on page 112 of his book *Led Zeppelin – A Photographic Collection*) there were still many questions unanswered – would Plant's fitness hold out?; could they still cut it musically?; was America's infatuation with them still intact?

The answer to all those questions was an emphatic yes.

'Led Zeppelin Lands Safely in Dallas,' reported the *Los Angeles Times*. Robert Hilburn wrote: "Led Zeppelin, generally conceded to be the world's most popular rock'n'roll band, has fond memories of this Texas city. It was here at the Dallas Pop

Led Zeppelin

Festival in 1969 that the English band climaxed a triumphant US tour that established it as a major new force in rock. It was also in Dallas four years ago that a local oil man's daughter hired a private jet to follow Zeppelin's plane out of town.

"But neither begin to match the importance – or emotionalism – of Zeppelin's appearance last weekend at the Dallas Memorial Auditorium.

"The band returned to live shows with a stirring performance that reassured both the group and its fans about Zeppelin's ability to continue.

"When the band stepped on stage just after 8pm, the audience roared its appreciation. Though much has been written about the aggressive nature of Zeppelin's audience in responding to the band's high-energy musical assault, the tone Friday was one of warmth. The audience, one sensed, was simply glad to see the band.

"Never a critic's favourite, Zeppelin played with an eagerness and joy that was contagious. I still think they'd be more effective – considering the limitation of much of their material – to cut an hour out of their set, thus shedding some of the excess. There were lots of rough spots in the band's first appearance in nearly two years, but there was only jubilation on the faces of the band after the three hour show, as they raced to limousines for the ride to the airport."

Plant told Hilburn the next day: "Sure it was emotional. We had just cleared the biggest hurdle of our career. It was a chapter in my life that I never really knew if I'd be able to see. I tried to keep a positive attitude in the months after the accident, but even after I was able to walk again, I didn't know how the foot would hold up on stage. Even rehearsals didn't prove it to me. I was so nervous before we went on stage last night that I almost threw up. I could feel the tenseness in my throat for the first couple of songs. I kept telling myself to loosen up.

"The whole show possessed an element of emotion that I've never known before. I could just as easily knelt on the stage and cried. I was so happy. I don't think I've ever sung better in America. I mean I'd have liked everybody who ever wanted to see us to have been there.

"You can't pretend last night's concert was the greatest thing we've ever done, but there was something between us after that long gap that enabled us – in certain songs, where we really got hold of it – to go far beyond where we had been before."

Sunday April 3 1977
Oklahoma City, Oklahoma
The Myriad

Set: The Song Remains The Same/Sick Again/Nobody's Fault But Mine/In My Time Of Dying/Since I've Been Loving You/No Quarter/Ten Years Gone/The Battle Of Evermore/Going To California/Black Country Woman – Bron Yr Aur Stomp/White Summer – Black Mountain Side/Kashmir/Moby Dick/Page Solo/Achilles Last Stand/Stairway To Heaven/Rock And Roll/Trampled Underfoot.

An Evening With … Led Zeppelin", as the tickets announced, the 1977 tour was the most lavish, large-scale tour the band would undertake.

The scale of the operation sometimes prohibited the spontaneity and improvisation of the past. Variations in the set lists were usually restricted to the encores.

'Black Dog' was now dropped as an encore in

favour of 'Trampled Underfoot'. The set structure of the Oklahoma show formed the template for much of the whole tour.

Traditionally Zeppelin tours were prone to problematic starts and this tour was no exception. The performance in Oklahoma was sloppy and technical problems abounded as the PA system tended to overpower the band.

There were also problems with ticket allocations, with demand far outstripping supply. *New Musical Express* reported that in Oklahoma City on January 29 … "A three day vigil of Led Zeppelin fans resorted to desperate measures as the cold became more intense and they began tearing down fence posts to feed the fires they had built in metal cans."

Bootleg CD References: *Fucking T.Y.* (Tattytura), *Fucking PA* (Tarantura)

Wednesday April 6 1977
Chicago, Illinois
Chicago Stadium
Set : The Song Remains the Same/The Rover (introduction)/Sick Again/Nobody's Fault But Mine/In My Time of Dying/Since I've Been Loving You/No Quarter/Ten Years Gone/The Battle of Evermore/Going To California/Black Country Woman/ Bron-Y-Aur Stomp/White Summer – Black Mountain Side/Kashmir/Out On The Tiles (introduction)/Moby Dick/Achilles Last Stand/Stairway To Heaven/Rock And Roll/Trampled Underfoot.

A barrage of firecrackers greeted Zeppelin's return to the Chicago stage, provoking Plant to make an announcement before even the first note was played: "Listen. Before we start, can we ask you one thing? Can you stop throwing those firecrackers? We want to give you a lot of music, but we're not going to fight with firecrackers! OK? Cool it with the explosives."

The American obsession with throwing firecrackers was a perpetual annoyance to Plant. "I don't know why the fans toss firecrackers. I think it's horrible. That's the element that makes you wonder whether it's better to be half-way up a tree in Wales."

The show was a vast improvement on the previous night. The acoustic set was warmly received, and John Bonham was cheered to the front of the stage but, again, technical problems abounded. However, this was a good show and the band were in party mood. Plant messed around with Elvis lyrics and teased the audience with snatches of 'Whole Lotta Love'. Page even spoke to the audience, a very rare occurrence indeed.

Technical problems persisted with Jimmy's guitar lead before 'White Summer', but Plant just laughed it off: "We're on a low budget this tour and we've only got one guitar lead! The man who looks after the guitars comes from Scotland where things are a lot slower, but he does speak English."

Bonham's drum solo was now being referred to as 'Over The Top'.

Press reaction to the first night in Chicago was favourable. Al Rudis of *Sounds* reported: "This is a new Led Zeppelin, a little older, a lot less brash and much more musical. They're still an exciting band however, still a band that gives the kids the best show their money can buy." Jimmy was particularly impressive: "Page was a wildman on stage, skittering here and there, overflowing with nervous energy. Even during the slow numbers his body moved with the speed of light. The fast, frenetic guitar parts came out well, and so did the more restrained parts."

'Jimmy's rampage keeps Zep flying' was the headline in *Rolling Stone*, which reviewed the show in their usual style: "Led Zeppelin comes on like a dragon whose tail slaps the air with haphazard but authoritative strokes. The heavy-metal beast, whether in concept or concert, shoulders a burdensome responsibility: the Zep must be an absolute testament to the liberating qualities of excessive hard rock. At the heart of the beast is Jimmy Page, his bone-thin body draped in silk and dwarfed by the totem of his art – the electric guitar. The high-decibel audacity of those six strings constitutes an image that is bigger than the band itself, and it is Zep's monument as much as their tool."

Bootleg Cd Reference: *Missing Night In Chicago* (Missing Link)

Thursday April 7 1977
Chicago, Illinois
Chicago Stadium
Set includes: The Song Remains The Same/Sick Again/Nobody's Fault But Mine/Since I've Been Loving You/No Quarter/Ten Years Gone/The Battle Of Evermore/Going To California/White Summer – Black Mountain Side/Kashmir/ Achilles Last Stand/Stairway To Heaven/Rock And Roll.

Chicago also experienced problems with ticket availability. Local press reported: "Thirty young men, including several juveniles, were arrested by police during a disturbance around Chicago Stadium, as thousands of people sought to buy tickets for a concert by Led Zeppelin – 'a rock group'."

Saturday April 9 1977
Chicago, Illinois
Chicago Stadium
Set: The Song Remains The Same/Sick Again/Nobody's Fault But Mine/Since I've Been Loving You/No Quarter/Ten Years Gone.

The second song performed this evening was never more appropriate, for Jimmy Page was indeed 'Sick Again' at this show. This resulted in the premature termination of the concert after only 65 minutes. It's clear there were problems from the start. Page's playing was erratic and after 'Sick Again' , he inadvertently launched into 'Since I've Been Loving You'. The rest of the band, expecting 'Nobody's Fault But Mine', didn't follow. 'Since I've Been Loving You' was then abandoned and the set proceeded as scheduled.

Firecrackers were again a problem, and after 'Ten Years Gone', Robert addressed the audience. "Jimmy has got a bout of gastro-enteritis, which isn't helped by firecrackers, so we're gonna take a necessary five minute break."

After much deliberation, road manager Richard Cole was despatched to make an announcement. "Jimmy does not want to do a half-hearted show tonight. If you watch the press on Monday, this show will be rescheduled. The band feel very bad about this, but please hang onto your tickets. All tickets will be honoured."

The next day Jimmy told *Circus* magazine: "They think it was food poisoning. The doctor says no solids. It's the first time we've ever stopped a gig like that. We always have a go, really, because we're not a rip-off band. But the pain was unbearable – if I hadn't sat down I would have fallen over. Anyway, we'll make it up to them. We'll do an all-request show."

Fate dictates that the rescheduled show would never take place.

A few minutes of silent colour cine film exists from this show

Bootleg CD reference: *Early Days Latter Days* (Early Days)
Visual Reference: *1977* (Unofficial DVD Cosmic Energy)

Sunday April 10 1977
Chicago, Illinois
Chicago Stadium
Set: The Song Remains The Same/Sick Again/Nobody's Fault But Mine/In My Time Of Dying/Since I've Been Loving You/No Quarter/ Ten Years Gone/The Battle Of Evermore/Going To California/Black Country Woman – Bron Yr Aur Stomp/Trampled Underfoot/White Summer – Black Mountain Side/Kashmir/Moby Dick/Page

Solo/Achilles Last Stand/Stairway To Heaven/ Rock And Roll.

The final show of the Chicago residency and there was a minor change to the set. 'Trampled Underfoot' was now inserted before 'White Summer' in the main set, instead of being reserved as a second encore.

Page had made a good recovery. Plant: "Jimmy was feeling ill last night, but it was only a false pregnancy, so that's alright." Plant also claimed that a local radio station insinuated that Page had been drinking alcohol and substances all day. "Mr Page neither smokes, drinks, takes women or does anything like that so we want an apology tomorrow and a crate of alcohol!"

At this show Page came on stage dressed in a striking Stormtrooper outfit complete with jack boots and cap. Photographer Neal Preston was in attendance and took a host of memorable photos which can be seen in his book *Led Zeppelin – A Photographic Collection.*

Fan Joe Schmidt recalled: "I attended all four Chicago shows – the last night was Easter Sunday and Page came out in that incredible outfit. He later changed into the white satin suit after Bonzo's 'Over The Top' solo. A friend and I shot some cine footage from a prime box seat."

Four minutes of colour cine film exists from this show

Visual References: *Latter Visions* unofficial DVD (Celebration), *1977* (Unofficial DVD Cosmic Energy)

Tuesday April 12 1977
Bloomington, Minnesota
Met Center

Set: The Song Remains The Same/Sick Again/Nobody's Fault But Mine/In My Time Of Dying/Since I've Been Loving You/No Quarter/Ten Years Gone/The Battle Of Evermore/Going To California/Black Country Woman – Bron Yr Aur Stomp/White Summer – Black Mountain Side/Kashmir/Moby Dick/Page Solo/Achilles Last Stand/Stairway To Heaven/ Rock And Roll.

Torrential rain and strong winds delayed the take-off of Zeppelin's private jet from Chicago's O'Hare airport. After finally landing at Minneapolis-St. Paul, the band's four rented limousines were escorted to the venue by three police motorcycles. However, the concert was still 75 minutes late starting and both band and audience were beginning to tire, resulting in a rather lacklustre show.

The ever-shifting 'Trampled Underfoot' had now been dropped from the set.

'Leaden playing grounds show by hard-rock band' is the next day's headline in the *Minneapolis Star*: "Led Zeppelin, arguably the world's most popular rock band, returned to Met Center last night with an unexpectedly versatile, well-orchestrated yet overlong show.

"The British quartet seemed distracted by firecrackers ignited by fans throughout the show and disturbed by the rain. For whatever reason, the band never seemed to get on track and the near-capacity crowd of 16,000 persons never gave Zeppelin the fuel to help it get off the ground."

Wednesday April 13 1977
St. Paul, Minnesota
Civic Center Arena

Set: The Song Remains The Same/Sick Again, Nobody's Fault But Mine/In My Time Of Dying/Since I've Been Loving You/No Quarter/ Ten Years Gone/The Battle Of Evermore/Going To California/Black Country Woman/Bron-Yr-Aur Stomp/White Summer – Black Mountain Side/Kashmir/Moby Dick/ Achilles Last Stand/Stairway To Heaven/Rock And Roll.

The second night of the Twin Cities shows was a much more accomplished performance.

John Bream of *Phonograph Record* reported: "Across the river in St. Paul, Page played with a renewed ferociousness and the undistracted Plant let loose, striking his familiar cocky poses and frenetically chopping his arms. The push-comes-to-shove-do-you-have-any-papers-man crowd of 17,500 roared at the powerhouse performance.

"Zeppelin understands the power of rock better

than any performer since Jimi Hendrix. Concertgoers don't tap their feet to Zeppelin's music, they ecstatically shake their heads."

'32,500 hear Led Zeppelin in 2 nights' reported the *Minneapolis Tribune*. Michael Anthony wrote: "The big one, Led Zeppelin, took over the Twin Cities this week, playing to a total audience of about 32,500. Only 'Up With People', the moral-uplift-through-song extravaganza, has tried the same kind of booking, playing the two biggest auditoriums in the Twin Cities on consecutive nights in 1975. But the attendance and proceeds in the latter instance were paltry compared with those of the Zeppelin events, which grossed about $280,000.

"Perhaps only the four Beatles reunited could command the drawing power of Led Zeppelin, though even in their peak earning years, The Beatles never achieved the record sales and atten-dance figures set by Zeppelin."

Unfortunately there were minor security prob-lems. 'As Fans Mob Civic Center, Zeppelin ride orderly' wrote Greg Hughes: "At least 34 persons were arrested for disorderly conduct and drinking in public. The four-member British rock group's appearance was twice marred by fans without tickets who attempted to rush entrances on both levels. A group of about 100 made a weak attempt to push across upper level ticket-taking aisles 30 minutes before show time. They were quickly and quietly turned away by three police officers and 13 Sims Security employees. Only moments before the concert began, a crowd of perhaps 200 stormed the lower level ticket-taking positions. Efforts by 18 of 45 policemen to repel the group quietly resulted in several verbal and pushing confrontations but no one was injured.

"While alcoholic beverages are not officially permitted inside, many concertgoers managed to smuggle in beer and liquor, also marijuana."

Friday April 15 1977
St. Louis, Missouri
St. Louis Arena
Set: The Song Remains The Same/Sick Again/Nobody's Fault But Mine/In My Time Of Dying/Since I've Been Loving You/No Quarter/Ten Years Gone/The Battle Of Evermore/Going To California/Black Country Woman/Bron-Yr-Aur Stomp/White Summer – Black Mountain Side/Kashmir/Moby Dick/Achilles Last Stand/Stairway To Heaven/Rock And Roll

Sunday April 17 1977
Indianapolis, Indiana
Market Square Arena
Set: The Song Remains The Same/Sick Again/Nobody's Fault But Mine/In My Time Of Dying/Since I've Been Loving You/No Quarter/Ten Years Gone/The Battle Of Evermore/Going To California/Black Country Woman – Bron Yr Aur Stomp/White Summer – Black Mountain Side/Kashmir/Moby Dick/Achilles Last Stand/Stairway To Heaven/Rock And Roll/Trampled Underfoot.

This arena normally held 16,500 but 'festival seating' added 2,000 to the gate. Tickets were $14 each though scalpers were getting as much as $50. Gates opened at 4pm and thousands of fans surged onto the arena floor.

A sound problem delayed Jimmy's intro to 'The Song Remains The Same' and 'Trampled Underfoot' now returned to its original role as a second encore.

H.P. Newquist in *Guitar* magazine recalled: "Three hours, $14, Les Pauls, 'Achilles Last Stand'. For the money and the memory, there was not a single guitarist in the 1970s who put on a better show than Page. He may not have invented lead guitar, but in concert Jimmy Page defined it as a visual art form."

Tuesday April 19 1977
Cincinnati, Ohio
Riverfront Coliseum
Set includes: The Song Remains the Same/The Rover (introduction)/Sick Again/Nobody's Fault But Mine/Since I've Been Loving You/No Quarter/Ten Years Gone/The Battle of

Evermore/Going To California/Black Country Woman/Bron-Y-Aur Stomp/White Summer/Black Mountain Side/Kashmir/Guitar Solo/Achilles Last Stand/Stairway To Heaven/Rock And Roll.

Violence again reared its ugly head, as local reports stated: "Led Zeppelin, a British rock group, again brought violence in its wake when about 1,000 fans tried to gatecrash a Zeppelin show in Cincinnati last night. Police arrested 100 youths during the mini-riot, which was punctuated by thrown bottles and fights."

The band's performance was obviously affected by tension in the air. After 'Sick Again', Robert attempted to diffuse the situation. "It's very difficult to play when you see crowds of people swaying. Keep it cool. Stand still. We don't want to see anybody get hurt."

Bootleg CD References: *Early Days Latter Days* (Early Days), *Cincinnati Kids* (H&Y), *Cincinatti 2 Nights* (Electric Magic)

Wednesday April 20 1977
Cincinnati, Ohio
Riverfront Coliseum
Set includes: The Song Remains The Same/The Rover (introduction) / Sick Again/Nobody's Fault But Mine/Since I've Been Loving You/No Quarter/Ten Years Gone/The Battle of Evermore/Going To California/Black Country Woman/Bron-Y-Aur Stomp/White Summer – Black Mountain Side/Kashmir/Achilles Last Stand/Stairway To Heaven/Rock And Roll

Billboard reported: "A fan was killed at Led Zeppelin's appearance at Cincinnati's Coliseum, when an unruly crowd pushed him from the stadium's third level. He plummeted into the street and was struck by a car."

Bootleg CD Reference: *Cincinnati 2 Nights* (Electric Magic)

Saturday April 23 1977
Atlanta, Georgia
The OMNI
Set: The Song Remains The Same/The Rover

(intro)/Sick Again/Nobody's Fault But Mine/In My Time of Dying/Since I've Been Loving You/No Quarter/Ten Years Gone/Battle of Evermore/Going to California/Black Country Woman/Bron-Yr-Aur Stomp/White Summer – Black Mountain Side/Kashmir/Moby Dick/Achilles Last Stand/Stairway To Heaven/Rock And Roll/Trampled Underfoot

This venue opened in October 1972 and was demolished in July 1997.

'Led Zeppelin Plays the Heavy, Best'- Scott Cain wrote: "Led Zeppelin gave an exciting show at the Omni Saturday night, reaffirming the group's position as the No.1 heavy-metal band in the world. In energy, enthusiasm and preparation, the concert met, and even surpassed, any possible expectation.

"Jimmy Page did not dominate the proceedings to the extent that might have been anticipated, although he used more guitars than Les Paul probably saw in a lifetime.

"Page gave a performance of manic intensity, however. His major solo was a rendition of 'Star Spangled Banner', done in the style made famous (or notorious, depending on your viewpoint) by Jimi Hendrix. Those who consider Hendrix's playing to have been masterful would have to accord Page the same status. Special effects helped make this section a spectacular triumph. Clouds of smoke billowed into the air and Page stood in the centre of a pyramid-shaped column of green laser light that revolved faster and faster as he picked up tempo."

Bootleg CD Reference: *Gone With The Wind* (No label)

Monday April 25 1977
Louisville, Kentucky
Freedom Hall Kentucky Fair And Exposition Center

Wednesday April 27 1977
Richfield, Ohio
Richfield Coliseum
Set: The Song Remains The Same/Sick

Again/Nobody's Fault But Mine/In My Time Of Dying/Since I've Been Loving You/No Quarter/Ten Years Gone/The Battle Of Evermore/Going To California/Black Country Woman-Bron Yr Aur Stomp/White Summer – Black Mountain Side/Kashmir/Moby Dick/Page Solo- Star Spangled Banner/Achilles Last Stand/Stairway To Heaven/Rock And Roll/Trampled Underfoot.

The night of *The Destroyer*. A much bootlegged performance, this was the first, and for a long period only, professionally recorded mixing desk tape to escape from the band's archives. It has been bootlegged many many times on vinyl and CD.

The show itself was not an exceptional performance, but it matched the general high standard on this tour, so far.

As the band approached the end of the first leg of the tour, Plant was still complaining of monitor problems during the acoustic set. Bonham was rather curiously introduced as … "A man who manages to wash my hair in 7UP". Page's solo now regularly featured 'Star Spangled Banner' and here also included snatches of 'Jerusalem'.

Plant dedicated 'Stairway To Heaven' to the audience for creating a nice vibey atmosphere, and "only one firecracker all night!"

The next day, *The Cleveland Press* ran the headline 'Led Zeppelin thrills packed house, 37 fans are arrested'. Bruno Bornino reported: "More than 20,000 hysterical fans in the Coliseum last night were transported into rock music ecstasy by the Led Zeppelin. A handful of the 20,000, however, were transported to jail. The Summit County Sheriff's Department reported 37 arrests for assorted offences including disorderly conduct, drug possession and possession of knives."

Bootleg CD References: *The Supreme Destroyer* (Empress Valley), *The Destroyers* (Tarantura), *Destroyer* (Achive)

Thursday April 28 1977
Richfield, Ohio
Richfield Coliseum
Set: The Song Remains The Same/Sick Again/Nobody's Fault But Mine/In My Time Of Dying/Since I've Been Loving You/No Quarter/Ten Years Gone/The Battle Of Evermore/Going To California/Black Country Woman – Bron Yr Aur Stomp/White Summer – Black Mountain Side/Kashmir/Moby Dick/Page Solo- Star Spangled Banner/Achilles Last Stand/Stairway To Heaven/Rock And Roll/Trampled Underfoot.

The band seemed much more animated tonight and turned in a more vibrant performance. Luckily audience tapes were rolling to get this one captured for posterity.

Bootleg CD References: *The Supreme Destroyer* (Empress Valley), *Destroyer II* (Last Stand Disk), *The Destroyer Strongest Edition* (The Diagrams Of Led Zeppelin), *Destroyers II* (SIRA), *The Destroyers* (Tarantura)

Saturday April 30 1977
Pontiac, Michigan
Pontiac Silverdome
Set: The Song Remains The Same/Sick Again/Nobody's Fault But Mine/In My Time Of Dying/Since I've Been Loving You/No Quarter/Ten Years Gone/The Battle Of Evermore/Going To California/Black Country Woman-Bron Yr Aur Stomp/White Summer – Black Mountain Side/Kashmir/Moby Dick/Page Solo- Star Spangled Banner/Achilles Last Stand/Stairway To Heaven/Rock And Roll/Trampled Underfoot

This show set a new world record for audience attendance at a solo indoor attraction. Some 76,229 people witnessed tonight's concert, beating the 75,962 that The Who attracted to the same venue in December 1975. Zeppelin's gross income from ticket sales to this gig was $792,361.

'Record Crowd Sees Zeppelin In Detroit' reported *Billboard*. "Police and stadium official

said they were amazed at the relative tranquillity of the throng, after earlier expecting the worst from the Zeppelin faithful."

"'We are pleasantly surprised,' said Pontiac police chief William Hangar as he watched the crowd saunter into the stadium's four gates Saturday afternoon. 'This is the first time in five big rock shows at the Silverdome that we've had no problems with crowds rushing the turnstiles or a major tie-up on surrounding roads.'

"'This is one of the smoothest shows we've ever had,' said Led Zeppelin's tour manager Richard Cole prior to the group's three hour set. 'For the amount of people, I'm pleasantly surprised. Frankly, we expected trouble.'"

The show was filmed for the venue's in house closed-circuit TV video system which showed footage of the gig on screen as it happened. The video tapes of this footage have never surfaced. A stunning photo of the band on stage with the cameraman in view can be seen on page two of Neal Preston's *A Photographic Collection* book.

A triumphant finale to the first leg of the tour.

The tour now breaks for two weeks. Jimmy flew to Cairo for a short holiday.

Bootleg CD Reference: *Hot Rods In Pontiac* (The Diagrams Of Led Zeppelin)

During the first leg of the tour London's Capital Radio began preparing a radio documentary to be titled *Led Zeppelin On The Road.* They conducted interviews in the US with Plant and Page plus various working personnel on the tour, including Swan Song's Janine Safker. DJ Nicky Horne trailed the programme on his *Your Mother Wouldn't Like it* show later in the year but for reasons unknown it was never completed or aired in any format.

Thursday May 12 1977
London, England
Grosvenor Hotel
NON PLAYING APPEARANCE
Plant, Jones, Grant and Page attend the Ivor Novello awards at the Grosvenor Hotel in London to pick up the prestigious award for Led Zeppelin's 'Outstanding Contribution to British Music'.

Led Zeppelin singer arrested

ATLANTA.
LED ZEPPELIN singer Robert Plant was arrested today on charges of drunkenness and carrying a knife at Hartsfield international airport.

Officer J. R. Kovsky of the airport police, who identified Plant said he was released after being fined 75 dollars at the city jail.

Police said Plant gave his age as 19, but records show that he is 29.

Atlanta police sergeant W. M. Adams said officers were called to a lounge at the airport and found Plant unconscious.

When Plant was awakened

On Monday May 16, the *Evening Standard* reported that Led Zeppelin singer Robert Plant had been arrested at Hartsfield Airport, Atlanta, for pulling a knife and being drunk. The incident was actually perpetrated by a 19-year-old youth impersonating Plant. The 'real' Plant was actually horse riding in Wales at the time. A retraction and apology was hastily inserted in the May 17 edition of the *Evening Standard*. That afternoon, Plant met up with the rest of the band at Heathrow Airport to fly out to Alabama for the start of the second leg of the tour.

Wednesday May 18 1977
Birmingham, Alabama
Jefferson Memorial Coliseum

Set: The Song Remains The Same/Sick Again/Nobody's Fault But Mine/In My Time Of Dying/Since I've Been Loving You/No Quarter/Ten Years Gone/The Battle Of Evermore/Going To California/Black Country Woman-Bron Yr Aur Stomp/White Summer – Black Mountain Side/Kashmir/Moby Dick/Page Solo – Dixie – Star Spangled Banner/Achilles Last Stand/Stairway To Heaven/Rock And Roll.

At the first show of the middle leg of the tour the band were greeted with hysteria. Zeppelin were the first act to play this new venue and the crowd were wild. Before the concert an MC was despatched to encourage the crowd to "Take one giant step back" and warned against the use of firecrackers during the performance.

Tonight's show was based on the first leg set; there were no rehearsals during the break. John Paul Jones had now taken delivery of the famous three-necked guitar that featured in the acoustic set. Plant referred to it as "His secret weapon – it only comes out at night!"

In recognition of the Deep South, Page included 'Dixie', the Southern anthem, in his solo show-case.

Bootleg cine footage from this show, shot by an enterprising member of the audience, illustrates how animated Page had become on stage. He is literally everywhere – duck walking, dropping to his knees, spinning, turning … the perfect foil for Robert to weave between.

Edits of this footage can be seen on the official DVD. It's featured on the bootleg montage extra of 'The Song Remains The Same' with the soundtrack from the June 21, 1977 *Listen To This Eddie* recording.

Bootleg CD Reference: *Dixie* (Antrabata), *Out Of The Way* (The Diagrams of Led Zeppelin)

Visual References: *Led Zeppelin* official 2003 DVD (Warner Music Vision), *Latter Visions* (Unofficial DVD Celebration), *1977* (Unofficial DVD Cosmic Energy)

Thursday May 19 1977
Baton Rouge, Louisiana
State University Assembly Center

Colour cine film of the Caesars Chariot private plane they hired for this tour arriving at the airport exists alongside some excellent on stage colour cine film – clips of this was used by Page for 'The Song Remains The Same' bootleg montage extra on the official DVD.

Visual References: *Led Zeppelin* official 2003 DVD (Warner Music Vision), *1977* (Unofficial DVD CosmicEnergy)

Saturday May 21 1977
Houston, Texas
The Summit

Ticket problems plagued this show. *Creem* magazine reported that on January 30, the day tickets went on sale: "Police had to call in fire trucks to hose down the 3,000 – 3,500 Led Zeppelin fans who tried to stampede Warehouse Records & Tapes to buy tickets for the band's concert. Store officials instructed the successful buyers to hide their tickets and leave by the rear entrance of the store, to avoid having them stolen by the crowd."

Again, all was not calm on the night of the show. 'Led Zeppelin concert results in about 40 arrests by police' was the following morning' headline: "Police hauled perhaps 40 persons including 20 juveniles, to the central police station Saturday night in the wake of the Led Zeppelin concert. One officer said maintenance personnel at The Summit estimated as much as $500,000 dam

off the solo virtuosity of the individual members. An hour or more of Saturday's three hour concert was devoted to solos.

"There is no way to make twenty minute solos by Jones and Bonham interesting. There are just so many things you can do with a drum or piano. Page's solos could be made interesting, but most of the time they were so loud they put Ella Fitzgerald's Memorex test to shame.

"But of course, the wildly fanatical Led Zeppelin crowd loved it all. I believe, however, they would have applauded wildly if the group had read from a telephone book. Saturday's show is both the first and last Led Zeppelin concert I will ever go to, unless I receive combat pay."

The band employed the arena's closed circuit TV system to show the action on screen. It was rumoured that the tapes of this video have survived and were in the hands of the company that operated the video system for the building, specifically in the hands of the owner who was described as "a former professional athlete". Footage from this venue of Kiss and Crosby Stills & Nash has circulated -however no footage of Zeppelin has yet surfaced.

While in Texas, Plant and Bonham found time to visit the Mother Blues club and Bonham ended up jamming with US act Kids.

ge may have been done in the form of broken glass and other vandalism."

The show itself was not well received by the local media, and produced some of the worst reviews of the whole tour. Bob Claypool wrote: "Indeed, the song does remain the same, and that's the whole problem. Led Zeppelin hasn't changed their music, and I haven't changed my opinions about it – so we're at something of a stand-off here. And, none of the crowd activities seem to have changed, either. Going to a Zep show is still an endurance test – picking your way over passed-out people in the halls, trying to avoid flying firecrackers and smoke bombs set off by audience members, and, of course, struggling vainly to retain your hearing in the cruel onslaught of decibels.

"In a nutshell, their music is still just what it's always been – tons of over-amplified sound and fury, signifying nothing and completely lacking in subtlety (including the acoustic set). I can only hope they stay away for at least another two years!"

'Bad Company punctures Zeppelin' read one headline. Steve Thomson wrote: "Two of rock's biggest attractions, Led Zeppelin and Bad Company, came to Houston within 48 hours of each other this week providing some very observable contrasts.

"In concert, Led Zeppelin has to be one of the most boring groups in all of music. Though they have some very powerful material, the group often by-passes that to do stuff that can best show

Sunday May 22 1977
Fort Worth, Texas
Tarrant Convention Cemter

Set: The Song Remains The Same/Sick Again/Nobody's Fault But Mine/In My Time Of

Dying/Since I've Been Loving You/Nobody's Fault But Mine/In My Time Of Dying/Since I've Been Loving You/No Quarter/Ten Years Gone/Going To California/Black Country Woman-Bron Yr Aur Stomp/White Summer – Black Mountain Side/Kashmir/Moby Dick/Page Solo – Dixie – Star Spangled Banner/Achilles Last Stand/Stairway To Heaven/Whole Lotta Love – Rock And Roll/It'll Be Me.

Another wild Southern crowd witnessed tonight's unusual show.

A mix up over time signatures at the start of 'In My Time Of Dying' forced Plant to call a premature halt to the song. "I tell you what we'll do – we'll start it again," he said, a rare admission of defeat and very much in the "tight but loose" vein of proceedings.

One can only wonder what excesses were occurring offstage when Bonham was introduced as ... 'A man who only last night was standing in a wardrobe, when a fist went right through it and hit him on the nose!"

'Whole Lotta Love' made its tour début tonight, albeit in a truncated form, segued with 'Rock And Roll' as a first encore.

Mick Ralphs, of Swan Song stablemates Bad Company, joined the band on stage for the second encore. As Plant said: "It's not like us to extend the warm hand of musical friendship to anyone, but this is a man who comes from the sticks like me and Bonzo. We're gonna try something. I don't know how it'll sound – it's what they call a jam!" They then romped through the old Jerry Lee Lewis classic, 'It'll Be Me'.

Bootleg CD References: *Polished Performance 1977* (POT), *It'll Be Zep* (Silver Rarities), *Song Of The South* (Capricorn Records), *Complete Tarrant Concert* (Wendy)

Wednesday May 25 1977
Landover, Maryland
Capitol Centre
Set: The Song Remains The Same/ Sick Again/ No-body's Fault But Mine/In My Time Of Dying/Since I've Been Loving You/No Quarter/Ten Years Gone/The Battle Of Evermore/Going To California/Black Country Woman-Bron Yr Aur Stomp/White Summer - Black Mountain Side/Kashmir/Moby Dick/Page Solo – Dixie – Star Spangled Banner/Achilles Last Stand/Stairway To Heaven/Whole Lotta Love-Rock And Roll.

Bootleg CD References: *Your Teenage Dream* (The Diagrams Of Led Zeppelin), *Landover 1977* box set (Electric Magic)

Thursday May 26 1977
Landover, Maryland
Capitol Center
Set: The Song Remains The Same/Sick Again/Nobody's Fault But Mine/In My Time Of Dying/Since I've Been Loving You/No Quarter/Ten Years Gone/The Battle Of Evermore/Going To California/Dancing Days - Black Country Woman-Bron Yr Aur Stomp/White Summer – Black Mountain Side/Kashmir/Moby Dick/Page Solo-Star Spangled Banner/Achilles Last Stand/Stairway To Heaven/Whole Lotta Love – Rock And Roll.

After the unpredictable Fort Worth show the set list stabilised for a while, with only minor changes. However, tonight the band attempted a semi-acoustic version of 'Dancing Days' prior to 'Black Country Woman', an experiment that would be expanded on at the last night at of the LA Forum shows.

Bootleg CD references: *Thunderous Break* (The Diagrams of Led Zeppelin), *Bringing The House Down* (Empress Valley)

Saturday May 28 1977
Landover, Maryland
Capitol Center
Set: The Song Remains The Same/Sick Again/Nobody's Fault But Mine/In My Time Of Dying/Since I've Been Loving You/No Quarter/Ten Years Gone/The Battle Of Evermore/Going To California/Black Country

290

Woman – Bron Yr Aur Stomp/White Summer – Black Mountain Side/Kashmir/Moby Dick/Page Solo/Achilles Last Stand/Stairway To Heaven/Whole Lotta Love-Rock And Roll.
Bootleg CD References: *Landover 1977* box set (Electric Magic)

Monday May 30 1977
Landover, Maryland
Capitol Center
Set: The Song Remains The Same/Sick Again/Nobody's Fault But Mine/In My Time Of Dying/Since I've Been Loving You/No Quarter/Ten Years Gone/The Battle Of Evermore/Going To California/Black Country Woman-Bron Yr Aur Stomp/White Summer – Black Mountain Side/Kashmir/Moby Dick/Page Solo-Star Spangled Banner/Achilles Last Stand/Stairway To Heaven/Whole Lotta Love-Rock And Roll/Trampled Underfoot.

Peter Grant recalled: "I was invited to dinner at the Russian Embassy and all the guests came to the gig. I think it was in Landover. They really knew their stuff. I was in the limo with one of the wives and she says 'What's the sound like for your group?' and I say 'Very good' and she adds that when they saw the Stones last year there was no bottom to their sound because all the amps were hung. Amazing. So then they met with the band beforehand and during the gig, instead of watching in the box they all want to sit on the side of the stage. Jonesy then plays variations from

Rachmaninov during 'No Quarter' and the Russian guests are just blown away. We planned to go to Russia but after Robert's tragedy we had to scrap it. Shame, as we could have been one of the first rock acts to go."

The band again deployed the arena closed circuit TV system to beam the concert on screen. However no footage of this gig has ever surfaced.
Bootleg CD References: *Destroyer III* (Tarantura), *Running On Pure Heart And Soul* (Diagrams Of Led Zeppelin), *Landover 1977* box set (Electric Magic), *The Supreme Destroyers* (Empress Valley)

Tuesday May 31 1977
Greensboro, North Carolina
Coliseum
Set: The Song Remains The Same/Sick Again/Nobody's Fault But Mine/In My Time Of Dying/Since I've Been Loving You/No Quarter/Ten Years Gone/The Battle Of Evermore/Going To California/Black Country Woman – Bron Yr Aur Stomp/White Summer – Black Mountain Side/Kashmir/Moby Dick/Page Solo/Achilles Last Stand/Stairway To Heaven/Whole Lotta Love-Rock And Roll.

Creem magazine reported: "In New York, rumours of a Led Zeppelin tour scheduled for Fall of 1979, spanning 30 cities in 28 days, has sparked off an unprecedented appeal for ticket information. Unhappy fans, when told that tickets were not yet available, resorted to sending plastic explosives to Ticketron offices across the USA."

The report was pure speculation.

Friday June 3 1977
Tampa Florida
Tampa Stadium
Set: The Song Remains The Same/ Sick Again/Nobody's Fault But Mine .

A disastrous event, both before and on the night, as *New Musical Express* reported: "Five hundred to 1,000 Led Zeppelin fans waiting in line to buy tickets, broke through the gates and began vandalising the Orange Bowl Stadium. Police had to use tear gas to break up that mêlée, and 16 policemen were injured as a result."

The *Miami Herald* ran the headline 'Black Sunday for Real at the Orange Bowl – Last time a Blimp, Now the Zeppelin'. The regular violent scenes at ticket outlets were both frustrating and upsetting for the band.

Plant: "I see a lot of craziness around us. Somehow, we generate it and we revile it. What we are trying to put across is positive and wholesome and people react in such an excitable manner that they miss the meaning of it, and that makes me lose my calm."

Robert's calm would again be shattered at the show itself. During the third number of the set, the skies opened and a thunderstorm erupted. The band were forced to leave the open-air stage for fear of electrocution. After a delay it was obvious that the rain would not stop, so a decision was made to reschedule the show on the next day (the "rain" day). However, the tickets clearly stated that they are 'Good This Date Only – Rain Or Shine'. Amid the confusion a section of the crowd rioted, barricades were broken, and 35 fans and six policemen were injured .

As a result, the local authorities banned Zeppelin from returning for a rescheduled show, a sad state of affairs in one of Zeppelin's favourite stomping grounds.

Peter Grant recalled the incident: "A big mistake. Possibly one of our biggest, and all because we never realised there should have been a rain date! It wasn't until we were on the plane flying from Miami to the gig that Richard (Cole) shows me the ticket which says on it 'come rain or shine' i.e. no rain date. I storm off to blast Terry Bassett from Concerts West. Steve Weiss, our lawyer should have caught it in the contract. I should have sent Richard out to check the place but he'd been sorting out some trip for Robert and Jonesy to visit Disneyland with the kids. All sorts of trouble. If Richard had gone, he'd have seen that they'd set up a canvas roof instead of a metal one which we always demanded. So when we get to the site there's something like 10,000 tons of water resting over the drums. So now I have to make a decision about them going on. You can't imagine the pressure. When they're about to go on, the rain has stopped. There's 70,000 fans gathered and we've got to get it on somehow. So I decided to let them start. Nearby overhead there's this big cloud looming. I thought at this rate it will be us who'll be leaving under a big black cloud and sure enough, after three numbers, it starts pouring. I quickly action to Robert to wind it up and off we run. One funny aside to this is Robert telling me later that as he's coming offstage, my son Warren shouts to Robert to pick up a Frisbee he's thrown on. As you can imagine, Robert told him in no uncertain terms to leave it there!"

The next day, the *New York Post* ran the front page headline '50 INJURED IN FLA. ROCK RIOT 19 arrested as Led Zeppelin is rained out' and reported that "4,000 people swarmed all over the stadium floor and stormed the barricade in front of the stage, chanting, 'We want Led Zeppelin'." Witnesses said tension had already been building up because of some drug arrests and a large contingent of police in riot gear also riled nerves by standing guard at highly visible points in the Amphitheatre.

"As police herded the rioters towards the exits, an announcement was made over the stadium's loudspeaker that the concert was rescheduled, but the message was garbled and failed to end the disorders. At 11 PM scattered violence continued a

two hospitals and outside a police station where youngsters gathered to protest the arrest of their friends."

Many other New York newspapers ran similar stories: 'Zeppelin Rainout Triggers Fan Riot', 'Thunderstorm, stormy fans end concert', 'Rain Grounds Led Zeppelin And Stirs Tampa Rumpus', '20 face charges in Fla. Led Zeppelin concert riot'.

New York was obviously very wary of the erratic harbinger of violence that would dominate their city for the next six shows. 'Boost Security For Rock Show' was the headline, "Led Zeppelin's Madison Square Garden engagement will be monitored by a force of security guards and city cops to prevent the riots that have marred other stops on the group's tour. Officials said the garden's 100-man security force will be bolstered by squads of cops and mounted patrols and that barriers will be erected around the building for crowd control."

Bootleg CD References: *Fucking T.Y.* (Tattytura), *Polished Performance 1977* (POT), *Killer Missile* (Flagge)

Tuesday June 7 1977
New York, New York
Madison Square Garden

Set: The Song Remains The Same/Sick Again/Nobody's Fault But Mine/In My Time Of Dying/Since I've Been Loving You/No Quarter/Ten Years Gone/The Battle Of Evermore/Going To California/Black Country Woman-Bron Yr Aur Stomp/White Summer – Black Mountain Side/Kashmir/Moby Dick/Page Solo (inc. Star Spangled Banner)/Achilles Last Stand/Stairway To Heaven/Whole Lotta Love-Rock And Roll.

After the disappointment of Tampa, the band were refreshed and ready for a marathon six-night residency in New York (enough ticket applications were received to sell out a further two nights, had time permitted). For this opening

night the band flew in their wives and children to see the show (they had earlier been brought in to see Disneyland and the ill-fated Tampa show).

The Garden was a battlefield. Explosions and firecrackers on a massive scale heralded their return to the Big Apple. In fact, *Melody Maker* refers to these shows, rather appropriately, as "The Six Day War". The band rose to the occasion and even dedicated 'In My Time Of Dying' to the Queen.

Plant: "Tonight is the beginning of the celebration of Queen Elizabeth II's Silver Jubilee, and that's a heavy thing for us, so we'll do this one for Liz!"

'In My Time Of Dying' now also featured snatches of 'You Shook Me' on the closing bars.

'Zeppelin: jetstream' was the headline of the *New York Daily News*. "With the sound like a 747 on takeoff, Led Zeppelin took over the Garden. No doubt about it, the Zeppelin are LOUD. Frequently so loud that you can't hear the music. There are so many pieces of equipment on stage that sometimes a listener has the feeling that they have amplifiers to amplify the amplifiers."

Demand for Zeppelin was so high that the black market thrived. 'Led is golden – Garden Concert A Smash'. Lou O'Neill Jr wrote: "The scene outside Madison Square Garden last night reminded onlookers of a real-live version of Ali Baba and the 40 thieves. Scalpers were everywhere and were having a field day hawking seats for sky-high prices. On several occasions we witnessed the highly valued brown tickets change hands for a steady $125 a pair.

"Beside the scalpers, every conceivable type of ware associated with Led Zeppelin was on sale. There were Zep T-shirts, posters, buttons, belt buckles and programs all available for ready cash. Business was conducted at a frantic pace and one

293

Led Zeppelin

T-shirt barker, just into town from Tampa, claimed it was possible to make a $200 profit per night strictly on T-shirts."

Not all reviews were complimentary, however. Mitchell Schneider wrote: "Ever step in a pile of turd and couldn't get it off your shoe, no matter how hard you scraped it against the cement, no matter how much you wished it would just go away? About the only thing you could do was search for a nearby puddle of water. Unfortunately, at the first of Zep's six shows at the Garden, there were no such puddles to remove the group's excrement, which goes under the name of heavy-metal.

"Robert Plant screeches as though he's got a fist lodged up his rear-end. And Jimmy Page: well, the guy's a great guitarist, everybody knows, yet tonight he was sloppy, and his hesitation rhythms were convoluted.

"Still, with a rock audience that never fails to confuse loudness for power and quantity for quality, the lumbering blimp can always reign supreme."

The *New York Post* also revealed that the band were not doing any sound checks on the tour ("Page feels any hall sounds measurably different once it's filled with concertgoers"); that Faye Dunaway was playing amateur photographer for the night; and that after the show John Paul Jones and his wife went partying with Dave Edmunds, Robert went to the Nirvana Indian restaurant, Jimmy Page sat down with a copy of *Newsweek* and Bonzo went straight to bed.

Bootleg CD References: *Back To The Garden* (Diagrams of Led Zep), *Mad Dogs Box* (Mad Dog)

Wednesday June 8 1977
New York, New York
Madison Square Garden

Set: The Song Remains The Same/Sick Again/Nobody's Fault But Mine/In My Time Of Dying/Since I've Been Loving You/No Quarter/Ten Years Gone/The Battle Of Evermore/Going To California/Black Country Woman – Bron Yr Aur Stomp/White Summer – Black Mountain Side/Kashmir/Moby Dick/Page Solo/Achilles Last Stand/Stairway To Heaven/Whole Lotta Love-Rock And Roll.

Peter Grant recalled: "One clear and very positive memory of '77 was when I realised just how much it had all come to mean. We announced the New York dates via Scott Muni's radio show. Whoosh! All tickets gone! The tariff for that Madison stint showed our advertising reading nil. It was the demand from the street and the fans that astounded me. There was no hype, no MTV or anything. It was pure demand. At that point I really did wonder how much bigger this all could get. From those humble beginnings in '69 to this in the space of seven years was just astounding."

Bootleg CD Reference: *Second Night In The Garden* (Diagrams Of Led Zeppelin)

Friday June 10 1977
New York, New York
Madison Square Garden

Set: The Song Remains The Same/Sick Again/Nobody's Fault But Mine/Over The Hills And Far Away/Since I've Been Loving You/No Quarter/Ten Years Gone/The Battle Of Evermore/Going To California/Black Country Woman – Bron Yr Aur Stomp/White Summer – Black Mountain Side/Kashmir/Moby Dick/Heartbreaker/Page Solo – Star Spangled Banner/Achilles Last Stand/Stairway To Heaven/Whole Lotta Love – Rock And Roll.

Some significant changes were made to the set for the third night in New York. 'In

My Time Of Dying' was dropped and replaced with 'Over The Hills And Far Away'. These two numbers would now alternate with each other for the rest of the tour, neither being played at the same gig. 'Heartbreaker' was also added, following John Bonham's solo.

'No Quarter' was used as a vehicle for improvisation between Page and Jones and was growing longer each evening. Plant: "Jimmy's solo tonight in 'No Quarter' was just fantastic, very well-constructed in such a manner, different from before, so that I can't help but respond differently to that."

Bonham's solo had now become an awesome spectacle of showmanship.

Roy Coleman in *Melody Maker* reported: "John Bonham is a titanic engine for the band, the appropriate personification of tastelessness, surrounded by a battery of tom toms, an artillery of drums and a gigantic gong, springing to life during his solo which brings him forward to the stage front on a moving platform, amid blinding lights, flames, dry ice and pandemonium from an elated crowd."

Page's performance also impressed Coleman in *Melody Maker*: "Page prowls the stage in a white silk suit and lopes between Plant and his amplifiers, with an undimmed reservoir of energy. His theatrical gestures of the rock guitarist do not rely on facial grimaces or stupid contortions but are patented and original."

Bootleg CD References: *Rock'n'Roll Circus* (Diagrams of Led Zep), *Riot In Thunderstorrm* (Electric Magic)

Saturday June 11 1977
New York, New York
Madison Square Garden
Set: The Song Remains The Same/Sick Again/Nobody's Fault But Mine/ Over The Hills And Far Away /Since I've Been Loving You/No Quarter/Ten Years Gone/ The Battle Of Evermore/Going To California/Black Country Woman – Bron Yr Aur Stomp/White Summer – Black Mountain Side/Kashmir/Moby Dick/

Heartbreaker/age Solo/Achilles Last Stand/ Stairway To Heaven/Whole Lotta Love – Rock And Roll.

Lisa Robinson reported that, while in New York: "Zep hung out in Trax – a local cellar disco – after the shows. In the same club, on a regular basis, were Keith Richard, Ron Wood and members of Kiss and Aerosmith – both in town recording.

"Robert Plant played soccer in Central Park and bought a Pink Lincoln Mark IV with red interiors (to be shipped back to England). John Paul Jones shopped in the Rizzoli bookstore, Jimmy Page visited The Rolling Stones at Atlantic Studios, and John Bonham stayed in the room a lot and watched TV."

Bootleg CD References: *Eat The Biggest Apple* (No label), *Coast To Coast* (Celebration), *Thunderstorm* (Electric Magic)

Monday June 13 1977
New York, New York
Madison Square Garden
Set: The Song Remains The Same/Sick Again/Nobody's Fault But Mine/Over The Hills And Far Away/Since I've Been Loving You/No Quarter/Ten Years Gone/Battle Of Evermore/Going To California/Black Country Woman – Bron Yr Aur Stomp/White Summer – Black Mountain Side/Kashmir/Moby Dick/Heartbreaker/Page Solo – Star Spangled Banner/Achilles Last Stand/Stairway To Heaven/Whole Lotta Love – Black Dog.

The penultimate night in New York saw them pull out a set list variation. For the encore, 'Black Dog' was segued with 'Whole Lotta Love' in a similar fashion to the 1975 tour.

Bootleg CD Reference: *Over The Garden* (The Diagrams Of Led Zeppelin)

Tuesday June 14 1977
New York, New York
Madison Square Garden
Set includes: The Song Remains The Same/Sick Again/Nobody's Fault But Mine/Over The Hills

And Far Away/Since I've Been Loving You/No Quarter/Ten Years Gone/The Battle Of Evermore/Going To California/White Summer – Black Mountain Side/Kashmir/Moby Dick /Page Solo/Achilles Last Stand/Stairway To Heaven/Whole Lotta Love – Rock And Roll.

Robert Plant: "The nights at the Garden turned out to be more exhilarating than I expected. But to be quite honest, I don't really like to keep returning to the same place. I thrive on perpetual motion, a new town, another time, another watch."

Five minutes of silent colour cine film exists from this show – clips of this were used by Page for *The Song Remains The Same* bootleg montage extra on the official DVD.

Another hour of various 8mm home movie footage exists from the New York shows alongside footage of all four band members filmed outside the Drake Hotel.

Bootleg CD Reference: *Strange Tales From The Road* (The Diagrams Of Led Zeppelin)

Visual References: *Led Zeppelin* official 2003 DVD (Warner Music), *1977* (Unofficial DVD CosmicEnergy)

Sunday June 19 1977
San Diego, California
Sports Arena

Set: The Song Remains The Same/Sick Again/Nobody's Fault But Mine/In My Time Of Dying/Since I've Been Loving You/No Quarter/Ten Years Gone/The Battle Of Evermore/Going To California/Mystery Train – Black Country Woman – Bron Yr Aur Stomp/White Summer – Black Mountain Side/

Kashmir/Page Solo – Star Spangled Banner-Dixie/Achilles Last Stand/Stairway To Heaven/Whole Lotta Love – Rock And Roll.

The band's first show on the West Coast found them in poor physical health. Plant told the audience that Jones was unwell: "He's got trouble with his back. He's been lying in bed all day. It's about time he had some sordid press. It should be noted that he doesn't just play backgammon!"

Although not referred to on stage, Bonzo was also having problems. Mistakes abounded in his performance and there was no drum solo. Despite all this, the performance was commendable and they even threw in Elvis's 'Mystery Train' during the acoustic set.

Bootleg CD References: *California Mystery Train* (Silver Rarities), *Mystery Train* (Badgeholders), *California Mystery Train* (Silver Rarities)

JUNE 21·23, 25·27
★★★ good seats available all shows ! ★★★
LED 278·6281 – 278·7638
9060 SANTA MONICA BLVD.
ZEPPELIN
THE ONLY ROCK GROUP IN HISTORY TO SELL OUT 80 SHOWS AT THE FABULOUS FORUM

Tuesday June 21 1977
Inglewood Los Angeles, California
The Forum

Set: The Song Remains The Same/Sick Again/Nobody's Fault But Mine/Over The Hills And Far Away/Since I've Been Loving You/No Quarter/Ten Years Gone/The Battle Of Evermore/Going To California/Black Country Woman – Bron Yr Aur Stomp/White Summer – Black Mountain Side/Kashmir/Moby Dick/

Heartbreaker/Page Solo – Star Spangled Banner – Dixie/Achilles Last Stand/Stairway To Heaven/Whole Lotta Love – Rock And Roll.

The first night of another six-show marathon, this time in Los Angeles, the sprawling city that was often described as Led Zeppelin's spiritual home. Posters for the event boasted 'The Only Rock Group In History To Sell Out 6 Shows At The Fabulous Forum!' In New York and Los Angeles alone, Zeppelin sold 240,000 tickets.

Bonzo's playing was impeccable throughout this show, as if he was trying extra hard to make up for his below par performance in San Diego. He was described by Pant as: "The man who fought food poisoning and drunk Heineken." The whole band was hot tonight. They were obviously enjoying being in the sun again. "It's very hard to see the sun in a basement in New York."

This was a landmark performance, famously captured on a superb audience recording issued on the bootleg set *Listen To This Eddie*. The title was allegedly a reference to Eddie Van Halen who, in interviews, was none too complimentary on Jimmy's playing ability. There are also claims that it's a reference to their recording engineer Eddie Kramer. Such is the clarity of this recording, Page even deployed the audio track of 'The Song Remains The Same' from this tape for the menu clip of 1977 cine footage on the official DVD.

Robert Hilburn of the *Los Angeles Times* reported on the show: "Most of the 18,700 persons were already in their seats when the seven limousines carrying Led Zeppelin and their entourage sped into the Inglewood Forum's tunnel entrance just before 8pm.

"But Loretta Villegas, 15, was among several hundred fans who had stayed outside the Forum to view the group's arrival. Loretta's seats were in the next-to-last row so the tunnel railing would be the closest to Zeppelin they'd be all night. The problem was, the cars had been pulling into the tunnel so fast that it was hard to tell anything about the people in them. When a police escort signalled Zeppelin's arrival, she began clicking her Instamatic furiously. Since no one exited until the seven cars were well beyond the girl's view, there was no chance for a picture of the band. But somewhere in the batch of 20 photos, Loretta would have a shot of the car that carried the band to the concert. That'd be more to show friends than just the ticket stub the other 110,000 fans who'll see Zeppelin during its unprecedented six-day Forum stand will have. With a little luck, Loretta might even find out from the guards the right car."

Bootleg CD References: *Listen To This Eddie* (Silver Rarities), *Listen To This Eddie* (Empress Valley), *Listen To This Eddie – Definitive Complete Version* (Jelly Roll), *Listen To This Eddie* (Wendy Records), *Listen To This Eddie* (Tarantura)

Wednesday June 22 1977
Inglewood Los Angeles, California
The Forum

Set: The Song Remains The Same/Sick Again/Nobody's Fault But Mine/In My Time Of Dying/Since I've Been Loving You/No Quarter/Ten Years Gone/The Battle Of Ever-

more/Going To California/Black Country Woman – Bron Yr Aur Stomp/White Summer – Black Mountain Side/Kashmir/Moby Dick/Page Solo – Star Spangled Banner/Achilles Last Stand/Stairway To Heaven/Whole Lotta Love – Rock And Roll.

Ten minutes of cine footage exists from this show

Bootleg CD Reference: *One Day After Eddie* (Immigrant)

Visual Reference: *1977* (Unofficial DVD Cosmic Energy)

Thursday June 23 1977
Inglewood Los Angeles, California
The Forum

Set: The Song Remains The Same/Sick Again/Nobody's Fault But Mine/Over The Hills And Far Away/Since I've Been Loving You/No Quarter/Ten Years Gone/The Battle Of Evermore/Going To California/Black Country Woman – Bron Yr Aur Stomp/White Summer – Black Mountain Side/Kashmir/Trampled Underfoot/Moby Dick/Page Solo – Star Spangled Banner/Achilles Last Stand/Stairway To Heaven/Whole Lotta Love – Rock And Roll.

"Good Evening. Welcome to three hours of lunacy." Plant wasnt joking.

Another truly outstanding show, again captured on the excellent bootleg – *For Badge Holders Only*. Plant dedicated songs all evening to various "Badge Holders".

'Trampled Underfoot' made a surprise return to the set (they hadn't played it for nearly a month), and Keith Moon of The Who ambled onto the stage during Bonham's solo and joined Bonzo on a drum duet – sharing the same kit. Moon also returned for the encores, lectured the audience on rock and roll and attempted to sing 'C'mon Everybody' before Plant finally reclaimed the mike. "LA. It's been very funny. Good night!"

'Keith Moon jams with Zeppelin'. Harvey Kubernik reported: "Led Zeppelin have been very well received in Los Angeles. The three and a half hour set has yielded some uneven media response but the paying public's applause has broken some eardrums. On Thursday night Keith Moon joined John Bonham at the drums and later announced:

THE TAPER – MIKE MILLARD

The superb audience recordings of the 1977 Los Angles concerts on June 21, 23, 25 and 27 featured on a variety of bootleg CDs were the work of local taper Mike Millard.

Millard taped many of the bands who came to the area including Pink Floyd, The Who, Yes, The Rolling Stones and Jethro Tull. Alongside the LA 1977 shows he also taped the Zeppelin's March 11/12 1975 shows in Long Beach, the March 24/25/27 shows at The Forum in 1975 and the San Diego June 19 1977 show.

Millard used a wheelchair as a prop to secure the best positions at shows. His taping equipment comprised a Nakamichi stereo cassette deck and AGK microphones. Millard hated bootleg companies and never willingly gave access to any of his tapes to be used. However the tapes he traded did find there way into the hands of various bootleg labels and were used for the vinyl bootlegs *For Badgeholders Only Vols 1 and 2* and *Listen To This Eddie* in the early Eighties. Sadly Mike suffered from depression and allegedly committed suicide in 1990. It is claimed that he destroyed some of his Led Zeppelin masters, though it is believed his family have possession of a bulk of the tapes he recorded of Led Zeppelin and countless other bands.

In 2003 Mike Millard's legacy as the most famous of all concert tapers was confirmed when Jimmy Page himself employed Millard's June 21 LA audience recording of 'The Song Remains The Same' for the audio track of 1977 cine film used as a menu on the official DVD

'I'll be back at the Forum later in the year with my back-up group'.

"A very healthy looking Jimmy Page earned the majority of the crowd's plaudits for some superb guitar playing. Following the performance, a reception was held for the band at a Stone Canyon residence. In attendance were Rod Stewart, Bernie Taupin, Dave Clark, Henry Edwards, Dennis Wilson, Swan Song's Detective, Karen Freeman, Keith Moon and Rodney Bingenheimer.

"'LA has always been our city,' offered Plant. 'We've drawn a lot of inspiration from this town.'"

Twelve minutes of cine footage exists from this show including footage of Keith Moon

Bootleg CD References: *For Budge Holders Only* (Cobra Standard), *Sgt. Jimmy* (Tarantura), *For Badgeholders Only* (Tarantura), *For Badgeholders Only* (Arms)

Visual Reference: *1977* (Unofficial DVD Cosmic Energy)

Saturday June 25 1977
Inglewood Los Angeles, California
The Forum
Set: The Song Remains The Same/Sick Again/Nobody's Fault But Mine/In My Time Of Dying-Rip It Up/Since I've Been Loving You/No Quarter/Ten Years Gone/The Battle Of Evermore/Going To California/Black Country Woman – Bron Yr Aur Stomp/White Summer – Black Mountain Side/Kashmir/Trampled Underfoot/Moby Dick/Page Solo – Dixie – Star Spangled Banner/Achilles Last Stand/Stairway To Heaven/Whole Lotta Love – Communication Breakdown.

The Los Angeles run continued to delight. Robert informed the audience that tonight they're celebrating "The Annual General Meeting of all the LA Badge Holders" and the party continued from the previous concert.

It was Saturday night, and appropriately Plant led them into an impromptu version of Little Richard's 'Rip It Up'. 'Whole Lotta Love' also segued into a riotous version of 'Communication

Breakdown' – the only performance of the tour.

Bootleg CD References: *The Battle Of Evermore Pt1 & Pt2* (Black Cat), *Last LA Forum 6/25//77 Budge Holders* (The Live Experience), *Delirium Tremens* (Tarantura)

Sunday June 26 1977
Inglewood Los Angeles, California
The Forum
Set: The Song Remains The Same/Sick Again/Nobody's Fault But Mine/Over The Hills And Far Away/Since I've Been Loving You/No Quarter/Ten Years Gone/The Battle Of Evermore/Going To California/That's All Right Mama -Black Country Woman-Bron Yr Aur Stomp/White Summer – Black Mountain Side/Kashmir/Moby Dick/Page Solo – Take The High Road/Achilles Last Stand/Stairway To Heaven/It'll Be Me.

The fifth night brought more set variation. Elvis's 'That's Alright Mama' was featured in the acoustic set and Page played 'Take The High Road', the traditional Scottish ballad, during his solo. 'It'll Be Me' was a rare encore and was introduced by Plant as … "Something from the new album"

Some 14 minutes of cine film exists from this show

Bootleg CD References: *That's Alright* (Tarantura), *Sundazed* (Silver Rarities)

Visual Reference: *1977* (Unoffcial DVD Cosmic Energy)

Monday June 27 1977
Inglewood Los Angeles, California
The Forum
Set: The Song Remains The Same/Sick Again/Nobody's Fault But Mine/Over The Hills And Far Away/Since I've Been Loving You/No Quarter/Ten Years Gone/The Battle Of Evermore/Going To California/Just Can't Be Satisfied – Black Country Woman-Bron Yr Aur Stomp – Dancing Days/White Summer – Black Mountain Side/Kashmir/Trampled Underfoot/Moby Dick/Page Solo – America –

Star Spangled Banner/Achilles Last Stand/Stairway To Heaven/Whole Lotta Love – Rock And Roll.

The final night in LA and the end of the middle leg of the tour. By now the show was over three and a half hours duration.

Tonight the acoustic set was extended to include 'Just Can't Be Satisfied' and 'Dancing Days'. Page's solo improvisation included Leonard Bernstein's 'America' from *West Side Story*.

In 1995 a Japanese 19-CD bootleg box set surfaced featuring recordings of all six of the LA Forum shows. *Yakuziï* was beautifully packaged but limited to only 150 copies and is a much sought after collectors item.

The Forum venue was purchased by the Faithful Central Bible Church in 2000.

Bootleg CD References: The Legend Of The End (Tarantura), The legendary End (Silver Raritites)

Sunday July 17 1977
Seattle Washington Kingdome

Set: The Song Remains The Same/Sick Again/ Nobody's Fault But Mine/Over The Hills And Far Away/Since I've Been Loving You/No Quarter/Ten Years Gone/The Battle Of Evermore/Going To California/Black Country Woman – Bron Yr Aur Stomp/White Summer – Black Mountain Side/Kashmir/Moby Dick/Page Solo/Achilles Last Stand/Stairway To Heaven/Whole Lotta Love – Rock And Roll.

This venue was built in 1976 and demolished in 2000. This was the first rock concert to be staged there.

The first show of the final leg opened with a fairly lacklustre performance. The band seemed not to have benefited from the three week break. Plant's voice was weak and all was not well with Page. Plant: "I've gone deaf in one ear and Jimmy's got a touch of sleeping sickness!"

True to form, monitor problems again plagued the acoustic set and Plant had to reprimand the audience about firecrackers. "I think it's the lousiest thing to do to throw firecrackers. We just wanna play acoustic without getting a heart attack."

Page broke a string during 'Bron Yr Aur Stomp' and Jones filled in with a lengthy impromptu jazz solo on the bass. "At least we know we can play in the hotel bar afterwards."

'Zeppelin conquers Dome' reported Patrick MacDonald: "For the first time since Wings, a rock show felt right in the Kingdome last night – but only because it was Led Zeppelin, the biggest band of them all.

"The sound was still pretty bad but that didn't matter much, because Zeppelin isn't the kind of band that requires careful listening most of the time. The rock they belt out is meant to jar your whole body, so the Dome's echo and reverberations hardly mattered. They almost seemed part of the show.

"Visually, the show offered an extra-large TV screen with good close-up coverage and clever replays. Laser beams were used a couple of times, but not nearly as effectively as they could have been.

"Hundreds milled around during the show and many were probably unhappy with their seats and the sound, but for an evening of good, loud, crude, raunchy rock, you couldn't have done better. It turned out to be one of the best rock shows of summer."

'Led Zep *vs.* The Dome Acoustics' reported the

Seattle Post-Intelligencer. George Arthur wrote: "Plant's attitude (which offstage might be called arrogant) and the power of Zeppelin's regal music promised a tight battle for supremacy between the band and the dome. Although the final bell hadn't sounded at press time last night, odds were the morning after talk would be about the Led Zeppelin concert and not the Kingdome spectacle."

'Led Zep Fill Dome' – "It was a mixed crowd coming to see the heavy metal group whose tours have been marked by violence. Heavy metal means the noise can blast you out of your socks at 100 paces. Plant had promised that the 1977 tour would be 'blood, thunder and the hammer of God'. A squad of paramedics was geared up for the blood and everybody else was geared up for the thunder and hammer part.

"By 7.15 pm, 22 paramedics from the Seattle Fire Department already had treated more than 50 patients. About 200 off-duty Seattle and King County police were on hand.

"The concert tickets originally sold for $10, but when some people saw the line to get in, they decided to give the tickets away for free."

Hugh Jones, editor of *Proximity* recalled: "Seattle was a town Zeppelin particularly enjoyed playing in, and was the site of at least two of the band's all-time legendary gigs (June 72 and March 75), thus the anticipation for their 1977 return was especially keen. As the day of the show approached, media coverage increased, both on the band themselves and their reputation for drawing problematic crowds, and by July 16, it seemed everyone in town was holding their breath as people started showing up in front of the Kingdome with their sleeping bags, lawn chairs and coolers.

"Led Zeppelin as a live band were prone to extremes. Either you got a super-charged, special performance or a lacklustre, excessive affair with sub-standard individual performances. Rarely did they put on a simply average concert, but this was the case at the Kingdome. The band just never really took off.

"When it was over, 65,000 people shuffled out of the stadium with their ears ringing, and the general reaction around town over the next few days was one of disappointment."

The whole of this show was videotaped via the venue closed circuit TV system and shown on screen. Peter Grant retained these tapes and took them back to the UK. However, at least the last half hour of the concert was allegedly copied by an employee of the venue who in turn gave it to a major Zep collector. This portion of the concert began circulating amongst collectors, initially as an audio tape and then video in the mid-Nineties.

The original video tape from this Seattle show was subsequently stored in Page's archives and years later excerpts from it were used for the 'Over The Hills And Far Away' promo video to promote the *Remasters* set, and also on MTV's *Whole Lotta Led* weekend 'Rockumentary' special screened December 8/9 1990.

Eventually the whole concert began to circulate and it finally appeared on a bootleg DVD in 2003. Page did revisit the footage for possible use on the official DVD but decided the quality and sound was not good enough for official release.

Bootleg CD References: *Kingdome Of Zep* (Silver Rarities), *Year Of The Dragon* (Empress Valley)
Visual Reference: *Heavy Metal* (Celebration), (Cosmic Energy)

Wednesday July 20 1977

Tempe, Arizona
A.S.U. Activities Center Arena

Set : The Song Remains The Same/Sick Again/Nobody's Fault But Mine/Over The Hills And Far Away/Since I've Been Loving You/No Quarter/Ten Years Gone/Battle Of Evermore/Going To California/Black Country Woman – Bron Yr Aur Stomp/Trampled Underfoot/Black Mountain Side/Kashmir/Page Solo/Achilles Last Stand/Stairway To Heaven..

The most bizarre performance of the tour. Jimmy didn't even bother with 'White Summer' and launched into 'Kashmir' after only a few bars of 'Black Mountain Side'. Surprised, the rest of the band joined in one by one. There were no encores.

Fan Ed Ortiz recalled:'' The show was due to start at 8pm but didn't start until nearer 9pm. Jimmy wore the black dragon suit trousers plus a white t-shirt and a white scarf for the first two numbers. He was not very animated, choosing to stand perfectly still for most of the show near Bonzo's drum riser. He seemed rather out of it and forgot to step on his guitar effect for 'Over The Hills' with Robert actually doing it for him. Things got stranger as it went on. Jimmy chose not to do 'White Summer' and instead went into 'Kashmir' after a few bars of 'Black Mountain Side'.

"There was no Bonzo solo and a pyrotechnic miscue went off after the opening bars of 'Achilles'. A loud explosion with a blinding white light. You could see Jimmy going over to the side of the stage and raising his fist presumably to a roadie. After the number, Robert announced the explosion was not meant to happen at the person responsible would be 'castrated'! Bonzo seemed to be in a hurry to get the gig over and he was off his drum stool and gone before Robert finished the last lyric of Stairway – so hence no cymbal tapping at the end.

"Over all it was a very uneven performance I was a bit disappointed but never the less happy that I'd got to see them and being only 75 feet from the stage it was a close encounter.''

HP Newquist from *Guitarist* magazine recalled: "The band cut the set short, eliminating Bonzo's drum solo entirely. Page also stood too close to the flashpots on 'Achilles' and was thrown back against the stage. At a brief meeting with Plant the next day he stated that Bonham had not been feeling well and his hand had been hurting."

Saturday July 23 1977

Oakland, California
Alameda County Coliseum

Set: The Song Remains The Same/Sick Again/Nobody's Fault But Mine/Over The Hills And Far Away/Since I've Been Loving You/No Quarter/Ten Years Gone/The Battle Of Evermore/Going To California/Black Country Woman – Bron Yr Aur Stomp/Trampled Underfoot/White Summer – Black Mountain Side/Kashmir/Page Solo/Achilles Last Stand/Stairway To Heaven/Whole Lotta Love – Rock And Roll/Black Dog.

Support from Judas Priest and Rick Derringer

For this date Plant wore a t-shirt with the slogan Nurses Do It Better! Page was back in the black dragon suit. These memorable images and shots of the remarkable stage set up can be seen via Dennis Callaghan and Michael Zagaris' photos in the book *The Photographers Led Zeppelin* (compiled by Ross Halfin).

"Good Afternoon. So this is what they call day light!"

The Oakland concerts were large outdoor after noon shows. A huge backdrop had been especial ly constructed featuring the Stonehenge design later to be lampooned in the rock spoof movie *This Is Spinal Tap*.

The concert itself was a strong performance and evidence that problems that plagued the other

July shows had been ironed out. They even threw in a rare second encore of 'Black Dog'.

However, backstage events would vastly overshadow events on stage. There was friction between Zeppelin's crew and employees of Bill Graham. The *San Francisco Chronicle* reported: "After the conclusion of the concert at 5.55pm, stagehand Jim Downey was assaulted over an imagined slight, and had his head banged against a concrete wall. Graham security man James Matzorkis refused the request of Grant's son for a sign affixed to a trailer. Matzorkis was kicked in the genitals, although not by Grant. Production Manager Bob Barsotti was struck in the head by a pipe. Finally, Matzorkis was cornered in Graham's trailer, Graham was ejected and Matzorkis was beaten."

Page was shocked by media reports: "I wasn't here, but I do know that it was nothing really heavy. Certainly nothing heavier than I'd witnessed out front during the concert."

Peter Grant recalled: "It could have got a lot worse. It was just a very regrettable incident. But we were up against Bill Graham's security guys with their gloves filled with sand. We didn't want to get into that. There were wives and children with us."

This incident prompted Bill Graham to state: "I could never in good conscience book them again."

Promoter Graham had previously enjoyed an excellent working relationship with Grant. Allegedly, he'd secured the Oakland dates by arranging a lunch for two in the deserted stadium for him and Grant – knowing of the latter's liking

for good food.

In February 1978, through their lawyers, John Bonham, Peter Grant, Richard Cole and John Bindon pleaded *nolo contendere* to the assault charges arising from the Oakland brawl. All four were found guilty and given fines and suspended sentences. Since they were not required to appear in Court, the civil suits against them were never heard. Bill Graham was furious with the apparently lenient sentences. "So they'll never learn!" was his comment at the time.

Twelve minutes of cine footage exists from this show

Bootleg CD Reference: *Confusion* (No label)
Visual Reference: *1977* (Unofficial DVD Cosmic Energy)

Sunday July 24 1977
Oakland, California
Alameda County Coliseum

Set: The Song Remains The Same/Sick Again/Nobody's Fault But Mine/Over The Hills And Far Away/Since I've Been Loving You/No Quarter/Ten Years Gone/The Battle Of Evermore/Going To California/Mystery Train – Black Country Woman – Bron Yr Aur Stomp/Trampled Underfoot/White Summer – Black Mountain Side/Kashmir/Page Solo/Achilles Last Stand/Stairway To Heaven/Whole Lotta Love – Rock And Roll.

Support from Judas Priest and Rick Derringer.

For this date Page was back in the jackboots as worn in Chicago. During 'No Quarter', a local dancer Betty made her way onto the stage. She danced with Plant and eventually ended up on Bonzo's shoulders. Photos of this taken by Dennis Callaghan and Michael Zagaris can be seen in the book *The Photographers Led Zeppelin*.

The band took the stage 90 minutes late for the second Oakland show. It was reported that they would not leave their hotel until Graham signed a waiver claiming a maximum of $2,000 damages in respect of the events of yesterday.

Whatever deals were going on behind the scenes, the band staged a professional performance, featuring 'Mystery Train' in the acoustic set. Plant even thanked Bill Graham from the stage for putting on such a spectacle.

As they were ushered away from the stage to face up to the violence that had occurred offstage, they did not realise it but Led Zeppelin's American journey which had begun in low key surroundings in Denver nine years before was at an end.

Bootleg CD References: *A Fighting Finish* (Silver Rarities), *Seventh Heaven* (Immigrant), *The Final Ever In The States* (Missing Link)

Tuesday July 26 1977
New Orleans, Louisiana
Robert Plant flew to New Orleans in preparation for his July 30 show at the Superdome, where Zeppelin were scheduled to play in front of 80,000. Then a call was flashed to Plant from England with the tragic news that his five-year-old son Karac had died of a virus at their Midlands home in England. Richard Cole flew with Plant and Bonham back to England via New York. The rest of the tour dates were immediately cancelled.

The tragedy, following hard on the heels of the Oakland incident, brought an untimely end to a tour that began with Led Zeppelin reaching new heights of musical prowess and popularity … and closed with them departing under the shadow of violence and tragedy.

Saturday July 30 1977
New Orleans, Louisiana
Superdome
CANCELLED

Tuesday August 2 1977
Wednesday August 3 1977
Chicago, Illinois
Chicago Stadium
CANCELLED

Monday August 8 1977
Buffalo, New York

Rich Coliseum
CANCELLED

Tuesday August 9 1977
Wednesday August 10 1977
Pittsburgh, Pennsylvania
Civic Arena
CANCELLED

Saturday August 13 1977
Pittsburgh, Pennsylvania
John F. Kennedy Stadium
CANCELLED

Sunday August 14 1977
Plumpton, Sussex
The Half Moon
GUEST APPEARANCE

Jimmy Page joins Ron Wood to jam with Portsmouth band, Arms And Legs. The concert is part of a charity golf event in aid of the Goaldiggers football charity to provide play area for underprivileged children.

Page (using a single neck Gibson SG) and Wood play in the pouring rain for about 45 minutes and raise £650. Around 150 witness the event including footballers Alan Ball, Peter Osgood and *Match Of The Day* pundit, Jimmy Hill.

Melody Maker parodies Hill's TV soccer analyst style in reporting the event: "Page had 14 riffs on target to Wood's 8. The controversial extended solo (which almost meant an early bath for the reckless Wood) was defended by Hill as a 'unparalleled example of superior virtuosity in deadball situation'."

Jimmy Page turned up as a guest at the annual WEA (Warner Elektra Atlantic) record company sales conference in Brighton. He took to the stage for the end of conference jam session, joining Phil Carson and Billy Kinsley of The Liverpool Express and Carl Simmons for a rock'n'roll medley.

Monday October 3 1977
London, England
Capital Radio
Your Mother Wouldn't Like It
JIMMY PAGE INTERVIEW
Jimmy conducted an interview with Captial Radio's Nicky Horne to dispel rumours that Led Zeppelin would be splitting up after the recent tragedies. Nicky Horne also trailed their scheduled four part *Led Zeppelin On The Road* documentary but it was never aired.

Thursday September 8 1977
Brighton, Sussex
Metropole Hotel
GUEST APPEARANCE

KNEBWORTH

A 24-month break separated Led Zeppelin's walking off stage in California on July 24, 1977, and their return to the concert stage in Copenhagen almost two years to the day on July 23, 1979.

For much of that period, the likelihood of Led Zeppelin ever performing again was under serious threat. Following the death of his son, Robert Plant retreated to his Midlands home to collect his thoughts in private. The glittering rewards that Led Zeppelin had brought meant nothing when compared to the life of his child. For months he questioned his role and his future. Close confidants believed him when he said he could never return to the group.

Slowly he began to pick up the pieces. He produced a single for local Midlands punk outfit Dansette Damage. Then, after constant cajoling from John Bonham, he agreed to a group rehearsal in May 1978 at Clearwell Castle in the Forest of Dean. After running through the familiar rock and roll standards that filled their onstage medleys, they turned their attention to a new Jones/Page/Plant composition entitled 'Carouselambra'. Relieved to be back with the band that had been his life for the past nine years, Plant agreed to the recording of a new album.

After making a series of cameo appearances with, among others, Dr Feelgood and Dave Edmunds, Plant joined the other three for rehearsals at Ezyhire Studios in London. On November 6 the band flew to Stockholm for a series of Monday through Friday sessions which would result in the *In Through The Out Door* album the following year.

As for the others, the lay-off produced mixed rewards. John Paul Jones emerged with various keyboard-led ideas and was anxious to apply them in the studio on his new GX1 synth set-up. Page, however, seemed distant, less enthusiastic

and not entirely comfortable, showing particular indifference to Plant's mellow leanings on songs like of 'All My Love'. "Jonesy started working more closely with Robert," recalls Page. "I wasn't that keen on 'All My Love'. It just didn't seem us. In fact Bonzo and I both felt it was a little soft that album. We wanted to make a more hard driving rock album after that."

His spark did rekindle for the new wave inspired 'Wearing And Tearing' – a number that didn't make the final album (it subsequently showed up on the posthumous *Coda* set in 1982). The sessions may have been tense but by early January they had ten numbers mixed and ready for release, and Page became more involved with the project at his home studios in Plumpton.

All that was needed now was some live performances to seal their return to active duty. At the end of 1978 it was rumoured that Peter Grant would work them back in with a series of low key gigs in Europe, and there was also talk of them playing unannounced club dates in the UK. The speculation finally ended in May 1979 when Grant announced that Led Zeppelin would top the bill at the giant Knebworth Festival on August 4.

"It seemed logical to me that if we were to regain our position as the world's top group, we'd better play the biggest place possible!" was Grant's typically arrogant ploy. The promoter of the event was Freddie Bannister who had staged the 1969 Bath Festival and also been involved in the 1974 Knebworth show when Grant declined Led Zeppelin's services. Ticket sales were so heavy when they went on sale in June that Grant asked Bannister to add a second Knebworth date for the following Saturday, August 11.

The stage was thus set for a spectacular return in front of their largest ever audience. The new album was held for release to coincide with the shows. The long lay off had done little for their confidence and even after a series of intensive rehearsals at Bray studios in June and July, they were far from ready when they flew to Copenhagen to play two warm-up shows on July 23/24 .

Problems with a power generator added to the nervousness of the first Falkoner Theatre date though the next night saw them recover to perform an intense show that hinted at some of the startling effects lined up for Knebworth, most notably Jimmy's laser etched violin bow pyramid light sequence

There was a hint of their caution in the set list that was devised for these dates. It retained a distinct feel of the last US tour, opening with 'The Song Remains The Same' and closing with the expected 'Stairway To Heaven'. Robert was by now contemptuous of Led Zeppelin's most celebrated song. "It was now getting (to be) a mill stone around our necks," he said. "In rehearsal we'd leave it until last and then do a reggae version. There's only so many times you can sing a song and really mean it."

From the new album only 'Hot Dog' and 'In The Evening' were premièred, attempts at the epic 'Carouselambra' having been aborted at the Bray rehearsals. Little effort was being made to market the new album, and there were further cracks in Grant's once unassailable planning strategy when the album, astutely titled *In Through The Out Door*, failed to appear on its scheduled release date of August 10 when it would have certainly benefited by their Knebworth exposure. It finally turned up a week later on August 20.

Only artists of genuine legendary status can disappear for two years and re-emerge with their popularity and status enhanced. So it was with Led Zep. Some 350,000 fans from all over Europe travelled to Knebworth House that August to pay blind devotion to the mighty Zeppelin. Their nervousness and the occasionally scrappy performance (Page in particular seemed very disjointed) was swept away on a mountain of emotion.

Time has been kind to Knebworth as can be seen by the stunning footage on the official DVD which was proof that when they were good, notably on 'Achilles Last Stand', the new track 'In The Evening' and vibrant encores of 'Rock And Roll' and a reworked 'Whole Lotta Love', 'Heartbreaker' (Aug 4) and 'Communication Breakdown' (Aug 11), they were still very good indeed, often reminiscent of the glory era and still capable of moments of sheer brilliance.

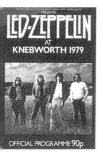

PRODUCTION/PRESENTATION IN ASSOCIATION WITH PETER GRANT
PRESENTS
LED-ZEPPELIN
AT
KNEBWORTH 1979

OFFICIAL PROGRAMME 90p

The press slated them, of course, but that had no effect on the Zep faithful who pushed the *In Through The Out Door* album to the number one spot the same week it was released. In America fans and industry alike were baying for the return of the Zeppelin. *In Through* boosted the whole US music business as no album had done in recent times, getting fans back into the record shops and shifting three million copies in as many weeks.

Grant's gamble to bring them back on the biggest stage available just about paid off. Behind the scenes there was a disagreement with promoter Bannister which resulted in Led Zeppelin taking the stage very late on the second date. Grant queried the actual attendance, and later had an aerial photo of the arena enlarged for studying by surveyors to prove his point. The final outcome was a liquidation order for Bannister's Tedoar company.

Knebworth remains one of the most notable landmarks in Led Zeppelin's career, not least because it was the only opportunity that many of their younger British fans ever had of seeing the group live. On a musical level it may have been somewhat inconsistent but they were at last back and working, and the occasion had touched them profoundly.

Plant: "It was an incredible thing really. I patrolled the grounds in a jeep on the night before the first gig and people had pushed down the stone pillars to get in early. It was a phenomenally powerful thing." Page's interviews of the time were littered with hints of them playing bullrings in Spain, and Plant had even mentioned from the Knebworth stage that … "We will go to Manchester around Christmas – should be pretty good."

But instead announcing an extensive UK tour, there was another prolonged period of silence. And, as the Eighties beckoned, there was no clear indication of where they might head next. Not that it mattered much to those loyal fans who filled in the voting slips in the annual *Melody Maker* poll that winter.

KNEBWORTH CONCERT 4th AUGUST 1979 GUEST PASS

ACHILLES LAST STAND

In his review of the *Presence* album for *Sounds* in April 1976, journalist Jonh Ingram noted that … "'Achilles Last Stand' will be a motherfucker played live". He wasn't far wrong. Such was their keenness to perform the piece live, when they reconvened for rehearsals for the 1977 US tour, this 10-minute epic was at the top of their agenda. Despite the mass of overdubs used in the studio, Page found he could adapt all the parts on the Gibson Les Paul rather than the double neck.

So it was that 'Achilles Last Stand' took its place in the latter part of their set from the 1977 American tour onwards. During these dates it was played immediately after Jimmy's guitar solo that sometimes encompassed the 'Star Spangled Banner'.

It's a track that inspired some of their most memorable onstage images: the stage bathed in clear white spotlights shining out behind Bonzo's kit and that classic Page/Plant stance for the 'Ah – Ah- Ah – Ah' refrain as they clustered together in archetypal rock star pose.

It was the DVD that provided conclusive proof of the sheer artistry of this track. The performance extracted from the Knebworth concerts was cited by Robert Plant as one of the outstanding moments of the entire set.

'Achilles Last Stand' demonstrated all the pomp and stateliness Led Zeppelin epitomised to its audience of the time.

Plant's pre-Knebworth quote that "We're not heroes anymore. Heroes are in books … old books" could be viewed as a rare moment of modesty after the turn-out in that field just outside Stevenage.

Led Zeppelin were still adored on both sides of the Atlantic. What they needed to do now was go out and justify this devotion, on stage, night after night.

Stage Set Up:
Full Showco PA and lighting rig including side panel lights and revolving light bins. The drum rostrum was also banked with lights. Bonham's drum mics were positioned differently for the two dates – one of the few noticable visual differences to their stage set up between the two Knebworth dates. White spotlights were used for 'Achilles Last Stand'. A giant backdrop screen behind the stage was used to show synched footage being shot by the film crew as it happened. Both Knebworth shows were filmed and recorded with George Chkiantz engineering in the Rolling Stones mobile. The band agreed to wear the same clothes for both shows to aid continuity for the filming should they decide to release it in some format in the future. In 2002 Page salvaged the footage and edited both nights for the 50-minute presentation released on the official DVD.

Equipment Notes:
For the 1979 comeback, Jimmy retained much of the set-up used on the last US tour with the addition of the Lake Placid Fender Stratocaster for 'In The Evening' and a Gibson RD Artist model for 'Misty Mountain Hop'. The Fender Telecaster was used on 'Hot Dog' and 'Ten Years Gone'. Jimmy' symbol on the amp was in evidence in Copenhagen but was absent by the time they got to Knebworth. John Paul continued with the Alembic basses and the Andy Manson Triple-neck for the August 4 'Ten Years Gone' performance. His keyboard set up included a white Yamaha CP 70B grand piano, and his newly acquired Yamaha GX1 synth. Plant still used a vocal harmoniser.

February 1978
Worcestershire, England
Old Smithy Studios, Kempsey
GUEST APPEARANCE
Not a live session but a significant return to working. This was Robert's first musical involvemen

since the tragedy. He assisted local punk band Dansette Damage to record at the studio near his home. Along with Zeppelin roadie, Benji Le Fevre, he produced both sides of their single and added backing vocals. Not wanting his involvement to be public knowledge, his production credit was listed on the sleeve as 'The Wolverhampton Wanderer'. A further credit listed thanks to 'Uncle Bob'. Unsurprisingly, the single was well reviewed in the *NME*, but made little impression outside of the West Midlands.

May 1978
Gloucestershire
Clearwell Castle,
Forest of Dean
REHEARSALS

Led Zeppelin regrouped for their first rehearsal sessions since the curtailed US tour. A month of rehearsals saw them working on, amongst other songs, the new 'Carouselambra' and an untitled riff number (dubbed 'Fire' on bootlegs) that was never completed. A spokesman for Swan Song commented: "We still don't know what will emerge out of the rehearsals – perhaps an album – it's too early to tell."

Page recalled: "That was basically a period of saying 'Hello' to each other musically once again. We hadn't played together for so long, and Clearwell was the first actual playing we'd done for what seemed like an eternity, although it was only about 20 months. It was really just limbering up."

Plant: "I started to play again, and I realised that I still possessed something that really turned me on."

Bootleg CD References: *Rehearsing* (CG), *Lost Mixes Vol 4* (Empress Valley), *Brutal Artistry Vol 2* (Empress Valley), *Missing Links* (The Diagrams Of Led Zeppelin)

June 1978
Birmingham, England
Tiswas *Central TV*
TV APPEARANCE

Robert's friendship with Chris Tarrant, then presenter of the popular Saturday morning TV show, led him to decide to drop in on the show. Dressed in a Wolverhampton Wanderers t-shirt he was seen on screen in a brief clip of him watching TV in the studio and then being caught out by the show's 'Phantom flan flinger' – a regular feature which had guests pelted with cream pies. Plant succumbed and photos of his appearance appeared in the press soon after. Robert returned to the show in 1981 for a brief interview.

Sunday July 16 1978
London, England
Royal Festival Hall

Rumours were rife for the past month that Maggie Bell's new line-up for this concert would contain at least one member of Led Zeppelin. Amidst more rumours that the band would play a series of pub gigs under an assumed name, it's also reported that they would play an opening set at this show before their fellow Swan Song artiste. This failed to materialise.

However, there was a smattering of truth in the rumours of live activity in the Zeppelin camp as Robert Plant stages three guest appearances over the next three months.

July 1978
Wolverly, England
Wolverly Memorial Hall
GUEST APPEARANCE

Plant sits in with local Midlands band Melvin's Marauders (aka Melvin Giganticus & The Turd Burglars). Songs performed include 'I Got A Woman' and 'Blue Suede Shoes'. Plant was also alleged to have provided backing vocals on their single, a cover of Freddy Cannon's 'Buzz Buzz A Diddle It'.

The Concert File

bus conductor in Wolverhampton and the ever rockin' Dave Edmunds. The only person Plant couldn't jam with was Tim Hinckley (who needs the publicity anyway) and the award was confirmed when Plant sang two verses of 'Poetry In Motion' with Johnny Tillotson, while shaking hands with Jake Riviera. This is a Robert Plant press release. PS Has any-one seen Rat Scabies' dad? All the best for 1979!"

August 1978
Ibiza, Spain
Club Amnesia
GUEST APPEARANCE

While on holiday in Ibiza, Robert jammed with Dr. Feelgood and Atlantic Records executive Phil Carson.

Stu Lyons, manager of the club, said: "Robert looked in great shape and sounded fantastic."

Saturday September 16 1978
Birmingham, England
Birmingham Town Hall
GUEST APPEARANCE

The day after attending Richard Cole and Simon Kirke's double wedding at Chelsea Registry Office and the reception at The Golden Lion in Fulham with Page and Jones, Plant returned to the Midlands and showed up at Dave Edmunds' gig in Birmingham, joining him for the encore.

Introduced by Edmunds as 'an old mate of mine', Plant joined them for performances of Chuck Willis's 'Mess O'Blues' and Arthur Crudup's 'My Baby Left Me'.

Plant also filed his own tongue-in-cheek review of recent events for the *Melody Maker*: "Creeping back from exhausting rehearsals for a triple album and a maxi single, Robert Plant managed to take the *Guinness Book Of Records* award for jamming with the most people over the weekend – from Bad Company, Richard Cole (who was so pleased with the harmonies that he also got married), to a

October 1978
London, England
Ezyhire Studios
REHEARSALS

The band re-convened in London to prepare material for their new album. They again returned to John Paul Jones's keyboard epic 'Carouselambra', added new Plant led songs 'In The Evening' and 'All My Love' and also ran down a punk inspired rocker titled 'Wearing And Tearing'. By early November they had ten new songs at the ready to record stage. Grant quickly did a deal with Abba's Polar Studios and by November they were in Stockholm for a three-week bout of recording that would produce the *In Through The Out Door* album.

October 1978
Shenstone College, England
GUEST APPEARANCE

In his book *Bonham By Bonham*, Mick Bonham revealed how John took a break from re-hearsal with Zep-pelin to attend a gig by Grit featuring on Move bassist Ace Kefford. John got on stage to jam with the band which included Johnny Hill, former member of his early pre-Zep band Way Of Life.

Tuesday October 3 1978
London, England,
Abbey Road No. 2 Studio
Paul McCartney & Wings Rockestra
Recording Session
GUEST APPEARANCE

Not an actual live appearance but a recording session that led to one. Paul McCartney invited John Paul Jones and John Bonham to an all star recording session at Abbey Road Studios. They joined McCartney's Wings and a host of musicians including Dave Gilmour, Hank Marvin, Kenny Jones, Ronnie Lane, Gary Brooker, Tony Ashton and Pete Townshend in recording two tracks as part of what McCartney dubbed the Rockestra. The tracks – 'Rockestra Theme' and 'So Glad To See You Here' – were later included on Wings' album *Back To The Egg*.

A year later McCartney would invite Jones and Bonham, along with Plant, to partcipate in the Wings' Concert For Kampuchea show at London's Hammersmith Odeon.

CD Reference: Wings – *Back To The Egg* (Parlophone)
Visual Reference: Paul McCartney – *Wingspan An Intimate Portrait* (Capital/MPL)
This documentary DVD includes the promotional film shot for the Rockestra Abbey Road sessions. John Bonham can be seen in several shots.

October 1978
Around this period John Paul Jones and Robert Plant attended a charity auction at the Golden Lion pub in Fulham.

November 1978
Stockholm, Sweden
Polar Studios
RECORDING SESSIONS

Working during the week and returning to the UK at weekends, the band spent three weeks at Abba's Polar Studios recording what would emerge as *In Through The Out Door.*
Known recording data:
Tuesday November 14 1978 – recording of 'Ozone

Baby' (released on *Coda*)
Thursday November 16 1978 – recording of 'Darlene' (released on *Coda*)
Friday November 17 1978 – recording of 'All My Love' (tape box labelled The Hook)
Tuesday November 21 1978 recording of 'Wearing And Tearing' (released on *Coda*)
Various outtakes and work in progress versions from these sessions have emerged on bootlegs. These include a superb 'All My Love' with full ending and isolated drum tracks of Bonzo in full flight on 'Carousalmbra', 'Ozone Baby', 'Fool In The Rain' and 'Wearing And Tearing'.

Bootleg References: *Studio Daze* (Scorpio), *In Through The Outtakes, All My Love* (Tarantura), *Lost Mixes Vol 4* (Empress Valley)

Friday November 24 1978
Stourport, England
Stourport Civic Hall
GUEST APPEARANCE

In his book *Bonham By Bonham*, Mick Bonham revealed that John got up and jammed with a local outfit known as the GB Band at the annual presentation of his local Scramble Club.

Saturday December 16 1978
News Report: The band returned to the UK, having completed the bulk of their new studio album at Abba's Polar Studios. It was rumoured they would undertake a series of dates in Europe at the end of February 1979. The album, tentatively titled *Look* had a provisional release date of February 12. It was also reported that Robert Plant would warm up for the tour by playing small club dates with local Midlands band, Little Acre.

These reports proved somewhat premature and nothing materialised until the spring.

Friday February 2 1979
London, England
Tommy Vance Friday Rock Show
RADIO BROADCAST

During his popular *Friday Night Rock show* DJ Tommy Vance aired the two March and in June

1969 BBC *Top Gear* radio appearances. It was the first time these sessions had been repeated in full since their original broadcast. At a time when there was still uncertainty to Zeppelin's long term plans, this broadcast did much to revive interest ahead of their Knebworth comback and was well received by fans old and new. Tommy Vance sadly died age 63 in March 2005.

Monday March 26 1979
Birmingham, England
Birmingham Odeon
GUEST APPEARANCE

Robert Plant joined Bad Company for the second show of their three night stint in Birmingham. He came on for the encore – an unidentified blues number with Paul Rodgers switching to guitar.

Tuesday April 3 1979
Birmingham, England
Birmingham Odeon
GUEST APPEARANCE

For this rescheduled date on Bad Company's *Desolation Angels* UK tour (the original March 27 was cancelled because Paul Rodgers suffered throat trouble), Robert was again on stage, but this time he brought John Bonham and Jimmy Page with him to perform 'I'm Going Down'. Page played a borrowed guitar belonging to Mick Ralphs, Bonham played a set of bongos alongside Simon Kirke's drums and Peter Grant watched yet another collaboration of his two finest acts from the side of the stage.

Wednesday May 16 1979
Stourbridge, England, Stourbridge Wine Bar
GUEST APPEARANCE

Robert Plant joined the Midlands part-time pick-up band, Melvin's Marauders, for an appearance at the local Stourbridge wine bar.

It's likely that Robert also jammed with another local band, Little Acre, around this period – though no specific dates have come to light.

Tuesday May 22 1979
News Report: Led Zeppelin formally announced their return to the UK stage. The news was exclusively revealed by Anne Nightingale on BBC TV's *Old Grey Whistle Test.* They would headline the Knebworth Festival to be staged within the grounds of the Stevenage stately home on August 4. Ironically, the promoter was Freddie Bannister who failed to book them in 1974. They would receive the highest ever fee for one single performance.

Subsequent ticket demand spurred Bannister to agree to a second date on August 11. Over the coming months speculation on the support bill was rife, undergoing several revisions. Van Morrison, Joni Mitchell, The Boomtown Rats and Dire Straits were all rumoured to be appearing.

The eventual line-up was somewhat lacking in major league names. Fairport Convention, Chas & Dave, Commander Cody (filing in for The Marshall Tucker Band who agreed to play and then dropped out), Southside Johnny & The Asbury Dukes, and Todd Rundgren's Utopia, were the first week's attractions.

Chas & Dave, Commander Cody, Southside Johnny, Todd Rundgren and Keith Richards and Ronnie Wood's part-time band The New Barbarians, was the August 11 line-up.

Saturday June 9
London, England
Rock On *BBC Radio One*
RADIO INTERVIEW

On June 9 Radio One's *Rock On* programme broadcast an exclusive interview with Robert Plant – his first in two years. It was conducted by Trevor Dann backstage at London's

Palace Theatre following a Dave Edmunds concert Plant had attended. Robert gave little way, deflecting the questions with ambiguous answers. "I think the music will stand up for itself. It will stand up there as it always has done. Things always change with Zeppelin… that's why after two years we can still get together and play. We are what we are when we walk on the stage and play. It's not a question of are we heroes anymore. Heroes are in books – old books."

Early June
Knebworth, Stevenage England
PHOTO SHOOT
In early June all four members of Led Zeppelin convened on the Knebworth site for a formal photo shoot with the Hipgnosis design team. It consisted of various front on and side on group portraits with the four members standing in an adjoining field to the Knebworth site. To spice things up, a pair of strippers were hired to ensure the band had a smile on their face. As tempers had been frayed early on, they soon mellowed. The old Zep frivolity soon kicked in and there exists an outtake from the shoot that clearly shows Plant dropping his trousers and exposing himself. The session produced the memorable images that were used on the official Knebworth poster and programme.

Late June/Early July
Bray Berkshire
Bray Studios
REHEARSALS
The group began intensive rehearsals in preparation for Knebworth. New lighting effects were set up. Video footage was shot for possible future use, including a sketch with John Bonham demonstrating the art of folding a tee-shirt which drew on his experience as a former menswear salesman. (This was later considered as a possible still for the *Coda* sleeve.)

The heat obviously got to them as pictures show Page, Plant and Jones wearing shorts. Photos from this session taken by Aubrey Powell of the Hipgnosis design team were used in the official Knebworth programme. Asked by a reporter from *NME* what they'd been up to, Plant retorted: "We've been checking the lighting and getting into shape. We've got some new stuff as well as some old favourites lined up."

Monday July 23 1979
Copenhagen, Denmark
Falkoner Theatre
Set: The Song Remains The Same/Celebration Day/Black Dog/Nobody's Fault But Mine/ Over The Hills And Far Away/ Misty Mountain Hop/Since I've Been Loving You/No Quarter/Hot Dog/The Rain Song/White Summer – Black Mountain Side/ Kashmir/ Trampled Underfoot/Achilles Last Stand/ Page Solo/In The Evening/Stairway To Heaven/Rock And Roll.

The venue chosen for the band's first gig in two years was the obscure Falkoner Theatre in Denmark's capital. The venue had previously played host to the likes of Abba and was also the venue where Judy Garland gave her last live performance on March 25, 1969.

Ticket price was Kr.105 (about £10) and capacity was only 2,000, and such was the low-key nature of these warm-up shows that it was still possible to buy tickets on the door. Peter Grant

Led Zeppelin

gave promoter Arne Worsoe just 14 days notice to arrange this warm-up stint for Knebworth, which takes them back to the scene of their first dates back in 1968.

New productions are prone to technical problems and this was no exception. The enormous lighting rig that the band had hoped to install was simply too big for the venue. This results in the persistent blowing of the generator, which led to long delays before punters were allowed admission to the auditorium. The show finished at just after 1 am the next morning.

The performance itself was rusty and under-rehearsed, but acceptable considering the circumstances.

No press were invited to these warm-ups, but a few managed to sneak in anyway. Erik Von Lustbaden, writing for *Sounds*, described the show as "Dazzling, staggering and sometimes awful. The subdued lights were still much better than most bands will ever have! The powerful ascending riff of 'Kashmir' and the group's sense of simple melody and repetition combine to at least give an inkling of why they've attained such legendary status. Dazzling. Another Page solo, all without any backing. I went for a piss, bought a bar of chocolate, ate it, had a sit down, made some notes, went back in, and he was still playing it!!"

Eric Kornfeldt, reporting for *New Musical Express*, was vitriolic in his criticism: "Dazed'n'Abused – They appeared sloppy and unrehearsed, sometimes seeming awkwardly lost bewildered, stiff and reluctant to play. They were no more than a quartet of uninspired old men, a relic from the past. There was so little feeling inherent in the set that for the most part it was like watching a fully automated factory producing an endless string of chords that neither musicians nor audience cared about."

Bootleg CD References: *Melancholy Danish Pageboys Remake* (Silver Rarities), *Copenhagen Warm Ups* (Tarantura), *Copenhagen '79* (The Diagrams Of Led Zeppelin)

Tuesday July 24 1979
Copenhagen, Denmark
Falkoner Theatre

Set: The Song Remains The Same/Celebration Day/Black Dog/Nobody's Fault But Mine/Over The Hills And Far Away/Misty Mountain Hop/Since I've Been Loving You/No Quarter/Ten Years Gone/Hot Dog/The Rain Song/White Summer – Black Mountain Side/Kashmir/Trampled Underfoot/Sick Again/Achilles Last Stand/Page Solo/In The Evening/Stairway To Heaven/Whole Lotta Love.

The auditorium was only three-quarters full for this second show. The Danish press (also refused admission) had slated the delays of the previous evening with the headline 'Led Zeppelin – Fiasko' which possibly affected ticket sales.

Tonight's show was a much more satisfying experience, although there were still some technical problems. Delays with Jones' effects pedals prior to 'Ten Years Gone' provoked Plant to comment: "We'll very shortly be doing 'Eleven Years Gone'."

Jon Carlsson gatecrashed the event for *Melody Maker* and was impressed by the effects during Page's solo. "The bow began glowing with an eerie green light that you could read a book by. It made Page look like a Crowleyite elf or perhaps Obe Wan Kanobe on exotic snuff. Page was then enclosed by a green pyramid of thin laser light, which on every fourth beat rotated through 90 degrees. It became faster in its rotations until it became a glowing green cone. Page stepped back into it and let the colour wash over him."

Bootleg CD References: *Copenhagen Nights Relived* (Black Swan), *Copenhagen Warm Ups* (Tarantura), *Copenhagen '79* (The Diagrams of Led Zeppelin)

Saturday August 4 1979

London, England
Radio One Rock On
RADIO BROADCAST

Radio One's *Rock On* programme with Tommy Vance hosted a live broadcast from the Knebworth site. There was a review of their Copenhagen warm up shows and Richard Skinner conducted interviews with fans from the site, building the atmosphere for their big return. However there were no interviews or live music from the band.

Saturday August 4 1979

Stevenage, England
Knebworth Festival

Set: The Song Remains The Same/Celebration Day/Black Dog/Nobody's Fault But Mine/Over The Hills And Far Away/Misty Mountain Hop/Since I've Been Loving You/No Quarter/Ten Years Gone/Hot Dog/The Rain Song/White Summer – Black Mountain Side/Kashmir/Trampled Underfoot/Sick Again/Achilles Last Stand/Page Solo/In The Evening/Stairway To Heaven/Rock And Roll/Whole Lotta Love/Heartbreaker.

Prior to going on stage the band held an official photo call in their dressing room caravan

Zeppelin's first UK show in four years was a truly emotional event, both for the band and the audience.

In retrospect even if the playing was hardly note perfect the sheer scale of the day pulled them through – proof that the spirit was still very willing.

Robert Plant: "Well, it's nice to see you again. I told Pagey one or two people would be here, but he said he doubted it very much. I can't tell you how it feels – I think you've got a good idea anyway."

The set opened fiercely with 'The Song Remains The Same' piercing the still of the night, and the audience reaction was sheer elation. However,

after a while, it became evident that the band were still under-rehearsed and that the magic wasn't quite there on some numbers.

'Over The Hills', however, was reminiscent of past glories and 'Since I've Been Loving You' was performed with passion. 'No Quarter' was scaled down from the marathons of 1977 to a mere 18 minutes of Jones/Page inspired improvisation.

Robert offered an apology for the delay in the release of the new album, and then proceeded to mess up the lyrics to 'Hot Dog'.

Plant: "So we get all the way here, and the equipment blows up! Never mind, it's got to be better than Earl's Court. Who's the person who owned that goat and the little wagon we saw two nights ago, camping out there. They must come round the back afterwards and write an acoustic set with us!"

Page's laser pyramid solo was an amazing spectacle of technology and musicianship, and it led directly into 'In The Evening' from the new album. Although the audience was unfamiliar with the track, it was received well. However, it was now very late and the audience were beginning to tire. 'Stairway To Heaven' sung by Plant with surprising conviction closed the main show.

The first encore of 'Rock And Roll' restored the balance and before the band returned for more, the crowd sang a heartfelt version of 'You'll Never Walk Alone'. Obviously moved by this, the group came back for two further encores, 'Whole Lotta Love', performed in a brand new arrangement akin to the original 'You Need Love' and

'Heartbreaker' which brought the proceedings to a glorious finale.

Plant: "All you people that have come so far. It's been kinda like a blind date. Thanks for eleven years."

Led Zeppelin were no longer fashionable as far as the now punk-dominated British music press made clear, but even their staunchest critics found something positive to say about Knebworth. Paul Morley of *New Musical Express*, perhaps the most hawkish of all young rock writers operating at the time, headlined his article "Ghosts of Progressive Rock Past" and wrote: "I'm considering them in a contemporary perspective, finding them not awkward or flatulent at all but in lots of ways exciting. In fact, I'm saying Zeppelin deserve some respect. When Zeppelin play rock'n'roll I can see why people call them the greatest. Led Zeppelin at Knebworth were A Triumph. I didn't expect or demand anything from them. I don't need them. I don't care whether they go away for another bunch of years. But over 140,000 people can't be wrong. And neither can I."

Hugh Fielder of *Sounds* (who were refused press passes for the event) wrote: "The sustained roar that greeted Led Zeppelin as they trooped onto the massive Knebworth stage at twenty to ten last Saturday said it all." Even David Hepworth, in a predominantly negative review for the same paper, was impressed when the band launched into 'Kashmir': "The twisting, Byzantine riff actually raising the spirits rather than riding roughshod over them like pre-Raphaelite boot boys. For about half an hour we had Led Zeppelin at their best. Tension, sheer power and spectacle."

Rolling Stone kept their readers up-to-date with a typically vitriolic review. "Two years ago when Zeppelin last played in America, this Knebworth performance might have been dismissed as merely the consequence of a temporary malaise, a below par enactment of the fake orgasm ritual so often acted out by groups and audiences at festivals of this size. But in the light of Zeppelin's prolonged lay off and the abrasive climate of the current British music scene to which they have chosen to return, the group sounded woefully complacent and anachronistic. Even obsolete."

Fan Joseph Whiteside managed to get a mention on stage from Plant. He recalled: "Just before 'Trampled Underfoot' Plant announces 'This is a small little uptempo ditty that we've been asked to do... some people in Vancouver it's all there in the end baby! The 'People in Vancouver' was a direct reference to my friend and I. My friend Roger Grais won two tickets to attend the August 4 show in England from CFOX FM, our Vancouver rock station, and knowing I was a massive Zep fan very kindly invited me along..

"The radio station gave us a contact at Atlantic Records – Danny Urweider. I phoned him and

316

asked him if he could get the band to do 'Trampled Underfoot' as this had not been played when I'd seen them in Seattle in 1977. I said it would be great if they could dedicate it to us not thinking for a minute he would pull this off. Sure enough Danny got the message through to Robert and amazingly he mentioned it before performing the track. We were over the moon when it happened!''

Fan Andy Banks took his cine camera along and came away with a lasting record of the day. The film begins with shots of hundreds of fans arriving at the campsite – the queues for the merchandise and toilets – and then cuts to inside the arena. It shows the Knebworth field filling up, fans dancing to the support bands and then cuts to the darkness before bursting into life as Led Zeppelin hit the stage. "I remember thinking I should save some film for 'Kashmir' and the lasers," recalled Andy. "I came away with about ten minutes of highlights and then shot the aftermath in the morning with all the cars leaving. Twenty years later I discovered the film again in my garage. It's a unique souvenir of a unique day. A snapshot of a moment never to be repeated."

Andy's film was later immortalised on the official *Zeppelin* DVD – it is one of the key contributions to the Knebworth section and indeed the entire DVD. Beginning with the crowds arriving it then adds real atmosphere to the Zeppelin performance as it intercuts within the main video film to remarkable effect.

Bootleg CD References: *Knebworth Parts 1, 2, & 3* (Flying Disc), *Knebworth 1979 Boxset* (Tarantura), *Lost Mixes* (Celebration)

Visual References: Official *Led Zeppelin* 2003 DVD (Warner Music Vision), *Knebworth 4* (unofficial DVD – Tarantura), *Latter Visions* (unofficial DVD – Celebration)

Saturday August 11 1979
Stevenage, England
Knebworth Festival
Set: The Song Remains The Same/Celebration Day/Black Dog/Nobody's Fault But Mine/Over The Hills And Far Away/Misty Mountain Hop/Since I've Been Loving You/No Quarter/Hot Dog/The Rain Song/White Summer/Kashmir/Trampled Underfoot/Sick Again/Achilles Last Stand/Page Solo/In The Evening/Stairway To Heaven/Rock And Roll/Whole Lotta Love/Communication Breakdown.

For this second date they seemed less nervous and more confident, leading to a more satisfying musical performance – though the day itself lacked the emotion of the earlier show.

Plant was quick to get one in on the press reaction: "Well, it didn't rain. But it rained on us during the week from one or two sources, and we're really gonna stick it right where it really belongs."

Early on there were technical problems. A faulty lead during 'Over The Hills' produced some unwanted sounds from the PA and provoked Plant to comment: "What's going on – must be the samosas!" The problem persisted through 'Misty Mountain Hop'. 'Ten Years Gone' was dropped from tonight's set and there was less improvisation in general, which resulted in a substantially shorter show than last week.

The new album still wasn't in the shops: Plant: "In the Neolithic caves in Peru, they've been finding a lot of drawings on the wall and along with the coloured drawings, they also found our new album cover. We're managing to get the album out in about two weeks. As you've no doubt read the reviews, it's tremendous. It's called *In Through The Out Door*, one of those methods of entry which proves harder than one would originally expect."

'Hot Dog' was dedicated to "The Texas road crew and all the people we found in the sleazy hang-outs around there." However, Plant still hadn't learnt the lyrics properly.

Plant: "Can you do the dinosaur rock? 'Whole Lotta Love' tonight also included the 'Boogie Chillun'' section and 'Communication Breakdown' was played as a final encore instead of 'Heartbreaker'.

Plant: "We'll see you soon. Very soon. Don't know about the Marquee, but somewhere soon."

Robert Plant and John Paul Jones talk about

LED·ZEPPELIN

PAST, PRESENT AND FUTURE

New Musical Express was one of the few papers that bothered to review the second show. Nick Kent wrote: "Zeppelin were perfection in sound, dynamics and note-for-note fastidious playing. For the first half hour one couldn't help but be impressed by Zep's powerdrive; at times they were breath taking. But the mixture of Robert Plant's frequent snipes at their less-than-totally-adulatory press coverage and the elongated virtuosity of the likes of 'No Quarter' and 'Dazed And Confused' (?) ultimately left me cold and bored.

"Zeppelin, for all their virtuosity, had very little to say beyond the bombastic power. Zep are like a behemoth, impressive but something from the past – almost a museum piece."

Robert Plant would later have mixed feelings about the comeback. "I wasn't as relaxed as I could have been. There was so much expectation there and the least we could have done was to have been confident enough to kill. We maimed the beast for life, but we didn't kill it. It was good, but only because everybody made it good. There was that sense of event."

Bootleg CD References: *Final Cut* (Celebration), *Knebworth November 11 1979* (TNT), *Knebworth 1979 Boxset* (Tarantura), *Lost Mixes* (Celebration)

Visual References: Official *Led Zeppelin* 2003 DVD (Warner Home Vision), *Final Cut* (unofficial DVD – Celebration)

THE AFTER SHOW KNEBWORTH INTERVIEWS/THE LOST PROMO ALBUM

Following the final two Knebworth shows Robert and John Paul Jones conducted two interviews from the Knebworth site – one for Australian Radio and the other for KLOS radio in Los Angeles with long time Zep supporter DJ JJ Jackson. There was a plan by Swan Song in America to use part of the JJ Jackson interview to publicise the *In Through The Out Door* album. To that end a promo interview album titled *Robert Plant and John Paul Jones Talk About Led Zeppelin Past Present and Future* was planned and allocated a US catalogue number (Swan Song PR 342). A

colour cover was designed depicting the famous Knebworth photo call side on shot. However the project never reached fruition and was shelved before the pressing went ahead. A handful of mock up sleeves were prepared and did get printed. These are amongst the rarest Zeppelin collectables. JJ Jackson sadly died age 62 in March 2004.

Friday December 28 1979
London, England
Radio One
Tommy Vance Friday Rock Show
RADIO BROADCAST

Tommy Vance aired a 53-minute edited repeat of Led Zeppelin's June 27 1969 Playhouse Theatre in concert *One Night Sand* recording. The repeat came about after a petition was raised by *Tight But Loose* subscriber Stuart Whitehead following an advert in the magazine. "Our most requested archive session – I hope all Led Zeppelin fans around the country are happy!" noted TV at the close.

Saturday December 29 1979
London, England
Hammersmith Odeon
GUEST APPEARANCE

Concert For The People Of Kampuchea – Three quarters of Led Zeppelin were in attendance for the final night of a series of concerts staged by Harvey Goldsmith, UN secretary General Waldheim and Paul McCartney to aid the relief operation in Cambodia.

This evening was headed by Paul McCartney & Wings, with support from The Pretenders, Rockpile and Elvis Costello, plus host comedian Billy Connolly.

Robert Plant joined Dave Edmund's Rockpile for a version of 'Little Sister'. Dressed in an oatmeal jacket, jeans and scarf, Plant's delivery was competent enough, though the ending was a little chaotic as Nick Lowe sang the chorus line of the song when everyone else has stopped. Plant laughed with mock embarrassment and exited after shaking hands with Dave Edmunds.

This cameo inspired Elvis Costello to comment during his set: "I never thought I'd see Rockpile play 'Stairway To Heaven'!"

Paul McCartney's climax to the Wings set was to reconstruct his Rockestra line-up that had recorded two tracks on the Wings' *Back To The Egg* album. John Bonham and John Paul Jones had been part of the studio sessions and had been asked by McCartney to do this show when Bonzo

attended the Wings show at the Birmingham Odeon a few weeks back. The mammoth line-up tonight included Pete Townshend, Kenny Jones, Tony Ashton, Dave Edmunds, Gary Brooker, members of The Attractions and The Pretenders, plus John Paul Jones on Alembic bass and John Bonham on drums. Robert also joined in, pretending to play one of Macca's famous Hofner bass guitars. All dressed in glittering tail coats (except Townshend), they performed the 'Rockestra Theme', 'Let It Be' (with Robert seated at the keyboards sharing backing vocal duties with Linda McCartney), and 'Lucille' (Plant sits this one out next to Linda on the keyboards).

The edited highlights of the four Kampuchea concerts, including all the Zeppelin appearances, are subsequently aired on the ITV network on January 4 1981, and issued on the double album set *The Concerts For The People Of Kampuchea*.

Visual Reference: *1979/1980* (unofficial DVD – Cosmic Energy)

EUROPE 1980

Led Zeppelin entered the new decade riding on the back of their triumphant showing in the 1979 year end *Melody Maker* Reader's Poll, in which they scooped a total of seven awards. Despite the lay offs, negative press reaction to their Knebworth shows, and the derision heaped down upon them by the newly popular punk bands ("Led Zeppelin? I don't need to hear their music – just looking at their album sleeves makes me want to throw up" – Paul Simonen of The Clash), the loyalty expressed by their following indicated that this particular dinosaur was far from extinct. The problem faced by Peter Grant was how to capitalise on their sustained popularity while Robert Plant refused to tour America.

"We had to go back if the group was to continue, as that was where a sizeable amount of the

market was," recalled Grant years later. To rejuvenate the camp, a plan was hatched to tour central Europe (avoiding the UK) over a two week period in the early summer.

The idea was to play the smaller places (the average venue held around 4,000) with a cut down PA and try to recapture the spirit of their tours in the early Seventies. By avoiding their homeland, they hoped to escape the press attention that had dogged Knebworth. And at the back of his mind, Grant hoped that being on the road again would act as an incentive for Plant that would eventually lead to a full scale return to the US.

Rehearsals took place in April and May at London's Rainbow and New Victoria Theatres and later at Shepperton. The mood was fairly optimistic, though their reluctance to rehearse

many of the new tracks from the recent *In Through The Out Door* album indicated an unwillingness to apply themselves as they had in the past. Page in particular was far from healthy. The baggy suits that would hang from his diminishing frame and the shades that hid his eyes at the beginning of many of the Europe shows were clear indications of his physical shortcomings.

There were also drug related problems. Grant's long serving right hand man, Zeppelin tour manager Richard Cole, was dropped from the entourage due to his heroin addiction. Phil Carlo from Bad Company's crew was drafted in to support Grant. "There were personalities around Led Zeppelin that I didn't take kindly to in the end," said Plant. "I found it very difficult to be a doting father on the one hand and have to deal with people like Richard Cole on the other."

After a couple of revisions to the itinerary (it was originally planned to open on May 22 in Vienna and then June 14 at the Palais Des Sportes in Paris), the tour kicked off in Dortmund on June 17 under the slogan "Over Europe 1980" and took in 14 dates spanning Switzerland, Holland, Belgium, and Germany.

The early shows displayed a strong air of determined rejuvenation as they romped through a streamlined set that effectively disposed of much of the excessive improvisation of the past. On stage Robert Plant was in jovial mood, taking the audiences through his music hall "Eye Thank Yew" catch phrase routine, a throwback to the "Badgeholders" sketches of 1977. There was a worrying night in Nuremberg on June 27 when they had to abandon the show after John Bonham collapsed with exhaustion after three numbers. This was a result of nervousness and bad eating habits more than any drink or drug related issues, but it was a bad omen nevertheless. Off stage, the road fever of previous tours, much of which had

been instigated by the now absent Cole, was no longer in evidence. Even Led Zeppelin, scourge of the world's innkeepers, could grow up, it seemed.

The halcyon days of the early Seventies were long past. This was reflected in the consistency of their performances, which towards the last days of the tour dipped towards a sterility that suggested their best days may indeed have been behind them. The spirit was still willing, but physically and mentally they were a long way off the peaks of earlier years.

Press coverage was minimal, draping a mystique over this tour (particularly in the US) that wouldn't evaporate until the end of the Eighties when a stream of soundboard recordings hit the bootleg market. The German *Bravo* magazine covered the opening shows, while the solitary UK review appeared in *Melody Maker*, a very favourable piece on the Munich show by Steve Gett, which pleased Grant enormously.

This Europe jaunt did provide enough motivation for Plant to reconsider his decision on America. "I didn't put any pressure on him and he kept saying to Bonzo, 'What's G said about America?' I hoped being up there on stage would give him the necessary lift to do it," said Grant.

Plant harboured secret reservations about the long term future of the group. "By the time we got to the *In Through The Out Door* album, I was so furtive," he admitted in 1995. "And I think Jimmy was too. Maybe if we had communicated then as we do now, perhaps we could have gone on working together. In that period, I was beginning to think that I could do fresh things outside of the group."

Torn between opting out and letting the others down, Robert decided to continue in the band. As they were walking across the airport tarmac on their return to the UK in early July Robert told Grant that he would be willing to tour the US in the fall – but for a maximum of four weeks only.

A relieved Grant set about getting the wheels in motion for a campaign that would be dubbed "Led Zeppelin – The 1980's Part One". The group split for their customary summer recess, ready reconvene at Page's Windsor house in September in preparation for their return to America. They didn't know it then of course, but as the tragic events of that month would dictate, they had already played their final gig as Led Zeppelin in Berlin on July 7. The flight was already over.

Equipment Notes:
Similar set up to 1979 – Jimmy again used the Botswana Brown Fender Telecaster for 'Hot Dog' and 'All My Love', and the Lake Placid Strat for 'In The Evening'. He also brought along an unused Gibson SG and a cream Fender Telecaster which made a rare appearance at the Brussels performance of 'All My Love'.

A radically cut down Showco PA and light show was used. The light show was cut back from 320 lamps to 120. A black drape curtain formed the backdrop. Bonzo's drums were mounted on a plain rostrum. The revolving side-stage light bins were used only during 'Trampled Underfoot'.

Noticably, on the reduced stage size Jones and Page came more to the front of the stage than on previous tours, especially on the encores.

Appearance Notes:
Robert Plant – similar attire for the entire tour, green capsleeve silk T-shirt, FU jeans and tennis shoes. The only jewellery on show was the silver necklace retained from the US '77 tour. His hair was back to near '68 length.
Jimmy Page – a variety of baggy suits were worn (pure white, grey and black pinstripe), green shirt, white and green scarves, green shoes, red slip-ons.
John Paul Jones – hair cut short in a 'Billy Fury' style, as Plant put it. Silk shirts and jeans.
John Bonham – shaved his beard for the two final shows.

Merchandise/Crew Wear: T-shirts and sweat shirts were made available featuring the Air Raid Warden design on the front and tour dates on the reverse. Warden badges were also on sale. There were two official posters – the Warden design and

a colour collage of individual photos taken by Aubrey Powell at the Rainbow rehearsals. A tour programme was planned but shelved. Crew wear included the official sweat shirts and Swan Song Over Europe tour jackets.

Note: The initial itinerary for the 'Over Europe' tour read: May 22 Vienna Stadhalle (rescheduled June 29); May 23 Munich Olympiahalle (rescheduled July 5); May 25 Dortmund Wesfalhallen (rescheduled June 17); May 26 Cologne Sporthalle (rescheduled June 18); May 28 Bremen Stadhalle (rescheduled June 23); May 29 Berlin Deutshlandhalle (rescheduled July 7); May 31 Mannheim Eisstadion (rescheduled July 2),June 1 Zurich Hallenstadion (re scheduled June 29) June 6 Forest National Brussels (rescheduled June 20)

A second revised itinerary had them down to play a date on June 14 in Paris at the Palais Des Sports. In the final tour itinerary that went ahead, it listed them planning on two nights in Berlin July 7 and 8 – this was also listed on the back of official tour T shirts. The date was later pulled for reasons unknown.

Sunday February 3 1980
Birmingham, England
Top Rank
GUEST APPEARANCE
Robert makes another guest appearance with Dave Edmunds' Rockpile joining him on stage for an encore jam.

Monday March 3 1980
Newcastle, England
All Right Now *Tyne Tees TV*
TV APPEARANCE
John Bonham was seen on screen in a rare TV interview for this edition of the Tyne Tees rock

show. Recorded in February at the Tyne Tees studios, it featured Billy Connolly asking John a few basic questions after the screening of a clip of the 'Moby Dick' sequence from *The Song Remains The Same* movie. A highly nervous Bonham chose to reply with basic one word answers, much to Connolly's embarrassment. Fans and subscribers of the Led Zeppelin magazine Sarah Brewin and Carolyn Longstaff were in attendance and could be seen standing behind Bonzo wearing Tight But Loose At Knebworth t-shirts.

April/May 1980
Rainbow Theatre/New Victoria Theatre
London, England
Shepperton Studios
Shepperton, England
REHEARSALS
The band spent over a month at these locations preparing a new stage set up and set list for the impending Europe tour. A surviving rehearsal tape from the Rainbow sessions included 'White Summe', 'Black Mountian Side', 'Achilles Last Stand' and 'Stairway To Heaven'.

During their rehearsal stint at the Rainbow Aubrey Powell of the Hipgnosis design team came in to take new photos of the band. It showed a pencil-thin, fragile looking Page in contrast to the fit looking Plant in Brazil soccer shirt with new shorter length hair. Photos from this session were used for the official Led Zeppelin *Over Europe* posters.

Bootleg CD Reference: *The Last Rehearsal* (Missing Link)

Tuesday June 17 1980
Dortmund, Germany
Westfalenhalle
Set: Train Kept A Rollin'/Nobody's Fault But Mine/Black Dog/In The Evening/The Rain Song/Hot Dog/All My Love/Trampled Underfoot/Since I've Been Loving You/Achilles Last Stand/White Summer – Black Mountain Side/Kashmir/Stairway To Heaven/Rock And Roll/Whole Lotta Love-Heartbreaker-Whole Lotta Love.

The rehearsals were obviously worthwhile. From the opening date they seemed enthusiastic and energetic. Problems often present at the start of Zeppelin tours were absent with the band already on top form and remarkably few equipment problems, probably because of the reduced size of the show and lack of acoustic set.

'Train Kept A Rollin'', an old Yardbirds favourite, was a surprise choice as opening number – the band hadn't played it live since September 2, 1970 in Oakland.

Another surprise for this tour – Jimmy actually spoke to the audience, something he did only rarely in the past. For this tour he introduced 'Black Dog', usually in a foreign language – tonight it's called 'Schwartz Hund'.

'All My Love', 'In The Evening' and 'Hot Dog' were the only new tracks from *In Through The Out Door* performed on the tour. The second encore was rather unusual: 'Whole Lotta Love' segued into 'Heartbreaker' and then back into 'Whole Lotta Love' again. It would not be performed again in this fashion.

Robert's parting comment was 'Goodnight Dinosaurs Rule! They would continue to refer to themselves as dinosaurs throughout the tour.

'Led Zeppelin Are Thundering Through Germany' reported the German magazine, *Bravo* "Seven years the fans had to wait for this German tour. It appears as if time has stood still. Led Zeppelin present their old songs and some of their new album. Everything seems clear as soon as Jimmy takes his slim fingers to the guitar and works himself into a solo. Led Zeppelin need no big show. Robert and Jimmy are all that is needed to release that old glitter and sparkle."

Bootleg CD References: *Dinosaurs Rule Pt 1 & Pt 2* (Flying Disc), *Dortmund* (Tarantura), *Return To Auschwitz* (Neptune)

Wednesday June 18 1980
Cologne, Germany
Sporthalle

Set: Train Kept A Rollin'/Nobody's Fault But Mine/Black Dog/In The Evening/The Rain Song/Hot Dog/All My Love/Trampled Underfoot/Since I've Been Loving You/Achilles Last Stand/White Summer – Black Mountain Side/Kashmir/Stairway To Heaven/Rock And Roll/Communication Breakdown.

Another strong performance. "There's quite a lot to be said for Dinosaurs."

The excesses of the past had now been shed; no more lengthy self-indulgent guitar, keyboard or drum solos. The shows were now usually just under two hours in duration, a far cry from the marathons of 1975 and 1977.

'Communication Breakdown' made its tour début tonight as a second encore.

"So this is what it's like being in a rock and roll band!" is Plant's parting shot.

Some 22 minutes of silent black and white cine footage exists from this show

Bootleg CD References: *It's Good To Be Seen* (The Diagrams Of Led Zeppelin), *Blitzkrieg Over Europe* (Tarantura), *A Close Shave Pt 1 & Pt 2* (Flying Disc)
Visual References: *Early Visions (unofficial DVD – Celebration)*, *1979/1980 (unofficial DVD – Cosmic Energy)*

Friday June 20 1980
Brussels, Belgium
Vorst National

Set: Train Kept A Rollin'/Nobody's Fault But Mine/Black Dog/In The Evening/The Rain Song/Hot Dog/All My Love/Trampled Underfoot/Since I've Been Loving You/Achilles Last Stand/White Summer – Black Mountain Side/Kashmir/Stairway To Heaven/Rock And

Roll/Whole Lotta Love (inc. Boogie Chillun).

"Eye Thank Yew" seemed to be Plant's catch phrase for this tour. He was continually urging audiences to repeat the phrase and make gestures with their hands.

There were very few changes to the main set on this tour with most variations occurring during the encores. Tonight 'Whole Lotta Love' was back as a second encore, but with a new arrangement featuring Page's Theremin battle, a funky new section and 'Boogie Chillun' (complete with the immortal line – "That little boy's reached the age of 31. I mean 24. Sorry!")

Bootleg CD References: *Brussels '80* (Tarantura), *The Belguim Triple* (Empress Valley), *Chien Noir* (Antrabata), *Brussels Affair* (Swinging Pig)

Saturday June 21 1980
Rotterdam, Holland
Ahoy

Set: Train Kept A Rollin'/Nobody's Fault But Mine/Black Dog/In The Evening/The Rain Song/Hot Dog/All My Love/Trampled Underfoot/Since I've Been Loving You/Achilles Last Stand/White Summer – Black Mountain Side/Kashmir/Stairway To Heaven/Rock And Roll/Heartbreaker.

Another good performance, though the Dutch audience were slow to react.

Many fans made the journey from England to Holland and afterwards one such fan, Barbara Rodermond, of London, wrote to the letters page of *Sounds*: "Dear Led Zeppelin, it was great to have had you playing in Holland. You were great! But the audience was a bore. I never went to a concert with an audience as uninspiring as this one in Rotterdam. It spoiled everything. What could have been a great show went down like a wet firework. As Robert Plant put it correctly, while speaking to the audience at the end of the show:

We've been here for two hours, where were you?' What a bore it must have been for you to play to the Dutch audience. So, Led Zep, I hope to see you playing over here in England soon – and I hope you play 'Whole Lotta Love'. I thought it was a bit ridiculous not playing it in Rotterdam."

Ten minutes of clear 8mm colour cine film exists from this show

Bootleg CD References: *Kashmir* (Seagull), *Not Guaranteed To Wake You* (The Diagrams Of Led Zeppelin), *Rotterdam '80* (Tarantura), *Live In Rotterdam* (Swinging Pig)

Visual References: *Latter Visions* (unofficial DVD – Celebration), *1979/1980* (unofficial DVD – Cosmic Energy)

Monday June 23 1980
Bremen, Germany
Stadthalle

Set: Train Kept A Rollin'/Nobody's Fault But Mine/Out On The Tiles (introduction)/Black Dog/In The Evening/The Rain Song/Hot Dog/All My Love/Trampled Underfoot/Since I've Been Loving You/Achilles Last Stand/White Summer – Black Mountainside/Kashmir/ Stair-way To Heaven/Rock And Roll/Communication Breakdown. .

A rather disjointed performance. John Bonham, surprisingly, ventured to the front of the stage to introduce 'Hot Dog'.

Some of their timings were suspect, but they recovered for a particularly potent encore, pairing 'Rock And Roll' with 'Communication Breakdown'.

Bootleg CD References: *Dinosaur* (Toasted Condor), *Moonlight* (Toasted Condor), *Bremen* (Tarantura), *Chien Noir* (Antrabata)

Tuesday June 24 1980
Hanover, Germany
Messehalle

Set Train Kept A Rollin'/Nobody's Fault But

Mine/Out On The Tiles (introduction)/Black Dog/In The Evening/The Rain Song/Hot Dog/All My Love/Trampled Underfoot/Since I've Been Loving You/Achilles Last Stand/White Summer – Black Mountainside/Kashmir/ Stairway To Heaven/Rock And Roll/Communication Breakdown. .

Similar performance to the previous night. 'Trampled Underfoot' and 'Achilles Last Stand' both contained ragged moments, but sheer enthusiasm pulled them through.

Bootleg CD References: *Messhalle Echoes* (Flying Disc), *Hanover* (Tarantura)
Last Tour (Forever Standard)

Thursday June 26 1980
Vienna, Austria
Stadthalle

Set: Train Kept A Rollin'/Nobody's Fault But Mine/Out On The Tiles (introduction)/Black Dog/In The Evening/The Rain Song/Hot Dog/All My Love/Trampled Underfoot/Since I've Been Loving You/Achilles Last Stand/White Summer – Black Mountainside/Kashmir/Stairway To Heaven/Rock And Roll/Whole Lotta Love.

Tonight's show was marred by audience problems. The crowd were noisy, rowdy and keep pushing the stage. Halfway through 'White Summer', Jimmy was hit in the face with one of Zeppelin's oldest enemies – a firecracker. The band left the stage and there was a long delay before the promoter of the concert took the microphone. He explained what had happened and said that the band wanted to talk to the idiot who threw the firecracker and that they would not return until they had seen him. Eventually the band did return and launched straight into 'Kashmir'.

Page later played a few bars of 'Deutschland Uber Alles' as the introduction to 'Stairway To Heaven'.

Bootleg CD References: *Deutschland Uber Alles* (The Diagrams Of Led Zeppelin), *Blitzkrieg Over Europe* (Tarantura), *Vienna 1980* (Tarantura)

Friday June 27 1980
Nuremberg, Germany
Messehalle
Set: Train Kept A Rollin'/Nobody's Fault But Mine/Black Dog.

After 'Nobody's Fault But Mine', Page warned the audience that two of the band were not feeling well. In fact, Bonzo only lasted one more number before collapsing. Plant referred to it as a slight technical problem. The show was abandoned.

There was press speculation that Bonham's problem was caused by too much booze and drugs. In fact, Bonham has simply eaten too much fruit. Peter Grant recalled: "They wrapped Bonzo up in a red blanket in the ambulance. So they strapped him in with this belt and he says 'How do I look?' and I said 'Like fucking Father Christmas!' and he says 'Don't make me laugh, it bloody hurts. But he'd had 27 bananas that night so it's not surprising he was ill."

Robert Plant: "Bonzo had a German belly. He had eaten, well, three thousand bananas!"

Bootleg CD References: *Air Raids Over Europe* (Tecumseh), *Fly Over Nuremburg* (The Diagrams Of Led Zeppelin), *Blitzkrieg Over Europe* (Tarantura)

Sunday June 29 1980
Zurich, Switzerland
Hallenstadion
Set: Train Kept A Rollin'/Nobody's Fault But

WRONG FUCKIN' GUITAR RAY!
FRANKFURT JUNE 30 1980

Mine/Out On the Tiles (introduction)/Black Dog/In The Evening/The Rain Song/Hot Dog/All My Love/Trampled Underfoot/Since I've Been Loving You/Achilles Last Stand/White Summer – Black Mountainside/Kashmir/Stairway To Heaven/Rock And Roll/Heartbreaker.

The band bounced back in style with one of the best performances of the tour. Robert's vocals were clear and sharp, while Jimmy's playing was fluent and inspiring.

They did, however, get a little bit lost during 'Kashmir' as Plant acknowledged: 'If anybody's bootlegging that, you'll have to scratch that number as it wasn't completely correct.'

'Stairway To Heaven' was a peerless performance and included Plant's regular "Over Europe" ad lib: "I keep chopin'n'changing."

Page was on peak form for the 'Heartbreaker' encore, turning in a performance that ran the whole gamut of styles that he has brought to the piece over the years. The end result was perhaps the most outstanding live performance of the post-1977 years.

This show was the first ever Zeppelin concert to be released on bootleg CD, in 1989. *Tour Over Europe 1980* on the Twin-Eagle label was sourced from an excellent quality soundboard tape. Superb mixing desk tapes have subsequently been released unofficially from nearly all the dates on this European jaunt.

Ten minutes of excellent clear colour cine film exists from this show

Bootleg CD References: *Tour Over Europe 1980* (Twin-Eagle), *Gracias* (Antrabata), *Zurich 80* (Tanrantura), *Zurich 80 "Tour Over Europe 80"* (The Diagrams Of Led Zeppelin), *Complete Switzerland Show* (Black Swan)

Monday June 30 1980
Frankfurt, Germany
Festhalle
Set: Train Kept A Rollin'/Nobody's Fault But Mine/Black Dog/In The Evening/The Rain Song/Hot Dog/All My Love/Trampled

Underfoot/Since I've Been Loving You/Achilles Last Stand/White Summer – Black Mountain Side/Kashmir/Stairway To Heaven/Rock And Roll/Money/Whole Lotta Love (inc. Boogie Chillun' and Frankfurt Special)

Another outstanding performance. The band was on top form and the crowd showed their appreciation. In fact they made so much noise during 'White Summer' that Jimmy had to stop the number to calm them down – he can't hear himself play!

Plant dedicated 'Trampled Underfoot' to Cooky, a local night club owner who had died a few days before.

Atlantic chief Ahmet Ertegun was in attendance for this date and after the show has some initial discussions with Grant regarding renewing their contract with the label. They tentatively shook hands on a new five year deal.

Back on stage, Phil Carson of Atlantic Records joined the band for the rare encore, the Barret Strong classic, 'Money'. He was introduced as "The man who used to play bass for Dusty Springfield" and Plant led the band into an impromptu version of 'Frankfurt Special' during 'Whole Lotta Love'.

'Professionals With Loveable Spleens!' was the bizarre headline in *Musik Express*. The German magazine reported: "The mood is relaxed, open and enthusiastic. The band gets a tremendous reception. The Frankfurter GIs guarantee the welcome in style."

Plant: "We can do it every night now – it's beginning to make Knebworth look a little puny."

Bootleg CD References: *Frankfurt Special* (Empress Valley), *Tour Over Europe* (Last Stand), *Blitzrieg Over Europe* (Tarantura), *Dinosaur* (Toasted Condor), *Moonlight* (Toasted Condor)

Tuesday July 1 1980
Frankfurt, Germany
Festhalle
GUEST APPEARANCE

Jimmy Page joined Santana for an encore performance of 'Shake Your Moneymaker'. Carlos Santana had attended the previous night's Led Zeppelin concert at the same venue and invited Page along to this show.

Bootleg CD Reference: *First Of July* (Empress Valley)

Wednesday July 2 1980
Mannheim, Germany
Eisstadion

Set: Train Kept A Rollin'/Nobody's Fault But Mine/Out On The Tiles (introduction)/Black Dog/In The Evening/The Rain Song/Hot Dog/All My Love/Trampled Underfoot/Since I've Been Loving You/Achilles Last Stand/White Summer – Black Mountainside/Kashmir/ Stair-way To Heaven/Rock And Roll/Whole Lotta Love.

The Mannheim shows were performed in a canvas covered arena. The crowd were wild and enthusiastic but the band seemed to tire and the urgency and excitement of the earlier shows was absent.

Curiously, Page was now introducing 'Black Dog' as 'Strangers In The Night'

Bootleg CD References: *Dinosaur Watching Pt 1 & Pt 2* (Flying Disc), *Strangers In The Night* (The Diagrams Of Led Zeppelin), *Eye Thank You* (Tarantura), *Mannheim 1980* (Tarantura)

Thursday July 3 1980
Mannheim, Germany
Eisstadion

Set: Train Kept A Rollin'/Nobody's Fault Bu

Mine/Black Dog/In The Evening/The Rain Song/Hot Dog/All My Love/Trampled Underfoot/Since I've Been Loving You/Achilles Last Stand/White Summer – Black Mountain Side/Kashmir/Stairway To Heaven/Communication Breakdown/Rock And Roll.

Plant had to continually urge the audience to calm down at both Mannheim gigs. "Stop moving like a snake!" he said. An average performance – again they appeared stilted at times compared to earlier gigs.

Bootleg CD References: *Mannheim* (Tarantura), *Motivated Dinosaurs In Mannheim Pt 1 & Pt 2* (Flying Disc), *Strangers In The Night* (The Diagrams Of Led Zeppelin), *Eye Thank You* (Tarantura), *Last Days In Mannheim* (Whole Lotta Live)

Saturday July 5 1980
Munich, Germany
Olympia Halle
Set Train Kept A Rollin'/Nobody's Fault But Mine/Out

On The Tiles (introduction)/Black Dog/In The Evening/The Rain Song/Hot Dog/All My Love/Trampled Underfoot/Since I've Been Loving You/Achilles Last Stand/White Summer – Black Mountainside/Kashmir/ Stairway To Heaven/Rock and Roll/Whole Lotta Love.

The larger surroundings seemed to prompt them back into top gear and a return to the urgency of the first few shows.

The second encore of 'Whole Lotta Love' featured Simon Kirke, the drummer from Bad Company, who joined Bonzo for a jam.

Melody Maker was one of the few magazines to review any shows from this tour. Under the headline 'Led Zeppelin Uber Alles!', Steve Gett wrote: "Just after a quarter past nine the house lights were switched off, the cue for Munich's Olympic Hall to erupt with more force than a volcano as Zeppelin were greeted with Teutonic fervour. This was indeed a magical moment.

"From the first few bars, Pagey leapt around the

stage like a madman, never standing still for more than a second throughout the whole show, cutting an image somewhere between Chuck Berry and AC/DC's Angus Young! Led Zeppelin, more than anything, were enjoying themselves and the true spirit of the band, somewhat lost by the showcase element of Knebworth, had returned.

"Indeed it was Jimmy, most of all, who epitomised the new-found enthusiasm of the group. His guitar playing was excellent – rough at times but any errors were covered by moments of inspired genius.

"It was one of the most enjoyable gigs I have experienced and certainly the best this year. The group enjoyed themselves as much as the audience."

At the after-show reception at Munich's Hilton hotel, Page and Bonham summarised the tour.

John Bonham: "Overall, everyone has been dead chuffed with the way the tour's gone. There were so many things that could have gone wrong. It was a bit of a gamble this one, but it's worked really well."

Jimmy Page: "Munich was the nearest feeling to that of the big American shows. There was a lot of energy and it was really exciting."

Ten minutes of clear colour cine footage including shots of Simon Kirke exist from this show

Bootleg CD References: *Munich 1980* **(Tarantura)**
Visual References: *Latter Days* (Unofficial DVD - Celebration), *1979/1980* (Unofficial DVD Cosmic Energy)

Monday July 7 1980
Berlin, Germany
Eissporthalle
Set: Train Kept A Rollin'/Nobody's

Fault But Mine/Black Dog/In The Evening/The Rain Song/Hot Dog/All My Love/Trampled Underfoot/Since I've Been Loving You/White Summer – Black Mountain Side/Kashmir/ Stairway To Heaven/Rock And Roll/Whole Lotta Love.

The final show of the tour and, as it turned out, the final show that Led Zeppelin would ever perform.

It was a rather unbalanced performance, with amazing highs like the beautifully constructed guitar solo in 'Stairway To Heaven' to some lesser moments such as a monotonous rambling 'White Summer'. 'Achilles Last Stand' was inexplicably dropped from the set, yet the concert was still the longest of the tour.

Zeppelin's final moments on stage were highlighted by two extraordinary performances – both delivered as if they intuitively knew it might be for the very last time. 'Stairway' found Page drifting off into a world of his own as he applied a lengthy lyrical solo that extended the piece to over 14 minutes. 'Whole Lotta Love' was also greatly extended, clocking in at over 17 minutes. The camaraderie of recent weeks seemed to will them to keep the flame burning for as long as they could on this tour. It triggered a nostalgic throwback to the experimental Zeppelin of the early Seventies as they battled out a lengthy Theremin vocal duel.

"Eye Thank Yew. Thank you very much Berlin. Thank you very much everybody who's worked with us and put up with us and all those sort of things and, er, goodnight!" was Plant's last formal address to a crowd as a member of Led Zeppelin.

A little over 80 days later, the group effectively ceased to be.

Bootleg CD References: *Complete Berlin* (Silver Rarities), *Final Touch* (Toasted Condor), *Last Stand* (Toasted Condor), *Heinekin* (Tarantura), *Eternal Magic* (Empress Valley), *The Last* (Immigrant)

POSTSCRIPT 1980

Following the European tour, the band split for a summer break. With Robert having finally agreed to go back to America, Peter Grant began negotiating venues for a US tour in the autumn. On September 5, Swan Song issued the following press statement under the heading "LED ZEPPELIN – THE 80's PART ONE":

"Peter Grant, manager of Led Zeppelin, announced today that Led Zeppelin will tour in the United States for approximately one month starting in the middle of October. Exact dates and information concerning the purchase of tickets will be announced within the next ten days."

Grant: "I knew we couldn't cover everywhere in four weeks which was Robert's condition, but once we got over there and got back into the swing I thought we'd be fine. So it was Part One of what I hoped would be further visits."

The basic plan was to cover the Midwest and North East of America in October and November and return to the US for a West Coast tour early in 1981. The UK was pencilled in for the spring. On September 11, Swan Song announced the first run of dates – the itinerary would take in 21 shows commencing in Montreal on October 17 and ending with four successive nights at Chicago Stadium over November 10, 11, 12 & 13. Rehearsals were booked for late September at Bray Studios, near Maidenhead.

On September 18 Jimmy Page visited the London Swan Song office to sanction a mock up

model of a new lighting rig and stage set up they would be using. This was a slightly larger rig than they had used in Europe with additional lighting effects to that used in Europe. A tentative set list was suggested with 'Carouselambra' heading the new numbers that had not previously been played live.

On September 24 John Bonham left his Worcestershire home with Rex King to meet up with the rest of the group for initial rehearsals at Bray Studios. He began drinking quadruple measures of vodka at a stop off in a pub on the way and this binge continued when the group assembled at Bray. Bonzo had been feeling tentative about going back to America – the Bill Graham incident still hung heavy on his mind – and as ever he was nervous about preparing for a tour.

Realising there would be little in the way of serious rehearsing completed that night, Page & Plant called an early evening halt. They all returned to Page's Windsor home. Bonham fell asleep around midnight. In the morning of September 25, Page's aide Rick Hobbs checked on Bonham's room at around 8am. He appeared to be sleeping fine. At 1.45pm roadie Benji Le Fevre entered Bonham's room to check on him again. He did not stir and on checking his pulse, John Bonham was found to be dead, a victim of waterlogging of the lungs through inhaling vomit following a drinking session that had included 40 measures of vodka. The verdict later recorded at the inquest was accidental death. He was just 32.

It was a tragic waste and the final premature chapter in the Led Zeppelin story.

Robert Plant: "John had a heart of gold. He was a beautiful man but he never really had an idea of how important he was, and he was very insecure because of it. It really was an exasperating loss."

In a bitter irony, at exactly the same time as these events were unfolding, thousands of Zeppelin fans were queuing in Chicago to obtain copies of the Thursday edition of the *Chicago Tribune* which carried mail order applications for the forthcoming November dates. Their quest was entirely in vain – the tour was immediately cancelled and the Led Zeppelin live experience was to become a memory in the minds of all those who had been lucky enough to catch them over the past 12 years.

Following John's funeral on October 7, the remaining group members and their entourage flew to their old haunt of Jersey to try to come to terms with the tragedy and decide what lay ahead. On their return Grant booked a room at the Savoy for a meeting. "They all looked to me and asked what I thought," recalled Grant. "I said it couldn't go on because what Led Zeppelin had been was the four of them and now one of them was no longer with us, it had to end. They were all relieved because that's exactly how they all felt."

In the weeks following the tragedy there had been much speculation in the music press that a replacement for Bonham would be sought. Names such as Bad Company's Simon Kirke, Carmine Appice, Aynsley Dunbar, Cozy Powell and Roxy Music's Paul Thompson were being cited, but there had never been any real intention to carry on and on December 4, 1980, Peter Grant handed Atlantic a press release for immediate distribution. It read as follows:

"We wish it to be known that the loss of our dear friend and the deep respect we have for his family, together with the deep sense of harmony felt by ourselves and our manager have led us to decide that we could not continue as we were."

Within three months of that statement Robert Plant was back on stage, returning to his pre-Zeppelin roots, fronting a pick-up R&B band known as The Honeydrippers. The stark reality of the events of the past few months was more than evident in his curt acknowledgement that his previous band was definitely a thing of the past. "As far as I'm concerned there is no more Led Zeppelin. No more Led anything. We got together and made the decision to call it a day. The band no longer exists."

Wednesday September 24 1980
Bray Studios, Berkshire, England
REHEARSALS

The last get together of the four members of

Led Zeppelin. Rehearsals for the forthcoming US tour were scheduled to start on the Tuesday but ran a day late. Bonzo's roadie Mick Hinton recalled, "We set up in Bray and did a lighting run through earlier in the day. Bonzo arrived looking well worse for wear. It was the first day so nobody was too worried though. He got on the drum stool and fell off it two or three times. I don't think much rehearsing was done. Robert suggested we call it a day and sort it out tomorrow. They all went back to Jimmy's. I went back to London as I was staying with a girlfriend. I heard the news the next day on the radio. I just couldn't believe it. I was in total shock."

John Paul Jones (1999): "I found him – me and Benji our roadie. It was at Jimmy's house in Windsor. It was like 'Lets go upstairs and have a look at Bonzo. Kick him out of bed'. We banged into the bedroom but there was no movement from him. It was drink. It could have happened to anyone. You drink too much and you end up on your back instead of your side. That's all it was. It was after our first day of rehearsals. I had to tell Robert and Jimmy and they had been in high spirits at the time because the band was almost in a rebirth situation. John could drink a lot but then we all used to take all sorts of things. I had some hairy nights with him. To be honest he hated being away from home. I was very fond of him. After his death we dissolved the band immediately. The band was such that it was four people. It wasn't a song-based band where the songs were famous with some musicians backing them. The whole point of Led Zeppelin was four members and how they interacted and the music we all made. It simply wasn't Led Zeppelin when there were only three of us …"

Robert Plant (1990): "To me the band didn't exist the moment Bonzo had gone.
Sometimes I still shout up there at that mass of blue and go 'That was not a very good trick.'"

Friday October 17 1980
Montreal, Quebec
Montreal Forum
CANCELLED

Sunday October 19 1980
Monday October 20 1980
Landover, Maryland
Capitol Center
CANCELLED

Wednesday October 22 1980
Philadelphia, Pensylvania
The Spectrum
CANCELLED

Thursday October 23 1980
Landover, Maryland
Capitol Center
CANCELLED

Sunday October 26 1980 &
Monday October 27 1980
Richfield, Ohio
Richfield Coliseum
CANCELLED

Wednesday October 29 1980 &
Thursday October 30 1980
Detroit, Michigan
Joe Louis Arena
CANCELLED

Saturday November 1 1980
Buffalo, New York
War Memorial Auditorium
CANCELLED

Monday November 3 1980 &
Tuesday November 4 1980
Philadelphia, Pensylvania
The Spectrum
CANCELLED

Thursday November 6 1980 &
Friday November 7 1980
Pittsburgh, Pensylvania
Civic Arena
CANCELLED

Sunday November 9 1980
St. Paul Minnesota
Civic Centre Arena
CANCELLED

Monday November 10,
Wednesday November 12,
Thursday November 13 &
Saturday November 15 1980
Chicago Illinois
Chicago
Stadium
CANCELLED

Led Zeppelin

Led Zeppelin may no longer have existed but John Bonham's untimely death left them with plenty of business to finalise. Atlantic in particular were most concerned that their single biggest selling act was no longer functioning. Contractually there was one album still to deliver. Grant had actually shaken on a tentative new deal with Atlantic supremo Ahmet Ertegun during the European tour.

During 1981, initial moves were made concerning a final album. Page was still keen on the live chronology idea he had mooted for the last five years. Plant was less struck on the idea. Instead it was decided that if enough out-take studio material could be found, a single album of leftover material would be issued. Page salvaged eight recordings: three from the *In Through The Out Door* sessions, one each from *Led Zeppelin III* and *Houses Of The Holy* periods, plus 'Bonzo's Montreux' – an all percussion excursion from mid-1976. The remaining pair of selections were mixed down from the live recording Page held of the famous Royal Albert Hall, January 9 1970 show. 'We're Gonna Groove' and 'I Can't Quit You' were easily the album's most impressive cuts and hinted at what in-concert riches might lurk within the Page archive. The album was duly released in November 1982 under the appropriate title of *Coda*.

By this time, Peter Grant had decided to relinquish all management ties with the remaining members and entered what he later described as "a period of blackness". Jimmy Page, Robert Plant and John Paul Jones had little alternative but to try and establish themselves as solo artists. Page himself sums up that period with this story: "There was a period after John died where I didn't touch a guitar for ages. It just seemed to relate to everything that had happened. But then one day I called up my road manager and instructed him to get the Les Paul out of storage. He went to get it and the case was empty! It had been borrowed without permission and it eventually reappeared.

But when he came back and said 'the guitar's missing', I thought 'that's it. I'm finished!' But thank God it turned up and I began to pick up the pieces."

The three of them set about establishing new careers. However, the pull of the past was never too far away and their respective paths continued to cross by way of guest appearances at each others' concerts and the occasional live gig. They were all adamant that there would be no major Led Zeppelin reunion. What they didn't bargain for was Bob Geldof's reaction to Michael Buerk's emotional report on the plight of the Ethiopians and Ahmet Ertegun's decision to throw an anniversary concert to celebrate the 40th birthday of Atlantic Records.

Wednesday May 12 1982
Munich, Germany
Sports Arena

Guest Appearance: Robert Plant and Jimmy Page guest with Foreigner – coming on for an encore jam of 'Lucille'.

Robin Smith reviewed the show for *Record Mirror*: "Six thousand fans gasp in disbelief and then scream for some action as Plant and Page amble out of the backstage shadows. Any bootlegger in the audience stands to make a fortune, as Lou Gramm and Plant settle down into a vocal powerhouse and Page's magic little fingers become a wicked blur over the frets of a borrowed guitar.

"For a while, it was touch and go whether they would be cajoled into this bit of fun. Plant trotted around undecided and Page tried a selection of guitars for size, before they both threw caution to the winds. The official explanation for their visit is that they're both on holiday and want a lively night out."

Lou Gramm, vocalist with Foreigner, commented: "I've always held Zeppelin in high esteem so it was great for me to be on stage with them tonight."

Sunday December 4 1983
Bristol, England
Colston Hall
GUEST APPEARANCE
John Paul Jones joined Robert on stage for the encore 'Little Sister' at his solo gig – a nostalgic return for the pair to a venue they last played with Zeppelin in 1970.

Tuesday December 13 1983
London, England
Hammersmith Odeon
GUEST APPEARANCE
Back from the ARMS tour, Jimmy joined Robert at his solo gig for an encore jam of 'Treat Her Right'. He used the cream Telecaster. Both attended the after show party at The Old Rangoon in Barnes.
Bootleg CD Reference: *Treat Her Right* (Wardour)

August 1984
Ibizia, Spain
Heartbreak Hotel
Robert Plant and Jimmy Page performed a short set in a small club with Phil May and various members of The Pretty Things accompanying them.

Jimmy played a white Fender Stratocaster and Robert played maracas.

Phil Carson of Atlantic Records was present and talked of his plans to re-form Led Zeppelin.

Saturday July 13 1985
Philadelphia, USA
JFK Stadium
Set: Rock And Roll/Whole Lotta Love/Stairway To Heaven.

Having missed out on the Band Aid single, Plant was more than happy to assist Bob Geldof at the Live Aid concert. Philadelphia tied in nicely with his Shaken'n'Stirred US tour. The initial plan was for Robert to hook up with Eric Clapton. "The event was far bigger than my determination to stay clear of something, so I called Jimmy up and said 'Let's do it'." Ex-Chic drummer Tony Thompson was roped in and John Paul Jones answered the call to join them. Paul Martinez from Plant's band also helped out. A morning rehearsal was all they had time for. Phil Collins, who had flown over after already appearing at the Wembley concert, completed the line-up. They took the stage at 8.13pm US East Coast time, 1.13am in the UK, following Collins' introduction: "I'd like to introduce some friends of mine. Would you welcome Mr Robert Plant, Mr Jimmy Page, Mr John Paul Jones, Mr Tony Thompson, Mr Paul Martinez."

Plant's voice was shot, Jimmy had trouble with his monitors and the drummers were out of sync, but none of this affected their impact on the audience and the millions watching at home on TV. Their three song set was the runaway hit of the Philadelphia concert. "Any requests?" called out Robert before Jimmy spat out 'Heartbreaker' riffs then broke into 'Whole Lotta Love' which was played in edited form *a la* the US hit single. Inevitably, it was 'Stairway To Heaven' that inspired the most emotional response from the 90,000 present, both out front and backstage, but also – and more importantly – in countless living rooms around the world. In the UK, when the set began the total monies pledged stood at £800,000. Within an hour of the last bars of 'Stairway To Heaven' being relayed via satellite, the total pledged had topped £2 million. Not only had thousands of fans stayed up late to see three-quarters of the mighty Led Zeppelin on stage again, but whatever its shortcomings their brief but moving appearance inspired a wave of generosity that more than doubled the day's takings.

All the band gathered for an interview for MTV

backstage. "It happened for about 20 minutes and it was great. This was the right reason to do it," said Plant. Asked the inevitable question would they play together again, Plant initially dismissed the question wit a curt: "Get out of get of it." Then, tellingly, he followed it up with: "Yes it would be great to do this more than once ... "

"I'd be lying if I said I wasn't drunk on the whole event," Plant would later reflect. "If we had the preparation that other people did we might have been able to hold our head up. But I was still very charged with the whole effect of it all."

A decade later he was less charitable: "Live Aid was a fucking atrocity for us. It made us look like loonies. I was hoarse and Pagey was out of tune. We had no monitors, no nothin'. The whole idea of playing 'Stairway To Heaven' with two drummers while Duran Duran cried on the side of stage – there was something really quite surreal about that. I thought 'Are we supposed to be Sinatra? Is this "My Way"?'"

In 2004 Page Plant and Jones refused permission to allow any of their Live Aid footage to be used on a special 20th anniversary official Live Aid DVD capturing the two concerts highlights. They informed Bob Geldof that they felt the performances to be substandard and not representative of the band. Instead they gave royalties over to the Band Aid Trust from sales of the just released Jimmy Page Robert Plant *Unledded/No Quarter* DVD and the proceeds of John Paul Jones' Mutual Admiration Society tour. This of course did not stop enterprising bootleggers from quickly pressing a DVD featuring the Zeppelin performance.

Bootleg CD Reference: *Still Flying* (Forever Standard)

Visual Reference: *Led Zeppelin – Minus One* (unofficial DVD, no label)

Tuesday July 23 1985
New Jersey, USA
Meadowlands Arena, East Rutherford
GUEST APPEARANCE

Jimmy Page joined up with Robert again for his solo Meadowlands concert. In the presence of Atlantic supremo Ahmet Ertegun, Jimmy joined in on the encore. Both had similar garb to that worn at the Live Aid show ten days ago. Robert repeated his "Any Requests?" taunt but resisted the obvious calls and the pair compromised with two old blues standards, 'Mean Woman Blues' and Roy Brown's 'Treat Her Right' (the latter was performed the last time Page joined Plant at the Hammersmith Odeon in 1983).

January 1986
Bath, Avon England
REHEARSALS

The Live Aid reunion sparked inevitable rumours that the three would reform on a permanent basis. This was not without credence and they all agreed to a period of rehearsal. In January 1986 Page, Plant and Jones converged on a village hall near Peter Gabriel's studio in Bath. Tony Thompson was again drafted in as drummer. They attempted to make new music together – with Jones on keyboards and allegedly Plant on bass. "Two or three things sounded quite promising," said Plant later. "A sort of cross between David Byrne and Husker Du." But the sessions were quickly abandoned. Page was not in good shape and had trouble tuning up. "For it to have succeeded in Bath I would have to have been far more patient than I have for years," admitted Plant. Matters were not helped when Tony Thompson was injured in a car accident. Page: "The second day we got to play, it really started to cook. And that very night Tony went out and got involved in a car crash. I just thought 'Wait a minute, this just isn't meant to be'. We tried playing along with drum machine after that and then a roadie took over drums for a bit. I just felt completely . 'What's the point ... y'know?' But before th

accident it had shown signs of really starting to get somewhere."

Friday December 19 1986
Stourport, England
Civic Centre
GUEST APPEARANCE

Jimmy Page joined Robert for a little publicised jam. Robert performed with The Honeydrippers at a benefit show in aid of the family of the late Midlands musician John Pasternak. Plant did two sets and during the second brought on Jimmy who used the Botswana brown Telecaster) to perform a few old blues standards. However they completed the evening with a blistering version of Rock And Roll'.

Sunday April 17 1988
London, England
Hammersmith Odeon
GUEST APPEARANCE

Jimmy joined Robert and his band for an extended cameo appearance that was an unexpected delight for all those lucky enough to be there. Originally scheduled to play on three encore numbers, Jimmy stayed on stage for half an hour, performing a stunning 'Tramped Underfoot', 'Gamblers Blues' (including snippets of 'I Can't Quit You' and 'Since I've Been Loving You') and Rock And Roll'. Page used the familiar Les Paul and played brilliantly throughout. This was in marked contrast to the next liaison with Plant.

Saturday May 14 1988
New York, USA
Madison Square Garden
Set: Kashmir/Heartbreaker/Whole Lotta Love/Misty Mountain Hop/Stairway To Heaven.

An opportunity to make amends for Live Aid. Page, Plant and Jones accepted an invitation from Ahmet Ertegun to re-form to headline Atlantic's 12-hour 40th Anniversary concert. They decided to bring in Jason Bonham to play on drums.

With Plant on tour, Page, Jones and Bonham junior rehearse at London's Nomis Studios. Between 15 and 20 Zeppelin numbers were put through their paces. Further rehearsals took place with Robert in New York, including a soundcheck at the Garden the day prior to the show. Here they ran through the Atlantic set plus 'I Can't Quit You'.

The concert, billed as 'It's Only Rock And Roll', included performances from The Coasters, The Rascals, Crosby Stills & Nash, Genesis, Wilson Pickett, Iron Butterfly, Emerson Lake & Palmer (reforming especially for the day), Ben E King, Foreigner and a solo spot from Plant and his band.

There were plans to close the show with a greatest hits all-star jam but that idea was shelved. As stage organiser Bill Graham (back in relative harmony with the reformed Zeppelin) stated: "No offence to anybody else on the bill, but nobody could follow Zeppelin!"

During the day a video of Zeppelin playing 'Heartbreaker' at Knebworth was screened between band changeovers.

But there were problems when the show ran late. Page arrived at the Garden at 11.30pm expecting to go on at midnight. They finally went on at 1.30am. This caused him great anxiety and the stress levels continued to soar when, with only minutes to go before they go on, Plant bemoaned

```
SG0514  57A    _D _J     K-CSNT ESG0514
100.00  TOWER C GATE 8         100.00
         COCA-COLA PRESENTS       CN 92424
57A_         ATLANTIC RECORDS      ! 57A
CA 226X     40TH ANNIVERSARY      :CA229MSS
_D _,7    IT?S ONLY ROCK & ROLL   ! _D
MSS1215.  MADISON SQUARE GARDEN    K 100.00
K29APR8  SAT MAY 14, 1988 1:30PM  !  7
```

the decision to perform 'Stairway To Heaven'. They eventually hit the stage and launched into 'Kashmir'. The whole event was being screened live on the HBO channel, and their problems were further compounded when the HBO TV feed completely lost Jones' keyboards. Plant mixed up some lyrics and was also a little unnerved when he had to dodge a blimp thrown onto the stage. 'Heartbreaker' found Page struggling badly with the solo, and his effect pedals seemed not to be working. This then led into a more spirited 'Whole Lotta Love', played in the arrangement they had used at Knebworth in 1979. 'Misty Mountain Hop' was more confident, probably due to its being part of Plant's current solo set. Finally, a perfunctory 'Stairway To Heaven' found Plant in trouble with the lyrics and Page rusty on the solo.

In the aftermath, only Jason seemed to emerge with any lasting pride. The other three were pleased for him but generally disappointed with their own performances and the HBO sound reproduction. Plant: "What happened? I can't tell you. I have no idea. But a lot of people thought they saw something great. The crazy thing is, at the soundcheck, it was spectacular."

Jimmy Page: "We had been asked to do it and it was Jason's dream to play with Led Zeppelin. It was so important to him, something he's always hoped for. I was looking forward to it too because I knew how good a drummer he'd become. Jones and I had rehearsed with Jason and it had gone particularly well. We'd agreed on what we want-

ed to play and the soundcheck at the Garden sounded really good because a bootlegger taped it and I got the tape. I listened to it with Jason and we both thought 'Hey, this is gonna be great!' Then at the eleventh hour or 11.59 so to speak, Robert decides he doesn't want to do 'Stairway'. So there's this running confusion and harsh words between us right up to literally the last minute and that shook me up quite a bit I can tell you. I don't think it was right for the spirit of things.

"The whole thing was one big disappointment. Especially since I knew I wasn't playing well. It was so upsetting because we really put work into it and it should have been really good. All the last-minute dramatics about not doing 'Stairway' suddenly threw the whole thing right up in the air. I was trying to cool it out at the end, but, it was like, 'thanks a lot, pal!'"

Robert Plant: "Page and I had our usual touchy vibration filled moment when I didn't want to sing 'Stairway To Heaven', and he said it was a necessity for the Western world and I said that I didn't think it was that important. So, the rehearsing was good, the soundcheck was good, the previous night was good … and the gig was foul.

"However, I must say that Jason Bonham was stunning. He was really good. I've always tried to clip him around the back of the head and tell him to get his act together and stuff, but he really was the kingpin of the whole delivery."

Bootleg CD References: *Still Flying* (Forever Standard)

After the moderate success of his 1988 solo Outrider Tour, Jimmy Page looked to consolidate his solo career, beginning an album project with a new band with, as he put it "A lot of young blood". A call from Atlantic at the end of 1990 put all solo plans on permanent hold.

They approached the remaining group members to sanction the release of a Led Zeppelin compilation box set drawn from the original studio albums. With the advent of the CD market such box sets were becoming *de rigueur* for most major artists. Page did much more than agree – he actively took control of the project and in the spring of 1990 spent hour upon hour in New York's Sterling Sound Studio diligently supervising the re-mastering of a bulk of the Zeppelin catalogue.

Page: "I did it primarily because the first release of CDs that were issued were from poor master tapes and generally sub-standard. It wasn't until I got into the studio and started work on them I realised how into it I was. I worked wherever possible from the original tapes. The essence of it all is in the re-sequencing of the tracks to get the same picture within a different frame. Sitting listening to it all was like reliving ten years of my life. A lot of memories came flooding back."

The end result was the hugely successful 54-track, four CD box set – issued in October 1990 alongside the condensed two CD *Remasters* set. The box set included the previously unreleased 'White Summer-Black Mountain Side' sequence from the June 27, 1969, BBC *In Concert* programme. The whole project enhanced the profile of Led Zeppelin almost overnight and registered a million sales in the States alone, ensuring its status as the best selling box set of its kind. Suddenly they were very much back in vogue – earning accolades for their innovation from a variety of sources and musicians. Their influence was echoed out loud from the sampling of The Beastie Boys, through the parodying of Dread Zeppelin to the then current practitioners of the art, Pearl Jam and Guns N' Roses.

A second box set package was duly released in 1993 after Page had remastered the remaining 34 tracks from their studio albums (also recovering a long presumed lost first album out-take 'Baby Come On Home'). Finally, this led to a full scale reissue programme of the 10 original Zeppelin albums, remastered and retaining their original sequencing of tracks. Initially only available as a box set, *The Complete Studio Recordings,* each album would later become available individually.

Unsurprisingly, offers for a full scale reunion were firmly on the table. During 1990 such rumours were further fuelled by the reunion of all three for a playful set at the wedding reception of Jason Bonham and the more public teaming up of Page and Plant for part of Plant's set at the much publicised Silver Clef awards show, nostalgically reuniting them at Knebworth – the scene of the last UK performances of Led Zeppelin. Jimmy

The Concert File

337

Page was very keen to get a full scale reunion up and running, as was the ever affable John Paul Jones. The stumbling block remained Plant who felt it would ultimately harm his solo career. He also seemed reticent to let Jason Bonham take up the drum stool. There were tentative meetings with Plant's manager, Bill Curbishley, to establish some sort of plan – Plant now favouring the involvement of Faith No More's Mike Bordin. Jones and Page were supplied with videos of the drummer but, according to Page, the very next day Plant changed his mind and decided against the idea. The reunion was off – at least for the time being.

This decision left Plant free to establish a new touring outfit and record the excellent *Fate Of Nations* album – the content of which echoed very much back to the folk and ethnic roots that influenced so much of the Zeppelin catalogue.

Page, in a quite astonishing move, then teamed up with former Deep Purple and Whitesnake singer, David Coverdale; astonishing not least because of the long running feud Plant had waged with Coverdale in the press regarding the latter being a sub-standard version of Plant himself. Even Page had criticised Whitesnake for ripping off his guitar style in the 'Kashmir'-like 'Still Of The Night'.

Page: "I'd been looking for a singer to work with and gone through scores of demo cassettes with no luck. Then someone from my record company, Geffen, suggested I team up with David.

Initially we just tried a few ideas and then the stuff began pouring out. We knew we had something good."

Against many odds, the resulting Coverdale/Page album, issued in March 1993, contained Page's best playing in years – returning to the wide-screen, multi-dubbed guitar army approach that really proved he could still cut it. Plant's own *Fate Of Nations* was released a month later. Both Plant and Page criticised each other in the round of promotional interviews at the time. However, under the surface it can be assumed with hindsight that Plant was extremely impressed with Page's musical rejuvenation because by the autumn of 1993 this rock soap opera took another unlikely turn.

Plant was asked to perform on the MTV *Unplugged* series, but rather than approach the show with his new band he saw it as an opportunity to reinterpret his vast back catalogue with his old colleague. A meeting was arranged with Page in Boston. They both agreed to get together after their respective solo tour projects expired to see if they could come up with the necessary chemistry. Page was in the throes of rehearsing for a run of concerts with David Coverdale in Japan. This seemingly stable relationship then petered out amidst inter-management hassles, leading to a cancelled US tour.

"It would have been incredibly facetious if I thought I could carry any thread of the Zeppelin history on my shoulders outside of a live gig," said Plant. "The only answer really was to see if I

could team up with the one bloke who knew where I was coming from."

"The MTV thing was a catalyst," said Page. "It gave Robert time to think about things and get in contact. And when we did, it was really the first time we had a chance to think about the future constructively. To kick it around, see how to do it, how not to do it. It also gave us a chance to write again to see if we'd still got the creative spark. And that was happening from day one."

In February 1994, Page and Plant began rehearsing in a studio in Kings Cross, working with a series of tape loop backing tracks. To their immense relief the old spark rekindled. "We initially worked with some North African tape loops made up by French producer Martin Meissonnier," said Page. "Just us and a backing tape and a big PA in a rehearsal room. It was instant."

A deal was quickly set up with MTV for them to produce an *Unplugged* style show, although rather than attempt to perform the obvious Zeppelin compositions acoustically, they saw this as an opportunity to breathe new life into the old songs, reinterpreting them in a way that was not possible in the previous four man format. At this point it's worth noting that no approach was made to John Paul Jones. Plant was adamant that this should not be seen as a Led Zeppelin revival but as a new Page/Plant project. Jones was understandably a little upset at not being informed of their intentions. "Nobody rang me to tell me they were doing it, which I found a little odd," he commented later.

In place of John Paul's contribution, they fleshed out the sound by using Plant's touring band rhythm section of Charlie Jones on bass and Michael Lee on drums. An Egyptian orchestral ensemble led by Hossam Ramzy was installed for their reworking of 'Friends', 'Four Sticks' and 'Kashmir'. A respected Pakistani vocalist Najma Akhtar, was sought for a fresh attempt at 'The Battle Of Evermore'. Hurdy gurdy player Nigel Eaton was another new recruit alongside ex-Cure guitarist Porl

Thompson. Musical arranger and keyboardist Ed Shearmur was brought in to look after the orchestral arrangements, working in London with the Metropolitan Orchestra.

The first visual evidence of the reunion occurred at the Alexis Korner memorial benefit show at Buxton, Derbyshire in April. The pair appeared with Lee and Jones to run through blues standards, including 'I Can't Quit You' and 'Train Kept A Rollin''. By August a filming schedule had been arranged with plans for location footage in Marrakech, and Snowdonia, Wales, both of which echoed the Zeppelin era.

On August 25/26, they duly recorded and filmed two performances in front of a specially invited audience at the London Studios on the South Bank. The resulting film titled *No Quarter – Jimmy Page and Robert Plant Unledded* was aired in both Europe and the USA in the MTV *Unplugged* slot in October. In America it registered the highest viewing figures ever for an *Unplugged* programme. An accompanying album soundtrack taken from the location and London filming was released in November. The album itself sold only moderately, no doubt hampered by its eclectic content and their refusal to trade on the Led Zeppelin brand-name.

In all but name though, this was a refreshing return to the original Zeppelin premise of moving ever onward. On their own terms they had solved the problem of reuniting outside of the corporate style that Plant wished to avoid by cleverly reinventing their catalogue in a style that drew heavily on the past, but also presented their music with a vitality and freshness, breathing new life into the Led Zeppelin legacy. The next logical step was to take it out on the road.

November 1989
Shatterford, England
Private Party

Jimmy and John Paul attended the 21st birthday party of Plant's daughter, Carmen, and reunited on stage for a jam. Together with members of Plant's band, including Chris Blackwell and Phil

Johnstone, they performed several numbers including 'Trampled Underfoot', 'Misty Mountain Hop' and 'Rock And Roll'.

Saturday April 28 1990
Bewdley, England
Heath Hotel

Page, Plant and Jones attended Jason Bonham's wedding to Jan Charteris at St. Mary's Parish Church, Stone, near Kidderminster. Peter Grant was also a guest. At the reception at the Heath Hotel, they provided the post-wedding entertainment with Jason on drums. The set consisted of 'Bring It On Home' (with Plant on harmonica), 'Rock And Roll', 'Sick Again', 'Custard Pie' (the first time it's been performed live in its entirety by the original composers), and Jerry Lee Lewis' 'It'll Be Me'. Page used the cherry red Gibson throughout.

Less than 200 guests witnessed this latest reunion, which unsurprisingly sparked off a new round of Zeppelin to re-form rumours.

Saturday June 30 1990
Stevenage, England
Knebworth Park
GUEST APPEARANCE

Jimmy joined Robert's band for a three song jam at the much publicised Silver Clef winners charity concert. Robert was the latest recipient of the award. The bill included Cliff Richard, Genesis, Phil Collins, Dire Straits, Pink Floyd and Paul McCartney. It was widely tipped in the week leading up to the show that all three ex-members will appear to re-form Zeppelin but this doesn't happen. Plant was introduced by Radio One's Gary Davies (the event was broadcast live) as "A singer who is no stranger to big crowds – he played to 380,000 on his last visit here eleven years ago". Plant strode onto the windswept stage at 4.45p.m. His set proceeded with 'Hurting Kind', 'Immigrant Song', 'Tie Dye On The Highway', 'Liars Dance', 'Going To California', and 'Tall Cool One'.

Before bringing on his guest he stated: "Well, this little award given to me last week, not particularly for anything I've done but for what has happened between 1966 when I made my first record and today. I've been working for the last four years with these guys and it's been a wonderful time and I owe a good portion of this to these chaps behind me. I also owe a major proportion to my good friend who has just joined me on stage ... Jimmy Page." With cherry red Gibson in hand, Page proceeded to add vast influence to enthusiastic work outs of 'Misty Mountain Hop', a superb 'Wearing And Tearing' (never before played live) and a rousing 'Rock And Roll'. They left the stage arm in arm.

Jimmy Page: "We were having a really good time. We'd had a rehearsal before we did it and that was great fun. It's really good playing all the old numbers ... especially 'Wearing And Tearing' ... it really was on a wing and a prayer that we went on with that at Knebworth. We were back to living dangerously again."

Rumours of a reunion abounded. It looked as though Plant was ready to relent. Much to Jimmy's surprise it didn't happen – at least for another four years.

340

Official CD Reference: *Knebworth – The Album* (Polydor)
Bootleg CD References: *Still Flying* (Forever Standard)
Visual References: *Live At Knebworth Parts 1, 2 & 3* (official DVD EagleRock)

Wednesday November 18 1992
London England
Park Lane Hotel
Q AWARDS
NON PLAYING APPEARANCE

At the annual awards of the UK magazine *Q*, Jimmy, Robert and John Paul reunited along with Jason Bonham representing his late father to accept the *Q* Merit Award. Plant took to the podium to make the speech: "So many of the songs we did we're still very proud of and they still stand up today. They were recorded in the least amount of time and often with the greatest amount of laughter. That's what this award is for, for having a ridiculously crazy time." During the ceremony, Page chatted to fellow winner B.B. King and Plant mingled with Neneh Cherry and Tori Amos.

Sunday April 17 1994
Buxton England
Opera House

Set: Baby Please Don't Go/I Can't Quit You Babe/ Untitled Jam I/ Untitled Jam II/ Train Kept A Rollin'.

Robert had long since volunteered his services for this Alexis Korner memorial benefit show. Also included on the bill were Paul Jones, Davy Graham, Pete Brown, Zoot Money and Chris Barber.

Plant's reunion with Jimmy at rehearsals in the preceding weeks fuelled speculation that they would perform together. Sure enough, in this most unlikely of settings, they were reunited for their first proper show in fourteen years. Appropriately, it was the blues influence of Alexis Korner that brought them back to their roots.

They took the stage just before 10pm and ran through 'Baby Please Don't Go' before a rousing and nostalgic 'I Can't Quit You'. Page employed the cherry red Gibson with much fluency. Two untitled jams hinted at the experiments of recent weeks with the rhythm section of Charlie Jones on bass and Michael Lee's drums already gelling. The second of the jams was a jerky off beat syncopated exercise with Page playing in the style of 'The Crunge'. After a five minute ovation from the small crowd, they returned for a spirited romp through 'Train Kept A Rollin'' – the set opener on the early Zep tours and their final excursion in Europe in 1980.

Their performance of 'I Can't Quit You Babe' was aired on regional TV.
Bootleg CD References: *Together Again* (no label), *The Story So Far* (Octopus)

Wednesday August 10 1004
Marrakech, Morocco
J'ma el FNA Square
FILMING

Not an actual gig but a public appearance in the famous 11th century market of the old city to film a sequence for the upcoming MTV *Unledded* show. Among the market traders, jugglers and snake charmers, Robert and Jimmy staged a 6pm filming shoot for their new composition, 'Loop' (later to be known as 'Yallah' or 'The Truth Explodes'). Playing against a tape loop, Jimmy plugged in the Gibson and proceeded to enthral and bemuse the locals as he used the effects box to add to the market square's ethnic and eclectic activity of sound. Unfortunately, Robert's voice seemed to have suffered from the climate change and several overdubs were required back in London.

They also ran through a communal version of 'Wah Wah' aided by many locals in the square.

While in Morocco they shot location sequences in Marakesh on August 9, capturing performances of 'Wah Wah' and 'City Don't Cry' with guest musicians Brahim El Balkani, Hassan Balkani, Hassan El Arfaoui, El Mahjoub, El Mathoun, and Abdelhak Eddahmane.

The next week the location filming switched to Snowdonia in Wales. On August 12 the 'No Quarter' sequence was filmed on the side of a mountain in Dolgorth. On August 17 they moved to the Corris slate quarry, near Bron Yr Aur to film a group location for 'Gallows Pole', 'Nobody's Fault But Mine' and 'When The Levee Breaks'. The line-up was Plant (vocals), Page (guitar), Michael Lee (drums), Charlie Jones (bass), Porl Thompson (guitar/banjo), Nigel Eaton (hurdy gurdy) and Jim Sutherland (mandolin). Despite the rain they managed to get the required takes by early evening.

Thursday August 25 1994
South Bank, London
Studio Two, London TV Studios
Set: Thank You/What Is And What Should Never Be/The Battle Of Evermore/Gallows Pole/The Rain Song/Since I've Been Loving You/Four Sticks/Friends/Kashmir/That's The Way.

Additional musicians used for the London filming are Charlie Jones (bass), Porl Thompson (guitar/banjo), Michael Lee (drums), Najma Akhtar (vocals on 'The Battle Of Evermore'), Jim Sutherland (mandolin), Nigel Eaton (hurdy gurdy), Ed Shermur (organ/string arrangements)

plus the Egyptian Ensemble and the London Metropolitan Orchestra.

Finally, after all the rumours, the MTV reunion became a reality. After an understandably nervous start they hit their stride, Jimmy and Robert turning back the clock with a superbly rehearsed set that more than does justice to the legacy. Highlights included the rarely performed 'Battle Of Evermore' with Najma Akhtar sharing vocals and welcome revivals for 'Gallows Pole' and 'Four Sticks', again both only rarely played live with Zeppelin. 'Since I've Been Loving You' was now given an extra dimension with the addition of strings, and the new arrangement of 'Kashmir' deployed the East and West orchestras take the song into uncharted territory. The whole atmosphere was one of joyous celebration. They have finally done it …

After the audience had left, Jimmy and Robert returned to the stage to run through various takes of a new song titled 'Wonderful One' – in preparation for the next night's filming.

Friday August 26 1994
Southbank, London
Studio Two, London TV Studios
Set: What Is And What Should Never Be/Than

BILL CURBISHLEY/ TRINIFOLD MANAGEMENT

The importance of Bill Curbishley in reuniting Robert Plant and Jimmy Page cannot be understated.

Curbishley, manager of The Who since the mid-Seventies, has been Robert's manager since 1986 and Jimmy's since 1994. After Robert's 'Shaken N' Stirred' tour, it was Bill who advised Robert to disband his current touring ensemble, start afresh with a completely new band and begin writing with different musicians. It was a brave move, and one which would result in escalating commercial success with the *Now & Zen*, *Manic Nirvana* and *Fate Of Nations* albums. While touring to promote *Fate Of Nations*, Robert met Jimmy at a show in Boston and discussed the possibility of a collaboration of some sort. Curbishley told *Talent/PM*: "I encouraged it, because I really felt it was a tragedy that these two guys who had written one of the best catalogues of songs in rock-'n'roll history weren't together."

There had, of course, been previous attempts to reunite the pair. Jimmy had generally appeared willing, but Robert was reti-cent. Curbishley: "Robert wasn't unwilling to work with Page; he was unwilling to work with Led Zeppelin because he didn't want to take a backwards step. Every time he worked with a band or unit, it became quite apparent to me that he was trying to turn the guitarist into another Jimmy Page. In the end, I said to him, 'Look, you can work with Jimmy without being Led Zeppelin. Besides, you two wrote all the songs, so there's no reason why you can't play them!'"

Plant succumbed to Curbishley's persuasion and the prospect of working with Page again became a reality. The result was the highly successful *Unledded* album, video and world tour and the 1998 *Walking Into Everywhere* tour.

Looking back on the achievement of bringing them together, Bill commented in an interview for *Tight But Loose* in 1999: "On a personal level I think they both walk with a lighter step now. The fact they got back together and started playing again unloaded a lot of shit and that's been very important to them. I think they came out of it with a wealth that was way beyond materialistic. It has equally benefitted them spiritually and they are both better people for it."

You/The Battle Of Evermore/Gallows Pole/The Rain Song/Since I've Been Loving You/Four Sticks/Friends/Kashmir/That's The Way/Wonderful One (two takes)/That's The Way (second version)/Nobody's Fault But Mine.

Plenty of fellow musicians were in attendance for this evening's performance including Mick Jones of The Clash, Bruce Dickinson, Dave Gahan, Hugh Cornwall, Aerosmith drummer Joey Kramer and Bryan Adams.

Unsurprisingly, the performance tonight was much more relaxed and provided the forum for Page and Plant to deliver an even more impressive performance. 'The Rain Song' was superbly played by Page and during 'Since I've Been Loving You' his playing was as fluent as any time in the past 20 years. They premiered the new song 'Wonderful One' during the encores. This found them working, without a band, to a tape loop – two arrangements were aired as they treated the audience to the intimate experience of the first public performance of their first joint composition in 15 years. Thankfully, the cameras got it all down as required and the result was the *No Quarter – Unledded* film, premièred on MTV in the US on October 12 and in Europe on October 17.

Robert Sandall was one of the few journalists present and commented in *The Sunday Times*: "They didn't play 'Stairway To Heaven', but then it wasn't that sort of a reunion. Having sensibly resisted the temptation to call themselves Led Zeppelin, Robert Plant and Jimmy Page were in no mood to treat their first joint venture in 14 years like a fan club outing for the faithful, or some elderly headbangers ball. The long awaited re-coupling of the Page/Plant partnership was a resolutely un-nostalgic affair. MTV originally commissioned this event to wind up its popular *Unplugged* series: what it got was something far removed from the standard mellow strumming of a famous back catalogue. Their performance constantly took off on extraordinary tangents. The finale was a magnificent overwrought account of 'Kashmir', Zeppelin's great late hippie nod to all things Eastern. From Plant's hoarse muezzin wail at the opening to the inspired improvisations of the Egyptian contingent that brought it to a thunderous close 10 minutes later, this was surprisingly risky stuff. Perhaps progressive rock, as such epic meandering used to be called, isn't dead. When Page and Plant take their remarkable show on the road in the new year, we shall find out."

Official CD References: *Jimmy Page Robert Plant No Quarter Unledded* (Fontana)

Bootleg CD References: *Robert Plant & Jimmy Page Reunion 1994* (Red Line)

Visual Reference: *Jimmy Page Robert Plant No Quarter Unledded* (Warner Music Vision)

* In 2004 engineer Kevin Shirley remixed the tapes of the *Unledded* film for 5.1 presentation on the DVD. He also prepared an acompanying remixed CD version which was released in the US only.

Wednesday October 12 1994
MTV America
Monday October 17 1994
MTV Europe
TV APPEARANCE
JIMMY PAGE ROBERT PLANT – NO QUARTER UNLEDDED
Programme: No Quarter/Thank You/The Battle Of Evermore/Gallows Pole/Nobody's Fault But Mine/City Don't Cry/Yallah/Wah Wah/ Wonderful One/Since I've Been Loving You/ Friends/Kashmir

The US and UK premiere broadcast of the original *Unledded* film. In America the debut broadcast achieved the highest viewing ratings ever for the *Unplugged* slot. The special earned a 2.4 rating beating the previous 2.3 rating for Eric Clapton's *Unledded* set in 1992.

Note: There was a second cut of the programme aired which included additional footage of 'What Is And What Should Never Be', 'The Rain Song' and 'City Don't Cry'. It was this version that was used for the official VHS release in 1995 and the 2004 release of the film on DVD. However for that project engineer Kevin Shirley was brought in to remix the sound for 5.1 presentation. The DVD also added the promotional interview with the pair shot on the streets of Camden, some additional Marakesh footage and the rehearsal version of 'Black Dog' aired on the American Music Awards in January 1995.

Tuesday November 8 1994
BBC Television Centre, London
Later With Jools Holland
TV APPEARANCE
With a scaled down Egyptian orchestra and band line-up, the pair record an opening jam on 'When The Levee Breaks' with fellow artists including Elastica, plus versions of 'Gallows Pole', 'Wonderful One' and 'Four Sticks' in front of the studio audience. The segment was transmitted on the November 19 edition of *Later* …

Bootleg CD Reference: *Together Again II* (No label)

Visual Reference: *Later With Jools Holland – The Giants* (BBC DVD, includes 'Gallows Pole')

Thursday November 10 1994
Tokyo, Japan
Tokyo News Station
TV APPEARANCE
Following the BBC filming, the pair began a promotional tour that took in Japan, Australia and Argentina. In Tokyo, they appeared on the Tokyo News station. Their musical contribution to the show was a surprise delivery of 'Stairway To Heaven'.

Sat on stools in a sparse studio setting with Jimmy playing a black Ovation acoustic, Robert sang the unsingable with surprising sincerity in a three-minute abridged version. This one-off delivery exorcised the negative stigma that has surrounded the song for so long and gave the much

maligned former anthem a renewed dignity.
Bootleg CD Reference: *Together Again II* (No label)

Wednesday November 16 1994
Sydney, Australia
TV APPEARANCE
Jimmy and Robert were interviewed on the Andrew Denton show. This is the show that instigated the 'Stairway To Heaven' spoof which resulted in the Rolf Harris cover version. After performing 'Black Dog' in front of the studio audience (accompanied by a local drummer and didgeridoo players) they joined in the 'Spin The Wheel' game where studio guests drew out at random a song to perform. Surprise, surprise the song was 'Sun

---

JOHN PEEL 1939–2004

John Peel's sudden passing from a heart attack on October 26, 2004, caused a deep sense of loss for millions of his listeners past and present. For 40 years Peel had influenced the nation's music taste with a maverick intuition that gave countless bands their first break.

Back in early 1969 it was his support of Led Zeppelin on the *John Peel Top Gear* Radio One programme that gave the group vital airtime and did much to spread their message. Evidence of this is of course now available first hand on the 1997 Led Zeppelin *BBC Sessions* album. Alongside the *Top Gear* appearances, Peel also acted as master of ceremonies on the famous April 1, 1971, BBC *In Concert* show and was involved in a humorous exchange with Plant before 'Whole Lotta Love': "I'm gonna sing on the next one. Say Mama," remarks Peel in homage to one of his and Plant's heroes Gene Vincent.

As the musical climate changed and Peel embraced punk, Zeppelin's airtime on his show was few and far between. 'Stairway To Heaven' did figure regularly in Peel's annual Festive 50 poll, attaining top position in 1976. Though it slipped considerably over the next five years, it was still in the list in 1980 sandwiched between Public Image and Joy Division.

Peel did relent in September 1979, playing 'In The Evening' from the then just released *In Through The Out Door*. At the *Melody Maker* Poll Awards a couple of months later, he mingled with Robert Plant, swapping soccer stories. When this author asked Peel how relevant he felt Zeppelin were and why he had given airtime to 'In The Evening' on his show amongst the indie and new wave bands, John replied "I played that track because it has that solo from Jimmy Page that sounds like a giant door closing. When they're doing interesting things like that then they are still relevant in my view."

Robert Plant represented Led Zeppelin at his funeral on November 12 2004 in Bury St Edmunds. He reflected on Peel's assistance in their early years. "In the early days of Zeppelin he gave us radio airplay when we were considered taboo by the flaccid BBC identikit DJs."

John Peel will be much missed and long remembered.

PETER GRANT 1935–1995

There can be little doubt that without the shrewd management of Peter Grant, Led Zeppelin would never have attained the level of success they did. His death from a heart attack in the back of a car *en route* to his home in Sussex on November 21, 1995, sparked a genuine feeling of grief within the music business as countless friends and business associates paid tribute. His funeral on December 4 (exactly 15 years to the day of the Zeppelin split announcement) was attended by, amongst others, Jimmy Page, Robert Plant, Jeff Beck, Paul Rodgers and Phil May.

In a book that deals with Led Zeppelin live, Grant's role cannot be underestimated. He was, after all, a roadie at heart, at home on road where he began his career. Unlike most managers he was hands-on, that is he only rarely missed a gig and was always on hand to sort out problems, watching over his charges from the side of the stage, ever alert to deal personally with trouble. It was his thorough knowledge of the American touring scene in the mid-Sixties, gleaned from touring with The Yardbirds and observing the Jeff Beck Group, that he was able to propel Led Zeppelin into the forefront of the expanding US rock market.

Grant's past experiences of handling stars such as Chuck Berry, Gene Vincent and Jerry Lee Lewis held him in good stead for dealing with the pandemonium that frequently surrounded Led Zeppelin. His management style broke every rule in the book: no singles, no TV appearances, wordless album covers and carefully planned touring schedules that built a mystique around the band that exists to this day. By insisting on retaining 90% of the gate receipts he also single-handedly pioneered the shift of power from the agents and promoters to the artists and management themselves.

Stories of his controversial heavyweight style of management are legion. His sheer size could be intimidating in itself and his capacity for 'verbal violence', as he called it, was enough to command respect from the most hardened business dealer. "They look after the music and I do everything else – and if it takes some strong measures to get our way, then so be it," was how he saw his role. There were many reports of his dubious heavy handed tactics but despite such stories he was generally held in high esteem by those with whom he came into contact.

Even in death his reputation preceded him. Just before his funeral it was revealed he had drawn up a small list of belongings he wished to be buried with him. "Who's on it?" joked a friend.

Grant was fiercely loyal to his artists, certainly the fifth 'unseen' member of Led Zepppelin. With that sort of devotion it's little surprise that following the death of John Bonham, Grant found it hard to cope, eventually relinquishing his control of the Zeppelin empire and entering what he described as a period of blackness. His battle with drink and drugs appeared to be over by the late Eighties but the legacy was heart trouble. By the early Nineties he emerged from semi-retirement and returned to the spotlight as an elder statesman of rock management, lauded by latter day peers such as Dire Straits manager Ed Bicknell and in big demand to address music business conventions such as In The City. Away from the rock-'n'roll madness of the Zeppelin years, Grant became something of a pillar of society around his Eastbourne home, tinkering with his collection of vintage cars and attending local charity events. He was even asked to stand as a Justice Of The Peace, an offer he politely declined.

During the last years of his life there was much talk of a biopic of his life story being put together by another music management Svengali, Malcolm McClaren. Although various scripts were put forward, by the time of his death it had still not entered production. Omnibus Press, the publishers of this book and Chris Welch's biography *Peter Grant: The Man Who Led Zeppelin*, regularly field calls from would-be film makers.

Biopics or not, Peter Grant will never be forgotten. His influence on the group members is readily acknowledged. "Peter Grant changed the rules. He did so much for us that in 1975 he had to turn around and say, 'Look there's nothing else I can do. We've had performing pigs and high wire acts. We've had the mud sharks and all the rest – there's no more I can do. Because now you really can go to Saturn.' I owe so much of my confidence to him because of the way he cajoled all of us to make us what we were," said Robert Plant. His last public appearance was at the final night of the Page/Plant tour at Wembley Arena in July 1995. Sadly it was to be his last glimpse of his former partners.

Summarising his time as their manager in 1993, Peter looked back with great affection on their relationship. "They played the most fantastic live music one could possibly wish for. There was a great camaraderie amongst us and even during the traumas we could always laugh afterwards. There were never any grudges. To be associated with them was a privilege because we made it into the biggest and best band there ever was. Working as Led Zeppelin's manager was a time of total magic."

Whenever and wherever the story of Led Zeppelin is told – Peter Grant will be remembered with awe.

Arise' (the Rolf Harris tune) which they performed in a fairly straight arrangement in tribute to Rolf – much to the amusement of the audience.

Clips of this were considered for the commercial video release of the *Unledded* film but did not make the final cut.

Bootleg CD Reference: *Together Again II* (No label)

Thursday January 12 1995
New York, USA
Waldorf-Astoria Hotel
ROCK'N'ROLL HALL OF FAME INDUCTION
Following lengthy and witty speeches from Aerosmith's Joe Perry and Steve Tyler, Jimmy Page, Robert Plant, John Paul Jones plus Jason and Zoé Bonham (accepting the award on behalf of their late father) stepped up to receive the award. Tension was high after Plant made a derogatory comment about Jones' association with Herman's Hermits and how he'd read in *The New York Times* that morning about Jones not being told of the

reunion. John Paul followed with a curt "Thanks to my friends for finally remembering my telephone number".

Feud or no feud they all took to the stage for the obligatory jam session. This featured the three of them plus Jason Bonham, and Perry and Tyler romping through a spirited, Page dominated, 'Train Kept A Rollin'', 'For Your Love', and 'Bring It On Home' medley before moving into a blues jam containing snippets of 'Prison Blues', 'Gamblers Blues' and moving into 'Baby Please Don't Go'.

A second jam had Michael Lee on drums and guest star Neil Young plus Jones, Page and Plant jamming on a lengthy and rather grunge-like 'When The Levee Breaks'. This fea-

Led Zeppelin

PAGE / PLANT PROJECT

DETAILED DAY BY DAY PROPOSED FILMING AND RECORDING
SCHEDULE FOR AUGUST '94

AS OF 30.6.94

AUGUST '94

FRIDAY 5TH	FLY TO RABAT, MOROCCO
SATURDAY 6TH	REHEARSE WITH MOROCCAN ORCHESTRA AT RTM STUDIOS IN RABAT
SUNDAY 7TH	RECORD WITH MOROCCAN ORCHESTRA AT RTM STUDIOS IN RABAT
MONDAY 8TH	DRIVE TO MARRAKESH
TUESDAY 9TH	PERFORM IN COURTYARD 'LIVE' WITH MOROCCAN ORCHESTRA AND FILM
WEDNESDAY 10TH	BUSK IN DJEMMA EL FNA SQUARE IN MARRAKESH AND FILM
THURSDAY 11TH	FLY TO LONDON
FRIDAY 12TH	DAY OFF
SATURDAY 13TH	DAY OFF
SUNDAY 14TH	DAY OFF
MONDAY 15TH	DRIVE TO MACHYNLLETH, WALES
TUESDAY 16TH	FILM AT DOLGOTH
WEDNESDAY 17TH	FILM AT CORRIS SLATE QUARRY
THURSDAY 18TH	RETURN TO LONDON
FRIDAY 19TH	REHEARSAL DAY
SATURDAY 20TH	DAY OFF
SUNDAY 21ST	DAY OFF
MONDAY 22ND	SET UP STUDIO SHOOT / ORCHESTRA REHEARSALS
TUESDAY 23RD	BAND REHEARSALS WITH CAMERAS IN STUDIO
WEDNESDAY 24TH	BAND REHEARSALS WITH ORCHESTRA IN STUDIO
THURSDAY 25TH	FILM STUDIO
FRIDAY 26TH	FILM STUDIO WITH ORCHESTRA

tured Plant donning Page's cherry red Gibson to add his three chords worth of fun. Plant also threw in a few lines from Young's old outfit Buffalo Springfield's 'For What It's Worth' before they left the stage. Most of the performance was screened on MTV.

Bootleg CD Reference: *The Story So Far* (Octopus)

Monday January 30 1995
Los Angeles, USA

THE AMERICAN MUSIC AWARDS

The second award within a month – this time award hosts Tom Jones and Queen Latifah paid homage to Led Zeppelin as winners of the International Artist award. It's only the third time the award has been handed out. Jimmy and Robert with Jason Bonham were seen accepting the award in London in the Depot rehearsal studio. This segment, previously filmed on January 25, showed the pair plus Michael Lee and Charlie Jones and accompanying didgeridoo players running through a riveting version of 'Black Dog', played in an arrangement that was subsequently discarded for the tour.

Back in Los Angeles John Paul Jones appeared in person to collect his award. His speech read as follows: "I'm very proud to be a part of, to my mind, the greatest band in the world and for working with the greatest drummer John Bonham – wish you were here. I'd also like to thank my wife Mo for being my inspiration and putting up

with me and rock and roll."

The show was aired in 170 countries by the ABC network.

Bootleg CD Reference: *Together Again IV* (No label)

Visual Reference: *Jimmy Page Robert Plant No Quarter Unledded* (Warner Music Vision)

JIMMY PAGE ROBERT PLANT
WORLD TOUR 1995/1996
US TOUR FEBRUARY TO APRIL
EUROPEAN TOUR JUNE TO JULY
US TOUR SEPTEMBER TO OCTOBER
SOUTH AMERICA JAPAN/AUSTRALIA
JANUARY FEBRUARY 1996

The year long Page/Plant tour commenced in Pensacola on February 26, 1995, and ended in Melbourne on March 1, 1996. Within a period of 370 days the pair performed 115 shows in 19 countries, easily their most intensive touring period since the early Seventies.

The staging of the tour was most ambitious, and aside from the nucleus of the MTV filming line-up, Porl Thompson (guitar), Michael Lee (drums), Charlie Jones (bass) and Nigel Eaton (hurdy gurdy), they took with them Hossam Ramzy's Egyptian ensemble (dubbed 'The Egyptian Phaorees' by Plant). At nearly all the shows a local string orchestra was hastily rehearsed by keyboardist and arranger Ed Shearmur to add support on various numbers. At the core, of course, it was Page and Plant, visually and musically rejuvenated, proving that within each other's company the special chemistry that had lit up their work with Led Zeppelin, was very much alive.

Plant's vocal performances were remarkably

348

consistent as he confidently approached the long deleted stage favourites of yore. Page was a man back in his element. These were the songs on which he had built his reputation and his desire to reinterpret them was more than obvious. His guitar playing was easily as good as anything he'd produced in the last 20 years, defying the advancing years with flair, vigour and commitment (and a pact with Satan). It was an exhilarating experience to see these two musicians so comfortable in each other's company after so long.

If there were criticisms, the most obvious was Jones' non involvement. It still rankles in some circles that his name was not linked to the reunion, particularly in the light of their naming the tour after one of John Paul's most famous compositions. As the tour progressed, the Zeppelin trademark was invoked in fairly blatant marketing tactics: posters for concerts carried the phrase 'The Evolution Of Led Zeppelin Continues', making something of a mockery of the original premise whereby Plant in particular refused to trade on past glories.

Such ethical blemishes aside, there was little to disappoint in the actual performances. The set lists delighted the faithful as they embraced the Zeppelin catalogue. 'Gallows Pole' and 'Four Sticks' had hardly ever been played live in the Zeppelin era but they were core elements of this show, clocking in over 100 performances each. Five Led Zeppelin songs, namely 'Good Times Bad Times', 'Ramble On', 'Custard Pie', 'Hey Hey What Can I Do', and 'Tea For One', were performed in their entirety for the first time and in keeping with tradition, certain numbers, principally 'Calling To You' and 'Whole Lotta Love', were used as vehicles for medley improvisation. This offered the opportunity to playfully resurrect parts of songs in a juke box manner; anything from a nostalgic 'How Many More Times' through 'In The Light' and 'Down By The Seaside' to covers of 'For What It's Worth', 'Break On Through' and even a stab at 'As Long As I Have You', the old Garnett Mimms song they used to play on the early Led Zeppelin

tours.

'Stairway To Heaven', however, was never performed.

As the tour moved into the final leg covering South America, Japan and Australia in early 1996, far from simply going through the motions as the project wound down, Page and Plant produced some of the most interesting performances of the whole tour. With Porl Thompson leaving the touring band Page took on all the guitar playing himself.

In yet another parallel to the Zeppelin era, it was the Japanese who were treated to all manner of set list variations as they spun the set list wheel to bring in the previously unsung 'Rain Song' and 'Tea For One' and changed the running order at will. In Osaka they also performed 'Ten Years Gone' for the one and only time since the Knebworth August 11 show.

'The Evolution Of Led Zeppelin Continues ... ' proclaimed the advertisements – aside from John Paul Jones' non involvement few would argue that on this tour Page & Plant did the legend justice.

The following Led Zeppelin songs were played live in full on this tour: Gallows Pole (112 performances)/Since I've Been Loving You (109)/The Song Remains The Same (109)/Four Sticks(108)/Kashmir(108)/Bring It On Home(107)/Black Dog(103)/No Quarter(102)/In The Evening(101)/Thank You(87)/The Wanton Song(81)/Friends(74)/Ramble On(69)/Whole Lotta Love(62)/Going To California(39)/Hey Hey What Can I Do(38)/Nobody's Fault But Mine(37)/Dancing Days(35)/Babe I'm Gonna Leave You(32)/Heartbreaker(270/Celebration Day(22)/Rock And Roll(21)/When The Levee Breaks(20)/That's The Way(15)/Wonderful One(14)/What Is And What Should Never Be(11)/The Rain Song(9)/Tangerine(8)/The Battle Of Evermore(7)/Tea For One(6)/Custard Pie(6)/Over The Hills And Far Away(1)/Good Times Bad Times(1)/Ten Years Gone(1)
Visual References: *Eternal Burning* (unofficial DVD, Fmpress Valley)

Saturday November 30 1996
Mumbai, India
Andheri Sports Complex
TV APPEARANCE

Robert and Jimmy flew to Mumbia to accept a Lifetime Achievement at the Channel V music awards show. They took to the stage to mime to the Led Zeppelin studio version of 'Rock And Roll' with Queen's Roger Taylor on drums and a local bassist named Remi.

Thursday May 29 1997
London, England
Grosvenor Hotel
IVOR NOVELLO AWARDS
NON PLAYING APPEARANCE

Jimmy, Robert and John Paul were reunited at the annual Ivor Norvello awards, twenty years after their last appearance at the prestigious ceremony when Led Zeppelin were recognised for their outstanding contribution to British music.

On this occasion they were presented with a Lifetime Achievement award, appropriately enough by Ahmet Ertegun, who initially singed them to his Atlantic Records.

JIMMY PAGE ROBERT PLANT:
WALKING INTO EVERYWHERE TOUR 1998
EASTERN EUROPEAN TOUR FEBRUARY TO MARCH
US TOUR MAY TO AUGUST
EUROPAN TOUR OCTOBER TO DECEMBER

Page and Plant continued their renewed partnership with the recording of a new studio album during 1997. It marked their first full songwriting venture together since the last Zeppelin album *In Through The Out Door*. Titled *Walking Into Clarksdale*, it was issued in the spring of 1998. To promote the album the pair undertook another touring campaign dubbed the *Walking Into Everywhere* tour – it took in another 89 gigs across 18 countries. After a Senior Tennis benefit date at the Cafe De Paris in December 1997, the tour kicked off in February 1998 in Eastern Europe. In contrast to the extravagant set up of the '95/'96

world tour, this time they went out in a stripped-down five-piece line-up, again enlisting the Michael Lee-Charlie Jones rhythm section plus Phil Andrews on keyboards.

The *Walking Into Clarksdale* album itself sold only moderately. Far from the expected riff fest, it was a rather understated affair. On the road, though, they continued to excel, the more simplistic approach on stage allowing them to attack the Zeppelin numbers with the power and sonic bombast of old.

Whilst they were initially keen to promote the new album, the quota of Zeppelin numbers performed increased as the tour took in America and a round of summer festival dates including a bill topping appearance at the Reading Festival. Set list highlights included a full revival complete with violin bow interlude of 'How Many More Times' – a track that had enjoyed renewed attention due to its inclusion on the 1997 Led Zeppelin *BBC Sessions* archive release. They deployed the track as the vehicle for off-the-cuff inserts as they had used 'Whole Lotta Love' on the 1995/'96 tour.

During the European tour in the fall they began inserting 'Night Flight', the *Physical Graffiti* track that had never been performed live with Zeppelin. Aside from isolated surprises like this, however, by the European stage of the tour in November 1998 the sterility of the set lists hinted at Plant's growing disenchantment with the Page liaison. This all came to a head at their final appearance of the year on an Amnesty International bill at the Bercy in Paris

''I began to feel intimidated committing myself to large parts of touring,'' he confessed soon after it was all over. ''All the big time trappings… it became exasperating and too demanding on my calendar. I mean I like 'Heartbreaker'… but I don't want to sing it forever.''

The plan was to take the tour on to Japan and Australia in early 1999, but much to Page's annoyance Plant opted out, cancelling all future plans Instead he returned to his Midlands roots to re-evaluate things, thus bringing this latest Page

Plant collaboration – which had started so positively four years earlier – to an abrupt end.

The following Led Zeppelin songs were performed by Page and Plant in full on the Walking Into Everywhere tour:
Rock And Roll (88 performances)/Babe I'm Gonna Leave You (87)/Gallows Pole(87)/The Wanton Song(86)/Heartbreaker(86)/No Quarter(86)/How Many More times (86)/Going To California (83)/Tangerine(81)/Ramble On (81)/Whole Lotta Love (77)/Bring It On Home(66)/Thank You (48)/What Is And What Should Never Be(20)/Black Dog(19)/Misty Mountain Hop(6)/Celebration Day(5)/Night Flight(4)/Trampled Underfoot(3)/In The Evening(1)/Over The Hills And Far Away(1).

Visual References: *The Paris Concert For Amnesty International* (Image Entertainment official DVD includes four Page & Plant performances: When The World Was Young/Babe I'm Gonna Leave You/Gallows Pole/Rock And Roll), *Walking Eastside/East European Tour 1998* (Eclipse unofficial DVD)

Saturday July 7 2001
Montreux, Switzerland
Stravinski Autitorium
A NIGHT OF SUN RECORDS
Set: Good Rockin' Tonight/My Bucket's Got A Hole In It/Heart In Your Hand/Candy Store Rock/Endless Sleep/How Many More Years/My Baby Left Me/Baby Let's Play House.

In August 2000 Plant enlisted the assistance of Jimmy Page to record a vintage Sonny Burgess track 'My Bucket's Got A Hole In It'. The project was Plant's contribution to an all star tribute album dedicated to the Sun Records label, *Good Rockin' Tonight/The Legacy Of Sun Records*. The sessions took place at London's Abbey Road Studios and were filmed for subsequent release on an accompanying DVD documenting the album's making.

On this night in July, co-incidentally 21 years to the day of their last show together in Zeppelin,

Plant and Page returned to the Montreux Festival to perform at what was billed as a Night Of Sun Records. It also rekindled their association with veteran promoter Claude Nobbs.

On stage they performed together for the first time since 1998, enlising the help of Bill Jennings of the Big Town Playboys on double bass and Mike Watts (formerly of the James Hunter Band) on drums.

After being introduced by Ahmet Ertegun, they ran through a mainly rockabilly set that featured the first ever live performance of the Led Zeppelin *Presence* track 'Candy Store Rock'.

The studio version of Page & Plant's 'My Bucket's Got A Hole In It' was released on *Good Rockin' Tonight – The Legacy Of Sun Records* (Sire) alongside a DVD with footage of them recording the track at Abbey Road.

Bootleg CD Reference: *Good Rockin'Tonight* (Empress Valley)

Saturday February 9 2002
London, England
Royal Albert Hall
TEENAGE CHARITY CONCERT
Set: Robert Plant – Strange Sensation: If I Ever Get Lucky/Morning Dew/Four Sticks/Hey Joe/Song To The Siren/A House Is Not A Motel; Jimmy Page – Dazed And Confused; also on the bill – Gary Moore, Paul Weller.

In one of the most bizarre evenings of their long careers, Page and Plant both agreed to perform on this closing night of one a series of now annual Teenage Charity Albert Hall shows staged by Who vocalist Roger Daltrey. Amid many rumours that they would get back together for at least one number, it did not happen – and for the first time ever the pair performed separately at a show they were both billed at.

For Plant this was a return to the famous venue for the first time in 32 years – since the now legendary Zeppelin January 9, 1970, show as seen on the DVD. Plant followed Gary Moore and delivered a six-song set with his band Strange Sensation. It included a version of 'Four Sticks' with the original co-writer somewhere in the vicinity of the hall, but not on stage to add a contribution.

Paul Weller topped the bill with a meandering set punctuated half way through with his surprise guest – Jimmy Page. Backed by members of Weller's band and Ocean Colour Scene, he enthusiastically delivered an instrumental version of 'Dazed And Confused'. Again there was the bizarre scenario of the original lead singer of the track being in the vicinity of the building but not on stage to add what would have been a much welcomed contribution.

Allegedly there was no animosity between them – in fact there had been a vague plan to perform 'Thank You' together but the strict schedule of the evening thwarted such plans. It left the many Zep Page/Plant fans who had travelled far and wide, to shuffle out reflecting on what could only be viewed as a missed opportunity.

Bootleg CD Reference: *Teenage Cancer Trust* (Flagge)

THE LED ZEPPELIN DVD AND HOW THE WEST WAS WON RELEASES, 2003

Jimmy Page had long harboured an idea to assemble a true record of Zeppelin's live act both on disc and film. After a concerted effort to assess the extent of their visual archive in 1997, which led to the production of the 'Whole Lotta Love' promo, he embarked on a serious plan to produce an official visual record of the group.

It was evident to Page that the advent of the DVD format with its enhanced sound capabilities finally offered a worthy medium to present the best possible sound and visual package. Significantly, Page had recently managed to acquire the rights and full masters of their 1970 Royal Albert Hall show which had been filmed and intended as a documentary of the band at the time.

In early 2002 Page enlisted the assistance of Director Dick Carruthers whose credits included The Who, Stones and Oasis. Together the pair trawled through the Zeppelin archive and painstakingly began the task of digitally matching visuals with the equivalent audio masters. To supervise the sound reproduction, Page brought in sound engineer Kevin Shirley who had previously worked with the guitarist on the *Live At The Greek* album with The Black Crowes.

During the search for archive footage, they also came across the multi-track tapes for the 1972 Zeppelin performances at Long Beach and the Los Angeles Forum. This would form the basis for a separate project, the live album *How The West Was Won*, which would be issued simultaneously with the DVD.

Though the initial idea was simply to present just the Albert Hall footage, when they uncovered the full extent of Page's archive Page a full career overview was possible. As well as the Albert Hall material, they had access to the masters from the 1973 Madison Square Garden show which had been filmed for their *Song Remains The Same* movie, two nights of videotape from the Earls Court 1975 shows (May 24 & 25) and extensive 16 camera multi-track footage from both of the 1979 Knebworth concerts. Armed with all this, Page and Carruthers spent over a year preparing the material for release.

They cleverly supplemented the main features with a series of short additional items, including the early black and white Danish TV film, the one-off 1969 *Supershow* film segment and the French TV *Tous En Scene* appearance. Page also put out a call for audience shot cine footage, a somewhat ironic request in view of Peter Grant's abhorrence of bootleggers, but as a result the DVD included the version of 'The Song Remains The Same' from the famous *Listen To This Eddie* bootleg cut to various cine film. Page and Carruthers also cleverly intercut cine film footage to add depth and perspective to the Madison Square Garden and Knebworth segments.

The finished package, simply titled *DVD*, was released worldwide in late May 2003. It became the fastest selling music DVD title up to that point shifting over 120,000 in the US alone in a matter of days.

The accompanying live set *How The West Was Won* was met with similar acclaim and took the band back to the top of the US charts when it

entered the *Billboard* listings at number one. These extraordinary sales feats took Zeppelin's stock higher than at any point since their mid-Seventies peak – an emphatic reminder of the lasting Led Zeppelin legacy.

All three ex-members reunited to promote the releases and attend premiers on both sides of the Atlantic. This situation again gave rise to familiar reunion rumours and was enough to put Page in an optimistic mood on that subject. "None of us have actually discussed reforming," he said. "If we got back in a room and played a Zeppelin number and there were smiles behind our eyes then maybe it could happen. It could be possible. Until that happens, it's hypothetical. I wouldn't discount it. I just don't know."

John Paul Jones added: "One quarter of Led Zeppelin is gone. He wasn't just a drummer. It couldn't ever be the same."

Ever reticent, Robert Plant summarised his feelings on the situation:

"I don't know if it could work in this century. You're talking about a lot of years later. I'm sure it would be evocative for people in the crowd, but I don't know if we could do it properly. If anything the DVD really opens and closes the issue because it's so explicit of what it was about. It's the epitaph of Led Zeppelin – stunning, a lot of energy, a rollercoaster ride, four guys melding in this great fusion of music … and it's gone."

Thursday May 15 2003
London, England
The Empire Cinema, Leicester Square
LED ZEPPELIN DVD UK PREMIERE
NON PLAYING APPEARANCE

Page, Plant and Jones all attended the London premiere of the DVD – a specially condensed hour and a half presentation. The three received a standing ovation as they appeared on stage before the showing. Page and Plant made short speeches. It was an emotional occasion for all in attendance. Speaking after the showing John Paul Jones reflected: "For me it was so great to see so much of Bonzo. It reminded me of how much of Led Zeppelin revolved around him. Sitting there watching him on the big screen at the premiere I really missed him. As people cheered at the end of his drum solo I joined in – it was like 'Play some more'. Everything revolved on stage around him. Whenever we started to improvise or change direction musically you'd see everyone move towards the drums."

Plant was equally moved: "Seeing Bonzo 40 foot high and across the screen doing his magnificent thing in front of all these people while sitting next to John's son Jason well, it was too much."

Tuesday May 27 2003
New York, New York
Loews Theatre 34th Street
LED ZEPPELIN DVD US PREMIERE
NON PLAYING APPEARANCE

A week later they all travelled to New York for another emotional premiere.

Wednesday May 28 2003 and
Thursday May 29 2003
New York, New York
NBC Tonight and Today Shows
TV APPEARANCE

Whilst in New York, as part of the promotional campaign for the DVD's release, Page, Plant and Jones appeared in a joint TV interview conduced by Matt Lorey for airing on NBC's *Tonight* on May 28 and the *Today* news programme on May 29. It was the first time all three had conducted a screened interview together since the brief backstage soundbite captured immediately after their Live Aid appearance in 1985.

Page did most of the talking, summarising it all: "It was a musical ESP. It just went off in a tangent when we were on stage. It couldn't go on after John – there were some drummers mentioned but with the best will in the world, how could we say 'Listen to this… this is how we improvise … now go off and learn that night after night.'"

Plant became animated while explaining their musical chemistry: "Look at 'Achilles' at Knebworth – the unity between these guys was unbelievable. If we couldn't get near that after John, then it would have been a real soulless experience."

John Paul Jones added: "Right from the Albert Hall footage we had such swagger and bravado. It was great to see that again just searing off the stage."

Plant had the last word.

Interviewer: "So what's stopping Led Zeppelin jumping back on stage."

Plant: "We don't know how good you are on the drums … "

Saturday February 12 2005
Hollywood California
Biltmore Hotel
THE GRAMMY SPECIAL MERIT AWARDS
NON PLAYING APPEARANCE
Led Zeppelin were acknowledged with a Lifetime Achievement at the 2005 Grammy Awards. Page and Jones together with Jason and Zoe Bonham accepted the award and crystal trophies. Plant failed to attend, instead sending a video message that explained he was rehearsing for an upcoming tour. Asked about his non appearance Page commented: "It wouldn't have taken much just to pop over here and meet everybody would it really?"

In accepting the award, John Paul Jones thanked Peter Grant and Ahmet Ertegun and "the other half of our rhythm section – John Bonham".

Jimmy spoke of how America spearheaded Zeppelin's success and how Atlantic's Ertegun signed them: "It's a feeling beyond words just to be in this illustrious company."

Zoe Bonham said: "It's totally overwhelming. The whole crazy thing is it's a lifetime achievement and my Dad isn't here – the legend lives on".

Jason Bonham added: "Fans still speak of Led Zeppelin in the present never the past … "

After the presentation, Page spoke with fellow inductee Jerry Lee Lewis and Jones was photographed with David Grohl and Steve Via amongst others.

Thursday March 17 2005
Austin Texas
SOUTH BY SOUTH WEST MUSIC AND
MEDIA CONFERENCE
As well as playing a showcase set with Strange Sensation, Robert Plant gave a keynote speech at this prestigious industry event. Introduced by a 15-minute career highlights film directed by Aubrey Powell, he ran through some tales of Zeppelin on the road, advice for new bands and thoughts on his new record.

Neil Portnow, president of the US Recording Academy, took the opportunity to belatedly present Robert with his Led Zeppelin Lifetime Achievement Grammy award. "It's been 37 years since Led Zeppelin released its first song," said Plant. "It will be 25 years since John Bonham died. Time goes very fast. Led Zeppelin has been a major part of my creative life and I thoroughly enjoyed it."

In the question and answer session with journalist Bill Flannigan, he was startled by a question from what he presumed was a journalist. "Do you still have groupies?" the lady asked. In fact the lady in question was the notorious LA rock star courtesan Pamela Des Barres, who had been a regular member of the band's LA entourage in the mid-Seventies. Recognising an old friend, Plant leapt over to hug her and quickly replied: "Yes, and I still have that same premature ejaculation problem!"

Commenting yet again on plans for a Led Zeppelin reunion he reflected: "It meant what it meant when it meant it. There's no other story. When Zeppelin peaked it was world beating. After that there was no going back. You can't do it again."

The following is a summary of the solo tours undertaken by Robert Plant, Jimmy Page and John Paul Jones since the demise of Led Zeppelin.

It chronicles the major solo tours and various guest appearances undertaken from 1981 up to 2005. It also documents the live interpretations of the Led Zeppelin catalogue the three ex-members have performed on stage.

ROBERT PLANT

1981
THE HONEYDRIPPERS
UK CLUBS TOUR MARCH – MAY

Robert's first tentative steps outside of Zeppelin saw him hooking up with local R&B musicians from the Midlands area to form a pick-up band known as The Honeydrippers (named after an old blues instrumental of the same name by Roosevelt Sykes). The nucleus of the line-up was a mixture of members of Ricky Cool & The Rialto's and assorted local musicians including Robbie Blunt and Andy Sylvester (guitars), Kevin J. O'Neil (drums), Ricky Cool (harp), Jim Wickman (bass) and Keith Evans (sax). Blunt, a former member of The Steve Gibbons Band, Savoy Brown and Bronco, formed a song writing partnership with Robert that would shape his first three solo albums.

The original Honeydrippers tour folded before they made their planned London début at Dingwalls. However, Plant retained The

Honeydrippers name for future 'one-off' R&B gigs and a mini-album released in 1984.

The Honeydrippers set list included a cross section of vintage R&B material, including Little Sister/Hey Mae/Lotta Lovin'/True Love/Deep In The Heart Of Texas/ Honky Tonk/How Many More Years/Cross Cut Saw/Bring It On Home/I Just Can't Be Satisfied/Born Under A Bad Sign/I Need Your Loving Every Day/Keep On Lovin' Me Baby/What Can I Do?/Tell Me How/ Little Sheila/I Got My Mojo Workin' /Stormy Monday/Queen Of The Hop/I Can't Get Next To You.

The only concession to Led Zeppelin were blues interpretations of 'Bring It On Home' and 'How Many More Times' (based on 'How Many More Years').

1982
July 21: London, Dominion Theatre

Prince's Trust Rock Gala. Robert appeared in front of Prince Charles in an all star line-up of Pete Townshend, Phil Collins, Midge Ure, Japan's Mick Kharn and Robbie Blunt to perform 'Worse Than Detroit' from his just released *Pictures At Eleven* solo album. He also performed in the all star finale of 'I Want To Take You Higher'.

August 22: Dudley, JB's Club

Honeydrippers appearance: Support from The Tygers Of Pang Tang and Melvin & The Marauders. The Honeydrippers' set list included Little Sister/Stormy Monday/Money/Save The Last Dance For Me/ Love Potion Number 9.

October: Ibiza, Sgt Pepper Bar, San Antonio

While rehearsing for the second album, Plant and band members Paul Martinez, Jezz Woodroffe, Robbie Blunt and Barriemore Barlow joined Chris Squire from Yes for two performances at the local Sgt. Pepper bar. Numbers performed included Save The Last Dance For Me/C'mon Everybody/Little Sister/Knock On Wood.

November 4: Kinver, Community Centre (rehearsal)
December 22: Leeds, Warehouse (cancelled)
December 23: Coventry, General Wolf Pub

1983
June 22: Newcastle, Tyne Tees Studio

Live recording for the *Midsummer's Night Tube* TV show. Robert's solo live début with the new band line-up: Robbie Blunt (guitar), Jezz Woodroffe (keyboards), Paul Martinez (bass), Bob Mayo (guitar) and Queen's Roger Taylor guesting on drums. Plant, however, was less than happy with his performance and refused to let it be screened, allegedly paying £7,000 to avoid legal action.

Set List: Little Sister/Treat Her Right/Sea Of Love/Pledge Pin/Other Arms/In The Mood/Big Log/Like I've Never Been Gone/Worse Than Detroit/Other Arms (take 2)/In The Mood (take 2)/Fat Lip/Burning Down One Side.

1983/1984
PRINCIPLE OF MOMENTS US TOUR
AUGUST TO OCTOBER
UK TOUR NOVEMBER–DECEMBER
AUSTRALIA -JAPAN
JANUARY FEBRUARY
1984

Robert took to the road with a line up that initially included Phil Collins on drums. Ex-Little feat drummer Ritchie Haywood took over from the UK tour onwards. There was a conscious effort to move away from Zeppelin but echoes of the past emerged in certain live arrangements, notably Other Arms which included lyrics from 'Trampled Underfoot' and 'Slow Dancer' which included lyrics from 'Since I've Been Loving You'. Additional guitarist Bob Mayo played on this tour – he sadly died in 2004 age 53.

On the UK tour on December 4 in Bristol Colston Hall John Paul Jones joined the band for the encore performance of 'Little Sister' and on December 13 at London's Hammersmith Odeon Jimmy Page joined Robert for the encore performance of 'Treat Her Right'.

1985
January 18: Monmouth, Rolls Hall

A benefit show with The Honeydrippers were billed as The Skinnydippers.

SHAKEN N' STIRRED US TOUR
JUNE TO AUGUST
UK DATES SEPTEMBER

Following the release of his third album, *Shaken N' Stirred*, Robert embarked on an ambitious tour that incorporated a Honeydrippers section complete with inflatable Cadillac backdrop. The band line-up was a five piece, retaining Robbie Blunt, Paul Martinez, Jezz Woodroffe and Ritchie Haywood and was supplemented by The Uptown Horns (dubbed The King Bees) and The Queen Bees backing vocalists.

The main concessions to Led Zeppelin occured on 'Young Boy Blues' which included the 'Boogie Chillun'' insert employed by Zep in the 'Whole Lotta Love' medleys) and Easily Led which included a 'Keep-A-Coolin'' reference from 'Whole Lotta Love'. A week after reuniting with Page and Jones for Live Aid, at the Meadowlands July 20 date Brian Setzer of Stray Cats and Paul Shaffer from The David Letterman Band (and a contributor to the Honeydrippers album) guested on 'Honey Hush'. Jimmy Page appeared on the encore performance of 'Mean Woman Blues' and 'Treat Her Right'.

1986
BIG TOWN PLAYBOYS SHOWS

In early 1986, Robert agreed to perform at the

Birmingham Heart Beat Benefit show with local Midlands R&B band The Big Town Playboys and added two warm up dates. The Playboys line-up included ex-Honeydrippers Ricky Cool and Andy Sylvester plus Michael Sanchez, Ian Jennings and John Spinetto. The material drew on the R&B catalogue previously favoured by The Honeydrippers.

March 12: Leeds, Leeds University
March 14: Norwich, University Of East Anglia
March 15: Birmingham NEC
Heart Beat Show in aid of the Birmingham Children's Hospital. Set list included: She Walks Right In/Come On/I Need Your Love So Bad/Mellow Saxophone/Lonely Avenue/ Drifting/Good Rockin' At Midnight/Honey Hush/So Many Roads. Robert's third on the bill appearance was a low key affair compared to headliners The Moody Blues and ELO. He took part in the all star finale, playing guitar with George Harrison on a version of 'Johnny B Goode'. Part of his set was later screened by Central TV.

August 9: Cropredy Festival, Oxfordshire
Guest appearance: Robert joined Fairport Convention at their annual outdoor festival to perform versions of 'Mess O' Blues', 'Nineteen Years Old' and 'Mystery Train'.

December 19: Stourport, Civic Centre
A Honeydrippers benefit in aid of the family of the late John Pasternak, a former Band Of Joy member. Jimmy Page joined Robert for the second half of the show, performing old blues favourites and they encored with a version of 'Rock And Roll'. Robbie Blunt also guested.

1987
NOW AND ZEN WARM UP SHOWS
During 1987 Robert assembled a new line-up and recorded his fourth solo set, *Now And Zen*. He commenced a series of low key warm up dates. The new line-up included Doug Boyle (guitar), Phil Johnstone (keyboards and guitar), Charlie Jones (bass) and Chris Blackwell (drums). For the first time Robert performed versions of numbers

from the Led Zeppelin catalogue. "I guess I am eating a sizeable proportion of my own words. But these are great songs and I think enough time has now lapsed. Some of them are sacred still, but if I want to romp through 'Misty Mountain Hop' again, well it's my prerogative."

December 17: Folkestone, Leas Cliff Hall
Billed as The Band Of Joy. First solo performances of Zeppelin tracks 'In The Evening', 'Trampled Underfoot' and 'Misty Mountain Hop'. Encores were 'Money' and 'Santa Claus Is Coming To Town'.

December 30: Stourbridge, Town Hall
A return to home base for this memorable show – encore numbers included 'Money' and 'Rock And Roll'. Andy Taylor of Duran Duran jammed on additional encores of 'Gambler's Blues' and 'Johnny B Goode'.

University of Essex Students N° 207
Union Entertainments *present*
Legendary "Led Zeppelin" singer
ROBERT PLANT
with THE BAND OF JOY plus Special Guest
PLUS DISCO AND LATE BAR
S.U. DANCE HALL   Saturday, 30th January, 1988
Doors open 8 p.m. On Stage 11.30   Tickets £6.00 advance £6.50 door
The Management Reserve the Right to Refuse Admission

1988
UK DATES JANUARY/FEBRURY
THE NON STOP GO TOUR UK LEG
MARCH TO APRIL
US LEG MAY TO JULY
SECOND US LEG OCTOBER TO DECEMBER
On the UK tour the support band was It Bites which includes Francis Dunnery who would later team up with Robert for the 'Fate Of Nations' tour. An easy listening cocktail version of 'Stairway To Heaven' was occasionally played as the outro music after the lights have gone up.

The following Led Zeppelin songs were performed in full across these tours: In The Evening/Misty Mountain Hop/ Trampled Underfoot/Black Country Woman/Rock And Roll/ Communication Break-down/. A cover of

'Dimple's included the intro of 'Heartbreaker'. 'Tall Cool One' included the intro to 'Custard Pie'.

1989
December 23: Kidderminster, Swan Centre
Guest appearance: Robert joined local band Out Of The Blue in Kidderminster's main shopping centre for a Day Of Awareness charity show in aid of Dr. Barnardos.

Robert performed cover versions of Bryan Adams 'Run To You', 'Spirit In The Sky', ZZ Top's 'She Loves My Automobile', The Police's 'Every Breath You Take', Dylan's 'All Along The Watchtower' and Zep's 'Rock And Roll'.

Plant: 'We're going to do Knebworth after this!'

1990/1991
MANIC NIRVANA TOUR:
EUROPE MAY
UK TOUR DATES JUNE
US TOUR JULY TO AUGUST
SECOND US TOUR NOVEMBER (The Tour That Time Forgot)
UK DATES DECEMBER
UK DATES JANUARY 1991

A new touring campaign commenced to support the release of his fifth solo set, *Manic Nirvana*. The same touring band was retained. The tour commenced with a trek around Europe – the first time Plant has ventured into mainland Europe as a solo artist.

The set list included a further new interpretations of Zeppelin numbers notably 'No Quarter', 'Wearing And Tearing', 'Livin' Lovin' Maid' and 'Ramble On'.

A date in March due to take place at the Salcombe, Cliff Trust Assembly Hall where Plant and band had been rehearsing had to be vetoed when the local council ordered the gig to be cancelled after they were led to believe a reformed Led Zeppelin would be appearing.

The following Led Zeppelin numbers were performed in full across these tours: Nobody's Fault But Mine (with Friends intro)/Wearing And Tearing/No Quarter/Going To California/Immigrant Song/Black Country Woman/Misty Mountain Hop/Livin' Lovin' Maid/Ramble On.

1992
April 20: London, Wembley Stadium
Freddie Mercury Tribute Concert. Robert joined the all star line-up to appear with the remaining members of Queen. His segment featured his rendition of Queen's 'Innuendo' complete with a middle section with lyrics from 'Kashmir' and a link piece featuring the opening lines from 'Thank You' that segued into 'Crazy Little Thing Called Love'. The concert was shown live on TV and Robert once again fell victim to the Zep TV curse – his mike failed to pick up for the first minute or so.

August 11: Banbury, Mill Theatre
Guest Appearance: Robert guested with Fairport Convention as a warm up for the Cropredy Festival. He performed 'Girl From The North Country'/'Babe I'm Gonna Leave You' (it's first live airing since 1969)/'In The Evening' and 'Ramble On'.

August 14: Cropredy Festival
Guest Appearance: Robert guested with Fairport Convention at the climax of their Friday night performance. The songs were again 'Girl From The North Country'/'Babe I'm Gonna Leave You (with a 'Stairway To Heaven' instrumental ending – this was retained by Jimmy Page for the 1995 Page/Plant tour version)/'In The Evening' (featuring an opening sample of the intro taken direct from the Zeppelin studio version) and 'Ramble On'.

1993
THE FATE OF NATIONS TOUR
EUROPEAN TOUR MAY TO JULY
US TOUR SEPTEMBER TO DECEMBER
EUROPEAN TOUR DECEMBER

There had been much fresh thinking in the Plant camp since his last tour. A new set of musicians was assembled – with only Phil Johnstone and Charlie Jones from the old unit retaining their places. New recruits were former Cult drummer Michael Lee and a duel guitar set up of Francis Dunnery (ex-It Bites) and Kevin Scott MacMichael (ex-Cutting Crew). In the UK Plant ended his long association with the Atlantic label and signed a deal with Phonogram. The first fruit of this alliance was the single '29 Palms' which was quickly followed by the release of the *Fate Of Nations* album. Easily his most accomplished solo effort to date, it mirrored the folk and West Coast

leanings that influenced his pre-Zeppelin career and found him in the best vocal form for years.

Robert Plant: "I feel much more at home with this album. This is the plot that I will keep now."

The initial European tour was a hugely enjoyable affair that combined major festival appearances, support slots for Lenny Kravitz and solo shows in their own right. The set list selection included a weighty input of Zeppelin numbers with 'Whole Lotta Love', 'What Is And What Should Never Be' and 'Thank You' new additions from the back catalogue. A cover of Buffalo Springfield's 'Bluebird' was also an occasional feature. The UK debut of the line up took place at two low key shows at London's Kings Head pub in early May where they were billed as Fate Of Nations and Band Of Joy.

There was a change of line-up for the US leg with Kevin Scott MacMicheal leaving the band to be replaced by Innis Sibun. MacMichael sadly died in 2002. The set list included various experiments and additions notably 'Babe I'm Gonna Leave You' and 'In The Mood'. The latter was extended to feature snippets of 'In The Light', 'That's The Way', 'Season Of The Witch', 'Justify My Love', 'Light My Fire' and 'Break On Through', amongst others. Another Zeppelin song 'Your Time Is Gonna Come' was performed on selected dates and 'Black Country Woman' was also played during the acoustic set. Long deleted early solo staples 'Just Like I've Never Been Gone' and 'Thru With The Two Step' were also recalled occasionally.

1994

SOUTH AMERICAN TOUR JANUARY

These dates were a hugely successful end to his most satisfying solo tour. They also signified the close of this stage of his solo career. Interestingly the set list for these dates included the addition of the rarely played Zeppelin favourite 'Rock And Roll'. The next time he would perform that song in this continent it would be in the company of the original co-composer.

January 15: San Paulo, Hollywood Rock Festival
January 17: Buenos Aires, Velez Sarsfield
January 19: Santiago, Veledrome
January 22: Rio De Janeiro, Hollywood Rock Festival

This superb performance was screened on the local TV network.

Set List: Babe I'm Gonna Leave You/29 Palms/Ramble On/Tall Cool One/Thank You/If I Were A Carpenter/Going To California/Black Country Woman/In The Mood (including snippets of Break On Through/Light My Fire/In The Light)/Calling To You/Hurting Kind/Whole Lotta Love/Encore: Rock And Roll.

January 25: Caracas
January 28 &29: Mexico, National Auditorium

The following Led Zeppelin songs were performed across these 1993/4 tours: Trampled Underfoot/What Is And What Should Never Be/Babe I'm Gonna Leave You/Ramble On/Going To California/Whole Lotta Love/Livin' Lovin'Maid/Black Country Woman/You Shook Me (included 'Dazed And Confused' insert at the NEC Birmingham July 14)/Your Time Is Gonna Come/Thank You/Rock And Roll.

1999

PRIORY OF BRION UK DATES

After deciding not to continue his collaboration with Jimmy, Plant went back to his Midlands base. In a move that mirrored his immediate post-Zep gigs with the pick up band The Honeydrippers, Plant began playing a series of low key club dates with a line up he dubbed

Priory of Brion. It included long time friend and ex-Band Of Joy guitarist Kevyn Gammond plus three local musicians Paul Timothy on keyboards, Paul Wetton bass and Andy Edwards on drums. The Priory set list was made up entirely of songs Plant had been influenced by or had performed before Zeppelin. This oddball concoction provided close proximity to the singer for the audience and was a virtual musical history lesson of the psychedelic rock era with covers of songs by the likes of Tim Buckley, Love, Buffalo Springfield and Jefferson Airplane. Initially gigs were advertised by word of mouth with no mention of Plant's name.

The only concessions to Led Zeppelin occurred in a performance of the original arrangement of Ben E King/James Bethea's 'We're Gonna Groove' which had briefly been the Zep set list opener in 1970 and eventually appeared on *Coda*. The Priory also performed a version of Garnet Mimms 'As Long As I Have You' which had been a staple part of Zeppelin's early 1969 set. He did finally relent at the close of the Priory's final tour, performing 'Thank You' on the last couple of dates.

2000
PRIORY OF BRION
UK TOUR DATES FEB TO APRIL
NORWAY UK AND IRELAND DATES
APRIL TO JUNE
UK AND EUROPEAN FESTIVAL DATES
JUNE TO AUGUST
UK AND ITALIAN DATES SEPTEMBER
UK AND EUROPEAN DATES
OCTOBER TO DECEMBER

During this year Plant continued his adventure with the Priory. Now comfortable enough to announce dates upfront and happy for his name to be tagged on, they combined small UK gigs with larger festival dates including appearances a Glastonbury, the Cambridge Folk Festival and the annual Fairport Convention bash in Cropredy. In Europe they played to larger audiences including appearances the Nice Festival and Pistoria Festiva in Italy.

After dates in Greece and three Christmas shows at Crewe, Derby and Wolverhampton, Plant decided to end the Priory alliance. They had played over 70 gigs in the space of eighteen months. However, management pressure to record a new album led Robert to regroup with a new set of musicians.

2001

STRANGE SENSATION
EUROPEAN TOUR APRIL TO MAY
US TOUR MAY TO JUNE
EUROPEAN TOUR JUNE TO AUGUST

Robert gathered a new set of musicians for his next venture. Under the banner Strange Sensation, it featured Charlie Jones on bass, ex-Jah Wobble guitarist Justin Adams, John Baggott on keyboards (ex-Massive Attack) and drummer Clive Deamer known for his work with Portishead. Former Cure guitarist Porl Thompson, who toured with Page and Plant on their 1995 world tour, completed the line up.

An altogether more serious affair, the band made their debut in Denmark. Their set combined elements of the Priory setlist with versions of Priory cover staples 'Morning Dew', 'Song To The Siren' and 'A House Is Not A Motel' with a smattering of Zeppelin numbers – namely 'Four Sticks', 'In the Light', 'Misty Mountain Hop', 'Night Flight', 'Whole Lotta Love' (in an arrangement that merged the Willie Dixon original 'You Need Love') and 'Babe I'm Gonna Leave You'.

Plant took the band to America for a series of spring dates and after a European tour which excluded the UK they began recording an album at RAK Studios. The plan was to capture on record their interpretations of several of the classic numbers that Plant had first introduced in the Priory. Whilst in the studio three new compositions, 'Red Dress', 'Last Time I Saw Her' and 'Dirt In A Hole', were also recorded.

2002

DREAMLAND TOUR WITH
STRANGE SENSATION

UK DATES FEBRUARY
PORTUGAL DATES MAY
UK DATES JUNE
US TOUR JULY TO AUGUST
US TOUR SEPTEMBER
UK TOUR OCTOBER
EUROPEAN TOUR NOVEMBER

Following dates in Bristol and at the Royal Albert Hall, Robert and Strange Sensation undertook a series of dates across Europe (including the Isle Of Wight Festival) and the US to promote the release of the resulting album *Dreamland*. Porl Thompson left the band in March and was replaced by ex-Cast guitarist Skin Tyson. The July and August leg of the US tour included a series of support slots to The Who. The year ended with a visit to Russia for dates in St Petersburg and Moscow.

The following Led Zeppelin songs were performed across these tours: Four Sticks/ Celebration Day/Going To California/Ramble On/Hey Hey What Can I Do/Misty Mountain Hop/Whole Lotta Love/Thank You/Rock And Roll (the latter two songs were a rare addition to the St Petersburg set list).

2003

FESTIVAL IN THE DESERT
ESSAKANE-MALIAN SAHARA

In January Plant accompanied by Justin Adams and Skin from Strange Sensation took part in the Festival Of The Desert in Mali. Plant performed on the last day of the festival with Skin, Justin Adams and a bass and percussion player from the French band Lo-Jo. Set: Win My Train Fare Home (If I Ever Get Lucky)/Girl From The North Country/Whole Lotta Love.

He also jammed with Ali Farka Toure and was interviewed by Andy Kershaw for BBC Radio. The track 'Win My Train Fare Home (If I Ever Get Lucky)' was issued on the live album from the event Festival In The Desert (World Village/Triban Union). An accompanying *Festival In The Desert* CD included 'Win My Train Fare Home'.

STRANGE SENSATION
UK TV DATES FEBRUARY
NORWAY/ITALY DATES APRIL/JULY
THE ARCTIC CIRCLE TOUR JUNE
EUROPEAN TOUR JULY AUGUST

The early part of the year saw the band play TV slots for BBC3's *Recovered* and BBC2's *Live Floor* show and perform selected dates in Norway and Italy. Charlie Jones left the band to be replaced by Billy Fuller on bass. In July they played an Arctic Circle tour covering four Norway gigs and summer festival dates in Italy, France, Estonia, Latvia, Ukraine and at Bristol's Ashton Court Festival and the Canterbury Fayre.

The following Led Zeppelin songs were performed across these dates: Gallows Pole/Going To California/Ramble On/Friends/What Is And What Should Never Be/Friends/Babe I'm Gonna Leave You/Four Sticks/Whole Lotta Love/Rock And Roll.

December 11: Oslo

Plant took part in the Nobel Peace Concert in Oslo. The set with Strange Sensation was Darkness Darkness/Morning Dew/Going To Califonia plus 'Imagine' (finale with Michael Douglas, Rosanne Cash and others).

2004

March 13: Stourbridge Rock Cafe

Guest appearance with Vanilla Fudge. Robert attended this show featuring early Zep tour mates Vanilla Fudge. When bassist Tim Bogert was taken ill, Plant took to the stage to jam with drummer Carmine Appice. Joined by support act The Lizzards, he performed 'Parchment Farm' and relayed tales of Zep and the Fudge's touring exploits to a crown of less that 100.

October

Plant was a guest vocalist in a line-up dubbed The RD Cruisers for two shows at Ronnie Scotts Club and The Cirque in London in aid of the Teenage Cancer Trust, a charity principally supported by The Who's Roger Daltrey. The ad-hoc band included Greg Lake, Gary Moore and Gary Brooker.

November 7: Leadbelly Tribute Concert.
Severance Hall. Cleveland. Ohio

Robert took part in a tribute concert for the blues legend Leadbelly. With Justin Adams on guitar/gymru), he performed 'Where Did You Sleep Last Night' (with Alison Krauss), 'Alabama Bound' (with the Cleveland Four), 'Red Dress' and 'Gallows Pole' (with Los Lobos).

2005

MIGHTY REARRANGER TOUR
US DATES
UK DATES
EUROPEAN TOUR
US TOUR

With the completion of *Mighty ReArranger*, a new album of new material written with Strange Sensation, Robert undertook a new tour to support the album. Now billed as Robert Plant & The Strange Sensation, they commenced with two tsunami benefit gis at Bristol Academy on a bill that included Massive Attack and Portishead.

In between the UK and US gigs Robert also made an appearance at the MAS Kidderminster College label launch at Kiddermister Town hall. He jammed with local blues band Blujuice on 'Parchment Farm', 'Hallelujah I Love You So', 'Mr Pitiful', 'Think', 'What I'd Say', 'Comin' Home Baby', 'Hoochie Coochie Man'.

Robert and The Strange Sensation then performed seven American dates, including a prestigious showcase at the South By South West Music Convention at which Plant also made a keynote speech.

April 1: Liverpool Academy
April 3: Warwick University
April 4: Royal Albert Hall, Teenage Cancer Trust show

The following Led Zeppelin songs were performed up to the April UK dates: No Quarter/Black Dog/ That's The Way/ Heartbreaker/When The Levee Breaks (including samples from John Bonham's original drum track)/Whole Lotta Love.

JIMMY PAGE

In October 1982 Page was prosecuted for drug possession. Conditionally discharged, he told the magistrates that he was currently forming a new band ready to tour Japan and America. There were rumours of him joining a new Whitesnake line-up. However, nothing much significant emerged from him until 1983.

1981
March 10: London, Hammersmith Odeon
Guest appearance: Jimmy joined Jeff Beck for an encore performance of 'I'm Going Down'.

1982
May 12: Munich, Sports Arena
Guest appearance: Jimmy and Robert Plant joined Foreigner for an encore performance of 'Lucille'. Guitar used: Black Gibson Les Paul.

1983
May 24: Guildford, Civic Hall
Guest appearance: Jimmy joined Eric Clapton for an encore jam on 'Further On Up The Road' and 'Cocaine'.

ARMS – UK TOUR
September 20 & 21: London, Royal Albert Hall
Three months after the Guildford jam, Jimmy answered Eric Clapton's call to perform at two special charity shows at The Royal Albert Hall. The first night was staged to raise money for the multiple sclerosis charity, ARMS, and former Small Faces bassist Ronnie Lane who was suffering from the disease. The second show was in aid of The Princes Trust and was attended by Prince Charles and Princess Diana. Page was supported by Simon Phillips on drums, Fernando Saunders on bass, Chris Stainton on piano and Andy Fairweather-Low on guitar,

Playing with Ray Cooper (percussion) and Steve Winwood (vocals), Jimmy's first major post-Zeppelin appearance was an emotional event. The

SOLO CONCERT PERFORMANCE ITINERARY
Page's early post-Zeppelin activities were limited to occasional guest appearances. He also established his own Sol Studio in Cookham, Berkshire. Visitors included George Harrison, Mick Fleetwood and Yes men Chris Squire and Alan White. The latter pair inspired rumours that Page would call in Plant to form a new band known as XYZ (ex-Yes and Zeppelin). This rumour was vehemently denied by everyone concerned. However, initial secret sessions by Page, Squire and White did produce seven new tracks, but management intervention, and Robert's apparent unwillingness to become involved, prevented the project from progressing further.

Instead, Page busied himself by recording the soundtrack to Michael Winner's film *Death Wish II*. Page recalled: "I was at a very low ebb, but then a great challenge came up – to do a film score. I had eight weeks on that project, that's all I had to deliver the whole thing. That's what got me back into it without a doubt."

Page then turned his attention to mixing and overdubbing tracks for the final Led Zeppelin album, *Coda*. Plant was also involved, overdubbing new vocals.

set list for both nights revolved around Jimmy's *Death Wish II* soundtrack for which he uses the Botswana brown Telecaster. The appearance of the famous Gibson double-neck signified a moving instrumental delivery of 'Stairway To Heaven'. On the second night Clapton and Beck assisted on the solo.

Set List: Prelude/Who's To Blame/City Sirens/Stairway To Heaven.

He also appeared in the All Star Finale with Beck and Clapton on 'Tulsa Time', 'Layla' and 'Goodnight Irene'.

ARMS – US TOUR

Flushed with the success of the London dates, the ARMS entourage moved to America for a nine date tour. With Steve Winwood unavailable, Jimmy asks Paul Rodgers to do the vocal honours. There had been tentative plans for the pair to team up earlier in the year for an album project. Page and Rodgers introduce a new composition on the tour, known as 'Bird On A Wing', later to be titled 'Midnight Moonlight'. This lengthy opus contained elements of Page's 'White Summer – Black Mountain Side' showpiece and was well received throughout the tour.

Set List Summary: Prelude/Who's To Blame/City Sirens/Boogie Mama (from Rodgers' solo album)/Bird On A Wing/Stairway To Heaven. Page also joined in for the finale numbers, 'Layla', 'With A Little Help From My Friends', and 'Goodnight Irene'.

November 28 & 29: Dallas, Reunion Arena
December 1, 2 & 3: San Francisco, Cow Palace
December 5 & 6: Los Angeles, Inglewood Forum
December 8 & 9: New York, Madison Square Garden

Page: "On the ARMS tour, I realised the fans wanted me back."

1984
February: New York

Page, with newly shorn haircut, jams with Eric Clapton, Charlie Watts, John Entwistle and Louis

Bertignac of French group Telephone, at a party for producer Glyn John's 42nd birthday.

May 6: Thetford, May Tree

Guest appearance: Jimmy resumed his friendship with Roy Harper, playing the first of a series of occasional shows. They also record an album together *Whatever Happened To Jugula?* Harper introduced Page as James MacGregor. Songs featuring Page: Highway Blues/20th Century Man/Hangman/ Elizabeth.

May 21: Lytham St. Annes, St. Ives Hotel

Guest appearance with Roy Harper.

Set List: Highway Blues/Commune/20th Century Man/Elizabeth/Hangman/North Country/Highway Blues.

June 5: Nottingham, Palais

Page joined Ian Stewart's Rocket 88 for an Alexis Korner tribute concert. Line-up included Jack Bruce, Dick Heckstall-Smith, Ian Stewart, Charlie Watts, Paul Jones, and Ruby Turner.

Set List: Bring It On Home To Me/How Long/Got My Money/Stormy Monday/ Splanky/Big Boss Man/Whole Lotta Energy/ Love And Money/Intuition/Page Solo/ King Of All I Survey/Got My Mojo Working/ Every Day I Have The Blues/Hoochie Koochie Man.

Page recalls: "When I played with Rocket 88 in Nottingham no-one was announced until half way through the second half. It was great because I heard people say, 'Oh, that guitarist wasn't bad', and they didn't know who it was. That meant so much to me. It helped me put things in proper perspective and see how things ought to be."

June 24: Dortmund, Westfalenhalle

Guest appearance: Jimmy joined Yes for an encore jam performance of The Beatles' 'I'm Down'.

July 16: Italy, Pistoia Blues Festival

Another Alexis Korner benefit with Ginger Baker, Jon Heiseman, Dick Heckstall-Smith, Barbara Thompson and Georgie Fame. Set List: Keep Your Mouth Shut/Gypsy/Train Kept A Rollin/Instrumental/Sitting Up Here/Mercy/Bring It On Home/See Me Coming.

July 28: Cambridge, Folk Festival

Roy Harper appearance: Jimmy joined Roy's band for two high profile sets at the annual Cambridge Folk Festival. Line-up is Harper, Page, Steve Broughton, drums, Nick Green, keyboards, Tony Franklin, bass. Set List (afternoon): Short And Sweet/Referendum/Elizabeth/Highway Blues/The Flycatcher/True Story/The Game. Set List (evening): Page joins Harper's set for 'Hangman' and 'Same Old Rock'. Guitars used by Jimmy: Brown Fender Telecaster, Ovation acoustic.

July 29: London, Battersea Park

Roy Harper appearance. Set List: Short And Sweet/Referendum/Highway Blues/True Story/The Game

November 24: London, Covent Garden Rock Garden

Roy Harper appearance: Jimmy joins from '20th Century Man' onwards. Set List: 20th Century Man/Guitar Solo From Same Old Rock/One Of Those Days In England/Same Old Rock/Hangman.

THE FIRM EUROPEAN TOUR

Alongside the Roy Harper project, Jimmy assembled a four-piece line-up with Paul Rodgers. Jimmy spent the first months of 1984 in London's Nomis Studios auditioning band members and rehearsing new material. Initially, drummer Rat Scabies of The Damned occupied the drum stool, then Bill Bruford, before he finally settled on former Manfred Mann Earth Band drummer, Chris Slade. Top session musician Pino Paladino was Jimmy's first choice as bassist. However, Paladino had prior touring commitments with Paul Young, so Page called on a recent member of Roy

Harper's band, Tony Franklin, to complete the line-up.

They rehearsed under the name The MacGregors. An album was quickly recorded and they announced a debut tour under the new name of The Firm. The set list avoided the past triumphs of Zeppelin and Free/Bad Company and was instead built around Page's *Death Wish II* soundtrack and Rodgers' solo album plus various covers.

The only concession to the Led Zeppelin catalogue was Jimmy's guitar solo which featured the violin bow episode from 'Dazed And Confused'.

Set list summary: Numbers performed during this tour – Holst Planets Suite intro/Closer/City Sirens/Make Up Or Break Up/Morning After The Night Before/Together/Cadillac/Prelude/ Money Can't Buy/Radioactive/ Live In Peace/Midnight Moonlight (including White Summer/Black Mountain Side insert)/You've Lost That Loving Feeling/The Chase (includes bass and drum solos and Dazed & Confused violin bow solo)/Someone To Love/Full Circle/Cut Loose/Boogie Mama/Everybody Needs Somebody To Love.

Guitars used during The Firm era: Brown Fender Telecaster, Gibson Les Paul, Lake Placid Blue Stratocaster.

November 29: Stockholm, Sweden, Gota Lejon
November 30: Copenhagen, Denmark, Falkonner Theatre
December 1: Lund, Sweden, Olympen
December 3: Frankfurt, Germany, Kongress Halle

Led Zeppelin

December 4: Ludwigshafen, Germany, Pfalzball
December 5: Hamburg, Germany, Audimax
December 7: Middlesborough, Town Hall
December 8 & 9: London, Hammersmith Odeon

Both Hammersmith Odeon dates are recorded and filmed professionally and later an edited version is aired on MTV in the US. Two performances from the December 9 show, 'City Sirens' and 'Live In Peace', are later issued as additional tracks on the 'Radioactive' 12 inch single.

1985
THE FIRM
US TOUR FEBRUARY TO MAY
UK TOUR

After rehearsals at Los Colinas in Texas, The Firm commenced a lengthy US tour to support the release of their début album. Set List Summary: Closer/City Sirens/Make Or Break Up/The Morning After/Together/ Cadillac/Prelude/ Money Can't Buy/Satisfaction Guaranteed/ Radioactive/ Live In Peace/Midnight Moonlight/You've Lost That Loving Feeling/The Chase/I Just Wanna Make Love To You/Someone To Love/Encores: Boogie Mama/Everybody Needs Somebody To Love.

A short UK return was slotted in. Ticket sales were slow and venues did not sell out.

May 18: Birmingham, National Exhibition Centre

Robert Plant attends this show. He later comments: "I thought Jimmy was great. He played so well. His solos just seared right across song structures that weren't always my cup of tea. But the way his presence and execution turned around quite ordinary Bad Company type songs was stunning. I suddenly realised I had never watched him play before. I'd always been beside him! So there I was at a gig shuffling around nervously not knowing if I was going to be excited or if I'd have to pretend I liked it … but

he played so well. He was skidding around the stage and the only thing that really upset me was that I wasn't doing all that. He could have bumped into me with pleasure."

May 20: Edinburgh, Playhouse Theatre
May 22: London, Wembley Arena

The venue was only three quarters full. Page does his best to save the night but Rodgers fails to match his enthusiasm.

July 4: Washington DC, Ben Franklin Parkway

Guest appearance: Jimmy joined The Beach Boys for performances of Lucille/Help Me Rhonda/Surfin' Safari/Barbara Ann/Fun Fun Fun.

July 13: Philadelphia, JFK Stadium

The Live Aid reunion with Plant and Jones. Set List: Rock And Roll/Whole Lotta Love/Stairway To Heaven.

July 23: East Rutherford, Meadowlands Arena

Guest appearance: Jimmy joined Robert Plant for an encore jam performing 'Mean Woman Blues' and 'Treat Her Right'.

August 28: Ibiza, Spain. 'Sun Power' Festival

Jimmy performs an energetic set with Jason Bonham, Chris Squire of Yes, and Mick Thompson on vocals. The fifty minute blues jam included several Muddy Waters tunes and the classic, 'Money'. Guitar used: Black Yamaha.

November 2: Waltham St. Lawrence, Neville Hall

Guest appearance: Page joined up for a 'Blues'n'Booze' benefit performance with John Coghlan, Mick Ralphs and Mickey Moody, plus Andy Powell from Wishbone Ash and The Moody Blues' Patrick Moraz. The concert was attended by 150 people (the maximum fire regulations allow) and raises £1,000 for the village hall restoration fund.

THE FIRM

NEC BIRMINGHAM
SATURDAY 18th MAY
8.00 p.m.

PLAYHOUSE THEATRE,
EDINBURGH
MONDAY 20th MAY
8.00 p.m.

WEMBLEY ARENA
WEDNESDAY 22nd MAY
8.00 p.m.

Page's involvement was via Roland guitar tech David Green whose wife Carol is Clerk to the Parish Council. Carol commented: "At one stage I announced the end of the concert but Jimmy Page got up and did another number – he didn't want to go home. It was an electric evening."

Guitar used: Brown Fender Telecaster.

1986
THE FIRM – US TOUR MARCH TO MAY

With a second album, 'Mean Business' just released, The Firm return to the US for what will be their final tour. For the first leg, the support band was Virginia Wolf with Jason Bonham. Set list summary: Fortune Hunter/Closer/Someone To Love/Make Or Break/Prelude/Money Can't Buy/Satisfaction Guaranteed/Drum Solo/Radioactive/Live In Peace/All The King's Horses/Bass Solo (includes snippet of Purple Haze)/The Chase/Midnight Moonlight/Cadillac/You've Lost That Loving Feeling/Tear Down The Walls/Spirit Of Love/Encores: I Just Want To Make Love To You/Everybody Needs Somebody To Love/Money.

May 28: Seattle, Centre Coliseum

The final Firm show in Seattle on May 28 was an eventful evening. After the first two numbers the band left the stage due to fighting in the audience and only returned when calm was relatively restored. The encores began with Phil Carson jamming on bass during 'Money' and continued with the usual 'I Just Wanna Make Love To You' and 'Everybody Needs Somebody To Love'.

Jimmy Page: "The Firm was originally going to be a one album project and then it went to two,

and then Paul and I agreed it had run its course really."

June 9: New York, Hard Rock Cafe

Guest appearance: Jimmy joined Les Paul for his 72nd birthday bash. Jeff Beck, Rick Derringer, Al Di Meola and Nile Rodgers were also in attendance. Guitar used: Cherry red Gibson Les Paul. John Paul Jones was also in attendance.

August 4: Ibiza, San Antonio

Page jams with Jason Bonham and Phil Carson in a club. Billed as 'Safe Sex'.

November 9: London, Hammersmith Odeon

Guest appearance: Jimmy joined an all star line-up with Brian May and Iron Maiden at the Bad News show in aid of NSPCC. Page is seen with Bad News on a spoof performance which involves him not being plugged in.

December 19: Stourport, Civic Centre

Guest appearance: Jimmy joined Robert Plant's Honeydrippers for a performance that included Zep's 'Rock And Roll'. Guitar used: Brown Fender Telecaster.

1988
April 17: London, Hammersmith Odeon

Guest appearance: Jimmy joined Robert for an extended encore appearance performing on 'Trampled Underfoot', 'Misty Mountain Hop', 'Gamblers Blues' (including snippets of 'I Can't Quit You' and 'Since I've Been Loving You') and 'Rock And Roll'. Guitar used: Gibson Les Paul.

May 14: New York, Madison Square Garden

Jimmy is reunited with Plant, Jones and Jason Bonham at the Atlantic 40th birthday bash. Set List: Kashmir/Heartbreaker/Whole Lotta Love/Misty Mountain Hop/Stairway To Heaven. Guitars used: Den Electro, Gibson Les Paul, Gibson double-neck.

OUTRIDER US TOUR
SEPTEMBER TO NOVEMBER

A new era – Page moved over to the Geffen label

for the release of his solo album *Outrider* where he was joined by various guest vocalists including Robert Plant, Chris Farlowe and John Miles. The album was originally intended to be a double set featuring one acoustic and one blues album, but the theft of songwriting tapes from Page reduced the project to a standard length disc.

Jimmy Page recalled: "The *Outrider* album project was fun to do, but I suppose looking back it was a bit like a glorified demo."

John Miles was chosen as the singer for the accompanying 'Outrider' tour. The line-up is completed by Jason Bonham on drums and Durban Laverde on bass. In line with Plant's current tour, Jimmy for the first time incorporates various Zeppelin numbers in the set, notably, 'Over The Hills And Far Away', 'In My Time Of Dying', 'White Summer', 'Custard Pie' and an instrumental 'Stairway To Heaven'. The set was presented as a *tour de force* of Page's entire career incorporating the Yardbirds arrangement of 'Train Kept A Rollin'', moving through the Zeppelin era and on to the *Death Wish*/Firm/*Outrider* material. 'The Chase' featured the usual 'Dazed And Confused' violin bow segment. 'City Sirens' includes a drum solo by Jason and featured samples of 'Bonzo's Montreux' played on a drum synth pad at the front of the stage. This cross section of material delights the audience and the tour is very well received throughout.

Set List Summary: Who's To Blame/Prelude/Over The Hills And Far Away/ Wanna Make Love/Rites Of Winter/Tear Down The Walls/Emerald Eyes/Midnight Moonlight (includes White Summer – Black Mountainside insert)/In My Time Of Dying/City Sirens/Drum Solo/Someone To Love/Prison Blues/The Chase (including Dazed & Confused violin bow solo insert)/ Wasting My Time/Blues Anthem/Custard Pie (including Black Dog insert)/Encores: Train Kept A Rollin'/Stairway To Heaven. 'Liquid Mercury' and 'The Only One' are occasionally performed.

The opening of the tour was slightly delayed when Jimmy was admitted to hospital with abdominal pains. This caused the rescheduling of some dates.

Guitars used during the 'Outrider' tour: Gibson Les Paul, cherry red Gibson Les Paul, brown Fender Telecaster, Dan Electro, Gibson double-neck.

OUTRIDER UK TOUR NOVEMBER

The tour moves to the UK and again the consistently good performances more than satisfy the home crowd. The set list was similar to the US.

Set list summary: Who's To Blame/Prelude/Over The Hills And Far Away/Wanna Make Love/Rites Of Winter/Tear Down The Walls/Midnight Moonlight (includes White Summer/Black Mountain Side/Kashmir inserts)/Emerald Eyes/In My Time Of Dying/City Sirens/Drum Solo/Someone To Love/Prison Blues/The Chase (includes Dazed & Confused insert)/Wasting My Time/Blues Anthem/Custard Pie (includes Black Dog insert)/Encores: Train Kept A Rollin'/Stairway To Heaven

November 21: Birmingham, Hummingbird

November 23: Newcastle, City Hall

November 24 & 24: London, Hammersmith Odeon

November 26: Manchester, Apollo

Jimmy Page: "The audience response was fantastic and that's an incredible charge that encourages you to continue … not that it would have stopped me anyway, if it hadn't worked."

1990

January 10: London, Hammersmith Odeon

Guest appearance: Jimmy joined Bon Jovi at their music therapy benefit show for an encore jam – performing 'Train Kept A Rollin'' and 'With A Little Help From My Friends'. Guitar used: Cherry red Gibson Les Paul.

June 30: Stevenage, Knebworth Park
Guest appearance: Jimmy joined Robert for the Silver Clef awards show performing on 'Wearing And Tearing', 'Misty Mountain Hop' and 'Rock And Roll'. Guitar used: Cherry red Gibson Les Paul.

August 18: Donnington Park, Monsters Of Rock Festival
Guest appearance: The first of two guest spots with Aerosmith. Jimmy joined them in front of the massive Donnington crowd, performing 'Train Kept A Rollin''. Guitar used – Cherry Red Gibson Les Paul.

August 20: London, Marquee Club
Guest appearance: Jimmy joined Aerosmith for their secret Marquee date performing on 'Ain't Got You', 'Think About It', 'Red House', 'Immigrant Song' and 'Train Kept A Rollin''. Guitar used: Cherry red Gibson Les Paul.

Page: "I'll be giving jamming a bad name soon. Aerosmith are such a good band to play with, let me tell you. They really know what it's all about, all right."

1991
March: New York, Fat Tuesday's
Guest appearance: Another jam with Les Paul.
March 23: New York, China Club
Guest appearance: Page jammed with a local band The Reputations for half an hour including a version of 'Further On Up The Road'. Guitar used: White reversed-headstock Charvell.
May 14: Reno, Lawlor Events Centre
Guest appearance: Page showed up with David Coverdale to jam with Poison. Despite falling into the stage pit, he recovered to assist ramshackle versions of 'Rock And Roll', 'The Rover' and 'Stairway To Heaven'.

Bret Michaels, the Poison vocalist, commented: "We had the honour of having Jimmy Page come up onstage with us. My mouth just hung open! It was one of our best nights."
May 29: Reno, Crystal Bay Club
Guest appearance: Page joined local band Solid Ground at a club. Set List: Spider In Your

Web/Steamroller/Johnny B. Goode/Hound Dog/Blue Suede Shoes/Smokin' Again/Slow Down/Old Time Rock And Roll/Kansas City/Louie Louie/Wild Thing/Hang On Sloopy and (again) Blue Suede Shoes.

November: Vancouver, Yale Club
While in Canada recording the Coverdale-Page album, Jimmy and David visited many clubs. At Yale, they indulged themselves in a brief jamming session which included a version of 'Dazed And Confused'.

December 7: Vancouver, Canada
Guest appearance: Page joined Long John Baldry for a 30-minute blues set which included an extended jam of 'Got My Mojo Working' That afternoon, Baldry appeared on CBC (an A.M. radio station) and announced that Jimmy could be playing with him tonight. However, few listeners took him seriously, as less than a hundred punters witnessed the performance.

1992
January 15: New York, Waldorf-Astoria Hotel
Jimmy attended The Yardbirds induction into the Rock And Roll Hall Of Fame. He joined Jeff Beck, Neil Young, Keith Richards, Mitch Mitchell, Noel Redding, Robbie Robertson and John Fogerty for an all star jam. Jimmy played a white Fender Telecaster and the highlight of the performance was a riotous version of Jimi Hendrix's 'All Along The Watchtower'

Jimmy Page: "It's certainly an honour, that's for sure. It's great … and it's really good to see all these old friends again."
March: Miami, Knight Centre
Guest appearance: Jimmy was a surprise guest at Harry Connick Jnr's show jamming on a couple of blues improvisations.

Page: "We met before the concert and Harry said, 'You should come up and play,' and I laughed. But I was sitting in the audience, and he suddenly said, 'We've got a good friend here … C'mon Jimmy, come up and play with us!' I went up and he put a guitar in my hands and said, 'Go ahead, it's your band.' So I did an improvised blues in B flat. I was so nervous! And he went over to the brass section and started singing these licks and cued them in."

1993

February 19: New Orleans, Muddy Waters Club
Guest appearance: Jimmy jammed with blues guitarist Mason Ruffner, who had previously opened for The Firm. Ruffner: "I can't say enough good things about Jimmy Page as a guitar player and as a person. He's a wonderful person. He's been wonderful to me. No one has taken it further on the rock guitar and he can still get out there and do it!"

February 21: New Orleans, Howlin' Wolf Club
Guest appearance: Jimmy jams again with Mason Ruffner.

COVERDALE/PAGE
After the release of the *Coverdale/Page* album in March, the pair set about making plans for a full scale tour. The initial idea was for them to play selected club dates around the world, including London's Marquee. This was vetoed in place of an arena tour and a US tour was scheduled for June. This was then shelved until October. Forty-five dates were arranged and due to commence in Miami on October 8 with the Vince Neil Band supporting. After rehearsals the tour was shelved with rumours of poor ticket sales reported. With the relationship obviously on borrowed time, they did agree to a lucrative Japanese tour with seven shows scheduled for December. The band line-up was Heart drummer Danny Carmassi, Guy Pratt on bass and Brett Tuggle on keyboards.

Guitars used for the Coverdale Page tour:

Gibson Les Paul, cherry red Gibson Les Paul, custom built Transperformance Les Paul, Dan Electro, Gibson double-neck, Ovation double-neck, Ovation acoustic.

COVERDALE /PAGE JAPANESE TOUR
The Japanese tour saw Page playing very confidently and alongside the usual Gibson Les Paul models introduced the Ovation double-neck which would play a major part in the Page/Plant reunion. The set list brought together tracks from the 'Coverdale /Page' album, a couple of Whitesnake staples and plenty of Led Zeppelin. David did a lot of swearing, Jimmy did plenty of inspired playing and when it was over they went their separate ways.

During soundchecks in Japan, the band experimented with 'For Your Life', 'Nobody's Fault But Mine', 'Dazed And Confused', 'Bron Yr Aur Stomp', 'Communication Breakdown' and 'Whole Lotta Love'. However, none of these made the final selection for performance.

December 14 & 15: Tokyo, Budokan Hall
Set List: Absolution Blues/Slide It In/Rock And Roll/Over Now/Kashmir/Pride And Joy/Take A Look At Yourself (acoustic)/Take Me For A Little While/In My Time Of Dying/Here I Go Again/White Summer – Black Mountain Side (includes snippets of Over The Hills And Far Away and Kashmir)/Don't Leave Me This Way/Shake My Tree (inc. Page Theremin solo)/Encores: Still Of The Night/Black Dog/Feeling Hot (including The Ocean intro).

December 17 & 18: Tokyo, Yoyogi Olympic Hall
'Rock And Roll' was played a second time as a final encore.

December 20 & 21: Osaka, Castle Hall
December 22: Nagoya, Nagoya Gym
A snippet of 'Stairway To Heaven' was played during 'Take Me For A Little While'. 'Shake My Tree' featured elements of the 'Whole Lotta Love' middle section.

June 16: Unicef Concert Banqueting Hall Whitehall, London

Jimmy appeared at a music industry event, performing an instrumental version of 'Dazed And Confused' with Michael Lee on drums and Guy Pratt on bass.

July 27: Cafe De Paris, London

Jimmy performed alongside an all star line up in aid of the charities Scream and ABC. With The Black Crowes he performed 'Shake Your Money Maker', 'Sloppy Drunk', 'Woke Up This Morning', 'In My Time Of Dying', 'Oh Well' and 'Whole Lotta Love'; with Michael Lee and Guy Pratt the instrumental 'Dazed And Confused'; then 'Train Kept A Rollin'' and 'Heartbreaker' with Aerosmith's Joe Perry and Steve Tyler; and finally 'You Shook Me' with Chris and Rich Robinson from The Black Crowes .

October 9: Net Aid, Giant's Stadium, New York

Jimmy performed at the Net Aid concert, teaming up with Puff Daddy to perform 'Come With Me' and then with Michael Lee and Guy Pratt for 'Dazed And Confused' and a new instrumental 'Domino'. Chris and Rich Robinson joined them for 'In My Time Of Dying' and 'Whole Lotta Love'.

BLACK CROWES US TOUR

October 12, 13, 14: Roseland Ballroom New York

October 14: Worcester Centrum Boston

October 18, 19: Greek Theatre Los Angeles

Following the London charity show Page was asked by The Black Crowes management if he would like to extend their liaison. With little chance of a reconciliation with Plant on the cards, Page saw this as an opportunity to perform Zeppelin material again, and their sets were predominantly made up of Zep numbers. Six initial US shows took place. At the Boston date Aerosmith's Joe Perry and Steve Tyler jammed on Fleetwood Mac's 'Oh Well' and 'You Shook Me'.

The following Led Zeppelin songs were performed during the dates: Celebration Day/Custard Pie/Sick Again/What Is And What Should Never Be/Ten Years Gone/In My Time Of Dying/Your Time Is Gonna Come/Lemon Song/Heartbreaker/Hey Hey What Can I Do/Out On The Tiles/Whole Lotta Love/ Nobody's Fault But Mine. Non Zep originals played: No Speak No Slave/Wiser Time/Mellow Down Easy/Woke Up This Morning/Shake Your Money Maker/Remedy/Sloppy Drunk/Oh Well/Shapes Of Things/Hard To Handle.

A resulting live album from the dates *Excess All Areas/Live At The Greek* was initially made available via the internet and then commercially released in 2000.

2000

BLACK CROWES US TOUR
JUNE TO AUGUST

On the back of the success of the live album Jimmy and The Black Crowes reconvened for a second US tour. However, continual back problems forced Page to pull out of a round of dates co-headlining with The Who in late summer and a planned 13-date late autumn European tour. It signalled the end of the short lived but well-received liaison with the Crowes.

The following Led Zeppelin songs were performed on this tour: Celebration Day/The Wanton Song/Misty Mountain Hop/Hots On For Nowehere (first ever live arrangement of this *Presence* track)/Sick Again/What Is And What Should Never Be/Ten Years Gone/In My Time Of Dying/Your Time Is Gonna Come/Lemon Song/In The Light/Nobody's Fault But Mine/Hearbreaker/Bring It On Home/Out On The Tiles/Whole Lotta Love. Non Zep songs performed included No Speak No Slave/ Horsehead/Oh Well/Remedy/Shapes Of Things /She Talks To Angels.

2002

February 9: Royal Albert Hall, London, Teenage Charity Concert

Jimmy performed an instrumental version of 'Dazed And Confused' backed by members of Paul Weller's band.

March 4: Epsom School, Rocking For Rio Benefit

Jimmy and wife Jimena attended an ABC charity event at Epsom Collage. Jimmy took part in a question and answer session and performed four numbers with the college student band including Bob Dylans' 'Subtrananean Homesick Blues'.

JOHN PAUL JONES

SOLO CONCERT PERFORMANCE ITINERARY

John Paul Jones spent most of the Eighties studio bound, building up an array of impressive production and arranging credits. These include The Mission, R.E.M., Michael Winner's *Scream For Help* movie, Ben E. King, Cinderella, The Buttonhole Surfers, Raging Slab, Peter Gabriel, plus a variety of world music projects. However, there were a number of 'one-off' appearances.

1983

December 7: Bristol, Colston Hall

Guest appearance: John Paul joined Robert Plant for the encore performance of 'Little Sister'.

1985

July 13: Philadelphia, USA

Live Aid reunion. Rock And Roll/Whole Lotta Love/Stairway To Heaven.

1988

March 27: London, Astoria

Guest appearance: John Paul joined The Mission playing keyboards on an encore performance of 'Shelter >From The Storm' which featured a snippet of 'Rock And Roll'. This performance was screened on Channel 4's *Wired* show and was issued as a free single with *Sounds* magazine.

May 14: New York, Madison Square Gardens

Reunion with Jimmy and Robert for Atlantic Records' 40th Anniversary Concert.

1991

January 18: London, Queen Elizabeth Hall

John Paul appeared on stage with vocal renaissance group Red Byrd. The group performed Jones' composition 'Amores Pasodas'. Jones plays lute, harpsichord and vihuela.

1992

May 8: London, South Bank

Jones attended the premiere of his new composition 'Macanda', at a night of world music billed as *Electrifying Exotica.*

1993

September: Los Angeles.

Jones joined the Lenny Kravitz band on bass for their appearance on the MTV Awards Show. They performed Lenny's hit 'Are You Gonna Go My Way?'

1994

August: Seattle, The Backstage Theatre

John Paul attended all five of Heart's residency at the Backstage Theatre. He was present to produce the subsequent live album *The Road Home* that emerged from these dates. As well as string arrangements and playing mandolin, he joined them on bass for a version of 'What Is And What

Should Never Be', though this is not featured on the album. The pairing was the idea of Capitol president, Gary Gersh. "It's a trillion thrills when you add John Paul Jones to this!" the band's Nancy Wilson stated: "It's a dream come true. He told us the whole band had gone out and seen Heart in the late Seventies and were like 'Whoa, look at these girls, they can play. Girls on guitar, wow!' They used to call us Little Led Zeppelin."

DIAMANDA GALAS:
THE SPORTING LIFE TOUR
EUROPEAN TOUR OCTOBER
US TOUR NOVEMBER TO DECEMBER

John Paul teamed up with the avant garde diva Diamanda Galas for the recording of an album, *The Sporting Life*. He played a variety of instruments including 4, 5 and 8 string bass and a lap steel guitar. He then undertook a tour of Europe and America in support of her album. The set includes a bass led encore version of 'Communication Breakdown'.

Set List Summary: Skotoseme/Do You Take This Man?/Dark End Of The Street/You're Mine/Devil's Rodeo/Tony/You Gotta Move /The Sporting Life/Baby's Insane/Let's Not Chat/Last Man Down/Hex/Encore: Communication Breakdown.

Guitar Player reports: "Wouldn't you know it? The year's wildest guitar solos emanate not from a guitar, but the extraordinary throat of avant-diva Galas. The best record by any former Zep member, hands down!"

1999
ZOOMA TOUR
IRELAND AND HOLLAND DATES OCTO-BER
US TOUR OCTOBER
EUROPEAN AND UK TOUR NOVEMBER

JAPAN TOUR
DECEMBER

To support the release of his first proper solo album *Zooma*, John took to the road with a touring unit that featured ex-Kajagoogoo bassist Nick Beggs on bass and Terl Bryent on drums (whose previous credits included work with Maddy Prior, Rick Wakeman and Roddy Frame). John played mandolin, bass guitar, lap steel guitar and keyboards. The set included the following instrumental versions of Led Zeppelin songs: No Quarter/When The Levee Breaks/Trampled Underfoot/Black Dog.

2000
US TOUR MARCH
July 14 & 15 Rome, Pistoia Blues Festival
The following Led Zeppelin songs were performed live across these dates: No Quarter/Going To California/Nobody's Fault But Mine/When The Levee Breaks/Trampled Underfoot/Black Dog. The intro to his own composition 'Bass'n'Drums' included elements of 'Heartbreaker'.

2001
US TOUR NOVEMBER TO DECEMBER
To support the release of his second solo album *The Thunderthief*, John undertook an American tour supporting King Crimson.

This tour saw him sufficiently confident to take on vocal duties, including a version of Zep's 'That's The Way'. The following Led Zeppelin songs were performed on this tour: That's The Way/When The Levee Breaks/Black Dog (with 'In My Time Of Dying' intro).

2002
January 27: Lyric Theatre Lowry, Manchester
John took part in the Mine Aid event along with Julie Felix, Roy Harper, Bill Wyman and Steve

Harley. Set list: When The Levee Breaks/Leafy Meadows/Freedom Song/ Black Dog. John also played mandolin on the finale 'Free The People'.

April 12: Borders Bookshop, London

John appeared at a special in-store benefit event for the Mines Advisory Group accompanying Julie on mandolin. He also stayed on to sign autographs.

2003

March 2: Queen Elizabeth Hall, London

Guest appearance: John joined Robyn Hitchcock for much of his set playing mandolin. He also took to the piano to sing his own composition 'Ice Fishing At Night'.

August 28/29: Akasaka Blitz, Tokyo
September 1: Namba Hatch, Osaka

John joined Steve Hackett, Paul Gilbert and Nuno Bethencour for three shows in Japan billed as Guitar Wars. His set comprised of Tidal/B. Fingers/Steel Away/When The Levee Breaks/ Nobody's Fault But Mine. He also performed with the whole band for the finale 'Communication Breakdown' and 'Rock And Roll'. A DVD and CD from this tour were released in Japan.

2004

March 13: Shepherds Bush Empire, London

Guest appearance with Seve Hackett. John joined Steve for a version of 'Los Endos' playing steel guitar.

April 29 – May 1/2: Merlefest Wilkesboro NC

John attended this festival jamming with Gillian Welch, David Rawlings and John Cown. His appearance with Cowan included a version of 'Dazed And Confused'.

MUTUAL ADMIRATION SOCIETY
US TOUR JULY TO AUGUST

John undertook this US tour in an amalgamation featuring Glen Phillips (ex Toad The Wet Sproket) and Nickel Creek. The set included 'Going To Califonia' and 'Gallows Pole'.

2004

November: Mandolin Festival Lunel South Of France

John attended this festival and jammed with Mike Marshall and Brazilian mandolinist Hamilton De Holanda on a borrowed double bass. "Lunel was witness to my first ever double bass solo," he reported on his website afterwards.

Led Zeppelin

4/06 (58545)